WALKING IN THE WAY OF PEACE

Walking in the Way of Peace

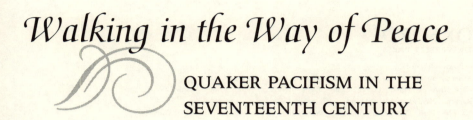

QUAKER PACIFISM IN THE SEVENTEENTH CENTURY

Meredith Baldwin Weddle

OXFORD
UNIVERSITY PRESS

2001

OXFORD
UNIVERSITY PRESS

Oxford   New York
Athens   Auckland   Bangkok   Bogotá   Buenos Aires   Calcutta
Cape Town   Chennai   Dar es Salaam   Delhi   Florence   Hong Kong   Istanbul
Karachi   Kuala Lumpur   Madrid   Melbourne   Mexico City   Mumbai
Nairobi   Paris   São Paulo   Shanghai   Singapore   Taipei   Tokyo   Toronto   Warsaw

and associated companies in
Berlin   Ibadan

Published by Oxford University Press, Inc.
198 Madison Avenue, New York, New York 10016

Oxford is a registered trademark of Oxford University Press.

Library of Congress Cataloging-in-Publication Data
Weddle, Meredith Baldwin, 1939–
Walking in the way of peace : Quaker pacifism in the seventeenth century / Meredith
Baldwin Weddle.
p.   cm.
Includes bibliographical references.
ISBN 0-19-513138-X (cloth)
1. Quakers—New England—History—17th century. 2. Quakers—England—History—17th
century. 3. King Philip's War, 1675–1676—Religious aspects—Society of friends. 4. New
England—Church history—17th century. 5. England—Church history—17th century.
I. Title.
BX7639 .W43   2000
261.8′73′088286—dc21   99-053089

9 8 7 6 5 4 3 2 1
Printed in the United States of America
on acid-free paper

All bloody principles and practices, we . . . do utterly deny. . . . And this is our testimony to the whole world.

A Declaration from the Harmles &
Innocent People of God, 1660

The Christian Soldier should love his Enemies; yet hate and destroy them as Enemies to God and his Country.

The Christian Soldiers Penny Bible, 1693

And they shall beat their swords into plowshares, and their spears into pruning hooks: nation shall not lift up sword against nation; neither shall they learn war any more.

Isaiah 2:4; Micah 4:3

Preface

Aware of the collaborative character of scholarly enterprise, it is with gratitude that I recall those who have contributed their knowledge, wisdom, time, care, and "mundane" everyday assistance to my efforts. John Demos, Edmund Morgan, and David Underdown have given me inspiration of transforming quality, enhanced by friendship. My appreciation of their magnificent teaching in the largest sense only grows as the years pass.

Critical, thoughtful, and challenging assistance from Jon Butler, Diane Kunz, and Phyllis Mack has enhanced this study substantially. The Barbara S. Mosbacher Fellowship made possible concentrated and extended study at the John Carter Brown Library, where the Fellows program under Library Director Norman Fiering promotes scholarly cooperation at its best. I learned from all of my colleagues there (and from none more than Wim Klooster). Travel grants from the Yale Graduate School History Department and the Council on West European Studies aided periods of essential research in England.

The librarians at many institutions were crucial to this study. I particularly valued the skill, good spirit, and unending patience of the staff of the Sterling Memorial and Beinecke Libraries at Yale University, especially Barbara Gajewski, Evelyn McLellan, Frederick Musto, Clifford Johnson, and Stephen Jones. Malcolm Thomas, Josef Keith, and Sylvia Carlyle at Friends' House Library, London, were generous with their specialized knowledge, so vital to accessing their fine collection. Norman Fiering, Susan Danforth, Gwen Jones, and the entire staff at the John Carter Brown Library in Providence, Rhode Island, exemplify excellence. Unusually helpful, too, were Richard Stattler and Rosalyn Cobb Wiggin, archivists of the New England Yearly Meeting Collection of the Society of Friends; Robin Flynn at the Rhode Island Historical Society; J. Stephen Grimes at the Rhode Island Court

Archives; Carol M. Treadway at Guilford College; and the librarians at the Newport Historical Society; the Rhode Island State Archives; Haverford College; and Swarthmore College. I appreciate the volunteers at the Yorktown, New York, branch of the Church of Jesus Christ of Latter-Day Saints, who made available its microfilmed records.

I have relied on the wise direction, example, encouragement, and friendship of Susan Amussen, Patricia Behre-Miskimin, Jennifer Gage, Judith Hunter, Maija Jansson, Robert McMullen, Jihad Mirza, Marie Morgan, John Stanley, and Wayne Tebrake. Their participation in this project took individual forms, each generous and vital in its own way; I am deeply grateful to each one. Clement Alexandre, Kenneth Carroll, Michael Mullett, and Ted L. Underwood guided early stages of this study. David and Susan Martynski and Mary and William Birkbeck provided warm English homes and companionship. Claire Fallender saved me from strangulation by footnotes; Joyce Griffen faxed and organized tirelessly; and Diana Valencia cheerfully provided auxiliary mothering. I have been well and truly sustained over many years by my friends Barbara and Bruce Coe, Fumiko and Stanley Feingold, Elizabeth Miller, Lan Phu, Carolyn and Harry Subin, Derek and Kathryn Wittner, Kathryn and Robert Wolfe, and lifelong friend Merwin Braxton Worth. My extended family of brothers and sisters remains my foundation: Allan Baldwin, Susan Stroh, and Shirley Waring; the Baldwin families, the Stroh family, Thomas Waring, and the Norton families.

I thank Christopher, Timothy, Justin, and Jamien; Ferrell, Melissa, Carmen, and Cassidy for the joy they have brought to my life. To Stephen S. Weddle, my husband, I owe everything, including my admiration, and possibility itself. To him, and to the memory of my parents, Arthur McDonald Baldwin and Margaret Price Baldwin, I dedicate this book.

Contents

Methods and Terms

The Religious Society of Friends (Quakers) is the proper modern name for Quakers. Originally an epithet, the term "Quaker" has become an acceptable, less formal name to present-day members of the Society. Seventeenth-century Quakers had not settled on a name for themselves. Some referred to themselves as "friends of Christ," or "friends"; more often they chose "children of God," or "children of the Light"; and most frequently to outsiders they called themselves "those (in scorn) called Quakers." As time has gentled the scorn, this study uses "Quaker" as most nearly appropriate and convenient.

There has been no attempt, however, to avoid anachronism in the matter of "pacifist" terminology. Whereas today terms such as *nonviolence, pacifism*, and *nonresistance* have discrete meanings and imply varying degrees of passivity, activism, and even force, such careful distinctions were not made in the period under consideration. Some terms used in the study—such as pacifism itself—are modern. This vocabulary has been used interchangeably, referring to beliefs and practices as yet indistinct, undefined, and varying. Indeed, one of the objectives of the study is to come to terms with the terms: to examine what these beliefs and practices meant in particular times and particular places.

Until 1752, England and its possessions used the Julian Calendar, in which the year began on March 25 instead of January 1. January, February, and some March dates, then, fall in the year previous to that which would be expected under the Gregorian Calendar, or "New Style," in use today. Dates in this study conform to the "Old Style" of the Julian Calendar. For dates in January, February, and March, contemporaries sometimes used the form "1675/1676" for increased precision, since the New Style calendar had already been adopted elsewhere in the world. This form has been retained when it was in the original source.

Quakers did not use "heathen" names of the months; instead, they numbered them: "first month," "second month," and so on; the first month, consistent with Old Style, was March. They numbered the days of the week, too: "first day" was Sunday. Throughout this study, Quaker dating appears wherever it appeared in the original source. Dates expressed in this manner are evidence that an individual may have been a Quaker; hence, Quaker form may be significant and has been retained. All dates originally in Quaker form have been standardized and abbreviated, however, as follows: 23/3M/1675, meaning the twenty-third day of the third month (May), 1675 (Old Style).

Quotations remain in original form, including spelling, except that obsolete and excessive punctuation and capitalization have been minimally excised for clarity; the modern letters "i" and "th" replace the archaic "j" and the symbol for "thorn," which resembles the modern "y." Certain contractions appearing as superscripts— notably "yt", "ym," "wch," where "y" is thorn—have been expanded and brought down into the text as, for example, "that," "them," "which." Early titles of written works were often long, sometimes filling most of a page; these have been truncated when no substantive loss is sustained thereby.

All references are to the Authorized King James Version of the Holy Bible. Abbreviations are as follows:

CSPC	Calendar of State Papers, Colonial
FHL	Friends' House Library, London
JCB	John Carter Brown Library, Providence, RI
JFHS	Journal of the Friends' Historical Society
MM	Monthly meeting: the local business unit of Quaker organization.
MS. Port.	Portfolio Collection, Friends' House Library, London
MS vol.	"Manuscript volume [no.]," a discrete collection within the manuscript archives of Friends' House Library, London
NEHGR	New England Historical and Genealogical Register
NEYM	New England Yearly Meeting, the largest geographical unit of Quaker organization. The comparable unit in England was the London Yearly Meeting
OED	Oxford English Dictionary
PMHB	Pennsylvania Magazine of History and Biography
PRO	Public Record Office (Great Britain)
RIHS	Rhode Island Historical Society, Providence, RI
"RIHSM"	"Rhode Island Historical Society Manuscripts," a discrete collection within the Manuscripts Collection
WMQ	William and Mary Quarterly

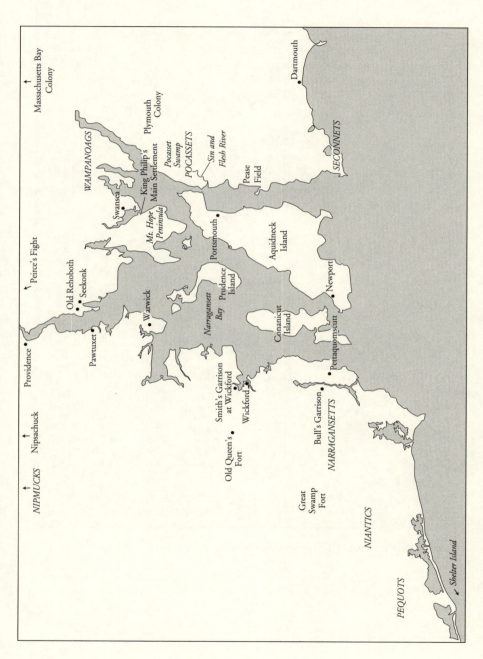

Narragansett Bay in the late seventeenth century

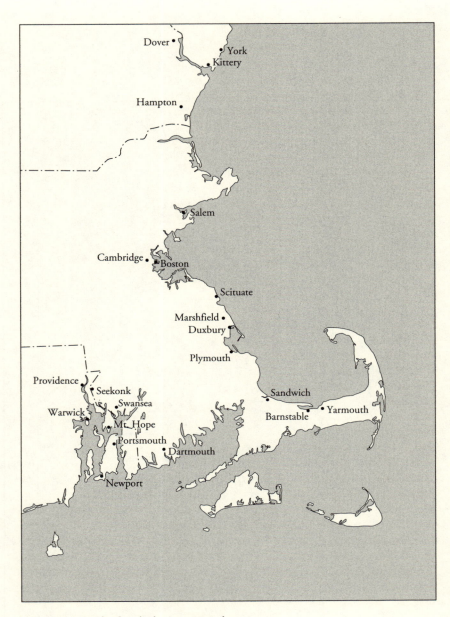

Eastern New England in the late seventeenth century

WALKING IN THE WAY OF PEACE

Introduction

come to walk in the Way of Peace . . . which is the Way to God.

George Fox
"Some Principles of the Elect People of God"

War is rudely obtrusive in history. Mankind has found war to be useful, justifiable, and quite unavoidable. Violence, in all its ugly forms, is unrelenting. Yet pacifism, the renunciation of violence, has also persisted in history. The voices of pacifism have come through the years faintly, whispering the failed programs of the evanescent, drowned out by the hollow echo of irrelevance. Impractical, ineffective, perhaps impossible—yet pacifism has endured. Occasionally, uncompromising voices have expressed the tenacity of pacifism in prophetic terms. The actions of these people have dramatized imagination and a search for moral excellence.

Such a people were those "in scorn called Quakers," in the last half of the seventeenth century in England and in her American colonies. Eager to quake before the Lord, "the people of God" stubbornly refused to quake before men, even and especially powerful men. Their supreme confidence, born of rigorous and painful conversion experiences and nourished by an empowering doctrine of God's potential availability within each person, was the core of a confrontational political and religious style. Their certainty encouraged them to challenge, their zeal obliterated caution: an itinerant country man lectured Oliver Cromwell; a mother of eight argued with Charles II; and a man filled with the love of God shouted "Dumb Dogs" at ministers of God in Cardiff. Quakers, by rude appearance, rude manners, rude carriage, exiled themselves from their society and were exiled for unyielding arrogance and unfathomable refusals, for imagined conspiracies and strange deviations.

Their style was provocative, their language on fire with military images, their method confrontational. Yet crucial substantive elements of their religious belief were in tension with this style, for from the earliest days many Quakers renounced violence as incompatible with the Kingdom of God. They maintained a testimony against offensive violence because it was contrary to the spirit of Jesus' new covenant and to his admonition to love one's enemies. Their trust in God's protection and their willingness to suffer rendered defensive violence unnecessary for them. At their best, they sought reconciliation, even with oppressors. Quaker renunciation of weapons, war, fighting, and violence gradually coalesced into a set of principles concerning peace, which became known as the peace testimony. As they developed, the principles of the peace testimony were vague and sometimes conflicting. From the beginning, Quakers displayed a range of beliefs about nonviolence, both civic and personal. Their actions, too, sometimes imperfectly expressive of belief, were arrayed along a continuum, from clear instances of violence, through indecision or indifference, to scrupulous disassociation from violence.

Such a pacifist continuum is not remarkable. Pacifism is complicated, because violence itself is complicated. Violence has infinite forms, which people have organized into various categories. They have distinguished among forms of violence on the basis of its purpose: for example, between force and violence, between force used to inflict hurt and force used to restrain. They have distinguished among types of violence, depending upon who is the agent: between state-sanctioned violence and individual violence; between killing by magistracy, called capital punishment, and killing by a criminal. They have differentiated on the basis of the initiator: between offensive violence and that which is reactive, or defensive violence.

Violence may be individual or collective, spontaneous or planned. One might develop countless categories of violence into which one's actions might fall and, evaluating them, validate one form of violence and invalidate another. Each human being, in fact, constantly faces decisions about violence within his life. What measures of force or violence will she sustain, and toward what forms of life (from the invading spider and field mouse to her rapacious neighbor; from the tax-collecting, armed democracy to the genocidal despot)? Upon these individual and collective decisions rest the very character of people and of the societies they establish.

Pacifism is not susceptible to easy understanding. As a way of organizing human interaction, it is organically connected to its historical setting and to inspired individuals, arising within a specific social culture, political system, legal and economic structure, and religious outlook. Thought impels its presence; events shape its characteristics; conflict challenges its consistency. Principles of peace are infinitely variable, changing in goals, rationales, and practical consequences. Each person must work out a definition of pacifism anew. At the same time, every pacifist has faced the same decisions. Varying in cultural details, these decisions answer the same question: Where does one's responsibility begin, and end? Can one stand watch for Spanish ships? Treat a wounded soldier? Spy on Indians? Designate the forts, when drawing up a map? Eat the king's food, while in the brig? Be a jailor? Redeem Quaker slaves from Morocco by selling arms?

The subject of this book is the character of early Quaker pacifism—of the Quaker peace testimony. In this work, I investigate the historical context, meaning, and expression of early Quaker pacifism in England and its colonies, asserting that historical context and individual witness are crucial in illuminating the very nature of pacifism itself. The book analyzes one discrete historical moment in detail, focusing on Quaker behavior during King Philip's War, a terrible war between settlers and Indians in Rhode Island and New England, 1675–1676. Through "observing" Quakers in this historical situation, it is possible to identify issues relating to the peace testimony, to discern motivations, and discover actual practice.

The history of the Quakers and their peace principles in England began in the years of the English Civil War, Oliver Cromwell and the Godly Commonwealth, and the Restoration of King Charles II, in the late 1640s to 1660. This study begins by setting forth Quaker religious belief, particularly those aspects that gave rise to and influenced the nature of the peace testimony. Quakers found the locus of truth to be the "Light within," source of continuing revelation from God. They located themselves within a present "Kingdom of God" on earth and subjected themselves to the rigors of its requirements, exemplified by the "new covenant" of Jesus, wherein love was the animating element of all human relationships and where the perfectibility of man, even while on earth, was possible. At the same time, Quakers remained fully engaged "in the world," under God's protection, acknowledging the legitimacy of worldly government within its sphere.

In the first years of the Quaker movement, one can trace individual expressions of the peace testimony arising from Quaker beliefs, followed by collective expressions of peace principles in response to significant governmental pressure. How Quakers explained and justified their testimony, using the spirit and texts of the New Testament Gospels and the doctrine of obedience to God, exposes the foundation of the early testimony, a foundation that had consequences for the choices Quakers made when confronted with violence. And these choices—how Quakers behaved in the English context and as they embarked upon the sea—in turn elaborate on their stated beliefs. The life experiences of such English Quakers as boatswain Thomas Lurting, serving on a frigate under Admiral Robert Blake; Edward Coxere, mate on board a merchant ship; and Henry Pitman, surgeon exiled to the West Indies after Monmouth's Rebellion illustrate the complexity by which pacifist principles are defined and absorbed into an individual's manner of living.

The second part of this book follows Quakerism to America and especially New England in 1656, where within only four years of its "gathering" in England the movement attracted local adherents, and where local experience would begin to demonstrate the importance of place to the nature and form of pacifist expression. Quakers represented an unwelcome challenge to New England Puritans of several persuasions, and Quaker peace principles were tested first in the context of persecution. Rhode Island, however, proved a sanctuary for these and other religious radicals, and by the time a party of the "founding" generation of English Quakers visited that colony in 1672, they found not only established Quaker religious institutions, but also Quakers beginning to exercise political power. New England was threatened during these years from Indian unrest within and Dutch depredations from without; in a period of increasing anxiety about war, all of the colony governments attempted to protect themselves from these threats in haphazard ways and to mobilize for war. A Rhode Island Quaker government did more in 1673, seeking to accommodate the peace principles of some of its residents through innovative legislation exempting them from military service, extraordinary measures allowing for refusal to serve for reasons of conscience, legislation that it justified in a subtle and revealing argument.

King Philip, or Metacom, sachem of the Wampanoag Indians, maintained his headquarters about a mile and a half from the border of Rhode Island. King Philip's War began in 1675, just over that border in Plymouth Colony, and spread throughout New England, confronting Quakers with the practical need to define the parameters of their peace testimony—to test their principles and the underlying foundation for those principles and to choose how they would respond to violence. Just before King Philip's War, moreover, Quakers had come to dominate the Rhode Island government. Here, Quaker peace principles would, for the first time anywhere in the world, be juxtaposed with the inherent demands of political office. These particular Quakers, as governors, had to reconcile their obligations to provide for the common defense with their own pacifist beliefs. It has been the common assumption that Rhode Island held itself aloof from the war because of its Quaker leaders and their pacifist beliefs. Thus an English Quaker visiting in Rhode Island in the closing months of the war later observed, "At that Time New England was at War with the Indians, except the Colony of Rhode-Island, the Governor of it being a Friend. . . . [He] could not give Commissions to kill and destroy Men."[1] And a modern historian has written, "Friends did not fight in this war although some leading Friends in Rhode Island helped direct defensive preparations."[2] A careful study of the war, however, shows the Rhode Island government, dominated by Quakers, taking initiative as well as defensive action. Such choices and maneuverings of Quaker magistrates impel us to analyze the wartime motivations and self-justifications of the Rhode Island government, in order to ascertain the influence of the peace testimony upon Rhode Island's choices. The assumptions that encouraged their participation in the war and the elements that limited that participation are relevant evidence in evaluating the conventional view that Quaker pacifism determined Rhode Island's role in King Philip's War. The self-interested accounts pressed by the other colonies describing Rhode Island's war efforts have also affected subsequent historical judgments about Quaker pacifism.

Certain Quakers within Rhode Island, not officeholders, disagreed with the wartime activities of their powerful brethren. These Quakers recorded their views in a document of compelling fervor, "A Testimony" from Rhode Island Quakers. This document contributes a unique voice to the understanding of early Quaker pacifism and its community. Elsewhere in New England, too, in Sandwich, Scituate, or perhaps Dover, Quakers had to reconcile their peace principles with mortal concerns. An Edward Perry had to decide whether to collect taxes for war, captain and Quaker Christopher Hussey whether principles against violence prohibited military service. Did Henry Dow wonder whether he should carry a gun as he worked his fields as his neighbors did? Did Richard Otis, fortifying his house, consider whether seeking security within a garrison betrayed doubt about God's protection? Was Patience Coggeshall among those who nursed the English wounded but not the Indian, and did she wonder if this signaled active cooperation with conflict? The implicit struggle in their situation has gone unrecognized and unanalyzed. Those who have only glanced at pacifism fail to see that it is not at all self-evident what behavior flows from pacifist belief. The choices foist themselves anew upon the conscientious in every changing historical circumstance, not because of any situational flexibility of the principles themselves but always because there is a line beyond which consequences and meaning are difficult and ambiguous. For even the most conscientious, the very location of that line may be disputable. Through incident, casualty lists, poetry, punishment, and other minutiae within a sparse historical record the individual Quaker makes his presence felt.

The experiences of early Quakers are useful in considering why pacifism remains opaque in theory and difficult in practice. The conclusion of this study points to the gulf separating secular and religious pacifists, a gulf that when unrecognized leaves them uncertain as to why they cohere so imperfectly and so temporarily. Pacifists of different perspectives may find common ground in policy, strategy, or even tactics, but when they fail to understand the grounding of pacifism in all its variety, their efforts may fragment and they drift apart.

Finally, the conclusion addresses unexamined assumptions about human nature that limit imagination and sap the courage to seek a peaceful path. The most potent of these is that human aggression is inevitable and overriding. This assumption early Quakers did not share. For them, dwelling in the Kingdom of God was possible and called forth the best that was in them. For their Quaker successors too, personal moral example could be a triumphant force, transforming evil into good.

Considering the unrelenting violence in history, it is strange that alternative paths have been so little pondered. Historical studies of pacifism have been few and have often suffered from oversimplification, a restricted scope, and insufficient detail. Even the Quaker peace testimony, hallowed by time, has drawn little systematic attention. Sometimes sentimentalized, the testimony has as readily been dismissed as foolish; its genesis was idealized in the past, and more recently its origins have been confined within strategic political manoeuverings. As historian Humphrey J. Fisher has observed, "[w]e live in rather sour, cynical days, reflecting perhaps as much the taste of the world in our own mouths as the superior perceptions of our historical analysis."[3] Most inquiries into the history and origins of the Quaker peace testimony have fallen within two streams of thought. The first has assumed that the peace testimony was an integral part of Quakerism from its earliest days in England and that it was an essential component of Quaker belief thereafter. Those within this tradition have thought about the peace testimony almost exclusively in "religious"—doctrinal or theological—terms.

Historians from the second stream of inquiry into the origins of Quaker pacifism have looked beyond Quaker sources and beyond doctrine and so have immeasurably enhanced the understanding of Quaker pacifism's historical seedbed. These historians, notably Christopher Hill, Barry Reay, W. Alan Cole, and James Maclear, found the origins of the peace testimony in the political turmoil surrounding the Restoration of Charles II to the English throne in 1660. Soon after the Restoration, one of the many religious sects born of the social upheaval, the Fifth Monarchists, staged a violent uprising. Lest they be mistakenly associated with this treasonous event, the Quakers issued a declaration setting forth their peace principles and disavowing violence, conspiracies, and plotting. This Declaration of 1660 became the normative expression of the peace testimony.[4] The peace testimony, according to this interpretation, then, was a self-defensive, reactive, strategic phenomenon arising from political necessity. In W. Alan Cole's memorable formulation, "[p]acifism was not a characteristic of the early Quakers: it was forced upon them by the hostility of the outside world."[5] This second stream of thought discounted the existence of peace principles before 1660, minimizing any earlier manifestations of peace principles as "prepacifist" or "premature-pacifist." Those who have relied on this political or sociological interpretation have deemed the peace testimony essentially "settled" after 1660. (After the Declaration of 1660, "no Quaker would knowingly engage in any livelihood or action which involved war or violence."[6])

The understandings about the origins of the Quaker peace testimony are important because they set up fundamental assumptions about the very meaning, function, and rationale behind peace principles. So it matters that both of the traditional streams of thought about early Quaker pacifism are inadequate. The first interpretation—that pacifism based on faith alone was an integral aspect of early Quaker practice—is overly pietistic, ignoring the confused and limited nature of the witness. Those in this tradition have made little effort to understand just what the peace testimony meant—what activities might be proscribed or mandated; what complex decisions might be required. Seeing the peace testimony solely as an element of religious faith, they have ignored political consequences of, and influences upon, that belief. They have not adequately appreciated the implications of historical context for the peace testimony. They have overlooked changes in the peace testimony: changes in its manifestations, in the choices people made, and in the underlying rationale for peace principles. In looking at the early years of the Quaker movement, these historians have sometimes read back the theologically elaborated, socially ritualized Quaker pacifism of later centuries. Historians and Quakers themselves have downplayed the range of belief and behavior among Quakers, justifying some who bore arms with odd excuses, relegating uncomfortable examples to footnotes, and defining out those whom they could not recognize as Quakers. They have assumed an ideological homogeneity that did not exist.[7]

Some historical misunderstandings within this tradition have arisen because early Quakers themselves did not address the implications of their developing beliefs about peace. Some of the Quaker reticence about matters of violence and peace may have reflected the thinking exemplified in the "advice" from the Yearly Meeting of English Quakers in 1757: "And as we are called out of wars and fightings, so let them be, *as seldom as possible*, the subjects of our conversation . . . the concerns of an unstable world . . . tend, as they are admitted into the mind, to lessen its trust on that rock which is immovable."[8] Some of the misunderstandings may have begun with early Quakers misunderstanding each other. In 1703, for instance, Samuel Bownas, an English Quaker traveling in the ministry near Dover, in northern New England, attended a Quaker meeting. "The Cuntry was all Allarm'd soe that it was a very Large meeting indeed," Bownas reported, "and it bieing warr time with the Indyeans[,] the peopel Brot such weapons as they had too Meetg." Bownas continued, credulously,

I was supprized too see soe maney fyer Armes and other Instruments of Warr Standing Against the Meeting house walle. However I was before tould that it was thee custom of other peopel too doo soe and I found that thoas fier Armes and Warrlike weapons belonged too other peopell (nott Fr[ien]ds).[9]

Even the work of the best Quaker historians suffers from a curious inadequacy in respect to the peace testimony. William C. Braithwaite's studies of early Quaker history, for example, still exemplify extraordinary scholarship, thoroughness, and fairness.[10] Braithwaite's consideration of pacifism was both accurate and nuanced: he warned, for example, that one must not expect early Quakers to have examined the implications of pacifism, without "our methods of historical . . . criticism"; that their priorities were different; and that they were primarily interested in issues involving the state church and religious liberty. His presentation of the spiritual experience leading to pacifism, of the initial absence of humanitarian concern, and of Quaker interest in obedience was balanced.[11] But even though he included problematical instances of Quaker speech or behavior that implied violence, he usually did not comment on them. He quoted "militant language" but did not attempt to explain its significance. Braithwaite described a Quaker who courageously stepped within a wrestling ring, for example, and gravely told the boisterous fighters that it was man's duty to fight only for Jesus. He later quoted the fiery words of the same Quaker, who incited his soldier audience to avenge the innocent against the pope in Rome; Braithwaite made no attempt to reconcile, or to understand, the two incidents.[12] Braithwaite's accuracy slipped, moreover, when he spoke about peace principles among Quakers in the colonies. Here he relied exclusively on the work of historian Rufus Jones and fell into oversimplification. "In Rhode Island," Braithwaite wrote, "Friends in the government were in every instance devoted to the maintenance of peace." To the extent that the pacifism of Rhode Island Quaker leaders was inconsistent, he assumed it was because their colonial status involved them in the foreign policy of England, their Indian policies had been "compromised" by their neighboring colonies, and some citizens were not pacifists.[13] Braithwaite's confidence that there was a "great gulf" between Quakers and others, because Quakers "resolutely excluded compulsion" as a possibility, led him to diminish Quaker responsibility when their practice violated his expectations.[14] While Braithwaite did not conceal the range of Quaker behavior and belief, neither did he grapple with the issues such diversity raises.

Rufus Jones, in *Quakers in the American Colonies*, excused rather than analyzed. When Quakers kept company with violence, he implied that such occasions were beyond their control. Thus the Quaker leaders of Rhode Island "found themselves compelled, by unavoidable conditions and circumstances, to perform public acts of a warlike nature."[15] Jones usefully pointed out the tension between the idealist, trying to remain true to his principles, and the practical leader, also principled, who must compromise in order to be effective. But while he was forgiving, he left much unquestioned. One of the more satisfactory treatments of Quaker pacifism remains that of Margaret Hirst, in *The Quakers in Peace and War*.[16] Her richly detailed study included extensive excerpts from documents of great interest. Like that of Braithwaite and Jones, however, Hirst's work was limited by her predominant attention to religious issues to the neglect of political and social causes or consequences of pacifism. She consistently slighted those who did not fit orthodox understanding of pacifism: "Some Quakers, or old soldiers with Quaker leanings," she wrote, joined military forces in 1659; Hirst dismissed them as "pseudo-Quakers."[17] Her treatment of pacifism in the colonies was fragmentary and derivative.

More recently, Peter Brock has written extensively on the subject of Quaker pacifism. While often presenting useful syntheses, Brock has not tested conventional interpretations of Quaker pacifism against detailed local research. The absence of this check against the traditional view of the peace testimony as an uncomplicated concomitant of Quaker belief from "then until now" permits some analyses of the early peace testimony to rest on the precarious grounds of modern assumptions. "From what I know of Quaker persistence, then and now," wrote Brock, for instance,

> I doubt if many of their young men falling into the clutches of the press-gang remained indefinitely a part of the Royal Navy. . . . Moreover, Quaker pressed men clearly made rather unruly—*though of course nonviolent*—tars, and thus the Navy was probably glad to get rid of them before too long.[18]

The second stream of thinking—that pacifism was a strategic reaction of persecuted Quakers to events of 1660—is also flawed, ignoring distinctions between spiritual and political motivations, between individuals and the group, between the private sphere and the public, between belief and method, between England and colonies.[19] The very energy of political interaction that it postulates, so resonant with modern assumptions, has tended to crowd out essential elements of Quaker spirituality and thereby reduce the dimensions of Quaker expression. In the course of more realistically evaluating the origins of Quaker pacifism, some have altogether diminished the potency of religious fervor by transmuting pacifism into self-serving politics, even into psychological pathology. The concentration on political exigencies has narowed thinking, too, by conceiving of "pacifism" mainly as opposition to war—to collective, or civic, violence—and ignoring other, more private, forms of nonviolence. This approach fails to allow for the individual Quakers who chose nonviolence before 1660, and chose it for themselves. The strategic interpretation assumes that most Quakers would be motivated to eschew violence for reasons requiring broad political consciousness. It assumes that pacifism is reactive, passive, and comes from weakness. But pacifism is instead often radical and revolutionary and demands extraordinary strength. And by assuming that pacifism was settled by document in 1660, such interpretation uncritically fails to take note of the great variety of scruples that Quakers developed one by one for decades to come and fails to note the failures to practice nonviolence as well. Ironically, a theory insisting on the ultimate importance of historical context for the origins of pacifism came to deny the importance of historical context thereafter. Perhaps most definitively, this second stream of thought does not comport with the development of the peace testimony in the colonies, where Quakers were refusing to train in the militias before 1660, where Quakerism did not mean withdrawal from participation in government, and where pacifism was not necessarily associated with political quietism.

Most histories only touch on the subject of Quaker pacifism, in one or two paragraphs—even one or two sentences—alluding to Quaker peace principles. The cumulative effect of such cursory reiteration of conventional thinking is to suggest that Quaker peace principles were uncomplicated, homogeneous, self-evident, and unproblematical. Otherwise excellent historical investigations have thus avoided, no doubt unintentionally, the messy challenges of a subject that is distinguished by its contradictions, its fundamental changes, and its sparse evidence. Careful study of how individual Quakers actually behaved when confronted with violence in specific historical situations can begin to redress oversimplification. While one need not go so far as to assert that questions themselves define reality, it is nevertheless true that a search for a more intricate understanding of pacifism yields few answers when the questions themselves are inadequately framed. Each historical circumstance should stimulate new questions about pacifism; in the aggregate, the questions may provoke reconsideration of earlier interpretations. The early Quakers—some more, some less nonviolent—stand as examples of the distinction between conscience and compromise, passion and indifference, commitment and calculation as they sought to walk in the way of peace.

PART I

The Peace Testimony

Prologue

The walking started in the North of England. A solitary figure arrived in a village, strode in upon the daily ritual, startling with his leather suit, or shocking with her bold summons.

The summons was to an age-old ecstasy: the soul could touch God. A listener might hear about God as a light within his own human person, a glorious infusion of joy toward which he might turn, and turn over his agonies. But, he learned, such an infusing light would inevitably cast into relief the darkest caches of sin, the evil elements of his being. So illumined, the darkness must be utterly recognized, utterly regretted, utterly renounced before the promise could be sustained.

The summons was to a profound and shattering struggle, and then to walk in the light of the Lord.

As they walked over the hills, once solitary figures recognized consonant purposes in each other and a certain resonance of spiritual impulse. As they walked they summoned themselves, too, to a great work, a great proclaiming, abroad into the southern counties of England, abroad into the papal continent of southern Europe, abroad into the American settlements and their surrounding wilderness. These summoners were those in scorn called Quakers; they began to call themselves the children of God.

I

"And the Shout of a King Is amongst Us"

George Fox was one of the first; surely he thought he was the first in centuries to understand that Christ was come to teach his people himself, that the Second Coming was fulfilled, fulfilled within each one who sought and found him.

Inspired enthusiasts in England found a new religious impulse within themselves and found each other as well. Men such as James Nayler, Francis Howgill, Edward Burrough, and John Camm burned a compelling message into crowds of a thousand or more gathered in the fields and hills of northern England in the early 1650s, or labored with one person at a time in an equally searing silence. Whispering quietly of grace or shouting with a trumpet voice the call to spiritual warfare upon the soul, they spoke a message at once dreadful and simple and joyous.

The message stretched out beyond the fields, beyond the hills of the North, to all people everywhere. For salvation was—in their view—potentially universal, not selective. Each person had the capacity to experience "that of God" within her, a manifestation of God's spirit, or even a presence of Christ's flesh; a potential for communication with the divine, a potential God would activate when the individual sought Christ within. Each person had access to his or her own source of revelation, which Quakers called the "Light within" or the "Light." The Light of Christ within was Truth's presence in present time, was a "universally bestowed light" and so represented the promised Second Coming of the Lord.[1] One might oneself spontaneously become aware of the Light by God's direct intervention, or one might become aware of the Light through the encouragement of someone else "answering" the unrecognized summons of God and pointing out this summons.

Early History

The personal religious seeking upon which the nineteen-year-old George Fox embarked in 1642 from the midland English village of Fenny Drayton in Leicestershire led him after some years to encounters with others similarly struggling to find a valid spiritual path, to inspired seekers such as Elizabeth Hooten, Richard Farnworth, James Nayler, Mary Fisher, and William Dewsbury. By 1652, the "creative moment" in Quakerism,[2] a cadre of dedicated people, later called the First Publishers of Truth, pushed out two by two from the North, on fire with the Truth: there is "that of God" within all people, a "Light within" that is the source of continuing revelation from God, revelation of the same nature and authority as an earlier collection of revelations, the scriptures. By acknowledging one's sin and surrendering totally to the will of God, one might have ongoing access to the Light, which leads to perfection and salvation even in this life. God's empowerment made available infinite possibility and necessitated infinite responsibility for living according to Truth itself. One might enter the Kingdom of God here on earth and live by its principle of love. This was at once the summons and the message.

Quakers were but one of the sects operating with blazing hope for godliness within the turbulence and strenuous opportunity of the Commonwealth and Protectorate periods, following the beheading of King Charles I in 1649. By the time of Protector Oliver Cromwell's death in 1658, Quakers already felt disappointed by Cromwell's betrayal of his own ideals, by his reliance on the army rather than the Spirit to bring about God's commonwealth. When deterioration of the political order galloped forward under Richard Cromwell and the "Rump" Parliament, many Quakers were energized into active intervention in political life; some experienced profound emotional disturbance; most came to terms with the impending restoration of the monarchy. An accumulating fear of Quakers and the disorder they represented, dramatized by Booth's rising and Monck's march south, contributed to the restoration of the monarchy in May 1660. Quakers encouraged the returning King Charles II to abide by his own Declaration of Breda of 1660, which offered freedom of conscience. But in January 1660 another sect, the Fifth Monarchists, rose with violence, initiating an infectious fear of sedition so intense that it was realized in a series of repressive measures, such as the Quaker Act of 1662 and the Conventicle Acts of 1664 and 1670. Until James II's Declaration of Indulgence of 1687 and William and Mary's Toleration Act of 1689, Quakers suffered great persecution. The movement's remarkable growth in the 1650s was proportionately slowed by the inhibiting chill of persecution and the imprisonment of thousands and death of hundreds.[3] In the colonies, where the Quaker vision had been carried a scant four years after its 1652 "gathering" in England—in 1656— Quaker experience was less homogeneous. While suffering under New England Puritanism and the Church of England in Virginia and the West Indies, Quakers found a measure of possibility in North Carolina, Maryland, the Jerseys, and even New York, and abundant opportunity in Rhode Island and, of course, Pennsylvania. What was the nature of Quaker belief and practice that at once enticed and repelled so many?

Figure 1.1. "Quackerifcher Mutter Mord," or "Quaker Mother Murder," reproduction of engraving in *Historia Fanaticorum*, 1701. Anti-Quaker cartoon, whose caption rehearses typical misunderstandings of Quaker doctrine, reading: "So the Quakers have the mother murder in common, But must the urge of spirit be the pretext even for this? This son wants to abolish the origin of sin, So his mother has to die by his hands." Reproduced with permission of the Library Committee of the Religious Society of Friends in Britain.

Others have ably explored the complexities and evolution of Quaker belief in general in its first half-century; to attempt a meaningful comprehensive account of these complexities would be superfluous. But to understand the peace testimony, it is essential to isolate and explore those particular aspects of early belief and practice—those particular assumptions, idiosyncratic interpretations, emphases, and experiences—that were crucial to its development as a part of Quakerism.

Underlying the Quaker insistence on an ostensibly simple religious construct—the Light within as the source for Truth—basic assumptions about truth itself began to assert themselves and to define and complicate Quaker belief. The assumptions fell within two realms: mankind's relationship with God and mankind's relationship with the world. Mankind's relationship with God was predicated on his experience of God, a conversation with God, that was both universally available and necessary. Four assumptions or beliefs emerged from the experiential nature of this relationship: the internal locus of religious authority, the internal source for teachings, the profound sense of human unworthiness, and the profound certainty about the availability of temporal salvation. All of these beliefs would be important in Quaker thinking about peace. In considering mankind's relationship with the world, beliefs about government, about God's protection of the faithful, and about persecution and suffering would be relevant to a nascent pacifism.

Conversations with God: Authority, Teachings, Reproof, Salvation

Authority: "Spiritually Discerned"

First, aspects of Quaker belief about the Light and unmediated access to the Light were to be of fundamental importance to Quaker pacifism, even as that pacifism has changed over the centuries. For Quakers, the Light within, synonymous with Truth, was *sufficient* for the teaching and salvation of sinful mankind. The Quaker, suspended in silence or leaping within an ecstatic moment, received directly the spirit of God. Revelation continues and is authoritative. She did not need any priest or minister to interpret God's spirit or to explain the meaning of scripture. Indeed, such intervention was absolutely a bar to the spirit of God, because priests or ministers could transmit only the forms of religion, not the substance. Their presence in the process was at best misleading, at worst fraudulent, for, shockingly, they were willing to "sell" that which must not be sold, the gospel message, through their acceptance of salaries. Nor was the earthly reason or learning the clergy relied on useful for understanding the revelations of scripture, for only the same spirit revealed in scripture could "open" scripture, a spirit that Quakers were certain the clergy had not experienced. "Take heed of the fleshly wisdom . . . take heed of thy reasoning or disputing; for these are the weapons wherewith the witness is slain," wrote Isaac Penington.[4] Because of this assumption, that the clergy had no function since authority and understanding were available within, Quakers assigned themselves a weighty responsibility: each was, alone, to find God.

Aspects of Quaker belief about revelation, scripture, and Jesus' new covenant were formative in Quaker pacifism because they harbored God's teaching. First, obedience to the principles of God was essential to maintaining a right relationship with God and so sustaining access to Truth and salvation. One of the ways in which God had revealed his principles, of course, was in scripture. Although the words of scripture came from the Light, the words alone could not transmit the substance of spirituality; "no creature can read the Scriptures to profit thereby" except the people "who come to the Light and Spirit that gave them forth." To understand scripture, to avoid "stumbling about the words," one must approach the words infused with the same Light that inspired and enveloped that earlier revelation.[5] Unlike the Light, scripture was not *sufficient* for teaching or for salvation. Isaac Penington explained this concept: "A man may read Scriptures, hear sermons, &c. and thereby gather a knowledge into the old understanding: but neither this understanding . . . nor the knowledge itself . . . is spiritual, but fleshly, and so cannot save."[6]

Nor was scripture *necessary* for teaching or for salvation, because the nature and authority of the revelations available to the converted were identical to the revelations inspiring the teachings in the Bible. The Light after all was the same Light that had illumined the words of the prophets speaking through scripture, that had guided their hands as they recorded their insights and the history of their peoples. The scriptures, then, were the words of God, but not the exclusive, preeminent, and final Word of God.[7]

The Light and the Spirit revealed in the gospel message about Jesus remained unchanged, unchanging, and approachable in an immediate, unmediated sense to all people, of whatever historical moment. Because revelation was ongoing, the inward Christ served the same function for those who had never heard of the historical Jesus as Jesus did in scripture; Jesus' Light continued to be the image of God's substance.[8] The revelation was at once eternal, because it was Truth, and temporal, because it came through a person located in history.[9] Through seeking and obeying God's will for herself by listening to God's voice within, each person might reach for her salvation, which, in fact, she might be certain of while living on this earth. Revelations from God were authoritative, were instructive, were not confined to scripture, and need never cease.

Reproof: "The Dreadful Day of the Lord"

Quakers did not naively suppose that human beings were only glancingly conversant with evil. They harbored no illusions that their developing ideas about nonviolence were unproblematical and thus subject to abandonment at the first sign of malignity in others. They found too much evil within themselves for that. For the same Light that illumined the way to salvation, according to Quakers, illumined also the evil within, which barred the way. With unrelenting clarity, each person convinced by the Quaker message could see his helplessness in the face of this evil. His convincement—the Quaker term for the intellectual acceptance of belief—was only the preliminary in a truly agonizing struggle on the way to conversion itself. He must first utterly acknowledge and regret the evil he shared with all human beings. Then, conversion would require surrender to the will of God. Part of this surrender involved a renunciation of earthly things: knowledge, earthly "comprehension," self-will, friends, and family. ("And then I separated from all the glory of the World, and from all my Acquaintance, and kindred.")[10] Renunciation was good preparation for the difficult paths Quakers would be called upon to walk.[11]

Salvation: "Be Ye Therefore Perfect"

For Quakers, the gospel message about Jesus was paramount in scripture because Jesus brought a new dispensation, a "new covenant," a new way of understanding man's obligations to God and his neighbor, which at once fulfilled and superseded the system of laws and the first covenant between the God of the Hebrew scriptures and the Jews.[12] They saw Jesus' coming as a return to higher standards, the standards from before the fall of Adam and before Mosaic law. "The Promise of the New Covenant," Margaret Fell wrote, is that of "the Law written in the Heart, and of the Spirit being put in the Inward Parts."[13] Penington noted that whereas the laws of the old covenant were written "outwardly in tables of stone," the laws of the new covenant were to be "written in the heart." Although in books one might read "some outward descriptions of the thing, yet here alone can he read the thing it self."[14]

Like most sectarians, Quakers demanded a new spiritual rigor, locating this heightened responsibility in the new covenant. While Jesus declared that he did not come to destroy the law and the prophets,[15] he introduced a distinction between the law of Moses, which said, for example, "Thou shalt not kill," and the law of the new covenant, which said "Thou shalt not be angry." He asserted the newness of his requirements when he explained, in words of special importance for the peace testimony,

[y]e have heard that it hath been said,
An eye for an eye,
and a tooth for a tooth:
But I say unto you,
That ye *resist not evil:*
but whosoever shall smite thee
on thy right cheek,
turn to him the other also.

. . .

Ye have heard that it hath been said,
Thou shalt love thy neighbour,
and hate thine enemy.
But I say unto you,
Love your enemies,
bless them that curse you,
do good to them that hate you,
and pray for them
which despitefully use you. . . .

. . .

Be ye therefore perfect,
even as your Father which is in heaven
is perfect.[16]

Quakers took seriously such extraordinarily difficult instructions from Jesus. They did not regard his admonitions as vague ideals but rather as moral commands under which they were to redirect their lives. They recognized in these commands the shout of a king[17] and saw that to obey them would necessitate a revolution in human moral character, one that could not be accomplished without the help of God. They were summoned into the Kingdom of God on earth.

And what of the Kingdom of God, where God's way triumphs? How might the Quaker live within this Kingdom into which she had been admitted while still living on earth, still only imperfectly transformed, still young in the faith? How might she accomplish a revolution in moral character, where her motives and feelings, too, must conform to God's requirements? Quakers felt themselves to have access to God and thus to his help. "Oh! His Replennishing Grace makes Us Strong," the Women's Meeting of Rhode Island gloried.[18] Added to beliefs about the Light, scripture, and the evil of man, the idea of access to God's strength was a fourth aspect of Quaker belief particularly relevent to the development of peace principles. Quakers believed that when a person had truly repented of the evil within and turned to God consistently to discern his will, that God would empower him to conquer his sin on this earth, to "the measure" or degree to which he had as yet discovered and acknowledged it. "And as he comes into puritie," wrote James Nayler, a person is changed "from glory to glory" into the image of God, "and he stands in the will of God improving that [which] he hath freely received of God . . . from grace to grace, from faith to faith, til he come . . . unto a perfect man, unto the measure of the stature of the fulness of Christ."[19] So did Jesus grow into the Christ. As a person "grew" in discernment, God would increase the measure of strength he gave in order to overcome sin, in a process that could lead to perfection in this life even "as your Father which is in heaven is perfect."[20] Redemption was not a promise to be fulfilled in the uncertain time after death.[21] "Salvation is wrought out here . . . for there is no working of it out hereafter."[22]

Edward Perry, a Quaker leader of Sandwich in Plymouth Colony, was one who interpreted "perfect" to mean utterly without sin: he contrasted "those that remain in their Sins, under a false belief that there is no other Estate attainable, while on this side the Grave" and those who "know Sin and Death slain in our mortal Bodies, and its Body put off."[23] He described his first encounter with the Quakers' testimony that obedience to Jesus "would lead out of Sin and save from Sin." "This is the thing which my Soul longed for," he wrote joyfully; it had been a thing he looked for outside himself, "and if this be so near unto me as within me, then am I a happy Man."[24] "Happiness" seems a pallid word to describe the exultation of believing that one might conquer sin in this life, even to become perfect while on earth. The sense of certainty, the sense of empowerment, the conviction that one could behave in a god-like manner, would determine the confidence with which one might approach even the most strenuous of demands outlined in Jesus' new covenant. When a Rhode Island Quaker unhesitatingly signed her name "Anne

Potter Whoe saith That the Time Is Now that Iniquity shall come to an End," her sense of boundless capacity is palpable.[25]

It had been, and continues to be, the common assumption that human nature itself is incompatible with the realization of the Christian ideals of the gospel message, prior to the Second Coming of Christ. But for Quakers, the millenium was within, attainable immediately by all people. They took seriously, then, the gospel requirements of pacifism and perfection in this life on earth, requirements that others were sometimes able to glide over as mere ideals far out of reach in a Kingdom of God to be established at some remote future time. Quakers were unwilling to be bound by the comfortable excuse that truly righteous behavior was, at last, inconsistent with human nature. Instead they were sure that they might transcend their human limitations with God's power. While personal and public experiences had made Quakers acutely aware of human sin and the darkness within, protecting them from an easy, sentimental naivete,[26] they did not become fixated on the inevitability of human depravity. Isaac Penington best expressed this carefully considered optimism: "When the principle of God, which lies hid in the hearts of men . . . shall be raised and come into dominion; righteousness, peace, and good-will shall spring up as naturally among men, as wars, strifes, divisions . . . now do."[27] This assumption that the nature of man was as potentially compatible with peace and goodwill as it was with aggression and violence was an assumption crucial to Quaker pacifism.

Yet in the World

A strong sense of the sources of his own empowerment affected a Quaker's assessment of the capacities of others to carry out the precepts of Jesus. If to the Quaker it seemed that he himself had been given extraordinary capacity to conquer earthly sin when he submitted to the Light within, the opposite was also true. To the Quaker it seemed that those who did not acknowledge their dependency on and capacity to consult the Light within for present-day revelation, and were instead hoping through faith or deeds to achieve a measure of redemption in a subsequent life, were helpless to accomplish the perfection demanded by Christ in this life. As humans, how could they hope not only to refrain from harming the bodies of their enemies, for example, but also remove the passion of hatred itself from their very hearts? Surely this was too much to expect of mortals, unaided by God. Quakers, then, while expecting much of themselves, could not expect much of their neighbors who were yet "in the world."

The Quaker hegemonic designs on a monopoly of moral authority were particularly odious to any regime that defined itself as the keeper of the cause of the Lord. To understand the resentment and fear—and awe and admiration—the potency of moral authority invoked in others, one need only visualize the lone Chinese student in 1989 Beijing, facing down an immense tank, which in the world's imagination stood helpless and puzzled before him. His eventual martyrdom, like others, has entered the common memory to lodge as a reproach and an inspiration, transmuting defeat into triumph. So Quaker ideas about continuing revelation, human nature, perfection, and the merging of spirit and the human soul not only challenged contemporary religious beliefs but also threatened political order, in a time when few were comfortable with a distinction between the two spheres. Moreover, Quakers had assumptions about worldly institutions as well, and their interactions with these institutions helped to codify and clarify belief itself. It is somewhat artificial to distinguish between realms of spiritual assumptions or beliefs, "worldly" assumptions and beliefs, and "worldly" historical experience, since they influence each other within time. For example, Quaker spiritual ideas conferred a certain power on Quakers within their own minds, a power that was acted out within society and at times was intimidating to others. When John Newland of Sandwich, in Plymouth Colony, was reported to have announced that "[I am] as holy as God is holy, and as perfect as God is perfect," the political authorities rightly might have seen such an individual as somehow unreachable, beyond punishment; such a person was mysteriously less vulnerable to sanctions imposed by earthly authority—and earthly authority rested on sanctions.[28] The sense of empowerment rendered Quakers psychologically less accessible to ordinary political controls. Their willingness to suffer, while suggesting superior moral worth, diminished political control; to be willingly vulnerable is to be invincible, the spirit withstanding and transcending force and violence. Their beliefs about persecution and suffering enhanced this spiritual strength. Nevertheless, it is useful to distill out from their religious worldview their reactions to institutions and events; to examine separately Quaker attitudes toward government and the state, the protection of God, persecution, and suffering so pertinent to Quaker beliefs about war, fighting, and carnal weapons.

Conversations with the World: Magistrate, Protection, Persecution, Suffering

The Magistrate

The Quaker view of government and Quaker interaction with the state were to help configure Quaker beliefs and practice concerning the use of violence, since governments by definition remain the ultimate repository of the use of violence in society, regulating, at least theoretically, the degree of violence permissible between members of the society both privately and publicly. Quaker attitudes concerning the source of governmental authority, the use of force both internally and externally, the duty of the Christian magistrate or office holder, the limits of authority, the duty of the Quaker citizen, and the service of Quakers in government were all relevant to the development of Quaker peace principles.

Quaker assumptions about the nature of earthly government and the earthly state were not anarchic. Quakers recognized that government was necessary and that its proper end was to further the righteousness of man. William Dewsbury, for instance, wrote that God spoke through him to Oliver Cromwell: "I chused thee out of the nations of the earth, to make knowne my power in thee."[29] The significant words "I chused," which Dewsbury attributed to God, were not reserved only for a Cromwell, a man outwardly committed to a godly society. Like other seventeenth-century Christians, Quakers believed that God appointed and installed all public officials, whom they commonly termed magistrates, however imperfect they might be, to further the righteousness of man and that God entrusted them with powers to accomplish their task.[30] George Bishop was typical in turning to Romans 13:1-5 for authority: "The Powers that be are ordained of God" was an oft-cited biblical text.[31] The powers and duties fell into two categories: the power and duty to control evil and the power and duty to reward good. Again and again in describing the role of the magistrate, Quakers used the biblical words "to be a terror to evil-doers, and a praise to them who do well."[32] Quakers themselves owed their "free and willing subjection in the things of this world . . . and our worke is not to weaken, but to strengthen the hand of the Magistrate."[33]

The implications of believing in the godly sponsorship of government were a source of complications for Quakers. Because government was not an outgrowth of man's reason and will or a social contract but was in a sense a contract with God, obedience to government took on enhanced importance.[34] Yet some of government's duties might apparently clash with some of Jesus' admonitions, especially those involving violence. Might the use of force and its implied violence in the service of regulating earthly society be taken to supersede other scriptural principles, such as the assertion that "all they that take the sword shall perish with the sword"?[35] Government itself, in its responsibilities to control evildoers, is virtually inseparable from the use of force. While force does not necessitate violence, the two are frequently partners. If force—the effort to persuade by physical means—is unsuccessful, then violence, the effort to impose hurt, will be enlisted to preserve power. Quakers, by associating the magistrate with a divine mandate and a divine appointment, recognized the validity of using force and, by extension, violence. That is, Quakers acknowledged the legitimacy of a police function to regulate society, as well as laws to direct the police function. Yet when one has acknowledged the legitimate power of the magistrate to use force, which may include violence, to control evil within the society—that is, when one has legitimized a police function—one has by no means eliminated difficult questions of authority and inconsistency. Aside from the obvious difficulty of agreeing about what constitutes evil and therefore about the proper reach of law, the scope and nature of the force and violence allowed to the magistrate is at issue. Does the maintenance of a defensive army fall within the definition of the police function of the state? Do preemptive strikes against a neighbor constitute police action? If the magistrate was a Quaker, as he would be during King Philip's War in Rhode Island in 1675, which of his religious obligations would receive priority: the obligation to shun the use of weapons, the obligation to rely only on the protection of God, or the obligation, as a magistrate chosen by God, to be a terror to evildoers? These difficult questions complicated and changed Quaker attitudes toward government, under the force of historical circumstance, even while their belief in God's ordaining the magistrate remained unchanged.

In the early enthusiastic days of Quakerism, Quaker eschatology sustained the hope for the imminent Kingdom of God on earth, through the universal and prompt recognition of the possibilities inherent in the Light within, and to some Quakers there seemed little need to spend energy focusing on an "interim ethic" to regulate human interactions on earth until the Second Coming. To such believers, worldly institutions such as government were of limited interest. After all, Quakers believed that the apocalypse was presently available, internally and individually available through the revelation of the Light. An apocalypse for the world at large awaited only the universal acknowledgment of this truth. In a sense, then, the timing of the apocalypse was dependent on human beings, its beneficiaries. In the 1650s context of a "Godly Commonwealth," it was possible to sustain theocratic hopes, hopes that God would immediately direct England's government.[36] God's government being imminent, the details and difficulties of earthly government seemed beyond the point to some Quakers, except as they might interfere with the understanding of the Light. Since the Quaker way was transforming, for themselves, and as a model for their opponents, as more people turned to the Truth, there would be less need for law itself: the righteousness they demonstrated in their lives would remove the very occasion for law. "'If they can Govern themselves, they have no need of your Government,'" a king's commissioner sympathetic to Quakers reassured an anxious Roger Williams of Rhode Island.[37] When coercion was no longer necessary, as righteousness prevailed, government would essentially disappear.

During the Commonwealth and Protectorate, other Quakers saw government as a potential ally in bringing about the Kingdom of God on earth. Hence Quakers were fervent about reform in the political, social, and economic spheres, for reform might bring a more just, less oppressive society. Such social utopianism held out a vision for a society that was not only good in itself but would ameliorate the strains that encouraged violence and so would create a more congenial environment for the peace principles. As the hope for this society-wide apocalypse waned, especially with the demise of the Cromwellian "Godly Commonwealth," Quakers were forced to pay more attention to the problem of earthly government, not solely because of its impact on their own religious opportunities but also in the matter of its righteousness "in the interim," before the realization of the Kingdom. As Quaker expectations of universal acceptance of the Light were disappointed, some began to speak of two standards of behavior—one for individual Quakers, one for those other Christians and their institutions still "in the world." For Quakers, it was the *universal acknowledgement* of the reality of Jesus' return that had been delayed, not Jesus' return itself. For themselves, then, there could be no justification for a less rigorous standard of Quaker behavior as citizens within civil society while awaiting the universal obedience to the Light. On the contrary, "God's people" were immediately responsible for acting according to the standards of the Kingdom of God.

Most other Christians believed that while it was important to strive for righteous earthly government, even Christians would be capable only of a lower standard of righteous behavior before the Second Coming; worldly rules and worldly institutions, under an interim ethic, would provide appropriate structure while awaiting the "parousia"—Christ's return. After the Second Coming, the rigor of Jesus' requirements would be fulfilled. Quaker Robert Barclay echoed this outlook in his *Apology* of 1678: there were those who called themselves Christians but were not yet "in the patient suffering spirit"; as people who were yet "in the mixture," they were not yet capable of the true rigors of Christianity. In regard to following Jesus' peace principle, for example, Barclay thought that magistrates "in the mixture" could be excused from its full demands: it was reasonable to expect that they "can not be undefending themselves, untill they attain that perfection. . . . [W]e shall not say, that warr, undertaken upon a just occasion, is altogether unlawfull to them." Barclay and others thus apologized for an interim ethic for non-Quaker Christian magistrates while maintaining that true Christianity was utterly incompatible with war.[38]

With the return of King Charles II, Quaker disenchantment with the possibilities of government grew in England. Indeed, by 1681, London Meeting minutes described the harm that might come from "unprofitable talking of Newes in Coffeehouses Tavernes Clubs & Alehouses . . . of matters Relating to the Governmt." All those professing "Truth," the advice continued, must be careful not to use "those reflecting disgustfull Termes of Distinction of [Whigg and Tory] . . . tending to provoke [one] Neighbour against another."[39] Quaker definitions of boldness, too, were mutating. Whereas the expression of "discontented spirits" had formerly been a Quaker duty in confronting authority, by 1672 a London epistle warned Quaker brethren to "stop all busy, discontented spirits . . . from reflecting upon and meddling with the powers . . . and all fruitless discourses of that tendency." Instead, mere peaceable and innocent living would constitute "true boldness and confidence."[40] In some of the colonies, on the other hand, Quakers still saw government as an instrument to further their own purposes and "meddled" with energy.

One Quaker belief about government did not change through the years: God endowed government with legitimacy but limited its sphere. While Quakers saw government, along with all other aspects of society, as expressive of religious meaning, the magistrate was only to deal with earthly, "natural" transgressions; God's preserve was that of spiritual transgressions. Religion was exempt from government by its nature, which was peace and love. "Caesar" could not make, nor give, faith; nor might he punish for spiritual error, for the ordering of the Church was God's.[41] Therefore Quakers agreed implicitly to act within the secular society according to its rules but reserved the right to disobey any regulation of religious belief or anything directly contrary to their religious consciences—and Quakers themselves would decide if government had intruded into these areas. "Christ never leads his people to disobey Just Laws, but to fulfil them (and Unjust Laws are to be obeyed at no times)," wrote Fox.[42] Instead, Quakers would patiently suffer the consequences of disobedience. They would resist but would not resist with violence. When laws were in accordance with the law of God, Quakers owed active obedience to government; when laws were not grounded in the law of God, Quakers owed passive obedience to government. The Quaker definition of passive obedience was of course not obedience at all. Citing the scriptural admonition "'Resist not evil; but whosoever shall smite thee on thy right cheek, turn to him the other,'" as well as instruction from the Light within himself, William Rogers asserted that it was against the doctrine of Christ to resist. Rogers was using this reference in a figurative and political sense; Quakers would use the same verse, understood literally, to warn against physical resistance.[43]

In spite of the Quaker characterizations of government as essentially benign, with a mandate for godly morality, it is understandable that seventeenth-century governments would see the hedging about of their reach as intolerably challenging of their authority. When coupled with the provocative behavior of the early Quakers and the virulence of their rhetoric, it is no wonder that magistrates of all levels of government felt threatened—threatened in an absolute physical sense, not just in a figurative, theoretical sense. And Quakers' refusal to swear oaths only confirmed their fears. The magistrates thought Quakers might be plotting overthrow or rebellion, planning to usurp power by force of arms. It was because this fear was so pervasive that Quakers were forced to defend themselves and explain their basically supportive posture toward government again and again. Indeed, the need to defend themselves in order to forestall greater repression may have by itself helped to modulate the Quaker stance toward government. "We are not Enemies unto Government it self, as these our Accusers do charge us," Burrough insisted in 1660, "but it is our Principle . . . to be subject to whatsover Government is set up over us, either by doing or suffering." He denied that Quakers would plot or rebel; rather, they would "walk in meekness and humility towards all."[44]

Magistrates might be forgiven if they failed to discern meekness and humility in the provocative actions of Quakers consumed with their own morality. Quaker missionaries William Brend and John Copeland left Scituate, in Plymouth Colony, and were on their way to Rhode Island in 1657, when the Plymouth magistrates arrested them. The magistrates required them to promise that they would be out of Plymouth within forty-eight hours. Although this had been the missionaries' original intention before they were detained, they discovered scruples to do so once it was a government order. The bench not surprisingly construed this disobedience as "contemptuous perverseness."[45] Alice and Thomas Curwen were traveling missionaries in New England in 1675 when they learned of a newly imposed law in Massachusetts, under which anyone found at a Quaker meeting would be jailed. "Then it opened in us . . . That We must travail thither, and break in upon their new Law"; when they went to Boston and attended Quaker meeting, they found that the law had not yet been published, so meeting was disappointingly uneventful. The Curwens roamed about in the provinces of New Hampshire and Maine until the law had been published, when they hastened to Boston, attended meeting, and were arrested.[46] Interacting with government in such provocative ways was not merely perverse but expressed religious convictions, established religious identifications, and revealed religious needs.

The First Publishers of Truth did not discount the possibility that Quakers themselves might be magistrates. A meeting of elders at Balby, Yorkshire, in 1656 advised "[t]hat if any be called to serve the Commonwealth . . . that with cheerfulness it be undertaken and in faithfulness discharged unto God, that therein patterns and examples in the thing that is righteous ye may be to those that are without."[47] Indeed, many Quakers continued in various offices, including the military, when their opposition to oaths did not interfere. After the Restoration, however, Quaker presence in office became untenable in England. Quaker disappearance from government did not imply a prior doctrinal opposition to the exercise of power. All Quakers did not feel compromised by political power per se, although their rhetoric in some times and places suggested so. On the contrary, many Quakers seemed fascinated with power, especially when it was susceptible to their influence or participation, and they showed a practical awareness of its usefulness in a worldly sense. Quakers actively used the legal system to protect their members and used political intrigue and political petitioning to further their causes.[48] Quakers had long had a lively agenda for reforming law and social relationships. Gerard Roberts and nineteen others, for instance, wrote to the Protector of "the great & heavy oppressions" of a legal system with "long delayes in Courts" and "great fees of officers," too often raising many to be "Excessively rich, out of the ruines of the poor" and bringing "an odium upon the law it selfe."[49] Within the movement, there was room both for the Quaker who justified his political interest by concentrating on God's appointment of magistrates and their role as punishers of evildoers and for the Quaker who was troubled by the notion that the duties of magistrates required actions apparently incompatible with other spiritual mandates. The idea of Quakers in government created a tension between the desire to remain pure (and thus to an extent irrelevant) and a desire to work for good (and therefore necessarily to compromise with "the world.") Unlike many Anabaptists, who saw government as irredeemably evil, most Quakers chose to stay "in the world." George Fox's changeability exemplified the ambivalence of their position. "Concern your Selves as little as may be with outward Government," he chastised Maryland Quakers who had written to Lord Baltimore. "It will be no ways Wisdom in Friends to concern themselves with him or his business."[50] Three years later he reminded Quakers, "therefore our Prayers be to him not to take us out of the World."[51] When Quaker power became a reality, Fox's enthusiasm overcame his hesitations.[52] Others sought a more retired "habitation":

> Peace wayward Soule lett not these various Stormes
> wch hourly fill the World with fresh alarms
> Invade thy peas nor Discompose that Rest
> wch thou mayst keep untoucht within thy brest
> Amidst those whirlwinds if thou keep but free
> The Intercourse betwixt thy God & thee.[53]

On the other hand, there was seldom ambivalence among non-Quakers: the prospect of Quaker magistrates was abhorrent. Having observed the early Quakers' confrontational style, Thomas Underhill voiced non-Quaker fears in *Hell Broke Loose,* predicting that should Quakers obtain civil power, "what Persecutors they would be, may be easily concluded from the sight of their teeth before hand."[54]

God's Protection: "So in the Lord's Power I Turned Them All"

From the earliest days, some Quakers renounced the use of violence. A constellation of beliefs fortified this choice; among them was the belief in the ultimate protection of God. In 1659, missionary John Taylor, aged twenty-two, diverted the ship on which he was a passenger from its intended route in the West Indies, a route later found to be infested with buccaneers, because "the Lord showed me there was great danger . . . so in the Lord's Power I turned them all."[55] Such extraordinary confidence was derived from the belief that once a person gave up his life to following the will of God, having acknowledged his own frailty, then he would truly become a child of God. Since he was doing God's bidding, God was responsible for his safety; God would give him strength. God was the only true protection—as long as Quakers trusted in him instead of the "fleshly arm." If they

THE PEACE TESTIMONY

failed to trust that God would take care of them, then this protection would be withdrawn.

Because Quaker beliefs and activities were provocative, they drew reprisals and violence to themselves. Experiencing violence, most chose not to retaliate, on the basis of scriptural admonitions such as "resist not evil," and "turn the other cheek." The conviction that God would protect them explains the fortitude and perseverance of the early Quakers, who often seemed undaunted at abuse directed toward them, returning again and again to challenge the forces arrayed against them. William Dewsbury, for example, described an occasion in York, when Quakers had been meeting for about two hours. The soldiers came "wth ther Muskitts and swards; and charged us to desparce." The Quakers did not obey but "dwelt in the power of god; wch struck to the hart." The soldiers called for their superior officers and reinforcements; they tried once again to break up the meeting. "Littel was said to them: god keept frinds in his power: & they Could Not do any thing that tim: but wthdrew again." Next, the soldiers "was sufered to lay hands [on] us and put us forth." As they were evicted one by one, the Quakers kept their meeting in the street; the Quakers apparently were uncooperative, for the eviction took about an hour. Finally, "the soulger wearied themselves, and went away." It is clear from this account, that no matter what happened, the Quakers felt that God was on their side and was directing events. In their view, when the soldiers were discouraged and withdrew, it was because of God's power within the Quakers; when the soldiers used force, it was because God had suffered them to do so.[56] The reassurance from these beliefs comes partly from the sense that there is a purpose to what happens to a person, if he has dedicated his life to God.

The early Quaker concept of God's protection should not be confused with a later Quaker notion, more humanitarian in nature, that, when a Quaker escaped disaster, gave credit to the positive impulse within another human being, to "that of God" speaking within another. William Caton's vocabulary, belonging to the earlier concept, illustrates the subtle difference. When Caton and other Quakers were released from a Haarlem prison, he commented that "thereby the handes of envyous men are as it were bound up, that they in their malicious wills cannot summons him as they have done." When men behaved well, Caton gave "credit" to God, for binding their arms. He did not emphasize God doing good within them but rather emphasized God preventing their badness.[57]

A less attractive side of the Quaker sense of themselves as an especially protected group—albeit a group open to anyone—was the attention they paid to the misfortunes of their persecutors. "What signal judgements have come upon persecutors?" asked early Quakers in a list of queries designed to record the condition of the various meetings. (By 1701 this kind of query had disappeared.) Quakers felt not only that God would protect them but that he would carry out congruent vengeance against those who opposed them. Quakers believed that the character of the misfortune befalling their persecutors was not merely coincidental; they carefully noted how a particular punishment seemed appropriate for a particular form of persecution. Fox himself wrote a whole treatise containing such examples, his "Book of Examples," never published but still available in 1694.[58] God's judgment fell upon Major-General Adderton (Atherton) of Massachusetts, wrote William Sewel, for scoffing at the hanged body of Quaker martyr Mary Dyer. *At the very place* where whipped Quakers were commonly loosed from the cart dragging them along, Atherton's horse was startled by a cow, and threw him, "so violently, that he died, his eyes being started out of his head, his brains out of his nose, his tongue out of his mouth, and his blood out of his ears."[59] Quaker accounts of God's revenge were not always free of malice but did reinforce their sense of being protected.

Persecution: "Blood-furrows on My Back"

Quakers excited opposition, and opposition resulted in responses that Quakers interpreted as religious persecution.[60] Persecution, for Quakers, was not just an external trial, sometimes a fatal trial, to which they were incidentally subject, but became incorporated into the movement itself, affecting Quaker attitudes, beliefs, and behavior. For Quakers, persecution had a specific meaning, and they made a virtue out of necessity by using persecution directed toward them for their own purposes. Because persecution spawned much of Quaker practice and belief about violence, the meaning of persecution and its consequences are of particular relevance to this study. Quakers were forced to decide how to react to persecution— whether violence was ever an appropriate response—and this first necessary decision led to a broader consideration of violence in other contexts.

Persecution of seventeenth-century religious sects took many forms: violent physical attack and injury, physical prevention of assembly, financial impositions, political disbarment, legal harassment, arrest and imprisonment, and other, more subtle, discouragement of belief and practice. Dreadful prison conditions assured that persecution was not a temporary inconvenience but often as dangerous as war itself. Quakers met all of these forms of persecution, at the hands of every segment of society. The clergy saw the Quakers as heretics, blasphemers, and religious competitors; Quaker preaching against tithes was only the final insult among many. Because of the common Christian heritage of persecution and suffering, Quakers thought that it should be obvious to every Christian that persecution was not effective as a means of religious persuasion. For Quakers, faith could come only from experiencing a relationship with God, a relationship that made possible and necessitated a profound "soul" transformation, which would then bear fruit in how one lived one's life. The assumption that even the most rigorous of religious forms could not fulfill God's mandate for the righteous life, without this soul transformation, confirmed the belief that any kind of force used to persuade someone else in matters of religion was useless. Transformation could not be accomplished through intimidation, deterrence, pressures to conform, threats of bodily harm, and other forms of force. When Quakers saw their Christian opponents using these methods in matters of religion, they not only deemed the methods to be of no utility but also saw such pressure as antithetical to the gospel of Jesus. Their outrage at persecutors grew in part from a sense of religious betrayal, not merely religious disagreement.

Government and judicial officials saw Quakers as seditious, potentially violent, and disorderly. Quaker behavior in the early days of the movement, during the Interregnum, often appeared defiant toward local governments and disrespectful, at a minimum, of the central government as well. Governments prosecuted Quakers under such laws as vagrancy laws, sedition laws, tithe laws, militia laws, blasphemy laws, and conventicle laws, those laws regulating religious assembly.[61] In turn, Quakers were able to justify most of their offensive behavior because they saw themselves acting out of the spirit of God and within the prescribed boundaries of religious matters. Some magistrates took full advantage of the controversy over Quakers as a source of money and goods, fining them and distraining their goods under the mask of law. Administering the oath to Quakers, knowing that they obeyed Jesus' injunction to "Swear not at all," served as the excuse to fine and imprison Quakers for a variety of offenses; it served as well for the sentence of *praemunire*. In Bristol, after Monmouth's Rebellion of 1685, the common council found it expedient to elect Quakers to the council, administer the oath of allegiance to them, and, when they refused to take the oath, fine them as much as two hundred pounds each. Thus were Quakers forced to pay for the defense of the city.[62]

Quakers stood up to political persecution. After the Restoration of King Charles II in 1660, Parliament passed a series of measures antithetical to Quakers, exposing them to a variety of legal prosecutions: the Corporation Act of 1661, mandating oaths and prohibiting "tumultuous petitioning,"[63] the Quaker Act of 1662, against meetings; and the Conventicle Acts of 1664 and 1670, prohibiting attendance at any other religious rite than that of the Church of England. Other groups subject to these measures sought to hide their activities to avoid punishment. But the Quaker challenge was deliberate, and their purpose reached beyond themselves, so they reacted by holding meetings in full view and in direct opposition to law. It was with a hint of triumph that Quakers noted: "Fd [friends] are bold. But the Independents meet in woods & privat places."[64] This behavior was mystifying to non-Quakers. When seventy Quakers were taken to Newgate Prison in August 1664, Samuel Pepys observed: "While we were talking, came by several poor creatures, carried by Constables for being at a conventicle. They go like lambs, without any resistance. I would to God they would either conform, or be more wise and not be ketched."[65] Quakers chose not to conceal their activities in order to express a view about their relationship to worldly government: that "he who submits to the punishment doth . . . really fullfil the Law."[66] Submitting without resistance constituted obedience to the state, even if they had violated a particular ungodly law.

Ordinary townspeople saw Quakers as libertines, divisive, and intrusive upon local habits and standards; the "better sort" saw them as undermining the system of deference so supportive of their rank.[67] Ordinary people enriched themselves by acting as informers. Persecutors might be motivated by their sense that they, too, were carrying on the work of the Lord and were cleansing their society lest they themselves be infected with contagion. "These populous places . . . have been miserably perplexed and much Dissetled by that unruly Sort of people called Quakers," complained a petition of 1659, "whose principles are to Overturn, Overturn, Overturn Magistracy, Ministry, Ordinances, all that which good men would keep up by their prayers."[68] And some, no doubt, were acting out anger or viciousness for their own peculiar pleasures under sanction of the community.

In common with other religious sects with millenial beliefs, the Quakers in the early stages of the movement prophesied in noticably confrontational rhetoric—a style that provoked persecution. Quaker prisoner John Wallis wrote to the minister he had deprived of tithes, "What now proud prelat; the Smoake of yor. torment is gonn upp; you have pouzened and bheated the People . . . Therefore you shall have worme-wood mingled with Gall to drinke, for vengance is mine saith the Lord."[69] Challenging accepted mores in multiple ways, many of them wasted no words in softening their message. "Come downe, come downe, thou painted beast, come downe," Mary Fisher interrupted while a minister was preaching in York. "Thou are but an hireling, and deludest the people with thy lyes."[70] Their method was nonviolent physically but far from timid or polite. Elizabeth Hooton, soon to carry the Quaker message to New England, was capable of commanding an assize judge, "Come downe, thou blynde beast."[71]

Quakers were provocative, unmovable, and anything but humble "in the world." While they were victims in a sense, they acted with the assurance of conquerors. "Have ye not plowed blood-furrows on my back for that already?" Edward Wharton challenged the Massachusetts Court.[72] In return, persecutors frequently punished in symbolic ways, coupling the violence of physical abuse to degradation and humiliation in an effort to associate Quakers with evil itself. Quaker accounts of their "sufferings" record being subject to abuses such as "daubing" with dirt and excrement, the grinding of their faces into the dirt, and being beaten with the Bible until they were bleeding.[73]

Suffering: "With Them Who Lived in Dens"

Although persecution thwarted Quaker goals and threatened their bodies, it also could be persuasively integrated with Christian belief. Because Jesus was persecuted, indeed because he was martyred, when any Christian suffered like treatment, he or she emulated Jesus' experience and participated with him in the redemptive aspects of persecution and martyrdom. ("We have suffered by them . . . being marked for the sheep of Christ, and bearing in our bodies the marks of the Lord Jesus."[74]) And there were important practical benefits from being a victim. Jesus, his apostles, and the disciples of the pure early church had all suffered, had all been persecuted for their beliefs. Suffering was valued in the Gospels and was inherent in Christianity from the beginning. Long before his own death, Jesus honored sufferers as people of increased capacity for spirituality. The poor, the despised, were not crippled by the distractions of earthly comfort and so potentially could move closer to God. Mary Magdalene, the leper, the "meek," the "poor in spirit" were "blessed" in a way the powerful persecutor could never be. Thus it was with a certain pride that William Bayly described his Quaker brethren as "his poore despised suffering harmless people; who waite in patience & long suffering upon god."[75] Through suffering, the Christian demonstrated humble dedication to God, a posture of love toward others, the strength of her confidence in God's protection and ultimate justice, her willingness to share in Jesus' ultimate sacrifice. "I have fellowship therein with them who lived in dens and desolate places in the earth, who through death obtained this resurrection and eternal holy life," wrote James Nayler.[76] To be persecuted and to suffer, then, were opportunities to serve God in another way; Jesus' suffering lent a holy significance to sacrifice and pain. The very word "persecution" implied that coercion was being applied to religious belief. It implied, too, a measure of injustice. The word admitted a sense of victimization, of martyrdom, and imputed righteousness. All of these implications served Quaker purposes.

As time passed, the usefulness of being seen as the victim was overwhelmed by disadvantages. The sect settled down into an acceptance that the millenarian promise had been deferred; and as Quakers contemplated the decimation of their leadership in harsh prison cells, and the discouragement that persecution left in its wake, they began to accept collective discipline and more organizational structure. By 1683, for example, the meeting of London's Quaker elders sent "advices" for good order to the London and Middlesex Quarterly Meeting "[t]hat all friends . . . keep in the peaceable spirit of Christ Jesus, And not enter into words of provocation Strife or contention with the persecutors, or others; to stirr up fury or strengthen the spirit of enmity in them."[77] Quakers realized that even without their acting provocatively and prophetically, they "stirred up fury" enough to injure their peaceful religious practice. Quakers, so often accused of being "ranters" in their earlier years, began to confer that label on to others who used the same provocative and theatrical methods they themselves had employed. In 1662, "with her face made black, and her hair down with blood poured in it, which run down upon her sackcloth," a Quaker woman had poured blood upon the alter in St. Paul's, London.[78] By 1675, when Quaker missionary William Edmundson encountered some Quakers in New Jersey carrying out similar demonstrations, he saw them as "tainted with the Ranting Spirit." Among them was Edward Tares, who came into meeting "with his Face black'd . . . also sung and danc'd, and came to me . . . and call'd me Old rotten Priest, saying, I had lost the Power of God." Edmundson told him he was mad. "He said, I lyed, for he was moved of the Lord, to come in that manner to reprove me."[79] Although sometimes troublesome, by the turn of the century such Quakers had been successfully tamed or disowned.

To Temper Enthusiasm

While in the early, heady days of the movement, the idea of individual revelation and the promise of an imminent apocalypse had given Quakers a somewhat careless sense of power and licensed their confrontational style, later Quakers grew more cautious and focused more on collective human relationships, valuing reconciliation and seeking consensus within the group. The early movement stressed the importance of the individual experience of God, which, although theoretically leading to one Truth, in reality encouraged individualism under a diffuse leadership. In many respects, early Quaker belief encompassed several characteristic themes of many cults or sects: a sense of the exclusive access to truth, a vision of absolute goodness and absolute badness, charismatic qualities of the leadership, millenarianism, and the sense of direct contact with God. Early Quaker behavior included common qualities of new religious movements as well: prophetic, provocative style; zealousness; and mystery.[80] As cults or sects mature, these themes and qualities usually drop out or are transmuted into new forms. As the Quaker movement matured and became organized into a sect, Quakers became more appreciative of the fact that religious revelation could be fostered by a collective search for truth and must be tested by that search. They began to redirect initial fervor into a more disciplined codification. But even as Quakerism became more institutionalized, and early fanaticism mellowed, it departed from the typical pattern. Quakers never abandoned the respect accorded to private inspiration, because the immediate revelation of God's will was the core insight itself. The possibility that each individual had access to Truth potentially inhibited the power of even the most admired leader and so saved them from one of the perils of cults. Similarly, the nature of Quaker authority—the inner Light, or direct and ongoing revelation—unlike a fixed authority, such as a text, discouraged the rigidity that often comes with the control of enthusiasm. The idea of the inner Light preserved a chance for continual revitalization.

"Our Ancient Testimony"

Even though Quakers located themselves firmly within the Christian orbit, seeking to retrieve the purity of the early church, and even though many elements of their belief were individually characteristic of other Christian sectaries, idiosyncratic interpretations and emphases combined with experience to define a distinct religious community. Some of these basic assumptions, idiosyncratic interpretations, and emphases received expression in formulations that the Quakers called testimonies.

Testimonies were not core beliefs, stated in creedal form with ruling force, but were, rather, principles derived from core beliefs. The Quakers often justified these statements of principle with the phrase "this has been our ancient testimony since we were a people," even when the movement was only a few years old. They reached for a nascent tradition to impute authority to these testimonies. Some of the early testimonies were the refusal to swear oaths, the use of "plain" language ("thee" instead of "you") for all people, straightforward business dealings, the eschewal of signs of deference such as "bowing and scraping," maintaining simplicity of speech and attire, and refusal to pay tithes.

Among the testimonies was a collection of ideas about the use of weapons and violence, an ongoing inquiry into the implications of gospel principles of peace. The peace testimony, as this collection of ideas came to be known in later Quaker history, grew from core beliefs about the relationship of God and the human being, from sensitivity to the "spirit" underlying the gospel, from the experiences of early Quakers, and from threat, opportunity, and disappointment. The peace testimony came from a variety of writings and speakings; one of the first collective expressions of the testimony was "A Declaration from the Harmles & Innocent People of God" of 1660—from Fox and others, who proclaimed, "this is our testimony to the whole world."[81] Although the foundation of the peace testimony would change through time, as would Quaker practice in regard to peace, the earliest Quaker beliefs, practices, and experiences gave rise to the words of the testimony, which would not change. The vocabulary, persisting even to the present time, includes such seventeenth-century constructions as "I lived in the virtue of that life and power that took away the occasion of all wars"; and "all wars and fightings with carnal weapons we do deny."[82] The New York Yearly Meeting "Book of Discipline" of 1974, for example, queries, "Do we 'live in the virtue of that life and power which takes away the occasion of all wars'?" and directly quotes the Declaration of 1660, "We utterly deny all outward wars," under the chapter heading "Peace and Civic Responsibility."[83] The peace testimony, especially, so unusual, so distinctive, so defining of Quakers, was but poorly defined itself. Its inherent complexity reflects the infinite variety of violence and echoes the complexity of Quaker belief.

The Whisper of the Soul

Quakers, contrary to common assumptions, did not separate themselves from others only when they "institutionalized." From the beginning, they separated themselves, in one sense, by virtue of the substance of their belief. Their initial withdrawal was not in order to avoid the "taint" of the world; this kind of sectarian separation would come later. Rather, the earliest Quakers saw themselves as united with God in the Kingdom, totally beyond the comprehension of those in the world. "The world cannot see or touch," wrote Penington.[84] The Kingdom of God for Quakers "is come," (and is also at the same time "coming," for those who have not yet turned to the Light). The peculiar and characteristic Quaker phrase "is come" (or "was come") was an expression of Quaker belief in the present and ongoing revelation of Christ.[85] "The presence of the Kingdom validates every moment of time," Richard K. Ullmann has written; the presence of the Kingdom represents God's transcendent reaching into time for his people.[86] For the Quaker in the Kingdom, then, every detail of daily existence had ultimate importance. One detail was *primus inter pares*: purity of heart. It was not enough to be righteous in behavior; one must be pure in heart as well.

Because purity of heart and feelings were crucial to Quakers, they were reluctant to prescribe or proscribe behavior for others. In regard to the peace testimony and beliefs about nonviolence, especially, Quakers could not urge others along too fast. Of all the testimonies, the peace testimony was most resistant to dogma. Because of the mortal implications of nonviolence, perhaps, the peace testimony could not be taught, and could not be learned, as a doctrinal formula. The peace testimony could not be worn as comfortably as an unadorned bonnet; the sword could not be discarded as readily as obeisance. In Quaker belief, peaceful principles were not goals but were the logical consequences of righteousness. The principles were not ideas but were the fruits of the soul. Transforming love could be the only genuine motivation, and the only restraint, that mattered. One sought to love perfectly; it was not enough to act *as if* one loved perfectly. In this sense, truth could not be passed along, except for one element: the need to heed the voice within. Quakers had confidence in the teaching nature of the voice within. They were patient, recognizing the nature of revelation as a process, a deepening. They tolerated a person's faltering steps toward the good; believing that God bestowed increasing capacities as he required increasing responsibility. In practice, they tolerated, then, those who continued to work in the king's shipyards, although they might not sail aboard the fighting ships they built; or tolerated those who carried guns to their cornfields. Often this patience led to an apparent anomaly: Truth was "postponed" in the service of seeking an unfeigned conviction. When each Quaker sought to love others in accordance with the requirements of God, each individual was faced with a psychological task, formulated, of course, in religious terms. Quaker principles of peacefulness were also to be worked out in social and political realms. Peace principles were extraordinarily difficult to develop, then, because the peace testimony was the fruit of attitude, not thought. But principles based on love—agape—once achieved, were unassailable in a way not available to a construct of the mind. A motion of the heart, profoundly established, is less susceptible to challenge than an intellectual frame.

Quakers believed that, one by one, laboriously, each person must find his or her own peace principles. The Bishopric Monthly Meeting urged in 1659 that "no footsteps may be left for those that shall come after." Instead, all must be left to the Truth, "that none may look back at us, nor have an eye behind them, but that all may look forward, waiting in the Spirit for the revelation."[87] But footsteps were unavoidable, and those who came after heard the echoes of both shouts and whispers.

2

"A Killinge Instrument We May neither Forme, nor Beare"

THE PEACE TESTIMONY

*All bloody principles and practices, we, as to our own particulars, do utterly
deny, with all outward wars and strife and fighting with outward weapons,
for any end or under any pretence whatsoever. And this is our testimony to
the whole world.*

—Declaration of 1660

"The whole world" listened, some with disbelief, some with scoffing,
some with patronizing kindness, some with contempt, some with wonder, a few
with admiration. Charles II listened, and his brother James; Voltaire listened, and
Abraham Lincoln, and Gandhi, and Martin Luther King, Jr. Nicholas Easton listened and decided not to mount "the great gun" upon the seawall in Newport. And
Quakers during the Vietnam War read these words, perhaps stitched into a quaint
wallhanging in an otherwise drab meeting house, or mimeographed in materials
used for counseling would-be conscientious objectors on a seventh-day morning,
and knew what the words meant and what they required. At least, each thought he
understood their meaning, until, perhaps, he attended more closely to the words
and was forced to join the company of all those in the past, whom the words thrust
toward difficult distinctions and decisions. Over the centuries, through such words,
outsiders came to associate Quakers with opposition to the use of violence. To
Quakers themselves, for whom it was an "ancient testimony since we were a people," the principles of peace were not self-evident when the time came to act upon
those principles.

Early Quakerism was an experiential religion, in which the mode of interpretation and expression fell within the realm of feeling rather than thought. Quakers in
these early years deemed reason to be a "carnal" process, an earthly, flawed human
capacity which was inadequate to fathom the nature of God and his creations.
Quakers saw intellectual processes as little relevant to the essential relationship of
God and man. So assumptions about what God required of man took the form not
of elaborate theological propositions, but rather of simple statements, often taken
from scripture, which seemed to be self-evident. "Swear not at all," and "put up
thy Sword into the Sheath,"[1] were declarative admonitions whose very assertive

brevity implies that further elaboration would be superfluous. Yet there is a difference between them: one is simple, one is deceptively simple.

"Swear not at all," for example, is indeed easy to understand. Oaths are forbidden, since oaths imply that one is not accountable before God for the truth of all speech. While one might inquire into the justification for this order, the order itself is clear. The same is not true for "put up thy Sword into the Sheath," "all bloody principles and practices, we . . . do utterly deny," or other formulations of nonviolence, for these statements cloak a complexity difficult to untangle. The complexity proceeds from the nature of violence itself.

Violence, unlike the relatively simple ritual of oathtaking, is complicated. The character of violence is infinitely variable. People have made judgments about violence depending on many factors, such as its purpose, who was inflicting it, who initiated it, and how severe its consequences were relative to its gains. Simple Quaker pronouncements about carnal weapons and the peaceable kingdom conceal intricate dilemmas about how people regulate their responses to fellow creatures, how they monitor their family lives, and what their attitudes are toward government itself. Therefore, the implications of the peace testimony were developed through the daily decisions confronting particular Quakers or groups of Quakers undergoing specific challenges to their witness against fighting, the use of weapons, and war. Yet in the meantime Quakers struggled to anticipate God's requirements and to articulate to themselves and to "the world" the foundation and justification for their disavowal of violence and its instruments. In attempting to further our understanding of why they abjured "wars and strife and fighting with outward weapons," then, I will first consider the meaning and rationale behind the early peace testimony through the words and explanations of Quakers themselves. Then I will show as best I can, how individual Quakers in fact acted when confronted with potential or actual violence. The careful analysis of behavior can clarify, modify, or contradict what Quakers said were their responsibilities respecting violence. A slow accretion of such evidence, however imperfect or idiosyncratic, may lead to another way to understand the development of principles in their formative period. So this study, which began with words of belief in general, turns in this chapter to words of belief about peace and nonviolence—before beginning, in the next chapter, to examine the choices Quakers made.

Early History: "I Was Brought to Stand Still"

The historical context of the first Quakers in England was that of religious, political, and social ferment, contemporaneous with an unprecedented confluence of civil war, governmental transformation, religious innovation, and challenge to accepted social hierarchies.[2] The Quaker "movement" was at first only an amorphous association of unconnected individuals with compatible religious impulses and insights, and it was as individuals that the earliest Quakers had to decide how to react to violence. Not only were they not yet an organized movement, but the very content of their developing beliefs gave preeminence to the individual, dependent on personal revelation and personal transformation; when they first expressed themselves about their response to violence, then, they spoke only for themselves as individuals.

John Lilburne, former lieutenant-general in the Parliamentary army and Leveller leader, wrote, "I shall never hereafter be an user of a temporal sword more, nor a joiner with those who do."[3] William Smith warned, "cease from Warring and Fightings, and Killing one another, and let [all men] follow that pure Principle of Light . . . which will teach them to put up their Swords."[4] "Our sufferings . . . stand a witnes against all violence," Fox wrote to Cromwell.[5] Sometimes we glimpse the peace testimony obliquely: two Quakers arrived in Boston in 1656 with books that were confiscated and burnt—"a few harmless Books, who like their Masters can neither fight, strike, nor quarrel."[6] "And they that Dept [depart] from his light, & trust in the Arme of flesh shall be rebuked."[7] "I lived in the virtue of that life and power that took away the occasion of all wars."[8] And memorably, Quaker William Ames and others quietly asserted, "a killinge Instrument we may neither forme, nor beare."[9] What were the conditions that prompted such utterances? Some Quakers when convinced were soldiers or sailors; others faced militia service. Subject as many Quakers were from the first to physical abuse, it was often in this context that they individually worked out what their responses would be. When a crowd attacked one or two Quakers, Quaker options were limited: fighting back would be futile. But when Quakers and adversaries were more evenly matched, a Quaker had to decide whether or not to retaliate physically. Forbearance was then significant. Quaker accounts of such forbearance occasionally contain the basis on which it rested and serve to elucidate early Quaker thinking about "carnal weapons" and fighting.[10]

Captain Melledge, captain of the *Sapphire* during Cromwell's war with Spain, had captured a "Brist man of War" sailing under Captain George Cod. After some time, and after turning Quaker, Melledge was visiting Quakers in prison when he fell victim to an unfortunate coincidence: as he was passing along in the prison, "there was the Captain and others of the Brist man of War . . . who knew me." The captive Captain Cod attacked him in a rage, he said, "and beat and kicked me, so that some of my blood was spilt by it, and he . . . had his wil of me, *for I was brought to stand still*, and not in the least to resist."[11] How were these early Quakers, in the words of Captain Melledge, "brought to stand still"? Some, like Melledge, did not say. Some, such as Lilburne, newly turned Quaker, gave, as he put it, "fulness of scope to that divine and heavenly voice of God speaking plainly in my heart . . . that . . . leads my soul by its divine and strong power."[12] Edward Burrough and Francis Howgill told Bristol magistrates in 1654 that rather than transgress "the righteous Law of God written in our Hearts" they would choose to suffer: "if by Violence you put us out of the City, and have Power to do it, we cannot resist."[13] Their own personal revelations brought these men to stand still.

Some spoke and acted in a manner that echoed scripture but without specific attribution. In a 1652 letter George Fox observed, "The peacemaker has the kingdom and is in it, and has Dominion over the peace-breaker, to calm him in the power of God." Here Fox was alluding to the Sermon on the Mount, "Blessed are the peacemakers: for they shall be called the children of God." In the same year, a "rude multitude" beat Fox into insensibility; he came to his senses, stood up, and invited them to "[s]trike again, here is my arms, and my head and my cheeks," an obvious echo of "Whosoever shall smite thee on thy right cheek, turn to him the other also."[14]

Some attributed their standing still to their presence in the Kingdom of God. Oliver Cromwell demanded in 1654 that Fox repudiate violence toward himself or the government; his order drew forth Fox's declaration that the Kingdom was different from "the world" and that Fox followed the ways of the Kingdom. Fox answered unambiguously, "I . . . doe deny the carryeing or draweinge of anie Carnall sword against any, or against thee Olliver Crumwell." His disavowal received added force from his self-characterisation as "George fox: who is the sonne of god, who is sent to stand a witnes against all violence." He continued, "My weapons are not Carnall but spirituall & my kingedom is not of this world. Therefore wth the Carnall weapon I doe not feight, but am from those thinges dead. from him who am not of the world called of the world by the Name of George Fox." Fox's claims for himself here ("who is the sonne of god," "my kingedom") were to seem immodest verging on the heretical to later Quakers. When this letter to Cromwell came to be printed, it was adjusted in various ways to reduce any embarrassment, but the original letter still exists to testify to Fox's confidence.[15]

Some explained their principles by giving actual scriptural references. In this connection, one must remember that although Quakers assigned priority to the continuing revelations of the Light within, most among them were imbued with detailed knowledge of the Bible, inherited from their prior religious history.[16] So although Quakers such as Samuel Fisher anticipated later biblical criticism, many did not as easily shed habits of mind and familiarity with forms of expression more appropriate to other Protestant movements.[17] Lilburne, for example, expressed a clear pacifist witness in 1656 (a change of heart for him), writing, "I am already dead, or crucified, to the very occasions, and real grounds of all outward wars, and carnal swordfightings & fleshly buslings and contests."[18] His reliance on scripture to undergird this pacifism is quite literally visible, for the margins of his book *The Resurrection of John Lilburne* are crowded from edge to edge with biblical citations: "Eph.5.7,8,9.Heb.12.22,23.&:Joh.1.5,6,7.Rev.6.24 [etc.]."[19] He supported his pacifism as early as 1656 with the particular biblical texts that would become traditional Quaker references. As in the Epistle of James, he found the source for "all the outward iron and steel sword war" and all the "wicked and fleshly fore-runners of it" in "the raging power of sin, or lust within" (James 4:1: "From whence come wars and fightings among you? come they not hence, even of your lusts"). He cited passages about the Kingdom being not of this world, the disciple Peter using the sword, spiritual weapons, perfection, and loving enemies and emphasized that the subjects of King Jesus were new creatures, each having become "spiritual & savory, yea even his very thoughts."[20] So Quakers attributed their "standing still" to the voice of God, which was the internal law; to the nature of the Kingdom of God; and to scripture, by both allusion and quotation.

Peace Principles Declared

Oliver died in 1658 and was succeeded by his son, the inadequate Richard Cromwell. In 1659, the "Rump" of the former Long Parliament was recalled, stimulating hope for a revival of the "Good Old Cause." Political power was unrooted, snatched from one institution, then another, through 1659 and the spring of 1660.

Many Quakers became active politically and militarily, energized within local communities or agitating in London, only to be once more disillusioned when liberty of conscience and social reform were not forthcoming. Instead, a readjusted Parliament itself recalled King Charles II from exile abroad and restored him to the monarchy in May 1660. Quaker leaders mobilized to prepare for the new regime. Margaret Fell, who, in her words, "was moved of the Lord to leave my House and Family," came "Two Hundred Miles" in June, the very next month, to deliver "into the Kings hand" her powerful declaration to the king dated 5/4M/1660 (5 June 1660, New Style); thirteen others had signed it as "witnesse to the Truth of this." Entitled *A Declaration and an Information From us the People of God called Quakers To . . . the King and Both Houses of Parliament,* the document was preemptive, designed to convince Crown and courtiers that Quakers were nonthreatening, before the old enemies had a chance to poison the king's mind against Quakers with old prejudices.[21] The document emphasized Quaker suffering, suffering that had been unjustly inflicted; catalogued Quaker habits that had been misunderstood in the past—their opposition to oath-taking, to paying for "Priests," to "respecting persons" (acting with deference according to rank); and then vigorously asserted their opposition to all manner of treachery and plotting. Reassuring the new government that Quakers honored them as governors, "so far as they do rule for God and his Truth," Fell hastened to explain that the Quakers had borne testimony "chiefly against the Priests" (not government).[22]

Within this explicitly self-protective document—issued by a group of leaders "on the behalf of many Thousands"—was a statement about Quaker peace principles. "We are a People," wrote Fell, who "do deny and beare our Testimony against all Strife, and Wars, and Contentions that come from the Lusts . . . that warr against the Soul." She explained their position with four biblical references: to Christ's kingdom being not of this world; to Christ having come not to destroy men's lives but to save them; to Christ's weapons being not carnal but spiritual; and to offering up one's body to suffering.[23] Highly significant because it was perhaps the first collective expression of Quaker ideas about peace, Fell's Declaration and Information has been often overlooked, probably because the peace principle was only one matter among many in the document; perhaps because it was presented by a woman; perhaps because it was only a trifle in the excitement of the king's return. The subsequent Declaration of 1660, given forth eight months later under the hand of George Fox and others, was the statement of developing Quaker peace principles that became the definitive expression of the Quaker peace testimony.[24]

The Declaration of 1660 was quickly issued on 21/11M/1660 (21 January 1661, New Style) to defuse the fear aroused by the violent uprising of Fifth Monarchy men a few days earlier. Five of the signatories had signed Fell's earlier Declaration and Information.[25] The Declaration of 1660 was both comprehensive and specific; it was directed exclusively to issues of nonviolence and so was clear and compelling. Intended to remove suspicion of sedition, the declaration stated that Quakers sought the peace of all and asserted that because Quakers had been redeemed out of the passions that give rise to wars and fighting, they renounced all "bloody principles and practices" for themselves. The statement defended the sincerity of the group against the skeptical opprobrium already attached to it, pointing to their history of refraining from violence when personally attacked as proof of this sincerity. "And whereas men come against us with clubs, staves, drawn swords, pistols cocked, and do beat, cut, and abuse us, yet we never resisted them."[26] As further reassurance, they alluded to the biblical teaching that the spirit of Christ was not changeable according to opportunity, so assuring that they would never be led to war—neither for Christ nor for a worldly kingdom.

Previous Quaker pronouncements had made declarations about Quakers generally but had been prompted by local events and had been issued on behalf of particular individuals. Both of these 1660 declarations, in contrast, were stimulated by the peril of Quakers as a group and were issued by a strengthening leadership on behalf of the group, transcending localism. It is crucial to note that it was not pacifism itself that was new in 1660; it was not pacifism itself that arose from a political strategy, but rather it was the collective expression of a collective ideal that was new, strategic, and reactive, stimulated by political considerations.[27] Furthermore, it is of utmost significance that even while speaking with an authoritative voice on behalf of Quakers as a group, the declaration said, "we, *as to our own particulars*, do utterly deny . . ." thus acknowledging the continuing obligation of each individual Quaker to transform herself in order to make nonviolence possible. Failure to understand this principle of individual transformation has led to historical misapprehensions that the declarations of 1660 "settled" the question of pacifism. The uncritical assessment has appeared in phrases such as "the Quaker peace testimony became indelible only in 1660"[28] and assertions such as that after the Declaration of 1660 "no Quaker would knowingly engage in any livelihood or action which involved war or violence."[29] The dissemination of these codifications of principle to the wider Quaker body would instead be gradual and partial; actions of individuals would define their parameters.

"Manslayers and Destroyers About Religion"

Both Fell's Declaration and Information and Fox's later Declaration of 1660 impute Quaker suffering to their insistence on following their consciences, in trying to cleave to the will of God. Had there been liberty of conscience, they felt, their innocent expression of religious belief would not have been misinterpreted. Their refusal to take oaths of allegiance, for instance, would not have been misinterpreted as disloyalty. After the restoration of the monarchy, targeted legislation perpetuated religious persecution. The Quaker Act of 1662 prohibited more than four Quakers from meeting in worship and made it a crime to hold an oath unlawful or even to persuade others not to take an oath. In 1664 the Conventicle Act forbade any convening for religious worship other than that authorized by the established church. The Second Conventicle Act in 1670 extended penalties to those preaching at a conventicle or harboring such a gathering. Penalties were severe under these measures, and for ten years (1662–1672) the Quaker movement was greatly weakened by wholesale imprisonments, the loss of those dying in prison, and "transportations" of Quakers to the West Indies. Denied liberty of thought, expression, and behavior, before Quakers even knew who they were as "a people," they knew they were not free. Liberty of religious conscience, then, became a paramount and fundamental value for Quakers, seen as inextricable from Christian perceptions and obligations. And because assertions of this liberty had been met with violence, it was connected explicitly and implicitly to their ideas about violence.

Not surprisingly, in an age when religious implications infused all of life and violence against Quakers was a reaction to religious ideas and practice, many of the earliest references to peace principles specifically connected nonviolence with the religious sphere and arose in a context of perceived religious persecution. Indeed, the peace testimony itself sometimes seemed restricted to the realm of persecution about religious belief. That fratricidal religious strife could lead to violence would have been no surprise to Isaac Penington, who warned Quakers not to go forth "into reasoneings & contendings about Matters of Religion . . . wch are apt to . . . lead to warre, & fightings, as carnall as those of the outward weapons."[30] When George Fox excoriated Massachusetts ministers in a tract directed to "New-England Professors, That Hanged the Servants of the Lord for Religion . . . Hating and Killing their Brethren about Religion," his outrage focused as much on the fact that Christians betrayed fellow Christians "about religion" as on the fact of the violent punishment itself.[31] Fox often directly associated his arguments against weapons and violence with imposing faith by force, as in his declaration to "Kings and Princes" in which he accused persecutors—"manslayers, and destroyers about Religion"—of betraying Christendom itself.[32] His argument against violence, limited in scope to violence about matters of faith, here depended on scriptural foundations. When the disciples wanted Jesus to bring fire down upon those who would not receive him, Jesus rebuked them, saying he came not to destroy but to save men's lives. Just as King David was a man of blood, Fox argued, and so was not allowed to build the temple, so too the "heavenly Jerusalem" could not be built with destroying hands, but only with saving hands. "[T]he Weapons of Christ's Followers and Ministers were to be Spiritual, and not Carnal, in all the matters of Faith, Worship and Religion, and they did not wrestle with Flesh and Blood." Paul, Fox noted, was "clear"—free—from the blood of all men.[33]

Richard Hubberthorne, too, chose his words carefully when he described "The Good Old Cause" in 1659 as "The Cause of God and Religion": those who remained faithful to the pure, undefiled religion (presumably the Quakers) did not contend for it with a "material Sword," for "[it] is the Work of God in the Light of Christ in the conscience, in the soul . . . who leads from such Acts of violence, (*upon that account*)." He then asserted the duties of the magistrate to use the "Sword Civil and Military" to punish evildoers and praise those that do well, and "not to justifie the wicked, nor condemn the just."[34] The sword had its proper uses in the hands of the magistracy, to secure "external Rights and Liberties" but not on the account of religion: "the conscience and soul of man is a place for the living God to dwel and walk in, where no Magistrate (as such) hath any business."[35] He seems to have objected to impressing men for foreign wars explicitly because most foreign wars were about religion.[36] Thomas Taylor in 1660 did "utterly deny" the Fifth Monarchy Men, a sect willing to bring in the Kingdom of God by force, because he denied that the Kingdom might be set up "with a Carnal Weapon, or that his Church can be preserved and kept clean by worldly Force."[37]

Even after the "official" statements about peace principles in 1660, then, individual comments about not using weapons or fighting were often ambiguous; that is, the comments may easily be understood to prohibit only fighting and the use of weapons in the cause of religion. The identification of nonviolence with the sphere of religion resurfaced explicitly as late as 1692, when Ambrose Rigge wrote to Quakers in the north of England: "And that religion is certainly false, which is either set up, or defended by destroying men's lives. Therefore touch not with it, but in the suffering seed of life let your dwellings be, so shall you be fortified with the munition of rocks, into which no destroyer shall enter."[38] By 1692, though, the admonitions against violence had long since extended to a broader sphere. If early pronouncements about violence had been primarily associated with religion, and if the fact that violence had occurred between Christian brethren had seemed more shocking than the violence itself, the dominant concern broadened to include questions of violence more generally, no matter the source or motivation.

Peace Principles Justified: When Quakers Spoke to the World

When Quakers increased in number and became visible in groups, others felt threatened in new ways; and Quakers had to explain themselves more carefully. It took some sophistication, after all, to distinguish between movements such as the Fifth Monarchists, willing to war for their goals, and the Quakers, especially when the Quakers were scarcely speaking with one voice. Few onlookers were able to draw such distinctions. Particularly, government itself worried about Quaker "plotting" and potential violence. Quaker leaders repudiated such expectations; in the course of allaying these fears, they left a record of their thinking about the role of violence within the political state—a record fairly established even before the restoration of the monarchy brought heightened disquiet in 1660.

In this effort directed toward non-Quakers, some who renounced violence, either for themselves or on the part of Quakers generally, argued primarily on the basis of both the words and the spirit of the scriptures. At times they were legalistic, adhering closely to particular texts. Others used the text to formulate a controlling "gospel spirit," at times concentrating on the nature of the Kingdom of God. Others stressed obedience to God. Underlying and controlling all these arguments was the idea that purity of soul was essential for ongoing revelation itself. But Quakers rarely mentioned the present and personal revelations of God within themselves, an authority not likely to persuade those outsiders whose fears they were attempting to allay. It is not possible to discern the degree to which the Quaker leaders pragmatically adjusted their reasoning because they realized that, for non-Quakers, scriptural authority would be more persuasive than individual revelation. For strategic reasons or not, when justifying their peace principles to "the world" Quakers stressed particular biblical texts, the "spirit" of the gospel, and obedience to God.

Biblical Texts

A variety of Quaker spokespersons gave voice to biblical authority, but they relied on relatively few biblical texts and concepts. In her address to the king, Margaret Fell gave a careful and typical exposition of Quaker peace principles and their biblical derivations. She testified with James 4:1 against "all Strife, and Wars, and Contentions that come from the Lusts," that is, from the passions of envy, covetousness, and enmity. Isaac Penington connected the "lusts" of the heart to the tenth commandment, Thou shalt not covet, for "covet" is the equivalent of "lust" in Greek. Passions derived from coveting, he thought, waged an inward war against man's soul and were the cause of outward violence.[39]

Margaret Fell quoted other biblical passages that were to appear constantly in Quaker explanations of their position on violence. "My kingdom is not of this world: if my kingdom were of this world, then would my servants fight," Jesus told Pilate, explaining why his followers were not protecting him from the judgment of the high priest and the Jews.[40] When disciples James and John suggested that Jesus might want to call down fire from heaven upon a Samaritan village that had spurned him, Jesus rebuked them, saying, "For the Son of man is not come to destroy men's lives, but to save them."[41] Emphasizing their paradoxical position as being in the world but not of the world, Quakers used the vocabulary of 2 Corinthians 10:3–5:

For though we walk in the flesh,
we do not war after the flesh:
(For the weapons of our warfare are not
carnal, but mighty through God
to the pulling down of strong holds;)
. . . bringing into captivity every
thought to the obedience of Christ.

Again and again Quakers pointed to God having ordained government and its functions, including the use of force: "the powers that be are ordained of God"; "submit . . . unto them that are sent by him for the punishment of evildoers, and for the praise of them that do well."[42] In his 1654 statement to Cromwell, Fox set forth his belief in the magistrate's godly mandate. But Fox's stated purpose was to bring people "from the occasion of the warr & from the occasion of the Magistrates sword." That is, a righteous people would be free of the passions giving rise to strife and would not require government regulation. He gave a warning to soldiers, viewed as "instruments" of magistracy, that they "noe false accuser must bee, noe violense must doe, but [must] be content wth their wages," a scriptural reminder no doubt welcome to their officers.[43]

Quakers often cited the story of Jesus in the Garden of Gethsemane, just before his death. There Jesus was betrayed and arrested and the apostle Peter drew his sword and struck off the ear of the high priest's servant. The Book of Matthew recounts that Jesus told Peter, "Put up again thy sword into his place: for all they that take the sword shall perish with the sword."[44] The Matthew version of the story, and the wording of this particular text, were mainstays of the Quaker justification for the peace testimony. A group of Quakers disavowing all "plotts & Conspireces" against the king, for example, explicitly connected the incident involving Peter's sword with the later saying of Jesus that his kingdom was not of this world and so his servants could not fight.[45] No doubt the words "All they that take the sword shall perish with the sword" were offered, and interpreted, on their face. But the succeeding verses, which Quakers sometimes omitted and sometimes included without comment, modified the literal interpretation of the incident. Jesus asked Peter, "Thinkest thou that I cannot now pray to my Father, and he shall presently give me more than twelve legions of angels? But how then shall the Scriptures be fulfilled, that thus it must be?"[46] Jesus was not condemning the use of the sword per se but rather showing Peter that if Jesus had wanted to be spared, he could have called upon God; instead, he realized his death was necessary to fulfill scriptural prophecy. Some Quakers used this incident with more subtlety, not depending on the literal meaning of the "sword" passage but instead stressing that, with Jesus, the "Saints" must "beare & suffer all things, knowing that vengance is the Lords [sic]."[47] Thus, God's people must not resist evil, "lest they should be found Opposers of that, which the Lord hath thought good to suffer to come upon his Heritage, for the Tryal of their Faith and Patience." God has ordained that Quakers must suffer, in order to test their faith; they must not therefore use violence. This way of thinking is unconcerned with the effect of violence on another person or the worldly destructiveness of war but rather is concerned with unquestioning obedience to the will of God, testing his people.[48]

Some scriptural texts were potentially problematic for pacifists, and non-Quakers used them to challenge the developing peace principles. One such text was Jesus' statement "Think not that I am come to send peace on earth: I came not to bring peace but a sword." Quakers explained away such difficulties by insisting that the passages must be figurative, because they were inconsistent with the spirit of the gospel. Thus, when Jesus said "I came not to bring peace but a sword," he was speaking of the metaphorical sword of the spirit, to be unsheathed against the sinful nature within man. (Quakers did not mention the forceful Jesus who drove out the merchants from the temple with "a scourge of small cords" and "overthrew" the tables of the moneychangers.)[49]

Gospel Spirit

The preeminent biblical lesson undergirding Quaker peace principles was Jesus' attitude toward enemies, an attitude that embodied the spirit of the gospel, the "new covenant." The spirit of the gospel was exemplified in "But I say unto you, Love your enemies, bless them that curse you, do good to them that hate you."[50] Finding the cause of violence in the "lusts" of the heart, Quakers emphasized the necessity of pure motives as well as pure behavior: "Ye have heard that it was said by them of old time, Thou shalt not kill . . . But I say unto you, That whosoever is angry with his brother without a cause shall be in danger of the judgment." In the First Epistle of John, the lesson is blunt: "Whosoever hateth his brother is a murderer."[51] For example, using both text and the "spirit" of the gospel, certain Quakers argued in the manner of this testimony to magistrates, "If any strike thee upon the one Cheake, hold up the other, & render to noe man Evill for Evill &c."[52] One who follows Jesus "hurts noe man"; "they that hath Enemyes, & hate one another, wee Cannot say they are of God." So the "Jewes outward sword, by wch they Cutt downe the heathen," was no longer an appropriate model; except as it was a "type" or symbol of the inward sword of the spirit, "wch Cutts downe the Inward heathen." Therefore, all those who "wrestle with flesh & bloud, & with Carnal weapons, are gone into the flesh, & out of the spirit."[53]

Quakers distilled the spirit of the gospel, as did Jesus himself, through the device of contrast, contrast in the first instance between the first covenant, made between God and the Jews, and Jesus' new covenant. "Ye have heard that it hath been said," said Jesus,

> Thou shalt love thy neighbour,
> and hate thine enemy.
> But I say unto you,
> Love your enemies,
> bless them that curse you,
> do good to them that hate you,
> and pray for them which despitefully use you,
> and persecute you;
> That ye may be the children of your Father which is in heaven.[54]

Thomas Maule, too, a Massachusetts Quaker writing in 1694, helped to elucidate the concept of Jesus as the "first Adam," who offered the world a return to a pure state before the Fall of man, the state that preceded the necessity of the Law itself. The first covenant, that of the Jews with God, was an "outward" phenomenon expressed in the Law and binding upon the activities of man in the kingdoms of the world. Under the first covenant, carnal weapons were appropriate to the task of creating "an outward holy Land for the Lords People to remain in." But the new covenant of Jesus meant the adoption of "the inward Sword of his spirit . . . against all the inward Enemies which would hinder the advancing of Gods Kingdom . . . to fight the Lords spiritual Battel against the Enemies of their soul." When Jesus heard his disciples say, in Luke 22:38, "behold, here are two swords," he said, "It is enough." Maule interpreted this passage to refer to the righteousness of the Law as the first sword and the righteousness of Jesus as the second sword, transfiguring the first.[55]

In contrast to the Jews, wrote Fox, who "were allowed to destroy" enemies, the Quakers would be free of that which "causes troubles, wars and fightings," for they were brethren, "not ruling in lordship, like Jews and gentiles, but the greatest shall be as the least amongst you for the Seed is one in all."[56] The children of God, in "these Gospel-Days," were not to participate in those things either "connived at, or suffered or commanded, before Christ Came."[57] (Other Quakers did honor those passages from the Hebrew scriptures that carried a peaceable vision, quoting Micah in a book for instructing children, for example: "And they shall beat their swords into plowshares, and their spears into pruninghooks: nation shall not lift up a sword against nation, neither shall they learn war any more.")[58]

It was William Bayly who articulated a more encompassing, less text-bound, less sectarian understanding of the spirit of the gospel and the significance of the "new covenant" embodied in the life of Jesus. He too saw Jesus as a redeemer—that is, a restorer—of that which preceded even death and hell: the beginning times, "before Death, Hell, Strife and Wars (or Enmity, the Ground of it) were, or before Disobedience, Transgression, Confusion or the Hardness of hart were." The great "Principle," the principle of peace, preceded the devil, "the Author and Ground of Strife and Mischief, of Plottings, Murders, Wars and Confusion"; and Jesus destroyed the works of the devil. And because Jesus' followers were "joyned unto him (the

Figure 2.1. [Swords into Plowshares], The Emblems of England's Distractions (detail) by Francis Barlow, pen and ink, 1658. "And they shall beat their swords into plowshares, and their spears into pruning hooks; nation shall not lift up sword against nation, neither shall they learn war any more" (Micah 4:3). Courtesy of the Huntington Library, Art Collections, and Botanical Gardens, San Marino, California.

Lord)," they partook of his spirit and partook of his power to remove the very grounds of enmity. The implications of Bayly regarding the peace principle as the very "foundation of God," recoverable through Jesus, are profound. In using the power of the Lord to remove the impure motions of their hearts, Quakers shared the capacity to transform even enemies, bringing about reconciliation through the example of righteousness.[59] Peace is the "fruit" of righteousness: if one stands before evil free of enmity, transfigured by love, evil itself melts away, transformed. Inspired example penetrates hatred to reach the heart, "for in the Strength of Love One chases a Thousand."[60] This is the intellectual source of the transforming power of peace.

To Do His Will: Obedience

For Margaret Fell, Jesus was a model especially in his obedience to his Father. ("Though he was a Son, yet learned he Obedience.") Quakers owed obedience to the principles of Jesus, one of which was obedience to God, and nonviolence was

the will of God. By 1677 in a testimony from Barbados Quakers, for instance, arguments based on biblical text and gospel spirit had joined with the precept of obedience to justify peace principles. Their testimony opened with the statement that
they dared not disobey Jesus Christ, the "Captain of our Salvation." Explaining
why they refused to serve in arms, Barbados Quakers cited the usual passages—
"my kingdom is not of this world," "I came not to destroy men's lives," "love your
enemies," "all they that take the sword shall perish from the sword," wars that de-
rive from the "lusts"—and concluded that they could not, "directly or indirectly,
war, fight against, kill nor destroy Men's Persons, neither be aiding nor assisting
therein." Instead, they must prepare to suffer with patience. The Barbadians recognized the need to slay wrath within with the sword of the spirit. "It is quick and
powerful, and sharper than any twoedged sword . . . and is a Discerner of the
Thoughts and Intents of the Heart," they quoted from Hebrews 4:12, reiterating
that it is thoughts and intents, even more than actions, that are crucial according to

Figure 2.2. [Spears into Pruning Hooks], The Emblems of England's Distractions (detail) by
Francis Barlow, pen and ink, 1658. "And they shall beat their swords into plowshares, and their
spears into pruning hooks; nation shall not lift up sword against nation, neither shall they learn
war any more" (Micah 4:3). Courtesy of the Huntington Library, Art Collections, and Botanical
Gardens, San Marino, California.

the spirit of the gospel. Throughout, the language of command and obedience controls their discourse, couched in the vocabulary of the sea, appropriate to this island community. If they should kill anyone in war, they "should do that we have no Command for from our Captain"; if the people remain "faithful to his holy Requiring," they will be preserved; they are unwilling to do anything without a command from Jesus, or he will say, "Who hath required these Things at your Hands?" God preserved the Israelites in Exodus, as long as they were obedient.[61]

Early Quakers saw their peace principles, however defined, whatever their source, whenever imparted, as derived from the wishes of God, and obedience to God required them to act accordingly. Whether a particular Quaker learned of this duty from the words and life of Jesus in scriptural accounts or from personal encounters with the Light is an individual matter. But it is clear that for "public" and "private" Quakers alike the principle of obedience relieved much of the necessity to justify the substance of the peace principles themselves. In attaching redemption so firmly to obedience, in this respect Quakers cleaved to a Hebraic tradition rather than to a Greek concentration on God's grace expressed in Jesus' sacrifice. For the earliest Quakers it was the immediate power of God that was crucial, for he had dominion over that which each person cannot control. George Bishop saw broken links in a great chain: "Here is the ground of all, the spirit that is in man lusteth to envy, boylings are in his heart, revenge is in his breast, he cannot bear an indignity . . . he would have, and he kills to have; he cannot rule his inordinate desires." Without each person seeking the Light within, "bringing into captivity every thought to the obedience of Christ," pacifism is impossible; it is obedience "which hath been wanting . . . and the want of this hath been the cause why there hath been such Wars." Bishop made it absolutely clear that he was not speaking of people in groups; each person must overcome himself, "which is greater prowess than to overcome strong Cities." For Quakers, the locus of the cause of war and the occasion of fighting and weapons was ultimately within the individual, not in impersonal societal forces. True valor, true courage, and the power of God were to be found in the one who subdues and destroys the spirit of wickedness within, not in he who "fights with mens persons, and kills, and slayes."[62]

The Changing Foundation for the Peace Testimony

Although Quakers held to "the testimony" over the centuries, the dominant reasons for which they renounced violence changed over time. The absence of theoretical Quaker concern in the early years about the *consequences* of avoiding fighting, war, and weapons reinforces the observation that obedience, and the resultant purity of soul allowing access to God's individual revelation, were the theoretical foundations of the seventeenth-century peace principles. The spirit that leads to wars and fighting with carnal weapons, wrote Edward Perry, "is the Soul's great Enemy."[63] In the power of the gospel, Fox advised Nevis Quakers, "you may all freely goe to god and in it feele nothing betwixt you and the Lord of hindering your pasage to him."[64] In this letter, Fox was reassuring Quakers that "standing watch" against invaders, *unarmed,* did not hinder the passage to God. Although some Quakers disagreed with his position, they shared his thought process—that the consequence that mattered from their actions was personal, not societal. The passions, Fell wrote, come from the heart, and the heart's defilement is washed with the blood of Christ.[65] It was the pure heart that rendered the soul open to God's revelation. In distinguishing between the soul, the conduit of a person's communication with God, and the heart, the governor of the impulses, and ignoring the mind, the locus of wisdom or earthly reason, Fell underscored the essential Quaker belief that one's actions would only be righteous when governed by a redeemed heart. A redeemed heart was a heart filled with love, love even of enemies, and was necessary before one might renounce violence.

Peace, then, was not a goal in itself but a byproduct of righteousness. Ambrose Rigge wrote, "Neither shall wars with flesh and blood complete true and lasting peace on earth, but righteousness shall deliver from death; the fruit thereof is peace."[66] War and peace were religious questions rather than social or political questions. "For Fox," noted Geoffrey Nuttall, "it was not war in itself which was out of the question, so much as the attitudes of mind and spirit which dispose men to war, and without which war would not be possible."[67] Quakers justifying their position, arguing from scripture, from spirit, from revelation, paid little attention to any but spiritual consequences, of either violence or nonviolence. "Victory" was defined by victory within, the condition of the individual soul. For Quakers the enemy within, not other people, was more relevant than life or death itself. Restraint, then, was for the sake of one's own soul, not for another's body. In addition to the irrelevance of physical life or death in itself, the irrelevance of both worldly striving and worldly conflict was a common motif, a motif useful in defusing the fears of Quaker violence toward authority. Addressing ambassadors meeting at Nimeguen in 1677, Robert Barclay argued that all outward reconciliation through treaties or other efforts would be in vain, without a true change of heart among the people, without removing "that evil ground of ambition, of pride, and lust and vain glory"; "all your articles will not bind them, but they will break them like strawes."[68] The blunt, utilitarian argument of another Quaker has enduring force:

> For all your great Workings, and toilsom Labour . . . you have wrought no Deliverance in the Earth; but your Souls Enemies still stand in strength. . . . [F]or all your Striving, and Fighting, and Killing, and Spoiling, and Destroying one another about Earthly Things, you have done no good at all.[69]

Some in these early decades occasionally did express profound grief at the consequences of war, notably Robert Barclay, when he lamented:

> They sheath their swords in one anothers bowels, ruin, waste and destroy whole Countreys, expose to the greatest misery many thousand Families, make thousands of Widows, and ten thousands of Orphans, cause the banks to over-flow with the blood of those for whom the Lord Jesus Christ shed his precious blood.[70]

And William Penn anticipated later Quaker preoccupations in his practical concern for worldly justice as a deterrent to war and fighting. But in the seventeenth century, such agonizings over worldly consequences were nearly invisible in the context of an overwhelming preoccupation with the state of the individual soul. As late as 1693, even after the influence of Barclay and Penn, the London Yearly Meeting addressed the problem of shipmasters: those "Esteemed Quakers" who carried guns on their ships in the mistaken belief that they could defend themselves thereby. The meeting warned that they endangered their own and others' lives by arming their ships (because they were depending on worldly weapons rather than on God's protection); and their confusing example made it more difficult for impressed Quakers to refuse to fight. Their home meetings were instructed to advise the shipmasters "that they may Seriously Consider how they injure their Own Souls in so doing." The shipmasters had misplaced their trust "thr'o disobedience and unbelief," which left them newly vulnerable. The meeting expressed concern for the shipmasters' "Recovery, and Safety from Distruction"; referring not to bodily safety but to spiritual safety, through relying on the power of God.[71]

In 1744 the same London Yearly Meeting referred to this very advice of 1693 in confirmation of a longstanding testimony against carrying guns for defense, when it criticized Quaker shipmasters and owners for their recent involvement with privateering and letters of marque. The new condemnation recommended again the proper Quaker faith in the protection of God rather than weapons but added a concern that privateering "may be attended with Injustice, Barbarity and Bloodshed."[72] Here the meeting went beyond the concern for the souls of the perpetrators to consider the victims.

By the 1790s, London Yearly Meeting admonitions became specific: Quakers were not to pay for exemption from militia service or for hiring substitutes; were not to pay any taxes if a portion of them was going for such purposes; were not to fabricate or sell "instruments of war"; were not to lend out or lease their vessels during times of war. And the "soul" is not to be found. "Beware of being induced . . . to give countenance to the destroying practice of war." "Behold the depth of misery into which war plunges mankind." They were to be "watchful" lest any otherwise promote "the destruction of the human species."[73]

By 1819, the London Yearly Meeting hierarchy of concerns bore but incidental resemblance to those of the seventeenth century. Its annual statement read, "Our refusal to bear arms is a testimony not only against the violence and cruelty of war" but also against confidence in the "'arm of flesh.'"[74] Quakers deplored the physical consequences of war but neglected to remind each other of the true task, as seventeenth-century Quakers had seen it—to "forme a killinge instrument" against the enemy within. God—and the soul—were only implied. Their cooler rationality looks outward from their eyes: how would they see their forebear, Thomas Taylor, who in 1672 (unusually) was equally concerned about the costs of war? He cried "Wo to the Rushing of Nations": "the Blood of the Slain cryes to God for Vengeance . . . and the Cryes of the Oppressed, even of the poor quiet-spirited People in all Lands groans by reason of the Burdens of the Souldiers, and excessive Charge of the Wars." But he concluded, "O! destroy that Spirit . . . which hath drawn the Hearts of people from the living God, after the Lusts of the evil World. . . . Come Lord Jesus . . . saith my Soul."[75]

3

"Fire at the Mast"

THE PRACTICE OF PEACE

William Coddington was governor of the small colony known as Rhode Island and Providence Plantations in June 1675, when just over its border in Plymouth, Wampanoag Indians had been provoked to burn and vandalize isolated farmhouses, then to kill settlers. Governor Josiah Winslow of Plymouth sped urgent requests for help to both Massachusetts and Rhode Island by overnight messenger. Governor Leverett of Massachusetts immediately replied to Winslow's request; if ever two small words could encapsulate fear, it was those he wrote on the back of his letter in his small pinched script urging haste: "hast hast." He sent three military officers down the path to Plymouth to investigate the rumors of Indian uprising and to intervene with the Wampanoag sachem King Philip; but when they came upon two grisly English bodies lying in the pathway, one head and both right hands missing, they retreated in horror. Governor Winslow asked Governor Coddington specifically for Rhode Island boats to surround and blockade the peninsula where the Wampanoags were headquartered, to ensure that none escaped while Plymouth troops approached from land. But Governor Coddington was a Quaker, well aware of the peace testimony. Did he struggle as he confronted competing responsibilities: to refrain from using "carnal weapons," to refuse to destroy enemies—to protect the citizens of his polity, to aid his fellow Englishmen? No record remains of any conscientious struggle; only the historical fact that Coddington deployed the boats as requested.[1]

Coddington's probable dilemma, while idiosyncratic to his historical circumstance, was in a broad sense emblematic of every Quaker's task of translating principle into practice. In England, on the high seas, in other colonies, and in other countries, Quakers had been "defining" the peace testimony through their actions as well. However ambiguous or truncated such individual anecdotes may be, in the aggregate they may be suggestive of how Quakers actually put abtract beliefs into practice. And however fragmentary the evidence, practice is more compelling than the most elegant theory, not least because the practice of peace involved the silent ones as well as the spokespersons of the movement.

Presented with relatively few "official" formulations of the Quaker peace testimony, such as the 1660 declarations of Margaret Fell, George Fox, and others, those studying early Quakers have reacted with comparably few understandings of the testimony, among which two have held sway. The traditional interpretation— that pacifism based on faith alone was an integral aspect of early Quaker practice—was overly pietistic, ignoring the confused and limited nature of the witness. The more current interpretation—that pacifism was a strategic reaction of persecuted Quakers after 1660—perpetuates flawed assumptions that the peace testimony was nonexistent before 1660 and that it was settled and operative after 1660.[2] Both of these interpretations suffer from their (unacknowledged) dependence on the English experience. The trouble with partial understandings of the peace testimony is not that they may be entirely wrong but that a doctrinaire view may prevent complex questions from being raised. The stories and behavior of particular Quakers challenge these interpretations of the peace testimony, reminding one of the questions that have not been asked and illuminating the density of Quaker experience and belief. How individual Quakers behaved when faced with violence, or with opportunities or requirements to commit violence, imbue the mellifluous formulations of the peace testimony with the messy cacophony of human choice. First, then, I will look at the practice of the peace testimony before 1660, in light of both the pietistic tradition asserting the existence of an uncomplicated, faith-based pacifism and the political interpretation asserting the absence of pacifism in these early years. Next, I will examine some of the implications of the political understanding of the peace testimony in 1660 and thereafter, measured against evidence of Quaker practice. Finally, I will turn to individual stories illuminating various elements of nonviolence.

"Crouching to the Spirit of the World"

The romantic notion that consistent and broadly defined pacifism accompanied the birth of the Quaker movement can no longer be sustained. In the earliest days, around the mid–seventeenth century, many people serving with the Cromwell's puritan New Model Army or sympathetic to the Good Old Cause of the Parliamentary side of the civil war had been among those attracted to what would coalesce into a Quaker movement. They were separating themselves from a Catholic-tinged monarchy, just as Charles I was separated from his head upon a scaffold in 1649. They shared a millenial vision of a godly society, guaranteeing rights and liberties conducive to a righteous and reformed community. They shared, too, a providentialism that led them to interpret the victories of the Parliamentary army and the ascendency of Cromwell as God's validation of the Cause. Many early Quakers, soldiers and nonsoldiers alike, thus fell within a "holy war" or "crusade" tradition, in which force might be enlisted in God's cause.[3]

The evidence that many early Quakers were sympathetic with military activities, and participated in military activities, is abundant.[4] Casual allusion shows how un-exceptional was the Quaker-military connection. An officer complained in 1657 that a "qaker" drummer from Major Hodden's company had caused a public disturbance "with much bitterness of spirit and revillings." The drummer was "the first qaker that hath given disturbance heere its good to nipp such spirits in the budd."[5] In the same year, Alexander Parker mentioned a "Corporall [who] stands pretty firme according to measure and one or two troopers and meets together on the first dayes."[6] Not only did many early Quakers continue to serve in the military, but others encouraged Cromwell in foreign military adventures and later enlisted in militias and cooperated with the restored Rump Parliament in military activity at home.

Some Quakers, however, even while approving of the Cause itself, including forceful means to its achievement, found themselves unable to use force themselves; being "redeemed" and already in the Kingdom the Cause was designed to "bring in," such methods were no longer available to them. They put aside the "fleshly arm." Yet in their eyes God himself was not a pacifist. God, in fact, might make use of imperfect, even evil, "instruments," such as an army, to further his mysterious purposes.[7] These Quakers, then, were comfortable not only in finding God's approval in temporal victories but in urging others to carry the Cause forward—against European Catholics, for instance—even, perhaps, with violent means. Later seventeenth-century critics delighted in reminding Quakers that during the Interregnum many had acted "outside" any peace testimony. Critics cited, for example, the Quakers' declaration to Oliver Cromwell, "Nor let any other take thy Crown:—And let thy Soldiers go forth with a free and willing Heart, that thou mayest Rock Nations as a Cradle." They quoted, too, Samuel Fisher's revelation from God, which he passed on to Oliver, in which God said he would overturn the existing order and put a two-edged sword into the hands of the saints, "and they shall Execute Vengeance upon the Heathen."[8]

During the 1650s, many Quakers gradually detected a perversion of the Good Old Cause, an abandonment of its aspirations, as seen in the religious oppression they themselves suffered, the unrelieved economic and social oppression of others, and the sinful grasping for power under the Commonwealth and Protectorate; so they began to distance themselves from their former allies and draw new lessons from the continued unsettledness of the English polity and the failure of the Kingdom to appear for all. God was still teaching through historical events, but the new lesson was that the army and the government had sinned; God had withdrawn his favor. Edward Burrough told Oliver Cromwell in 1657 that had Cromwell only obeyed the Lord, "then would he have made thine enemies to have bowed under thee, and the force of their policy and arm should never have prevailed against thee."[9]

Meanwhile, all did not "crouch to the Spirit of the World"; countless other Quakers had already chosen to refrain from violence when abused, had refused militia service, and had renounced the use of weapons.[10] William Caton remembered a 1659 voyage when a pirate ship bore down upon his ship. As was customary, all made ready to fight and "the passengers . . . were furnished with Arms so well as the rest"; but as for Caton, "I could not touch any of their Weapons, as to shed blood with them."[11] Captain Peter Foote of the *Mermaid* reported with palpable frustration that his master gunner had "conffined himselfe to his cabbinne" and declared that "noe powre shall command him to fire a gunn as that frm thence blood might be spilt."[12] That some Quakers had already seen violence as incompatible with their faith prior to the 1660 declarations is as obvious as the fact that other Quakers had not. Regarding the origins of the peace testimony, then, both the pietistic tradition finding the peace testimony as an integral witness of Quakerism from its beginning and the political tradition asserting the appearance of the testimony only in 1660 are simplistic and are gainsaid by early Quaker practice. One anecdote might stand witness to the ironic ambiguities of Quaker practice: Quaker John Hall challenged the local priest in Aberdeen and preached to the people in the "steeple house." Hall was lodging with a military officer, one Cornet Warde, also a Quaker. When the priest and another man came to Warde's quarters in a threatening manner, Cornet Warde declared in support of Hall that if he or any of his soldiers should be likewise moved of the Lord, they might do as Hall had done and "they should not seek the carnall sword to maintaine them."[13]

Pragmatism and the Peace Testimony

Historian W. Alan Cole in 1956 asserted memorably that "[p]acifism was not a characteristic of the early Quakers: it was forced upon them by the hostility of the outside world."[14] Those, like Cole, who find the true origin of the peace testimony in the 1660 declarations at the time of the restoration of the monarchy in effect stress the strategic, political impulses behind its expression, often ignoring its prior expression derived from faith. This political argument, associated in its most elaborate and subtle form with Barry Reay and Christopher Hill and so useful as a historical corrective, is inadequate in important ways.[15] First, it concentrates on the peace testimony as a collective phenomenon. Yet even those early Quakers most closely identified with a collective expression of the peace testimony based its realization on the individual. It was the individual heart that must be transformed, and the individual relationship with God that must be sustained through obedience to Christ's commands. It was not sufficient to reform social or political institutions. Quakers were indeed interested in the reform of society, in order to bring it closer to the qualities of God's kingdom, but they were under no illusions that institutions might become righteous without the prior righteousness of individuals. The grace of God was to be bestowed on individuals, empowering them one by one to transcend "the world" and participate in the spiritual Kingdom. But random people in groups—in society—are by definition "in the world" and by definition sinful. While not removing themselves from "the world," Quakers were well aware of the "world's" limitations. It is an anachronistic, materialist, secular view that postulates reform or revolution coming about through human power alone or through anonymous societal forces, economic or political. Rather than institutions having the capacity for righteousness or perfect justice and so imparting these qualities to individuals, Quakers could see no such shortcuts, even in regard to themselves as a group. The Declaration of 1660 is worded, significantly, "we, *as to our own particulars*, do utterly deny," making clear that they were speaking as separate actors, assembled into a group but not subsumed by the group. Therefore, to overstress the importance of collective proclamations and to validate political maneuvers more highly than personal insights is particularly ironic and inappropriate. Early Quakers would not comprehend such a position.

Among other misunderstandings and simplifications introduced by the emphasis on 1660 as an irenic fulcrum is the assumption that Quaker practice largely fell into compliance with the official pronouncement after 1660. Both before and after 1660, Quaker comments show clearly that Quakers by no means universally observed peace principles, even in their most basic, simple form. The comments show just as clearly that some did. A 1690 history of early Quakers during the Commonwealth and Protectorate, for example, described how Cromwell, the Independents, and others in power removed Quaker justices of the peace, officers, and soldiers from their positions. "And besides," the account continued, "many lay down their arms for conscience sake when they came to be convinced, and many broke their swords and their pistols and weapons to pieces and could not lift up sword nor learn war."[16] The (no longer surprising) implication of this description is that adoption of even minimal peace principles was partial among Quakers from the beginning. There is little difference between this observation about the first days of Quakerism, before 1660, and the implications of John Burnyeat's 1670 observations. Writing from Barbados, Burnyeat referred obliquely to his having refrained from meddling or judging a matter "wherein Friends have somewhat differed." This matter, unmistakably, was "Sending Men, Horse and Arms to the Training, Trooping or Playing." Burnyeat had come to feel, along with those who had refused to send men and arms and had therefore been punished, that to send arms was "folly" and belonged among those activities that "would put a bushel over the lighted Candle, and by degrees would put it out, and would lead us to crouch to the Spirit of the World, until its large wing of Darkness would over-shadow us."[17] Regardless of his own hardening convictions, he revealed inadvertantly that Quakers still differed in their belief and behavior about the peace testimony. Indeed, in the same year, the Turks captured a ship under Quaker command armed with eight guns.[18] In 1675, fifteen years after the public, collective Declaration of 1660, the Morning Meeting in London, a group of Quaker "elders in the faith," found it necessary to admonish those "in the severall Countyes they that find arms."[19] The London Meeting for Sufferings in 1690, learning that a Liverpool Quaker shipmaster carried guns, reminded Quakers that "our weapons are not carnal but spiritual; and that it hath not been the practice of Friends to use or carry carnal weapons."[20] And the minutes of a Devonshire meeting in 1692 noted that "the support of souldiers is inconsistent with Truth" and "some have neglected this advis."[21]

Even those practicing pacifism in some ways retained interesting tolerances after 1660. Fox corresponded with William Penn in 1674 about the earl of Salisbury's younger son, the commander of a troop of soldiers. In a classic letter of recommendation and introduction, Fox said of the earl's son that he was "convinced in his judgement [of] the truth," and "hee goes often to bull and mouth meetinge" (the primary London meeting). Fox asked Penn to get to know those officers of Salisbury's son's troop who lived in the town where Penn was living and in the town of Guilford, "on truths account." Fox did not seem fazed by the son's occupation and did not question his conviction on the basis of his occupation.[22] Fox also recommended the physical punishment of children in 1665.[23] James Claypoole, seemingly oblivious to that corollary of the peace testimony, the absolute trust in God's protection, energetically brokered insurance for the maritime trade. "Enclosed I send thee copies of the two policies on which have gotten £800 subscribed," he wrote, using "plain" language. And he secured a policy to insure another "personally against capture by the Turks, at 2%." He booked passage for Quaker emigrants on the *Concord*, five hundred tons, twenty six guns, mentioning that the captain, apropos of the guns, "which may be in our way," had "promised to stow about 1/3 part of them in the hold."[24] One Robert Grassingham was a shipwright who continued to provision transport ships, refit navel vessels, and repair gunships after he became a Quaker.[25] The struggle to define the disavowal of weapons was scarcely resolved in 1660, or in 1960; the foundations for the definition would change, and change again.

The most misleading implication of the political argument is that the peace testimony was a conservative, reactive, and passive doctrine. While it might have had all of those qualities as a strategy in a particular time and a particular place, in its substance, it potentially requires activity and initiative of radical proportions. The Quakers surely became more conservative in many respects, or at least less ranting, which is not necessarily the same thing, after 1660; but in the course of doing so, the leadership enunciated in the peace testimony a doctrine of profoundly revolutionary implications. By attributing pacifism to defeat—by association, an expression of weakness—the 1660 emphasis denies the dimensions of pacifism that arise from strength. Sometimes pacifism proceeds from moral strength alone; sometimes it is even associated with political strength. The argument fails to take into account that political advantage was not immutable; when Quakers gained access to political power, although some were apparently seduced to ignore pacifist principles, others were not. And even if one sees pacifist behavior as misguided, there is no mistaking the extraordinary physical courage pacifism sometimes requires. In contrast, wrote John Milton, war is an "argument / Of human weakness rather than of strength."[26]

Finally, the political argument assumes a broad and sophisticated political outlook; such an outlook was doubtless the province of relatively few Quakers. So attributing the origin of the peace testimony to the political exigencies of 1660 is an inadequate formulation because it fails to explain the behavior of many Quakers before and after 1660. It is unlikely that early Quakers, largely simple people, were conscious of what would be beneficial on a national scale to defuse the widespread fear of Quakers as a subversive group; it is unlikely that individuals based their choices of whether or not to use violence on such considerations. The stories and the practices of individual Quakers, then, are crucial to a rounded understanding of the peace testimony.

"Above the Arm of Flesh"

Individuals deciding how to apply peaceful principles were sometimes formulating a moral response to the ultimate challenges of life and death, a task of extreme complexity and danger. They were confronting immediate choices about how to behave in a particular situation. They were not necessarily equipped to record either their motivations or their actions. They did not necessarily all make the same choices in similar situations. As the historical situations changed, so also did Quaker responses. Influencing their responses, too, were the idiosyncratic characters of countless individual Quakers; here combining to fire up a holy courage, there isolated so that few were inspired to depart from the safe way. Because peace principles arose out of different places and over time, it is not surprising that a range of interpretations about the peace testimony should develop, as well as a continuum of behavior. Similarly, when assumptions underlying Quaker belief changed, so once again would the range of responses. Changing meanings, rationales, and behavioral traditions have accrued over nearly three hundred and fifty years, masked in the original vocabulary of the first Quakers.

Most of the early Quakers confronted violence on a local field, face to face; dragged down a street and beaten, for example, for preaching near a market. Many probably reacted to violence or were violent themselves, flinging their fists much as they always had in the rough-and-tumble of seventeenth-century life, unaffected by their new religious direction. Thomas Holmes, for instance, was standing on a chair in a house in Durham, declaring the "Gospell of Truth," when a "rude multitude" violently pulled him down "in great Rage & fury," but he was "providentially rescued out of their hands by some Friends."[27] How violent was this rescue? William Penn and William Mead were indicted for holding a tumultuous assembly "with force and arms" in 1670. One Read, a constable, testified that he and his men had endeavored to pull Penn down from his preaching, but he could not get near him, "the people [Quakers?] kicking my watchmen and myself on the shins." (Mead insisted the indictment was a bundle of lies, for while "time was, when I had freedom to use a carnal weapon; and then I thought I feared no man; but now I fear the living God; and dare not make use thereof."[28]) William Ward, a Quaker, scrupulously had a new ship built for himself without guns and traded safely and profitably in the Mediterranean. Later, seduced by worldly esteem and worldly goods, he replaced his unarmed ship with a newly built ship which he fitted out with eighteen guns.[29] But one hears about others behaving in unexpected and mystifying ways. A sailor might suddenly refuse to man a gun on deck, or Quakers might not resist when young boys and soldiers attacked their gathering. Ellis Hookes, compiler of two books of Quaker sufferings, delivered a letter to his mother at the house of William Waller, the Parliamentary general. Waller's wife "fell a beating the said E. H. About the Head and pulling him by the Hair in a cruel manner." Hookes bore the abuse, saying only, "Woman, I deny thy Religion that cannot bridle thy Tongue nor thy hands."[30] Notably, George Fox never used violence himself, in spite of all the many provocations he endured from 1649 on; and several times he refused military office.[31] God's arm, he wrote, is "above the arm of flesh."[32] We read of a trooper who, as early as 1651, had rebuked his two colonels after coming to understand "Truth." The colonels repaid his insolence when the royalist and Parliament armies confronted each other at Worcester, sending him and one other to fight against two royalist soldiers. The companion was killed; the trooper reported that he "drove" his opponents away without firing his pistol; then, seeing "the deceit and hypocrisy of the officers," he "laid down his arms and saw to the end of fighting."[33] Many in England and its colonies refused to appear on mandatory militia training days or to serve in "trained bands." This tendency was infamous: when a Quaker missionary was not permitted to land at the island of Nevis, an official explained that since the coming of the Quakers to the Caribbean, "there are seven hundred of our militia turned Quakers; and the Quakers will not fight, and we have need of men to fight, being surrounded by enemies."[34] The listing of such Quakers refusing militia duties sometimes seem tedious, until the suffering is personified in homely example: a Captain Thomas Luxford refused to send in arms "from year to year," suffering penalties to the value of twenty or thirty pounds; one year "they took away his wife's bed and bedding, as soon as she was risen out of it, for one year's tax for drums and colours."[35]

"How If I Had Killed a Man?"

Mariner Thomas Lurting's "enlightenment" of the mid-1650s in regard to violence falls within a pattern of experience remote from the defeat and disillusionment that current historiography recognizes as the primary conditions giving rise to pacifism; remote, too, from the self-conscious purposes of Quaker leaders. Lurting was an English seaman serving under Admiral Blake about 1654; among his duties as boatswain was the responsibility to make sure that all two hundred sailors aboard his ship attended worship services and to punish those who did not. He had energetically beaten a small group of six Quakers for their absence from services. After having experienced four providential "deliverances" from extreme peril at sea, Lurting recounted, he became sensitized to religious concerns. Becoming troubled by the remembrance of these manifestations of God's protection, he stopped beating the Quakers and withdrew (as best he could on board ship) into private spiritual contemplation that continued for many months. Most of Lurting's religious struggles took place in solitude; he experienced God without outside instruction. His isolation and distraction made him an oddity: "Many came on Board to see me, thinking the Shape of my Body was alter'd, and I heard some say, that . . . I look'd like a dumb Saint."[36] But communing with God, Lurting to his surprise felt himself instructed to join with the Quakers, and approached one amongst them. "[A]nd before he opened his Mouth, the Hand of the Lord was upon me, and melted my Heart, and brought me into great Tenderness, and then he spake but a few Words . . . hitting the Mark to a Hair's Breadth."[37] Lurting began to associate with the Quakers. They were freed from much persecution, temporarily, when some who had abused them met with death, and when the Quakers survived an epidemic that killed forty sailors; these providentialist "deliverances" were apparently seen as God's favor, even by non-Quakers.[38]

As yet all the Quaker seamen continued to fight with courage, "we seeing then no farther"; Lurting noted, however, that they refused to take any plunder. They were aboard ship, far from political controversy, carrying out their duties in the navy. None of these new Quakers had ever heard that any Quakers refused to fight. Then, Lurting wrote, during a bombardment God "in a Minute's Time so far chang'd my Heart," that while he had been striving with all his capacity to kill, in the next minute, he could not have killed "if it were to gain the World": "as I was coming out of the Fore-castle Door, to see where the Shot fell, the Word of the Lord run through me, 'How if I had killed a Man': And it was with such Power, that for some Time I hardly knew whether I was in the Body, or out of it."[39] Meeting with the other Quakers, who bargained that if God saw them safely home, they would no longer fight, Lurting in contrast came to the position that his "testimony" could not be deferred; "inasmuch as we had been so great Actors in it, now we must bear our Testimony against Fighting." It was no lightly held conviction, for the printed ship's orders provided that "[i]f any Man flinch from his Quarters in Time of Engagement, any may kill him." Lurting did not lay his testimony "as an Injunction upon any one" but left his fellow Quakers "to the Lord, to do as he shall direct you." In spite of the captain's threat that "he that denies to fight in time of engagement I will put my sword in his bowels," all eventually came to a similar position, and the individual testimony became collective.[40]

The Lurting example does not fit within the parameters of pacifism as a self-defensive, strategic choice. Far from protecting him, in a worldly sense Lurting's pacifism exacerbated the menace he posed to others. Unlike the signers of the Declaration of 1660, whose renunciations of violence had the potential to defuse the threat they posed and the persecution they endured, Lurting and his fellow sailors aboard the man-of-war posed a greater threat to those about them by opting out of battle and so invited greater persecution—indeed, mandated punishment. While suggesting the process leading to nonviolence, Lurting's case also demonstrates the insufficiency of the political explanation for pacifism; it is too narrow to encompass Quaker heterogeneity.

We Might Fire at the Mast

Edward Coxere, a seaman aged about twenty six, attended a debate at Dover in 1659 between the local priest and Quakers Burrough and Fisher, where his interest in Quakerism was piqued. The experience stimulated a crucial question in Coxere's mind. "The first remarkable opening I had . . . was concerning fighting or killing of enemies." Whether or not this was "lawful" under God was naturally a great concern to him, "because it struck at my very life" (and livelihood). So Coxere visited the two Quakers at their lodgings and asked them, in view of his responsibilities as a seaman, if he could fight and yet be righteous.

> They, being very mild, used but few words . . . but wished me to be faithful to what the Lord did make known to me . . . so did not encourage me to fight, but left me to the working of the power of the Lord in my own heart . . . so that I did not lay down fighting on other men's words, but the Lord taught me to love my enemies in his own time.[41]

It is easy to interpret Burrough's and Fisher's reticence as stemming from their own possible lack of interest in pacifism, but it is highly significant that Coxere himself explained it as the traditional Quaker respect for individual revelation.[42] When Coxere was still coming to terms with his doubts about fighting, he consulted his shipmate, Quaker Richard Knowleman, about how they should act if their ship were attacked. Knowleman, who had been a gunner on a man-of-war but had left that position because of Quaker scruples (not about fighting but about deference), had felt free to sign on board a merchantman. He answered that what they must do was to fire not at men but instead to "fire at the mast." Coxere rejected this "deceit." Coxere reported the development of his peace principles as a process:

Figure 3.1. Edward Coxere's Ship *The Diligence,* of which he was gunner.—"An Inglish marchant
[merchant] man."—"A Spanish man of war in which I was a prisoner in the time of the
figh[t]."—"The Dilleience [Dillejence] of London of which I was Guner." "After we got of[f]
from the shore we had fitted our ship with foure [a fore] mast then the Spanish man of war
above tuck [took] us." Seaman Edward Coxere became a Quaker c. 1659. His diary with
his drawings of ships was written c. 1685–94. *Adventures by Sea of Edward Coxere,* forward
H. M. Tomlinson, edited E. H. W. Meyerstein, 1946, by permission of Oxford University Press.

"I saw I had a very heavy cross to take up, and it was indeed: it was so heavy that I could not soon take it up; I was yet too weak." Years later, he was still struggling with the question, seeking out Quaker captains to serve under.[43] Coxere and Knowleman serve as examples of two conscientious people struggling to interpret their obligations in regard to fighting; the distinctions they were forced to draw were not laid out for them in words.

James Strutt, a Quaker ship captain, renounced his livelihood over concern about fighting, but his reasoning bore little resemblence to Coxere's. England had promised the king of Spain that England's fleet was no threat to Spanish shipping; the English fleet then received explicit instructions to waylay the Spanish plate fleet. In Strutt's eyes, this betrayal rendered all his duties unjust: "I stood a servant unto my Nation in an evil cause." He laid down fighting, far more conventionally, because his cause was unjust.[44] In Quaker eyes, God would instruct each Quaker, each might understand his duties differently, and each might persuade others by example and suffering, not promulgations. Quakers, then, could be tolerant even of other Quakers serving as soldiers or as sailors obliged to fight. Rather than necessarily reflecting ambivalence, early pacifist statements and behavioral restraints were personal, in a process of individual clarification, consistent with belief in the necessity of each individual's personally discovering God's will. Even when tempered with collective discipline, this individualism persisted within Quakerism, eventually receiving protection in the idea of concensus decision-making.[45]

Some Scruple of Conscience

Quakers continued, long after 1660, to struggle with what nonviolence meant in practical terms. Some expressed their beliefs in especially careful, idiosyncratic ways. Alexander Somervaile was a mariner from Aberdeen, Scotland. In 1672 he was vulnerable to being impressed for the war against the Dutch. Most of the other Aberdeen seamen had fled the press. Somervaile's wife consulted with the Aberdeen Meeting as to whether it was appropriate for him to flee the press, given his unwillingness to serve because of conscience. The meeting decided it was safest for him not to flee but left it to Somervaile's own judgment. He decided to "come in and run the hazard"; he was arrested and imprisoned. The magistrates offered him liberty upon payment of a bond, that apparently the other seamen had paid (and forfeited). The meeting advised him to refuse, because giving a bond would plainly imply "an engagement on him to . . . list himself for the war" that might "mar his peace and reflect on Truth."[46] One Richard Forde of Barbados was commissioned to draw an official map of the island for the governor to send to the Lords of Trade and Plantations. Governor Atkins of Barbados had to apologize to the lords, for Forde had neglected to draw any "places of fortification" on his map, because of his religious scruples.[47] Captured Quakers were among those held as slaves in Morocco, in dire conditions. The Dutch redeemed Dutch slaves similarly held in 1686 by exchanging them for a captured Moor and thirty muskets per prisoner. The wife of one of the Quaker slaves appealed to the London Meeting for Sufferings to similarly intervene on behalf of her husband; the meeting in response wrote to captive Quakers warning them against using arms to buy their freedom.[48]

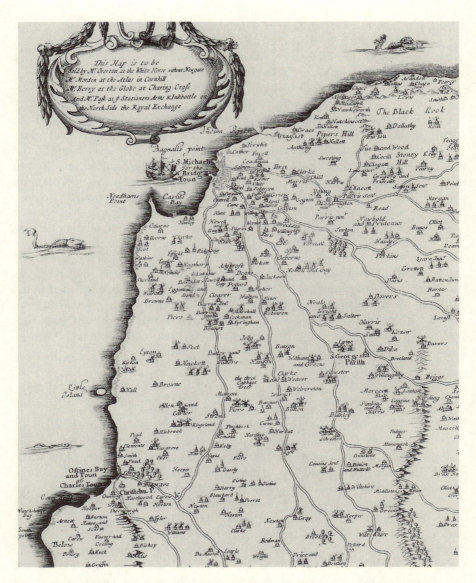

Figure 3.2. [Richard Forde], A New Map of the Island of Barbadoes. . . . (detail), London, 1675–76, Blathwayt Atlas # 32. Richard Forde's "Quaker" map. Note absence of fortifications and cannon at Carlisle Bay and absence of watch houses at Watch-House Bay. Compare with Ligon and Ogilby maps (figs. 3.3, 3.5) and with "A Prospect of Bridgetown" (fig. 3.4). Courtesy of the John Carter Brown Library at Brown University.

In the course of telling his story, Thomas Lurting alluded to several scruples connected with the peace testimony. When he was pressed to go aboard the ship *Mary* in 1662, he would not willingly step aboard and so was hoisted aboard with tackle. As he refused to do the king's work, so he refused to eat the king's food, fasting for five days before he spoke with the captain of the ship. The captain offered him several tasks: to stand with him and repeat his orders to the men; to "hand beer" with the coopers; to "stand by the fore-braces" and receive the captain's orders—"this is not killing men to haul a rope." Lurting replied, "But I will not do that." The captain then suggested that Lurting might act as assistant to the doctor, "when a man comes down, that hath lost a leg, or an arm, to hold the man, while the doctor cuts it off. This is not killing men; but saving their lives." Lurting answered, "But I will not do that; for it is all an assistance."[49]

Perhaps the clearest example of an individual working out his scruples regarding violence is the case of Henry Pitman.[50] Henry Pitman had just returned from Italy in 1685 and went to visit his relations in Somerset. There was another, more prominent, visitor to Somerset during these days: the duke of Monmouth, on the march with an army to challenge the reign of his uncle James II. Henry Pitman, a Quaker surgeon, went with friends to see the duke's army. Compassion led him to attach

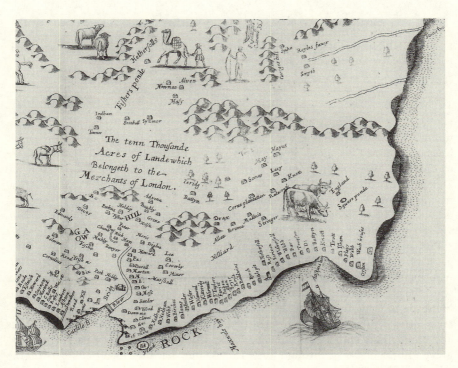

Figure 3.3. [Richard Ligon], A Topographicall Description. . . . (detail), 1673, in *A True & Exact History of the Island of Barbadoes*, London, 1673. Note cannon at Carlisle Bay; note watch houses. Compare with Forde map (fig. 3.2). Courtesy of the John Carter Brown Library at Brown University.

Figure 3.4. A Prospect of Bridgetown in Barbados, drawing, London, 1695. Detail of Needham's Fort, Carlisle Bay. Courtesy of the John Carter Brown Library at Brown University.

himself to the troops and to treat the wounded. Pitman justified his actions in his journal. "But as I was never in Arms my self, so neither was I wanting in my care to dress the Wounds of many of the King's Soldiers, who were Prisoners in the Duke's Army, using the utmost of my care and skill for both."[51] When Monmouth's army was routed, Pitman was captured and condemned to be hanged, drawn, and quartered; partially reprieved, he was transported to Barbados and involuntary servitude.

Pitman masterminded an escape from Barbados in a small boat with seven companions, making landfall on the island of Tortuga. In describing his adventures, Pitman included several details relevant to an examination of Quaker attitudes toward the use of force. He mentioned, for example, that he ordered his companions in escape to bring their weapons. When they were surprised by a canoe of privateers, he said, "my Companions provided their Arms, and charged their Musquets and Blunderbuss with pieces of Glass-Bottles (for we coming from Barbadoes in so great a hurry and fear, through forgetfulness they left their Bag of Bullets on the Wharf.)"[52] The privateers invited the group to join them; Pitman refused, explaining his decision as his being faithful to God.[53] When the shipwrecked Pitman and companions broke their knives trying to separate turtle shells from their meat, they made new knives from the swords "my Companions brought with them."[54] A

THE PEACE TESTIMONY

steady diet of tortoise meat and eggs gave the group a violent flux; Pitman cured them with an opium tincture,

> for before we came from Barbadoes, I thought of a way to deliver ourselves out of our Enemies Hands (in case we should be taken) without shedding of Blood; and it was thus, I dissolved a sufficient quantity of Opium in a Bottle of rich Cordial Water . . . intending to give it to those Persons that should take us.[55]

His design was that the drink would so overcome the enemies with sleep that the group could escape. Pitman overcame any scruples about marauders and went aboard a privateer that was heavily laden with prize, eventually making his way back to England.

Pitman found it necessary to explain and distinguish his behavior whenever he was proximate to violence or potential violence. Clearly, he felt that fighting in the army would be wrong. Wrong, too, would be partisanship of a kind that would cause him to treat an enemy casualty less humanely than one "on his side." He was careful to point out that he did not himself wear a sword or carry weapons. He would not have done violence to those thwarting his escape, going to some pains

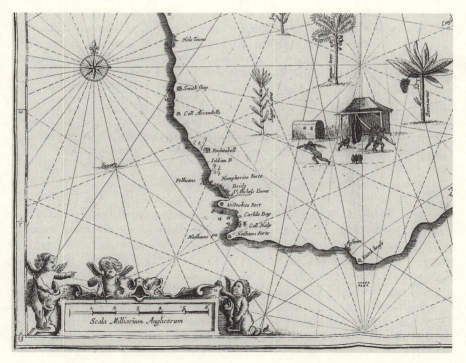

Figure 3.5. John Ogilby, Novissima . . . Barbados, (detail), in *America: Being An Accurate Description of the New World.* . . . London, 1670. Note: "Humpheries Forte," "Willowbies Fort," "Needhams Forte"; watch house. Compare with Forde's map (fig. 3.2). Courtesy of the John Carter Brown Library at Brown University.

to develop an alternative protection (the opium potion) for himself. He would not participate in piracy directly.

Yet Pitman did in fact associate himself with an army. He demanded that his companions bring their arms for the escape; although not bearing arms himself, he saw a necessity for the group to be armed, and heavily armed, with cutlasses and blunderbusses. He stood by while others mobilized these weapons against privateers. He welcomed rescue by violent men, as long as they were en route to cashing in their prize rather than garnering it. Pitman, then, absorbed in his own goodness, felt no responsibility for the goodness of others. His pacifism was intensely personal; it was consistent with contemporary Quaker understanding of obedience to God, without emphasis on the victims of violence.

Though of Course Nonviolent

Other related difficulties persist. Many Quaker historians, for example, recognizing from their own religious experience the traditional words of the peace testimony that still serve today, mistake the familiar words for familiar meaning, failing to see the philosophical chasm between peace principles based on obedience and considerations of soul purity and peace principles based instead or additionally on a later concern caring for worldly justice and the physical lives of others. Some assume Quaker actions were based on principle when they may merely have been the only feasible option. The Quaker historian Howard Brinton offered one such interpretation of the shipwreck of a party of Quakers. When Jonathan Dickinson's ship ran aground in what is now Florida in 1696, he and his shipmates sat on the beach, surrounded by excited and looting Indians gesticulating with knives. The stranded party sat still, some held from behind, and the menacing and commotion of the Indians stilled as well. Dickinson himself attributed their deliverance to God's preservation; Brinton saw their behavior as "a chance to put their pacifism into practice." They may have indeed been practicing their pacifism, but they may also have had no other choice.[56]

Understanding of the peace testimony has been muddled, too, because Quakers so often used militant rhetoric associated with the Lamb's War. The Lamb's War, a concept drawn from the apocalyptic Book of Revelation, anticipated a war in which Jesus Christ, "the Lamb of God," would lead the forces of absolute good against the forces of absolute evil—a war fought exclusively with spiritual weapons, such as the sword of the spirit that was the Word of God.[57] Quakers saw themselves as engaged in the Lamb's War, an inward war against their own unrighteousness and wills and an outward war against God's adversaries, including the churches, because they were false churches. Most historians have recognized the difficulty many contemporaries had in distinguishing between the metaphorical and the literal in the militant Quaker vocabulary of the Lamb's War. The 1659 tract "A Declaration From the People Called Quakers" illustrates the apparent contradiction seen in the frequent juxtaposition of militant language and disavowal of carnal weapons:

the Sonn of God . . . might command thousands, and ten thousands of his Saints at this day, to fight in his cause, he might . . . give them victory over all their Enemies . . . but yet . . . neither is his warrfare with carnall weapons, neither is his victory by the murthering, and killing of mens persons.[58]

Moreover, Quakers themselves sometimes seemed uncertain of their course, as in this declaration with its strong suggestion of temporizing: "neither can we yet beleeve that he will make use of us in that way, though it be . . . our Heireship . . . to possesse the uttermost parts of the Earth, but for the present we are given up to beare, and suffer . . . without the Arme of flesh."[59] Is the battle of good and evil fought with weapons or without? Is any measure of violence justified when "the sword of the Lord is in the hands of the saints"? Lamb's War rhetoric complicates the understanding of the peace testimony, not only because of its generalized warfare imagery but also because of the flexibility of the phrase "carnal weapons." At times the "carnal weapons" vocabulary is purely figurative, meaning any weapons of the earth, such as the mind and human reason; at other times it means physical instruments of coercion. Fox, for example, described people after the Fall (of Adam) as warring with each other with carnal weapons; he continued by describing this weaponry as "inward foul weather, storms, tempests, winds, strifes, the whole family of it in confusion, being all gone from . . . the witness of God in themselves."[60] Robert Barrow described Fox himself as God's "Battle Axe and weapons of War to break through the will worships and rudiments of the world."[61] Thomas Taylor saw magistrates as the carnal weapons of the ministers.[62] A Catholic friar on Malta demonstrated the ultimate flexibility of carnal weapons language, as a tortured Quaker prisoner of the Inquisition recorded. She asked the friar, who had insisted he was in the same spirit as the apostles, "why they did abuse their Power then, and make use of Carnal Weapons. He said they did not, they were all spiritual, their Inquisition, & their Chains and Irons, and all is spiritual."[63]

Historians have neglected to notice that much of the violent language is applied to the intentions of God himself. "Oh, England . . . you must be cut down. . . . The Lord will pluck you down."[64] The omnipotent God was judge and revenger, in Quaker eyes. "For your Whoredoms in the city of *London,* is the hand of the Lord stretched forth against thee, and the Sword of the Lord God drawn to hew thee down."[65] It was not necessary, and indeed not possible, for God to be a pacifist. Much of the warlike language, then, even if literal, need not indicate that the particular Quaker was not a pacifist; he could hold to nonviolence himself while believing that God was not a pacifist. In addition to admitting a double standard on earth—between redeemed Quakers already living in the Kingdom and unredeemed others—Quakers could accept another double standard: between people, commanded to live according to the spirit of the gospel, and God, responsible for justice. "And therefore [it is] just with the Lord to give them as A prey unto their Enemies."[66] And the "light in all your consciences"—the very Light "centering" Quakers—"shall . . . make you confess his judgments just, his wrath just, his vengeance just, his plagues just, his destruction just . . . in the day of the Lord's slaughter."[67]

The paradox resulted from lingering Quaker providentialism. Quakers had seen God's hand in the victories of the Good Old Cause; when they saw the Cause as betrayed during the Interregnum, they interpreted continuing instability as God's warning to the leaders and army to repent; they interpreted the Restoration as God punishing the nation for its sins, as the defeat of hope. The belief that God intervened in the details of life for didactic purposes, and to mete out justice, necessitated a concentration upon people as "instruments" of God. It was but a short maneuver, then, to thrust the responsibility for violence onto the will of God, in spite of gospel ordinations. Not even the most conscientious pacifist among the early Quakers adequately reconciled providentialism with pacifism; those who tried, by using "spiritual weapons" vocabulary, did not abrogate God's having ordained the violence of the Civil War.[68]

Some historians, Quaker and non-Quaker alike, have misunderstood the scope of the peace testimony because they have defined out of the religious society those early Quakers who chose paths inconsonant with later understandings of the peace witness. They thus followed, perhaps unthinkingly, those Quakers who held that if a fellow Quaker erred, by definition, he or she was no longer a Quaker, and the group should not be tainted by the errant activity. Francis Howgill, for example, testified in court in 1663/1664 that it was "reseaved principall" among Quakers that Christ's kingdom could not be established with carnal weapons. "If I had 20 lives," he said, "I durst ingage them all for the body of Quackers for ever having any hand in war . . . for all such as wear found in any thing of that nature I did disowne them, nay further I sayd if their wear any such they wear not of us."[69] Nevertheless, Howgill was privately far less certain a few months later. Some Quakers had been associated with plotting an abortive uprising in Yorkshire, the so-called Kaber Rigg Plot of 1663. "I have borne a greatt weight many monethes upon my backe about this plotting," Howgill confided in Fox. But Howgill found it impossible to "wholy rejecte" those "that weare to[o] much inclined . . . to it," because they were, he knew, "beleveing in the treuth." Furthermore, he was unable to "justisse" (rule or govern) them, "so that I have been as upon a racke betwixt my freinds & enimies."[70] Howgill was typical of the reluctance to discipline in the area of peace principles, when their implications had been as yet so little considered. The reluctance was to persist into the next century and to revive periodically throughout Quaker history. When a few Quakers were unmistakeably involved directly in violent episodes, such as the Northern Plot of 1663 and the Monmouth Rebellion of 1685, the response of fellow Quakers was to attempt to disassociate the movement from both the activities and the Quaker credentials of the perpetrators. But their disavowals sometimes seemed halfhearted, temporary; perhaps because 1660 and its declarations were less definitive than they, and their descendants, would like to conclude.[71]

The Foundation of God

"And as for our Principle," wrote William Bayly of the peace testimony in 1676, it is "without Beginning or End; it is the Foundation of God." For Bayly, the peace testimony was "Everlasting and Universal," "steadfast and Unmoveable"; necessarily so, as he saw Quakers "joyned unto him (the Lord) . . . one Spirit with him."[72] Yet within the historical world it is perhaps the very dynamism of the peace testimony, in its changing rationale, its multiple manifestations, and its radical risk that has preserved a distinctive dimension to a sect that might otherwise have been only one among many comfortably unchallenging communities. Instead, within Quakerism, the very disquieting unsettledness of the peace testimony has kept alive a spirit of inquiry and vitality. Within the larger society, the peace testimony has challenged convention and conscience to force a glancing confrontation with the intrinsic value of human existence. For Quakers, the way of Jesus was the way of worldly risk. There were few places of greater risk than New England, during the war known as King Philip's War. Survival was at risk for all New Englanders, old and new, Indians and settlers, in 1675 and 1676. Quakers would risk both their lives and their principles.

PART II

New England

4

"Bold Boyes and Blasphemers"

QUAKERS IN EARLY NEW ENGLAND

He built a small ship, small even for a coaster; although he was a coastal mariner from Holderness near the sea in the north of England, he had never before made an ocean voyage. Manned by only three men and three boys, the *Woodhouse* sailed from London in June 1657, making for the New World. Its builder and captain, Quaker Robert Fowler, knew nothing, of course, of navigation, nor of latitude and longitude. Instead, he and his eleven Quaker passengers met daily on deck in a meeting for worship, to seek God's course, their spiritual sextant, which they followed to landfall at Long Island at the end of July 1657 ("and the word was from Him, 'Cut through and steer your straightest course, and mind nothing but me.'").[1]

Other Quaker missionaries had carried "Truth" to these far lands on the winds of spiritual fervor the summer before.[2] Ann Austin and Mary Fisher had landed at Boston, in Massachusetts Bay, in summer 1656; eight others arrived shortly thereafter, on 27 July 1656, in the *Speedwell*.[3] Because some of the *Speedwell* Quakers, such as the twenty-five-year-old Christopher Holder, were educated and cultivated, they may have been especially threatening to Boston magistrates, whose shock at their message and method was not to diminish for more than two decades.[4] It had taken only a few months until the magistrates could bend their outrage to legislation—the first Quaker Act of October 1656.[5] This act banished all Quakers from the colony, including Christopher Holder and the others, and imposed heavy penalties on anyone transporting Quakers into the colony. Even the sympathetic Nicholas Upshall, a local resident who only protested the act, had been thereby rendered a Quaker adherent and banished to Rhode Island, where a Newport Indian gave him shelter.[6] It was the act, then, that had forced six of the banished missionaries plus five others to seek passage the following year with the unlikely Captain Fowler aboard the *Woodhouse*, because no ordinary shipmaster would risk taking them back to Boston.

Christopher Holder and Nicholas Upshall were among the first of many Quakers—foreign and local—to excite outrage in New England. The faith of the missionaries was to be severely tested throughout the colonies, and some would lose their way. "Plantation Work is full of Snares and Cares," wrote William Loddington soberly. "I have had a taste of it, and have known some lose even lovely Gifts and Testimonies . . . among Woods and Bogs."[7] The woods and bogs were the unavoidable natural features through which the missionaries would struggle from the Great Dismal Swamp in Carolina to New Quechawanah in Maine; they were also the metaphorical woods and bogs of hostility, misunderstanding, fear, and excess—rising from within themselves and facing them down from without.

Within a few years of its rise in England, then, the Quaker movement had disciples on the other side of the Atlantic Ocean. A religious movement in its formative and typically zealous and tumultuous phase was defining itself on both sides of the Atlantic concurrently—an unusual phenomenon in history, surely. The content of the message carried back and forth across time and the ocean was apparently suited to this pattern of dissemination, for it was simple in its outward frame. But this simplicity hid a potential complexity that was to challenge the unity of spirit so fundamental to the Quaker religious assumption.

Answering the Witness of God

The visiting Quakers saw their task as one of literal, not figurative, enlightenment—of teaching people to turn to the Light within themselves. Rather than an elaborate theology, with structured forms of belief and worship, the Quaker missionary brought with her the plain instruction to turn within to God and Christ: "the Lord was come to teach them himself."[8] In 1659, George Fox wrote to six missionaries in New England and Virginia, charging them to "answer the Witness of God in everyone and be a dread to nations." In spite of its vagueness, this charge theoretically gave adequate guidance for Quaker missionaries, because the content of the Quaker message was contained in the method of teaching, which the letter prescribed.[9] The missionary was not to impart a programmatic Truth but was only to point out where each person must seek truth.[10] The central assumption was that spiritual authority and revelation were accessible in an unmediated sense to anyone willing to acknowledge her profound error and to submit her will to the will of God. Given this core belief, the missionary was theoretically called upon to transmit knowledge of a method, a process, rather than substantive content, creed, or dogma. Early Quaker missionaries personified an ideal: that they were not evangelizing with the purpose of converting others, but rather were travelling in search of like-minded souls who would discover their convincements within themselves. George Fox, for example, in Barbados, preached and prayed, and closed his messages with "And so frends I leave you all to the wittnes of God in your selves."[11] When a group of listeners in Narragansett, Rhode Island Colony, indicated that if they had had money enough, they would have hired Fox to remain with them as preacher, Fox replied, "it was time for me to go away, for [if I stayed,] then they would not come to their own teacher . . . for we brought every one to their own teacher."[12]

"I Perceived a Small Path"

In actuality, in the course of bringing each person to his own teacher within, the traveling ministers stressed aspects of the gospel message—teaching about the Kingdom of God, enlarging upon Quaker spiritual obligations—and so transmitted fundamental assumptions about the nature of God and man's relationship to him. In this way, among a highly individualized search for truth, there grew nevertheless a community with peculiarly Quaker habits and assumptions. Just as the missionaries themselves had absorbed common themes from their own experiences among Quakers, so too they carried common themes abroad. While it is impossible to know what particular missionaries did actually bring as their messages to a new region, the character of Quakerism as it developed within the new region might suggest some of their priorities. Since from early days, for example, New England Quakers refused to swear oaths, unlike their Puritan neighbors, one may be confident that this Quaker testimony was included explicitly in missionary messages. Sometimes the message the itinerant ministers apparently took to a region such as New England shed light on the nature of belief in Old England. When early converts in New England made reference to renouncing war, it suggests that this was a concern for Quakers in Old England as well. When they made such references before 1660 and the Restoration of King Charles II, they showed that peace concerns had held a greater pride of place in England than has lately been assumed to have been true; before, that is, their beliefs about peace became useful to defend against monarchical persecution.

The initial commonality of belief, as English Quakers offered a new faith to colonists, would have seemed natural to Quakers themselves, who could have expected nothing less even from a completely undirected search for truth, since in their eyes truth was one truth; and a sincere search on the part of any number would yield a unified Truth. Quakers were sure that the Truth was unfailing and was one Truth. If each were true to her own leadings, then what she taught would be consonant with the teaching of any other Quaker messenger. "Speak the Word of the Lord faithfully, neither add to it with your reason nor diminish from it with a disobedient mind," warned George Fox. "The Light is but one. All being guided by it, all are subject to One and are one in the unity of the Spirit."[13]

But religious beliefs do not take hold and are not maintained in a merely spiritual realm, unaffected by their historical and geographical locations, unaffected by the example of particular individuals. Societal contexts may influence both style and content of belief.[14] Yet it has been a persistent assumption of Quaker historiography that Quakerism, developing as it did nearly simultaneously on both sides of the Atlantic in America and in England, transmitted by traveling ministers, sustained by interlocking family and commercial relationships, and disciplined by a copious correspondence between Quaker centers and widespread meetings maintained a homogeneity of belief and practice in remarkable harmony with the Quaker conviction that Truth itself is one.[15] When Welsh Quakers reluctantly bade goodbye to those emigrating to the colonies, they wrote, "Tho the Branches be many running over the walks, and extending themselves to the utmost parts of the earth, yet one is the root and the same is the body that bears them."[16] But in studying the peace testimony—one particular aspect of Quaker belief—one notices differences in emphasis, underlying meaning, and behavior in different times and places, and it becomes difficult to ignore the effect of varied cultural requirements on the manifestations of belief itself. Presented with challenges to their peace testimony peculiar to one location and one situation, Quakers reacted in ways distinct from Quakers challenged in other times and in other situations. Individuals influenced and sustained those about them in idiosyncratic ways. Quakers themselves did not often acknowledge—or perhaps even detect—these differences, because the vocabulary in which they expressed their convictions continued to be shared among all Quakers. Quakers continued to seek opinions from London, for example, even when it should have been apparent that those opinions, in the absence of knowledge about the local situation, were of dubious relevance.[17]

Historians, too, have generally failed to take into account some of the local influences acting on belief and its expression, taking at face value the shared idiom of Quakers throughout their history. But it is not enough to assume that a continuity of words signifies a continuity of meaning. To understand the peace testimony fully, one must pose consistent questions about its manifestations within a historical context, looking for the specific meaning, specific requirements, specific leaders, and specific responses arising from a particular society.

The Particulars of Place

While politics, the economy, the character of a society, and events all would affect the nature of Quaker belief after it took root in a new place, a prior factor—the way Quakerism arrived and was sustained in a region in the first place—assured a certain divergence from the beginning. As Quakerism walked its way from the north of England to the south, for instance, it found congenial ground among some in a society fractured by change, floundering for a new certainty in a culture where old certainty had been beheaded. But others saw the Quakers as exacerbating uncertainty, as further eroding the safe hierarchies of earthly authority. When a Quaker shouted "Dumb Dog and Hireling" at the priest during the Sunday service in the town church, he was disturbing more than the calm of prayer and reason of the sermon. When Soloman Eccles marched into Westminster Hall in London with a pan of burning coals on his head, he challenged the self-esteem of the English polity.[18] In the eyes of people all over England, Quakers were corroding the primacy of scripture, they were brimming over with a chaos of personal revelation, they were preening an arrogance of perfectibility, and they were destroying the structure of deference. So the people of England reacted in a fury of persecution, reviling, stoning, beating, hounding out of town, fining, imprisoning, and torturing to death. Quakerism emerged out of England's turmoil, opportunities, and needs and was shaped immediately by its turmoil, opportunities, and needs. Quakerism was defined from its beginning by its origins.

The early traveling missionaries of the 1650s sent accounts of their travels to Margaret Fell and George Fox at Swarthmore, the Fell home, letters preserved in the Swarthmore Manuscripts. Although suffused with an enobling sense of mission, these letters also betray a siege mentality, sparing little overt love for "enemies"; rather, they evoke a vengeful God treading upon their enemies' necks. The Quakers constantly urged each other to revisit an individual or a village and revisit again, making it clear that local work was very dependent on the visiting missionaries for the perpetuation of the initial response to the Quaker message.[19]

As these early Quakers traveled from village to village, from countryside to London, from market square to Parliament, from sheepfold to coffeehouse to ship's hold, their assurance, sense of prophetic mission, and sense of besiegement lent an abrasive edge to a message already inherently challenging to the very foundations of religious, social and political institutions. The Lamb's War metaphor permitted a harsh and militant rhetoric apparently difficult to harmonize with a Christian ideal of reconciliation or with the pacific spirit traditionally associated with the Quakers:

> Put on your Armour, and gird on your sword . . . sound an Alarum, and make their ears to tingle. . . . Appear in your terror as an Army with Banners, and let the Nations know your power, and the stroke of your hand: cut down on the right hand, and slay on the left, and let not your eye pitty . . . and dash her children against the stones."[20]

Blunt, harsh rhetoric indeed made ears tingle as Quakers challenged all people to renounce their evil souls, abandon comfortable ways of worship, and instead risk the immensity of experiencing God. But like others with prophetic messages, Quakers justified scathing speech because it was ultimately redemptive for their hearers. As opposed to a flattering, worldly love, wrote James Nayler, God's love "consists of Reproofs, Judgment, and Condemnation, against all that defiles the Creation, and against the Creature who yeelds to that pollution." In "declaring its condition," it is a "pure love to the Soul."[21] Their mission was not to "sooth up People in their Sins, nor sow Pillows under their Arm-holes."[22] The weapons of the Spirit—the armor of God, the breastplate of righteousness, the shield of faith, the helmet of salvation, and the sword of the Spirit, the word of God—were to "wrestle not against flesh and blood, but . . . against spiritual wickedness in high places."[23] At the same time that their proselytizing was extraordinarily successful, then, Quakers excited fear, antagonism, persecution, and punishment. All of Quaker experience—initial insights, "minding" the Light, fervor, joy, spiritual companionship, throngs of listeners, throngs of sneerers, conversions, hatreds, violence, "laboring" with Protector, Parliament, soldier, judge, jailor, and jailed—all elaborated the nature and content of Quaker faith.

Quakerism in Pennsylvania was another matter. Quakerism sailed to Pennsylvania in the souls of immigrants. Pennsylvania Quaker settlers carried with them religious conviction and practice already established in another place. The experiences that these settlers would undergo in their new land would in time influence their religious lives, but upon their arrival they looked about them with a set of religious assumptions that were bound to affect the way they interpreted and acted within their new environment. These Quakers were used to thinking of themselves as outsiders: their countrymen had persecuted and misunderstood them in England, resenting them as problematical and disturbing to the larger English society, ridiculing them as bewildering clowns. When their ships dropped anchor in the Delaware River, they knew what they were about: to find a better life, to finally become insiders within the boundaries of a Holy Experiment. Moreover, they were many in number from the beginning; their Quakerism was not mediated by a few missionaries who appeared for a few days and then moved on. They had, too, by 1682, when they started settling Pennsylvania, the benefit of hindsight, of having watched from a distance the experience of Quakers in other colonies who had lived their religion in America for as long as twenty-six years.

In contrast, one may consider the way in which Quakerism took hold in Carolina, in what is now North Carolina. The original settlers of Carolina, backwoodsmen and their families slogging their way from Virginia through the Great Dismal Swamp, had little to lose by striking off into wilderness—a wilderness still populated by bison.[24] No defined faith sustained them in their ventures; no spiritual leader arose among them, until isolated Quaker missionaries, William Edmundson in early 1672 and George Fox some months later, found their way to isolated farmhouses and stimulated religious interest. Edmundson's coming was typically onerous: "I perceiv'd a small Path, which I follow'd till it was very dark, and rain'd violently . . . I walk'd all Night . . . I durst not lie down on the Ground, for my Cloaths were wet to my Skin." In this sodden condition, he found the home of the one Quaker couple, from New England, who had not seen another Quaker in seven years. When many people came, "smoking their Pipes" during the ensuing meeting for worship, "in a little time," Edmundson reported, "the Lord's Testimony arose in the Authority of his Power, and their Hearts being reach'd with it, several of them were tender'd and received the Testimony." He held a meeting the next day and left on the third day.[25]

Fox came in like manner in November, to see if what had been sown had taken root: "we were much wet in the canoe, the water came upon us in waves . . . the boat being deep and the water shoal that our boat would not swim."[26] Fox spent eighteen days bailing boats upon the rivers and swamps of Carolina, making "a little entrance for Truth."[27] Three years later, Edmundson returned; several seem to have remembered him well, and when he left again, "Friends were finely settled."[28] How fleeting the Carolina introduction to Quakerism was, and how remote and cut off the early adherents were from the wider Quaker community—yet on such a foundation several meetings in Carolina prospered and their members became the leaders in the new colony.[29] From the evidence that remains, these small Quaker gatherings received visitors for only a few days over a period of several years, yet nevertheless coalesced into a self-conscious community. Quaker testimonies from the Quaker community in England had been imparted to them, for the Carolina Quakers articulated some of them in succeeding years, even before correspondence with Quakers in England became practical.[30] But to some degree, Quakerism had to find its way again and again in the wilderness, unaided by any Valiant Sixty.[31]

In this setting, Quakerism meant something entirely different within the community from its meaning in England. Here in the wild and lonely Carolina backwaters Quakerism meant order, not disorder. It represented stability, discipline, a binding influence on neighborly relationships rather than a licentious fracturing of community. The manner in which Carolina Quakers received the new religious belief and their experience as organizers of a community would later influence the way they expressed their Quaker convictions in their lives. Here Quakerism drew to itself only the advantage of a quiet self-confidence, not the defensive confidence of the persecuted.

Missionaries transmitted Quaker religious belief to New Englanders in a quite different manner. Here, missionaries from Old England, still imbued with the fervor of a nascent religious enthusiasm, influenced already established settlers, many of whom had already expressed active religious deviance from traditional Puritanism of either the Separatist or non-Separatist forms. The missionaries were welcome to those who chafed under the ambitious vision of Puritan theocrats, welcome to those who had excited the attention of the courts for years for absenting themselves from religious meetings or for making disparaging remarks about ministers. Unlike the Carolina settlers, the New England converts suffered not from an absence but from a surfeit of order and discipline. Quakerism represented a freedom from external, earthly ministerial authority, even while it demanded extraordinary faithfulness of another kind. Some of these exiles from the Puritan religion, such as William Coddington or Nicholas Easton, had become sectarian vagabonds, passing through several forms of religious expression, from Puritans to so-called antinomians, or to Baptists, or to Gortonists, or to other personalized forms that remain unidentified. Some were vagabonds in fact as well as metaphor, moving from town to town in search of more compatible surroundings. For some, like Benjamin Newbury and Daniel Gould, Rhode Island was the last of successive moves: from Massachusetts, perhaps, to north country settlements such as Dover or Hampton; or from the Plymouth north shore to Dartmouth on the south shore; or from Massachusetts towns such as Salem, traditionally a place of less religious control. To the extent that many of the settlers who listened sympathetically to missionaries had a history of questioning dominant religious modes, a history of seeking, a history of claiming for themselves alternative ways of spiritual existence, they resembled those groups of Seekers, Baptists, and other innovators in Old England who were especially receptive to the Quaker message as introduced in the north of England.[32]

Unlike missionaries and their adherents in Old England, those in New England were more easily able to go elsewhere when threatened, although many chose not to. They could retreat temporarily to sanctuary in Rhode Island or the West Indies and return to more strenuous work in less welcoming colonies again and again. Although fewer in number than those in England, there were many missionaries in New England compared to Carolina, some staying within a community for months at a time until some infraction drew the attention of authorities.[33] Some finally settled in the colonies, such as Robert Hodgson and Christopher Holder, who settled in Rhode Island.

The nature of the particular society into which Quakerism was introduced was bound to affect the nature of Quakerism in that particular place and time. Who carried the message, the character of the society hearing the message, and how that society responded to the message could all shape the direction of Quakerism itself. The testimonies, those shared principles that, by insight and experience, had gradually become important to Quakers, were not codified into any program or creed. They were subject, then, to changing interpretations and changing importance, according to the challenges presented by local circumstance. The New England experience would force its own definition of the peace testimony.

Persecution: "Knock Him Down, It Is a Wolf"

Puritan governments of New England greeted the Quaker missionaries and their new adherents with a familiar persecution. As in Old England, persecution was significant in both shaping and making visible early principles of nonviolence. Reacting to the Quaker provocation of gathering together and testifying, of luring others away from the Puritan dogma, colonial governments arrested and imprisoned Quakers, beat them and exiled them, fined them and ruined them. The prophetic style of Quaker missionaries, as much as the substance of their message, stimulated an immediate horrified reaction on the part of Puritan churchmen and their governmental allies. Fear and disgust mingled with their anger as political and religious leaders faced the simultaneous challenge to their authority and their cherished vision of absolute truth. Quaker George Wilson's description of his prior encounters with the "priests" of New England illustrates this fear, disgust, and anger, betrayed through their virulence: they did "push and hitte & exceedingly abuse me, som saying hang him Quakeing dog, others Roague & some blasphemer, witch & devill."[34] Plymouth Colony promulgated a Day of Humiliation in 1658 because it detected a sign of God's displeasure in "leting loose as a scourge upon us those freeting gangreinlike doctrines and persons commonly called Quakers."[35] If a Quaker refused to remove his hat, "persecutors" might say, reportedly, "Knock him down, it is a wolf." Charles Chauncey, the "chief teacher" at Harvard, was remembered to have said in a sermon that Quakers could be knocked down as wolves.[36] And the Boston Court of Assistants sneered at Quakers as "Bold Boyes & Blasphemers."[37]

Vilification was codified into command. The governments rushed into the formulation of laws against the Quakers, only to repeal them and enact yet more rigorous laws in a vain hope to contain the contagion. The escalation of these measures and punishments, culminating in the Boston hangings of four religious martyrs in 1659–1660, signifies that the missionaries were to a measure accomplishing their design and successful in convincing new believers.

The Plymouth Quaker Law of 1657, for example, outlined the judicial duties of citizen and court officer alike. Any Quaker "entertaining" a "foreign" Quaker was to be fined an exorbitant five pounds and whipped; a citizen was obliged to report any visiting Quaker to the constable or be censured. The constable was required to escort the Quaker to the magistrate. The magistrate was to take the Quaker to jail—the costs of jail and transport out of the colony to be borne by the prisoner. For holding a religious meeting, local Quakers were fined as follows: any speaker,

Figure 4.1. "Die Quacker Schiesen noch viel Menschen," or "Quakers still [fight with] many people," reproduction of engraving in *Historia Fanaticorum,* 1701. Available in London in 1660 as *A Fanatick History.* Many were skeptical of Quaker peace principles, as this anti-Quaker cartoon illustrates. "Shall we rationally question," Roger Williams asked rhetorically, "whether their hands . . . will not be as fierce and cruel, if the most holy and only Wise permits Whips & Halters, Swords & Fagots to fall into their Hands?" Courtesy of the John Carter Brown Library at Brown University.

forty shillings; the host, forty shillings; any attender, ten shillings.[38] Quakers reacted with some discretion: in Sandwich for instance, having learned that local authorities would threaten a religious meeting, the local Quakers slipped after Christopher Holder, climbing over a ridge through the forest and down into a hollow by a stream—to meet in a place called Christopher's Hollow to this day.[39]

A Massachusetts Quaker law of 1657 took notice of the frustrating habit of banished Quakers to return. Any male "foreign" Quaker returning to the colony after banishment for the first time would suffer the loss of one ear; for the second time, the other ear; for the third, his tongue would be bored through with a hot iron. A returning female Quaker would merely be whipped.[40] Such severities did occur; such was the fate of Christopher Holder, the "Mutilated," who sacrificed his right ear to authority. (Holder took his one ear back to England to plead for colonial Quakers before the king.)[41] Less dramatic encounters also dotted the colony records of the early Quaker years. The records preserve the order to search the house of Nicholas Davis of Barnstable for Quaker writings; the fine imposed against Edward Perry of Sandwich for using threatening speech against the marshall; the petition from the inhabitants of Dover complaining about the spread of Quakerism; the imprisonment of Robert Whetcombe and Mary Cudworth for having been married "irregularly"; the seizing of Joshua Coggeshall's horse, because, as a Rhode Islander, he violated the law against any strange Quaker riding a horse within Plymouth Colony.[42] Even the powerful were not immune: Captain James Cudworth of Scituate was dismissed from military office and disenfranchised merely for having allowed Quakers to meet in his house, even though, as he wrote, "the Quakers and my self cannot close in divers things."[43]

Persecution is a well-known story, an embarrassment to later Americans who would rather remember a purely noble history.[44] It is a well-known story partly because the meticulous accounts of all persecutions—"sufferings"—that New England Quakers reported back to Old England have preserved the character and details of the persecution. Fox's summary of New England persecution for one twelve-month period detailed, for example, that

> [e]leven strangers which are free-born English received 22. whipings, the stripes amounting to 350. Eleven inhabitants and free-born English received 16 whippings, the stripes amounting to 160. Fourty five imprisonments of strangers and inhabitants, amounting to 307 weeks; two beaten with pitch ropes, the blows amounting to 139.[45]

Jonathan Chu has continued Fox's distinction between "stranger" and inhabitant Quakers, pointing out that because the General Court of Massachusetts Bay was separated from ecclesiatical power, it cited Quakers for sedition, not heresy: as a threat to authority because they would not obey laws. The General Court devolved its responsibility for Quaker management upon local jurisdictions after the Restoration, in order to insulate itself from too much unfavorable attention from the Crown to its harsh treatment of Quakers. Local control mitigated the severity of measures against resident Quakers, for it was readily apparent that these neighbors obeyed laws and did not threaten the kind of seditious challenge to order that visiting Quakers seemed to. Visiting Quakers, in the old English tradition of wariness toward "vagabonds," were subject to greater punishment, then, than inhabitant Quakers.[46]

The scale of persecution, in relation to the number of Quakers, seems to have been similar to that in England, but in England the mortal consequences of persecution were greater, as Quakers by the hundreds perished, many in foul prisons. Prisons were absent from many small towns in New England, and most people were reluctant to expose other people, no matter how odious their behavior, to prolonged detention in faraway facilities or to prolonged detention in makeshift places nearby. For their own convenience and profit, then, New England authorities often relied on economic sanctions rather than physical sanctions. William Newland and Ralph Allen were exceptions: for holding Quaker meetings and "entertaining" foreign Quakers, they were imprisoned thirty miles from their Sandwich homes, in winter.[47] The Boston prison housed a steady, if changing, population of Quakers, especially before King Charles ordered in 1661 that Massachusetts authorities transfer any Quakers in jeopardy of capital punishment to England to be tried there.[48] Perhaps the most cruelly treated was William Brend, an older

Figure 4.2. "Patience on force is a Medicine for a Mad Horse," "Proverb Card," Cary Playing Card Collection. A whipping at a cart's tail, a common punishment for Quakers in both England and New England, is here illustrated on a playing card. Notice the victim is stripped to the waist. "And make them fast to the Cart's Tail, and driving the Cart through your several Towns, to whip them on their Backs" (Order of Richard Waldron, 22 December 1662, Dover in New England). The Beinecke Rare Book and Manuscript Library, Yale University.

man. He had not had food for five days when he was tied "neck & heels" for sixteen hours, then beaten so grotesquely that there was "Blood hanging as in Bags under his Arms."[49] Only the four Quakers hanged in Boston in 1659–1660 joined the list of actual martyrs that Quakers kept fresh in Quaker chronicles as a tribute to their sacrifice.

Because New England punishments did not result in more deaths does not diminish the physical horror many had to undergo in the early years of Quaker presence in New England or the unremitting hardship arising from constant official theft from the small stock of Quaker household goods, a hardship that persisted for decades. On 9/10M/1676, for example, Edward Wanton, shipbuilder of Scituate, lost five pewter platters for failing to contribute to the "priest;" on 19/8M/1677 he lost broadcloth worth six shillings per yard; in 4M/1677 he lost a cow for failing to support the Puritan meeting house.[50] Punishment tended to be highly arbitrary, dependent on the predilections of a particular constable or official. Governor Bellingham of Massachusetts Bay represented the viciousness of the man with power; Constable Barlow of Sandwich, Plymouth, the no less vicious depredations of petty authority; the people of Dover, now in New Hampshire, the maliciousness of the mob. It was Governor Bellingham who took the time to visit Quaker John Stubbs imprisoned in Boston and whispered to him "(John thinking that he had some great oracle to tell him) that the devil had sucked John's blood and with his blood had sealed to the devil."[51] Constable Barlow's activities centered around using his Quaker neighbors as his source of livelihood, taking a kettle, cows, corn, cloth, and horses in a nagging and debilitating harassment that continued for years.[52] In Dover, a church elder named HateEvil Nutwel presided over cruelty toward three Quaker women missionaries. In wintertime, local constables dragged Alice Ambrose out of meeting, face down in the snow for nearly a mile, "over stumps and old trees." The next day, Mary Tompkins was dragged "on her back over the stumps of trees." Alice Ambrose was "plucked violently into the water, and kept . . . swimming by the canoe, so that she was in danger of being drowned or frozen to death." The weather was so cold that her clothes were "frozen like boards."[53] Quakers as a group did not retaliate with violence for their punishments, and it is only rarely that records show individuals lashing out toward their taunters, harassers, or whippers.

The Uses of "Suffering"

Quakers carefully preserved their "sufferings" for several purposes: in order to edify and inspire Quaker posterity; in order to shame the persecutors; and in order to persuade non-Quakers of the "Truth."[54] John M. Murrin has commented that in these compilations Quakers "may have been trying to add their own book to the Bible," almost another "Acts of the Apostles."[55] They recorded persecution carefully to be "as a continuall weight and burthen on the heads of the persecutors," to encourage persecutors to repent of their iniquity and so find mercy.[56] However, one Quaker admonished, it was essential that Quakers be circumspect, so that "there may not bee the least addition in the relation of those things" that would mar the expression of truth. Apparently, some Quaker had exaggerated "freinds sufferings in New england" through "publicke misrepresentation." This was a "matter of greife" to English Quakers, who felt the necessity of reminding their Rhode Island brethren of the Christian principle of forgiveness toward enemies, the principle that should have prompted them "rather to extenuate" the description of the enemies' crimes than to aggravate them.[57]

Elizabeth Hooten expressed the explicit Quaker connection between suffering and proselytizing when she voiced regret that after the hanging of the Quakers in 1660, she "found their blood ly cold in the streets, & *none regarded.*" She was discouraged, for "so much suffering & bloodshed as there had been in Boston, *and nothing brought forth.*"[58] While the hope that undergoing persecution by itself alone would advance their witness undoubtedly somewhat assuaged the physical and economic pain they suffered, the Quakers were also right—the example they set of endurance and patient principle did attract others to Quakerism. Edward Wanton is an oft-cited example: Wanton was a guard at the execution of the first martyrs in 1659, and the experience rendered him a fervent adherent to the sect.[59] Eleven-year-old Patience Scott, traveling from Rhode Island to Boston in protest at the persecution of Quakers, became a particularly potent witness, especially when the Boston magistrates foolishly threw her into prison with William Robinson and Marmaduke Stevenson, who were to be hanged later that year. One can imagine her impact as she preached to the curious, her innocent fervor contrasting usefully with the embittered posture of the magistrates.[60] The court saw fit to discharge her after three months; although the governor had discerned a spirit in her preaching "beyond the spirit of a woman," he ascribed the spirit to the devil.[61]

The Quakers under persecution did more than offer themselves up to repeated punishment, instead vigorously defending themselves in many venues—court, legislature, public streets, church, town meeting.[62] In 1677, for example, Alice Curwen greeted a warrant from Massachusetts Assistant Simon Bradstreet that ordered that his agents were to bring "every Person found at a Quakers Meeting." She quick-wittedly answered, "This Warrant takes not hold on us; we *are* the Meeting; this Warrant is to bring such Persons as are *found* at a Quakers Meeting."[63] A non-Quaker happened upon two Quakers in 1660; the Quakers disclosed to him that Quakers knew what "writings" were sent to England about them because "they had active men, whoe brake up theire letters and tooke coppies of them, and sealed them up againe."[64] This system of intrigue contradicts a conventional portrait of Quakers as helpless victims.

In the Context of Religious Dissent:
"Did He Leave Any Precept?"

In New England as in Old England, persecution defined the first field on which Quakers would explore pacifist ideas, and Quakers interpreted the persecution as based solely on religion. Like George Fox and others, they often seemed to define "enemy" as the person who persecuted on the basis of religion, the person who was a religious opponent. (Secular enemies such as the Dutch or the French were often termed "enemies to the King.") Writing about the Massachusetts banishment of its Quaker inhabitants Southwick and Buffum, George Bishop stressed that

Quakers reached out to "that of God in every mans Conscience, thereby to lead them" rather than resorting to the "Outward Sword," the weapon of Antichrist. Quakers, he said, relied on other weapons, spiritual weapons, "mighty through the Spirit," to influence the consciences of others; they did not use carnal weapons, which he defined expansively as "Prisons, Whipps, Cutting off Ears, Fines, Famishings, Stocks, Burnings, Beatings, Banishment, Death."[65] Clearly, Bishop used "carnal weapons" in a figurative sense, not solely a literal sense, by including in his list fines and banishment, which were not necessarily violent in character. "Carnal weapons," in this sense, were any of man's devices for "persuasion"; they included force but were not restricted to physical force. Carnal weapons were thus connected to the means of persecution, whatever they might be.

Christopher Holder, John Rous, and John Copeland, three missionaries in Boston who suffered the removal of their ears in 1659, judged their persecutors by enquiring rhetorically whether Jesus had acted so toward his religious opponents. "Did he leave any Precept that his servants should do so?" they asked, alluding to Jesus' rebuking Peter when Peter smote the servant of the high priest and cut off his ear. The three men argued further against violence, intoning as they did so the phrase "innocent blood":

> nothing defileth a land or people more then the shedding of innocent blood; and nothing brings down the judgements of God sooner . . . then the cry of innocent blood . . . God hath no union . . . with such that acteth violence, and gather themselves together, and condemn the innocent blood.

While warning that "He that sheds mans blood, by man shall his blood be shed," they especially condemned persecuting violence directed against the innocent, in this case the Quakers. Because they laid emphasis on the key word "innocent," they seem to have been concentrating still on that violence having to do with religious persecution.[66] As late as 1674, Governor William Coddington of Rhode Island explicitly conflated persecution and carnal weapons when he wrote, "For the Weapons of our Warfare are not carnal, 2 Cor. x. 3, 4, 5. but Fines and Imprisonments are." His words extend the meaning of the words "carnal weapons" beyond mere physical objects to instruments of metaphorical force, suggesting that rhetoric about doing violence may be figurative as well as literal. As other Quakers had done before him, Coddington saw the prohibition of violence in the context of religious dissent. Coddington wrote of Jesus: "For there were Dissenters in his Time, his Disciples saw it, and would have commanded Fire to come down from Heaven and destroy them, but he rebuked them, and said . . . 'the Son of Man is not come to destroy Men's Lives, but to save them.'"[67]

Just how awkward it was for Quakers and Puritans to interact as Christian competitors, both claiming the authority of Christian precepts, is apparent in the case of Quaker Eliakim Wardel, who was tied to a tree to be whipped. "I pitty thee for thy Fathers sake," one magistrate said to him, and turned to the whipper and said, "Whip him a good." The Quaker recounting this incident remarked parenthetically, "such a kind of Kim Kam Generation one shall hardly hear of."[68] Even more convoluted was the reasoning of the Massachusetts General Court in 1659, trying to justify its execution of three Quakers. If the Quakers had been persecuted (which the court denied), the Quakers had not followed the example of Jesus and his "Saints," who, when persecuted in one city, fled to another. Since Quakers refused to stay banished and returned again and again to the scene of their persecution, "theire actings are not the same, but quite contrary, so that Christ and his saints were led by one spirit, and those people by another."[69] The court seemed willing even to identify itself with Christ's persecutors in its eagerness to condemn the Quakers. Ann Coddington, in 1660 the wife of William Coddington, Rhode Island's wealthiest settler and future governor and former Massachusetts councilman, wrote to Governor John Endicott of Massachusetts and reminded him that his hanging of Quaker Mary Dyer was un-Christian, even had she been a heretic (which Coddington of course denied), for Jesus himself did not command that heretics be put to death. Jesus said that "gainsayers" should be persuaded with sound doctrine—with spiritual weapons, not carnal weapons. "Do you not build up your Church with Blood," she warned. "For Blood is a crying Sin: It cries loud in the Ears of the Lord for Vengeance."[70] In contrast to the hanging of Mary Dyer "as a flag,"[71] we can see in our imaginations the ridiculous scampering about of Quaker John Burnyeat and a sexton in a Connecticut church in 1672. Burnyeat after the morning service tried to speak to the departing congregation in the churchyard, but no one stayed to listen. Undaunted, he returned to the afternoon service, listened to the "priest" again, and then stood and asked the people to remain and hear his message. The vigilant sexton "drove the People away." When Burnyeat attempted to follow, the sexton "got to the Door, and shut the Door to keep me in." Burnyeat hastened down an aisle to another door, but the sexton scrambled over the seats and cut him off at that door too. Uncowed, the Quaker "made for a third Door; he also got to that before me, and shut that; and so made their Meetinghouse a Prison."[72] Dignity and decorum departed Hartford that day.

The Peace Testimony in New England

By using "carnal weapons" in a figurative sense and by associating scriptural renunciations of violence with persecution and religious dissent, these early Quakers left room for an ambiguous and confused formulation of the peace testimony. Some might understand the peace testimony in a more restricted way, as only applying to Christian violence against Christian, for purposes of religious persuasion, or as only applying to violence against the innocent. If any punishments could be termed carnal weapons, meaning earthly measures as opposed to spiritual measures, whether physically abusive toward the body or not, then the renunciation of carnal weapons could refer to renunciation of force as well as of physical violence. An understanding of the peace testimony as encompassing a renunciation of force as well as of violence could imply an altogether different interpretation of Quaker obligation.

Quaker nonviolence at times appears flexible, both simultaneously principled and pragmatic depending on the audience. Elizabeth Hooten, George Fox's first convert and missionary to New England, left a complicated yet revealing account of such pragmatism. In 1665 Hooten was one of four Quakers who had come to Boston to speak with the king's commissioners, who were "inspecting" the Massachusetts Bay Colony. The colony's government, which intensely resented the oversight of the commissioners, had the Quakers arrested and brought before the governor. Here the Quakers heard an astounding admission: "they said they would whip the Comissionrs upon the Quakrs backs, & so they whipt us very grievously at 3 towns & out of their Jurisdiction they put us." The Quakers served literally as whipping boys, as a way to express antagonism against the commissioners. Hooten apparently was privy to the reaction of the commissioners, who, she wrote, "were grieved at wt they did unto [us], because they knew that their enmity was to them as well as to us." According to the commissioners (in Hooten's account), the Massachusetts government did not dare to punish the obnoxious commissioners, because the "Country" would have risen against the government, so it punished the Quakers instead, knowing that it was safe to do so because "or [our] Kingdome is not of this world, therefore his servts could not fight, but we have comitted or [our] Cause to God who hath & wil defend it to his glory."[73] Hooten here enunciated the Quaker peace testimony in scriptural, religious diction, referring to the Kingdom of God.

Subsequently she encountered some non-Quakers from "New England" who, opposing the commissioners, "made a decree against them, to rise in foure & Twenty houres against them, to fight with them." She made it clear that she had advocated nonviolence to these impatient militants on practical grounds. When Hooten learned of their intentions, she went to some of their church members, warning them that if they fought they would invite the retaliation of the commissioners' supporters and thereby destroy themselves and their country. "And I said to them you had better (as we have such an example) to suffer rather then fight."[74] In this practical warning, Hooten tailored her reasoning to her audience, using an argument that she judged they had the capacity to respond to, while reminding them as Christians of Jesus' example.

Had New Englanders readily accepted the Quakers within their midst instead of having proceeded against them, the Quaker peace testimony, however defined, would have been even less visible to historians than it is, because the response of authorities in Massachusetts, Plymouth, and Connecticut to the Quakers through punitive and preventative legislation and in court records tracks the activities and provocations of the Quakers. For instance, the United Colonies sent a letter to the Rhode Island government in 1657/1658, warning it explicitly that Quakers posed a threat to New England, and obliquely that should Rhode Island continue to harbor Quakers (allowing them to make forays into the other colonies) the United Colonies would cut off all trade. The Rhode Island response to this warning gives unwitting access to early Quaker belief. In its reply dated 13 March 1657/1658, the Rhode Island assembly sturdily reiterated its charter protection of liberty of conscience in regard to religion and promised within the parameters of the charter provision to be vigilant about Quakers. "And in case they the said people called Quakers," they wrote, "do refuse to submit to the doing all duties aforesaid, as training, watching," duties essential to the preservation of civil society, the assembly would consult England about how to reconcile freedom of religion and social order.[75] Obviously, Quakers were already associated with refusing civic responsibilities of a military nature. In October 1658, the Rhode Island General Court of Trials was still concerned about this threat, calling a court of commissioners to "Tranceact such affayres as are of greate nesessity . . . viztt Touchinge obstructions and Discoragements in trayneinge" and writing to England about the United Colonies' letter concerning Quakers.[76] This striking evidence that Quakers had early reservations about military participation undermines the validity of the thesis that Quaker pacifism was largely self-defensive in response to the Restoration of King Charles II. Although the subscribers to that thesis have acknowledged that individual Quakers expressed pacifist beliefs before the Declaration of 1660, clearly the Quaker missionaries had integrated these beliefs into their message to a greater extent than they might have surmised. Clearly, too, the colonial experience of pacifism would follow a different timetable from that of Old England.[77]

It was around the issue of militia training that early peace principles primarily excited notice. Within Plymouth's 1658 Quaker law was the provision that all those opposed to military service were disenfranchised, again evidence that Quaker opposition to training was well known to the Plymouth court two years before the Restoration.[78] Massachusetts records of 1663 describe inhabitants who "make it much of theire religion" to "not yeild obedience to authority . . . & refuse to beare armes under others."[79]

It is difficult to assess the proportion of Quakers who stayed away from military training. Since the various militias were under local jurisdiction, any instances of Quakers abstaining from militia training would normally appear in local militia records, rarely preserved. But other records occasionally documented the fines imposed on such Quakers. In 1658, Magistrate William Hathorn of Ipswich, Massachusetts, was attempting to prove that Quaker Samuel Shattuck was one who "condemned Authority" by saying that Shattuck had "denyed [refused] training in a Writing to him, beginning thus, 'Be it known to thee, we will not follow thee in training.'" Shattuck meticulously corrected the magistrate, saying that his actual words had been "We cannot," not "we will not follow thee."[80] Whatever the wording, Shattuck's principles were clear. In October 1659, two sons of the soon-to-be Quaker martyr Mary Dyer were indicted for larceny against the state, "whereas the matter rose at first about Nontrayneinge." The General Court of Trials in Portsmouth, Rhode Island, exonerated the Dyer sons—Samuel Dyer and Mahorshalelhiashbash Dyer—because they conformed "unto order."[81] Humphrey Norton in 1659 recorded fines assessed against Thomas Ewer, Edward Perry, John Jenkins, and Robert Harper, all of Sandwich, for refusing to train. Even Peter Gaunt—"a man of great age . . . although his natural strength be much spent"—was required to train, "which for conscience sake he could not do."[82] Quaker Daniel Butler of Sandwich was fined the great sum of eight pounds for being a delinquent soldier during wartime.[83] Personal witness, official notice, and popular perception in New England, then, testified to some Quaker association with peace principles before 1660 and the political strategy of the Quaker leadership in England.

In respect to the peace testimony, the understanding of New England Quakers developed erratically and varied according to individual interpretation. Thus, Quakers continued to serve in militias, continued to express anger through physical violence, and failed to abandon old, violent methods of achieving their ends. Christopher Hussey remained a militia officer in 1664 after his conversion.[84] It was William Sabine of Rehoboth in Plymouth who, traveling along a path, fell into the company of two Quakers just after the hanging of Mary Dyer in Boston and asked them why they had not taken steps to rescue those Quakers put to death. "Soe they would," they answered, without any disavowal of violence, "but they wanted a leader."[85]

In the first years after Quakerism appeared in New England, accusations of physical violence occasionally enlivened the records of court proceedings against Quakers. In Plymouth, for example, Thomas Greenfield's name was included in a list of fines assessed against Quakers for refusing the oath in 1658; in the same year he was fined three pounds for striking the infamous marshall George Barlow. Two years later Quaker Daniel Butler "attacked" the marshall, who had captured the "foreign" missionary Wenlock Christopherson, and set Wenlock free; Butler was whipped.[86] One must make allowance for self-interest and hyperbole in these accounts, however. The case of Arthur Howland of Sandwich is illustrative. According to Plymouth court records, Quaker missionary Robert Hodgson was ranging from town to town, attempting with some success to convince his hearers. Constable John Phillipes of Sandwich, equipped with a warrant to apprehend him, went on Sunday to Arthur Howland's house, where Hodgson was staying and where a meeting for worship was to take place. However, the meeting having been forewarned, no one was there. The next day, with a warrant extended to cover Howland as well as Hodgson and two others, the constable returned and demanded that Hodgson go with him. Howland, one of the founding Quakers of Marshfield, prevented Hodgson's arrest, on which the constable "pulled him to goe alonge with him; and then the said Arthur Howland thrust the said John Phillipes out of his dores." Howland continued to threaten the constable, warning him that "hee would have either a sword or a gun in the belly of him."[87] George Fox's rendering of this incident, not surprisingly, included no mention of the Quaker's violent threat. In his account, he specifically said that the constable had no warrant, and thus Howland's refusal to yield up Hodgson appears less provocative. Moreover, Fox described Arthur Howland as being an ancient man of seventy years, a fact that considerably alters the menace of Howland's threat as presented in the court version, no matter how intemperate it may have been.[88]

When the Sandwich town council ordered James Skiffe, in 1660, to distribute two pounds of powder from the town stock to each member of the militia who mustered at Yarmouth, the occasion incidentally created one of the few extant lists of town militias. Skiffe was to deliver the powder "to every musgetere of the Millitary Company that went to the generall Muster at Yarmoth," and the minutes carefully listed all those "musgeteres" who so served. "Fransis Allen," "Steven Wing," "Luddes Hake," "Henry Sanderson," "Isack Turner," and of course the officer of the company, "Leiftenant Ellis," were among those who had made their way loyally to Yarmouth, to meet up no doubt with militias from other Cape towns.[89] All were Quakers. Plymouth records frequently mention John Ellis as an officer of the militia: he was approved in 1653 as the lieutenant of the Sandwich military company, engaged to train the military company for a season in 1660, nominated to be a trooper for the town in 1662—and presented before the Plymouth court for "tumultuous conduct," in the company of other Quakers, including Stephen Wing, in 1657.[90] Ellis, Wing, and the other tumultuous men had probably been at the meeting of Quakers when missionary Humphrey Norton was seized and marched to the colony border in October 1657.[91] Wing was prevented from acting in town meeting along with eight others, all Quakers, in 1658, among whom was "Henery Saunders," likely to be Sanderson.[92] Allen refused an oath in 1658, along with twelve others, all identifiable Quakers.[93] "Luddes Hake," variously styled "Ludue Hakes," Lodowick Hawkes, or, more correctly, Lodowick Hoxie, became a prominent Quaker in Sandwich, as did both Sanderson and Allen. It is likely that Hoxie became a Quaker during the time of great Quaker conversion in Sandwich—in 1657 and 1658, although verifying evidence does not exist. Ellis, Wing, Sanderson, Allen, and probably Hoxie were thus associated with the Sandwich Quaker community from its earliest difficulties with the colony authorities yet had continued their military service as late as 1660 or beyond. Isaac Turner signed marriage certificates in 1679 and 1683; whether he was already a Quaker when he mustered at Yarmouth is unknown.[94]

Ensign John Williams, Jr., of the Scituate militia company, appointed to train the company in 1657 and a member of the Council of War in 1658, found himself standing before the Plymouth court in 1660 to answer for having entertained foreign Quakers and for permitting Quaker meetings in his house. The court fined him a substantial forty shillings but did not degrade him as an officer, in the hope that he would reform.[95] Perhaps its judgment was valid, for Ensign Williams does not appear in later Quaker documents. Nor does Anthony Needham of Salem, Massachusetts, continue to appear in Quaker documents, although he was a documented Quaker from 1658 until 1664 and the husband of an active Quaker. But historian Jonathan Chu continues to identify Anthony Needham as a Quaker even in the 1670s, in spite of the fact that he was a militia captain in 1665.[96]

In the first few years of Quakerism in New England, Quakers confronted the concept of nonviolence largely in association with persecution and with the requirements of military training. Military training would become increasingly significant for the remainder of the century; its background to a greater drama will become evident in the pages ahead. Although persecution toward Quakers was to continue in Massachusetts and be at least legally feasible in Plymouth for decades, it is rare that one finds comments on Quaker nonviolence, either from Quakers themselves or from non-Quaker observers. After pressure from England in the form of a letter from King Charles to the Boston government in 1662, brutal physical persecution subsided and persecution took the form of prohibitions against residence, fines and distraints, and bars against Quaker civic activity. Perhaps because the more overt violence was curtailed, the Quaker focus on physical coercion was deflected in new directions; talk about Christian use of force toward other Christians, about physical force for purposes of religious persuasion, and about spiritual weapons replacing carnal weapons seems to have lessened—at least such discussion has not been preserved to any extent. Similarly, because refusal to train could be anticipated and was therefore less shocking, perhaps because the colony towns reached local accomodations toward Quaker non-participation, and perhaps because early Quaker zealotry diminished as there were more local Quakers than "foreign" missionaries, evidence of what Quakers decided about militia service remains sparse. A letter to fellow Quakers from Edward Perry is an oblique exception: it seems to address some trouble that had fallen upon Quakers because of the peace testimony. Referring to a "present case & condition," Perry reassured them that God would preserve them against their enemies—enemies created by the

Quakers keeping "your testimony for the Lord: & for the peaceable kingdome." Perry warned that they should not rely on reasoning against their enemies with words but rather "keep to the truth of the testimony," which would be to the praise of the "peaceable Lord & king" who came "to save mens Lives & not to destroy them."[97]

One rare document still preserved came from the hand of missionary George Wilson, who arrived in Massachusetts in 1661. He was not long tolerated; exiled, he went south to his eventual death in a Virginia prison. From prison, he wrote a letter to the authorities in 1662 in which he explained the Quaker peace testimony—a letter that may reveal some of the ideas about violence that missionaries brought to the colonies. The Quaker sword, he explained, was the word of God; Quakers testified against other carnal weapons. "Wee wrestle not, with flesh, & blood, neither doe wee strike att the person of any," Wilson continued, categorizing the earthly human body as a carnal weapon because it was capable of physical violence. Instead, with the Quaker spiritual sword, the word of God, Quakers struck at the principle of spiritual wickedness, which must be killed before people can be witnesses with Christ. As his justification for Quakers not fighting, Wilson pointed to the phrase "my kingdom is not of this world" from scripture, emphasizing that scripture said that God would retaliate against all "fighters": "for he that killeth with the sword, shall be killed by the sword." In this observation, Wilson was not making a practical observation—that violence begets violence—but was warning of spiritual judgement. Through faith in the Light, he wrote, Wilson could clearly see that "no murderer nor man slayer . . . shall enter into the kingdome of God." Finally he appealed to God's mercy toward "those blinde persecutors wch banished mee."[98]

Wilson's letter is an invaluable expression of the meaning of the peace testimony in the early days of Quakerism. Its focus is on obedience to God, on the ways one may be admitted to the Kingdom of God and the ways one may be disbarred from it. Carnal weapons, including earthly weapons, while effective against "flesh," were deemed useless in killing true wickedness, which must be destroyed to live with Christ. Scriptural passages buttressed his efforts to show his captors their disobedience toward God; he sought to frighten "fighters" by stressing punishment. The punishment, according to scripture, would be death. Finally, Wilson closely associated the peace testimony with persecution. He was thinking specifically about persecutors "fighting & [?], or conspireing, how to kill, slay, or distroy, any mans life" rather than about impersonal killing during a war, for instance, although this kind of killing would also be reprehensible.

This understanding of pacifism proceeded from a quite different motivation from that which would later animate the discussions of nonviolence. Quite simply, early Quakers renounced the use of carnal weapons and fighting out of obedience to scripture. Because Christ's message was clear that one must love one's enemy and turn the other cheek and that he who lived by the sword would die by the sword, it was also clear that to remain in right relationship to God one had to obey these new imperatives.

The omissions from early interpretations of the peace witness are telling: what was absent was a direct concern for the victim of violence. These early formulations did not mention the sacredness of human life or the destruction, dislocation, misery, and suffering of war as reasons to refrain from violence. The phrase "that of God in every man," so closely associated with the rationale of the peace testimony in latter years, was occasionally used in these early days, but it was virtually never used to explain why physical harm should not be done to another. In sum, the foundation of early Quaker pacifism expressed a concern about the subjective state of one's own soul and one's relationship with God. The objective safety of another's body was only incidental.

In Wilson's document, the state of the soul as the reason for nonviolence is implied; in later years, it was sometimes made explicit. For example, in Rhode Island in 1675, a group of Quakers wrote that people involved in war "wound their own Souls."[99] In 1678, Quakers in Sandwich, Plymouth, explained the ground of their failure to fight as the command of Jesus, to do unto others as they would have others do unto them. "For they well know that the Eternall well being of their imortall soules is Conserned in it."[100] As late as 1693, as already noted, the London Yearly Meeting advices took Quaker shipmasters to task for arming their vessels. Their home meetings were to warn the shipmasters "that they may Seriously Consider how they injure their Own Souls in so doing."[101] This emphasis on the individual's soul and his relationship with God, derived from the words of scripture, shaped and limited the requirements flowing from the peace testimony. Obedience to the words and concentration on their literal meaning allowed a limited definition of how Quakers should act in relation to violence. They might fulfill the scripture solely by refraining from personally using weapons to kill another.

The "Bold" and the "Blasphemers" at Home

Rhode Islanders were exempt from most of the difficulties facing other New England Quakers, and many of the "bold" and the "blasphemers" helped to influence its character. Rhode Islanders were proud of and preoccupied with liberty of conscience, and Quakers in Rhode Island were to take particular interest in how liberty of conscience as a civic principle intersected with military requirements. The contest between civic and religious duties, equally compelling, gave rise to innovative arrangements. Rhode Island was first a haven for those of independent religious minds, was then a refuge for the despised, and, as a result and not without a struggle, was to become an incubator for imaginative civic solutions. The Quakers were a catalyst in this history.

5

"The Habitation of the Hunted-Christ"

RHODE ISLAND AND PROVIDENCE PLANTATIONS

The Massachusetts, Plymouth, and Connecticut colonies sourly failed to appreciate the missionary zeal of Quaker Humphrey Norton, proselytizing his way among the Puritans and should-be Puritans in those settlements in the late 1650s. Consequently, Humphrey Norton spent the winter of 1657 chained by the leg to a log in an open-air New Haven prison. When he attempted to argue in court with the esteemed minister John Davenport, he had to endure a "great Iron Key athwart his Mouth so that he could not speak." Finally, the Connecticut authorities burned him deeply in the right hand with an H for heresy and banished him.[1]

"The habitation of the hunted-Christ," Norton called Rhode Island and Providence Plantations, where he found security and succor.[2] By intoning this deeply grave phrase, he perhaps was inspired by Rhode Island's foundation as a refuge for religious dissidents, remembering the few Quakers and many others who had preceded him in a search for sanctuary. Perhaps he compared his own mission symbolically to Christ's, in the not-always-modest terms common to religious certainty—thinking of himself as a "type" of Christ, seeking refuge in Rhode Island. Or perhaps he considered the essence of Christ to be within his body: that he himself incorporated the "hunted Christ," in a kind of "celestial inhabitation," coming close to confirming the judgment he could not discard from his own hand.[3]

Given a society hospitable to sincerely held religious beliefs, what did Rhode Island Quakers do with their liberty in regard to the peace testimony? In the absence of violent persecution, did Quakers have to consider the nature of the peace testimony at all? And when the liberty of the ordinary person combined with political power, when Quakers became governors, how much impact did the peace testimony have on their decisions? As elsewhere, the particular place, people, events, and beliefs would in a measure shape the nature of the Rhode Island Quaker response to violence. A heritage of religious liberty, the particular missionaries who came there, the prominence of the local Quaker converts and the practice of local Quakers all influenced Quaker belief about nonviolence. An imposing visit of England's Quaker leaders in 1672 and the impact of their teachings intersected with the empowerment of home-grown colonial Quakers in government for the first time, providing a unique, untried opportunity to work out what the peace testimony would mean when Quakers were in power. The authoritative aura of visiting Quaker founders from England at once dramatized inherited tradition and nascent divergences. How Rhode Island became the "habitation of the hunted-Christ" and what its Quaker residents came to think about their obligations to "follow the path of peace" within this sanctuary would lead to novel accommodations to the peace testimony.

"A Place of Security . . . A Place of Peace"

Beginning with Roger Williams, who was the first religious dissident to tramp on a lonely way through the woods from Salem, Massachusetts, to the shores of Narragansett Bay, the territory later to become Rhode Island and Providence Plantations became a haven for Anne Hutchinson and her accused antinomians, for Samuel Gorton and his quest for the "mysteries of Christ,"[4] and eventually for stragglers from the small ship *Woodhouse,* people "in scorn called Quakers" who as a group as yet had no polite name. By the 1660s the colony included mainland settlements and settlements on the island of Aquidneck, in Narragansett Bay. It was a mysterious harmony that the name "Aquidneck," derived from "Aquidnet," meant "a place of security or peace" in the Algonquian language.[5]

The heritage of Rhode Island encompassed in the phrases "the habitation of the hunted-Christ" and "a place of peace" arose from its geography and early history; in turn, this inherited sense of itself as both metaphorical and geographical sanctuary had a profound influence on the political structure and culture of the new colony. A sensitivity to the religious concerns of others, a sophisticated awareness that coercion of religious belief led to shallow spirituality, and an ability to separate religious difference from threats to the social order were qualities that distinguished seventeenth-century Rhode Islanders from others, and these qualities were expressed in a religious liberty and political restraint remarkable for the time.

Rhode Island's charter of 1663 ensured religious liberty in a provision that echoed the restored king's Declaration of Breda and directed the terms of debate for years to come: "That noe parson [person] within the sayd Collony at any time hearafter, shall be in any wayes molested, punnished, disquieted or called in question for any differance of opinion in matters of religion, and doe not actually disturbe the civill peace of the sayd Collony."[6] While those in other colonies saw Rhode Island as a sinkhole, a receptacle for the maladjusted and malevolent of the other colonies precisely because of this liberty, Quaker missionary Elizabeth Hooten quietly observed, "And allwayes they drive us toward Road Isl being a place of liberty to us."[7]

"Woalves . . . Made A Path": Missionaries

Elizabeth Hooten had listened to a very young George Fox in England and early took up his journey as her own. Her description of traveling from Boston to Rhode Island and back at the age of sixty-five years dramatizes that the walk for dissenting settlers and Quaker missionaries to Rhode Island was daunting.

> "I was necessitated to goe three score Miles through the woods a foote among the wild beasts with a woman freind that was bigg with Child . . . and coming back againe myselfe through the woods, and the snow pretty deep, a Company of woalves had gon before mee and made a path."[8]

By 1658, at least ten missionaries had made similar passages to Rhode Island, one of whom was William Brend, an "aged person" (about forty years old),[9] some walking, some arriving by boat. Among William Brend's first converts were two prior dissenters who thus typify Quaker conversion: Catherine and Richard Scott of Providence. Catherine Scott was the sister of antinomian Anne Hutchinson, whose intelligence had caused severe religious trauma in Boston in 1637. Richard Scott had been a founder of the Baptist Church in Providence.[10] Another missionary was Robert Hodgson, who had first landed at New Amsterdam in 1657, where he provocatively called a prayer meeting in a public garden. His unconventional demeanor had alarmed the Dutch magistrates there; "taking Hodson [,] upon whom besides a Bible in his hand, they found a Dagger in his Bosom, and since that seem'd to be a Weapon more fit for Offence than Defence, they ty'd his hands."[11] After severe whipping and harsh imprisonment under Governor Peter Stuyvesant, he too made his way to Rhode Island, using it as a base for travels about New England, and eventually settling at Portsmouth on Aquidneck. Thomas Thurston, "with extraordinary long hair hanging over his shoulders," was another who took advantage of Rhode Island's safety: he set out for America aboard the *Speedwell* in 1656 and was imprisoned and shipped back to England but had returned to the colonies with Josiah Coale by 1657.[12]

One missionary was in fact a Rhode Islander. Mary Dyer had been a longtime friend of Anne Hutchinson; Massachusetts authorities saw divine retribution for her unorthodoxy visited upon her in the form of a "monstrous birth," the premature birth of a deformed child assisted by Hutchison acting as midwife in 1637.[13] Dyer accompanied her husband and Roger Williams on a visit to England in 1652 as they sought a charter for the colony. She remained in England three years longer than her husband and fell under the influence of the Quakers.[14] When she returned in 1656, she frightened and frustrated the authorities in Massachusetts with her proselytizing and refusal to stay banished, until they hanged her in Boston in 1660.

"A Sort of People": The Political Condition

"A sort of people, called by the name of Quakers . . . are come amongst us," the Rhode Island General Assembly tentatively wrote to its representative in England as early as 1658, "and have raised up divers, who seem at present to be of their spirit."[15] "A sort of people" could as well describe Rhode Island Colony itself, still only loosely tied together and to remain fragmented for decades to come.[16]

The colony by 1672 included four towns: the town of Providence, on the main; a small settlement at Warwick, on the main; and the towns of Portsmouth and Newport on Aquidneck Island. The Narragansett lands to the west of Narragansett Bay were home to some scattered English settlers (mostly Baptists) at what is now Westerly but were abundantly populated with the Niantic and the Narragansett Indians. In addition, Richard Smith had a trading post at Wickford and Jireh Bull a home at what is now Kingstown, each home substantial enough to serve as the local gathering place and garrison. A few Puritans from Massachusetts lived at Shoreham, now Block Island. At this time, Quakers were concentrated on Aquidneck; a few lived in Warwick and a few at Providence and elsewhere.[17] Sydney James has estimated that during the years 1670–1695, Quakers were about half the voting population in Rhode Island—about five to six hundred voters out of eleven to fourteen hundred total.[18] The total land forces in Rhode Island were estimated at the time to be potentially about one thousand men.[19]

Under the royal charter of 1663, the colony government, seated at Newport, was vested in a governor, a deputy governor, and ten assistants, called magistrates, who together formed the council. These magistrates, with the powers of justices of the peace, by tradition were distributed among the towns: Newport had five, Providence three, Portsmouth and Warwick two each. The council, meeting together with eighteen deputies—four town deputies each from Providence, Warwick, and Portsmouth and six deputies from Newport—constituted the General Assembly. (Sometimes representatives from Westerly or Block Island were included.) Under normal circumstances, the council members were elected annually in May and deputies were selected two times a year, and they met together as the General Assembly twice a year in May and October, but "normal circumstances" were rare, and extra sessions were called in times of danger. The council, which advised the governor, served also as the council of war and as the court of trials. The assembly not only was the legislature enacting general laws but also issued orders of a private nature, established courts, appointed officials, and constituted a court of appeals.[20]

Quakers had served in various governmental capacities prior to 1672, notably early comers Nicholas Easton, John Easton, William Coddington, Walter Clarke, Philip Shearman, and Caleb Carr, who came to America at age eleven alone with his brother. But on 1 May 1672, Rhode Island held its annual elections, and Quakers and their supporters came to dominate the government.[21] Governor Nicholas Easton, assistants John Easton, Joshua Coggeshall, Thomas Harris, and Benjamin Smith were Quakers. Among the town deputies to the assembly in May were at least seven more Quakers: Walter Clarke, Henry Bull, Peter Easton, Edward Thurston, Weston Clarke, William Wodell, and John Gould. By October 1672 Quaker Daniel Gould had replaced Weston Clark, and two more Quakers were added: Thomas Borden and innkeeper John Anthony; with possibly one or two more.[22]

It is seldom a straightforward matter to identify who was a Quaker. The Quakers had no formal membership as such—and no membership rolls. What they did keep were birth and death records, and marriage certificates, which attested to a

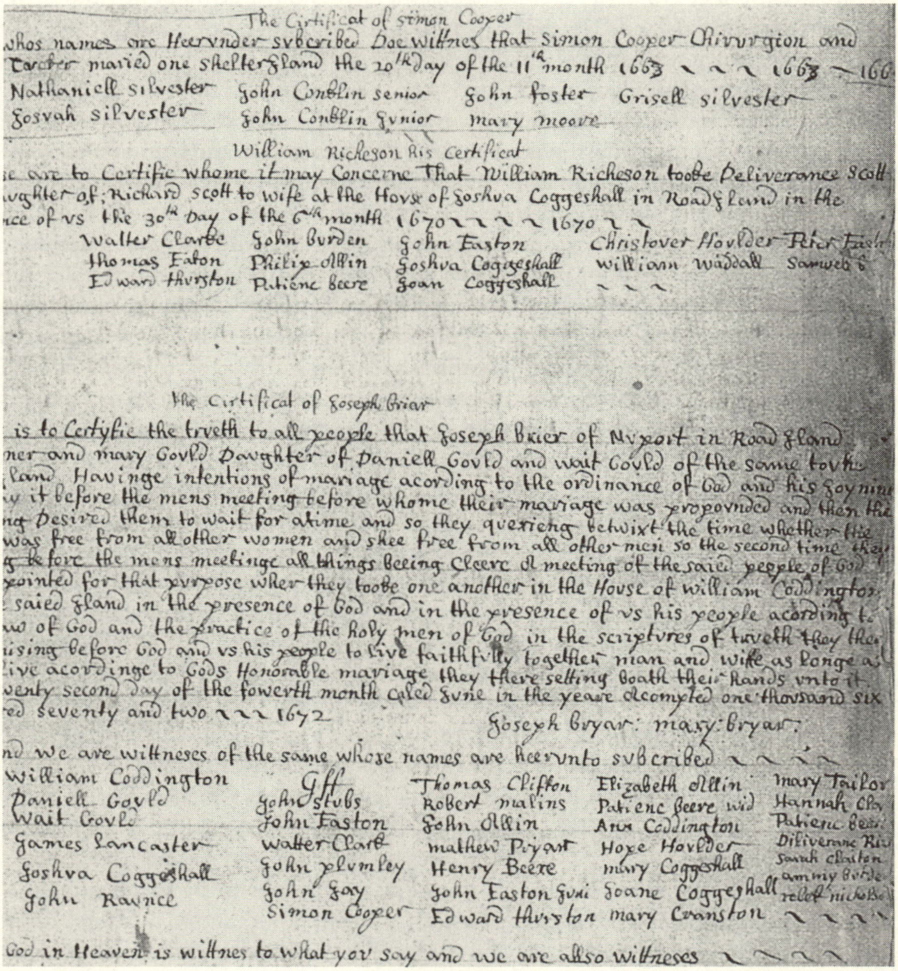

The Certificat of simon Cooper

whos names are Heervnder svbcribed Doe wittnes that simon Cooper Chirvrgion and
Tacter maried one shelter gland the 20th day of the 11th month 1663 ~ ~ ~ 1663 ~ 160
Nathaniell silvester   John Conblin senior   John foster   Grisell silvester
Josvah silvester   John Conblin Gvnior   mary moore

William Richeson his Certificat

we are to Certifie whome it may Conceerne That William Richeson toobe Deliverance Scott
wghter of: Richard scott to wife at the Hovse of Joshva Coggeshall in Road gland in the
nce of vs the 30th Day of the 6th month 1670 ~ ~ ~ 1670 ~
    Walter Clarke   John Burden   John Easton   Chrislover Hovlder Rier Tash
    thomas Eaton   Philip ollin   Joshva Coggeshall   william waddall   samveb ?
    Edward thvrston   Patience Beere   Joan Coggeshall   ~ ~ ~

The Certificat of Joseph Briar

is to Certifie the trveth to all peeople that Joseph Brier of Nyport in Road gland
ner and mary Govld Davghter of Daniell Govld and wait Govld of the same tovh
gland Havinge intentions of mariage acording to the ordinance of God and his Goynin
y it before the mens meeting before whome their mariage was propovnded and then the
ng Desired them to wait for atime and so they qveriehg betwixt the time whether the
was free from all other women and shee free from all other men so the second time the
g before the mens meetinge all things beeing Cleere A meeting of the saied peeple of God
pointed for that pvrpose wher they toobe one another in the House of william Coddington
saied gland in the presence of God and in the presence of vs his peeple acording to
w of God and the practice of the holy men of God in the scriptvres of trveth they the
ising before God and vs his peeple to live faithfvlly together man and wife as longe as
live acordinge to Gods Honorable mariage they there setting boath their hands vnto it
venty second Day of the fowerth month caled Gvne in the yeare decompted one thovsand six
ed seventy and two ~ ~ ~ 1672   Joseph bryar: mary bryar:

nd we are wittneses of the same whose names are heervnto svbcribed ~ ~ ~
William Coddington   Gff   Thomas Clifton   Elizabeth ollin   mary Tailor
Daniell Govld   John stubs   Robert malins   Patience Beere wid   Hannah Cla
Wait Govle   John Easton   John ollin   Ann Coddington   Patience Beer
James Lancaster   walter Clark   mathew Pryart   Hoxe Hovlder   Dilivenne Riu
Joshva Coggeshall   John plvmley   Henry Beere   mary Coggeshall   Sarah clinton
John Raynel   John Gay   John Easton Gvni   Joane Coggeshall   amniny Borle
                                  Simon Cooper   Edward thvrston   mary Cranston   ~ ~ ~
God in Heaven is wittnes to what you say and we are allso wittneses ~ ~ ~

Figure 5.1. Marriage Certificate of Joseph Briar–Mary Gould, 1672, Records of Marriages,
Society of Friends, 1643–1775, (detail). Marriage certificates provide evidence of Quaker
affiliation through the signatures of witnesses. At this wedding were Quaker visitors to Rhode
Island, including George Fox [Gff], Stubbs, Lancaster, and John Jay of the "broken" neck.
Courtesy of Library Special Collections, Newport Historical Society.

marriage and which were signed by the witnesses who were present at the wedding. Marriage certificates provide some of the best evidence for who was a Quaker by a particular date. Although George Fox mentioned that those "of the world," or outsiders, would sometimes set their hands to a certificate, these occasions are rare, obvious, and seem restricted to the presence of known colony officials at particularly important weddings. Their signatures appear in a prominent position and are often identified by title; they are therefore not subject to being mistaken for Quakers.[23] Other Quaker records are the minutes of monthly, quarterly, and yearly meetings. These records tend only to mention leaders by name, as they are appointed to various duties. Others mentioned in minutes are those who were falling short in some way and were desired to amend their behavior. While some discount such individuals as Quakers, as long as the meetings did not "deny" them, I consider them Quakers, for the meetings would not have struggled with them unless they viewed them as such. The place of burial is revealing when there are Quaker burial grounds. Quakers are identifiable, too, when they appear in court records, having run afoul of the laws, for example, by refusing to take oaths, refusing to pay for the local minister, or refusing military training. These transgressions varied, of course, with the particular colony. Occasionally other more random sources such as letters or government documents, identify Quakers.

But garnering a Quaker name is an incomplete accomplishment. A single reference carries insufficient information with it. When did he or she become a Quaker? Did she remain a Quaker? How central was Quaker belief to his life? There are rarely sufficient references to a particular Quaker to answer these questions. For some the Quaker identification is obvious; for some, probable; for more, possible or peripheral; for many, obscure. The nature of the claims made for individuals and the conclusions drawn must be proportional to the limitations inherent in the available evidence. When Quakers are identified in this study, then, limitations underlie and necessarily qualify such judgements, however carefully and thoughtfully made. Conversely, because the work of particular Quakers can so seldom be discerned, it does not follow that particular individuals were not crucial to the directions chosen. Because we cannot recapture the details of personal leadership and the quality of personal inspiration does not imply a geopolitically determinist view of how things happened.

"A Cage of Unclean Birds": The Religious Condition

In 1661, a short five years after the first appearance of Quakers in a largely hostile New England, English visitor George Rofe called Quakers from different parts of New England to gather in a "genrall meeting" on the island of Aquidneck.[24] "A very greate mettinge & very pretious & Continued 4 dayes togeither," this was the first such "general meeting" (meeting once a year) of Quakers anywhere, including England. "There is a good seede in that people," Rofe wrote, but he noted too that the "Enemy Keepes some under through their Cruell persecution."[25] His mention of persecution signals the presence of Quakers from the Puritan colonies at the general meeting. John Bowne, the New Amsterdam Quaker who brought religious liberty back from exile in Holland, also attended.[26]

The splendid Rhode Island freedom from the civil enforcement of religion did not preclude vigorous religious rivalry, which at times became virulent. In 1676, for example, Roger Williams himself described a Quaker adversary as "loud and clamorous, simple and knowing nothing . . . a Face of Brass, and a Tongue set on fire from the Hell of Lyes and Fury." He called George Fox "this proud swelling Bladder puft up with a Timpany of Wind and Vanity."[27] Neither did Quakers shrink from invective; William Coddington retaliated, "Here is a lying, scandalous Book of Roger Williams. . . . His Inveterate Malice was so great against the Truth, that he would have put us in a Lion's Skin, and set Dog's to worry us; but the Lord Reproved his Madness."[28] The dislike, even perhaps hatred, arose from political concerns, social snobbery, and land disputes as much as from theological differences, although couched in religious identity. After Quakers and their sympathizers had captured the electoral victory in 1672, for example, a visiting Quaker wrote back to England that "the Baptists here are full of Rage against us."[29] Roger Williams, stung by the same defeat and doubly insulted by Fox's charismatic presence in Rhode Island, wrote on 30 July 1672 to his former friend John Throckmorton, now a Quaker, "I heartily wish that your hands were washed from the bloody trade of Liquors to the Indians, which even the Quakers have practiced." Even worse, not only did Quakers trade in the debilitating substance, he complained, but they were especially successful at it, using unfair tactics: "telling the Indians that the Quakers only know God, and therefore would sell them Powder and Liquours cheaper, and they would not mix water with Rhum as others did."[30] And when a Quaker asked Roger Williams to translate a paper about the inner Light into Indian language, to be printed in England and distributed among the Indians, he refused, because he said it wasn't the truth.[31] As late as 1709, a prominent Rhode Islander wrote in disgust of the Narragansett region: "It is a Quaker mob Government. The meanest sort rule their betters. I much question whether two persons in the ruling part of their government can write true English, or forme a writeing in any methodical way."[32]

In spite of the Quaker expectation that the Spirit would assure unity within the community, reinforced by oversight from visiting Quaker ministers, dissension existed even among Quakers in New England and Rhode Island. "Peopel heare is very loveing if the other bad spirits [Quakers] weare not," Quaker Joseph Nicholson remarked in Rhode Island in 1660, predicting that "the truth will take place beter in other places then heare." He criticized fellow Quakers such as Robert Hodgson, who had interfered with Nicholson's staying with a wealthy family, and Humphrey Norton, who had a bad spirit.[33] Some of the rivalry may have been reflected in the settlement of the two towns, Portsmouth and Newport, on Aquidneck.

"Thundering Lungs"

But religious tensions were temporarily suspended upon the arrival at Newport on 30 May 1672 of the "weighty" English Quakers from the founding generation: George Fox, John Burnyeat, John Stubbs, William Edmundson, and their companions from the West Indies and Maryland.[34] Welcomed, entertained, admired, and listened to with "ardent affection," the visitors were energized at the enthusiasm of their large gatherings. People of "all Religions in the Island . . . went away rejoyceing." For John Stubbs, "it was a glorious time as ever I saw Since I owned the truth." Stubbs recounted how he and others would go first to "settle" the meeting each day, and then Fox himself would appear, "for all expectations and eyes were upon him and for him."[35]

The expectations about George Fox were beyond the ordinary. Elizabeth Hooten had written about the miracles of healing Fox had performed, upon Quakers and non-Quakers alike; undoubtedly she included such stories in the messages she carried around New England.[36] The nature of these expectations may be extrapolated from the account of the "miracle" of 2 September 1672, which, although the incident took place just after Fox's visit to Rhode Island, was typical of many stories circulating among Quakers. One John Jay was thrown from his horse in New Jersey, and thought to be dead of a broken neck. His companions laid out his body on a "tree." "I came to him and felt on him," wrote Fox, "and saw that he was dead." Sorrowing with the others, Fox took him by the hair and saw that he had a broken neck: "his head turned like a cloth it was so loose." Fox seized his head in both hands, braced himself against the tree, and "wrested his head." Repeating his thrusts, Fox aligned his neck, and Jay began to breathe ("rattle"). Jay lived, and became a Quaker minister. Fox himself wrote about this event and clearly viewed it as miraculous. He, too, had great expectations of himself, as a conduit for the "wonders" of Jesus.[37] "Wonder" stories—and there were many—combined with Fox's imposing presence, amplified by magisterial drama like his late, solo entrance into meetings, were potent sources of his authority. His authority had the potential, then, to profoundly affect local Quaker testimonies and their observance. A guest in the home of (Quaker) Governor Nicholas Easton, Fox was apparently a figure of widespread fascination for Quakers and non-Quakers alike, holding forth at many meetings throughout the colony during June and July.

The schedule was ambitious: in the first week were daily, large "public" meetings open to all; in the second week, the annual "great meting of all new england" drew Quakers from the several colonies. Fox stood up in each meeting and preached "severall houres together." William Rogers, perhaps envious, would later disparage Fox's "thundering lungs";[38] such lungs could only have been an advantage, as "the body of the whole Island as it were came in to heare, of all sorts high and low."[39] Fox and his companions had ample opportunity to elaborate on Quaker beliefs and testimonies. Although few records detail the content of his preaching and praying in this colony, it is possible to postulate with some confidence at least some of what Rhode Islanders had been exposed to, even if only through a hostile conduit, Roger Williams. We know that Roger Williams read aloud from one of Fox's works—*The Great Mistery of the Great Whore Unfolded*—for a day and a half in 1672, in order to argue, as it were, with Fox's religious tenets. Williams, in so "exposing" Fox's book in 1672, ironically drew attention to its pertinence and tied it to Rhode Island theological interests, if only negatively. It is of interest, then, to note that Fox's book, itself a meticulous refutation of various anti-Quaker writings, concentrated on the doctrine of the inner Light, the possibility of perfection, and the oneness of Christ and believer. Because in this book Fox was responding to the concerns of his critics, he framed his argument within the ideas that interested them;

unfortunately for our purposes, Quaker testimonies such as those on oaths, plain speaking, and nonviolence were not among them and so received little or no attention.[40]

Orderly Walking

In between the large meetings, Fox was working with each individual Rhode Island meeting—men's and women's—"about the church afaiers."[41] Some of these "afaiers" involved Quaker practice. Humphrey Norton had taught at Newport that meetings were to be utterly silent, unless a Quaker "minister" came among them. If meetings at Newport were silent, a few miles away at Portsmouth they were filled with "Singing and Toning and Humming many at once." Fox, on the other hand, encouraged any to speak in meeting as led by the spirit. And unlike William Brend, who had apparently held rigidly to the early Quaker avoidance of superfluous social niceties and misplaced deference such as greetings, bowings and scrapings, and especially removing the hat, Fox, as Roger Williams observed, was more

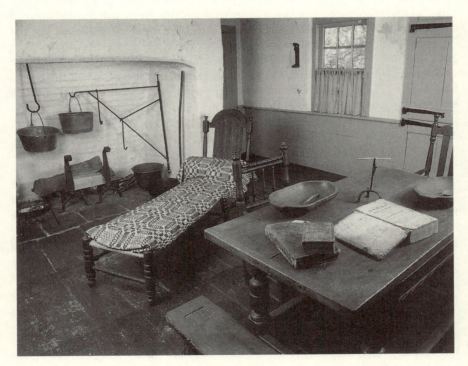

Figure 5.2. Kitchen, the John Bowne House, Flushing, New Amsterdam/New York, 1661. Quakers of Flushing met in this kitchen. George Fox stayed with John Bowne in 1672 on his way to Rhode Island and by tradition used the oak and leather day bed. The open book is Burrough's *Memorable Works of a Son of Thunder and Consolation* (1672), the small book is Bishop's *New England Judged* (1667). Photo by Scott Rosenberg. The Bowne House Historical Society, Inc.

relaxed, "more sociable and manlike," so that many Quakers even began to "speak in Salutations." Fox himself demonstrated the new style at Providence, "uncovering his Head and bowing to the People"; even passing among them with "his Hat in his hand." (Those Quakers who had suffered in prison for not removing their hats would have been stunned.)[42] Under Fox's direction, the general meeting established men's and women's meetings in "all other parts" of New England. Although a measure of structure within the wider Quaker community already was in place, the structure supportive of collective activities, oversight, and discipline was enhanced. "There is to be a generall womans meting set up twice a yeare at boaston," wrote Fox, "to look to the poor & church affaiers & to see that all walk according to the glorious gospell of god."[43] Fox thus assigned an explicit responsibility to the meetings, both new and established: the responsibility to judge each other to make sure all were living according to the Light. This responsibility of oversight and discipline would become increasingly important in Quaker self-definition and in their concept of membership—a responsibility to come to agreement about what constitutes "gospel order." And discipline, too, might be a window into the contemporary understanding of the peace testimony.

Although meetings had already dealt with problematic members through collective discipline, Fox's mandate focused increased attention on this function. By regularizing the meeting structure and assigning a disciplinary function to the collective bodies, then, Fox strengthened a preexisting strand of Quakerism, best exemplified by the testimonies themselves: the developing codification of idiosyncratic Quaker attitudes and behavior at the expense of an emphasis on individual revelation. In carrying out this responsibility, the difficulty, of course, was to discern the will of God—to explicate what it meant to walk according to the gospel. When a meeting became responsible in this way for an individual in its midst, it was forced to define "orderly walking" as understood at the time; the very process of definition, and the later discipline enforcing it, helped to shape future understanding as well.

But it was a fine line to walk between reproving those who strayed from the "Truth" and judging them in a way that encroached on the proper province of God alone. Fox tried to distinguish the duty from the error at the women's meeting while he was in the colony. He carefully regulated the manner in which discipline was to occur. He told the women that they must reprove "backsliders": "you are to admonish them." But they were not to publicly judge these backsliders in the time of meeting. In England, during the "schism" known as the Wilkinson-Story controversy, conflict within the meeting in Bristol had become so pronounced and public that William Rogers, the Quaker separatist, said the meetinghouse had become "a Stage of Scolding." Apparently some of this unfortunate public judgment had been taking place in New England, for Fox wrote, "Let this thing bee amended, & done soe no more." Nor should a Quaker make known to just anyone the failing of another; rather, she should speak privately to the offender, and then two or three from the meeting would be appointed to visit with the offender and seek his repentance. Fox emphasized the reluctance of Quakers to give up on one of their members. "For wee cast none out, but they cast themsellves out, and when they are out then wee endeavour to bring them In Againe."[44] The meetings in New England heeded the advice; the accounts of endless visits to a recalcitrant member, sometimes lasting for years, show both patience and confidence in the efficacy of repentance.

With a new attention to Quaker discipline, one would expect to find in the Quaker minutes increased information about the developing peace testimony in New England. That this was not the case also reveals something about the peace testimony. Either there were no such infractions; or the meeting could not come to agreement about what constituted disorder in relation to the peace testimony; or the meeting did not feel that the peace testimony came under the purview of collective responsibility but was a matter of individual revelation.

When a meeting recorded disciplinary actions against a member, it recorded inadvertently the range of uncertainties, disagreements, and convictions within the meeting. It is a disappointment, then, that the Quaker records in New England contain only a few references to discipline pertinent to the peace testimony before the 1690s.[45] Yet clearly the peace testimony in various forms was abroad among Quakers, as was noncompliance with it. At the same time, one may track the gradual increase in disciplinary activities centering around other failings. The absence of disciplinary measures in reference to weapons, wars, or fighting could imply that either the Quakers had achieved unchallenged unity about their obligations, as well as perfect compliance with those obligations, or variations of the opposite.

Foxes and Firebrands: Government and Violence

Government

Fox and Stubbs took special notice of the "high sort" of people they attracted to their meetings, each of them delineating which meetings the governor attended, which the justices, which the deputy governor. To take such careful note of the dignitaries was not necessarily a preoccupation with worldly status as a matter of vanity, for, as Stubbs explained, their presence was a strong enticement for the people "to flock in" from all parts.[46] Nevertheless, wherever he went, Fox had consistently seemed well aware of who were the powerful and the prestigious, knowing that frequently Quaker destiny could be determined at their hands. His sojourn in Rhode Island was illustrative of this preoccupation with power, both secular and religious. He had an intense, and practical, interest in the "magistracy," especially coinciding as it did with Quakers coming to dominate the colony government. Fox was gratified at his reception by the colony leadership, political as well as religious (in many instances the leadership overlapped). No doubt stimulated by the particular opportunity of Quakers in Rhode Island, here especially Fox's teachings on government carried a significance and immediacy scarcely even contemplated before, unless in the confident years, the early 1650s, when Quakers anticipated universal acceptance of the Kingdom of God on earth, when government itself would no longer be needed. So, too, the teachings must have also had bearing on issues of force and violence, the concomitants of government.

In Rhode Island, then, Fox's view of the role of the magistrate was both dramatic and relevant—dramatic because he was staying in Governor Easton's home and relevant because of the recent Quaker electoral success.[47] While Fox was in Rhode Island, he gave a sermon, preserved only in summary form, that directly addressed the opportunities and duties facing those Quakers newly in power.[48] The sermon demonstrates vividly just what George Fox thought about the prospect of Quakers holding governmental power in this time and place. "What an Honor is itt that Christ should bee both Priest, Prophett, Minister, Shepherd, & Bishop, Councellor Leader, & Captaine & Prince in your Colony," he rejoiced.[49] Telling them bluntly that their mission as magistrates was to glorify God, he urged upon them specific measures and attitudes that would do so. His enthusiasm extended to proposing measures focused on worldly matters, such as laws against drunkenness, selling liquor, fighting, and swearing; establishing a weekly market and a "house" to hold it in; and recording births, deaths, and marriages.

Fox suggested other measures, still practical but more lofty: a tallying and burnishing of the "ancient Liberties . . . & Priviledges & agreements concerning your Divine Liberty & Nationall Liberty," as well as internal liberties; a pattern of fair judgment, whether of matters, or words, or persons, wherein the magistrate would listen to both parties without prejudice and then render judgment: "doe not give both your Ears[,] lett him have one, and Reserve the other for the other." Some measures were spiritual charges: to follow the law of God "that answereth that of God in every one," thus fulfilling God's plan for his appointed magistrates; to "Stand up for the good of the people which is for the good of your Selves"; "Double your guards against Sin & Oppression." The divine liberty of Jesus, making his adherents "f[r]ee in Life, Glory & Power," was to be their guide in governing; should they act outside of the Lord's boundaries, they would be "the unworthiest Men upon the Earth." They were to stand for God: for divine liberties derived from their religious convictions, and for temporal liberties, the heritage of their colony.[50]

Clearly, George Fox was excited that Quakers were to govern the colony; so excited, indeed, that the local pastor of the First Baptist Church and politician Thomas Olney, Jr., deemed him nakedly ambitious.[51] It was unseemly, Olney pointed out, for Fox to be so anxious for the Quakers in power to exceed the former governors in wisdom and right action, for fear that otherwise the new government would be mocked. Olney intimated that such a competitive concern was unworthy of "some greate one." Olney argued one point at a time from Fox's sermon, sometimes with effect and sometimes slipping over into misunderstanding because he took words out of context. One of his arguments is of special historical interest because it illuminates the contemporary understanding of the traditional Quaker attitude toward serving in government. "This is new Doctrine," he wrote in June 1673 of Quakers serving in government. "There was none of this in old time; for when Quakerisme was first broacht in these parts he that was found to be acting in Civill Govournment (after his Conversion) was not Counted worthly to be a friend."[52] Moreover, Quakers had "preached up as Gospell amongst us"— to Quakers and non-Quakers alike—the idea that those who converted were not to serve in civil government, and had in fact held debates on this topic. Olney saw Fox's sermon as proposing an unholy alliance between civil government and matters of the spirit, surely antithetical to Rhode Island's prized culture. Even if a converted person served solely in a civil capacity, not meddling with religion at all, according to the earlier Quakers, said Olney, "If any were found defileing themselves with a portion of that meat, they were accounted as polluted persons."[53] Unless Olney was referring to New England Quakers before 1660, his observations may validate Barry

Reay's and Christopher Hill's emphasis on Quaker political quietism in England after the Restoration.[54] Olney was aware that Fox had at times discouraged Quaker participation in government. He seized the opportunity to inquire why, if Fox had attained "perfection," he could reverse himself.[55] In any case, Fox's enthusiasm in Rhode Island shows that any former quietism was more likely a strategy than a principle—that millenarian hope might live on in appropriate climates.

One might have sympathy for the new Rhode Island governors, "polluted" if they accepted office at all (a convenient argument for political rivals to throw up from Quaker heritage) and the "unworthiest Men upon the Earth" if they did not succeed in establishing a sufficiently hospitable climate for the glory of God. In the essence of his instructions, however, Fox equated the good of all the people with the good of the government. This standard undoubtedly justified, if not influenced, the way Quakers in government would reconcile their religious beliefs and their civil obligations.

Violence

According to Fox, all in Rhode Island were "migh[t]ily affected with trueth beyond what can be written & expressed with words."[56] His perception was faulty, however, because as the two months of the visitors' presence in Rhode Island passed, so did, apparently, some of the initial euphoria. Thomas Olney, Jr., was not the only mocking skeptic. Resentment coagulated too in the mind of Roger Williams, who challenged Fox to a debate. Fox did not receive the offer before he left on 26 July, so Edmundson, Stubbs, and Burnyeat debated Williams in a two-day marathon. (After "rowing all day with my old bones," wrote the seventy-three-year-old Williams, "I got to Newport toward the midnight.") Instead of clarifying differences, the debate served only to inflame passions between Williams and the Quakers. The Quakers seem to have attempted to drown out Williams's arguments by sheer volume: while he was speaking, Henry Nichols resorted to loud singing and Ann Easton prayed aloud in an annoyingly vigorous voice.[57]

Each side sought to confirm what it insisted was its victory through continuing the debate by other means. After the visitors left Williams wrote his book *George Fox Digg'd Out of His Burrowes;* his arguments with an invisible Fox derived from his experience of their presence. Williams seemed to metaphorically retake his beloved colony from the usurpers—his colony, whose seal portrayed an anchor, whose motto was "Hope." "How many painted Anchors and painted Hopes are there?" he enquired, accusing the Quakers of counterfeiting false anchors and false hopes. The false anchor was the Quaker's Christ within, the true anchor the historical, outward Christ. The false hope was the Quaker idea of true glory here on earth; the true hope the transcendent hope of glory in heaven. In his book Williams took note of Quaker claims not to "meddle" with carnal weapons but expressed his opinion that these were hollow claims when Fox reserved to Quakers alone the capacity to evaluate who was a true Christian magistrate, justifiably wielding the "Carnal and Material Sword" to "terrifie" evildoers. "Shall we rationally question," Williams asked rhetorically, "whether their hands . . . will not be as fierce and cruel, if the most holy and only Wise permits Whips & Halters,

Swords & Fagots to fall into their Hands?"[58] The book was published in 1676; Fox's equally rancorous refutation, *A New-England-Fire-brand Quenched,* was published in 1678–1679, King Philip's War having delayed its publication. Williams had accused Fox of hypocrisy for his "prating against Carnal Weapons" and suggested that Fox only had to get a sword and "most of the Popish and Protestant and Pagan-world will easily be brought to dance after him." Fox protested in rebuttal that Quaker weapons were only spiritual and told Williams that "Quakers abhor thy words."[59] Fox's words are reminiscent of the original thinking about the peace testimony when it developed in the context of religious persuasion and persecution.[60]

No other evidence exists that Fox directly addressed issues of violence when he was in Rhode Island. He had reason and opportunity to consider these issues, but there remains no record of his having done so. Nor did Rhode Island Quakers later refer to any direct Foxian influence on their decision-making about war and violence. Because Rhode Island had felt itself threatened by attack for two years, however, and because of Quaker governmental power, it is scarcely conceivable that he ignored such issues entirely. While Fox and the other visitors were actually in residence, moreover, the Rhode Island council received the king's proclamation of 17 March 1672 declaring war against the Dutch—the third Dutch war. The council, including the three Quaker members present at a meeting on 25 June 1672, wrote to Governor Bellingham of Massachusetts, as well as to John Winthrop of Connecticut and Thomas Prence of Plymouth, proposing joint consultation and defense against possible Dutch attack. Quaker Henry Bull carried the letter to Boston, as well as a request for him to purchase and return with ammunition from Massachusetts, in spite of its existing prohibition against the transport of ammunition. The councilors ordered the magistrates and militia officers of the respective Rhode Island towns to "putt the Inhabitants of each Towne into the best posture of Defence . . . and Especially to take Care for powder shott & ammunition."[61]

With George Fox not publically mentioning military responsibility, the unavoidable conclusion is that Quaker magistrates, carrying out military measures, did not offend his own interpretation of the peace testimony. God's imprimatur upon magistrates excused them from scriptural strictures against violence. In fact, this public silence suggests that Fox would have approved of the Quaker magistrates identifying themselves with military measures that were for the benefit of the colony as a whole. He proposed neither a legal exemption from service, such as that to be developed in Rhode Island in 1673, one year later, nor the rationale on which this might rest. No hint of these appeared in his instructional sermon.[62] When faced with the possibilities inherent in political power, then, Fox abandoned whatever reluctance earlier New England—or Old England—Quakers had displayed toward participating in government, even when that government faced immediate military tasks. Fox had resisted the seduction of power in 1659 England (in contrast to some Quakers), perhaps out of conviction or perhaps out of realism. But power seduced Fox in Rhode Island. Its opportunities may have seemed overridingly blessed in the heady days of the summer of 1672.

Violence had always been a part of colonial experience, accompanying the fishermen in their pinnaces along the coasts of the northern waters and the explorers wading ashore with their crosses in southern waters. But war itself was threatening New England in 1672, in ever more menacing dimensions, threatening from without and from within. For Rhode Island Quakers, the responsibilities of governing in wartime would dilute the possibilities of power that had enthralled the 1672 visitors, would threaten Quaker stewardship of an exalted habitation, and would blunt the welcoming of the hunted Christ.

6

"Times of Motion and Danger"

REACTING TO FEAR OF WAR, 1667–1673

New England colonists were chronically anxious about Indians making plans to overrun their settlements and farms and about invasion by the Dutch and French during the Anglo-European wars. The Indian scares of 1667 and 1671 and the major Dutch and French invasion scares of 1667 and 1672 had energized the colonial governments to make plans, both defensive and offensive, plans that would have been haphazard and inadequate had the threat of attack materialized.

The response of the Rhode Island government to these abortive crises provides a useful comparison not only to the responses of the other colony governments but also to the response it itself would make to King Philip's War in 1675, when the threat became a reality and war between the United Colonies and various Indian tribes took place in part on Rhode Island territory and devastated Rhode Island Indian peoples and Rhode Island property. The important factor for this study is the religious composition of the various Rhode Island governments, in comparison to each other and to the United Colony governments, with their different religious characters. Did non-Quaker governments respond differently to these crises from governments dominated by Quakers? Did either form of Rhode Island government react differently from other colonial governments to common threats? If there were material differences, were they in any way determined by the Quaker peace testimony? To address these questions, the first step is to compare and analyze the varying reactions to rumors of war from 1667 to 1673.

1667: "Native Treachery" and "Enemies By Sea"

Rhode Island

To better understand the reaction of the Rhode Island government to crises, it is appropriate to set forth certain pertinent conditions within the colony. The king's commissioners, appointed to evaluate and order the governmental arrangements of the various New England colonies, presented five directives to the Rhode Island assembly in 1665, two of which bore upon military affairs. The first relevant directive was that all householders take an oath of allegiance to the king; the other ordered the colony to see to its own defense. Since Quakers held to a scruple against swearing oaths on scriptural grounds, the practice of oath-taking had always caused them disadvantage and harm. Not only were Quakers thereby barred from legal procedures such as witnessing documents, barred from becoming freemen and thus often barred from voting, and punished in courts for not swearing, even if acquitted of any other fault, but those in power chose to interpret their refusal to swear allegiance to the king as a threat to the security of the realm. Their loyalty was called into question, in turn subjecting them to confiscation of liberty and estate. Quakers, of course, regarded the imposition of oaths not as a political test, but as an affront to liberty of conscience in the realm of religion ("swear not at all").[1] In ostensibly agreeing wholeheartedly to the directive mandating the oath of allegiance, the Rhode Island assembly simultaneously and pointedly referred back to Rhode Island's 1663 charter from King Charles II, in which it was granted certain dispensations for its tradition of liberty of conscience. The assembly had undertaken to adhere to laws and customs of England, it reminded the commissioners, "as neare . . . as the constitution of the place will admitt"; that is, as far as liberty of conscience in matters of religion would permit. While the assembly unanimously agreed to observe the commissioners' directive, in fact in the same sentence it transfigured the oath into an "engagement." Expressing its gratitude for the commissioners' (nonexistent) accommodation, the assembly according to its own lights allowed those who scrupled to swear the alternative of "engaging" to their allegiance to the king. The minutes of the assembly session set forth the form of this engagement in which an individual would "sollemly and sincearly engage true and faithfull aleagiance unto his Majestye" and engage to obey the laws of the colony.[2] The significance of this accommodation was that the issue of Quaker disloyalty was defused—they were not as a group tainted with disloyalty and sedition—so if they in turn asserted scruples about military activities, their loyalty was not immediately impugned, as it was in England and other colonies. And no oath impeded their civic participation in voting and holding office. (In contrast, note the case of Quaker Nicholas Shapleigh, of Kittery, now Maine: "a man every way fit for the employment," enthused Joseph Mason of Shapleigh, but remembering that he neither took nor imposed oaths, pronounced him "therefore . . . unfit for a magistrate or governor.")[3] In order that the engagement might carry the same weight with the general populace as an oath, the assembly made it retroactive and mandatory for all freemen, past and future, to take the engagement of allegiance. Even those who had previously sworn the oath had to reestablish their allegiance through the engagement, thereby obliterating differences caused by religion in this respect. Rhode Island was establishing a pattern of carving out domains of difference for itself.

The commissioners' other relevant directive ordered that the colony put itself into a posture of defense sufficient for its own readiness and to come to the aid of neighbor colonies in case of invasion. In response, the assembly set out its plans for defense. These arrangements form a background, then, for measures taken in times of alarm. The basic plans were these: all men from sixteen to sixty were listed as soldiers in the several militias of the towns. They would assemble in each town on six days per year for training, well-armed and with ammunition, for which they would receive an allowance of nine shillings per year. These men would choose their officers from among the freemen, all having a vote for this purpose if eighteen or older, regardless of whether or not they were freemen of the town or colony. We can discern the evident unpopularity of training duties from the detailed fines the assembly felt called upon to provide for penalizing those who failed to perform, from householders who did not adequately supply their servants to officers who neglected to call out the trained bands to towns that failed to tax themselves and establish the required magazines. Although the military plans preserved a localized system of defense, the assembly did hold in reserve for itself, or for the governor and council in its absence, the power to "order" the various militias for the defense of the whole colony in extraordinary situations.[4]

Ironically, the impetus for the five directives had come in the first place from the prodding of Quakers in regard to oath-taking. William Coddington had apparently written to the commissioners laying out the Quaker difficulty with oaths. We see the result in the assembly minutes: the assembly ordered Governor Benedict Arnold to assemble Coddington, Nicholas Easton, and "those concearned (called Quackers)" to receive the commissioners' reply in the form of the five directives. The minutes noted (twice) that the reply to the letter was delivered in the presence of the assembly, for the Quakers to "mind and obaye accordingly."[5] But as we have seen, the assembly graciously appeared to accept the commissioners' five points, while redesigning the oath to fit its own condition. Whatever the contents of Coddington's letter, the assembly had taken the initiative to protect its scrupulous inhabitants.

In 1667, the Rhode Island assembly, governor, and council prepared to counter both invasion from abroad—England was at war with the Dutch and the French and her colonies were consequently vulnerable to her enemies—and "native treachery" from within. In May the assembly called for the activation of a council of war in each of the four towns of the colony: Newport and Portsmouth on the island of Aquidneck and Providence and Warwick on the mainland. Each council of war was to consist of the town council plus the captain and the lieutenant of the trained band (the local militia). Each town was responsible for procuring ammunition—fifty pounds for Newport, twenty pounds for the others. Again the assembly doubted whether self-interest would be sufficient to motivate the towns; it imposed a fine on each town for failure to comply, the proceeds to go to the general treasury of the colony.[6]

The Rhode Island governor and council directed its attention to Newport and ordered a house-to-house inventory of arms and ammunition, repair of all arms, a tax of one hundred fifty pounds for defense, and the mounting of the great guns in Newport.[7] At this time, Deputy Governor Nicholas Easton and Assistant William Reape were the only Quaker members to sign the regulations, since the other Quaker, Assistant John Easton, was absent. But although concurring in the other measures, Nicholas Easton found himself unable "to consent as to command" the mounting of the guns. His scruples were illustrative of the peace testimony's ambiguity: he was able to associate himself with preparing for and financing war, tasks presumably to be carried out by others, and was unable to be directly involved with those weapons whose only purpose was to kill people. The directives were obviously to affect other Quakers as well. "Sett against [aside] all excuses," the council warned the Quaker gunsmith Emanuel Wooley, among others, ordering them to repair all the arms and "utensills of warr" of the inhabitants.[8] Quakers Nicholas Easton, Peter Easton, John Coggeshall, John Gould, and Daniel Gould sat on the committee organizing the war tax.

The council also empowered any town magistrate acting alone, in time of danger, to raise an alarm, to press any persons, horses, or vessels, and to commission any person for assistance. All English men and boys over the age of sixteen were *prohibited* from departing the island of Aquidneck without a license, in case they were needed for defense. In contrast, the council ruled that Indian men and boys over the age of sixteen *must* depart the island unless they had a license to remain; all Indians on Aquidneck were to be disarmed, and any Indians found walking at night were to be detained. A committee was formed to meet with the Narragansett sachems and demand from them information about rumored Indian conspiracies and combinations with Philip, sachem of the Wampanoags.[9]

By July 1667, the fear of the enemy "as if he were even at our doors" led the General Assembly to reiterate that town councils and councils of war had full power to provide for defense of whatever kind. The assembly gave the governor and council power to procure ammunition and weapons from Massachusetts or elsewhere, to establish a magazine accessible to the whole colony for supplies, and to treat with neighboring colonies for the safety of the whole. (In fact, the council minutes of 21 May already had taken notice of a letter from Plymouth reporting rumored Indian conspiracies and recorded the intention to reply to this intelligence.) The councilors also asserted their right to provide for the defense of outlying regions such as Hog Island, Narragansett, and the King's Province on the mainland, regions without town government. They were made responsible for setting up a system of warning beacons across the country. A poem about beacons is in the Newbury-Richardson Commonplace Book at Newport, probably written by Quaker Benjamin Newbury:

> if you that succeed us in the ward [watch]
> will go on as we have begunne
> that for good Designes have any Regard
> then lend a hand Each one
>
> A pile of wood will be very good
> On Beakon hill to Raise
> our neighbors to alarm to Shun the harm
> And our Enimys for to maze
>
> for if fired Right in time of night
> when Danger Seemes to be [Nigh?]
> twill make a Show may Feare our [foe?]
> And Draw our frand more nigh[10]

The council were empowered to impress "all the vessells great and small," as well as horses, and to raise a troop of horse on Aquidneck. Quakers were not loath to volunteer for the troop of horse: John Easton volunteered, along with William Reape, Francis Brayton, and Hugh Parsons; volunteers Henry Dyer, son of Mary Dyer, and Ralph Earle, Sr., may also have been Quakers.[11] The assembly of July 1667 enacting these measures included Quakers Nicholas Easton, John Easton, William Reape, John Coggeshall, Philip Shearman, Walter Clarke, and Edward Thurston and, possibly, Benjamin Smith and John Throckmorton.[12]

The Rhode Island colony government in 1667, as in prior years, although having a modest proportion of those who happened to be Quakers, was a non-Quaker government. But both non-Quaker- and Quaker-dominated governments in Rhode Island responded to threats of attack in these years in ways that shared several broad characteristics. In the first place, military responsibility was highly decentralized within the colony. The central government was responsible for the foreign relations aspects of preparedness: securing weapons and cooperation from other colonies and petitioning the king for port fortifications.[13] This decentralization of military authority corroborates Bruce C. Daniel's thesis that in Rhode Island, citizens would be more loyal to their towns than to the colony for many decades to come.[14] Military decentralization may have been purely pragmatic, given the geography and history of the colony, or may have been a deference to the fierce independence of the towns or may have been an unwillingness of the stronger towns of Newport and Portsmouth, with their dominance of political power, to sacrifice on behalf of outlying regions.[15] Even within the localities, power was individualized: a single magistrate was able to use his discretion, for example, about returning arms to an Indian or punishing a "night walker."

Second, the Rhode Island government, whether Quaker or not, often appeared to direct itself to the needs of the island of Aquidneck, as if it were the government of that island alone rather than the seat of the whole colony. The people of Aquidneck perceived their island as a sanctuary or as a fortress, depending on whether they looked to the continent or to the ocean. Geography offered this choice: Aquidneck was safer than the mainland from land-based attack, but the island was more vulnerable than the mainland from sea-based attack. The government exploited the fortress concept through such measures as licensing people to come and go, demanding that masters of vessels report to a senior officer ashore. The people of Aquidneck pressured the government for protective resources because of their vulnerability to sea-based attack but offered only hospitality instead of resources to people of the main.

Third, the colony's government, whatever its religious composition, only minimally sought King Charles's participation in its military mobilization, expecting and desiring little practical support from England against either internal or external threat. Although from time to time it reminded the king that the Dutch threat menacing its shores was a consequence of the Anglo-Dutch war, the government did not act as if entitled to significant help from the king; to the contrary, the government found occasion to cite its charter responsibilities to provide for itself. After all, soliciting the king's help would only invite interference with its own jealously guarded autonomy.[16]

Fourth, the various Rhode Island governments interacted with the Indians in similar ways, unrelated to their religious persuasion. There is no evidence that Rhode Island Quakers viewed themselves as having a special relationship with, and therefore special influence over, the various Indian tribes within their borders. Neither is there evidence that their fellow colonists perceived them in this way. None of the four men charged with treating with the Indians in 1667, for example, were Quakers.[17] The common assumption that Quakers served as exemplars of harmonious Indian relations is probably a projection backward of the later Pennsylvania experience. Indeed, it is likely that the Rhode Island experience with the Indians served as a caution and a spur to the Pennsylvania colonists. Finally, the governments were alike in their reluctance to do more than recommend, encourage, mandate, and mobilize, devoting remarkably few actual resources to defense preparations.

Plymouth

"It is determined," wrote the Plymouth court in April 1667, "that Duch and French be looked upon as our common enimie whiles soe to our nation." The Plymouth government responded to the threat of outside attack by issuing orders and warnings to its people, as did the various Rhode Island governments. It established a central council of war, called for an inventory of all weapons, developed the form of military commissions, and urged each town to set watches and make troops available to carry intelligence. It encouraged the towns to designate safe houses where women and children would be protected, so that men might better fight, without the distraction of worrying about their families. The towns were to help each other in case of attack, lending each other up to half of their men. Three musket shots would serve as a universal alarm in the night; shooting pigeons or game, by day or night, was therefore discouraged.[18] In June the court summoned Philip (Metacom) to account; they suspected that this chief of the Wampanoags had offered to help the French or Dutch against the English in return for repossessing their Indian lands and acquiring English goods. Philip maintained that his enemy Ninigret, a Narragansett sachem, had been the source of this false report.[19]

The Plymouth colony government reaction to threat was similar to that of Rhode Island in that it, too, did not solicit significant help from the king and devoted few material resources to its people, but it did add a centralized element to its military resources, the council of war for the colony. Most important, the colony had the capacity to call on its all-colony regiment, headed by a major, to which the various towns were required to supply troops and officers for the colony's service. The colony raised a cavalry company as well.[20] In this as in other emergencies, it was more activist in its monitoring of the neighboring Indian population and issuing peremptory summonses and impositions. Plymouth settlers and Indians had a history of shared territory and close living, of unresolved land rights that might have made the English feel more threatened, less secure, hence more controlling.

Massachusetts Bay

In May, the Massachusetts General Court expressed a sense of vulnerability when it spoke of "times of motion & danger, from enemies by sea & land." Massachusetts Bay had a nominally well-developed military structure in which each county had organized the various town companies into a regimental order, with regimental officers. The various regiments, led by majors, were under the leadership of the major general for the colony, a member of the General Court. Three counties together raised a cavalry company.[21] But its additional preparations in the 1667 emergency were even less adequate—had threats materialized—than those of Rhode Island and Plymouth. To counter the motion and danger, the court merely called on the "country treasurer" to buy nine barrels of powder for the country's stock, from which the towns might purchase their supplies. And the court urged each town militia to use its training days to erect a fort for women, children, and the aged, "whereby the souldjers may be more free to oppose an enemy."[22] Such a meager response from the central government of the colony permits no generalizations.

As each of the three colonies reacted to military danger, its provisions for defense were haphazard and tentative. Consider, for example, just the inadequacy of "great guns." Although New England had three or four ironworks, William Harris reported in 1675 that he "never heard that they cast any Guns there"; rather, "in these Iron-workes they formerly cast Iron pots to boyle meat in." Boston was best prepared, having more than twenty great guns "planted on the Bulwarke neare the Town," but the guns protected only from attack from the sea. Meanwhile, in Rhode Island, Roger Williams had planted two "murderers," or small cannon, facing Narragansett Bay in front of his trading post at Wickford.[23] The uncertainty and failure to prepare of the colonial leaders was more reflective perhaps of a lack of power than a failure of will; of rudimentary roads than an absence of concern; of a lack of surplus than an ungenerous spirit. An act of the Rhode Island assembly six years later may be held emblematic of the colonial conditions: after designating the specific authorities who were to respond in case of alarm—commissioning the governor, or deputy governor, and whichever assistants were available to consult with the chief captain, captains, lieutenants, and ensignes—the provision peters out with the nomination of "any other knowinge, discreete men in such matters."[24] It is as if the government were conscientiously formulating correct legal provisions but then recognized that legal forms might be irrelevant in the time of danger and so empowered almost anyone to exercise authority. The governments of all the colonies, too, all too aware of their own incapacity, pragmatically gave most responsibility to local towns to make military arrangements. Each was anxious about where the money for defense would come from; each volunteered little or no concrete financial assistance; none were looking to the king for support. Each placated, tried to bring to account, and punished Indians.

1671: "Then Lend a Hand Each One"

In 1671, Rhode Island and Plymouth again feared Indian attack. They reacted by passing new resolutions, still reflecting their inability to plan a concerted resistance, or at least their reluctance to do so. Manpower was inadequate: men could not leave farming or fishing on the strength of rumors alone. Once again the measures were oddly fragmentary and vague, but there is some evidence that the central governments were becoming more assertive.

In Rhode Island, the council commanded the two Aquidneck towns to send their town councils of war to meet at George Lawton's house in Portsmouth.[25] Each town was to furnish ten armed horsemen to guard this meeting. The council sent word to the towns on the mainland to set watches, provide ammunition, establish a posture of defense, and watch the activities of Indians so they could give notice of danger to the colony.[26] (Two or three Quakers were members of this council.) The Plymouth court reacted in much the same way. The court enlarged and activated its centralized council of war, again urged the populace to establish watches and to carry arms to meeting, and "solicited" engagements of fidelity from various Indian clans. The Plymouth government responded more vigorously than did that of Rhode Island, using the threat of military force to secure these agreements and actually pressing men for a possible expedition.[27] The Massachusetts General Court apparently took no preparatory measures at this time. In 1671 the colonies' central governments continued to swat at gnats; showing little less reliance on the informal willingness of its English settlers to "lend a hand each one."[28]

1673: Rhode Island

With the election of Nicholas Easton as governor, William Coddington as deputy governor, six Quaker assistants, and at least seven Quaker deputies in 1673, it was a Quaker-dominated government that responded to the news that the Dutch had taken New York in July 1673 and might well have designs on Rhode Island. In August, the assembly, at least half of which was Quaker, appointed a committee of five to consider this danger and to encourage the militia. Quakers John Easton and Peter Easton served on this committee. The assembly named a captain-in-chief for Aquidneck, empowered to order the inhabitants to "assemble, exercise in armes, martiall array, and put [themselves] in war like posture;" empowered the governor, deputy governor, and assistants to direct this captain; established sanctions for disloyal behavior; and provided that the whole colony bear the charge for soldiers and trained bands. They established an elaborate plan of compensation for those killed or wounded. The reach of these provisions is exemplified by the provision that the colony would assume support even "if a nephew or kinsman be slaine . . . that hath an uncle or aunt or other neere of kin, who had dependancy on him." Further, they enabled survivors to sue the colony government if compensation were withheld or inadequate.[29] The legislation was silent about how the colony might fund these obligations.

The extraordinarily detailed provisions for compensating the families of the maimed or slain were expressed in language of great concern, suggesting that the authors were sensitive to the consequences of their military efforts, were perhaps ambivalent toward those preparations, and saw a practical need to recruit troops. In the absence of explicit explanation, however, one cannot discern their motives, let alone attribute to Quaker "virtue" their heightened analysis of the consequences of war.

It is already apparent that there was little difference between how the governments of the United Colonies and the government of Rhode Island reacted to threats.

Nor was there appreciable difference between the non-Quaker governments and the Quaker-dominated government within Rhode Island itself. Indeed, the Quaker-dominated Rhode Island assembly enacted mobilization measures at least comparable to—indeed, perhaps more comprehensive than—those enacted by non-Quaker governments, whether in Rhode Island or Plymouth. Its members were not apparently inhibited by pacifist belief from endorsing active if still feeble and scattershot military preparation. It is hard to see reluctance to provide for the defense of the colony. Different religious beliefs did not apparently influence government behavior in different ways—with one remarkable exception.

The exception was an extraordinary provision in Rhode Island's August 1673 acts: this assembly wrote into law measures exempting men from training or fighting for reasons of religious belief; such men were to suffer no penalty. While Quaker magistrates could apparently accommodate their duties as legislators with the pacifist demands of their faith, in the 1673 Exemption they used their power to accommodate those of their faith who could not comply with the very military activities the government itself mandated. Indeed, the Exemption itself was an essential element in the reconciliation between pacifism and magistracy. In a time of motion and danger from without, the Rhode Island government moved to protect liberty of conscience from the danger of its suppression within.

7

"Fighting against the Minde of God"

THE 1673 EXEMPTION

Liberty of conscience was an ideal that defined Rhode Islanders in their own minds. The ideal tamped down even fierce contention and commanded a loyalty transcending the empty protestations of contemporaries whose interest in liberty of conscience waned at the boundaries of their own beliefs. However imperfect was its realization, however sporadic and short-lived, the passion for liberty of conscience stimulated innovative ways to live in community. By any measure, one of the efforts to honor their ideal was extraordinary: in 1673 the General Assembly of Rhode Island provided for exemption from military service on the basis of conscience.[1]

The General Assembly convened in an emergency session on 13 August 1673 at Newport, in response to the Dutch having just retaken New York at the end of July; the Rhode Islanders feared that they might next "unhapely assault and fall upon us." Two thirds of this council and a majority of the assembly were Quakers.[2] As its first act, the assembly appointed a committee of five, including Quakers John and Peter Easton, and perhaps John Tripp, "to prepare matters for this Assembly" concerning several issues: Indian drunkenness, the "encourragement of the mallitia," the new threat occasioned by the Dutch taking New York, and other "publick matters."[3] The assembly showed its sense of urgency by ordering the committee to return its report to that very session. The alarm had been building in the assembly at least since May, when "Dutch men of warr" were supposed "to be Intended for this Cuntry"; the assembly had anticipated the need to call the emergency session and had stipulated the procedure for so doing. It is likely, then, that the vote to "establish" the committee was merely pro forma; the committee

Figure 7.1. "The Dutch Re-Take New Amsterdam, formerly New York, August, 1673," detail from the map Totius Neobelgii Nova et Accuratissima Tabula, Reinier and Josua Ottens, 1673. Engraving on copper. This inset view shows the magazine (G); troops in formation; cannon (R); Fort Amsterdam. This event so alarmed Rhode Island that its government enacted new military provisions, as well as the 1673 Exemption. Courtesy of the Map Collection, Yale University Library.

had already prepared its "report." In any case, the assembly was ready to mobilize against attack from the sea.

A program addressing these particular concerns (except for Indian drunkenness) follows immediately in the minutes—a program of such formal and careful detail, and of such scope, that one must conclude that the program was, in fact, the committee report. The first item in the program called for the appointment of Captain John Cranston as captain-in-chief of the forces on Aquidneck Island "to order direct appoint and putt in warrlike posture all the forces . . . for the defence." As soon as attack was imminent, those members of the council on the island were to gather in order to advise the captain and to answer any "summons of the enemy." The assistants from Warwick or Providence, together with their respective town councils, were to be empowered in like manner. Military officers were given the power to restrain any residents so foolish as to "gitt on board the enemies shipp . . . to informe or serve the enemy." Next, the assembly voted that all charges incurred for defence were to be borne by the whole colony. There follows a careful and detailed plan for indemnifying any persons serving in the military forces who might be maimed or killed during hostilities (or their relatives).[4]

In short, these provisions project the government's sense of fear and danger, its preparation for actual assault. All the more courageous, then, is the section of the legislative program that follows these preparations, the unusual legislative initiative of the 1673 Exemption. The Exemption provided for exemption from military service on the basis of a person's conscience:

> No person (within this Colony), that is or hereafter shall be persuaded in his conscience, (and by him declared) that he cannot nor ought not to train, to learn to fight, nor to war, nor kill any person nor persons[,] shall at any time be compelled against his Judgment and conscience to train, arm or fight, to kill any person nor shall suffer any punishment.[5]

As if this provision were not sufficiently remarkable on its own, the legislation also includes within its complete text the justification on which it rests. Its content, language, and argument unmistakeably reflect the influence of Quakers and their peace principles.

The Exemption

"For this present occassion," the assembly found it "needfull" to address itself in this legislative act to a strain of "strife and unproffitable Contention" within the colony itself. The fierce insistence on the part of some that God forbade them to fight or kill tugged destructively at the jealous incredulity of others who wondered why they needed to bear the entire burden of serving in the militia. The assembly did not flinch. Because the colony had from the beginning enacted laws for the protection of liberty of conscience, it wrote, those who for reasons of conscience (declared by themselves) could not train or learn to fight or to war or to kill were excused from doing so, just as "men are by any other debillety." Those men who "takeinge themselves forbidden of God to learne war any more" were to be thought of as having no ability to fight, as if their disability were visible and physical. "As, aged, lame, sick, weake, deafe, blinde, or any other Infirmety exemptith persons in and by law," so the aforesaid men must be seen as having no capacity to fight, as if they had an internal infirmity, as valid and substantial as any other. Note, too, that to train, to arm, to fight, to war, and to kill are delineated as discrete activities, as if recognizing that persons might have individual parameters to their scruples about violent activity. Including "to war" as a separate category from fighting and killing, for instance, suggests that scruples might encompass activities associated with war as distinct from fighting, such as paying war taxes. None of the exempted persons could be compelled to serve in a military capacity by any official, whether civil or military, or by any former law. They were to be subject to no punishment whatsoever—neither imprisonment or another like physical penalty nor a fine or distraint of worldly goods.[6]

The act established a form of alternative civil service for those exempt from martial service. In this service, exempt persons might conduct "weake and aged impotent persons, women and children, goods and Cattell" out of the reach of an approaching or assaulting enemy. They were required to watch, though they were permitted to do so "without armes in martiall manner nor matters."[7] Any civil officer might require them to do any other civil service for the good of the colony. The act was explicit that the exempt men only had to respond to the orders of civil officers, acting in a civil capacity. The wording suggests that the same individual might be both a military and a civil officer; it was only in his civil capacity that he might regulate alternative service. This careful distinction anticipates that those opposed to fighting might also be opposed to taking any orders, however benign, from a military officer.

Furthermore, the act exempted from alternative civil service those whose consciences forbade even this indirect association with military matters. The original record required as follows:

> Such said persons who cannot fight nor destroy men it beinge against their Conscience, *and is not against their Conscience* to doe and perform civill service to the Collony though not martill service, and can preserve *(soo farr as in them lies)* lives, goods and cattell . . . then it shall be lawfull for the civill officers . . . to require such said persons . . . to conduct or convoy [impotent persons] out of the danger.[8]

This generous provision has been overlooked, because the crucial phrase ("and is not against their Conscience") was omitted from the printed records, leaving the impression that all of those excused from fighting must perform alternative service.[9] But the assembly in fact excused from civil, alternative service those who, on the basis of conscience, could not participate even to this extent in war. The assembly was quick to assert that this act would not excuse any who were not persuaded that God prohibited them from fighting; all such men would be subject to command as if the act had never been made.

Snaking around these legislative clauses were the justifications that gave them conviction. The defense and justification, carefully and imaginatively attached to the frame, revealed far more than secular policy or pragmatic reasoning. One strand was Rhode Island's own proud liberty; other strands were religious; some recalled the rights of Englishmen. The sinuous argument is difficult to follow, sometimes satisfyingly clever and sometimes twisting into a lame heap. Its twists and turns may have bewildered others besides historians. In any case, because the substance of the legislation—the idea of military exemption—is in itself so innovative, it is exclusively this aspect that has received historical attention. The defense and support for the exemption has been left alone. One historian wrote, for example, that "Individual Friends had been exempted in 1673 from the military service that continued to be obligatory in the colony even after the Quakers came into virtual control of its government," went on to note that the Exemption was the first of its kind in America, and then outlined only its provisions for alternative service.[10] Another called the act "the most favorable law for pacifists in seventeenth-century New England" and mentioned only that the assembly "adopted a biblical justification for pacifism."[11] Rufus Jones described the actual exemption clause and its appearance in "a very curious and quaint document full of odd Scripture texts" but found the document too long to address further.[12]

Aside from brief allusions to the assembly's reasoning, historians have neglected to analyze carefully the associated features of the exemption itself. Containing, as the official record does, a virtual legislative essay explaining the rationale for allowing conscientious objection to military training or fighting, it supplies a rare glimpse into the nature of belief and debate. This major departure from the usual governmental response to threats was not only innovative in its prescription but was curiously inventive in its underlying justifications. The justifications were not of pacifism itself but of the validity of excusing pacifists from military service.

The Justification

While the exemption from military service explicitly recognized that there were "divers persons of severall societies" who judged themselves unable to participate in some military activities for religious reasons, the assembly, through its committee, appeared eager to explain why it validated this position, to forestall criticism from those compelled to serve. As noted, the legislators introduced their discussion by acknowledging the "strife and unproffitable Contention, which hath too long contineued" between those whose consciences forbade "Trayninge and fightinge to kill thereby" and those "not willing to allow or permitt" this liberty.[13] That such an exemption should be formulated in a time of perceived danger suggests that the conflict within the community over this issue seemed in itself to be a danger that had to be resolved. It is no surprise that these provisions for military exemption were enacted in 1673 when one recalls that in June 1672, just after the Quakers became dominant in the government, George Fox himself and other prominent English Quakers visited Rhode Island and stayed for two months. The heightened religious climate of renewal and proselytizing, of persuasion and fierce debate, must have fired the thinking, energies, and confidence of the local Quakers. Surely, these issues of religious conscience toward the military must have demanded consideration within the Quaker bodies and perhaps stimulated the "strife and unprofitable contention" to which the assembly was reacting.[14]

Tradition

The assembly justified the Exemption, in the first place, with the familiar, with a reminder that the Rhode Island Colony had always honored liberty of conscience. The colony had already, for example, accommodated those whose beliefs prohibited them from taking oaths by accepting alternative means of establishing allegiance or good faith, even though it was "contrary to the customs of our nation [England] and our neighbours the Rest of the Collonys."[15] Implicit in this observation was the fact that the king had left them unmolested in this regard. Their new military exemption on the basis of conscience, they implied, was not an inappropriate novelty but was part of a respected tradition of freedom of religious conscience.

The assembly went on to argue from the literal text of the Hebrew scriptures that God himself did not universally compel men to fight in his wars. Rather, he excused "Fearefull [men, and] they that had built houses and not dedicated them, [or had] newly married a wife, or planted a vinyard and not eaten the fruites thereof."[16] This reference was to Deuteronomy 20:5–8, in which God excuses a man from fighting lest he die in battle and by doing so leave room for another man to reap those first fruits rightly his: the enjoyment of his new house, his bride, and his first harvest.[17] God excused, too, the man who was afraid, "lest his brethren's heart faint as well as his heart."[18] This scriptural passage makes clear that the fainthearted is excused not for his own benefit but because his faintheartedness might be contagious and demoralizing for the other soldiers. The purpose here is to keep God's army strong. But the Exemption only said that "the fearefull . . . had a liberty not to goe" to war, neglecting to include the scriptural reason for excusing the man who was afraid.

By leaving out the reason why God had excused the fearful men—that they might influence others adversely—the Rhode Islanders either deliberately or by accident offered a new interpretation of the passage. They implied that God excused men who were afraid of dying because of that fear—solely for their own benefit and relief. Thus "If persons are excused then of God from war because fearefull of looseing their lives present," they argued, how much more should they be excused "for feare of looseinge everlastinge life, by fightinge against the minde of God (as they are perswaded)."[19] One could be excused on the basis of fear alone—the fear for the fate of one's own soul. By taking this direction, rather than following the textual association of fear with demoralization and weakening of the army, the assembly lost the opportunity to capitalize on the fact that those who believed that fighting jeopardized eternal life would surely be even more persuasive in undermining the will to fight of their compatriots than if they were merely concerned about their earthly bodies.

The Exemption did not address the discrepancy between the two portrayals of God: the God encouraging men to fight, as in the Deuteronomy passage, which they truncated; and the God who would deny men everlasting life if they should fight. To choose this passage, in which God urges on his army, in support of excusing men from fighting, without explaining this apparent difficulty, seems a surprising choice. It at first seems curious that the Quakers on the committee and in the assembly did not choose to support the unwillingness to fight by the more usual Quaker explanation—that Jesus' new covenant replaced the old and demanded a new attitude and standard of behavior toward enemies. But their explanation was directed toward those who drew different implications from Jesus' teachings, who did not agree that belief in Christ necessitated a posture of nonviolence. Thus, perhaps, they stretched for support, however disconsonant, elsewhere in scripture. Moreover, the use of the Hebrew scriptures was to support granting military *exemptions,* not, as one historian said, to justify pacifism itself.[20] They did not seek to persuade others that pacifism was legitimate but merely to argue that excusing pacifists from military service was legitimate.

The authors seized scriptural authority to justify excusing men from war and systematically expanded its meaning, moving from the use of the literal text to the use of metaphor. In Deuteronomy, God excuses a man from war lest he be slain and another should "dedicate" the house he built. How much more, the Rhode Islanders asked, should men be excused who believe that by learning to war, by fighting to kill they will be destroying "that house of clay, or Tabernacle which God hath built . . . beinge the Temple of God?"[21] Here they equated the tabernacle of God with the human body itself. It is a powerful metaphor—if God accords respect to human houses, human creations, then how much more must people accord respect to those for whom it is impossible to destroy God's "temples," God's creations: other human beings.

Similarly, the authors extended the literal scriptural meaning of "wife" to a metaphorical relationship between the believer and his "spouse," Jesus Christ. "If marryinge of a wife shall Excuse a man from war," they asked, how much more should any be excused who believe that they are espoused to Christ and who are convinced that their learning war "would occassion [create] a differeance and distance between them forever?"[22] Again, it would be difficult to deny that the relationship between believer and Christ takes moral precedence over that between bridegroom and bride.

Finally, the authors argued that if God has excused from war the man who has not yet eaten the fruit of his vineyard, how much more readily would he excuse the man who, by fighting, would cut off a branch from God's vineyard: his own conscience and understanding, planted in him by God himself.[23] This somewhat strained metaphor, equating man's sensitive conscience with God's vineyard, suggests that as man deserves to reap the fruit of his labor, so he deserves to reap the fruit of his obedience to God.

The King

Having enlisted God's authority to support excusing some men from fighting, the legislators turned to the authority of the monarch. In spite of the requirements for his subjects in England, the king "hath soe highly Indulged his Subjects of this Collony" to excuse them from taking the oath, even in matters united with life and death. Similarly, the legislators pointed out, the king "doth not soe universally compell all, but permitt some, yea very many not to trayne or fight or war for him" whose consciences persuade them that they ought not to "learne war nor war at all." If the king himself showed such toleration, must not his subjects show such indulgence for one another?[24]

"Reasons Expressed with Many More Implyed"

The legislation sheds light on varied aspects of Rhode Island society and beliefs. In justifying its Exemption, the assembly chose its words with care, thereby establishing who would be eligible for the exemption and who would decide eligibility; putting forward a variety of supporting authorities; and betraying the pressure the assembly was under. First, as already noted, the legislation asserted that "there are divers persons of severall societies" who as a matter of conscience could not train nor fight to kill.[25] It is significant that the Exemption was directed toward individuals within "severall societies," not toward the societies themselves. The conscientious position, then, was an individual position, not a collective position. We must assume that it was individual Quakers who were led to this belief and that it was not a position required of all Quakers or upheld by all Quakers. Further, there is an implication that members of other religious groups held these beliefs. Some Baptists in 1654, in fact, when Roger Williams was president of Rhode Island, had criticized the government for approving the use of force by passing a law concerning militia service. Roger Williams's brother Robert was one objector who asserted that it was against the rule of the gospel to judge transgressors, and so all violence was invalid, even governmental violence. This anarchistic posture vanished along with pacifism, however, when the group took up arms to protest the government's approval of official force.[26] All Baptists were not as extreme; indeed, looking backward in 1721, a Rhode Island Quaker, arguing with his Baptist friend, admitted that Baptists were advanced from popery in many respects, "many . . . were, yea and still are . . . against all Swearing and Fighting."[27]

It is a measure of trust, too, that each individual would establish his own eligibility for exemption merely by declaring his conscientious position. In 1696, in contrast, Carolina exempted Quakers from military service, but the governor himself, a Quaker, was to judge and establish the religious sincerity of each refuser. The Carolina statute read: "all such whom the present Governour John Archdale Esq; shall judge that they refuse to bear Arms on a Conscientious Principle of Religion" would be excused from bearing arms only "by a Certificate from him."[28]

The assembly declared that those who held these beliefs relied on "divers places of Scripture the letter thereof for their said conscience." While one cannot know which among the "divers persons" in several societies relied on which particular literal texts to validate their objections to military service, one may presume that the legislation itself reflected the threads of that reliance. If Quakers were among those who relied upon passages from the Hebrew scriptures for their justification, they would be departing from the usual Quaker reliance on the idea of "the new covenant" of Jesus as fundamental to their peace testimony, the covenant that was to lead out of the first covenant—the Law—into the Kingdom of God. One may speculate that the reference to the letter of scripture was deliberate and was meant to be more persuasive than an appeal to the "spirit" of the gospel message would have been. In contrast, latter-day Quaker pacifists rely primarily on the spirit of Jesus' message and its implications for the Kingdom of God to support their nonviolence rather than on any particular scriptural quotation, which too often can be countered by a conflicting citation. For the emphasis is not on pacifism as an idea, in the realm of reason, but rather on pacifism as an attitude, in the realm of feeling. The document did say that in addition to the reasons given in support of exemption, there were "many more Implyed, and others for brevety concealed."[29]

The anticipated objections to military service, while extremely significant, were narrowly construed in that the objectors were assumed to be concerned for their own actions, not the actions of others. There was no suggestion, for instance, that opposition to fighting carried with it a duty to observe neutrality or to persuade others not to fight. It was an objection specifically to training, to learning to fight, to taking orders from military officers, to fighting to kill, to warring oneself. It was a willingness to "loose their owne lives rather than distroy other mens lives."[30] Although particular individuals may in fact have broadened their own parameters for military nonparticipation, the legislation focused on an unwillingness to engage directly in violence; it hinted at an unwillingness to participate indirectly in defense.

One senses, finally, the conviction with which the pacifist beliefs of some people must have been held. In the course of explaining that to compel these men to fight against their consciences would cause them to be hypocrites, the authors parenthetically mused "(if they would be Compelled)." In this phrase, the legislators hinted that they anticipated stubborn resistance, a posture as awkward to manage in the seventeenth century as in our own. Indeed, according to the Exemption, the king also accepted the futility of "compelling" those willing to die rather than to kill.[31] To the extent that the Exemption was a pragmatic recognition of reality, then, it appears less an accommodation of principles held by those currently in the government themselves. Indeed, the records of this particular assembly session reveal Quaker magistrates preparing for war. They showed themselves to be men who drew fine distinctions between those acting in a military capacity and those acting in a civil capacity. It is likely that the Quaker magistrates drew a parallel distinction between acting in their capacities as magistrates and acting as private citizens. The elaborate legislation betrays no evidence that they struggled over any conflicts between their governmental role and their religious predilections. Their Exemption legislation did, however, protect Quaker magistrates from having to order unwilling Quaker civilians to fight.

Ironically, the legislation giving Quakers protection for their beliefs may have in fact allowed some Quakers latitude to be less rigorous about their peace principles. In other places, in the face of hostile outsiders, Quakers warned each other about the importance of remaining consistent in refusing to fight, for example; for if some Quakers were willing to perform military service, it undermined the credibility of the Quaker who refused service, and in such places, a monolithic consistency protected the peace testimony. In Rhode Island, in contrast, legislation protected the peace testimony, and Quakers were perhaps freed up accordingly to a broader individual interpretation of its requirements. The protective legislation hides this possible consequence from view.

In this 1673 provision for "conscientious objection," to use an anachronistic phrase, the Rhode Island Quaker position grew from a parochial plant. The legislation was a local and original solution for competing interests within a polity. Its rationale for exempting pacifists unintentionally pruned the Quaker experience in a new direction: calling on unfamiliar justifications, reaching for relevance to a particular set of circumstances in a particular place and time. Far from England, far from the leadership of the founding generation of Quakers, far from the minority status of Quakers elsewhere, the Rhode Islanders defined for themselves a zone of protection for the pacifist position and a rationale to honor that protection, tailored to local conditions. Freedom of conscience, a creative but sometimes inapt appeal to the precedent of the Hebrew scriptures, and a recognition of power realities within the colony were the arguments derived from local needs and expressive of peculiarly Rhode Island qualities supporting the moral necessity of an exemption provision. English influence, while in the broadest sense inherent in any Quaker formulation faithful to its tradition, was insignificant in the efforts of faraway Quakers, on their little island, to cope with the knowledge that their moral choices might cost them their very lives. The peace testimony was seeking definition in colonial circumstances by a people struggling to articulate and apply the spiritual implications of their beliefs.

It was one small hint of divergence, of the cultural and intellectual distance between colonists and Englishmen. Among Quakers, this distance would at times stretch out and at times shrink but would be a nexus of flexibility in a doctrine anticipating nothing but oneness. Although seen from another perspective as inevitable, for Quakers such distance was and remains an uncomfortable concept. Some of this discomfort might be reduced by heeding the words of Isaac Penington, who set forth his understanding of unity as unity of spirit, before codification dragged unity toward uniformity of practice: "It is not the different practice from one another that breaks the Peace and Unity, but judging of one another because of differing practises."[32]

8

"Sin and Flesh"

THE NEW ENGLAND TRIBES:
ENGLISHMEN AND INDIANS

Indians killed Quaker Zoar Howland near the ferry in Pocasset in 1676. According to tradition, they threw his body into a brook, which was henceforth known as the Sin and Flesh River.[1] Sin and flesh—an apt pairing that might stand as a metaphor for a war that included plenty of both.

Sin

The war would be known as King Philip's War, but both the Indians and the English regarded each other as "sinners."[2] King Philip himself, sachem of the Wampanoags, gave forth a chronicle of grievances against the English when he was meeting with John Easton of Rhode Island just before war broke out; not the least of which was the English failure to treat the Indians as the Indians under Massasoit had treated the settlers, when the Indians were stronger and the English were "as a litell Child." "The English should do to them as thay did when thay wear to strong for the english," the Indians observed, recommending a burnished way of living that the English should have recognized from their own scriptures.[3]

That the English viewed the Indians as "sinners" needs no elaboration here. Even the fair-minded John Easton, who listened so well to Philip, wrote "it is true the indians genaraly ar very barbarus peopell" before he admitted, "in this war I have not herd of ther tormenting ani but that the English army Cote [caught] an old indian and tormented him."[4] Many colonial Englishmen felt entitled to this new land and therefore interpreted Indian misfortunes as being for the Englishmen's benefit. George Fox himself implied as much: "The Indians at Dalaway [Delaware] lay in waite to cut of[f] some of our Companie as they passed that way

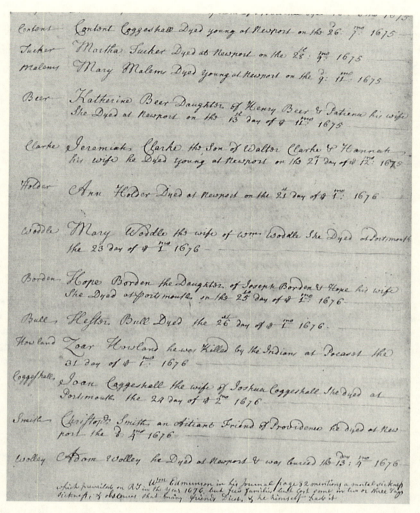

Figure 8.1. Zoar Howland's Death Record, 31/1M/1676, "A Record of the Death of Friends and their Children," Friends Records, Births, Deaths, 1638–1812, (detail). One Manasses Molasses was implicated by hearsay in the death of Zoar Howland at Sin and Flesh River at a court-martial after the war. He escaped execution, but probably was sold into slavery. Courtesy of Library Special Collections, Newport Historical Society.

but their designe was discovered one being hanged at Dalaway Two or Three days before wee came Thither. The Lord gave us power over all."[5] And when writing about the settlement of Carolina, John Archdale observed that "the Hand of God was eminently seen in thining [thinning] the Indians, to make room for the English."[6]

The English of some New England colonies similarly viewed each other as sinners, going so far as to accuse each other of bringing the retribution of God upon them all for various religious failings. Quaker Easton was "perswaided" that Puritan ministers were "so blinded by the spiret of persecution" and by their interest in maintaining their livelihood that "thay have bine the Case [cause] that the law of nations and the law of arems have bine voiolated in this war."[7] Baptist Peter Folger of Sherborn, Nantucket, echoed this charge in verse, attributing the war to the sin of religious persecution:

> But if that we a smiting go
>   of Fellow-Servants So,
> No marvel if our Wars encrease,
>   and things so heavy go.
> 'Tis like that some may think & say,
>   our War would not remain,
> If so be that a thousand more
>   of Natives were but slain.
> Alas! these are but foolish thoughts,
>   God can make more arise,
> And if that there were none at all,
>   he can make War with flies.[8]

The Indians here appear as incidental passive agents of an angry God. Quakers in Boston, silently in the night, raised a tomblike structure over the graves of two Quaker martyrs, hanged from a tree in 1659. This theatrical display was meant to dramatize that "the destroying of those good people, is that which hath brought the Displeasure and Judgment of the Lord upon this Countrey." The martyrs were made to give voice from the grave:

> Although our Bodyes here
>   in silent Earth do lie,
> Yet are our Righteous Souls at Rest,
>   our Blood for Vengance cry.[9]

Even a Quaker voice from England chimed in to the chorus of blame: "and therefore thou must drink of the Cup of terrible Amazement and Astonishment, poured out by a Just Hand, as from God upon thy Inhabitants, oh New-England!"[10] Similarly, in November 1675, the General Court of Massachusetts excoriated the Quakers, "whose damnable haeresies [and] abominable idolatrys" led to the "provocation of divine jealousie against this people."[11] In order to deflect God's wrath from Massachusetts, the court once again ordered the arrest, imprisonment, forced labor, and fining of Quakers. Although the colonists disagreed about whose sin God was punishing through the Indian rising, then, they did not doubt that the war was in fact God's vengeance against sin. And concealed beneath religious self-righteousness on all sides was the greedy lust for land.

Flesh

King Philip's War was indeed profligate of human flesh. In the fourteen months of its course in southern New England—from June 1675 until August 1676—angry and fearful people visited slaughter upon many portions of New England.[12] War decimated Indian tribes, which lost over half of their population and suffered two-thirds of the war's nine thousand killed.[13] Another recent source concurs: an estimated 1250 Indian warriors out of a total of 2900 warriors were killed, out of a total population of 11,600 Indian belligerents. Three thousand more died of exposure or disease, one thousand were sold into slavery, and two thousand went into exile. Of the total population, 10.8 percent were battle casualties and 57.1 percent were lost to other causes.[14]

One modern estimate has close to 10 percent of the English adult males killed in battle.[15] Half of the English towns in New England suffered burning or other damage; twelve were destroyed. Historians Richard Slotkin and James K. Folsom pointed out the startling reality that "King Philip's War was (in proportion to population) the costliest in lives of any American war." They estimated that one in sixteen English men of military age—and most were of military age—were killed or died as direct result of battle; the civilian population lost lives as well.[16] What war devastation meant in material terms is chillingly clear in the case of Stephen Dexter, who had settled in Providence before the war and had planted orchards and built a house. Providence was one of the towns destroyed during the war, and when Dexter's son returned to the land after the war, he found nothing left but the orchards. "He built him a Cave under Ground, and lived in it four years."[17] Settlers from Narragansett wrote after the war of returning home and finding "very dangerous living in sellers and holes under ground."[18] The town of Yarmouth in Plymouth Colony collected 297 pounds from ninety-nine people in 1676, at a time when the value of a cow was two pounds. Barnstable before the war collected twenty four pounds in taxes; in 1676 the assessment was 351 pounds.[19] Members of the king's council estimated after the war that the war had cost the colonial governments one hundred thousand pounds.[20]

English Tribes and Indian Tribes

The wider New England context giving rise to King Philip's War, then, was one of conflict and fear. Fear of attack from abroad and from within caused each individual colony government to think about military preparedness. Their insecurities drove them, too, to consider ways of relating to the other English colonies, whether natural allies or not.

The generalized insecurity had, in 1672, prompted the governments of Massachusetts, Plymouth, and Connecticut to renew a loose alliance called the United Colonies,[21] periodically exchanging commissioners to confer on matters of mutual concern. Sharing a similar religious heritage, although differing in matters such as church government, the United Colonies mistrusted Rhode Island as a repository for misfits who could not accommodate to the religious requirements of Puritanism. Rhode Islanders returned this dislike, and a well-founded fear of territorial encroachment reinforced their religious resentments. In spite of intersecting interests, the three United Colonies had obvious problematical relations, not only with the Indians but also with each other; for example, they competed for the clientage of Indian groups in order to secure rights to purchase land and they had conflicting claims to the same territory.

At intervals the fears of Indian attack were sufficient to overcome the mutual antipathy of Massachusetts, Plymouth, and Rhode Island long enough for them to make overtures toward mutual aid. Imperial jealousies, quarrels over land, economic resentments, and religious hatred all lost a certain potency when the Englishmen considered their separate and collective vulnerabilities to Indian, Dutch, and French violence. In 1671, for example, the Plymouth government had warned Rhode Island of Indian danger. Repeating an overture of 1667 to Plymouth, the Rhode Island government answered that it had had similar suspicions of Indian menace and was "bound by the highest obligations with united hearts and hands to use our uttermost indeavours to resist and defeat (through the assistance of the Almighty) their bloody and perfidious designes."[22] Proposing a joint conference, the Rhode Island council had appointed the governor and four others to meet with Plymouth officials.[23] But as fears periodically faded, so did ideas of begrudging ethnic cooperation, and the United Colonies and Rhode Island resumed mutual distrust and boundary disputes. Exemplifying the tension between dependence and suspicion, the Rhode Island council in 1672 requested permission from Massachusetts to buy powder and shot, in a letter delivered by Quaker Henry Bull, the council assuring Massachusetts that it was "only for the defence of this place, and for noe other end or intent,"[24] lest Massachusetts suspect that the ammunition would be turned against itself.

Indian resentments toward the English grew inexorably, for they had been but poorly protected by English law,[25] often unfairly compensated for land, and felt the pressure of gradual encroachment on their long-term well-being, even if individual land agreements had been fairly made. Yet because the Indian tribes had historically competed among themselves, they had severally allied themselves to various colonial governments in order to enhance their strength. In 1669, for example, the Rhode Island council summoned Ninigret (Ninicraft) to appear before it; Ninigret was the sachem of the Niantics, a subject tribe of the Narragansetts, occupying the southwestern portion of the Narragansett territory. The council suspected Ninigret and the Niantics of a plot or "combination" to "cut off" the English. Ninigret denied any such Indian alliance; on the contrary, he reminded his interlocutors, he and his tribe had subjected themselves to King Charles in 1662 within the scope of the Rhode Island colony. Because he saw himself in the same polity alongside the English, he said, he anticipated that the Rhode Island Englishmen would help the Narragansetts if they were menaced, and that the Indians would aid the English if any should invade the colony.[26] These alliances and submissions to the protection of the English king, Charles II, did not fulfill their promise and indeed eventually exacerbated Indian vulnerability in the face of English encroachment, replacing one danger with another as Indians came to participate in the enmities of their patrons. Although the English through the early years of the 1670s constantly dreaded Indian combination against them, their very attempts to control Indians may have pushed adversarial Indians toward each other by physically bringing them together and thus inadvertently allowing their common interests to become obvious. The Rhode Island assembly in 1673, for instance, had established a large committee to treat with Indian sachems about the problem of Indian drunkenness. Led by the governor himself, the committee summoned traditional rivals Mawshup and Ninigret of the Narragansetts, Philip of the Wampanoags,

Weetamoo of the Pocassets, and Awashonks of the Seconnets to a joint colloquy at Newport.[27] It is unclear, however, whether these and other sachems had in fact submerged hostilities and formed alliances to counter English imperiousness before June 1675.

On the Path to War

Slights and insults, duplicity and threat had particularly characterized the relations between Plymouth Colony and the Wampanoag Indians. When in June 1675 the Plymouth authorities hanged three Wampanoags for murder, New England could no longer contain its volatile tribes—both English and Indian—and its people turned conflict into killing. Small groups of Indians made appearances on the edges of English settlements in Plymouth, near the boundary with Rhode Island, killing some cattle and burning an occasional house. The English were tense from the ominous rumors flying along the paths between the colonies: rumors that Wampanoags were watching the route between Swansea and Taunton, that Indian women were being sent across Narragansett Bay for safety, and that warriors were massing. Benjamin Church, Plymouth adventurer and soldier, attended a dance near present-day Little Compton at the invitation of the squaw sachem Awashonks of the Seconnets and reported that six war-painted men of King Philip's were his fellow guests. (Church felt of their shot-bags and found them full of bullets.)[28]

The leaders of each party mobilized. King Philip led the Wampanoags, counseled by Annawon, and in addition to Awashonks and Tuspaquin, his eventual southern New England allies would be the Narragansetts Canonchet, the great war sachem, old Canonicus, and Pomham of Shawomet, now Warwick; Weetamoo of the Pocassets who married the Narragansett Quanopen (Quinnipin); and Matoonas and other local leaders of the fragmented Nipmuck tribes of central Massachusetts. It is questionable whether Philip ever exerted any authority over the other Indian combatants: the River Indians of the Connecticut River valley or the "eastern" Indians of the provinces of New Hampshire and Maine. To an extent, Philip as enemy commander was an imaginary creation of the English, who saw him as the paramount leader of all Indians combined against them. This attribution was surely overdrawn. Indeed, he disappeared for portions of the war, perhaps detained or undercut by other groups of Indians such as the Mohawks of New York. There were no verified reports of ever seeing him in battle with his warriors.

Various bands of Indians, less easily identifiable or verifiable, would from time to time join Philip's cause, such as contingents of Christian or praying Indians and Niantics. Other Indians would mobilize or be mobilized on behalf of the English, some more ambiguously, some less, drifting in and out of allegiance and conflict both. Among these were the Mohegan Indians under Uncas and the Pequots of eastern Connecticut; bands of the Seconnets of Plymouth; the Christian Indians of Massachusetts; and perhaps some from the eastern Wampanoags of Cape Cod, Martha's Vineyard, and Nantucket. By war's end, they would be joined by defectors from Philip's cause.

John Leverett, a veteran of Cromwell's wars, was governor of Massachusetts.

On the eve of war he wrote urgently to Josiah Winslow, the first native-born governor in New England and governor of Plymouth, that he knew of the increased "insolency" of Philip and his confederates and that he had "ordered the Convening of the Council instantly and doubt not but shall have men ready at an hours warning for theire march." Just under the address of his letter he wrote "Hast Hast" (haste haste).[29] John Winthrop, Jr., was governor of Connecticut; his close friend, Quaker William Coddington, was governor of Rhode Island. None of these leaders would be exempt from a measure of defeat in this war.

To Governor Winthrop, Coddington's Quaker faith was neither mysterious nor threatening, for the Winthrop and Coddington families had been friends for years, beginning with Coddington's friendship with John Winthrop, Sr., the revered father of the Bay Colony.[30] Long before, Coddington had been treasurer and an assistant of Massachusetts Bay. Coddington had corresponded with the younger Winthrop about his new-found faith over the years. In 1660, Coddington learned that Winthrop had just recovered from a sickness, and took the opportunity "to do the office of a trew frind to putt you in rememberanc to mind him who is life from the dead." He continued with fervor, "Oh, be not affraid to recaive the gosple."[31] When George Fox was in Rhode Island, he also corresponded with Winthrop, expressing the hope, in fact, that Winthrop would come to the faith of his brother, Quaker Samuel Winthrop, governor of Antigua.

But even a comfortable familiarity with the Quaker faith could not equip anyone—even the Rhode Island Quakers themselves—to predict if, or how, that faith and its accompanying peace testimony would influence their response to an actual war. King Philip's War would be the first encounter anywhere of a Quaker-dominated government with wartime responsibilities. The Quakers in the newly elected Rhode Island council who confronted these responsibilities in June 1675 included the governor, Coddington; the deputy governor, John Easton; and assistants Walter Clarke, Henry Bull, Edward Thurston, Thomas Harris, Thomas Borden, John Tripp, Benjamin Barton, and Joshua Coggeshall. Thus, ten of the twelve council members were Quakers. Treasurer Peter Easton and general attorney Weston Clarke were also Quakers. In the assembly were Quaker deputies Thomas Clifton, Gideon Freeborne, John Coggeshall, Sr., Peter Easton, William Wodell, George Lawton, and probably William Austin. One or more others may have been Quakers.[32] Of the thirty men in the assembly, then, at least sixteen were Quakers, and the leadership structure was overwhelmingly Quaker. Quaker dominance is even more striking when set against the number of assembly members who probably actually attended: twenty to twenty-three, fourteen of whom were probably Quakers.[33] It is these men, then, whose decisions, words, and actions point the way to understanding the influence of the peace testimony on Rhode Island's role in the New England crisis. Observing these leaders, one may try to isolate the factors determining their motives and choices.

The Rhode Island colony government had limited itself in its centralized military powers, consigning detailed responsibilities to the councils of war in the individual towns. Whereas the colony government periodically ordered the local councils of war to see to their own defense, established the days on which the militias were to train, and the fines to be levied for not training, each town "regulated" its own militia (trained band), whose soldiers voted for their own officers. Military power was local but subject to amendment during emergencies. During the Dutch scare of 1673, the assembly had provided for enhanced authority in emergency situations when the assembly was not meeting: the governor or the deputy governor plus a majority of the assistants were empowered to appoint as many military officers as deemed necessary to lead Aquidneck's militias. John Cranston had been appointed "Captaine in chiefe" over all forces mustered on the island of Aquidneck; it was probably anticipated that the councils of war for Newport and Portsmouth would meet together, although the legislative record is ambiguous. In case of Dutch threat to the mainland, the mainland assistants of each town had been similarly empowered to join together and give advice to the militia officers. If forces had been mobilized to meet an external threat, the colony as a whole would have borne the consequent costs. As the immediate Dutch threat subsided, so too did attention to military preparedness in the legislature. The locus of military responsibility apparently became so murky that Captain Cranston himself would demand clarification when war came with the Indians.[34]

"Rhode Island, although it gave some assistance from time to time, remained technically neutral in the struggle." This statement reproduces the conventional view of Rhode Island's role in King Philip's War, the view that Rhode Island was only minimally involved because of its Quaker leadership. "The Quaker officials in the Rhode Island Colony were in every instance devoted to the maintenance of peace" is another example of a common theme, a theme that must be tested by revisiting the history of the war.[35]

About the middle of June 1675, Quakers John Easton, deputy governor, and John Borden, with two Rhode Island magistrates, met an unarmed King Philip and forty of his armed men at Tripp's Ferry.[36] There they "sate veri frindly together," attempting to resolve disagreements and defuse resentments. Easton reported, "we told him our bisnes was to indever that thay might not reseve [receive] or do rong. thay said that was well thay had dun no rong, the English ronged them."[37] It is unclear whether or not the Rhode Islanders were official delegates of the colony; there is no such commission in the assembly records, but the council records are lost for this period. The length and detail of Easton's account of the meeting suggests that he was leading an official delegation; but as it was an inherently interesting encounter, this is not certain. One detail suggests that if Easton was an official negotiator, it was only on behalf of Rhode Island. In the course of the meeting, Easton suggested to King Philip that New York governor Edmond Andros and an Indian king arbitrate the dispute between Plymouth and the Wampanoags and commented in his later account of the conference that had this been "proposed," the Indians would have accepted the offer. Easton implied that his suggestion was not in fact a proposal, indicating that Easton had been given no power to propose on behalf of any other colony, or at least that Rhode Island had not secured Plymouth's agreement to arbitration.[38]

Often historians imply that John Easton's Quakerism was particularly significant in this peacemaking initiative. Rufus Jones, for example, wrote: "It was always the Quaker way to endeavour to prevent war by removing the occasion for it, and the Quakers in authority at this crisis made a vigorous trial of their method."[39] Yet it was not a Quaker method alone; arbitration and mediation had been honored New England procedures for resolving conflicts, both privately between individuals and publicly between groups, beginning among the Englishmen in John Winthrop's Massachusetts. In fact, the Rhode Island "Combination" of 1640 had made government by arbitration compulsory in Providence.[40] Roger Williams had long been a trusted negotiator with the Indians, negotiating a treaty of neutrality with the Narragansetts when the United Colonies declared war against them in 1645—a way of protecting Rhode Island and its Narragansetts that would be imitated less successfully thirty years later.[41] Boston had mediated the differences between King Philip and Plymouth Colony in 1671, to the advantage of Philip; Williams offered himself as hostage to the Wampanoags on this occasion. And just before Providence was destroyed during King Philip's War, he would come forth unarmed from Providence to talk with the Indians, carrying only a staff.[42] Social and political tradition may have provided the impetus for Easton's efforts as much as Quaker tradition. Or the initiative for the meeting may in fact have come from Philip.[43]

On 24 June 1675, Captains Savage and Oliver and Mr. Brattle from Boston were making their way southward, also "with an intension to speeke with Philipe," when they came upon "2 englishmen killed in the way & a horse shot ded the men wer striped off ther uper garments one having his hed Cut off & caried a way the other his hed fleed; the skin & heare off from his scull & both thar right hands Cut off & gone." The captains and Brattle also heard about one man being killed at Mattapoiset and a sentinel being killed at the Miles garrison house at Swansea and recognized that they "had litell ground to incorage them to adventure to goe to Philipe & so they returned home warde."[44] Sin and flesh, shrieks and moans: King Philip's War had begun.

PART III

War

9

"Midnight Shrieks and Soul-Amazing Moanes"

THE RHODE ISLAND GOVERNMENT AND KING PHILIP'S WAR

The great Narragansett Bay penetrated the Rhode Island colony—surrounded its islands, gave it purpose through trade and food for sustenance, protected it from easy access, and opened it to the seas. The bay dominated the colony's outlook. Rhode Islanders had to come to terms with the sea—even the mainlanders, whose government was harbored at Newport. For them, Narragansett Bay was a bridge, a highway. For others, it was a barrier. The bay would facilitate both Rhode Island's participation in King Philip's War and its retreat from the war. It is fitting, then, that Rhode Island's first encounter with war would be on the water.

"So by turns for our own safety": thus John Easton expressed inadvertently both the motive and the method of Rhode Island government policy in King Philip's War. The safety of the colony motivated its policy; to achieve safety, the government had to turn and turn again. Of course, all governments seek safety, when their territory and people are in danger. Usually they think of themselves as acting only defensively. Quickly, however, defense comes to include offensive measures. Rhode Island was no different in its reflexes. The early events of the war took place technically in Plymouth but near enough to the Rhode Island border—only a few miles from Providence—that the threat was concrete. During the war, as the threat ebbed and flowed, government policy reflected the understandable ambivalence of a people whose geography permitted a certain amount of distancing from the war and who lacked an ideology and an economy of surplus that would drive them to fight when it was not absolutely necessary for survival. Government policy shifted and turned, then, from enthusiastic cooperation with fellow Englishmen in June, diluted by corroding suspicion in the summer and fall, through reengagement and reorientation in the time of the Great Swamp Fight, into a fresh tide of military ef-

fort in the spring and summer of 1676. To what extent did the Quaker peace testimony influence the Quakers helping to make this policy and affect the shifts in
their management of King Philip's War? To answer this question requires a detailed account of actual government activity during the course of the war—a war
that was, like all wars, to call forth "midnight shrieks and Soul-amazing moanes."[1]

War

June: "All of Us Being Englishmen"

By the third week in June, news of Indian violence had traveled the paths to Warwick, alarming the English settlers sufficiently so that they convened a town meeting to decide on precautions. Plymouth troops under Captain (later General) James
Cudworth moved to Plymouth's western frontier to reinforce the Swansea settlement. "We had [a] leter from Plimoth governer," wrote Quaker John Easton, "to
desier our help with sum boats if thay had such ocation and for us to looke to our
selefs." Rhode Island learned from Cudworth, Easton wrote, "of the day thay intended to Cum upon the indians and desier for sum of our bots to atend, so we
tooke it to be of nesesety for our Ieslanders one half one day and night to atend
and the other half the next, so by turens for our oune safty."[2] The Plymouth
council, Governor Winslow, and Captain Cudworth unambiguously asked that
Rhode Island supply boats to blockade the Mount Hope peninsula, Wampanoag
land just north of Aquidneck, on the specific day when the Plymouth forces intended to attack the Indians by land. When Quaker Governor Coddington of
Rhode Island wrote back to Governor Winslow offering his support, then, he was
unambiguously choosing sides in the conflict and agreeing to active participation
in securing the victory of the English: "I intend (God willing) to get out boats and
watch the shore to oppose the common enemy, all of us being Englishmen and
subjects of our King and proposing to serve one and the same end."[3]

Moreover, Rhode Island help was not to be confined merely to standing watch.
In writing to Captain Cudworth, Coddington promised that his sloops would surround the Mount Hope peninsula, where Philip's forces were, and prevent their escape by sea. Cudworth, in turn, reported this close collaboration to Winslow: "the
26th day in the morninge I received a letter from govornor Codington signifienge
they have vessells warned to prevent the Indians escape."[4] The offer was crucial,
because the combination of the Plymouth army blocking the neck of the peninsula and Coddington's naval blockade would cut off Philip's escape.[5] Roger
Williams confirmed this sequence: "Rhode Island hath set out some sloops to attend Philip's motions by water and his canoes; it is thought he bends for an escape
to the Islands."[6] While a circling of Aquidneck Island might have been arguably a
defensive maneuver, blockading Mount Hope was a clearly offensive tactic carrying with it no hint of reluctance. Nor was there a suggestion that the Rhode Islanders would not have prevented Philip's escape from Mount Hope by force of
arms. Meanwhile, Samuel Dyer, the son of the Quaker martyr Mary Dyer, sailed in
his ketch to the western shore of the bay to remove Jireh Bull's wife and children as
well as others from the garrison at Pettaquomscutt, in Narragansett territory, to

Aquidneck Island. On 27 June, Quaker Caleb Carr sailed back and forth bringing intelligence from Swansea.[7] Coddington reported that Rhode Islanders were seeing to "publique defence those that are soldiers are in Armes & others to do the best they cann." And the Plymouth commander was assured that the Rhode Island governor wanted to hear from him "that they may a ford us the best assistance they cann."[8]

Word of Rhode Island activity surprised a Boston merchant named Benjamin Batten. In an intriguing letter to the Navy Office in London, dated from Boston, 28 June, Batten wrote "that thaire was 300 of the English of Plimoth & Road Iland besides our forces which ware just gott up [to the Indians]." Then, two days later, in the same letter, he wrote with deliberate irony that "thay of Road Iland had newly sent a hundred quakers men well apinted with Carnall weapons to fight the Infidells, most of them and Road Iland being such." The *London Gazette* of 16–19 August 1675 drew upon Batten's letter to publish news of the war datelined 30 June, Boston in New England. The *Gazette* truncated Batten's 28 June report of "300 of the English of Plimoth & road Iland" to "they of Plymouth had 300 Men in Arms." Batten's colorful account of Quakers and carnal weapons was rendered drab in the *Gazette's* straightforward report that "they of Rhodes Island, had sent out 100 Men well armed."[9] Batten's observations contradict the conventional view of both Quaker and Rhode Island Colony participation in the war. They state that Rhode Island participation included troops and was formal rather than ad hoc, solely defensive, and spontaneous.

Moreover, Batten's somewhat sarcastic use of the "Carnall weapons" phrase shows that "quakers" was a specific group for him rather than a generic term for all Rhode Islanders. Similarly, in the phrase "most of them and Road Iland being such" Batten differentiated between the group of soldiers and the population of the Rhode Island colony as a whole. He used "Rhode Island" here to refer to Aquidneck Island and its two towns Newport and Portsmouth, which had many Quaker settlers; the rest of the colony, Providence Plantations, had many fewer Quakers. Since troop mobilization was the local responsibility of town councils of war, if Rhode Islanders of Aquidneck had mobilized these "hundred quakers men," it is all the more significant. Batten's letter is thus revealing in several respects: it shows that the peculiar vocabulary of the Quaker peace testimony had become well known, albeit subject to suggestions of hypocrisy. It asserts the presence of Rhode Island troops among those fighting the Indians. Finally, it states that a substantial number of Quakers were among those Rhode Island troops. Rarely do the written accounts of this period allude to Rhode Islanders specifically, however; those manning the blockade boats and those transporting Plymouth troops to Rhode Island are only implied, and soldiers disappear under the names of their individual leaders. Instead, corroboration would come from Narragansetts challenging Rhode Island's partisanship.

During these early days, John Easton was still involved in pragmatic efforts to resolve the quarrel with the Indians without war. He learned that "queen" Weetamoo of the Pocasset Indians on the eastern shore of Narragansett Bay in Plymouth Colony was interested in peace, holding herself and the Pocassets apart from Philip's Wampanoags, even though she was Philip's sister-in-law. On the recommendation of Governor Winslow, she proposed coming to Rhode Island with six of her men to encourage the effort toward peace. Some of the Rhode Islanders protested her coming, being "allso in fury against all indians," so Easton took upon himself the charge to guarantee the safety of both Indians and settlers on Aquidneck Island. The joint meeting was not to take place, however, first because Easton was prevented "acsedentaly" from sending for her, and then because relations deteriorated between the Pocassets and the English, both eventually incinerating each other's houses. Contributing to the deterioration of relations were a pair of provocations: one for each side. Rhode Islanders "had seased [seized] sum Cannos on hir side suposing they wear Philops," although they in fact belonged to Weetamoo, thereby undermining Coddington's promise that Rhode Island would be "patient."[10] But Weetamoo had perhaps already put canoes at Philip's disposal: "the squa sachem at pocasset has neare about 18 or 19 canoues & 2 of them hid in a swampe one of which will Carry 40 men; & tho she seemes to Carry faier to you yet it is Aprehended she is all one with Phillipe."[11] Weetamoo's canoes paddled on behalf of Philip would completely undermine the current strategy of containing Philip within the Mount Hope peninsula by means of a Rhode Island blockade: " & it will be to Litell purpose to improve Rodiland men to Cut off mount hope Canoues, if so many are in a redines on pocasset sid to give them a passage."[12] Even while Easton endeavored to avoid war by negotiating with Indians, other Rhode Islanders had simultaneously committed acts of war in seizing canoes belonging to those Indians. He did not disassociate himself from this activity. Although he regarded peaceful relations as most desirable and urged both sides to respect each other without oppression or usurpation, Easton did not express an ideological pacifism; his approach was practical and not distinguishable from that of well-meaning non-Quakers who sought to avoid war.

On 30 June, having been delayed by storms, Massachusetts and Plymouth troops penetrated the Mount Hope peninsula by land, but Philip and his men had already slipped away undetected. Rhode Island boats transported the disappointed Cudworth and his rain-soaked forces to Aquidneck Island for rest and provisioning.[13] Although the historian Douglas Leach wrote that the Massachusetts troops may have refused similar help because of old hatreds,[14] Easton's account of this episode contradicted this suggestion, asserting that the Massachusetts troops did not want to "return" in the morning before the Rhode Islanders had fed them; the foot soldiers "wear free to acsept as we wear willing to relive [relieve] them."[15]

At the same time, the Rhode Island government sought to deflect danger from its territory by assuring the neutrality of its traditional friends the Narragansetts, who, if they combined with the Wampanoags, would pose a great threat to its mainland colonists. The Quaker governor and council had "invited" Canonchet, the chief warrior leader of the Narragansetts, to come to Newport under safe conduct. Begging off, Canonchet nevertheless forewarned that the English settlers in Narragansett country should fortify their houses, or flee, since he was having trouble controlling the Narragansett youth and common people who were restive to join Philip.[16] Rhode Islanders also hoped to divide Weetamoo and the Pocassets from Philip. Perhaps it was in this reply that the "naroganset kings," as Easton called them, tried to exonerate Weetamoo, informing the settlers that Weetamoo must "be in a thicket a starving or conformed to Philop" but that the Narragansetts knew she would not have joined him willingly; Easton wrote that Rhode Islanders gave the Narragansetts "incuredgment to get hir and as mani as thay Could from Philop."[17] Some settlers, particularly women and children, chose this time to sail for Newport. Among them was Esther Smith, wife of Richard Smith (owner of Smith's garrison at Wickford), whom Roger Williams described as "too much favoring the Foxians."[18]

Roger Williams led emissaries from Massachusetts Bay in late June to meet with four Narragansett Indian leaders, who "demaunded us why the Massachusets and Rode Iland rose, and joynd with Plymmouth agnst Phillip." Williams did not deny this characterization of Rhode Island activity, echoing Coddington by explaining that it was the duty of "one English man to stand to the Death by Each other in all parts of the World."[19] Although at this early date the "rising" of Rhode Island had not yet actually involved military violence, the Indians clearly perceived Rhode Island as partisan rather than neutral in the conflict. In combination with peremptory summonses directed toward the Narragansetts and the disarming and exiling of the Aquidneck Indians, with whom it had previously had mutually advantageous relations, Rhode Island's partisan behavior may have helped to bring about the very circumstance the colonists most feared—Indian coalition.

While Williams was away from home, negotiating, he heard about "some hurt they did about Providence, & some say John Scot, at Pawtucket ferry, is slaine." Hubbard was more specific (and less accurate), asserting that eighteen houses were burned at Providence on 28 June, 1675. About ten days later, Williams wrote of many farmhouses that had been burned around Providence, and that three had been wounded. Violence had visited Rhode Island territory for the first time.[20]

Summer: "With Out Our Consent"

As the Narragansetts so perceptively recognized, the Quaker government in those early days of the war recognized a mutual interest with Plymouth, as Massachusetts had recognized its own interest with Plymouth. Not only did the Rhode Islanders choose sides in the conflict, but they were active allies. When five Rhode Island men went to Pocasset territory "on the Main" to look after cattle and were assaulted by Indians, "those of Road-Island were hereby Alarmed to look to themselves."[21] Sloops from Rhode Island ferried Plymouth soldiers to and fro and rescued them when they ran into difficulty.[22] On 8 July 1675, for example, Captain Goulding from Portsmouth spotted twenty Englishmen under the command of Benjamin Church of Plymouth besieged behind a rock in a "pease field" on the shores of Pocasset. Without powder, and facing about three hundred Indians, Church's men were taken out of peril two at a time in a lone canoe belonging to Goulding's sloop. The next day, Church secured provisions for his company at Rhode Island.[23]

When the war began to encroach upon Rhode Island territory, new strains arose within the English coalition. Rhode Island's unquestioning and energetic cooperation with its neighboring colonies would gradually give way to increasing doubt, but for political, not religious, reasons. On 8 July, a contingent of Massachusetts troops met with Narragansett leaders and a military force within Rhode Island territory on the western coast of Narragansett Bay. Joined there by a modest Connecticut force, the Massachusetts army sought more positive guarantees than the promises mere negotiators had secured. They pressured the Narragansetts to sign a treaty in which the Indians agreed to look upon the Wampanoags as enemies and to reaffirm all grants of Indian land including old claims of Massachusetts and Connecticut overturned by the king's commissioners.[24] The Narragansetts agreed to turn over any Wampanoags to Massachusetts or Connecticut; the English would pay them for either live captives or for heads. Four Narragansetts were taken to Boston as hostages to guarantee Indian good faith.[25] The Rhode Island government was outraged. Since Rhode Island had long defended the ownership and sovereignty of Narragansett lands against groups from both Massachusetts and Connecticut, to have these colonies discussing land claims directly with the Narragansetts was alarming indeed to the Rhode Island government. That these discussions took place within Rhode Island's very borders under the auspices of army contingents was a further abomination. Moreover, under the terms of the Rhode Island charter of 1663, no colony was permitted to invade or punish the Narragansett Indians without the consent of Rhode Island.[26] In 1665, the royal commissioners had confirmed Rhode Island's jurisdiction over the Narragansett area, and Rhode Island could well argue by extension that for other colonies to conduct independent treaty negotiations within its territory would surely require the consent of the Rhode Island government as well. On the occasion of the treaty negotiation, neither the Massachusetts nor the Connecticut forces had made any effort to secure consent from Rhode Island, unless they felt that by inviting Roger Williams along they had implicitly fulfilled this requirement.[27] Since Williams was by this time no admirer of the Quaker government in power, nor the Quaker members of him, his presence at the negotiations did nothing to reassure the government that its sovereignty was safe. Governor Coddington suspected that the preeminent purpose of the Massachusetts expedition was to seize territory, not to neutralize the Narragansetts; a conservator of the peace in Narragansett, Thomas Gould, verbalized this suspicion and was swooped up, sent to Connecticut, and imprisoned.[28]

The Rhode Island government had shown no signs as yet of having been constrained by Quaker peace principles. It had raised troops (or had allowed the raising of troops), prepared to contain the Indians at Mount Hope by force, seized Indian canoes, and supplied transport, provisions, and a haven for English troops. In a letter to Governor Edmond Andros of New York dated 21 July 1675, Quaker Governor Coddington described the war between Plymouth and the Indians and referred to Rhode Island's "being in a warlike Posture of Defence."[29] In August, Andros "though unasked sent six Barrells of powder and some match to Roade Island, which they thankfully accepted."[30] Coddington impressed arms sent to William Dyer, sent again to Massachusetts for powder and lead, and laid an embargo upon an English ship with a cargo of arms and ammunition bound for New York.[31] These activities must be interpreted in the context of what powers the central government actually had at this time to organize the military. Military power was still decentralized and located in the towns, with a measure of consolidation between the two towns on Aquidneck. Although during the last military scare, of two years before, a superior military officer was appointed for all of Aquidneck, when the assembly next addressed the military issue, in October 1675 during the war, he was not reappointed. The assembly decided to "referr the consideration and conclusion of the matter unto the Councill of Warr in each towne to order; and what each

Councill shall soe order, shall stand and be authentick." Until April of the next year, then, the central government, if it wished to accomplish anything of a military nature, appointed ad hoc commissioners to fulfill particular missions, such as organizing watchs, gunboats, and garrisons. In April 1676 the central government finally centralized command and commissioned one major to be in command of all colony forces, and the colony government thus assumed power over the military.[32]

It is an error, then, in the absence of other evidence, to read pacifist motives into the failure of the colony government to raise a colony-wide army; before spring of 1676 it was not organized to do so. Nor is there evidence that pacifist motives restrained the government from so organizing. Each town was a potential and partial stand-in for the colony, and given the colony's geography, the arrangement seemed practical. But town deliberations and decisions are unknown to us; no records of the towns' councils of war exist. Fragmentary evidence sometimes emerges from other sources. The minutes of the Portsmouth town meeting of 16 July, for instance, show one aspect of the local mobilization for war. The minutes refer to a 12 July joint meeting of the governor, deputy governor, and councils of Newport and Portsmouth that levied a "rate" of four hundred pounds upon the two island towns, to be raised "with all Convenient speed." Portsmouth's share of the assessment was to be 120 pounds. Comparing this levy to two previous non-wartime assessments of 51 pounds (by the General Assembly, 1670) and 40 pounds (for the poor and the town, 1672) makes vivid the sense of emergency.[33]

A summer engagement at Nipsachuck, about twelve miles northwest of Providence, well illustrates the fluidity and localism of military efforts under these near-wilderness conditions, where a single woodland path might be the most sophisticated route of communication. It may illustrate, too, the initiative of a town council of war, for a company of thirty Rhode Islanders from Providence took part in the engagement. Philip and his Wampanoags, together with the Pocassets, had been bogged down in the swamps around Pocasset but had managed to distract and elude Massachusetts and Plymouth forces, moving north and west at the end of July, crossing a river into Rhode Island territory near Providence "at the wading Place." A local minister reported their movements to Lieutenant Nathaniel Thomas of the small Plymouth garrison at Mount Hope, urging that the garrison force "Apprehend them before they swamp themselves and while theire Wearines is upon them."[34] Lieutenant Thomas sent word to Captain Henchman of Massachusetts, who was building a fort at the edge of Pocasset swamp, then set out in pursuit of Philip. Thirty men of Stonington, Connecticut, forty or fifty allied Connecticut Indians, and thirty Providence men under Captain Andrew Edmunds were already in pursuit of Philip; Thomas and his Plymouth soldiers caught up with them about sunset. These contingents joined together and "Called A Counsell of Warr." They dispatched Indian and English scouts, discovering the whereabouts of the "enemy" by "hering them Cut wood," left their horses and a few to guard them, and marched about three miles to Nipsachuck and made camp in a field— one of Philip's fields.[35] At dawn, they moved forward, then once again stopped "to Consult" about how to surprise the enemy without endangering each other. When they engaged the Pocassets and Wampanoags, "Philips men upon our runing toward them disperced them selves For shelter in fighting & so in like maner did we the ground being a Hilly plaine with some small swamps betwen as advantagus for us as for them." They fought until nine o'clock, killing about twenty-three of Philip's men. Their Connecticut Indian allies "stript & scined their heads"; three heads were later taken to Boston.[36]

Meanwhile, Henchman and his sixty-eight troops slowly mobilized. Christopher Almy of Portsmouth, whose wife was the daughter of Quakers and whose father, William, brother, Job, and son were Quakers, ferried the Massachusetts troops from Pocasset to Providence in his sloop. From there Henchman marched overland, arriving after the battle at Nipsachuck, with a letter saying that he would take command. Lieutenant Thomas, his garrison soldiers, and the Providence men returned to Providence, arriving at midnight, carrying the wounded and intending to get provisions and ammunition. The wounded were sent on to Aquidneck to a Plymouth officer there. The next day, five Plymouth men and twelve Providence men returned with supplies, only to find that Henchman had fatally delayed in his pursuit and the Wampanoags had escaped. A captive reported later that Philip had only forty men, thirty guns, and ten bows and arrows. As for Henchman, the disgusted Thomas wrote, "before he came we all agred togethr as one."[37] This episode exhibits an extraordinary degree of cooperation between Englishmen of two colonies and their Indian allies—of flexibility and local improvisation. It demonstrates, too, the irrelevance of distant central control and the pertinance of local decision. It makes explicitly visible the role of Providence soldiers. The case of Eleazer Whipple, one of the wounded men at Nipsachuck, only confirms the sense of local responsibility—in this case of Providence. Whipple was cared for on Aquidneck; as late as 1680 he was asking the town of Providence to pay Aquidneck the money he owed "for my Diett when I lay under Cure, being wounded by the Indians in the Troublesome warr." Apparently, he had "often [been] Called upon for the same, Saing they have great need of the same."[38] Whipple's service was to his town, which owed him support. He did not look to the colony government for his succor; rather, the colony government was dunning him for payment.

Late Fall: "Fals and Perfideouse"

Violent encounters between English and Indians moved to other theaters during the summer and fall of 1675, from Plymouth Colony to central and western Massachusetts, to the Merrimac Valley, and to what is now Maine. No large-scale Indian violence had yet taken place within the colony of Rhode Island and Providence Plantations—these months formed a "Parenthesis of peace."[39] When the General Assembly met for one day, 27 October, it heard the petition of Captain John Cranston for the "settling" of the "mallicia" and putting the colony "in a Sutable posture of defence." The assembly once again left all military decisions to the councils of war in each town, declaring that all such decisions should be deemed "Authentick." It ordered the Newport and Portsmouth councils of war to meet in one week's time, and dissolved. This assembly was once again decisively dominated by Quakers.[40]

Meanwhile, Richard Smith of Wickford, south of Warwick, had been serving as an informer for the United Colonies, reporting on the supposed failure of the Narragansetts to comply with the summer agreement. The Narragansetts had not, for example, turned over any of Philip's forces to the English as they had promised,

Figure 9.1. Richard Smith's Cloak, wool and silk, c. 1670s. Richard Smith served as informer for United Colonies. His house in Wickford, now called Smith's Castle, was headquarters for settler armies. Troops stayed here before and after the Great Swamp Fight, during freezing aftermath "sheltred onely by little hutts under a Stone wall." Courtesy of the Rhode Island Historical Society, RHix3 9280.

and repromised on October 18 at Boston.[41] (They had, however, brought sixteen Indian heads to Richard Smith in September and had been paid with two yards of trucking cloth per head.)[42] On 2 November 1675, the commissioners of the United Colonies responded to Smith's reports and compiled a list of Narragansett offenses, accusing them of harboring warring Indians and succoring their women, children, and wounded; stealing or killing English cattle; and momentarily seizing Smith's house and family. The commissioners were further irritated when they learned that the Narragansetts, upon receiving the news of an Indian victory near the town of Hadley, "did in a very Reproachfull and blasphemouse manor triumph and Rejoyce theratt." Consequently, the United Colonies authorized an army of one thousand additional men to march into Narragansett country "to proceed against them as our enimies," provided that the sachems did not inconveniently deprive the armies of this opportunity by an "actuall performance of theire Covenants made with the Commissioners."[43]

The commissioners of the United Colonies wrote to Rhode Island on 12 November 1675 about a general Indian plot, striking at the interest of all the colonies, and averred that "god calls all the Colloneys to use their utmost indeavers to defend his Majestys intrest and their owne." Because the Narragansetts were "fals and perfideouse," Narragansett territory would be the next seat of the war. Informing Rhode Island of their troop mobilization, the commissioners requested Rhode Island to give "so[me] addition to our numbers, and give us such asistance by your sloopes and vessells as wee may stand in need of."[44] While giving notice of their proposed intrusion into Rhode Island territory, the letter did not seek Rhode Island's permission to intrude. Strangely, on 3 November, just a few days before, the Massachusetts court had chosen one more time to condemn Quakers in harsh terms, in order to expiate the failings of the people of Massachusetts before God; believing that because the people had been insufficiently zealous in rooting out Quakerism from their midst, God was punishing them through the Indian war. Nevertheless, the court was at the same time (falsely and perfidiously) applying for military assistance to the Quakers dominating the Rhode Island government and was probably somewhat inhibited in its actual treatment of its Quaker population. For example, in later months the Massachusetts General Court could not punish Coddington's commercial agent, Quaker Nicholas Moulder, and other Boston Quakers for holding meetings in violation of a 1676 law for fear of alienating Coddington at a time when his cooperation was sought in war.[45]

John Easton reported that upon receipt of the request for troops and boats, "our governer sent them word we wear satesfied naragansets wear tretcherous, and had ayded Philop, and as we had asisted to relive ther army before so we should be redy to asist them still."[46] Easton implied that military action was justified by Indian provocation—that military action could in fact be just. By implication, too, the rest of the Rhode Island Quaker government subscribed to a just war argument.[47] By pleading for the joint forces to set terms for the Indians in advance of moving against them and thus offering compassion to those pledging not to engage in war, so that "ther might be a separation betwene the gilty and the inosent which in war Could not be expected,"[48] the government implied that war against the guilty is justified. Again, there was no hint of ideological opposition to war itself; they justified war if it was defensive or if it was waged against the guilty.

Walter Clarke, Quaker assistant, wrote to the Providence magistrates about the United Colonies' request for support of arms, men, and boats, "that you may be awakned to Look to yourselves." He reported that Coddington's response to the request was to offer "that when we know the Certaine time of theire Comeing forth our Sloups shall be ready: to secure ourselves & give such Assistance to them by Transportating theire men: & other wayes as need may require (as wee did to plimmoth)."[49] In Clarke's rendering, Rhode Island offered generous support, no longer qualified by political uncertainty or excess loyalty to the Narragansetts; a stronger self-interest temporarily overcame its previous resentment at outside incursions into its territory. Through its offer, Rhode Island "consented" to outside troops coming into its territory, in the terms of its charter. The governor and council signed an order on 19 November 1675 requiring the Providence council of war to establish and furnish garrisons in Providence or "else where in this Collony," taking care that "provissions & Amunition be In garission."[50] (Funding, however, was still to be local; the council offered no money or supplies.) This order was addressed to Captain Arthur Fenner, Thomas Harris, Thomas Borden, "& the rest of the Councell of warr in the Towne of Providence." It is significant that Harris and Borden, both Quakers, found it possible to serve on the council of war.

The colony government dispatched sloops to transport the Plymouth and Massachusetts troops mustering at Seconk and to transport supplies. Communicating with Winslow, Coddington assured him that he had warned the "Commander in Chief" of these sloops, John Olney, against tipping Plymouth's hand by prematurely eliminating any Indian canoes to be found near Pawtuxet. Rather, "the blow shall be struck" and the "service of destroying all their canoes" would be performed when it fit best into the "designs" of the Plymouth command.[51] Coddington's words—"commander in chief," "blow . . . struck," "destroying"—all suggest his military frame of mind. One of the Rhode Island sloops, loaded at Newport with thirty barrels of beef and pork, was also carrying the ammunition General Cudworth had stored at Portsmouth—in the care of Robert Hodgson.[52] This was the very Robert Hodgson, "traveller in God's truth,"[53] who had ventured on the small bark *Woodhouse* with some of the first Quakers to come to the colonies, sailing from Portsmouth, England, in 1657 and astonishing New Amsterdam two months later. No lukewarm Quaker, Hodgson was punished for his faith (and for the dagger in his bosom?): "they caused a Negro to beat him with a pitch rope nigh four inches about, till he fell down twice as one dead . . . [He then was] tyed up by the hands, and a log of wood tyed to his feet."[54] This was the Robert Hodgson whose name appears frequently in the Quaker minutes, to whom George Fox sent a personal greeting in 1677,[55] and who died in 1696 apparently comfortable in worldly estate and as "an ancient minister" in spiritual estate.[56] Hodgson and Cudworth had long been acquainted. Cudworth had been relieved of his militia command in 1657 because he had "entertained" Quakers in his home, one of whom was Robert Hodgson.[57] Obviously a substantial and respected Quaker, Hodgson was to be one of the "judicious inhabitants" consulted by the political leaders in 1676 and was to serve on the commissions for securing boats and for regulating the watch. Such contributions to the military effort were arguably defensive, hence more justified in the eyes of some Quakers, but storing ammunition for soldiers on the march comes perilously close to even a narrow understanding of warring and fighting with carnal weapons.[58] Moreover, Hodgson could not rationalize his behavior on the basis of his being a "magistrate" and having an official duty to defend the colony. Hodgson's case suggests that governmental officials were not the only Quakers who found their duty in abetting the conquests of others and that some Quakers felt free to foster military enterprises.

About seven hundred foot soldiers and two hundred horse from Massachusetts and Plymouth had gathered near Seconk on the eastern side of the bay by 10 December, according to a contemporary estimate.[59] Under government direction, in a massive military deployment, Rhode Islanders guided and carried the English combined armies twenty-three miles over land and water to Smith's garrison at

Wickford,[60] where the supply vessels met the main body of the troops on 13 December.[61] Historian H. M. Dexter stressed that "a 'considerable number' of recruits joined the expedition from the Rhode-Island Colony." Another wrote of a force of about eleven hundred, attracting volunteers as they marched through Providence and Warwick.[62] While recognizing that there was no way of knowing the number of recruits, S. G. Arnold concurred that "it must have been considerable, for the people were roused to a full sense of the mortal struggle at hand by the massacres which had already commenced."[63] Even though the central government did not muster troops, he continued, it is entirely possible for Rhode Islanders to have been involved, since the government had delegated such matters to the various town councils of war, for which there are no records.[64] Benjamin Church had preceded the arrival of the main force at Smith's garrison and "proposed to the Eldridges, and some other brisk hands" that they hunt down some Indians. The Eldridges, at least, were residents of Narragansett.[65] Some of the "considerable number" may have been Quakers.

While we see the hands of at least some Quakers behind the government directives, a letter from Roger Williams to John Winthrop, Jr., forces us to acknowledge a more complex situation and to detect the insistent beat of other Quaker hearts. Writing on 18 December, just as the combined forces were marching against the Narragansetts, Williams was musing to his friend about the necessity and justness of the war's expansion, musing about what he found to be the "mind and voice of the most [H]igh amongst us." To those who thought "clear contrary" about the war, Williams said, "Let them take the pains with God" that he himself had taken to discover the differences between them; let them suffer as long as he had suffered "for their Beliefe & Conscience." Let them debate calmly, without "the pope's sword which Christ commanded Peter to put up in his matters." Winthrop had always been known, Williams wrote, for tenderness to men's souls in matters of conscience, to men's bodies and estates, even to the Indians; but Williams presumed that even such a caring man would be satisfied that the present hostilities "with these barbarous men of Bloud" were necessary and just, as just as against wolves that assault the sheep. Continuing his shadow argument against his shadow opponents, he wrote, "But God (*against whom only is no fighting*)" had put this iron yoke on their necks. While not identified by name, those who had so tested Williams's patience, who had spoken against fighting, against any war being just, perhaps who had even acknowledged the humanity of the Indians, surely included some of his neighboring Quakers.[66]

In their planned attack against the Narragansetts, the New England forces, augmented by about three hundred Connecticut troops, next intended to march south and headquarter at the garrison home of Jireh Bull, near present-day South Kingston.[67] But Indians had burned this house, "killing ten English men and five women and children, but two escaping in all."[68] Having spent a freezing night in the open, before dawn on 19 December the New England forces struggled through deep snow to the hidden swamp fortress of the Narragansett Indians. They came upon an extensive palisade constructed of tall stakes that enclosed five or six acres. The wall was, in turn, protected by heaped brush and tree limbs outside, several yards wide, as well as by blockhouses. Inside the palisade were about one thousand men, women, and children intending to shelter there for the winter and all their homes,

Figure 9.2. Cock's Head Hinge, iron, c. 1670, Jireh Bull's Garrison House. Site of meetings during English Quaker visit, 1672. Burned just before Great Swamp Fight, King Philip's War, 1675. Site of settler troop encampment on the way to the Great Swamp Fight. Courtesy of the Rhode Island Historical Society, RHix3 2667.

winter food, and goods.[69] After finally breaching the not-quite-completed fortification and after hideous combat, the English prevailed. As earlier New Englanders had burned the Pequot fort in 1637, so "then we fired about 500 Wigwams . . . and killed all that we met with of them, as well Squaws and Papooses . . . as Sanups (i.e. Men.)"[70] Cotton Mather, the Massachusetts cleric, wrote that the Indians had been "Berbikew'd." (It was Quaker "E. W.," probably Edward Wharton, who had two months before described the Indians as "Barbarous enraged Natives . . . on Fire, flaming forth their fury," a sad irony.)[71] Governor Leverett of Massachusetts was all cool righteousness: "our men by the good hand of God, became masters after some houres spent in a hot dispute." The English suffered about seventy-five dead and one hundred twenty-five injured in this battle, which came to be known as the Great Swamp Fight; the Indians lost perhaps six hundred killed.[72] Lieutenant Robert Westcott, of Warwick, Quaker, was killed in the Great Swamp Fight.[73]

Douglas Leach has suggested that the Great Swamp Fight, the first major engagement on Rhode Island soil, restimulated Rhode Island disenchantment with the United Colonies.[74] How this disenchantment was expressed illuminates moral calculations about war itself. Quaker John Easton, for example, deplored the fact that in attacking the fortress, the English army had struck first, initiating the war against the Narragansetts; not only because Easton himself had promised the Indians that the English would never attack first but also because it was "brutish so to do." His discomfort seemed to come from a sense of being ungentlemanly rather than un-Christian. He felt personally embarrassed, too, because he had assured the Indians who had been exiled from Aquidneck Island that "if thay kept by the water sides and did not medell that how ever the English wold do them no harem alltho it was not save [safe] for us to let them live here." His promise was ignored. Moreover, United Colonies forces had killed Indians without warning outlying Rhode Islanders, exposing nearby settlers to retaliation from Indians without the settlers being aware of their increased vulnerability. As a result, these Rhode Island settlers did not know that they ought to keep their garrisons "exactly" and were killed when Indians retaliated. Easton once again attributed the war against the Narragansetts to the United Colonies' hunger for land and desire to deprive Rhode Island of its territory. He pointed out pragmatically that the English army, by killing Indian women, children, and "decrepit" persons in the Great Swamp Fight made it all the easier for the remaining able Indians to do the more "mischief" because they were left unencumbered and might range freely without the care of dependents.[75] He did not deplore the killing on humanitarian grounds.

In addition to his feelings of personal betrayal, Easton's rage, which he directed toward New England ministers, may have stemmed in part from guilt at participating in injustice. He as an Englishman had been "ingadged" by the "blud" that was spilt, "for we wear to be all under one king," engaged to take part in a war in which the "laws of arems" had been and were being ignored.[76] He did not suggest, however, that the very laws of arms themselves should not have been necessary, only that they had been disregarded. Instead, Easton raised practical objections to this war and this killing, not expressing global revulsion to war itself but deploring simply the injustice of this particular war. He suggested that this war might have been unnecessary had the proper procedure been activated—consultation with the king himself.[77] Easton conjectured that Massachusetts had failed to solicit the support of the king because Massachusetts had lost respect for the king's power to act; after all, wrote Easton, the king had not redressed the wrongs Massachusetts imposed on those it had persecuted for nonconformity, including, presumably, the Quakers.[78] While Quaker Easton clearly expressed a preference for peace and an activism in seeking peace, underlying the lessons he drew from this war was the basic assumption that wars can be just. In deploring English aggression, English violence against noncombatant Indians, English failure to observe laws of war, Easton implied that war itself might be just: when defensive, when waged against a guilty foe, when regulated by laws of war, and when consonant with reasonable ends. His contemporary William Harris spoke for those who determined that this was a just war, reasoning that the Wampanoags' taking up arms against the king was high treason, "therfore the war Just."[79]

Apart from Easton's account, the historical record is silent about what reasons propelled the Rhode Island government to overcome its traditional suspicions toward Massachusetts and give crucial assistance in a major military engagement—only to become quickly disillusioned with its alliance once again.[80] One might conjecture that the leaders came to regret their participation because they saw the destruction of war; they realized that the danger to their own settlers had increased rather than diminished; they resented that Rhode Island's welfare had apparently not been a consideration in United Colony plans; they were disturbed by the thought that this catastrophic attack against their former friends, the Narragansetts, might have been avoided; they foresaw renewed competition for newly cleared Narragansett lands. Perhaps their cooperation fell off when they noticed that the operation was a preemptive strike. Perhaps, too, tensions with the United Colonies revived because of disputes over payment for the wounded soldiers sheltered and treated on Aquidneck Island.

It is possible, too, that the Quaker government viewed its participation as a police action to enforce a treaty rather than as a military action when it supplied transport for United Colonies forces before the Great Swamp Fight; either the treaty between fellow English colonists and Indians or the implied allegiance owed by Indians to the English monarch. In the Quaker understanding of magistracy, the magistrate was justified in using "the sword" to be "a terror to evil-doers." The police function, then, legitimized the use of force in the Quaker mind and might override any prohibitions against wars and fighting. Just ten years hence, a Quaker explained how a people believing in the necessity of loving their enemies, a people whose principles were against wars and bloodshed, could come to live (and rule) in safety among the Indians in Pennsylvania and New Jersey. Predicating his argument on consenting and just covenants between the two peoples, he claimed the lawfulness of using the magistrate's sword against "such as raise Rebellions and Insurrections against the Government of the Country, be they Indians or others." Otherwise, he said, Quakers should not "pretend" to government.[81] Here the police function was explicitly considered applicable to fighting on a scale that we would term war. Yet perhaps, when hearing about the great destruction of the Great Swamp Fight, in which women, children, and the old people alike were burned in their homes, the Rhode Island governors found the violence exceeded the necessary force allowed for police enforcement.

The English soldiers struggled through deep snow fifteen miles back to Smith's garrison after the Great Swamp Fight, where most spent the night "sheltred onely by little hutts under a Stone wall."[82] The English wounded who survived this trek had their wounds dressed at Smith's and then were "removed to Road-Island, where they have good Quarters provided, and care taken for their Recovery."[83] The combined armies of the United Colonies lingered at Wickford for about six weeks, as new recruits and supplies restored their strength, which they applied to raiding and burning out clusters of Narragansetts scouting nearby. Captain Fenner of Providence and his "party," too, went out against Indians, at one point fighting in an Indian town with many wigwams.[84] Finally they moved out to the northwest at the end of January, leaving behind a legacy of slaughter as well as unprotected English settlers. At about the same time, Indians raided Pawtuxet, killing a few settlers and stealing cattle.

In addition to caring for the wounded, Aquidneck offered a safe harbor to mainland English families or to English women and children whose men stayed behind to protect their homes. The only direct references to King Philip's War in the Portsmouth town records, for instance, were taxes assessed by the council of war and two provisions: one for expelling Indians and prohibiting Indians from entering the town and another for setting aside common lands for the relief of mainland refugees.[85] While Aquidneck's hospitality was without question generous, it was at the same time exclusive: the Islanders only provided care for English casualties, not for Indian casualties; only provided sanctuary for English families, not Indian. (When Governor Edmund Andros of New York issued a proclamation encouraging the building of blockhouses, it was "for a Retreat to the Women and Children, into which our Indyan Women and Children, to bee also received and protected if they desire it.")[86] Rhode Islanders provided another kind of "sanctuary" in December 1675—Captain Davenport's Indian prisoners were sent to Aquidneck for "safekeeping."[87] Perhaps Quakers under the stress of war had forgotten the ideals that Coddington had expressed in 1672, when he explained the Quaker view to Connecticut:

> wee (the people of God which are in scor[n]e called Quakers) . . . honnor all men as our bretheren by Creation, & made after the similetude of God. And therfore we cannot hurte any man, therfore have indevered to prevent in our owne Jurisdiction what might tend to the hurt of others.[88]

The "habitation of the hunted-Christ" was sometimes the "habitation of the hunted." Even the "habitation of the hunter."

"A Bulit out of Everi Bush"

WAR, CONTINUED

Like a bullet from ambush, a desperate letter found its mark in the body of the Rhode Island government, sometime before March 1675/76, from "wee that Are Left in this towne of Warwicke, (yett Alive)," otherwise unsigned. In rage and disbelief, the letter said that the townsmen had already told the colony government of their peril; told it that Mr. Wickes (one of their deputies!) had been slain; told, too, that Francis Budlong, his wife, and his four children were nowhere to be found but their house and everything in it had been burned to the ground; told of their abandonment by the strongest and wealthiest among them, who packed up their arms and all their treasure and moved to Newport, where they "Abide with you, with ther Estates." They did not mention that they had had to bury John Wickes twice: on the first day, his head, found impaled on a pole; on another day, his body, when they could find it.[1] Nor did they mention the agony of a Warwick family whose three-year-old had been a hostage of the Indians until the Indians returned him in January.[2] Only a few yet able to bear arms were left to guard nearly sixty old men, women, and children. Outrage garbled their next words: "you sighned a commition As it was said, directed to Captaine Captaine ~~Latham~~ Weston Clarke . . . sighned by your selfe"—a commission that Weston Clark and twenty soldiers had brought to Warwick. His was but a temporary mission; the Warwick citizens were incredulous that it was within Clark's discretion to "settle" the town in fortified houses of his choosing. His "mannagment" did "noe wayes Answer" their needs: not only did his power void that of their council of war (whose orders had already been disobeyed by those who fled), but, if the townspeople did not concur with his choice of garrisons, he could destroy any competing fortifications. Although he did stand guard for two weeks while they put up their hay and offered to transport the women and children to Aquidneck free of

Figure 10.1. A Map of New England New Yorke New Jersey (detail), sold by Robert Morden and William Berry, (1676), Blathwayt Atlas # 12. "King Philip's Country" and other place names associated with King Philip's War. Courtesy of the John Carter Brown Library at Brown University.

charge, the townsmen could not possibly afford to maintain their families in such an expensive place—whereupon the letter groans to a confused close in midsentence.[3] Weston Clarke, captain of this company of twenty soldiers, was a Quaker, brother of Walter Clarke, next governor of Rhode Island.[4] His presence under such conditions implied multiple inconsistencies with the peace testimony: he was a military officer, leading others; he was undoubtedly armed; he was prepared to harm and kill; and he placed his faith in fortifications, not God's preservation.

Men at Providence, too, felt that their government owed them more than distant shelter for their families and wrote to the government on Aquidneck in February 1675, asking for soldiers as on-site reinforcements and complaining harshly about the lack of help from the central government. Quaker Walter Clarke, an assistant, seems to have been the target of their anger; in his 28 February reply to them he referred to "your evell suggestions conserning us in athority Espetially: my selfe, (as if not worthy to live.)"[5] Clarke disclaimed his government's responsibility for not having sent any soldiers; although it had tried to do so, he assured the mainlanders, the harsh weather had obstructed its plan. In fact, he continued, it was fortunate for Providence that no soldiers had found their way to Providence, for otherwise the soldiers' wages, ammunition, and provisions would have "eaton" up Providence as they had Newport. Clarke clearly revealed that soldiers had been mustered at Newport and that the government had soldiers it might have despatched to Providence but for the "weather." Clarke told the Providence men that they were expected to secure themselves and whomever they could not secure should be transported to Newport. After all, Clarke reminded them, the government had expended eight hundred pounds partly for their security—through an imposition from which Providence was exempted. Although "wee are not of ability: to keepe soulders under paye having not provitions:, as bread," he explained, nevertheless he warned Providence not to seek help from other colonies. Having perhaps sensed the weakness of his explanation, Clarke lapsed into fatalism and told the people of Providence that it did not matter what efforts they made to save themselves: "wee know the lordes hande is against new Ingland and noe weapon formed will or shall prosper tell the worke be finished: by which: the wheate is puled up with the tears [tares]: and the Inosent soufers with the Guilty."[6] It is important to notice that Clarke's rationalization depends on no pacifist doctrine. Clarke was not reiterating the Quaker view that no weapon, ever, could "prosper," only that in this particular case, since God had levied a judgment upon New England, weapons were useless. The wintry weather, the fact that the government had already appropriated money, and the inability of the colony to provision Providence all explained government inaction, which in any case may have been irrelevant since God was visiting his judgment upon New England.

The confusion of Clarke's explanation reflects a certain theological confusion. It mirrors the confusion of Warwick. It probably mirrors, too, the confusion of people confronted with uncertain perils. Having only a few resources of men or materiél, they were reluctant to share with those to whom they felt only loosely connected, such as the mainlanders; yet they felt some obligation to protect those under their authority. Even though Clarke obliquely expressed one element of his belief, shared with Puritans, that man is impotent in the face of God's war, he left unexpressed the more active element in Quaker belief—man's responsibility to take himself out of that war.

On 13 March, the assembly convened an extraordinary session "by Especial Warrant," whose first order of business was to draft an official reply to Warwick and Providence, more sympathetic and tactful than Walter Clarke's but no more forthcoming. After effusively commiserating with their inhabitants, recognizing that "the present troubles with the natives is and hath been great, very hazardous" and that the sense of danger was fully "upon the hearts of the Governor and Councill" and that it viewed itself "soe neerly related to you, and in duty bound for the good of his Majesty's interest," the assembly declared anticlimactically "that wee finde this Collony is not of ability to maintaine sufficient garrisons for the security of our out Plantations."[7] While reiterating that it advised the inhabitants to come to Aquidneck, where, if needy, they would be supplied with land and be able to keep one cow per family on the commons, the assembly indicated that it would not "positively oppose" them should they think they could protect themselves where they were. It strongly urged, however, that the inhabitants "take the occasion from the enemy" and leave their towns, for by remaining they would "make themselves a prey" to the enemy and be offering up their goods as a relief to the enemy. They would be fatally vulnerable, unless "more than ordinary providence prevent." By not tempting the enemy, then, the inhabitants could take some responsibility for their fate; while they should not passively trust that God would preserve them, such a possibility—"more than ordinary providence"—was not ruled out entirely. The assembly was less pessimistic than had been Clarke, who seemed in despair, at least temporarily, because he thought God had resolved to punish all of New England. Crucially, the assembly included no explicit pacifist argument when it attempted to justify its denial of overt on-site military protection to Providence and Warwick, even though it was still dominated by Quakers.[8] Of course, if the leaders' Quaker beliefs demanded only that they themselves refuse to use weapons or fight or that they refrain from coercing others to fight against their consciences, then what the Providence and Warwick men did would pose no moral problems to Quakers. In such a narrow understanding of the peace testimony, then, it would be irrelevant and would not have influenced government decisions.

Yet a Quaker hand may have penned the assembly letter, for the phrase "take the occasion from the enemy" echoed vocabulary typically associated with the early Quaker peace testimony. When in 1650 George Fox had refused the offer of a commission in the Parliamentary army, he explained his refusal by saying, "I lived in the virtue of that life and power that took away the occasion of all wars, and I knew from whence all wars did rise, from the lust."[9] Subsequently, Fox and other Quakers again and again described his mission and the mission of Quakers generally as being to take away the occasion of war. "God is my witness," he wrote in 1654/55 to a suspicious Oliver Cromwell, describing himself as a man "who is sent to stand a witness against all violence . . . and to turn people from the darkness to the light, and to bring them from the occasion of the war and from the occasion of the magistrate's sword."[10] In Fox's understanding, the occasion of war, the cause of war, was man's evil, particularly his covetousness. Inappropriate and excessive desires—"lusts"—of all kinds created the opportunity for war, just as man's evil behavior created the necessity for law, symbolized by the magistrate's sword. Only the power of the light of Jesus could subdue and remove the cause of war and the necessity of worldly law. Living in the Kingdom of God was incompatible with strife, as love was incompatible with enmity, as righteousness was incompatible with socially destructive behavior. Taking away the occasion of war, then, was being obedient to God, was a purification of one's soul. An internal transformation, and only an internal transformation, removed the possibility of war.

When the Rhode Island assembly used this language, recommending that the "out Plantations" take the occasion from the enemy by leaving their homes for sanctuary on Aquidneck, it was only recommending a practical strategy for saving lives.[11] Its suggestion, although employing Quaker phraseology, embodied nothing of the Quaker concept of harmony with the Kingdom. It was the Quaker view that only those accepting the Kingdom could bear a true testimony for peace; non-Quakers, like most of the people of Providence and Warwick, would not yet in Quaker opinion have had the capacity to order their lives in accordance with peaceful principles. The best they could do was to remove the occasion from the enemy in a secular sense by physically removing their bodies.[12] It is not "the way of the gospel," Isaac Penington taught, "to give forth precepts of holiness . . . before mens minds are turned to that which enlighteneth, and giveth power to believe and obey."[13] It was not their peace principles that checked the hands of Quaker governors.

Spring: "Daingerous Hurries with the Indians"

Seventy houses and thirty barns in Providence and all but one house in Warwick were destroyed by the end of March. "Tis happy for them, if their filth and dross / Be cleansed off, though by a common loss," wrote a Boston poet unsympathetically only two weeks later, implying that the burning of Providence, "a miscellaneous nest," was well deserved.[14] The destruction of its mainland towns and of nearby Plymouth towns made danger an ominous reality for the assembly, which responded on 4 April with renewed military efforts, sloughing off its ambivalence yet again. It commissioned four gunboats, having five or six men each "well furnished," that is, well armed, to patrol the waters of the bay. Those in charge of this operation—Quakers John Easton, Walter Clarke, John Coggeshall, Caleb Carr, and Robert Hodgson and three others—were authorized to order more boats and men if needed. These were patrol boats, not transport boats. Portsmouth, being closer to danger, was assigned a barrel of powder and two great guns, pressed for the purpose; the powder and the guns were put under the control of four non-Quakers.[15] The assembly, aware of the crucial importance of its decisions in this emergency, voted to solicit the "advice and concurrance of the most juditious inhabitants," naming sixteen men not in government, of whom six to eight were Quakers.[16]

We can assume that it was with the impetus of the "juditious inhabitants" that the assembly took the next significant step: on 11 April 1676 it finally centralized military responsibility by naming John Cranston as the major for the whole colony, with authority over all local forces and officers. Cranston's commission came from above rather than below. This appointment removed the arms-length distance between the central government and local military decisions. Now it was the Quaker Governor Coddington himself rather than a town council of war who signed Cranston's commission to "use your utmost endeavor to kill, expulse, expell, take and destroy all and every the enemies of this his Majesty's Collony."[17] Walter Clarke, Caleb Carr, and Robert Hodgson—again, Quakers all three—were among those the central government appointed commissioners of the watch, with full power to assign and regulate watches and impose penalties for dereliction. In an earlier Indian scare the Warwick town meeting described a version of the watch: "to consist of fower men every night with gunns well fixed & charged with powder

& that they have bullet or shot ready to clap in to ther gunns in case the watch or any of them be in any danger when they walke rounds."[18]

Whether or not to watch at all and whether or not to watch "with gunns well fixed" were dilemmas Quakers considered in other places, such as the Caribbean islands and North Carolina. Since the 1673 Exemption already allowed for watching without arms for those opposed to arms on religious grounds, Rhode Island Quakers too had considered the possible conflict between their peace principles and their community obligations. The 1673 Exemption, still in force, required all eligible people to watch, regardless of their conscientious objection to fighting, if it was "not against their Conscience to doe and perform civil service to the Collony though not martill service." "Watching" was but one of the activities the legislators listed as civil services the objectors might perform. By their definition, watching was a civil function, not a military. Those constrained by their consciences not to fight might stand watch unarmed—"without armes in martiall manner nor matters"—and need only respond to orders coming from civil rather than military authority; the watch commissioners appointed in 1676, then, were civil officers, not military, and thus might order Quakers to watch unarmed. But the legislation also recognized and allowed that the conscience of some would not suffer them to perform even civil service.[19] The Quaker commissioners appear to have had no scruples about supervising, and indeed recruiting, those who would watch armed. An Indian comment from June 1676 suggests that the commissioners were effective in their mobilization; some Indians from Plymouth sought to go to Aquidneck, but "the younge men there kept such a strict watch that wee could not get over in saftey."[20] Whether any Rhode Island Quakers refused to watch even without arms is not known.

By May, a new government, still preponderantly Quaker under a new Quaker governor, Walter Clarke, met in the kitchen of Henry Palmer's house in Newport and revisited some old military issues; they revisited with enhanced, centralized power that they had bestowed on themselves (by extension) in the appointment of the major. The legislators voted to procure ten barrels of powder and two thousand weight of lead, took note that some of the military officers were deceased, and sent two Quakers, John Easton (assistant) and George Lawton (deputy), to Providence to evaluate a new request for relief and for garrisons for that town, now largely destroyed. The assembly delegated full authority to Easton and Lawton to negotiate and decide whether, how many, and where situated any garrisons to be funded by the colony government might be.[21] Upon reconvening in June, having received the recommendation of Easton and Lawton, they decided to fund one garrison, with eight soldiers—the king's garrison—"for the maintaininge of the King's interest." They made any additional garrisons that might be established at the expense of the town subject to the command of Captain Fenner, captain of the king's garrison; but, respecting local sensitivities, they carefully denied Fenner authority over the local trained band. Quaker Governor Clarke signed Fenner's commission, which not only directed him to "expulse" the enemy but also, reverting to old distrust, to defend against any attempt by the forces of the United Colonies to unlawfully intrude or establish garrisons of their own in Rhode Island jurisdictions temporarily "left voyd."[22] This remarkable commission dramatized again Rhode Island's anomalous position, caught between the depredations of the

Indians and the depredations of their fellow Englishmen. Although the Rhode Island government had recently whittled away at its own hesitation to intervene actively in the military arena, its bifurcated enmities and loyalties may explain some of that hesitation.

On 30 June the assembly whittled away, too, at the generous terms of the 1673 Exemption from military service. "Findinge that severall, under pretence decline their duty," they took up the complaints of the trained band militiamen, who were suspicious that some of those seeking relief from military service were not motivated by religious convictions or by the sense that they were "forbidden of God" to fight but were common everyday malingerers or had other reasons not to fight. Echoing the vocabulary of the new legislation, William Harris, a non-Quaker assistant, shed light on who these others seeking relief from service might be: "Others hold the war unjust, as no war is just, and have some temptation to this pretence, as not aiding or willing in the defence."[23] Other people who refused service denied that they were self-interested malingerers but presented themselves as people who viewed this war or perhaps any war as unjust, not necessarily for reasons of religious conviction, as the 1673 Exemption had taken for granted. (Harris disallowed this possibility by using the word "pretence.") Repealing that aspect of the 1673 law that excused objectors from paying any penalty for refusing to serve, the legislators decided instead that "all persons in this Collony are to be observant actively or passively . . . in millitary affaires."[24] Passive observance meant that an individual who wished to be a noncombatant because of religious belief would now be forced to participate "passively," by paying a fine or having goods distrained, instead. Religiously conscientious objectors, now subject to penalties, were relegated to a new category of men; no longer were such objectors to be regarded as men exempt for "any other debilety; as said aged, lame, sick, weake . . . or any other infirmity."[25] The "just war" objectors were not specifically addressed.

The new restriction undoubtedly served to diffuse criticism from some quarters, to spread the costs of war more equitably, and to demonstrate religious sincerity by ascertaining whether or not an objector was willing to "suffer." That the new stringency came about at this particular time was perhaps because the assembly was newly elected, with new members shifting the balance of toleration; or because the assemblymen were affected by the increased proximity and heightened reality of the war; or because, as they explained themselves, they were responding to pressure from the population. The modification of the Exemption did not result solely from any dramatic change in the number of Quakers in this assembly. Quaker Walter Clarke had replaced Quaker William Coddington as governor, Major John Cranston replaced John Easton as deputy governor as well as serving as chief military officer, and the number of Quaker assistants were reduced to four, from a previous eight.[26] Although the new council, the leadership, had thus lost five Quakers, the new assembly had only one or two fewer Quakers than the old, having doubled the number of Quaker deputies. Numbers alone, then, do not reveal a religious dynamic for the new policy decision. The focus of the fighting, however, had returned to Rhode Island and Plymouth from the western Massachusetts frontier. Receiving the refugees from the two burned towns, the outlying farms, the survivors of Peirce's Fight,[27] and many skirmishes, the central government on Aquidneck could not escape a sense of increased danger, any more than it could ignore the comings and goings of the armies, which once again relied on Rhode Island for rest and provisions, transportation, and intelligence, and even reinforcements.

Summer: "Seasonable Prey"

Spring had been a fearsome time in a New England despoiled with death; summer brought a more one-sided violence. Connecticut troops of English and Mohegans, for example, killed Indians seemingly at will in Narragansett. In the summer months of 1676 the Indians lost more and more power as English confidence gradually grew in proportion. Weakened by disease, hunger, surrenders, treachery, and depredations of the English enemy, the Nipmucks, Wampanoags, Narragansetts, and other allies sought to minimize their losses and to position themselves advantageously in case of eventual defeat by negotiating with colony governments. Indian attempts to contact the English governments in order to discuss peace often met with bad faith. By sometimes promising mercy, the English effectively encouraged divisions among the Indians but frequently betrayed their promises, chasing down remnants of fighting units and either slaughtering the Indians or taking them prisoner for eventual sale as slaves.[28] The Rhode Island government had prohibited the enslavement of Indians on 13 March 1675/1676, obligating them merely to serve for terms, albeit stringent terms. (Quaker William Edmundson, visiting from Ireland, wrote to New England Quakers from Newport six months later: "And many of you count it unlawfull to make Slaves of the Indians, & if soe, then why the Negroes?")[29]

Rhode Island boats were still active in transporting Major Bradford's Plymouth soldiers in June and early July: "The Rhode Island boats, by the Major's order, meeting them at Pocasset, they were soon imbarked." Note that the boats were organized into a unit subject to orders from a Plymouth commander, not just serendipitously available from individual volunteers.[30] In corroboration, we find the example of one William Clarke, who with his company captured several Indians when he was "Commander of one of the sloops in the yeare 1676"; the Indians were taken from him by the government. Here again the telling words are "company" and "commander."[31] In August, Plymouth and allied Indian troops rested and regrouped at Portsmouth, refreshed most of all by the news that Philip himself and his Wampanoags had returned to their land, the Mount Hope peninsula, in a tragic and desperate quest for renewal. On 12 August, under Captain Benjamin Church of Plymouth and Captain Peleg Sanford of Rhode Island, English troops crossed to Mount Hope from Portsmouth, a half-mile away by water. They hunted down and killed Philip: "this seasonable Prey was soon divided, they cut off his head, and hands, and conveyed them to Rhode-Island."[32] Alderman, the "friendly" Rhode Island Indian who actually killed Philip, later charged money to view Philip's scarred hand, which he soaked in rum and carried around in a bucket; Philip's head was mounted on a pole at Plymouth, where it was still a ghoulish caution twenty years later.[33]

Considering the Indians to be in rebellion against the sovereign and therefore treasonous,[34] the colonies felt justified in subjecting the Indian leaders taken as prisoners of war to trial and punishment. The Rhode Island government, too, had its own trials to conduct as the war ebbed away. In August 1676, just after the death of Philip, a court-martial tried about nine Indian leaders for various offenses, ranging from treason to murder.[35] In the colony at this time, the council was not only an executive body, but also could constitute itself as the General Court of Trials, a court of original jurisdiction for important cases, and an appeals court for lesser cases. The council had become uncomfortable with the irregular punishment of the Indians and others by various commissioned officers, who proceeded against them "as in warr."[36] Joshua Tift, for example, had been tried, hanged, drawn, and quartered with unseemingly dispatch. This is another hint that a kind of martial law prevailed in the colony; the first indication was the fact that Benjamin Church was supposed to secure a permit from the colony government to go from Aquidneck to visit Awashonks in Seconnet on the eastern coast of Narragansett Bay. (It refused his request, and he went anyway.)[37] The council voted to correct the embarrassment of irregular punishment of Indians by constituting a proper court-martial; the addition of seventeen military officers transmogrified the usual General Court of Trials into a court-martial, distinguished from a civilian court by the absence of a jury. Losing no time, it convened the next day. The civilians on this court probably included five Quakers—although only Joshua Coggeshall may have actually appeared—joined by two Quaker officers, Walter Clarke's brothers. Ensign Weston Clarke was a Quaker; Lieutenant Latham Clarke may have been a Quaker, but this is not clear. Lieutenant Jireh Bull also was a member.[38] Although a certain list of those who actually appeared to judge the Indians does not exist, a letter written from the court-martial to Walter Clarke during the trial, asking for his attendance at court on the morrow, suggests that he had absented himself from the deliberations that were to end in the execution of four Indians.[39] One Indian, Manasses Molasses, accused of killing "Low" (Zoar, Zoeth) Howland, the corpse in the Sin and Flesh River, was tried before this court-martial. Evidence against him was hearsay and inconclusive, although Molasses himself admitted that he bought the coat of the dead man for some ground nuts. He was turned over to Captain Church of Plymouth with other captives for removal from the colony; Plymouth empowered Church to sell the captives for life terms of servitude, or less, as he judged appropriate.[40]

Some historians have inferred from Clarke's absence that not only did he scruple to appear with a military body because he was a Quaker but that some or all of the other Quakers did also. If the Quakers did so scruple, it was because the judicial body had assumed the military nature, not because they shrank from capital punishment. Capital punishment, after all, was only another of the "terrors to evil-doers" which the magistrate was allowed, indeed appointed, by God to apply. Rhode Island Quaker governments had not shirked such duty in the past, ordering and carrying out executions, such as that of one Thomas Cornell, found guilty of setting his mother on fire in 1673 and hanged with the Indian Punnean by order of the Quaker government.[41] Peter Easton, George Lawton, Ralph Earle, and Thomas Cornell had participated in the unanimous verdict and sentencing of Thomas Flounders to be hung for manslaughter in 1670.[42] Nor did the government hesitate now. It found Quanopen, Sunkeecunasuck, Wenanaquabin, and Wecopeak guilty and sentenced them to be shot two days hence.[43]

The war ended. The issues it raised continued. As the Rhode Island boats had tacked back and forth across the bay, so too the Rhode Island government acted "by turens" in policy and succeeded in preserving the "safty" of most of its English population, although the mainlanders had suffered severe property losses and most islanders were significantly poorer for the war. The pattern of vigorous involvement in military affairs, alternating with periods of resentful reluctance, reflected ambivalence toward prosecuting the war when war was not immediately threatening Rhode Island territory. Many factors contributed to this ambivalence; the Quaker peace testimony was virtually indiscernible among them. And finally, the council itself said, 23 August, 1676, "this Collony, and all the publick officers thereof have proceeded as in warr."[44]

II

"To Looke to Our Selefs"

ASCRIBING MOTIVES TO A QUAKER GOVERNMENT IN WARTIME

Governor Winslow meant to be generous. As the killings began in June 1675, he had not only requested help from his Rhode Island neighbors but had urged them to be alert to their own peril. As John Easton recounted Winslow's warning, Winslow had written to Rhode Island "for us to looke to our selefs [selves]."[1] The simple phrase signaled a brotherly concern, an auspicious attitude between those who would become allies. But "for us to looke to our selefs" became a phrase more aptly characterizing the self-interested quality of the relationships that developed among the colonies, both during the stress of the war itself, when all were seeking survival, and in the aftermath of the war, when all were seeking advantage. To look to oneself became the silent assumption motivating governments in New England. To consider Rhode Island's part in King Philip's War, then, requires an understanding of the motives driving the government's wartime decisions, motives that carried out the mandate of looking out for oneself.

Any analysis of motive on the part of a collective body such as a legislature, an administrative council, or a discrete grouping within such a body must be only a gross assessment, unless extraordinary documentation exists. When surviving documents are as patchy as they are in the case of King Philip's War, subtlety and precision are far out of reach. One must acknowledge emphatically the oversimplification inherent in treating the Quakers in the Rhode Island government as a monolithic group of men unvisited by differences in outlook, temperament, capacity, or belief. Nor is it likely that the slight Quaker majority always cohered in their decisions or consistently prevailed over others. One must acknowledge this inadequacy—and then must move beyond a fatal hesitation to one's best approximation.

From a review of the Rhode Island Quaker government's participation in King Philip's War several significant features emerge: the colony was not neutral in the conflict; the colony at times carried out active military maneuvers; and the level of its involvement was different from that of its fellow New England colonies in some respects. It is appropriate to analyze how, and if, the Quaker peace testimony was related to the significant features of Rhode Island performance. Essential to this analysis is an identification of other feasible motives for government decisions and an examination of the interests animating those who interpreted them.

Rhode Island's Response to War: Partisanship

There is no doubt that Rhode Island unhesitatingly chose sides in the conflict. "Wee fortifyed ourselves against the Indians as necessity required," Rhode Island would reply to inquiries from the English government after the war.[2] Douglas Leach has seen it otherwise: "Rhode Island . . . had remained officially neutral during the war."[3] "Rhode Island was not a party to the war and raised no armies," echoed a modern historian, reiterating the common judgement.[4] But failure to raise an army is not the equivalent of neutrality. And there is room to define "army" in more flexible ways. (Was the Providence contingent at the Nipsachuck battle not an army, while the Plymouth contingent was?) Even while Rhode Islanders attempted to avoid war through negotiation, there was never a question as to where their sympathies would lie should war break out. Yet the Quaker government did even more than verbally express support for fellow Englishmen: it acted on its allegiance. When it offered sanctuary to the wounded, it was only to the English wounded. In contrast, only ten years later in England, a Quaker surgeon emphasized that his religious conviction led him to treat soldiers from both sides in Monmouth's rebellion.[5] Rhode Island exiled Indians, supplied boats to the Plymouth and Massachusetts armies, blockaded Philip on Mount Hope, rescued English soldiers, provisioned and provided a safe haven for colonial troops, raised and dispatched soldiers, stored ammunition, transported troops across Narragansett Bay to battle, encouraged the mobilization and training of the local militias, deployed gunboats, manned an official garrison, contributed troops to the final search for Philip himself—and, at last, tried and executed prisoners of war. This is scarcely the record of either a neutral government or an inactive one. At the end of the war in southern New England, the Rhode Island council itself laid out evidence for its participation in the war, as it sought to justify establishing a court-martial to try its adversaries. After rehearsing the constitutional provisions for its past military actions, hence for the court-martial, the council wrote of its "Just Cause to invade and distroy the Native Indians and other Enemys of the said Collony." The council asserted that it had identified and imprisoned "principle actors and contrivers"—that is, leaders—of the "late Rebellion and Murthers and other outrages committed against his Majesties Authorety." It found it necessary to recite, too, the evidence that "this Collony, and all the publick officers thereof have proceeded as in warr," but since its purpose was to justify an internal proceeding (for an internal audience), the council could not rely on those activities merely in support of the military activities of its neighbor colonies. The evidence the officials cited were the rates their predecessors had imposed, the commissions granted to military officers, the watches that were constituted, and "all the proceedings that have been against the Indians hitherto."[6]

Rhode Island's Response to War: Limitations

The very fact that the Rhode Island council found it necessary to establish for the persuasion of its own citizens that Rhode Island had just fought a war signals a limiting ambiguity. This is a strange thing to do. Yet the Rhode Island government before the beginning of hostilities had reacted to the "motions" of the Indians much as the prior, non-Quaker, governments had in the past and much as Plymouth and Massachusetts were reacting on this occasion, even actually mobilizing troops. ("Those that are soldiers are in Armes.")[7] As it perceived danger approaching, the Rhode Island government tightened restrictions on the Indians and joined in the informal offers of mutual defense circulating among the colonies. The colony government had no reserved troops of its own; military authority was parceled out among the towns. Each town had its own council of war, responsible for its own militia and its own defense. Portsmouth and Newport had at times combined their councils of war. The authority to train, arm, provision, mobilize, and deploy troops; to choose officers; and to tax for their maintenance was thus decentralized, no novelty in itself. Not until the final months of the war, on 11 April 1676, did the colony government order and centralize its military affairs under one commander, Major John Cranston, although it is difficult to see any appreciable difference that this decision effected. For much of the war, then, the central colony government's activities seemed fragmentary: issuing individual commissions for particular occasions, trying to stock its magazine at Newport, and moving about the few "great guns" it had impressed. Because the records of the individual councils of war have been lost, the activities of military units are lost as well. To some degree, then, the question of the Rhode Island Colony's engagement in King Philip's War is a matter of definition: whether town forces such as those of Captains Fenner and Edmunds are deemed to count. And it is legitimate to question whether centralization under the duress of war was delayed because decentralization of military authority was more convenient for pacifists within government. The government did not hint at this possibility in explaining its own actions, nor did accusations about its inadequacies seize upon this specific element. We are left without evidence.

Rhode Island's Response to War: Distinctions

Yet the Rhode Island colony government acted differently from the governments of neighbor colonies in some important respects. Failure to raise a colony-wide army under central command differentiated Rhode Island's posture from that of the United Colonies. Although undoubtedly Rhode Island men fought in the war's larger engagements and also defended their own homes, they were probably acting not as agents of their own colony-wide government but rather as agents of the individual towns; with the overstated exception of Batten's "hundreds." Moreover, unlike its quasi partners, Rhode Island's involvement was restricted to its own territory and immediate environs; Rhode Island's interest flagged at its periphery. It did not press its men for service outside the colony. More than the other colonies, as individuals and collectively, the leaders made efforts to diffuse enmity through direct contact with various Indian groups. The government saw itself as having a mission to care for some of the casualties of war. The kind of rhetoric exemplified by Cotton Mather a few years later was notably absent from Rhode Island discourse: "Yea, when once you have but got the Track of those Ravenous howling Wolves, then pursue them vigorously; Turn not back till they are consumed: Wound them that they shall not be able to Arise. . . . Beat them small as the Dust before the Wind."[8] Most significant for the purposes of this study, in an unprecedented way Rhode Island acknowledged and supported those whose consciences did forbid a wider range of military activity, even during the times of greatest danger.

Governance and the Peace Testimony

Historians' Interpretations

The usual interpretation of the actions and inactions of the Rhode Island government has been that its members were inhibited by the pacifist scruples of the Quakers among them. Historians have not cited, nor have I found, evidence on which to base this belief. Such scruples were not expressed, at least not in any extant records, but modern historians have been untroubled by the lack of any specific evidence regarding Quaker scruples and have confidently assumed that the peace testimony motivated Quaker behavior. In the absence of evidence for such an assumption, one would have to believe that Quakers had either found it politic deliberately to conceal their pacifism, or that all expressions of pacifism were detached from written records and lost; or believe that because they were Quakers, they did not need to express their pacifism—it could be assumed. The latter explanation for the common unquestioned assumption is the most likely, but unpersuasive.

James Bowden's 1850 analysis exemplifies the misinformation and oversimplification of the more common historical judgment. Bowden wrote that the government spurned an invitation from the other colonies to unite against the Indians, a proposal to which the government could not "conscientiously accede"; and "in dependence on the protecting care of Him who hath the hearts of all men at his disposal, they refrained from engaging in the war."[9] Bowden relied in part on William Edmundson's *Journal*, first published in 1715; Edmundson, who had been visiting Rhode Island in the summer of 1676, wrote (in error), "But the Governor being a Friend, (one Walter Clark) could not give Commissions to kill and destroy Men." Bowden repeated the mainlanders' accusation that the Aquidneck government refused to issue commissions and to give them protection. While not attributing the outcome to God directly, he pointedly called it "remarkable" that "the habitations of the peaceloving settlers on Rhode Island itself remained safe, and not a settler thereon received personal injury," while settlers on the main (non-Quakers who requested military assistance) were subject to devastation.[10]

Moreover, he wrote, the Indians were aware that the governors were "guided by principles of peace," had been interested in the "welfare of the natives," and had allowed Indians to serve on juries, and so the Indians had no "incitement" to kill these benevolent friends.[11] Responding to the evidence that Quakers had not uniformly abstained from self-protective defenses because they used armed boats to patrol against Indians, Bowden counters with a nonsequitur: there was no evidence that the Indians in fact attempted forcefully to land on Aquidneck—as if the absence of Indian aggression exonerated the government from having taken potentially violent measures. He concluded that such governmental measures were necessary, that their omission would have constituted "culpable neglect," and that they did not violate "in the slightest degree the doctrine which holds in abhorrence the slaying of our fellow-creatures."[12]

Rufus Jones wrote in 1911 that "[t]he Quaker officials in the Rhode Island Colony were in every instance devoted to the maintenance of peace," although he did acknowledge the compromise necessary for government officials whose ideals conflicted with their civic duties, when "they found themselves compelled, by unavoidable conditions and circumstances, to perform public acts of a warlike nature."[13] His pragmatism renders Quaker magistrates indistinguishable from any other and "devotion to the maintenance of peace" an empty phrase.

More recently, Arthur J. Worrall discussed the dilemma of Quaker leadership in time of war, concentrating particularly and usefully on the relationship between Rhode Island and Massachusetts Quakers.[14] Echoing Rufus Jones's assumption, Worrall described the activities of the Quaker government leaders in terms implying their passivity, their lack of choice, and the inevitable quality of their involvement. He wrote: "Suddenly *thrust into war*, Rhode Island's Quaker leaders *had to participate* at least *indirectly* to the extent of placing the colony on a defensive footing"; "Friends . . . *found themselves* participating indirectly in hostilities"; "Quakers . . . *had to participate*."[15] Although Worrall cites the "essentially defensive" measures the Quaker government took, he does not consider other possible explanations for its behavior, nor does he cite evidence for pacifism contributing to the limited nature of its measures, nor does he consider the nature of pacifist belief at that time and place. He does acknowledge an increasing rigor in a more general sense toward pacifist witness in New England.

Peter Brock, another historian who has touched upon pacifist issues in King Philip's War, wrestled more directly with the inconsistencies of Quaker behavior and the peace testimony and concluded that Quaker magistrates in Rhode Island felt compelled to take "forcible measures" because they were magistrates of a "non-Quaker polity." He presented no evidence to support his assumption that pacifist principles restrained their activities or to support his conjecture that a non-Quaker polity accounted for the differences between Rhode Island Quaker governors and their Pennsylvania counterparts of later years. Jonathan Chu is an exception among historians, however, fully appreciating the unsettled quality of early pacifism, and carefully drawing appropriate distinctions.[16]

The common assumptions and beliefs need to be readdressed. First, it strains credulity that people willing to risk their own lives for a principle would have no courage left over to defend their principle openly. Second, just because later Quaker magistrates might be bound by their peace testimony to avoid warlike activities, it is not valid to make assumptions about seventeenth-century motives in the absence of evidence. Such reading back of later Quaker understandings of the peace testimony obscures not only other wartime motives but the nature of the peace testimony as it was understood in this particular time and place. Third, in many respects the government activities do not appear to have been constrained.

Fourth, other plausible motives for constraint do emerge from the evidence. Modern expectations about how Quakers would act have led to the downplaying of any actions that contradicted those expectations and have led to a failure to consider other motives for their actions. And others had an interest in minimizing Rhode Island activities. The question of Rhode Island motivation is far more complex than easy assumptions have allowed.

It is of course possible that the peace testimony deterred the Quakers in government from actually using weapons themselves to fight or kill—governors Coddington and Clarke did not lead an army into the field, for example, as did Governor Winslow. If their understanding of the peace testimony was limited to a narrow, specific, and literal sphere of activity—a testimony against actually using weapons themselves to fight or kill—their wartime activities would have been fully compatible with such a peace testimony. They could have in good conscience procured, stored, and distributed weapons (as they did), as long as they did not personally use them.[17] Without violating their consciences, they could have made it possible for others to fight, including Rhode Island men; they could have defended their colony and commissioned military leaders; they could have taxed and paid for these measures; they could have eschewed neutrality for partisanship. The 1673 Exemption may have eased any qualms about such decisions, since magistrates would not be compelling others to violate their consciences. Whether or not it was religious conscience that prohibited the individual Quaker leaders from bearing arms themselves—whether or not they were acting within the constraints of the peace testimony—is unknowable and is not a firm basis for explaining the extent of Rhode Island participation in the war.

Just as there are no governmental debates, no papers from governmental officials—no explanation whatsoever on the part of those in government suggesting that religious conscience stayed their weapons on an individual basis, other than the implications of the 1673 Exemption—neither is there any evidence that the peace testimony affected the collective military choices of the government, other than the choice to maintain the Exemption. On the contrary, there is evidence that the Quaker politicians were willing to entertain the concept of just war and the validity of defensive war and to take ethnic cohesion for granted. While it is not possible to assess at this remove the precise motives animating the Rhode Island Quakers in government during King Philip's War, it is possible to reject assumptions unsupported by contemporary evidence.

But whatever the leaders' understanding of their obligations under the peace testimony, it is finally unimportant, for these obligations would be superseded by the seventeenth-century Quaker understanding of the obligations of the magistrate. Their personal hesitations about wars and fightings would become irrelevant because they were magistrates. Quakers believed that God directly empowered and required magistrates to be "a terror to evil doers and a praise to those that do well."[18] To Quaker magistrates, having identified the Indians as the evildoers, as treasonous, their duty was plain; the decisions they made were made in the light of a magistrate's responsibility and might include activities not available to the ordinary Quaker. They might separate themselves from ordinary Quaker discourse and dilemmas. Their own religious obligations—however broadly or narrowly each might have construed them—might influence their decisions but need not determine them. This most plausible interpretation of their posture, after all, was consonant with the posture of George Fox himself, seeing a necessary and great power belonging to the magistrate, limited of course by righteousness and limited as well to "Caesar's" sphere, not God's.[19] The only "evidence" that adherence to the peace testimony influenced the government's response to war is the plain fact that Rhode Island indeed engaged in this war in a somewhat marginal way.

The perpetual difficulty with justifying a broad range of actions as part of a magistrate's duty is to determine what actions, if any, should be excluded from the allowable area swept by the magistrate's sword. What police powers involving force are considered righteous? Is war always unrighteous? Might this justification legitimize fighting with carnal weapons even by Quakers? The Baptist Confession of 1677, issued in London, for example, declared that wars instituted by civil magistrates were just, because God had set up the magistrates.[20] Defining the legitimate sphere for magistrates implied a moral flexibility of such extent that to serve would become untenable for many Quakers in the next century, a matter that continues unresolved today. The Rhode Island Quaker leaders, at least those serving in the government in October 1677, did come to terms with defining the magistrates' duties in the face of their religious duties. They apparently displayed no unease at allowing the Quaker view of magistracy to override concerns derived from the peace testimony, while at the same time safeguarding the options of those who were not magistrates, even the most scrupulous of their brethren.

Fortunately for the historian, the Quaker leaders themselves put forth some explanations for their actions, and others may be deduced from the circumstances. Both during and after the war, those Rhode Islanders most involved in the events and decisions of the war had an interest in explaining themselves to their own constituencies. It was in their interest, too, to explain themselves to other New England colonies. Explanations sent to the king had perhaps the most potential to shape history to their own benefit. Other colonies, too, discovered that they might use Rhode Island's wartime record to their own preferment. Since the resulting contemporary evaluations of Rhode Island's wartime choices have influenced later historical judgements, the interests of those who made them become important in assessing the accuracy of their accounts.

Justifications: Rhode Island to Itself

The terms by which the wartime government leaders explained the limited posture of Rhode Island fell into several categories, none of them religious. Some of their hesitations, as was apparent from the narrative of the war, resulted from political considerations: allied encroachment on land, allied treaty intrusions, the precarious hold on sovereignty, and resentment at disloyalty. They also mentioned economic constraints: the incapacity to provide materiél and the shortage of manpower. They talked about moral qualms: the breaking of promises to Indians, the killing of the innocent. They had come to comfortable equilibrium with the Narragansetts before the war; they had no particular quarrel with the Wampanoags. Other unexpressed factors may have contributed to their decisions: a residual adherence to Roger Williams's principles respecting the rights of the original proprietors of the soil;[21] fear; doubt that this particular war was either justified or their problem; chronic lack of money; reluctance of people to leave their homes, their fields, and their boats if not directly threatened; or a lack of commitment on the part of Aquidneck to outlying parts of the colony. Samuel Hubbard of Aquidneck wrote in November 1675, after all, "This island doth look to ourselves as yet, by mercy not one slain, blessed be God."[22] Any residual qualms were either unexpressed, suppressed, or subsumed in a fatalism leaving everything to God. Without direct explanations tied to principles of peace from the magistrates involved, then, the influence of the peace testimony on their decisions, if any, is both invisible and irrelevant.

Revisiting the Exemption of 1673

The Rhode Island government continued to struggle with military requirements for its inhabitants after the war. The legislation it promulgated offered explicit explanations of how the Quakers and their fellow colonists found ways to coexist and how the Quakers in government found a way to coexist with their own testimonies. An account of assembly actions in the year following the war sheds additional light on Rhode Island's controlling motives for its wartime military behavior. In October 1676, the assembly restored the privilege of refusing military service without incurring a penalty. The assembly appointed a committee to consider the militia, and when the three Quakers—John Easton, Job Almy, and William Wodell—and the one non-Quaker submitted their report, the assembly, with about three more Quakers than in May, reinstated the full exemption from service for those conscientiously opposed to war. Its reasons were probably the obverse of the previous repeal, when penalties had been imposed for those objecting to military service: the war was over, and it saw a need to respond to popular pressure—this time from the Quakers.

The assembly's expressed reasons for restoring the full exemption are fascinating. The assembly first deplored the injustice that had arisen since the imposition of fines for not serving in the militia. Those deputized to collect the penalties made no distinction, it found, between those who "by their neglect, or in contempt of authority" failed to serve and those who could not conform for conscience's sake. The conscientious refusers, the assembly insisted, were as anxious to further the good of the colony as any responsible citizen and so were just as concerned as any others that no one refuse service under the *pretense* of conscience; such "practicers" of contempt should suffer the full penalty of the law. To fine conscientious refusers, however, was to deprive them of their rightful liberty of conscience guaranteed by fundamental laws and the king's charter.[23] But those who collected the fines did distinguish, in one way, between the two groups who did not serve, the assembly went on to contradict itself: the collectors distrained from the conscientious refusers goods "sometimes five times the value" owed and "often excused for a small matter" the careless or rebellious refusers. Furthermore, the amounts collected were frivolously spent, in "company keepeing" and other wasteful ways, rather than having been applied to strictly military supplies.[24]

The assembly recognized two groups within its own body as well: those who for conscience's sake "cannot prepare for war, or fight with carnal weapons, and doe desire that all were brought to the same understanding" and those who found it their duty "to prepare for war and defend themselves by carnall weapons."[25] Here is the indirect evidence that members of the government were among those constrained by conscience. Because those members who renounced war and weapons were at the same time civil officers, the reasoning continued, it was their duty to maintain the laws under the king and charter: to "order, authorize and require such [nonobjecting] persons to act in millitary discipline" and to penalize those who were "neglectinge" or were "in contempt of authority." Even though they might personally be unable to prepare for war, when they acted as civil officers, as magistrates, they not only were able to prepare for war and to defend with weapons but were positively obliged to do so.[26]

The majority, including Quakers, decided that "it would be persecution to hinder any from that way of defence, which they thinke in conscience is their duty." Just as Quakers had been freed of persecution on the basis of belief in nonviolence, their religious belief, they granted freedom from persecution to others on the basis of their belief in military protection. The Quaker majority's commitment to Rhode Island's historical liberty of conscience overrode a possible impulse to encourage others in "the same understanding" by significantly relaxing military requirements in the colony. The assembly did, however, reduce the number of training days per year from six to two, a relaxation later prompting one James Barker, who had been "sick unto death" and so missed the assembly session, to register his dismay in the official court records. He was enraged that the "People called Quakers, and their Adherants" had repealed the "good and wholesome Law . . . mainetaineing of the Kings Millitery forces" as the charter required.[27] The Quaker reasoning in this restoration of the Exemption found an echo in the "Fundamental Constitutions" for the province of East New Jersey, in 1683. Among the proprietors of that colony were several who had "no freedom to defend themselves with arms, and others who judge it their duty to defend themselves." They agreed, therefore, "that they will not in this case force each other against their respective judgments and consciences," and, whether proprietor or planter, those conscientiously prevented from bearing arms were excused, and excused as well from supplying a substitute. Those not so constrained had liberty to bear arms for the public defense "in a legal way."[28]

In explaining the restoration of the full exemption in Rhode Island, the "People called Quakers, and their Adherants" enunciated three remarkable principles: they found it appropriate that they maintain the military strength of the colony through mandatory service and proper supply, in spite of a (Quaker) religious belief that such strength was inefficacious; they saw the right to bear arms as a matter of liberty of conscience as much as the right not to bear arms; and they allowed their status as civil officers to justify their own active pursuit of military preparedness. The latter rationale is the clearest extant articulation of how the Quakers in the Rhode Island government were able to reconcile their Quaker beliefs with their participation in the military activities of King Philip's War.

By June 1677, the Quakers had been voted out of office. James Barker, newly elected assistant, and the rest of the non-Quaker assemblymen lost no time in addressing once more the inadequate and undisciplined character of the colony's militia. The new assembly paid homage to the charter's liberty of conscience "for the reall worship of God," but in the same sentence assigned equal importance to the charter's mandate to obey the king's laws, which were of course upheld by the military power. In fact, the assembly declared, the military power was the very grounding of all civil power, the protection of all freedom and privileges. In a familiar refrain, however, the members accused "some under pretence of conscience" of so undermining military authority and strength by disobeying the militia laws that the colony was "in effect wholly destitute of the millitary forces" and might thereby be vulnerable to the "weakest and meanest" of enemies. Stepping up firmly to ameliorate this problem, the new assembly restored the six training days and enacted several provisions relating to militia leadership and organization, to fines and distraints for not appearing on the training field, and to the elimination of corruption from the distraint process. Most important, the assembly established that no (male) person between the ages of sixteen and sixty could be released from training, except civil officers or those whose work might excuse them or a person who had a valid excuse for a specific occasion.[29]

Historians have always labeled this act of the 1677 assembly a full "repeal" of the 1673 conscientious refuser exemption, and this it seems to be upon hasty reading. One clause, however, adds considerable ambiguity to the act. Qualifying all of the detailed and strict provisions it contained, the act renews once more an allegiance to freedom of conscience: "Provided alwayes, and this Assembly doe hereby declare, that it is their full and unanimous resolution to maintaine a full liberty in religious concernments relateing to the worship of God." Arguably, the Quaker testimony against "learning war" does not relate to the worship of God, in a narrow sense. But the act continued: "noe person inhabitinge within this jurisdiction shall bee in any wise molested, punished, disquieted or called in question for any differences of opinion in matters of religion, whoe doe not actually disturbe the civill peace of the Collony."[30]

The peace testimony perhaps was a "matter of religion" within the meaning of this clause. Unless the holding of pacifist belief constituted "disturbing the civil peace," then, it might be argued that pacifists had retained their privilege of exemption. Moreover, in justifying strengthened military requirements, the act explicitly stated that the new requirements were necessitated not by those who for reasons of conscience refused militia service but rather by those who were "under *pretence* of conscience."[31] Although the vocabulary of the religious liberty clause in the 1677 act is the stock formula governments elsewhere used to guarantee liberty of conscience, in Rhode Island, with its history of connecting this liberty with pacifist convictions, the words might at least have provided a cover for any lax enforcement of military requirements that may have prevailed after the war. It would seem, then, that sincerely conscientious Quakers might still have made a case for refusing militia service without penalty, thus explaining why the Rhode Island Quaker records, which do exist, are silent on the matter of fines until the 1690s. The absence of local militia records or treasury records that might have recorded fines and distraints precludes determining whether, or for how long, this exemption might have continued.

In 1686 the Rhode Island colony was under an order of "quo warranto," its charter under threat of being vacated, its authority about to be swallowed in the new but short-lived "Dominion of New England." Rhode Island Quakers sent Robert

Hodgson to deliver a petition to the new king, James II. The petition begged that Quakers and "others Conscientious amongst us" might be exempt from training or bearing arms. The petitioners sought to protect the "indulgence" contained in the old Rhode Island Charter "in matters of Religious Concernments," specifying two areas of privilege: oaths, and bearing arms and learning war. In coupling these two areas the petition implies that Quakers were free of bearing arms and learning war, since it is certain that they were free of having to swear oaths.[32] But by the 1690s, with the resumption of war with the Indians, the Quaker records begin to note sufferings on account of not training. Clearly whatever concessions Quakers may have enjoyed were at an end, and they were subject to punishment for their pacifist scruples.

Justifications: Rhode Island to the King

Too often historians and others have assessed the degree of Rhode Island's participation in King Philip's War by accepting the partisan observations of some participants in the war and by almost cavalierly discounting others. After the war, all the colonies characterized their own behavior and that of others for particular purposes having nothing to do with moral necessity and everything to do with self-interested gain. It was most convenient for the United Colonies, for example, to stress Rhode Island's hesitations rather than its contributions, blaming the hesitations on the hated Quaker religion deluding its governors. Even the Rhode Island government itself vacillated between emphasizing its cooperation with the war effort and its distance from it.

"Butt this your Majesties Collony not being Concerned in the said war," Rhode Island wrote to the king, defending itself against King Charles's rebuke for not having given him an account of the war, acted "only as Necessety Required, for the defence of their lives, and what they could of their Estates." Perhaps thinking better of appearing too detached, they continued, "and as Cuntrymen and fellow subjects did with Our boates and provissions, Asist and relieve our Neighbours." Improving their case, they

> [were] bold to informe your Majestie, that Sachim Phillip the beginer of the warr was slaine (in Mount hope neck where the war began) by an Indian belonging to this your Majesties Collony; he was one of a small Company under the Comand of a Captaine of Rhode Island . . . who was then in that Ingagment with a Captaine of Plymoth forces as volenters.[33]

Those preparing this report to the King were eager to establish their claims to the now vacant Mount Hope peninsula, arguing that Rhode Islanders had bought land there from the sachems, that the colony needed growing room, and that it had been more loyal to the crown than the United Colonies in the past, having "ever had a lothing to any usurped power."[34] Its role in ridding Mount Hope of its Indians might be an additional boost for its land claims.

Responding at about the same time to a Massachusetts allegation that Rhode Island had given no assistance in the war, Rhode Island agents Randall Howlden and John Greene countered with a different portrayal: the colony did "assist them with several sloops well-Manned when the Warr was begun in Plimouth Colony, to the utmost they could doe, and to the great damage of the Enemy." Furthermore, they implied that Rhode Island, left alone, would have maintained its friendly relations with the Narragansett Indians. Instead, because the United Colonies had violated its patent by intruding without authorization and because it had not been consulted "as to the Lawfulness or necessity of that warr," Rhode Island had been drawn into the hideous destructiveness unnecessarily.[35] Rhode Island was desperate to establish its unquestioned rights to the Narragansett territory.

In answer to the questions of William Blathwayt, the secretary to the Committee for Foreign Plantations, Governor Peleg Sanford in 1680 wrote, "in the late Indian Warrs wee fortifyed ourselves against the Indians as necessity required, but as for fortification against a forreigne Enemy as yet Wee have had no occasion but have made as good Provision as at present Wee are capacitated to doe."[36] A non-Quaker government in 1680 seemed to be no more "capacitated" than its Quaker predecessor; nor did this non-Quaker governor express any criticism that its measures had been inadequate during King Philip's War.

The government's was not the only explanatory voice emanating from Rhode Island. Some of the English residents of Narragansett—a territory that was imperfectly reconciled to being under the authority of Rhode Island and that flirted periodically with bestowing its allegiance upon Connecticut—petitioned the king to settle their land dispute by making Narragansett part of Connecticut. To justify their dissatisfaction they wrote indignantly about their experience in King Philip's War:

> the petitioners sent to the Government of Road Island for their Protection and defence, which was absolutely denied them, the then Governour of Rhode Island being a Quaker and thought it perhaps not lawfull either to give Commission or take up armes, so that their Townes, goods, Corne, and Cattell were by the Salvage Natives burnt.[37]

Again Howlden and Greene, Rhode Island agents in England, undercut these assertions, pointing out to the Lords Committees of Trade and Plantations that the petitioners had tried to "bring in" Connecticut while denying the jurisdiction of Rhode Island. They continued: "And for what hee alleges that the then Governor of Rhode Island being a Quaker, thought it not lawfull to grant Commissions; wee answer, there were Commissions given forth in the beginning of the Warr with the Sachem Philip."[38] Quaker governors did indeed sign commissions: responding to later accusations that the colony was a reluctant participant in the war because of the religious principles of its Quaker administration, the deputy governor, John Easton, attested in an affidavit that "he never was against giving forth any commissions to any, that might have been for the security of the King's interest in this Colony."[39] John Callender pointed out that military commissions, signed by Coddington and Easton, the governor and deputy governor, were still in existence that authorized several men to "go in *an armed sloop to visit the garrisons at Providence,* &c."[40] The Rhode Island agents defending Rhode Island in England then presented a familiar list of ways in which the colony had supported the war effort, with transport, sanctuary, and "oftentimes venturing hard on shore to fetch off their Men, when they were in danger to bee surprised."[41] The self-interest of all parties again colored the description.

Connecticut accused the Rhode Island government of neglecting to protect Rhode Island's Narragansett residents during the war, without, however, mentioning Quakers. The two governments traded veiled threats of force back and forth in 1677, whereupon Connecticut snidely commented, "it is apt and easy for us, to be [as] resolute and violent in our doings, as yourselves: and such a spirit in you would have been as useful formerly against the common enemy as now against your friends."[42] Connecticut deplored too the niggardly relief offered to their wounded soldiers at Aquidneck: "we were forced to pay dearly for what releife they had there."[43] Connecticut dismissed as unjust a bill Rhode Island presented for this care, although they begrudgingly paid ten pounds, "seeing possibly you may have shewed some kindness to some of our souldiery."[44] These interactions show that Quakers were not always designated targets of a generalized antipathy, although the indiscriminate use of the term "Quaker" might carry with it its own useful disparaging implications.

Plymouth, after the war, allowed its hunger for "conquest lands," such as Philip's Mount Hope lands, to erase the memory of how Rhode Island came to its assistance during the war. It hoped to strengthen its rights to these lands in competition with Rhode Island by telling the king: "The truth is the authority of Rhode Island being all the time of the Warr in the hands of Quakers they scarcely shewed an English Spiritt either in assisting Us their distressed Neighbours or releiving their own Plantations upon the Mayne."[45] Furthermore, when the Plymouth forces had almost routed the enemy, "they tooke in many of our Enemyes that were flying before Us, thereby making profit by our expence of blood and Treasure."[46] Plymouth was suggesting not that Rhode Islanders were succoring these enemies, but rather, as is apparent from the word "profitt," that they were exploiting them for gain, either selling them to other colonies or using them as servants. That Rhode Islanders were not loath so to profit may be deduced from the General Assembly minutes of 8 November 1678, which reported that the towns of Newport and Portsmouth might profit from those Indians who "came in" to each respective town, "for the defraying of their charge of the late Indian warr."[47]

The "Agents of Boston" answered the complaints of the "Men of Warwick" after the war, who complained about the withdrawal of the United Colonies forces leaving them exposed and vulnerable, by writing

> [t]hat the Government of Road Island unto which they belong would never yeild any joynt assistance against the common Enimy, noe, not soe much as within theire owne bounds upon the Maine, nor Garrison these theire owne Townes of Warwick and Providence, soe that if upon the necessary withdrawing of the forces to pursue the routed Enemy up into the wilderness, they suffered damage, the blame must lye upon their owne Government.[48]

All of the participants knew well how to look to—to look out for—themselves during the war. In judging each other after the war, they also knew how to look to themselves. It was useful for many to stress Rhode Island's relative inactivity during the war—even at times useful for Rhode Island itself—and to attribute its government's inactivity to Quakers and by implication to their peace testimony. It was a potent way to denigrate the government, because in most places, to be a Quaker was to be despised. Whether or not they believed their own propaganda is less important than the fact that their accusations have influenced the way others have interpreted Rhode Island's motives. The various accusations show, too, that the peace testimony was well recognized as a Quaker requirement, although its nuances were but poorly understood. That onlookers displayed imperfect understanding cannot be surprising, for the Rhode Island Quakers themselves, dominating government for the first time, were working out with each event the nuances of the peace testimony.

Rhode Island Quakers who were onlookers to government, too, had to work out nuances. Often they came to different conclusions, and the different conclusions threatened to destabilize the Quaker community. An extraordinary document, the subject of the next chapter, illustrates the distance some Quakers perceived between themselves and their brethren in government. The document, dated 24/6M/1675, or August, 1675, was entitled "A Testimony from us (in scorn called Quakers but are) the Children of the Light" and was signed "From our mens-Meeting att Rhode-Island att Joshua Coggeshalls."[49] The authors do not further identify themselves. This is among the most important testimonies of Quaker belief from early colonial days, particularly as it arose in response to the actual and active hostilities of war. The testimony was not a theoretical tract but sprang from a situation demanding decisions of mortal significance of both a personal and community nature; lives were at risk. Seemingly prepared by "ordinary" Quakers and directed toward Quaker magistrates, the testimony serves as a bridge between those Quakers who bore responsibility for the community at large and those who bore responsibility only on a personal level. They looked to themselves for spiritual articulation.

"Witnesses to the Life of Innocency"

A TESTIMONY FROM RHODE ISLAND QUAKERS

"Shine forth more, & more" exulted the authors of "A Testimony from us (in scorn called Quakers but are) the Children of the Light."[1] Although they did not record their names, the authors limned an intimate portrait of their central religious preoccupations and assumptions. Their ardent souls spilled forth a spirit infused with religious joy and the consciousness of a fearful duty, with an immediacy and definition that indeed shines through the intervening centuries.

The testimony is invaluable because it clearly represents the thinking of a group of Quakers who considered themselves the true Quakers, the people of God. Their vocabulary, their prophetic zeal, their piety, their depth of conviction, all suggest that this group exemplifies those most serious and devout Quakers, those who attempted to inform their lives with the consciousness of the Kingdom, those most likely to demand the most of themselves in regard to Quaker testimonies. Some of them interpreted the peace testimony in a rigorous and radical way.

Although the testimony, dated 24/6M/1675 (24 August 1675), appears to have been written in Rhode Island during King Philip's War, it may have originated elsewhere. Quakers had a practice of exchanging testimonies between meetings and copying them into local records, sometimes without noting their origins. Almost five years later, for example, the general meeting of Quakers at Dublin, Ireland, heard the identical testimony "given forth." When the Irish Quakers absorbed it into their records, they replaced "From our mens-Meeting att Rhode-Island att Joshua Coggeshalls" with "Given forth at the nationall mens & womans meetings being met . . . at Dublin the 30 day of the 3d month 1680." Fifty Quakers signed the testimony on behalf of the Irish meeting; one of them was William Edmundson, who had been in Rhode Island during King Philip's War, from May to August 1676, where he had undoubtedly had access to the Rhode Island testimony. The testimony found its way from Ireland to the Chuckatuck Meeting, in Lower Virginia, and was copied into its records as an Irish document.[2]

But corroborating its Rhode Island provenance is a copy of the testimony, still dated 24/6M/1675, found among the Winthrop Papers, now at the Massachusetts Historical Society, Boston. It is unsurprising that its Rhode Island authors would send such a testimony to a contemporary leader such as John Winthrop, Jr., governor of Connecticut and ally of Rhode Island in the current "troubles" with the Indians. It would be surprising indeed to find such a parochial document residing in the Winthrop Papers had it originated in a distant Quaker venue; its relevance, after all, derived from its local origin and its implications for local policy. So while a measure of caution is appropriate in interpreting the testimony, internal and circumstantial evidence render it nearly certain that Rhode Island Quakers created it.[3]

"This Is Our Testimony"

"We are Witnesses this day," the anonymous authors of the testimony began, "And therefore this is our Testimony unto all people, that the gospel of our Lord Jesus Christ is come near in us, & we brought near in Measure to God in it." Thus they established their authority, relying on their acceptance of the gospel of Christ, which gave them access to God to a certain degree—"in measure." They were brought near to God because they dwelt in the Kingdom of God on earth and could testify to all people about the nature and requirements of the Kingdom.

It was the "Peaceable Kingdom" of God that the authors described first in the document: who dwelt within it and how they came to do so; the rewards of being in the Kingdom; the special knowledge available to those in the Kingdom; and the qualities defining both the Kingdom of God and the kingdom of the devil or Antichrist. Second, they set forth the requirements that the peaceable kingdom imposed regarding the use of force. Finally, they measured lapsed Quakers, their friends and acquaintances, against those requirements, outlining how they had failed in word and deed. The authors closed with a judgment of condemnation.

The document reveals disagreements about the peace testimony among Quakers: between Quakers in government and their critics and, more subtly, among the critics themselves. If the testimony originated in Rhode Island, the exposure of these disagreements may have reflected and contributed to that ongoing turmoil within the Rhode Island Meeting that is oddly and only obscurely visible within Quaker records in the postwar years. Just as oddly, while Quakers in England were aware of these tensions and did not hesitate to comment on them, they apparently ignored the pacifist issues raised by the war in New England—the issues explored in the testimony. We cannot avoid struggling with the significance of their avoidance and selective intrusion.

"Christ Jesus the Light of the world, & Prince of peace is come." So the authors introduced their leader and their testimony. In the authors' understanding, Jesus had called the "Sons of men" to turn from the way of death to the way of life, and a "remnant"—the Quakers—had answered. The remnant were those who submitted to Christ and were obedient to the righteous government of Christ and whose belief fulfilled the "Righteousness of the Law" and drew them into the Kingdom of God on earth. The testimony asserted that the gospel of Jesus had the power to bring believers near to God and to reconcile believers with him. Believers bore testimony to God's truth and walked "in the Light" with him; their unity with God enhanced their fellowship with one another as well. Jesus had "given an understanding that is true" to those in the Kingdom; this belief was the source of the testimony's confident and authoritative tone.

In its first section on the Kingdom of God, the testimony included three distinct descriptions of the peaceable kingdom, each of which embodied a slightly different interpretation of peace principles. Curiously, the authors of the testimony first defined the peaceable kingdom by default, by describing what it was *not*. Instead of listing the righteous qualities of God's Kingdom, they listed the spiritual evils that defined Satan's kingdom. Thus, the peaceable kingdom was "where Strife, Envy, Pride, Covetousness, are not." These spiritual failures were a generalized and abstract catalogue of the "lusts of the heart" that lead to violence. They listed, too, evil acts proscribed in the Kingdom. The Kingdom was where

Fighting,
Killing Blood-shed Murther with Carnall Weapons,
rendering Evil for Evil,
   are not;

Revenge,
Robbing for Concience sake;
watching with Guns or Swords to kill the Bodys of Men, though Enemies;
Offending,
or defending
with Carnal weapons of whatsortsoever to preserve att Liberty Body or Estate
   are not.[4]

All of these sinful actions were related to violence. Not only did killing and murder proceed from Satan's kingdom, so did fighting and bloodshed. (Whether fighting without weapons was proscribed was ambiguous.) Standing watch while armed was evil, as was the reprehensible practice of fining or distraining ("robbing") the goods of those who, for conscience's sake, would not fight. All use of weapons to protect one's life or property, whether for offense or defense, was deemed to be evil. This first description of the peaceable kingdom thus served to proscribe specific attitudes and activities as incompatible with the Kingdom. It especially emphasized the evil of weapons—broadly defined as "weapons of whatsortsoever."

The testimony's second description of God's Kingdom was positive rather than negative; was more philosophical, concerned with general spiritual attitudes rather than particular actions—with one exception. God's Kingdom contained "Humility, Charity, Brotherly Kindness, Peace, & Love . . . Faith, Hope, watching for the good of all, & good will towards all, both Friends & Enemies." This emphasis on spirituality underscored their belief that purity of soul was crucial; correct behavior, wrongly motivated, was by itself not righteous. Spiritual purity, on the other hand, would necessarily result in godly behavior: when one stood watch out of benevolent motives, "for the good of all," for example, a potentially hostile activity became benign. Weapons were not mentioned.

The third description of the peaceable kingdom was both positive and negative. It set forth the reward of the Kingdom, that one's presence in the Kingdom brought "Wisdom, & Life Eternall, with the peaceable Fruits of Righteousness." The fruits of righteousness were peace, joy, and preservation through "great Tryalls inwardly & outwardly." One's preservation would come through Jesus, not one's own worldly efforts. The authors condemned the "Murthering hurtful Spirit, Blood-shed, warrs outward, killing men or women, God's workmanship, Death & him which hath the power thereof the Divel." In this reiteration of the evils connected with violence a new element appears: the description of human beings as God's workmanship. Killing, then, would be robbing God himself of his creation and so would be an ultimate affront both to the victim and to God.

Violence and the Gospel

The second section of the testimony set forth scriptural authority for the peace testimony and addressed its implications for believers. The authors formulated pacifist doctrine on the basis of familiar scriptural passages: "Our Testimony is, that this Kingdom of Christ . . . is not of this world, for if it were, we (his Servants) could (with carnall weapons) fight; but 'tis of another World." Although not cited explicitly, the scriptural source for this formulation is John 18:36: "Jesus answered, My kingdom is not of this world: if my kingdom were of this world, then would my servants fight." By including the phrase "with carnall weapons," the authors parenthetically inserted themselves and their particular situation into the scriptural model, clarifying and limiting the meaning of fighting. In so pointedly modifying scripture, they seemed to hesitate to forbid all fighting, as long as weapons were not involved.

They elaborated on this theme: "we (his Servants) cannot (with Swords, Guns, or any carnall Weapons) fight, or make use thereof to hurt or kill our Enemies, or defend our Bodies therewith from our Enemies." In this passage, the authors made explicit the impossibility of fighting with weapons, whether for preemptive attack or personal protection. Lest there be any ambiguity, each prohibition was specifically qualified: each clause included an allusion to weapons. They could not fight with weapons, use weapons to kill enemies, defend themselves with weapons. The discussion, then, was directed to a narrow field: violence committed with weapons. This is particularly significant since the scriptural passage serving as inspiration for this discussion includes no mention of weapons. To speculate about why the prohibition against fighting was limited in this way is difficult. This more restricted understanding of the peace testimony was common among early Quakers, including

George Fox himself on occasion. Yet the qualification tying weapons to conscience had not been part of the 1673 Exemption.

The authors then proceeded to modify scripture again, transferring a practical admonition from one place in scripture—"put thy Sword up into the Sheath"—into a listing of Jesus' commands for spiritual purity: "Love Enemies, bless them that curse you; put thy Sword up into the Sheath; doe good to them that hate you; pray for them that despightfully use you, & persecute you."[5] The amalgamation of the two scriptural passages manifested the relatedness the authors saw between attitude and behavior.

Their reason for not fighting "with weapons," as expressed in this section of the testimony, was that fighting was incompatible with the nature of Christ's kingdom as defined in scripture. No other justification seemed necessary to them, nor did they offer any. They did not even mention God's workmanship. They did not consider, for example, that life on earth might have value for its own sake, nor did they consider preserving life because of the potential in each human to discover the Light within. Such reasons for nonviolence would be advanced only when the millenium receded as an imminent possibility and the importance of the Kingdom of God became less exclusively central to Quaker belief, with a consequent increased valuing of people's lives in and of themselves on earth.

However, by renouncing the use of weapons, and by following a benevolent course toward those who would do harm, a person would inevitably put himself in the way of danger. "Christ our Lord . . . left us an Example," the authors of the testimony continued, and the example was to meet danger in the same way Christ did: through suffering. They would seek to "outlive Cruelty through Suffering," knowing that if they were to suffer, the suffering itself was the will of God for them. Although God was able to change the hearts of all people, he often chose not to do so; "We know [this], yet we say his will be done." The authors applied this reasoning to the concrete case of King Philip's War:

> If he permit the Heathen . . . to come forth against us, & outwardly spoile us, yet with any carnall Weapons, we may not them resist, nor put Confidence in the Arm of Flesh, but in the Faith, & Patience of our Gods Hand . . . to perfect our Dominion over Destruction & Death, through Suffering.

The implications for the peace testimony of this worldview are profound. If one thinks that God is determining every detail of men's hearts and that he need only to change the enmity in some hearts to affect the behavior of men in an immediate way, then one is relieved of the responsibility to worry about the fate of others. God is willing their fate. It allows one to concentrate upon one's own relationship to God and the Kingdom—the contents of one's own heart and the destiny of one's own soul. It is up to God to change the spirits of others, and until the spirits of men are changed, little can be expected of their behavior.

Thus far, the testimony implied that a Quaker had only to renounce the use of weapons for himself, out of love, to comply with peace principles and remain in right relationship with God. In a violent situation, he had but to remove himself from participation; it was not his concern what might happen to those remaining in conflict. He might thus maintain his own purity, even if he assisted others who would achieve their purposes through violence.

It is the third section of this testimony that serves to document how certain Quakers had participated in war; probably, in fact, King Philip's War. After describing once again how Christ, the "Prince of Peace," ruled in his Kingdom over "the Children of Peace," leading them "in & out in the Way of Peace," the authors wrote forcefully of those in the Kingdom who had accepted Christ as the "true Light," had followed him and had dwelt with him, "yet notwithstanding goe out into the dark Spirit of the world again." This was an acknowledgment that even Quakers who had once benefited from living in the Kingdom could fall away and return to the ways of the unredeemed world. The testimony accused such Quakers of specific errors, who by their actions had betrayed an apostate spirit. The errant Quakers had succumbed to the dark spirit of the world through their "lust after the use of Carnall Weapons, in the Kingdom of Contention, & Strife (as Guns Swords &c.) to defend their own, or others Bodys, Lives, or Estates, by threatning to Wound; or kill, or by wounding or killing, the Bodyes of their Enemys." The primary failing of these Quakers was their willingness to rely on weapons and to threaten physical harm. Significantly, they were not necessarily accused of bearing arms themselves—just of putting credence in the utility of weapons. The testimony strongly suggested that among these darkened Quakers were those holding political power, those who were making decisions trying to protect others. The testimony, furthermore, accused them of "makeing Laws or grant[ing] forth Writeings, thereby to Rob, Spoile, or Imprison, any that out of Concience to God-wards, cannot make use of Carnall weapons."[6]

The testimony next issued a particularly sweeping condemnation: the "fallen" Quakers had been willing to "Justify, or encourage, by Word or Practice, Killing, Blood-shed, use of carnal Weapons, to preserve Life by takeing away Life; & Warrs outward either offensive; or defensive, or plead for, or live in, that faith which stands in Carnall Weapons." Here the authors of the testimony broadened the field of forbidden activity to include any furthering of military activity, whether by Quakers or others. It is obvious that many of the Rhode Island government's activities would have fallen within the definition of "encouraging" war. Many of the government's rationalizations for assisting the United Colonies were "justifications" within the meaning of the testimony, such as their arguments that all English subjects of the king were obligated to help each other or that they mobilized for defense in order not to infringe the religious consciences of those who felt it was appropriate to fight or that the "naragansets wear tretcherous."[7] In the course of the war, the Quakers in the government had indeed seized the opportunity to "encourage" war, to "justify" war, to establish armed watches, to place confidence in the "arm of flesh," and eventually to legislate against religious conscience.

With powerful simplicity, the testimony described the consequence of this forbidden activity. Those in complicity with war "wound their own Souls . . . & pierce in themselves affresh the Righteous Life." The consequence of unrighteousness was the wounding of their own souls. There were no reminders about the value of men's lives, no laments for the destruction war necessarily inflicts. The focus of concern was on the actors, not the victims.

Finally, the testimony declared with quiet intensity that all such works were

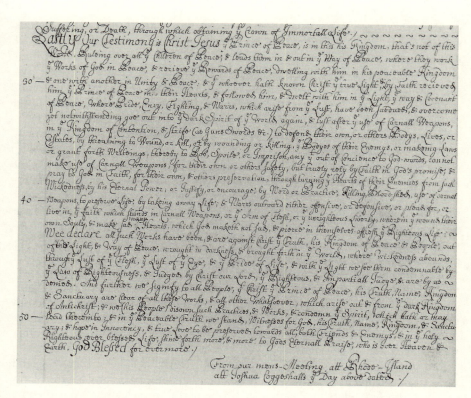

Figure 12.1. The Rhode Island Peace Testimony: The Final Section, New England Yearly Meeting, Ancient Epistles Minutes and Advices, 1672–1735 (detail). The Rhode Island Historical Society, RHix3 9281.

against truth, and "are by us denied." Such works "arise out & from the dark Kingdom of Antichrist; & we (his People) disown such Practices, & Works, & condemn the Spirit, which hath or may lead thereinto." The impact of such an uncompromising condemnation within a single monthly meeting in the close Quaker community must have been severe. The authors of the testimony—"his People"—consigned their neighbors to the kingdom of the Antichrist. Assuming the testimony originated in Rhode Island, the authors witnessed against both their religious and political leadership, for the leadership of the two spheres overlapped.

The testimony was a unique document, setting forth a rare exposition of Quaker peace principles. Yet even within this short and apparently cohesive treatise there were internal inconsistencies that exposed the range, variety, and complexity of Quaker peace principles. At some points the testimony seemed to define the peace testimony narrowly, emphasizing only the prohibition against carnal weapons, amending scripture to do so. At others, the testimony added "wars and fightings" to the prohibition but with the meaning of the words left vague and perhaps flexible. At still others, the document specified that "wars and fightings" included both defensive and offensive war. Sometimes the peace testimony applied to the details of life: watching while armed, fining others for remaining true to their religious convictions, and making oppressive laws. Some passages explained that personal renunciation of weapons was enough; that each person was responsible for himself, because God was overseeing the hearts and actions of others. Yet other passages criticized magistrates, not for bearing arms themselves but just for threatening or allowing their use. The testimony recognized no special adjustments in the peace testimony for Quaker magistrates carrying out civic duties. Finally, emphatically, the testimony defined the peace testimony as prohibiting any encouragement of warlike activities by others.

The inconsistencies demonstrate unwittingly how diverse the interpretations of the peace testimony were even among those for whom it was supremely important. The authors of the testimony seem untroubled to have included such variations in interpretation—indeed, they seem unaware of having done so. These internal inconsistencies, combined with the reiterations of the Kingdom descriptions, suggest that the testimony may have been pieced together from shorter versions and may have incorporated the drafts of several different authors. Even though the point of the testimony was to deny the validity of individual interpretations and to stress the unity that truth exemplifies—to insist in effect that truth could not be all-forgiving—the testimony's own nuances mirrored in microcosm the range of ideas that the peace testimony encompassed in the wider Quaker movement. The testimony condemned backsliders and so bore witness to conflict within the wider Quaker body.

The internal evidence that Rhode Island Quakers, or at least New England Quakers, wrote the testimony is unmistakeable. The setting was probably a colony, for the testimony refers to "heathen" ("[i]f he permit the Heathen . . . to come forth"). It was probable that the testimony was inspired by imminent danger, rather than being an intellectual exercise. It was explicitly directed against Quaker brethren, those who had once accepted the "true Light" yet went "out" into "the world" again. Clearly, too, the testimony was directed to Quaker magistrates, the only persons in a position to "make laws." There were few opportunities for Quakers to become magistrates in 1675–1676 other than Rhode Island and the West Indies. Quaker magistrates in Rhode Island, by August 1675, had in fact already engaged in partisan spying and other assistance to Plymouth forces; Rhode Island men had already taken the field. Finally, William Edmundson lived in Rhode Island at the end of the war and signed the copy of the testimony read in Dublin five years later. He had the opportunity to be a conduit.

There is one anomaly. The testimony accuses the magistrates of making laws against those conscientiously unable to bear arms. There is no evidence that by August 1675, the date of the testimony, the current colony-wide Quaker government had threatened the 1673 Exemption, or that they had attempted to enact other prejudicial measures that the testimony deplored. The assembly had last met in May 1675, before the beginning of the war, and would not reconvene until October 1675, after the testimony was issued. However, by August 1676 the Exemption had indeed been questioned and had been modified in the same particulars as the testimony condemned: to "rob, spoile, and imprison" those refusing military service. Between June and October 1676, if an objector refused to pay the fine, his goods were subject to distraint; presumably, if he had no goods to distrain, he would have suffered imprisonment. The assembly that modified the Exemption in June 1676 still included twelve or thirteen Quakers, perhaps those who were the targets of the testimony. The "making laws" phrase calls into question the dating of this document and allows one to speculate that when the original testimony, undoubtedly written as a discrete document, was copied into the book of disciplines, it was misdated. If it had been written in August 1676—a year later than dated—the Exemption would have already been impaired, the government would have engaged in another year of compromising activity, and Edmundson would have had two months to reinvigorate Quaker scruples, as he did during Bacon's Rebellion in Virginia.[8]

There is a less extreme interpretation, however. It is highly likely that the governor and at least part of the council met on an emergency basis after war began. Since there are no council records between June 1672 and January 1677 (New Style), their deliberations are unavailable, and we are aware of a few decisions only through the fortuitous preservation of letters and casual allusions. Council of war records are also missing, but we know that Quakers served on at least three local councils. Town governments, too, had Quaker magistrates. The testimony could have well referred to Quaker magistrates and their activities below the level of the colony-wide government, where indeed many responses to the war were formulated. The words of the assembly minutes of May 1676 confirm the unceremonious nature of decision-making: the "Multiplicety of urgancy" arising from sudden Indian assaults, they said, gave rise to many "Suddaine meetings of Towne Councells, [and] councells of warr," as well as "privet orders from officers, commissions, and verbal orders." The assembly, acknowledging the good intent of all such improvisations, voted them formal retroactive approval.[9] Amid such fluidity, the relevance of the testimony may have gained an entrance. Finally, Governor John Winthrop, Jr., died in April 1976, and was succeeded as governor by William Leete. It is far more likely that the testimony found its way into the Winthrop Papers after August 1675 when Winthrop was still alive, than in August 1676 after his death: strong evidence that the document was written in 1675, as dated.

"Rash Hasty Expressions"

The testimony was a form of discipline. Quakers in the colonies and in England had begun to evaluate each other's behavior. In the 1670s the testimony was almost unique in addressing the peace testimony as a matter of discipline; certainly no other explicit discussions of the peace testimony appear in New England Quaker records during King Philip's War. What other issues did capture the attention of Quaker oversight during the time of war in New England?

The testimony revealed divisions among Quakers within Rhode Island meetings, difficulties alluded to in meeting minutes. The earliest extant minutes of the Rhode Island Monthly Meeting date from December 1676, a year and four months after the date of the testimony. In those and subsequent minutes, there are oblique indications of a serious split in the meeting, a splintering that had been an inheritance from English schisms and that was to continue for many years around issues that remain obscure. While the testimony's spirit of judgment and condemnation may have prolonged and exacerbated resentments and hurt, preparing fertile ground for the growth of later dissension, it is not possible to directly connect the content of the testimony with later contentions within this meeting. It was a meeting at Joshua Coggeshall's house in Portsmouth that endorsed the testimony, for example, suggesting that he might have been of the more strict group of Quakers. Yet he was an assistant in the Rhode Island government all during the war—and thus potentially one of those too-lax Quakers the testimony witnessed against, unless he had voted against the prevailing measures.

Joshua Coggeshall did receive specific criticism, however; his difficulties reveal the focus of Quaker disciplinary efforts during a significant time. In December 1676 he condemned himself for his hasty "proceed[ing] About mariage after his wife was dead."[10] His self-condemnation was apparently inadequate, however, for two months later, Coddington and Hodgson were deputed to invite Coggeshall to the meeting, the meeting place having been moved from Coggeshall's house unless he "gave satisfaction" that he had repented. The minutes spoke of his "rash hasty expressions" and reflections "Contrary to truth: and that hee had binn much Troble & hoped: he should be more Carefull: for time to Come."[11] At this meeting, too, a committee was formed to "labor with" Henry Bull for his offenses.[12] At the next meeting, held at his own home, Coggeshall submitted a "paper of condemnation" for his former "miscarriage," or inappropriate behavior.

During these controversies, Quaker Robert Hodgson of Portsmouth, the keeper of ammunition for General Cudworth, was acting as the agent for the meeting to bring Coggeshall to repentance. By 1678, however, Hodgson himself had to give satisfaction for hasty words.[13] By the end of that year, Hodgson was defending Joshua Coggeshall, and Joseph Nicholson's proposed trip to England was termed "contrary to truth." Hodgson was several times accused of charging Friends falsely and speaking abusively of Friends.[14] By 1681 a group of separated Quakers "in opposition to truth" were meeting at Joshua Coggeshall's, including Hodgson, Bull, Adam Mott, Peter Easton, and his wife, who had sequestered the Quaker records, and others.[15] The shifting alliances of these years complicate an attempt to understand the turmoil and its causes. The turmoil in Rhode Island meetings may in fact have merely echoed the schisms roiling up the Quakers in England, in which fierce disagreements about the locus of churchly authority caused years of unpleasantness. There is no indication in the minutes that discipline had anything to do with military issues.

English Quakers sometimes commented on New England affairs. The matters they thought important, their understandings and misunderstandings, hint at English attitudes as well as the colonial condition. When English Quakers commented on the events in New England affecting Quakers, they often seemed to be out of touch. George Fox wrote to his "Brethren" at Newport in November 1675, when the war had been underway for five months—probably long enough for Fox to have been aware of the war when he wrote his letter. The substance of his message was to urge Quakers to keep their testimonies. Included in his reminder were such testimonies as that of opposition to the "antichristian ministry" and tithes, opposition to the world's fashions and customs, maintaining "sound" language, both singular and plural, being mindful of the cross of Christ, and keeping men's and women's meetings in good order.[16] One might forgive the Newport Quakers had they been impatient with such an irrelevant list.

After the war, George Fox became aware of the turbulence in the Rhode Island Meeting and on 15/4M/1677 he wrote the meeting a pastoral letter, in which he reminded Quakers to avoid hasty marriages and to keep to good order and in which he chastised Henry Bull for killing his neighbor's trespassing horses instead of dealing directly with the offending neighbor. "Such actions brings a Reproach upon the Goverment," Fox warned, " and the Governors should take notice of such things & I am sorry that any such ill action should have been done in your Government."[17] The particulars of the dissension, and of Fox's letter, are less important than the fact that in a letter written only ten months after the end of the war Fox still did not mention the actions of the Quaker government in relation to war. Killing horses and hasty marriage received his warning attention; "encouraging" war did not.[18] He was preoccupied with how the horse incident would reflect on the Quaker government—the "image" of the government—and betrayed once again his intense interest in having that government succeed.[19]

It is understandable if Fox, at a distance, had not been accurately informed of Rhode Island activities. He could not know, for example, that by the time his letter had reached Rhode Island in 1677 the Quaker government was no longer in power. Harder to understand, however, is William Edmundson, who roamed about New England during King Philip's War. His journal entry for his visits to Rhode Island between May 1676 and August 1676 shows that his physical presence did not assure an accurate appraisal of the local situation:

> [In] . . . Rhode-Island, where great Troubles attended Friends by Reason of the Wars . . . and the People, who were not Friends, were outrageous to fight: But the Governor being a Friend, (one Walter Clark) could not give Commissions to kill and destroy Men.[20]

On the contrary, both governors Coddington and Clarke signed military commissions. Edmundson's misstatement may have resulted from his having written his *Journal* some time after the fact. The local Quakers may not have wished to bring the military commissions to Edmundson's attention and so invite his correction. His observations suggest that he and George Fox differed in their expectations about the obligations of Quaker magistrates in relation to peace principles. Fox allowed latitude for Quakers as magistrates because he concentrated on the fact that magistrates were agents of God, with specific obligations "in the world," while Edmundson seemed in this comment to have assumed that Quaker magistrates shared the obligations of any other Quakers.

Edmundson was aware of some difficulty among Rhode Island Quakers. He wrote that "the Faithful and Honest-hearted among Friends were much help'd and strengthned by my being there," implying that there were some Friends who were not faithful and honest-hearted; and after he had been stricken with a great sickness,

> some loose Spirits, that I had dealt with for their Looseness, were glad, and thought their Curb and Reins were taken off . . . and altho' my Body was thin and weak by reason of Travels and Troubles with wrong Spirits, loose Livers and false Brethren, yet the Lord's Power carried over all.[21]

It is curious that Edmundson, who saw himself as "Curb and Reins," did not explicitly comment on the choices facing Quakers in a wartime government.

Nor did other wartime travelers direct any concern toward peace issues. After having visited the troubled Rhode Island Quakers, a Quaker admonished from Barbados, "a necessity is upon us to write unto you, That no Prejudices, nor Evil Surmisings, nor Whisperings, nor Back-bitings be or remain among you"; "stand in Awe . . . and sin not."[22] The men's meeting of Newport itself requested George Fox's advice in 1679, the meeting apparently not having been sufficiently awed and free of sin. They wrote a testimony against several of their members for "ranting," "disorderly marriage," sheltering disorderly walkers, and disorderly houses.[23]

Official Quaker oversight was institutionalized in a meeting of English Quaker ministers in London, who met in a body called the Second Day Morning Meeting to consider which Quaker writings should be published and to edit them as appropriate. The minutes of the Second Day Morning Meeting in December 1675 ordered that

> the paper (conteyning two letters from E. W.) printed by B. Clerk being a Relation of the Warr in New-England be not dispersed, but brought to John Osgoods there to lye till freinds see meet to deliver them back for waste paper & that B. C. print no bookes for the future but what are first read & approved of by this Meeting.[24]

This disapproval was directed to letters from Edward Wharton signed "E. W.," dated Boston, in the eighth and eleventh months, 1675, and printed in London. In the letters, Wharton spared no gruesome detail in reporting atrocities of the Indians "as a Scourge in the hand of the Lord" and predicted that the Indians were so wise in military strategy that they might "roul up the rest of our Nation, as a burdensome, and menstruous Cloth, and cast it out of their Land."[25] Neither of these observations would have been shocking in New England; that London Quakers found them fit only for waste paper is another manifestation of the distance between the English and American Quakers.

On careful reading, Wharton's letters differ from non-Quaker accounts of the war. He wrote as one distanced from the conflict, almost as a third party witnessing the "dolesome" scene: "This may inform thee, that a most bitter Spirit is entred the English, and Indians; in which they greatly endeavour the utter destruction one of another: so that the Face of the state and condition of this Country, to all that sees, seems very sad." Here the English and the Indians were equal in intention, driven by an identical spirit. When he wrote of Indian torture, he made it clear that he was reporting rumor: "it is reported"; "came news to mine ear." He credited the Indians with intelligence and forethought unsullied with the usual diabolical associations when he wrote, "Great is the Policy, and Wisdome the Natives do Act withal," describing their strategy of attacking outlying settlements and gradually pushing the English to greater and greater concentration and consequent starvation in the major towns. Wharton made clear, too, the differences among the English in Massachusetts: the confusion of the secular leadership, "like as men in a maze"; the ministers disagreeing about the cause and direction of God's visitation of wrath, some even finding the fault within themselves, all wondering why the Lord seemed not to go forth with their soldiers; the "concourse of people" who witnessed Wharton's construction upon the grave of the Quaker martyrs hanged in Boston, susceptible to Wharton's message that the destruction of the Quakers had brought down God's judgment onto the land; the General Court confiscating

Quaker George Bishop's book in a futile repression. While Wharton took note of the rumor that "some of the Indians did say to some Englishmen, That they did not think the Quakers would come out against them: I have not yet heard of much hurt they have done to Friends," he acknowledged that "it is likely to be a time of great tryal to all here." He could not separate himself, either, when he found himself a member of "our Nation."[26]

In short, Wharton's account departed from the self-justifying accounts that historian Jill Lepore explores so usefully in *The Name of War*. His account, and the London Quaker's disassociation from it, do not fit within her Puritan pattern of "reclaiming civility" through the very capacity to write about and define the qualities of those who fought the war, thereby triumphing twice, in a measure, through literacy. As we have seen, Quaker self-explanation was notably absent, even to themselves in their own records; and those accounts that do appear, such as Easton's, Wharton's and the Rhode Island Testimony are driven to establish their cultural distinction from fellow Englishmen rather than from Indians. If the Puritans of the United Colonies were indeed as reliant upon the power of the written word as Lepore's analysis suggests, it is no surprise that Quakers did not share in this endeavor. The Puritans, after all, were people of the Book, looking to the scriptures as final authority, and consequently venerating literary study, knowledge, and training. The Quakers were not Protestants, not people of the Book; although the first generation were steeped in the vocabulary and knowledge of the scriptures, they did not assign them the religious authority they found in the ongoing revelations of God. Consequently, these early Quakers actively disavowed dependence on the literate, on education, training, the priesthood. For them the written word did not carry such power, was not a crucial cultural difference setting them apart from others.

The experience of the Quakers in the Rhode Island government demonstrates that the Quaker peace testimony was ambiguous, variously interpreted, and variously applied. The peace testimony did not absolutely constrain Quakers in the understanding or performance of their governmental responsibilities. Some among Rhode Island Quakers found this reprehensible and chastised their brethren in the testimony. Meanwhile, Quakers in England only sporadically and imperfectly commented on issues confronting the Rhode Island Quaker magistrate, who was responsible for the survival of his colony, the survival of his family and himself, and the survival of his soul.

There were other Quakers in New England who faced danger without the responsibility for the collective safety. Such people rarely recorded private struggles and choices; only an occasional incident speaks for them. Freed from the constraints of official duties, and able to act as individuals, with worldly responsibility only to themselves and to whomever they cared for, they may nevertheless have been constrained from acting according to peace principles. Their convictions may have been weakened by a hostile and unforgiving environment in the other colonies, which were far from tolerant of religious deviation. Some may have been constrained by a shallow faith, careless ignorance, or mortal danger. Although they did not burst forth with any inspired effusions of religious fervor, many nevertheless modestly maintained a scrupulous disengagement from violence. All Quakers faced similar challenges; each Quaker had finally to confront alone his or her own conscience and courage and be ultimately responsible for his or her relationship to God. A few of their experiences appear in the historical record. The difficulty of their moral choices forces us to witness the fate of "innocency."

"Run the Hazard"

THE INDIVIDUAL QUAKER IN KING PHILIP'S WAR

Upon any incursion: "Three Muskets distinctly discharged, and a Herauld appointed to go speedilie threw the Towne, and crie, Alarum! Alarum!! and the Drum to beate incessantly."[1] "Major Nicholas Shapleigh, Quaker." "Violent in their carriage."[2] "Could not take up armes it was against our conscience."[3] To integrate these various phrases and properly to appreciate the moral task facing each Quaker during King Philip's War, it is essential to imagine the immensity of the danger threatening the people of New England; the fear of violence shredding all certainty and all expectations, just as sword and hachet shredded the bodies fallen in their way. "For all there were in an Uproar, Killing, and Burning, and Murdering, and great Distress was upon the Peoples Minds."[4] The imminence of death alone would have been enough to shake each vulnerable settler or Indian; when death itself was dressed up in atrocity, whether real or rumored, it would be the rare person who could be sure that principle would not yield to terror or rage. For the Quaker, alone in his small house, miles perhaps from a neighbor, fear and horror faced down the ordained love for his enemies. Moreover, he might rationalize, if perhaps men were not quite men, could they even qualify as "enemies"? To the extent that the danger and fear can be approximated from the security and predictability of modern America, to this extent no hesitation can be seen as remarkable or shameful.

Quakers were familiar with the promise of the new covenant, as they understood it: if they turned from wars and fightings, turned from reliance on the "fleshly arm," God himself would protect them, indeed, could be the only perfect protection. "Except the Lord keep the city, the watchman waketh but in vain."[5] Perhaps some felt infused with weakness as they considered the corollary to this promised outcome: if God did not preserve them from bodily harm, then they would be heirs to the suffering of Jesus. Suffering would not only teach others the majesty of Truth and be a rebuke to the unthinking or the fainthearted but would console the one who had the courage to seek the Kingdom of God through the narrow gate.[6] But could the honor and obligation such a person might feel in sharing Jesus' fate supersede the human love of parent for child, of wife for her husband?

On the dilemmas of conscience rested the possibility of death or life, of slaughtering or being slaughtered, of a severed head or a severed soul. "In thaire Jorney thay had mett with the bodys of sum english without heads," wrote one correspondent from Boston, and later in the same letter, "thay had Executed one Indian spie . . . [and] his head was plaiced at the govenors dore."[7] The Quaker soul hungered for a union with God, that could be severed if he should "live in that faith which Stands in . . . the Arm of Flesh . . . wherein they wound their own Souls."[8] The dilemmas of conscience gave birth to the familiar continuum of Quaker choices. If a particular Quaker had discovered the testimony against wars and fighting, against carnal weapons, and taught himself to rely on the protection of God and the companionship of the suffering Jesus, one might neverthless understand him if he forgot such considerations in the reality of a burning shed or an abducted child. This hypothetical Quaker may have remembered the testimony but dismissed its implications as too difficult. Another may have tried more strenuously to reconcile two conflicting dangers: the danger over the next hill stimulating her human impulse to save herself and her family and the danger a violent course would pose to her soul. Trying carefully to define the peace testimony, she might conclude that certain actions were impossible, certain actions were regrettable but necessary, certain actions were well-justified; the person she sat next to in meeting each First Day would come to a different list and a different set of priorities. Some few Quakers would be of sufficient spiritual capacity to define their religious scruples in the broadest way and to remove themselves from any connection with wars and fighting, however remote and indirect.

All New England Quakers must have been aware that there was a peculiarly Quaker testimony about wars and fighting, even if its mandate was unclear. Even a non-Quaker official visitor reported back to England just before the war in April 1675 that in New England "all men that are able beare Armes, except some few Anabaptists, & the Quakers, who will not beare any."[9] The renunciation of weapons, wars, and fightings called both for acting and for refusing to act "in the world," but the nature of action and inaction was undefined. Because the mandate was unclear, no Quaker could retire into passive acceptance of doctrine. In this particular time and place, a time and a place of wars and fighting, the time had come for each Quaker to define how he must act, or refuse to act; to translate belief into practice.

A Time and a Place of War:
The Historical Context

Quakers responded to the violent imperatives of war within a religious, social, and political context, a context that undoubtedly in some measure shaped their decisions. The religious or moral context was one of some unease, where non-Quaker ministers found justification for war in scripture and encouraged soldiers from the pulpit. "The Lord is a Man of War, the Lord is his name," taught Chaplain Samuel Nowell of the United Colonies armies.[10] The assertion "To be good souldiers is a matter of praise or honour" gave voice to a common Puritan understanding. Mystified by an intruding deviation from this norm, Nowell continued, "It is a strange piece of dotage befallen this crazy-headed age, that men should not use the sword."[11] And it was less than twenty years in the future that the *Christian Soldiers Penny Bible* would instruct: "The Christian Soldier should love his Enemies; yet hate and destroy them as Enemies to God and his Country."[12]

In the social sphere, the non-Quaker was deeply affected by his Quaker neighbor refusing fully to participate in military matters. If one person in a town refused to fight, his place would have to be filled by another, equally unwilling to leave his apples half-gathered and his family without fish. If his place was not filled, the remainder of the community suffered increased danger. Such separating out of some men within a community undermined the crucial reality of mutual dependence, sometimes already compromised nearly to extinction by an exchange of condemnation and persecution in an atmosphere of religious superiority. Misunderstanding saw only malingering, resentment reinforced contempt. It is little wonder that non-Quaker anger and bewilderment sometimes sputtered out in conflict and retribution, particularly on an interpersonal level.[13]

Political and legal arrangements became ever more onerous as obligations increased and corn stood unharvested in perilous solitude. In Plymouth, for example, the council of war anticipated that the several towns would be responsible for home defense, each town directing its local militia, each militiaman to supply his own arms. The duties of the militia were crucial, including such activities as watching, scouting in the town environs, relieving other towns, repelling Indians, and surprising lurking Indians in order to preempt attack.[14] For colony-wide service, the central colony government impressed a certain number out of the town militias to serve in a colony regiment under colony officers. Plymouth in addition assessed each town for charges arising from war. The council set forth in December 1675 a system of sanctions for noncompliance. The punishment should a man refuse to watch or ward with arms was a fine of five pounds or to be tied "necke and heeles" for a half-hour, at most.[15] Should any man neglect or refuse impressment, he was to be fined ten pounds or was to suffer imprisonment, not to exceed six months. Because men had tried to escape the press by exiling themselves from the colony, the council warned that any such emigrant would forfeit his entire estate.[16] By June 1676, the council of war was perhaps becoming more realistic about collecting fines, for they reduced the penalty for not complying with the press to being "compelled to run the gantlett" or pay five pounds or both; if the delinquent failed to refuse the press early enough for another to be pressed in his place, he would be fined an additional five pounds. Those who refused to secure adequate arms for themselves would have their goods distrained sufficient to supply them with arms, and if they "will not performe service with theire guns . . . [the arms] shalbe kept . . . for the use of them that will serve with them."[17] While the fines were substantial, the tone of the regulations in Plymouth Colony was restrained and surprisingly free of outrage.[18] In practice the penalties took idiosyncratic forms. Quakers Joseph, Zachariah, and Thomas Colman of Scituate, for example, had refused to train during the fifteen years prior to the war, for which they had paid fines "sum times 3 pound and sum times less." In wartime they lost to distraint forty-six sheep and twenty lambs worth twenty-four pounds eleven shillings, "wee being prest & could not take up armes it was against our conscience."[19] Each town imposed local requirements on its inhabitants.

In Rhode Island, men between the ages of sixteen and sixty were expected to serve in the militia but might exempt themselves without consequence from military service on the basis of religious belief under the 1673 Exemption. After May 1676, they were subject to fine and distraint for not serving, until October 1676 and again after May 1677. All were subject to taxes, whatever their purpose, and all to the watch, although the religious exemption excused Quakers from watching armed or unarmed.[20] In addition, since the council of war in each town had the authority to order the "settlinge of the millitia" and to put its town into "a suitable posture of defence," Quakers would have been subject to particular local obligations, of which no record remains.[21]

The Task

King Philip's War offered a multitude of specific challenges to the Quaker peace testimony: war taxes due; committees staffed; militias exercised; soldiers pressed; watches kept, armed or unarmed; ammunition and firearms distributed; troops transported and cared for when wounded; homes and livestock defended; blockades set; and garrison houses established and furnished. Then there was the enemy; or was he the enemy? Was it not possible to be neutral? Might one treat individuals on both sides equally? Must a combatant be killed, or captured? As for the prisoner of war, might he be sold into slavery? into limited servitude? tried and executed? or confined on behalf of another Englishman? It was in a confusing moral atmosphere, a resentful social atmosphere, and a punitive legal atmosphere, then, that Quakers tried to meet these challenges and answer these questions—to define their own peace testimony.

The historian is rarely privy to the feelings, reasonings, or prayers of any particular seventeenth-century New England Quaker as he or she struggled with how to react to King Philip's War. Only a few results of these imagined deliberations—the actions he or she took—remain in the records, unexplained, perhaps even anonymous. But in the aggregate, the actions taken by individual Quakers can in their variety help to define the parameters of the early peace testimony in this particular time and place, when its testing was infinitely practical rather than theoretical. Such imperfect glimpses can show the surrender to violence, the weakness and fear that people fear in themselves, the foolishness and glory of the good, the mystery of impenetrable belief, and the magnificence of a people whose time has not yet come. They illustrate the ambiguity of the peace testimony.

"A Tender Conscience Towards God":
Quaker Noncombatants

Quakers who interpreted their peace testimony literally and seriously knew that they could not use weapons in war. At the least, then, they could not be soldiers potentially involved in battle. Refusing to be soldiers threatened the mutual responsibility crucial to English survival, and some town and colony governments reacted accordingly, thereby inadvertently preserving a historical record of the refusals. In one such instance, the Plymouth court fined eighteen men for "not goeing forth being pressed" on 10 March 1675/1676, of whom nine were Quakers from Sandwich and Scituate.[22] Perhaps it was the substantial Quaker community in the town of Scituate that provoked Josiah Winslow's remarks in a letter of 23 May 1676: "The people in all our towns (Scituate excepted) are very desirous to be ranging after the enemy." Even though Indians had killed four at Taunton, burning a house and barn, "not a man from Scituate would stir to remove them."[23]

Pacifists and Petitions

Within one Plymouth community, Sandwich, outrage at the Quakers who refused military service was disguised in political reprisal and was at a pitch high enough to resonate even two years after the end of the war. The Plymouth council of war minutes of February 1675 had reported that several Sandwich men had refused a muster call, being pressed, and had ordered that they be fined.[24] Although the council minutes had included no names, the Sandwich Quaker Meeting minutes document Quaker refusals at this very time. Then in 1678, "Divers of the Church & towne of Sandwich" addressed a petition to the court at Plymouth, complaining that the Quakers had failed to help in the maintenance of the minister and the town church.[25] The angry petitioners seemed especially to resent the permissiveness of the town of Sandwich, which before the war in April 1675 had circumvented colony disfranchisement of Quakers by "recording" the names of all inhabitants who had successfully argued their rights to town privileges. The Quakers would normally have been excluded from being townsmen because they refused to take the oath of fidelity, but those who had taken the oath and become freemen before they became Quakers were able to vote. Fifteen such Quakers were included on the listing of townsmen in 1675 and thus could vote and participate in the property interests of the town. The Quakers, their critics thought, had been "violent in their carriage & voating" and had displayed a "turbelent spirit."[26] In July 1678 under colony edict a town meeting was held to readminister the oath of fidelity, and the fifteen Quakers disappeared from the list. Peter Gaunt, William Newland and John Jenkins protested on behalf of fellow Quakers, for they would lose more than their votes—they would lose their rights to town lands.[27]

But the petitioners' bitterness toward their Quaker neighbors had deeper roots; talk of the minister's maintenance and the right to vote was mere distraction from a matter that they regarded as an affront to the Crown and to Jesus himself: "their declineing to preserve his majesties intrest: their neighbours & their owne: as is well known to many of late times: & that such persons should have a kind of liberty by voating impleyeth to trample under foot the instant waies of jesus christ in his ordinances."[28] "To preserve his majesties intrest" meant, of course, fighting against the Indians in the "late times" of King Philip's War. Both sides in the controversy claimed righteousness on the basis of Jesus' "ordinances." The petitioners saw those who refused to fight as denying the authority of the king, who was the magistrate God had appointed; as denying the legitimacy of "Caesar." In their view, too, those who refused service violated Jesus' ordinance requiring love for one's neighbor—one's English neighbor. By refusing to fight, the Quakers might as well have actively overthrown their neighbors, the petitioners thought, through their "censorious & violent selfe seeking carriages."[29] The Quakers had the same biblical ordinance in mind but defined "neighbor" to include the "enemy."

It was Quaker refusal to contribute to the common defense that stimulated the disgust on this occasion; withholding the vote and concomitant property interests was the town's eventual retaliation. Sandwich Quakers were well aware of the true nature of their neighbors' anger. In responding to the petition, they focused on the particular accusation that Quakers had betrayed the king's interest by refusing military service.[30] They had, they insisted, declined to do those things thought to be for the preservation of the king's interest "absolutely from or in the sence of the command of christ jesus & a tender conscience towards God." In contrast, the Quakers averred, those non-Quakers who refused service and betrayed the duty to the king's interest had done so because they had concentrated on their "owne bodily intrest" and thus "must needs be farr more Guilty." While they themselves had avoided the press through obedience to Jesus, the Quakers asserted, some of the petitioners sought to "avoyd their sons being prest to goe out to the warr" for a base reason: "for their owne perticuler intrest which at most could be but the feare of the losse of their outward life." The ground of Quaker refusal was the command of Jesus that is more binding on the conscience "ten thousand fold" than either the fear of losing one's life or any commands given contrary to the ordinances of Jesus. Drawing a parallel between the "lost state & condition" of their neighbors in New England and "Judah" of old, the Quakers remembered the words of the Lord himself, uttered through his servant Jeremiah: "Cursed be the man that trusteth in man. and maketh flesh his arme."[31]

"Let all people take heed how they instigate or stir up rulers to punish those: who for conscience sake cannot doe that which others can," the Quakers warned, "for their so doeing provoakes the Lords anger." Indeed, they pointed out, the Lord's hand had already "touched" some concerned in this matter, making reference to misfortunes that apparently had already been visited upon the community. "Take heed, take heed," they intoned, for there is "nothing more certaine than that he will avenge their cause."[32]

The Sandwich controversy, by stirring Quakers to respond to angry accusations, led them to explain why they refused to go to war. The Sandwich Quakers explained that they did not participate in war because "they well know that the Eternall well being of their imortall soules is conserned in it." They restrained themselves in order to preserve a right relationship with God, without which their souls would be imperiled. Although the ground of their failure to fight was Jesus' command to do unto others as they would have others do unto them, they focused not on the "others" but inward on their own spiritual conditions. Their pacifism, then, reflected a concern about the subjective state of one's own soul; the objective safety of another's body was only incidental. "O that all people would consider as touching their imortall soules," the Quakers wished aloud.[33] The controversy illuminates, therefore, not only the fact that a group of Quakers acted in accordance with the peace testimony but, most unusual, the rationale for that testimony. It is the rationale that is usually most illusive; the behavior is more often accessible.

The Sandwich experience cautions against assuming that high-minded pacifism motivated all those refusing military service. Just as the Sandwich Quaker records showed that Quakers refused service, they also revealed that non-Quakers refused service, when Quakers impugned their motives for doing so. The town records, too, make "reforance to all those persons as refused or neglected" to serve.[34] It is not appropriate to conclude, then, that Plymouth officials were referring exclusively to Quakers when they complained, "many of the souldiers that were pressed came not to goe forth, especially Scituate and Sandwich proved very deficient . . . they did not agree to goe forward in any thinge for publicke good,"[35] even though both Sandwich and Scituate had substantial Quaker communities. John Smith, Jr., for one, the son of the Sandwich minister, was fined for not going to the Indian war.[36] The requirements of defense at home must have been a compelling deterent to joining the fighting companies that would be fighting elsewhere, especially for Sandwich, the gateway to Cape Cod. In another instance, during the Massachusetts mobilization for the Great Swamp expedition, a Boston correspondent wrote, "Several Men, some whereof are Quakers, will not go out on Command, and for their Disobedience thereunto, are forced to run the Gantelop."[37] If only "some whereof are Quakers," then "some whereof" must not have been Quakers as well. In fact, it became increasingly difficult as the war went on for Massachusetts and Plymouth to find soldiers to man the garrisons and go out after the Indians. The governments imposed more and more orders restricting movement out of the frontier towns lest they be abandoned, as well as restricting movement from town to town lest men succeed in avoiding the press. Not only did the Massachusetts government impose fines for failing to "practice scouting," and for not answering the press—four pounds for foot, six pounds for troopers—but "if their neglects . . . be accompanied with refractorines, reflection or contempt upon authority, such persons shall be punished with death."[38]

Nor is it accurate to assume that only Quakers refused service on a moral or religious basis. The Quakers judged their defaulting Sandwich neighbors as acting from base motives, but some who refused, here as elsewhere, surely acted from principles informed by other, non-Quaker, moral or religious convictions. Consider, for example, the astonishing case of the only man killed in the destruction of Providence, a man named Wright, who, while not a Quaker, behaved in a way reminiscent of the tales that are handed down in Quaker tradition. A contemporary account marvels at his convictions:

> he was a Man of a singular and sordid Humour; of great Knowledge in the Scriptures, but of no particular professed Sect . . . one that derided Watches, Fortifications, and all publick Endeavours and Administrations for the common Safety. [H]e refused . . . to shelter himself in any Garrison, but presumed he should be safe in his own House.

Moreover, he believed that while he held the Bible, he would be impervious to violence. The Indians finding him so protected and deriding his folly, "ript him open, and put his Bible in his belly."[39] In every respect, except in his faith in the literal protection of the Book, Wright might be a Quaker of the more scrupulous kind, one whose belief in God's preservation met the Quaker ideal. There was more than one path to pacifism.

"Going Forth": Quaker Combatants

There were Quakers who bore arms during the war. Captain Weston Clarke, who was sent to relieve Warwick, Lieutenant Robert Westcott, who was killed in the Great Swamp Fight, and Abraham Mann of Providence, who was wounded are three examples. But to conclude with certainty that particular combatants were Quakers or that particular Quakers were combatants is usually out of the question. There were no membership lists—indeed no such designation among the Quakers—and individual Quakers were mentioned only haphazardly in the records: if they were assigned a duty within the meeting, for example, or attended and witnessed a marriage, or wanted to move and sought the meeting's endorsement, or were admonished by the meeting, or were brought up before a court. The names appearing most often in Quaker minutes are those of the most "weighty" Quakers, the ministers or "Public Friends," the "elders in the faith"; the more "ordinary" Quaker rarely appeared. When comparing known Quakers or Quaker families with military rosters and finding a Quaker name on the roster, one cannot be certain that there was not a non-Quaker with that name in the same town. Often it is not known whether it is a father or son who appears in a record, and it is precarious to assume that all members of a family will be Quakers on the basis of one member's Quakerism, even though one Quaker member is strongly suggestive of familial affiliation.[40] It is impossible to know, sometimes, whether or not a person had become a Quaker by the date his name appeared on a military list. Typically, if a military roster exists for a particular time or place, Quaker records will be nonexistent, or vice versa. Nevertheless, with careful judgment, suggestive correlations may be teased out of the few sources. In this process one must establish both the relationship of a particular individual to Quakers and the involvement of that person in fighting.

Sandwich

Lieutenant John Ellis, Sr., of Sandwich may serve as an example. Lieutenant Ellis had been brought up before the Plymouth Court in 1657/1658 for "tumultuous carriage" in the company of other men who were known Quakers.[41] Before 1661 an infamous local constable distrained some whale oil from Ellis, for attending meeting.[42] During these years, Ellis continued to act as lieutenant of the militia.[43] In 1672, John Ellis appeared again in the records—this time in Quaker meeting records, for *not* attending meeting. Because Ellis was cited in the minutes for being absent from meeting, it is clear that the meeting considered him to be a Quaker. An elder visited him to enquire about his absence; Ellis told him that "his ground & reason was knowne unto himselfe: & he was not willing that it should goe any further at present."[44] Two years later, the meeting elders were still visiting and "laboring" with Ellis, who told them that he could not come to meeting "untill the power did move him or work it in him." That his absence reflected a difference in religious doctrine rather than indifference is better expressed by Peter Gaunt, a highly regarded Quaker in the Sandwich meeting who was absenting himself at the same time, explaining to his meeting visitors that he didn't believe in "visible worship of God in the world." In July 1678, Peter Gaunt was still officially representing the meeting. In 1682, he continued to absent himself from meetings; but as it had been to Ellis, the meeting was still tolerant of Gaunt, reporting in the minutes that Gaunt "valued not public worship."[45]

The relationships of Ellis and Gaunt to the Sandwich Meeting exemplify the ambiguity of Quaker membership. It is easy to see how later Quakers in looking at their behavior might disavow any military aspects on the basis that Ellis and Gaunt were not "really" Quakers, yet it is unlikely that Ellis and Gaunt would have defined themselves out in this way. Indeed, their vocabulary is consonant with an individualistic thread that had been part of Quakerism from the beginning. Their own meeting obviously sustained its connection with these nonconforming Quakers; it did not abandon them. Lieutenant Ellis, then, may be considered a Quaker, identifying himself as such by his associations, behavior, and words. Others identified him as a Quaker as well—hostile non-Quakers as well as other Quakers.

Ellis, a Quaker militiaman, was also in some form, at some time, a Quaker soldier. Ellis and his son John, Jr., both died during King Philip's War. John Ellis, Sr., most likely was killed as a soldier, for his widow, Elizabeth, subsequently moved to Sepican, a new community whose lands were distributed to the veterans of the war.[46] During the war, the Sandwich Meeting recorded no criticism about "disorderly" activities connected with fighting; it only criticized one Francis Allen for "bad carriage" toward his wife.[47] Judgments about the range of Quaker behavior, then, are dependent on the definition of *who* was a Quaker. It is important that one not make such judgments retroactively, using as standard a particular tendency within Quakerism that eventually won out and became the predominant understanding.

Yarmouth and Barnstable

Ananias Wing, his brother Joseph Wing, and Richard Taylor, of Yarmouth in Plymouth Colony, were all soldiers who participated in military expeditions to Rhode Island during the war. The names of Ananias Wing and Richard Taylor may be found on Yarmouth rosters for two of the expeditions to Mount Hope and Narragansett.[48] Ananias and his brother Joseph were identified in a contemporary source as sons of John Wing, Jr., and described as "inhabitants of Yarmouth who lost horses in the first expedition to Mount Hope against King Philip in 1675"; Ananias served as a soldier again under Captain John Gorham in the second expedition of 1676.[49] There is persuasive evidence that all were Quakers. Ananias and Joseph Wing were the nephews of Stephen and Daniel Wing, prominent Sandwich Quakers; their father was the John Wing who was building a house near Yarmouth in 1659 and who signed several Quaker marriage certificates beginning in 1675.[50] The names of both Ananias Wing and Richard Taylor of Yarmouth, Plymouth Colony, appeared on Quaker marriage certificates in 1684, 1686, and 1682; a Joseph Wing was married in 1710. Richard Taylor, "Now Liveing in the township of yarmouth," was the father of the bride in the 1682 Quaker marriage; it is likely that the soldier was also a Quaker.[51] Ananias Wing, Richard Taylor, and John Goodspeed of Barnstable were granted land in the township known as Narragansett No. 7, land granted to those who had fought in the Narragansett campaign. A John Goodspeed signed a marriage certificate in 1679.[52]

Plymouth

The Plymouth court commissioned a Lieutenant Joseph Howland to guard Indian prisoners in June 1675, and a Joseph Howland of Duxbury signed a Quaker marriage certificate in 1676 and was married under the care of Quakers in 1683.[53] These men were cousins, one a Quaker and one not; such are the difficulties in this analysis. Such suggestive but inconclusive examples abound: a Benjamin Woodworth of Scituate is listed as a soldier during the war and as a soldier to be paid in land after the war; a John Woodworth of Scituate signed a Quaker marriage certificate in 1675. Although the name is not common, it would be foolish to do more than wonder if Benjamin were a Quaker.[54]

The Plymouth court did commission one known Quaker, however: John Smith, originally from Plymouth. There he married Deborah, the daughter of Quaker Arthur Howland of Marshfield. He became a Quaker and was fined in Plymouth for holding Quaker meetings in his house and "entertaining" foreign Quakers.[55] Smith moved to Dartmouth about 1665, and the Plymouth court appointed him lieutenant of the Dartmouth military company in March 1673/74.[56] His activities during King Philip's War are unknown.

Hampton

Hampton, in Massachusetts (now New Hampshire), was home to several families of Quakers by the 1670s. Men whose names appear as Quakers in various records were known to have been in military service in 1675 and 1676: Caleb and his brother Ebenezer Perkins; John Stanyan; Henry Dow; Ephraim, James, and William Marston; John and Christopher Hussey; and perhaps Captain Benjamin Swett.[57] Caleb Perkins appears on a scrawled roster of recruits from Hampton and on a military company wage list from 24 August 1676, for his wages due of one pound, fifteen shillings. Caleb Perkins was convicted before a Salisbury court for holding a Quaker meeting in 1674.[58] John Stanyan is on the same list of military recruits and is designated on that list "to conduct this party to your honour." Stanyan, too, was convicted for meeting with Quakers in 1674. He was at the yearly meeting at Salem in 1682.[59] Thomas Cram and Abraham Chase were on the military list, as well as the list of those convicted for meeting with Quakers.[60] A Henry Dow was listed with fellow townsman Benjamin Swett for the Narragansett campaign and was a military officer for many years, serving as well in King William's War beginning in 1689. Henry Dow was later thought to be a Quaker, but whether he was a Quaker by 1675 is not known. His nephew Henry was an active Quaker.[61] Three other soldiers share a family name with families later listed as Quakers. Soldiers Ephraim, James, and William Marston are most intriguing. Ephraim "Matson" was credited with service at the Chelmsford garrison in February 1675 and again for wages in August 1676. James and William Marston were listed with Hampton soldiers in

February 1676.[62] William Marston, Sr., was prosecuted in 1656 in county court for "keeping two Quaker books and a paper of the Quakers." George Fox identified the Marston family of Hampton as Quakers, taking notice of Marston and his "two small books which declared against sin"; Marston was fined the exorbitant sum of ten pounds for their possession.[63]

The Swett and Hussey families were important in Hampton leadership. Captain Benjamin Swett is problematical: he was an active military officer, recruiting for the Narragansett campaign and fighting and dying in a major battle at Black Point, Maine, in July 1677. There is no direct evidence that he was a Quaker, but the fact that his two sons Benjamin and Moses, young adults at the time of his death, were active Quakers is strongly suggestive. Stanyan and Captain Swett's son Benjamin signed the marriage certificate of John Hussey's daughter at Hussey's house in 1683. His son Moses Swett appeared in meeting minutes after the turn of the century and was also listed as a soldier in King William's War.[64] Christopher Hussey was a leader in the Hampton community and beyond, in spite of his having become a Quaker in 1664. He was listed as militia captain in 1677, before the war was over in New Hampshire, as well as in 1681, the same year he was a member of the New Hampshire council. As Captain Christopher Hussey he was convicted of attending the same Quaker meeting in 1674. John Hussey appeared frequently in the minutes of the Salem meeting but not in military records.[65] Hampton is a convincing example of how important the influence of a particular meeting is for the peace testimony in these years. Clearly, in this community, Quakerism and military service coexisted. In another community, such as Sandwich, a strong leader like Edward Perry might bring about altogether different understandings.

Kittery

Several Quakers of Kittery in the province of Maine had connections with the militia. Quaker missionaries had visited Kittery in October 1659, probably converting about this time Major Nicholas Shapleigh, commander of the militia.[66] Two others who continued to serve as ranking members of the Kittery town militia were Quakers James Hurd (ensign) and Michael Thompson (sergeant).[67] Shapleigh served as ranking member of the militia after his conversion and before his dismissal in May 1663, when his commission was annulled—annulled for political, not religious reasons.[68] While identified as a Quaker, he was simultaneously called "Major"; for example, Quaker George Bishop, writing in 1667, continued to call him Major; and Edward Cranfield referred to him in 1682 as Major Shapleigh, a Quaker, now dead.[69] While continuing to be known by his military title, Major Shapleigh held Quaker meetings in his home; received Quaker ministers Colman, Tompkins, and Ambrose after they had been whipped through three towns in the dead of winter; showed his Quakerism again in 1667 by using the plain language, thee and thou, in a letter to a "Worthy Freend"; and was dismissed from being a townsman ostensibly because he was a Quaker in 1669.[70] Major Shapleigh was a wealthy merchant, a powerful supporter of Ferdinando Gorges the younger, and a leader apparently respected by Englishman and Indian alike.[71] Although his wartime military role is obscure, his leadership was unmistakeable during King Philip's war. Major Richard Waldron, leader of New Hampshire province, men-

Figure 13.1. John Foster, A Map of New-England, (detail), in William Hubbard, *A Narrative of the Troubles with the Indians in New-England,* Boston, 1677. Known as the "White Hills" map, showing Dover, Hampton, Scituate, Sandwich, Yarmouth. Courtesy of the John Carter Brown Library at Brown University.

tioned to military leaders on 8 November 1675 that he expected to meet them at Major Shapleigh's. Along with Waldron, Shapleigh was appointed 21 February 1675/76 to treat with the Indians and on 5 May 1676 was appointed to approve all charges for the militias in the county.[72] William Edmundson, the missionary from England, stayed with Shapleigh in spring 1676, holding meetings at his house; in his words, Shapleigh was "a Man of Note in that Country (he and his Wife were both honest Friends)."[73] Edmundson allows an unusual look into the tense interactions of that time and place. He held a large meeting a few miles away, then returned to Shapleigh's for a few days, during an interval of peace. "There came in fourteen lusty Indian men, with their heads trimmed, and faces painted for war; they looked fierce." He would have talked with them, but "they were churlish, and their countenances bloody," Edmundson warned Shapleigh; they left peaceably enough. It was Shapleigh's turn to warn his visitor, the next day, that he had heard of an insurrection stirring, but Edmundson carried out his plan to have a meeting on Great Island. After he had left, he learned that the Indians did rise and "murdered about seventy Christians."[74]

Shapleigh was one of three English signatories to a treaty with the eastern Indians on 3 July 1676. He was involved, too, in the treacherous events of September 1676, when four hundred of these Indians somehow "surrendered" of whom two hundred were sent to Boston for disposition, and most of these were sold into slavery, in spite of treaties. Shapleigh signed the transmittal letter about these captives 10 September 1676. Still, "as most acceptable to the Indians," he acted for the English in concluding peace at Casco in spring 1678.[75] He was fully engaged in matters concerning the war, especially in bringing it to an end; but also even so far as to host and perhaps collaborate with its military leaders.

Peirce's Fight

One trace of Quaker combatants appeared in a surprising source: a contemporary verse commemorating a lopsided battle. In February and March 1675/76, Philip's Wampanoag troops were back in Rhode Island, Mount Hope, and Plymouth. Plymouth Colony impressed a company of about sixty-three men under the command of Captain Michael Peirce of Scituate, reinforced with a group of about twenty "friendly" Cape Cod Indians, in order to confront the renewed danger.[76] Peirce's company encountered a small group of Indians near Seekonk on 26 March, seemingly trying to escape. Lulled into carelessness by the prospect of capturing them, Peirce and his men chased them directly into an Indian ambush. According to the English sources, as many as five hundred Indians surrounded the vastly outnumbered Plymouth company. In desperate defense, Peirce's men formed into a "double-double ring"; fighting back to back, all but a few of the company were killed. Contemporary poet-soldier Benjamin Tompson memorialized this battle in verse and suggested that some of the fighters had been Quakers:

> Here Captious ones, without their Queries lie,
> The Quaker here, the Presbiterian by.
> The Scruple dormant lies of thee and thou,
> And most as one to Deaths dominion bow.[77]

In the poet's eyes, fault-finding, sophistical Quakers and all their foolish scruples were among those who succumbed to death, all earthly controversies rendered irrelevant. If there were Quakers in Peirce's company—and it seems an unlikely detail to fabricate—they apparently had no scruple about fighting. Once again, nonexistant military rosters, the unsystematic nature of the Quaker records, and the fact that Quakers did not keep lists of their members defeat certainty, but the incomplete evidence is nevertheless suggestive.[78] Almost by definition those who chose to fight were less likely to have appeared in Quaker minutes, which recorded the activities and concerns of Quaker elders, those likely to be more rigorous about their faith. A Quaker soldier was perhaps a young man, not yet established in his own household; or he may have been one among those lukewarm adherents found in any religious group, hence not readily identified as a Quaker except by a chance circumstance or by being criticized.[79] The example of Stephen Wing, Jr., of Sandwich, killed in Peirce's Fight, illustrates the problem.

Even though the Wing family included Sandwich Quaker leaders, trying to verify if a particular Wing was a Quaker is typically difficult for those individuals more peripherally involved and for those who were young. Stephen Wing, Jr., is not mentioned in meeting minutes, so his connection with Quakers must be established through his family. His name appears in the Sandwich Meeting birth records as the son of Stephen and Sarah Wing, born 1656.[80] Stephen's uncle was Daniel Wing, the notable and early Quaker who signed his name to a Quaker document in 1658 and who is mentioned frequently in Quaker records.[81] The religious affiliation of Stephen Wing, Sr. (1621–1710), brother of Daniel and father of the slain man, is only slightly less obvious. His was not among the eighteen names usually listed as the first Sandwich converts; but his name does surface in association with Quaker leaders in court records. He and his brother Daniel were among those whom the Plymouth court accused of being Quakers in 1657, citing their "tumultuose carriage."[82] On this occasion (probably the apprehension of the very "tumultuose" missionary Humphrey Norton), most of the Quakers seem to have refused to remove their hats in court. Stephen Wing, Sr., was cleared, with Lieutenant Ellis and one other, because he was "not found soe faulty"; the three probably were willing to stand uncovered in deference to the court. A year later his name appears again as one of nine men, all Quakers, disenfranchised by the Plymouth court.[83] His next appearance was again among nine other known Quakers—this time they were to be prevented from acting in town meetings.[84] The best recent authority, in a listing of the earliest Sandwich converts, connects him to his brother John, saying that they both "later" became Quakers.[85] A former curator of the Sandwich archives wrote that Stephen Wing, Sr., heard missionaries Christopher Holder and John Copeland in 1657 and "quaked."[86] Three other Wings living in Sandwich had already appeared in records as Quakers: Samuel, his nephew, cited in meeting minutes in 1673, and John and Ebenezer, undoubtedly his sons, in a marriage certificate of 1675.[87] The Sandwich Meeting named both Stephen Wing, Sr., and Daniel Wing as "disorderly" in 1681. Thus, Stephen Wing, Sr., was clearly a Quaker, as certainly was his young son, born just before Quakers came to Sandwich and his father "quaked." Stephen Wing, Jr., would have been about nineteen in 1676 when he was killed in battle.[88]

Samuel Bourman (Bowerman) of Barnstable was another casualty of Peirce's Fight who probably was a Quaker.[89] According to one historian, Bourman's father, although otherwise qualified, was not admitted as a townsman in Barnstable, perhaps because he "favored the Quakers." The historian vaguely said that the Bourman family "early" joined the Quakers.[90] More specific evidence of the family's affiliation is the name of Thomas Bourman (Samuel's brother) in the Sandwich Meeting minutes of 1678 and 1688 and on a marriage certificate in 1679.[91] Casualty John Sprague of Duxbury may be connected to the Quaker William Sprague of Duxbury, who signed a marriage certificate in 1675.[92]

Enough isolated examples of Quaker soldiers exist to counteract an overly simplistic view of Quaker pacifism in New England at this time and must not be forgotten in appraising the extent and character of pacifist belief, lest important questions remain unexamined. Still, the examples are few and fragmentary; clearly the dominant thread in Quaker belief was the refusal to fight in war. Philip Walker of Rehoboth, in his odd and obscure poem probably written soon after Peirce's Fight, enunciated the common perception others had of Quakers—a reminder to maintain a sense of proportion while striving to acknowledge diversity. His poem off-handedly revealed that the very word "Quaker" was synonymous with someone who absconds from war in a shameful manner:

Elikssander thou to mars trew born
    [Alexander thou to Mars true-born]
whos multituds soupt Meedyanders dry
    [whose multitudes supped—consumed—the Medes]
thayd shak ther tressis turn tany in scorn
    [they'd shake their tresses, turn t'any in scorn]
quockwish say they & so away thay fly
    [Quakerish say they & so away they fly—like a pacifist say they][93]

Quakers may indeed have fought in Peirce's Fight, and elsewhere, but such occasional participation did not apparently counteract the prevailing understanding exemplified in Walker's poem, as well as the prevailing fact, that Quakers were more likely to refuse to fight. Both noncombatants and combatants ran the hazard.

14

"The Rectification of the Heart"

AROUND THE PERIPHERY OF WAR

Some felt "a tender conscience toward God" and were noncombatants. Some "went forth" as combatants. Some were visible around the periphery of war: seeking protection in garrison houses, offering sanctuary to others. As yet the Quaker meetings spoke with no collective voice about violence; the choices were still a private matter. Fear and anger, the belief in God's preservation, and the acceptance of suffering were all private adjuncts to the peace testimony and necessarily associated with it. Fear and anger resulted from violence and also established the occasion for violence; they had to be overcome to fulfill the peace witness. The belief in God's preservation and the acceptance of suffering assuaged the fear and made possible for some the renunciation of carnal weapons, wars, and fightings. The belief in God's justice assuaged the anger and made room for reconciliation. These beliefs made possible the "rectification of the heart."[1]

The last section of the Rhode Island Testimony of 1675 on peace gave voice to a strict—a most encompassing—interpretation of the peace testimony in asserting that to have any connection to war was "encouraging" war and was prohibited by the gospel. There were many who might be said to have encouraged war under this interpretation, aiding one side or the other without being combatants, such as Quaker Caleb Carr, who sailed back and forth across Narragansett Bay gathering and reporting intelligence for the government.[2] Among their number, too, were other Rhode Islanders about whom the authors of the testimony complained. Some who might be deemed "encouragers" found it possible to act within their communities in a civil capacity, serving on committees often immediately connected with the war. In Sandwich, for example, residents did not give way entirely to resentments caused by Quaker pacifism: they several times chose William Newland and Edward Perry to establish taxes for Sandwich—taxes that concerned the war "just past." The town chose Newland to "order the lands" set aside for those who had had to leave their own homes and land to shelter in garrisons during the war. A respected and capable man, he was called on for civic service in spite of the fact that he had exercised the role of legal counsel to his fellow Quakers, beginning with the earliest confrontations between Quakers and the Plymouth court.[3] And Daniel Wing was on a town committee "to take an account of what ought justly to be satisfied for in referance to our present warr" and to settle the town debts due to Plymouth "for divers perticler that hath fallen out by the warr."[4] Skirting the periphery of war, these Quakers were staying within the letter of the peace testimony; they were not actually bearing arms themselves.

Three major issues on the periphery—extraneous to bearing arms and fighting—confronted Quakers during King Philip's War. The first was the question of how far a Quaker might seek protection for himself and his family by worldly means—what defensive measures might be consonant with submission to the will of God. The struggles to assess the legitimacy of self-protection and self-defense, by setting Quakers apart from others in their own minds, stimulated a correlative question: were Quakers somehow immune from violence if they put aside weapons? Did God stay Indian hatchets on their behalf?

The second major issue arose around offering sanctuary—to civilians or soldiers, the able-bodied or the wounded. Finally, the third area of inquiry concerned what oversight or judgment the collective body of Quakers should exercise, if any, upon individual Quakers. Did the discipline of the meeting encompass responsibility for interpreting the peace testimony? Who bore the responsibility to "rectify the heart?" Although peripheral in some sense to the main objective of war, seeking protection "in the world," offering sanctuary, and bearing the responsibility of discipline were matters of serious consequence to people of conscience.

Seeking Protection "in the World"

Garrison Houses

The peace testimony was pertinent to both offensive acts and defensive acts and depended on different justifications for each. The testimony witnessed against offensive acts, such as bearing arms and fighting, because such acts contradicted Jesus' instruction to love enemies and were incompatible with the Kingdom of God. The testimony witnessed against defensive acts, such as seeking refuge in fortified houses and watching armed, not only because these acts potentially involved violence and were against the spirit of Jesus but also because such activities betrayed a lack of faith in God's protection. God, after all, penetrated the density of human society to the very details of each individual life, to reward his people and to "Thunder out of Heaven" upon his adversaries.[5] A male Quaker had to decide whether or not to bear arms offensively, whether or not to share in the wider tasks of war. A female Quaker, with her family, had to come to terms with that aspect of the testimony that impinged on defense: the belief in God's overriding protection and the concomitant belief in the futility and faithlessness of any human effort to protect oneself. In practice, the latter aspect of belief determined whether or not

Quaker families took any measures of protection; especially whether or not they would go to garrison houses, either semipermanently or only at night, either armed or unarmed.

Some scrupulous Quakers categorized as carnal, as "of the world," not only weapons, wars, and fightings but also spiked fences and barred doors, which were therefore to be "put off." Such means of protection, they thought, should have no relevance to those absorbed in achieving a right relationship with God. God reserved to himself the task of regulating the world as well as his Kingdom, even though it was beyond man's capacity to understand how and for what purposes he did so. The care of his people, the Quakers, was part of this regulation. Struggling men and women were struggling in vain in trying to protect themselves with physical means, when the only true protection could come through spiritual means and through God. Baptist Peter Folger expressed similar ideas during King Philip's War:

> But if that we do leave the Lord,
> and trust in Fleshly Arm,
> Then 'tis no wonder if that we
> do hear more News of Harm.
> Let's have our Faith and Hope in God,
> and trust in him alone,
> And then no doubt this Storm of War
> it quickly will be gone.[6]

To rely on one's own strength was an abrogation of God's rule, a sign that the person did not wholeheartedly give up his life to the will of God. Of course, New England Puritans shared just as intensely the belief that God constantly intervened in the world but did not think that individual efforts at self-protection betrayed a disbelief in God's power. Quaker leaders emphasized that God would protect the Children of God, either by protecting their physical bodies or by preserving their greater interests, even if those greater interests required their suffering and death. Seeing defensive arrangements as well as carnal weapons, wars, and fighting as incompatible with the message of Jesus, Quakers were to renounce these methods of operating in the world in the belief that it was God's task to "save" them.

The writings of early Quakers make clear their anticipation not only that God would protect them but also that he would carry out any appropriate vengeance against wrongdoers in their behalf. "Vengeance is mine; I will repay, saith the Lord," thereby eliminating, Quakers affirmed, one of the primary justifications for men to use violence.[7] The protecting God was also the just God; he would not only make a believer truly safe but would also avenge him perfectly. As George Fox described the judging God in 1652,

> He will plague the beast,
> burn the whore,
> plague and torment the disobedient
> and rebellious backsliders very sore.[8]

The early missionaries who came to New England were particularly fond of expostulating upon God's recompense of the guilty. Although many of their prophetic words about God's revenge were provoked by persecution, not fighting or war, the habit of thinking about God as protector and revenger took root with immediacy both in England and the colonies; they had after all suffered persecution in England and could not escape its severity in New England either. "Thomas Prince . . . thou . . . hatcheth thy hatred in thy cecrett chamber," Humphrey Norton wrote bluntly to the Plymouth governor in 1658. "The anguish and paine that will enter upon thy reignes will be like knawing worms lodging betwixt thy hart and liver . . . the God of vengance [sic] is our God."[9] Speaking "truth to power" in 1660, Mary Trask and Margaret Smith prophesied to Governor Endicott, "the Lord our God is rising as a mighty terrible one, to plead the Cause of his People."[10] Those who put to death two Quakers in Boston "shall howl and lament," Joseph Nicholson warned; "good it had been for them they had never been born, or that a millstone had been hanged about their neck, and that cast into the Sea."[11] Quaker vengefulness could be assuaged in words because Quakers were confident that God would punish in their names.

A myth developed among Quakers that the early New England Quakers were immune from Indian violence because the Indians knew about and admired their nonviolence and therefore did not feel threatened by them.[12] The Quaker correspondent from New England repeated a rumor in his letter to London in 1675 that Indians had told some Englishmen "that they did not think the Quakers would come out against them" and added, "I have not yet heard of much hurt they have done to Friends."[13] "The Indians rose in Arms and murthered about Seventy Christians," reported William Edmundson, adding, "but I did not hear of one Friend murther'd that Night." Again, still reporting from King Philip's War, "for at that time most of the People in those Parts, except Friends, were in Garrisons."[14] Quaker John Farmer built on the same tradition in a later war, writing:

> For I have been cridditably Informed that som friends . . . have refused to make use of Garrisons & carnall weapons for their defence . . . & have Insteed thereof made uce of faith in god . . . & hee hath saved them from beeing destroyed by Indians. Who oftimes destroyed their neighbors.[15]

God, he suggested, rewarded their faith through controlling the Indians. Moreover, the myth went, should a Quaker abandon his peace witness by carrying a weapon, he would be immediately rendered vulnerable again; in fact it almost seemed that he would be more vulnerable than others, for having violated his own belief. Farmer continued: "And also the Indians destroyed som friends who did incline to the uce of a Garrison or a carnall weapon . . . perticulorly 1 man whome his neighbors perswaded to carry a gun. . . . But the Indians seeing him with a gun shot him deadly."[16] The nascent myth articulated in King Philip's War was later elaborated on and reinforced by a thrice-told tale: in the first version, Farmer recounted a story he had heard while traveling in New England, of a Quaker mother, her daughter, and the daughter's husband, who disagreed about whether or not to go to a garrison in 1704. Although they had been "Exposed to the Incurtions of the Indians . . . the Lord had preserved them from destruction." The daughter refused to remove the family to the garrison, trusting instead in God; eventually the husband prevailed and moved his family, including his mother-in-law, and the mother was "killed by Indians a fue days after their said removeall." After continual family strife, whose intensity is not pleasant to imagine, the family returned home, "where the Lord hath saved them."[17] Traveling Quaker Thomas Story recounted the story in a second version with a few differences: he attributed the desire to go to the garrison to the mother herself; the family moved to a house near the garrison in town, not the garrison itself; and the same day that the mother was killed, the daughter took her two children into the swamp, where she felt safe from the Indians. But his conclusion was clear:

> The People . . . were generally in Garrisons in the Night-time; and some professing Truth [Quakers] also went into the same with their Guns, and some without them: But the faithful and true, trusting in the Lord, neither used Gun nor Garrison, Sword, Buckler, nor Spear . . . and great was their Peace, Safety, and Comfort in him.[18]

Notice that even those who chose to go into a garrison had different scruples: some would be armed, inplying that they would actively fight, and some would be unarmed, implying that they sought safety but were unwilling to use weapons. Thomas Chalkley supplied yet another version of this story, reprinting what he identified as the actual letter of Mary Dow, the daughter, to her children, in which she herself described the episode. Mary Dow wrote that her husband, Henry, repeatedly disparaged her certainty that she would offend the Lord by seeking safety elsewhere, telling her that she had been "deluded by the devil" and "took a wrong spirit for the right." When she relented and the family went into the town of Hampton, she wrote, "But O the fear and trouble that I felt! . . . [I]t seemed as if we were going into the mouth of the Indians." She depicted her mother as being in a "beclouded condition," unable to decide on whether or not safety lay in trusting God or in the garrison. The mother, in her confusion, left the garrison to move to a friend's house nearby and was killed. When the family moved back home, Henry Dow still doubted his wife's wisdom until Thomas Story himself validated Mary Dow's revelation.[19]

The three versions of the story, although differing in details, stress the same point: that trusting in God's protection is the only surety; trust in garrisons or the greater safety of towns was not only misplaced but somehow stripped Quakers of God's protection. Inadvertently, moreover, the story revealed that Quakers themselves were still divided on this principle a quarter-century after King Philip's War and required a morality tale to persuade them to a more consistent practice. That which more scrupulous Quakers assumed was received principle was as yet insecurely established. Yet the myth persists: Howard Brinton continued this tradition when he wrote: "The Quakers remained in their homes during Indian raids and were unmolested while the remainder of the population sought the protection of stockades."[20] While undoubtedly this was at times true, to generalize the myth to all Quakers diminishes the real danger and the harsh choices they were forced to make. Logically, if the myth exempted Quakers from Indian depredations, it therefore rendered Quaker moral choices completely facile and of shallow worth.

The garrison house during King Philip's War was sometimes no more than an ordinary house, minimally improved to offer more protection to its inhabitants, to which neighbors might repair if their houses were less well fortified. "Our people are so extremely frighted," wrote John Pynchon to John Winthrop from Springfield, that "in the very heart of the town" people leave their own houses for stronger ones, "as this very night three families are come into my house."[21] Sometimes, people would band together to construct more adequate fortifications to a large house, sufficient to protect as many as fifty or sixty men, women, and children, plus their most important possessions, supplies, and food.[22] Two decades later, Thomas Story described in detail even more elaborate garrison houses; it is likely that the description fit earlier houses as well. The strongest dwellings in an area would serve as garrisons, and their exteriors were "impaled with small Trees, sharpen'd like Stakes at the upper Ends, and higher than the Indians could climb over." The houses themselves were fortified with "Imbattlements of Logs at two of the reverse Corners," providing a platform from which to command the ends and sides of the houses.[23] Garrisons were effective; in many cases, while the rest of a town was destroyed, few or no lives were lost.[24] One contemporary letter-writer reporting on the sack of Providence in April 1676 noted that all residents who were in "forts" were saved. However, one Quaker woman was not so fortunate: "Elizabeth Sucklin was preparing to goe from Her own Hous to A Fort but delaying they Killed Her."[25] The significance of her case is complex. Her intention to go to the "fort" rather than totally trust in God's protection, as well as her death, simultaneously fulfills and belies the Quaker myth: it might be argued that, because she sought worldly protection, she became vulnerable and was killed; or the incident shows that Quakers in fact did seek worldly protection and were not invulnerable to Indians.

It was all very well to believe in God's protection, a New England Quaker might have argued, but to fulfill God's plan did not necessarily require that one must be perfectly passive. Were not fortified houses a way to "take the occasion" from violence, for example, a prudent action helping God along in his protection of his people? Most Quakers did seek safety in garrisons and seemingly suffered no misgivings about doing so. All of the constituent villages within the town of Sandwich had to build defensive centers, and Spring Hill, where many of the Quakers lived, was no exception. The defense at Spring Hill, home of Stephen Wing, was known as the "Wing fort." As Stephen Wing's house was small, the "fort" no doubt referred to a palisaded area.[26] Two Quakers traveled "east" into present-day New Hampshire and Maine "and came to a Friend's House beyond the River, where there were about two hundred people (some Friends, and others) who were come thither for Safety, and had fortified the House very strongly about for fear of these Bloody Indians."[27] "It was a needful time," they went on, for Indians had killed two Quakers not three miles from that place; "and the Power of the Lord was with us, and was our Support."[28] They felt God's support for their missionary efforts; they did not think of his support as preserving their lives, and they joined their friends in the garrison house. One reads of two garrison houses belonging to Quakers in the subsequent Indian wars. A 1690 list of garrison houses in Kittery listed that of Richard Nason; a Richard Nason was thought to be a Quaker contemporary of Shapleigh's.[29] Quaker Richard Otis of Dover may have garrisoned his house as early as King Philip's War. The Otis family probably suffered greater loss than any other English family in the Indian wars: he was killed with two children in his garrison house in 1689; two more children and a son-in-law were killed subsequently; his wife, four other children, and three grandchildren were captured, and two of them did not return.[30]

Quakers were among the first purchasers and settlers in Dartmouth, Plymouth Colony, where garrison houses would prove crucial to survival. Henry Howland of Sandwich was one of the first settlers; it was his son Zoar or Zoeth who was killed at Tiverton in 1676.[31] At the time of King Philip's War, Baptists and Quakers had built substantial two-story dwellings in the town, three of which were garrisoned. Indians attacked and burned the town in July 1675. "At New Dartmouth (. . . most of them Quakers) they burnt all their houses but one, viz 29, and slew several persons."[32] Most Quakers, then, must have made use of the garrison house. John Russell's garrison was located in the Quaker section of town, and those defending Russell's garrison took Indian captives.[33]

In May 1676 Indians attacked Scituate, burning houses on their way to the garrison house at Charles Stockbridge's. A Quaker woman, Mrs. Ewell, was alone in her house with her infant grandchild John Northy. Seeing Indians rushing down the hill to her house, she distractedly fled to the nearby garrison house, leaving the infant behind. Indians entered her house, took bread from the oven, ignored the sleeping baby, and went on to attack the garrison. Astoundingly, during the battle Mrs. Ewell managed to leave the garrison, return home, retrieve the still sleeping baby, and take him safely back with her to the garrison.[34] This John Northy appears in Quaker minutes of the next century.[35]

Quakers were not immune from the violence all around them. A Quaker woman who had been imprisoned at Boston for about a month, with "John Eston's Son," disproved the stereotype that Indians would leave Quakers alone: "I cannot now give you an account concerning my Mother and Brothers, who were taken Captives by the cruel Indians some Moneths; but the Lord hath delivered them."[36] Nor did Indians single out only Quakers for merciful treatment. King Philip had known and admired a Captain Thomas Willett and had ordered that his family not be harmed. When by mistake "stranger" Indians killed Willett's son Hezekiah and brought his head to Philip, probably expecting praise, Philip in grief took the head and combed the hair and adorned it with wampum.[37]

Those Quakers who were more strict with themselves and stayed clear of garrisons were more courageous or fatally foolish, depending on who was making the judgment. Farmer's judgment was unambiguous: "Blessed bee the Lord for his goodnes to those that trust in him with all their Harts & do not lean to their own understandings nor to any other besides the Lord for defence & teaching & all other good things."[38] Others, non-Quakers, found the failure to take defensive precautions foolhardy, and their concern for their friends had them trying to persuade them to another course. Matthias Nicolls and his friend Governor John Winthrop, Jr., had obviously worried together, while both were visiting in Boston, about the safety of two of their Quaker friends, Governor William Coddington and Nathaniel Sylvester of Shelter Island in New York. Nicolls subsequently wrote Winthrop about his effort "according to your direction" to convince Sylvester to "make some sort of fortification about his house." The argument he used with Sylvester, dressed in his "best Rhetorick," was the example of his Quaker "brother" Coddington, who, reported Nicolls, if he "did not cause it to bee done himselfe" would nevertheless "permitt his wife to Sett a pallisadoed fortification about his house." Nicolls thought Codding-ton's compromise would be convincing, deeming Sylvester "not altogether averse from it," but Sylvester's polite demurral, if unstated, is obvious: he "pleaded want of hands for defence," implying that fortification would be pointless, and he hoped to have enough warning of any trouble so that he might "fly with his family." (Nicolls was skeptical of this maneuver, with Sylvester's wife "big with Child" and their hav-ing ten small children.)[39] This small kindliness among friends illuminates great mat-ters: it shows that Nicolls and Winthrop knew Quakers to be opposed to "carnal" measures of defense; it suggests marital discussion and perhaps disagreement in the Coddington family; it shows Coddington's fear leading him to contorted legalisms; and it shows Sylvester seeing danger realistically but standing firm on his principles. In a later war, traveling Quaker Thomas Story delimited the parameters of the issue by commenting on reality while upholding an ideal: "most [Quakers] went into Gar-risons to lodge in the Nights, and some not, but trusted in the Lord; and we kept clear of all Garrisons, always lodging without their Bounds, and Protection of their Guns or Arms."[40] A single standard of behavior, in this as in many aspects of the Quaker peace testimony, did not prevail. It is this continuum of behavior among the Quakers that is significant and, defying easy expectations, renders their community far more complex and intriguing than it sometimes appears.

Sanctuary

Individual Quakers who lived on Aquidneck Island were involved in a particularly vital way with the consequences of war, because Aquidneck became a sanctuary for refugees and casualties of the war. Although the Rhode Island government un-doubtedly sponsored the provision of sanctuary, individual civilians, including Quakers, were the people bearing the burden. When the residents of Aquidneck Is-land offered sanctuary to Rhode Island civilians from the mainland, as well as to wounded soldiers after battle and to tired troops preparing for battle, it involved a major effort, requiring the sustained participation of many people over many months. A Newport man suggests the magnitude of generosity—and the crowd-ing—that must have been required: "my wife and 3 daughters . . . are all here by reason of the Indian war, with their 15 children."[41] For the Quakers as well as oth-ers, sanctuary did not always take the form of unadulterated humanitarianism in one respect; it was, after all, only offered to one segment of Rhode Island human-ity, unlike the Quaker practice in the Revolution and since, when Quakers treated the wounded from both sides in the same facility.[42]

After the Great Swamp Fight alone it was a considerable task to care for about one hundred fifty men who were lodged in private homes; General Winslow wrote from Smith's garrison "I understand the number of oure woun[d]ed are soe many & Chyrurgions soe few that some will suffer."[43] The Plymouth General Court after the war reimbursed Quaker Simon Cooper, a Newport surgeon, for "surjery exer-cysed on William Die and others, of Dartmouth." In submitting a bill to Connecti-cut, Cooper described his services in terse understatement; for instance: "Edward Shippy of seay Brooke shot through the mouth & his upper Jaw brocke which the Surgions would not dress because they said he was a deade man. Cured."[44] A non-Quaker of Newport, Peleg Sanford, submitted a substantial bill of 103 pounds, 9 shillings, and 9 pence to Plymouth for his costs sustained in treating the wounded, showing the scale of the effort. Part of these costs included "damage sustained in my beding & other household stuffe, with things perloined by incomers."[45]

Such "perloining" surely soured the spirit of generosity and obligation that must have motivated many of the Aquidneck settlers who opened their small homes and provided prolonged nursing care for battle casualties from neighbor colonies and hospitality for refugees from the Rhode Island mainland. Not only was the Christian gratitude of the wounded occasionally found wanting, however. Roger Williams called Christian succor into question as well, harshly criticizing his rival Governor Coddington for niggardly treatment of Providence refugees. Caring "nothing for publick but all for himself and private," Coddington, according to Williams, refused to let refugees use his windfall trees to fence their planting grounds; prohibited them from planting a second crop on the common lands set aside for their use; and cruelly charged a poor man a week's work for a bushel of corn to feed "his poor Wife and Children in great want."[46] And refugees from Narragansett country complained after the war that island charity was "cold," made colder no doubt by the taxes imposed on them, even as they were living "[in cellars and holes] underground."[47]

A Massachusetts account of the events of 1675 portrayed Coddington in a more complimentary light. After the Great Swamp Fight, the wounded were sent to Aquidneck, as "the best place for their Acommodation, where accordingly they were kindely received by the Governour, and others." The commentator contrasted Coddington's initial welcome with the despicable behavior of "some churlish Quakers [who] were not free to entertain them, untill compelled by the Governour." The commentator could not conceal his outrage at the Quakers, writing "of so inhumane, peevish and untoward a disposition are these Nabals, as not to Vouchsafe Civility to those that had ventured their Lives, and received dangerons [sic] wounds in their defence."[48] The words "not free to entertain" suggest that these Quakers were not merely acting selfishly but rather were constrained by a compunction somehow connected with their religion—perhaps as simple as resentment against Puritans. Why did they feel "not free to entertain"?

To offer sanctuary appears to be a purely benevolent service, expressing sacrificial love, and so appears an appropriate replacement for military participation. In the context of the Quaker peace testimony, however, several possible qualifications intrude. First, the purity of sanctuary would be compromised if it were not offered to both sides in a conflict and offered without regard to the justice of their causes. Because the residents of Aquidneck offered sanctuary only to the English and not to the Indians as well, some Quakers might have considered the moral value of the sanctuary diminished. Some might have seen partisanship as a form of participation in war, in fact or in spirit; as such, it would represent a betrayal of the new covenant, a failure to love one's enemies. Second, to offer any sanctuary and to offer any care, whether to soldiers or to civilians, whether partisan or not, might be considered a contribution to the war, however peripheral, and thus a compromise of the peace testimony. Some might have deplored the housing of soldiers as a form of military participation. If indeed these Quakers who "were not free to entertain" the soldiers from the Great Swamp Fight were uncooperative because of their religious scruples, then this is yet more evidence that there was by this time significant disagreement among the Quakers themselves about the proper degree of participation in the turmoil that was all around them.[49]

Even the extremely sparse evidence of the actions of individual Quakers during King Philip's War discloses that Quakers were far from uniform in their interpretations of, interest in, or commitment to the peace testimony. The expectation of outsiders that Quakers did not bear arms suggests that the peace testimony in this

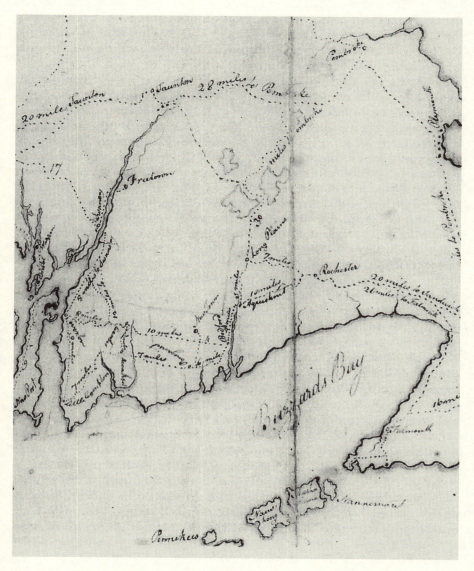

Figure 14.1. A Map of all Friends Meetings belonging to the Yearly Meeting of Rhode Island, 1782 (detail). A road map showing distances and routes between Quaker meetings a century after King Philip's War. Undoubtedly for the use of traveling Quakers. Courtesy of the John Carter Brown Library at Brown University.

limited sense was dominant among the Quakers. But more peripheral aspects of the testimony's implications were uncertain, to outsiders and to Quakers alike. New England Quakers were in the process of defining for themselves their obligations under the peace testimony—defining by default or by serious consideration, by omission or commission, by reference to scripture or to tradition. Often, in a preference for purity, later Quakers and other observers have defined out of the Society of Friends those early Quakers who chose paths inconsonant with later understandings of the peace witness. Finding discordant behavior, in modern terms, these writers have assumed that by definition these persons must not have been Quakers. It is as if they have chosen to retroactively read out of meeting those whose choices make them uncomfortable.[50]

In contrast, even the more pious New England Quakers themselves did not read these people out of meeting, did not exclude those with different understandings of their obligations under the peace testimony. The virtual absence of any issues occasioned by the war in Quaker records of this period, except for the Rhode Island Testimony of 1675, and especially the absence of any sign that meetings imposed any disciplinary measures connected with war, reveals in a most compelling way that no certainty about the parameters of the peace testimony had developed. The sole reference to the war in the Sandwich Meeting minutes during 1675 and 1676, for instance, was a concern for one Samuel Hicks of Cushnett, because of "his Great Loss by reason of the indian troubles."[51] None of the extant meeting minutes for the war and immediate postwar period mention any condemnations of individual Quakers for war-related activities. Even the complaints appearing in the Rhode Island Testimony issuing from the "men's-Meeting att Joshua Coggeshall's" did not identify or hold accountable particular individuals, although the authors clearly had particular individuals in mind. Their complaints did not result in meeting action, unless they were reflected in the temporary separation of some Quakers from the larger group in Newport. Yet this seems unlikely, since some from each group were implicated in the war effort.

An epistle from the general meeting held at William Coddington's in June 1676, during King Philip's War, epitomizes the lack of official Quaker attention to the responsibilities of Quakers under the peace testimony.[52] The epistle, a pastoral letter directed to all Quakers, discussed the principle of collective discipline and the duty of each meeting to admonish its wayward members. Resting its prescriptions on the belief that God "hath . . . taught us to deny the Customs, Fashions, & Words, of the World, which are evil, & to bear a Testimony against it," the general meeting recognized its own responsibility "to stir up the pure mind in one another, that the Principles of the blessed Truth, be allways stood in" and assigned to each particular men's and women's meeting the duty to admonish "all that shall walk disorderly." The epistle then defined the offenses that constituted disorderly walking. Keeping in mind that the epistle was written during King Philip's War, the list of offenses is instructive:

not to keep the form of sound words,
or use or wear needless Attire
or to oppress or defraud any man in his dealings . . .
or that doth not endeavour to bring up their Children . . . in the fear of the
    Lord,

& [rather] that they use plain language,

& wear plain & decent Cloathing,

& demean themselves (in all things Acording to the Truth, which they make a Profession of . . .)[53]

The list included nothing specifically having to do with the peace witness: no admonitions about not bearing arms, transporting soldiers, fortifying houses, training, paying fines for avoiding the press, or any other activities that New England Quakers might have seen as incompatible with the peace testimony. The omission is persuasive evidence that New England Quakers were not sufficiently in accord on the peace testimony to standardize its practical meaning. The requirements flowing from the testimony were too variously understood for meetings to pass judgment upon particular Quakers. Thus, even Quaker soldiers were not admonished, at least not officially by the meetings. Far from being established by the time of the Restoration of Charles II in 1660, the peace testimony, while certainly existing among some in rigorous form in New England, was not yet settled.

Some of the silence may be attributed to the fact that the disciplinary functions of the meeting were as yet rudimentary, and meetings were perhaps reluctant to discipline their members, especially since lapses into military association would not have drawn the criticism from the outside community that Quaker discipline was often designed to forestall. In Quaker understanding, while each Quaker was to "keep watch" inwardly over his spirit, each was to take responsibility, too, if a fellow Quaker seemed to be straying from the truth. The form this responsibility should take was not established. As late as 1704, an English Quaker visiting the meeting at Hampton remarked that a meeting for discipline was only recent there and that the elder people were "of an old separate sort, and against it."[54]

In the early days of Quakerism, scripture provided "gospel order," the model of how to correct someone who had departed from the true way: "tell him his fault between thee and him alone. . . . But if he will not hear thee, then take with thee one or two more . . . And if he shall neglect to hear them, tell it unto the church."[55] In the words of the epistle from the General Meeting of New England, 12/4M/1676,

> If after they are admonished (according to Gospel order) they still continue in the practice as aforesaid, then the men & womens meetings is to be informed of it, & further enquiry to be made concerning it, that Judgment may stand upon the heads of the willfull & disobedient.[56]

Early minutes, such as the Sandwich minutes, record many instances where it was necessary for the meeting to admonish a member for a fault. If such a person did not repent or give public satisfaction that she understood the nature of her offense, scripture again showed the way—to shun her as a heathen. In the "gospel order," if a person should refuse to "hear" the church, "let him be unto thee as an heathen man and a publican."[57] The meetings did readily impose some "Judgment"; for judgment to be carried as far as to "disown" a member at this time was rare, but possible. Quakers on Long Island, for instance, disgusted with a small group of Ranters going by the name of "New Quakers" who engaged in "confused practices," bore public testimony against the New Quakers and finally in August 1676 "utterly" denied them.[58] This ultimate discipline was available to New England Quakers; a clear sense of collective obligation and a clear sense of what constituted "disorderly walking" in the military sphere may not have yet been available, and so the meeting records are silent. Yet even if formal collective judgement was not yet applied in this sphere, the normative conduct of different communities of Quakers in New England varied sufficiently to suggest that informal local influence was potent. Thus, Sandwich Quakers mostly stood free of military service; Hampton Quakers mostly entered into military service.[59]

When the peace testimony was more fully acknowledged as part of the body of "truth" was uncertain. Not until 1M/1678/79 did the Meeting for Sufferings in London resolve that sufferings on the account of not bearing arms and similar actions were indeed "suffering for the Lord and his Truth." Henceforth fines, distraints, and other punishments on behalf of the peace witness were to be recorded and preserved with the other sufferings for the inspiration of Quakers and the shame of the persecutors.[60] That it could not have been assumed before this time that the peace testimony and sufferings on its account were central to Quakerism and not peripheral is a possible indication why discussion and discipline regarding the testimony were rare. Not until the 1690s and early 1700s in New England did reminders about the testimony find their way into letters; and controversies over paying for substitutes, paying war taxes, and training find their way into minutes of meetings. In 1700, Salem Monthly Meeting exhorted all Friends to "Stand clear in there Testimoneys Against wars . . . and also Against paying directly or indirectly for not . . . Trayning." In 1704, Quakers John Smith and Thomas Maccomber of Dartmouth were in prison, having refused the press to fight in Canada against the French and Indians.[61] Rhode Island Quakers began to consider in 1702 whether "Friends could pay a tax . . . for the building a fortification." In 1706, discipline was intensifying: the yearly meeting asked those who "can take up armes and goe to training" to withdraw from meetings for business until they "give sattisfaction for such theare miscarriage."[62]

Perhaps because of their faith in individual revelation, the central core and emphasis of radical Quakerism, still a fresh notion, the first Quakers were to a measure comfortable tolerating a range of different opinions about the peace testimony, giving latitude for each Quaker to interpret his "leadings" from God, and thus they may not have considered individual behavior in this complex sphere to be a matter for collective review. The authors of the Rhode Island Testimony stretched toward the Kingdom. The Quaker soldiers remained Quakers, and the Quaker families sheltering behind reinforced walls remained Quakers. And the implacable conviction of some that they must not do violence shone the creative possibility of the Exemption into being. Whatever the reason, in the realm of war and fighting, these New England Quakers left each other to rectify their own hearts. "My Soul Cries with yours," wrote Edward Perry, "that the Lord will be pleased to open your Understandings."[63]

15

"All Things Have Their Beginnings"

Early Quakerism was an amalgam of contradictions. For those interested in the peace testimony, the first contradiction is that Quakers were dramatically steadfast and rigorous in many aspects of their spirituality and its translation into a coherent way of living. But some dimensions of belief and behavior were incoherent; unresolved contradictions contributed to the intractable incoherence of the peace testimony. The experiences of a group of New England Quakers struggling to work out beliefs when the reality of violence crashed against principle have raised questions that may help to penetrate the incoherence. Many questions remain unanswered. Even these can point to a more valid way of thinking about the peace testimony.

A fundamental contradiction of Quakerism concerned its very identity. From the beginning, Quakers were aware of themselves "as a people"; their sense of already being in God's Kingdom subjected them as a group to different requirements, a different way of walking in the world. In this sense, Quakers thought of themselves as separate; they were a self-conscious entity, the primary identification of its members. They craved coherence.[1] In common with other "chosen people," they demanded more of themselves and saw themselves as beneficiaries of unusual rewards. Their chosenness did not come from God's preference but rather their own choosing to be chosen, to respond to that which is available to anyone. They chose to be a people.

Yet, paradoxically, this was a people without a name, a people whose only specific name was assigned as an epithet and who were defined by others. "Those in scorn called Quakers," they called themselves most frequently in the early years. Their lack of a name reflected their expectations of an imminent, universal turning to "Truth" and, simultaneously, both reflected and sustained a highly individualistic society.[2] They did not always name their meetings. North Carolina Quakers, for example, spoke of "a meeting held at Henry Prows' at Little River," an open and amorphous designation, instead of "the Little River Meeting," a more defining designation. They were at once separate and undefined.

Quaker peace principles were dependent on their understanding of truth. Quaker beliefs about truth incorporated an ambiguity found in the New Testament. They believed in the unity of Truth, in the Greek sense of believing that there exists a body of eternal realities that can be known and by which each person is judged. The opposite of this truth is error. Simultaneously, the Quaker emphasis on the relationship between a person and God is reminiscent of a Hebrew understanding of truth: that which is to be trusted. A right relationship with God ensured access to that which is absolutely reliable. Right relationship leads to truth; one approaches truth through trust. The opposite of this truth is deceit—the destruction of trust, the breaking of relationship. When Quakers condemned their opponents, they as often pointed to "deceit" as to "error." Quaker Anthony Holder conjoined Hebrew and Greek concepts in the very subtitle of his tract *A Discovery of Two unclean Spirits,* in which he condemned two "Priests" for "working deceitfully the Works of Errour."[3]

"Deceit" is a more complicated word than "error"; "deceit" carries with it an implication of will, of volition.[4] This interpretation of truth is compatible with Quaker insistence that motivation is crucial—that intention, a "pure heart," matters. The Hebrew idea of truth as that which is trustworthy converges with the Christian idea that motivation is as crucial as correct behavior. William Coddington sent a letter to Richard Bellingham, who ordered his servant to tear it up; he took a candle "and burntst all the Writing without . . . reading any of it." When Coddington chastised Bellingham for "thy Untrustiness and Wickedness," he demonstrated his conflation of truth and trust.[5]

Quakers personally forswore justice by being willing to suffer; at the same time they took precise notice of what they saw as God's satisfyingly swift justice visited upon persecutors. In fact, they saw God's vengeance as the reward for their own trust in him. In the manner of Psalm 36, they were confident of God's "lovingkindness unto them that know thee" and pointed out "the workers of iniquity fallen: they are cast down, and shall not be able to rise." They were willing to defer earthly justice for themselves for the sake of ultimate justice. While their suffering and martyrdom may have at times looked humble, in reality they presupposed a healthy self-regard, a sense that one was valuable enough to make one's martyrdom significant.

A strong sense of purpose, combined with beliefs in God's protection and swift justice as a reward for trust, made pacifism easier. Eschatological belief also enhanced the capacity to forego violence; if Christ was soon coming to do battle, mankind was excused from battle. On the other hand, some Quakers seized on the same anticipated Coming as a call to battle, a justification to "bring in" the Kingdom. The same eschatology could promote nonviolence for some and justify violence for others.

For early Quakers, pacifism was vocational. Their duty was to obey, and God ordained love for enemies. Quakers did not muse about *why* God thought killing was sinful. Obedience for its own sake was enough; revelation was its own reason.

They thought in a tautology: it was revealed that they could not fight. Why? Because it was revealed. They obeyed, because they wished to preserve the purity of their own souls, to maintain their personal relationship with God, so that they might receive his immediate leading and redemption from sin. This outlook was consonant with early Quaker devaluation of intellect, of "airy notions," of theories, which, for them, were associated with a carnal mind. Ironically, they were more comfortable with their carnal bodies, whose behavior would reflect the righteous soul and which contained a spirit capable of *experiencing* Truth, not *thinking* about it. The body lent Quaker language its extraordinarily sensual imagery, used to describe spiritual experience; organic, bodily imagery of taste and smell, especially, validated spiritual truth.[6] Some have speculated, in fact, that pacifism itself is reactive, concealing a fear of too much physicality, an attempt to contain heightened sensuality and passion.

The absence of one element from the early history of Quaker pacifism is startling, an example of history's silence sounding significance. Many accusations were leveled at Quakers; notably absent were any accusations of cowardice or effeminacy, so basic to the opprobrium directed to later pacifists. This curious difference stimulates reexamination of assumptions about definitions of masculinity. Why did hostile contemporaries, eager to discredit dissenters, not seize on such accusations to disparage Quakers? Why would effeminacy be an impotent insult? Indeed, on one occasion, at least, a Quaker labeled violence itself unmanly, when a raging man threatened another Quaker with a drawn sword. The Quaker told the violent man that he "unmanned himself in offering to strike at one that would not strike again."[7] John Burnyeat identified those Quakers who complied with, or kept silent about, military requirements such as training and sending men to arms as having a "cowardly" spirit.[8] Again, cowardice was identified with violence; courage with nonviolence. The word "effeminate" itself stood out only rarely in the hundreds of documents consulted for this study, once when a non-Quaker used it in reference to himself. General James Cudworth, in the course of turning down a military appointment when he was an old man, assured the Plymouth governor that he was motivated by personal considerations, not by "an effeminate or dastardly spirit." Even here, "effeminate" may mean "luxurious" or "soft" as much as "unmasculine."[9] One might speculate that seventeenth-century critics did not see refusal to bear weapons, to fight, or to war as cowardly or effeminate because they did not really believe that Quakers were nonviolent; they believed that Quaker ideas about peace were a fraudulent cover for sinister or self-interested intentions. Or, seeing the physical torment Quakers stoically endured, they had difficulty finding them cowardly or weak. Or they did not use violence to define masculinity in as pronounced a way as do other cultures. For example, a 1993 radio broadcaster offhandedly announced that it was easy to establish one's masculinity in America—one need only register with Selective Service at age eighteen. The careless jest conceals a cultural truism, the equating of violence and masculinity in contemporary America.

The history of Quaker pacifism inevitably raises issues about masculinity and femininity when those issues are currently entwined with questions about aggression and violence. What was behind these anonymous lines in a New England Quaker account book?

Give Not thy Strength to women
Nor thy ways to that which destroyeth
Kings Nither latt pation overcom the[e]
but let Vertue guid thee in all thy ways.[10]

Without becoming caught up in the biology-versus-acculturation debate, one must at least recognize that features of early pacifism may reflect contemporary assumptions about men and women. One might postulate, for example, that Quaker emphasis shifting from the vertical concern with the personal transaction between God and the believer to a more horizontal concern with the lives of others represented a feminization of peace principles. One modern opinion holds that young males are historically most closely identified with military service and with violence because they are more "bounded" than females—are freer from involvement with family and caretaking and feel less responsibility for solidifying human relationships, until their own fatherhood. Females, on the other hand, have the model of caretaking mothers responsible for others. Morality to a young man, then, consists of restraining his own impulses. Morality to a woman is thought to extend to refraining from hurting someone even indirectly.

It is crucial, however, to separate that which is temporarily true from that which is necessarily true. The Quaker peace testimony stimulated new possibilities for women and men. Courage, for example, has long been associated with violence, hence a virtue more available to men. The peace testimony amputated this association because it took great courage to be nonviolent. It established a new connection between women and physical courage. It established a new connection between men and caretaking. Both men and women became aware of a transforming power, derived from the best within themselves, that called forth the best in others. Yet women were not impressed for military service, and men were governors. Did the peace principles have different meaning for men and for women? Contrary to common assumptions that women's domestic role made them more personal and parochial in outlook, may it not have been true that their slight distance from the practical concerns of conscription, exemption money, and war taxes freed them to look beyond the personal, even to relations between nations?[11] Hester Bidley, before Queen Mary died and while England and France were at war, visited her, asking for the right to carry a letter to the king of France at Versailles. She told the Queen "[t]hat it was very great grief of Heart to her, as she was a Woman . . . that so great and tedious a War was waged . . . and such great Calamities and Slaughters of Men."[12] The Quakers Hannah Bernard and Lucretia Mott, too, exemplify such global thinking about peace.

A dramatic contradiction within early Quaker pacifism arose from the conflict between private belief and public duty, between a testimony against weapons and war and a testimony about government. Especially troubling when Quakers themselves became magistrates, the conflict forced them to choose between two inherently incompatible duties—the duty to forbear and the duty to protect. Their rationalizations pleased no one. Early Quaker magistrates chose to reconcile political duty and religious duty by elevating the idea of the magistrate above the individual and relying on providentialism to assuage their unease. Many saw this choice as endowing the state with too much sanctity. Quaker magistrates themselves must have suffered discomfort from their private religious views because they disguised some of their activities behind subterfuge. Magistrates complied with military taxation but rationalized their compliance by asserting that the use to which taxes were put was not their responsibility. In Pennsylvania, for example, in 1709 during Queen Anne's War, the Quaker legislature granted money "for the Queen's use" with full knowledge of what that use would be. Others commissioned non-Quakers to oversee military activities.

A Pacifist Continuum

The complexity of violence itself, the vast differences between cultures, both geographical and through time, the alternating periods of relative war and peace, and the influence of a shining integrity have, with underlying contradictions, rendered Quaker pacifism far less coherent than it has appeared. The major coherence, in fact, has been the persistence of a continuum of belief and behavior even when the very basis of pacifism changed. At any particular time in history one can find examples of the whole continuum of Quaker understandings—understandings about why violence was evil, the very basis of peace principles; about what kind of violence is evil; about responsibilities of government and the use of force; about weapons; and about where to draw lines to separate oneself from the violence of others. The dominant or mainstream understanding of pacifist obligation has shifted along the continuum from the individualist concern for the soul to the collective concern for human life; from refusing to bear arms to refusing forms of alternative military service; from paying war taxes to withholding taxes. The dominant understanding has not necessarily moved in one direction, toward greater coherence, conscientiousness, or commitment. Consistent with the complexity of pacifism itself, shifts have taken different directions in different aspects of pacifism. The spiritual undergirding of belief, for example, may have slackened at the same time that people have become more scrupulous in behavior. One might be less concerned about discovering the will of God, in an immediate sense, and at the same time decide that one could not carry pails of water in a prison camp. The existence of a pacifist continuum reflects the fact that the renunciation of violence is a great deep, containing within it schools of sources and justifications and reefs of contradictions and requiring a tide of action and restraint.

The dominant strain of early Quaker pacifism was that of individual renunciation, negative in character, essentially turned inward toward one's own soul. Quakers concentrated on removing "the occasion" of wars and fighting from their own hearts. The Quaker could not bear arms or fight, even to defend himself. Gradually, the circle of duty expanded, with an increased focus on the potential victims of violence and on the consequences of violence on the bodies of others. Quakers spoke more and more about "that of God" in every person—honoring the potential for relationship with God, as well as its realization. Accompanying this awareness was a heightened conscientiousness about not abetting other people's violence, a reluctance to act even on the periphery of violence. Finally, pacifism became predominantly more actively assertive, as Quaker attention turned to the prevention of violence, to removing "the occasion" of wars and fighting from society itself through social reform. Quakers began to encourage all people to renounce war.

An uncharacteristic silence in Quaker records has veiled the complexities of Quaker pacifism. Quaker record-keeping, historically so comprehensive, has, in the area of pacifism, been minimal. The very incoherence of pacifist belief and the uncertainty about its meaning and requirements ensured its lack of written definition. When people cannot agree, they may conceal that disagreement for very practical reasons. Quaker recording of history was a witness of the unity of Truth for outsiders and to a degree was meant to be instructive for Quakers as well. To display the variety of approaches to issues of peace undermined the presumption of unity; it also compromised the ability of Quakers to plead that they were a special case the next time a Quaker attempted to refuse military involvement. Even when a particular group did seem to adhere to common standards, they may have been tempted to leave any "backslidings" obscure.[13] They were torn between two needs: recording an offense, in order to reinforce the standard, and not drawing attention to the offense, in order to avoid bringing a "reproach" upon Truth. The offender, too, needed time to repent.

Conversely, when a particular meeting did record sufferings resulting from pacifist choices, it did not necessarily imply that the meeting agreed on rigorous standards for everyone. While the members might admire rigorous observance of the peace testimony, they might not require it of all. Remembering that early Quakers, particularly, believed that nonviolence was for the redeemed; that magistrates and people "in the mixture" would still need to defend themselves; that religious seekers must not be hustled beyond their own leadings; and that coming to principles of peace was a process and thus unlikely among new or lukewarm Quakers, it is obvious that tolerance within a meeting was itself tolerable. Because behavioral conformity was important for a noncreedal, laicized body such as Quakerism, many have interpreted the absence of "disownments" having to do with violence as proof of the absence of violence itself. Often, historians have concentrated on who was defined out, or excluded, at the expense of attention to who was defined in and so have made the mistake of generalizing about a core of deeply committed elders and forgetting about those drifting around on the periphery. Formal exclusion, after all, was reserved for those unambiguously defined in.

The contradictions surrounding magistracy were an important part of the Quaker pacifist continuum. Some Quakers seized the opportunity for Quakers to become magistrates; not only had God ordained magistrates but righteous magistrates were essential to a righteous order, one that incorporated freedom of conscience. From the beginning, other Quakers saw magistracy as inevitably corrupting, because government necessarily must calculate the utility of its activities. These Quakers found their duty in forbearing to use violence, regardless of consequences. Pacifism was a demand, not a path to reward. Some Quakers thus brushed up against an interpretation of Christianity as *essentially* countercultural. They thought that the gospel itself required being in opposition to culture by definition, because culture was "the world." Perhaps, then, the conflict for Quaker magistrates was deeper than it seemed. Conflict may have resided less in any specific aspect of their duties, such as defense, than in a more fundamental and abstracted difficulty: the impossibility of being Christian and simultaneously co-opted by the ordinary. A peculiar directive from the non-Quaker *Christian Soldiers Penny Bible* of 1693 remarkably and starkly epitomizes the dilemma: "The Christian Soldier should love his Enemies; yet hate and destroy them as Enemies to God and his Country."[14]

Over time, Quakers based their renunciations of violence on different foundations. The changing basis of pacifism—*why* one held particular beliefs about violence—had consequences for the choices they made about how to act. While none of the underlying rationales for pacifism excluded others—they were of course intricately interwoven—nevertheless, concentrating on one's own soul or another's body did influence the choices one made in how to behave. In fact, *why* one renounced violence affected how one thought about the importance of behavior itself. When pacifism rested on a foundation of obedience to God and soul-purity, although a Quaker believed that righteous behavior necessarily flowed from a pure heart, motive was more important than behavior. "Right" behavior was not enough in itself; the consequences of one's behavior were irrelevant, and did not define success. One needed to love one's enemies because it was right to do so; the rest was not one's business. Consequently, one was not responsible for the activities of others. One might transport soldiers destined for battle, for example, because those soldiers were responsible for their own transactions with God. It was enough to remove oneself from the battle. One need not overly concern oneself with Indian victims—God's will would determine their fate. This understanding was associated with belief in God's regulation of the moral order and with a more passive reliance on God's justice. Earthly existence was insignificant in comparison with life in God's imminent kingdom. Virtue defined morality.

When millenarian expectations seemed distant and the preservation of earthly life was consequently more highly valued, humanitarian impulses crowded in upon otherworldly preoccupations and constrained behavior in additional ways. Instead of concentrating on the harm that violence does to the soul of the perpetrator, concern shifted to the harm done to the victims of violence, and the results of violence appeared more damaging. Merely to refrain from acting violently oneself was not sufficient. Peripheral activities that led to other people's violence became reprehensible. It was as if the definition of violence itself broadened: transporting soldiers became part of the battle, as it were. Behavior, then, assumed more importance and could be separated from motive. This basis for pacifism was associated with a belief that manmade justice could be efficacious in taming worldly chaos. It was this form of pacifism that deemed Jesus a pacifist-revolutionary and that required proselytizing for peace and prevention of strife. As a decision about how to conduct oneself in the midst of society, pacifism was thus sometimes associated with rebellion and sometimes antithetical to rebellion.[15]

With the increased attention to behavior and its consequences, conduct defined morality. Outcome defined success. Pacifism became susceptible to secularization. When pacifism became secularized, it became dependent on results. If refusing to fight resulted in worldly defeat, there was little residual reward for the pacifist, except, perhaps, his own physical survival.

Assuming that the tools of violence are ever more perilous, on the sidewalk and in the post office, from mountain artillery installations to heat-seeking missiles, a careful and deeper consideration of the goals and methods of pacifism is urgent. In the first place, those thinking about pacifism must recognize the vastly different premises for pacifism and their effect on behavior. The varied approaches must be harmonized. The obvious difficulty for secular pacifism, compared to pacifism based on religious obedience, for example, is how to motivate people to choose nonviolence when the method fails to accomplish the goal. A pacifist animated by spiritual belief does not necessarily anticipate a just outcome. Quaker John Woolman warned that not fighting when "wrongly Invaded" would require "great self-denial and Resignation of ourselves to God."[16] What kind of secular restraints can equal the power of religious belief? Can secular fears—of societal disorder, of retaliation, of annihilation itself—control choices as effectively as does the fear of God? What kind of moral commitment or legal authority can equal "the rectification of the heart"?

The greatest initial impediment to peace in the present day is an unexamined assumption—a prior assumption that is rarely even raised, let alone challenged: that the psychological nature of human beings is incompatible with sustained avoidance of fighting and war. It remains virtually unquestioned that human aggression is necessarily and inevitably dominant within human nature.[17] It is this assumption that underlies the common perception that pacifism itself is faintly—or militantly—pathological. To renounce the use of violence invites suspicion that one harbors repressed maniacal rage, unnatural cowardice, antisocial eccentricity, or dimwitted naivete. Especially, perhaps, in a psychologically oriented modern world, people have come to believe in "the existence and overriding authority of a human fighting instinct."[18] Concomitantly, modern wisdom holds it not only futile but a positive danger to repress emotions too vigorously. The notion of emotional health promotes the honoring of emotion, tolerating even excessive and odious emotions, as long as *conduct* is appropriately restrained. Through an insidious alchemy, pride becomes self-esteem, hatred becomes identity, nationalism becomes a god, and God guides the smart bombs. Violence is innate, dominant, and inevitable.

The assumption was not always so. Early Quakers in England, while supremely aware of human capacity for evil, assumed that a conversion experience had the power to change a life and that human nature was susceptible to fundamental transformation. Quakers who crafted a "peaceable kingdom" in Pennsylvania seemed to have a more optimistic view of human nature. Their very designs for a new society implied that humans had a natural capacity "to conduct themselves in the way of the kingdom" and that human nature was innately capable of sustaining "an essentially ethical realm of brotherhood, peace, and love."[19]

The assumption that the violent nature of human beings eventually will prevail sets up conditions to fulfill the expectation. As long as the assumption goes unexamined, it is likely that humans will continue to structure their societies accordingly—to structure "a world organized for despair," in the words of William Hubben. "Man must not be reconciled to himself," Hubben continued, "lest he lose his spiritual destiny."[20] In a profoundly skeptical age, many may deny a "spiritual destiny"; in an age of vast destructive capacity, none can afford to be reconciled to unquestioned and unproven assumptions about human nature.

Why, if aggressive instincts are so invincible, is it necessary to intimidate military recruits, to yell, to cow, to humiliate, to drill, to march, and to plunge bayonets into straw men again and again—to build "morale" with hate? To train? Why, if modern warfare is detached, "surgical," and "cool," is it imperative to demonize an enemy and to foment hatred, even among civilians? To dress up slaughter in yellow ribbons?

Different expectations empowered early Quakers. Well acquainted with evil, they transcended a lazy surrender to the strength of evil, in their aspirations at least, through belief in the present Kingdom, perfectibility, "celestial inhabitation," God's protection, redemptive suffering, acceptance of the idea that the way of Jesus was the way of risk, and, finally, the transforming power of love. Their particular empowerment cannot be recovered, of course, but their different assumptions about humankind prompt consideration of alternative expectations. Their example, while not transferable, may at least stimulate a search for new sources of empowerment to control whatever propensity for violence is undeniable. It is by no means certain that sources of empowerment can be mobilized that will adequately encourage peaceful resolution of conflict and constrain a militarized, heterodox world, whose people include religious zealots, secular zealots, and vast companies of the apathetic. Indeed, some of history's certainties, empowering at one time for peaceable ends, have become in themselves threats to peace. Yet it is certain that, occasionally, the moral force of individual integrity stills the thunder of physical mayhem. It is this quality that infuses nonviolence with power and renders nonviolence ultimately more powerful than violence, for it is capable of transforming the heart of the enemy. It is this phenomenon that demands to be explored more fully.

Some are moving beyond assumptions about a priori hierarchies of primitive drives—assumptions that inhibit imagination—to think about alternative understandings of human interaction. It is obvious that physical force and self-interest do not exhaust the forces to which people respond. From time to time, individuals demonstrate such personal moral incandescence that ordinary expectations for human behavior may be overturned. Although even the cynical can sense this form of strength, its power is not conventionally measurable, and adequate language to describe new spiritual connections among people does not exist. The early Quaker experience shows that the incompatible language of power and might, when applied to nonviolent struggles, not only obfuscates peace principles but may encourage their compromise. Here then is the challenge: to be set free from stifling assumptions, dispiriting structures, controlling vocabulary, and acceptance of defeat in order to find a better way. "All things have their beginnings," even "the struggle without end."[21]

The early Quakers accepted a challenge; the questions with which they struggled, however imperfectly, and even their failures nag at the consciences of those who suspect that war does not work.

The Quaker path, erratic and stony, measured the limits of moral imagination. It traces a vision: that the walk might become a dance. That each of us might become a habitation for the hunted.

Appendix 1

THE 1660 DECLARATION

A Declaration from the harmless and innocent people of God, called Quakers, against all plotters and fighters in the world, for the removing the ground of jealousy and suspicion from both magistrates and people in the kingdom, concerning wars and fightings. And also something in answer to that clause of the King's late Proclamation which mentions the Quakers, to clear them from the plot and fighting which therein is mentioned, and for the clearing their innocency.

Our principle is, and our practices have always been, to seek peace and ensue it and to follow after righteousness and the knowledge of God, seeking the good and welfare and doing that which tends to the peace of all. We know that wars and fightings proceed from the lusts of men (as Jas. iv. 1–3), out of which lusts the Lord hath redeemed us, and so out of the occasion of war. The occasion of which war, and war itself (wherein envious men, who are lovers of themselves more than lovers of God, lust, kill, and desire to have men's lives or estates) ariseth from the lust. All bloody principles and practices, we, as to our own particulars, do utterly deny, with all outward wars and strife and fightings with outward weapons, for any end or under any pretence whatsover. And this is our testimony to the whole world.

And whereas it is objected:

'But although you now say that you cannot fight nor take up arms at all, yet if the spirit do move you, then you will change your principle, and then you will sell your coat and buy a sword and fight for the kingdom of Christ.'

Answer:

As for this we say to you that Christ said to Peter, 'Put up thy sword in his place'; though he had said before, he that had no sword might sell his coat and buy one (to the fulfilling of the law and Scripture), yet after, when he had bid him put it up, he said, 'He that taketh the sword shall perish with the sword.' And further, Christ said to Peter, 'Thinkest thou, that I cannot now pray to my Father, and he shall presently give me more than twelve legions of angels?' And this might satisfy Peter, after he had put up his sword, when he said to him he that took it, should perish by it, which satisfieth us. (Luke xxii. 36; Matt. xxvi. 51–53.) And in the Revelation, it's said, 'He that kills with the sword shall perish with the sword: and here is the faith and the patience of the saints.' (Rev. xiii. 10.) And so Christ's kingdom is not of this world, therefore do not his servants fight, as he told Pilate, the magistrate who crucified him. And did they not look upon Christ as a raiser of sedition? And did not he say, 'Forgive them'? But thus it is that we are numbered amongst transgressors and numbered amongst fighters, that the Scriptures might be fulfilled.

That the spirit of Christ, by which we are guided, is not changeable, so as once to command us from a thing as evil and again to move unto it; and we do certainly know, and so testify to the world, that the spirit of Christ, which leads us into all Truth, will never move us to fight and war against any man with outward weapons, neither for the kingdom of Christ, nor for the kingdoms of this world.

First:

Because the kingdom of Christ God will exalt, according to his promise, and cause it to grow and flourish in righteousness. 'Not by might, nor by power [of outward sword], but by my spirit, saith the Lord.' (Zech. iv. 6.) So those that use any weapon to fight for Christ, or for the establishing of his kingdom or government, both the spirit, principle, and practice in that we deny.

Secondly:

And as for the kingdoms of this world, we cannot covet them, much less can we fight for them, but we do earnestly desire and wait, that by the Word of God's power and its effectual operation in the hearts of men, the kingdoms of this world may become the kingdoms of the Lord, and of his Christ, that he may rule and reign in men by his spirit and truth, that thereby all people, out of all different judgements and professions may be brought into love and unity with God, and one with another, and that they may all come to witness the prophet's words who said, 'Nation shall not lift up sword against nation, neither shall they learn war any more.' (Isa. ii. 4; Mic. iv. 3.)

So, we whom the Lord hath called into the obedience of his Truth have denied wars and fightings and cannot again any more learn it. This is a certain testimony unto all the world of the truth of our hearts in this particular, that as God persuadeth every man's heart to believe, so they may receive it. For we have not, as some others, gone about cunningly with devised fables, nor have we ever denied in practice what we have professed in principle, but in sincerity and truth and by the word of God have we laboured to be made manifest unto all men, that both we and our ways might be witnessed in the hearts of all people.

And whereas all manner of evil hath been falsely spoken of us, we hereby speak forth the plain truth of our hearts, to take away the occasion of that offence, that so we being innocent may not suffer for other men's offences, nor be made a prey upon by the wills of men for that of which we were never guilty; but in the uprightness of our hearts we may, under the power ordained of God for the punishment of evil-doers and for the praise of them that do well, live a peaceable and godly life in all godliness and honesty. For although we have always suffered, and do now more abundantly suffer, yet we know that it's for righteousness' sake; 'for all our rejoicing is this, the testimony of our consciences, that in simplicity and godly sincerity, not with fleshly wisdom but by the grace of God, we have had our conversation in the world' (2 Cor. i. 12), which for us is a witness for the convincing of our enemies. For this we can say to the whole world, we have wronged no man's person or possessions, we have used no force nor violence against any man, we have been found in no plots, nor guilty of sedition. When we have been wronged, we have not sought to revenge ourselves, we have not made resistance against authority, but wherein we could not obey for conscience' sake, we have suffered even the most of any people in the nation. We have been accounted as sheep for the slaughter, persecuted and despised, beaten, stoned, wounded, stocked, whipped, imprisoned, haled out of synagogues, cast into dungeons and noisome vaults where many have died in bonds, shut up from our friends, denied needful sustenance for many days together, with other the like cruelties.

And the cause of all this our sufferings is not for any evil, but for things relating to the worship of our God and in obedience to his requirings of us. For which cause we shall freely give up our bodies a sacrifice, rather than disobey the Lord. For we know, as the Lord hath kept us innocent, so he will plead our cause, when there is none in the earth to plead it. So we, in obedience unto his Truth, do not love our lives unto the death, that we may do his will, and wrong no man in our generation, but seek the good and peace of all men. And he that hath commanded us that we shall not swear at all (Matt. v. 34), hath also commanded us that we shall not kill (Matt. v. 21), so that we can neither kill men, nor swear for nor against them. And this is both our principle and practice, and hath been from the beginning, so that if we suffer, as suspected to take up arms or make war against any, it is without any ground from us; for it neither is, nor ever was in our hearts, since we owned the truth of God; neither shall we ever do it, because it is contrary to the spirit of Christ, his doctrine, and the practice of his apostles, even contrary to him for whom we suffer all things, and endure all things.

And whereas men come against us with clubs, staves, drawn swords, pistols cocked, and do beat, cut, and abuse us, yet we never resisted them, but to them our hair, backs, and cheeks have been ready. It is not an honour to manhood nor to nobility to run upon harmless people who lift not up a hand against them, with arms and weapons.

Therefore consider these things ye men of understanding; for plotters, raisers of insurrections, tumultuous ones, and fighters, running with swords, clubs, staves, and pistols one against another, we say, these are of the world and this hath its foundation from this unrighteous world, from the foundation of which the Lamb hath been slain, which Lamb hath redeemed us from the unrighteous world, and we are not of it, but are heirs of a world in which there is no end and of a kingdom where no corruptible thing enters. And our weapons are spiritual and not carnal, yet mighty through God to the plucking down of the strongholds of Satan, who is author of wars, fighting, murder, and plots. And our swords are broken into ploughshares and spears into pruning-hooks, as prophesied of in Micah iv. Therefore we cannot learn war any more, neither rise up against nation or kingdom with outward weapons, though you have numbered us among the transgressors and plotters. The Lord knows our innocency herein, and will plead our cause with all men and people upon earth at the day of their judgement, when all men shall have a reward according to their works. . . .

O friends offend not the Lord and his little ones, neither afflict his people, but consider and be moderate, and do not run hastily into things, but mind and consider mercy, justice, and judgement; that is the way for you to prosper and get the favour of the Lord. Our meetings were stopped and broken up in the days of Oliver, in pretence of plotting against him; and in the days of the Parliament and Committee of Safety we were looked upon as plotters to bring in King Charles, and now we are called plotters against King Charles. Oh, that men should lose their reason and go contrary to their own conscience, knowing that we have suffered all things and have been accounted plotters all along, though we have declared against them both by word of mouth and printing, and are clear from any such things. We have suffered all along because we would not take up carnal weapons to fight withal against any, and are thus made a prey upon because we are the innocent lambs of Christ and cannot avenge ourselves. These things are left upon your hearts to consider, but we are out of all those things in the patience of the saints, and we know that as Christ said, 'He that takes the sword, shall perish with the sword.' (Matt. xxvi. 52; Rev. xiii. 10.)

This is given forth from the people called Quakers to satisfy the King and his Council, and all those that have any jealousy concerning us, that all occasion of suspicion may be taken away and our innocency cleared.

Given forth under our names, and in behalf of the whole body of the Elect People of God who are called Quakers.

George Fox	Gerrard Roberts	Henry Fell
Richard Hubberthorn	John Bolton	John Hinde
John Stubbs	Leonard Fell	John Furley Junr.
Francis Howgill	Samuel Fisher	Thomas Moore
		21/11M/1660

(Abridged.) George Fox, *The Journal of George Fox*, ed. John L. Nickalls (Philadelphia, 1985), 398–403.

Appendix 2

THE 1673 EXEMPTION

At the Remeetinge of the Generall Asembly Called by the Governors
Warrant to Sitt Att Newport the 13th of August 1673

Voted   that Mr. John Easton, Mr. William Harris, Mr. John Tripp, Mr. Peter Easton, and Lt. William Cadman are Chossen a Committee to prepare matters for this Asembly Concerninge the Indians Drunkenness, Encourragement of the Mallicia, the Danger wee are in by the late Enterprize of the
Dutch takeinge New-Yorke and such other publick matters Relatinge to
this Asembly and make their Returne to this Asembly. . . .

Voted   And Further needfull to be Considered for this pressent occassion a
more certaine peaceable setlement for the ending of strife and unproffitable Contention, which hath too long continewed as to the liberty of
some mens Consciences, which others are not willing to allow or permitt
concerninge Trayninge and fightinge to kill thereby: – : And forasmuch as
from the begininge of these plantations law hath been Enacted as to Liberty of Conscience then sinceable of others opression of their owne Conscience.

And Consideringe that every one, ought both toward God and man to
have a Conscience unspotted by doeing that which God Requireth to be
done, or not doeinge that which he Requiers not to be done toward man,
and pure Religion before God the Father is to vissitt the fatherless and the
widdow and to keep our selves unspotted of this world or worldly things.

And Considering that Generally the Inhabitants of this Collony hath a
Conscience or understandinge even about Temporalls contrary to the cus-

238

toms of our nation and our neighbours the Rest of the Collonys their Inhabitants, even about the highest things of that nature, vizt Jurisdiction to which an oath is alwaies joyned to the Authentiquety of their proceedings thereabout, which is not ussed here in this Collony, as being Contrary to the Conscience (as it seemith[)] of the Inhabitants even about such high ~~things~~ occassions as Reach life or death : And Consideringe that God himselfe did not soe univrsally compell to his war (though soe undoubtedly warranted) but that the Fearefull, they that had built houses and not dedicated them, newly married, a wife, or planted a vinyard and not eaten the fruites thereof, had a liberty not to goe to (or returne home) from the said War. Alsoe Consideringe the Kings Majesty hath soe highly Indulged his subjects of this Collony to Excussinge them from an oath it being about Temporall things Notwithstandinge by the lawes of England united to all such proceedings in soe high matters as of life and Death, Alsoe Consideringe that the Kings Majesty in the way of his wars doth not soe universally compell all, but permitt some, yea very many not to trayne or fight or war for him, whose consciences are that they ought not learne war nor war at all, yea notwithstandinge his Majesty have great waringe and ussith men of other understandings to fight, yet not those against whose Conscience it is to fight, That they who will loose their owne lives rather then distroy other mens lives can noe waies nor by noe meanes be compelled to fight to kill.

And Consideringe there are divers persons of severall societies, who are one in that point of Conscience of not Trayninge and not Fightinge to kill, and have in divers places of Scripture the letter thereof for their said Conscience, contrary to which to compell them (if they would be compelled) were to compell them to be hypocrites alsoe Now consideringe as afore-said if persons are Excussed then of God from war because fearefull of loossing their lives pressent, how much more for feare of loossinge Everlastinge life, by fightinge against the minde of God (as they are perswaded[)]: If persons Excussed from War least they be slain and an other dedicate their house they built, how much more Excussed from learninge war and waringe Least thereby and in their Consciences then beleive they should, if learne war and fight to kill and distroy that house of clay or Tabernacle which God hath built be Excussed from war and destroyinge it beinge the Temple of God.

If marryinge of a wife shall Excuse a man from war how much more any such who are perswaded in their Consciences that they are Espoussed to Christ, and that if they should learne war or war would occassion a differeance and distance between them forever:

Or he that hath planted a vinyard be Excussed fom war because he hath not eat of the fruit, how much more rather, a man Excussed from war, then whereby he is perswaded if warringe against his Conscience and understanding, h[e] cutts off a branch or limb (which Gods Ri[g]ht Hand hath planted) from the vinyard and destroys it:

And seeinge the Kings Majesty is pleassed to forbeare to Compell such to warr who are, perswaded in their Consciences they may not fight to kill, how much less may such compell them, that have Consciences that need and Receive a Tolleration from the King even in the highest temporall things in Jurisdiction as to life and death, and cannot take an oath of Aleagiance though annexed thereto, yett his Majesty dispenceth with his law, how much more ought such men to forbeare to Compell or Endeavor to compell their Equall neighbours against their Consciences, to trayne, to fight and kill by force of any by-law of theirs but rather Consider, that if the Kings Majesty Indulge us all even in Temporalls, how much more ought his subjects to Indulge one an other.

Bee It Therfore Enacted, and hereby is Enacted by his Majestys Authorety that noe person nor persons (within this Collony) that is or hereafter shall be perswaded in his or their Conscience, or Consciences (and by him or them declared) that he nor they cannot nor ought not to trayne, to learne to fight, nor to war, nor kill any person nor persons -

That neither he nor they shall at any time be Compelled against his or their Judgment and Conscience to trayne, arme, or fight to kill any person nor persons by Reason of or at the Comand of any officer of this Collony civill nor millitary, nor by Reason of any by-law, here past or formerly Enacted, nor shall suffer any punnishment, fine, distraint, pennalty, nor Imprissonment, who cannot in conscience traine, fight, nor kill any person nor persons for the afore-said Reasons ~~Rendored~~ Expressed with many more Implyed and others for brevety concealed, such said men of such said understandings shall be Exempt from Trayninge, Armminge, Rallyinge to Fight, to kill, and all such martiall service as men are by any other debillety, as, aged, lame, sick, weake, deafe, blinde, or any other Infirmety exemptith persons in and by law, soe the afore-said men, have noe abillity to fight haveinge noe Knowlidge soe to doe, nor Capassety soe to learne, they takeinge themselves forbidden of God to learne war any more

provided never the less, that all those who are perswaded in their understandings and consciences, that it is lawfull and noe ofence against God to fight to kill enemys in hostillity against the King and his subjects, That such said persons of lawfull age and not Exempted by any other debilletys may be compelled and ought to obay, and not to deny obedience to such said service as if the afore-said act by which the afore-said Exempted had never been made.

Provided never-the-less that such said persons who cannot fight nor destroy men it beinge against their Conscience, and is not against their Conscience to doe and perform civill service to the Collony though not martill service, and can preserve (soe farr as in them lies) lives goods and cattell &c, That when any enemy shall aproach or assault the Collony or any place there of that then it shall be lawfull for the civill officers for the time beinge, as civill officers (and not as martiall or Millitary) to Require such said persons as are of suffitient able Bodye and of strength (though Exempt from Arminge and fightinge) to conduct or convay out of the Danger of the enemy, weake and aged impotent persons, women and children, goods and Cattell, by which the common weale may be the better maintained, and works of mercy mannifested to distressed weake persons, And shall be Required to watch to informe of Danger (but without armes in martiall manner nor matters) and to performe any other civill service by order of the civill officers for the good of the Collony and Inhabitants thereof:

And the afore-said or by-law to stand in full Force and every clause therein (in this Collony) any other former by-law, act or acts, clause or clauses in them or either of them to the Contrary hereof in any-wise notwithstandinge.

Voted   Because the acts of this Asembly at the sittinge thereof (this adjournment) is of soe great necessety for the preventinge of eminnant Danger, Be It therefore Enacted by his Majestys Authorety that the acts of this meetinge upon adjournment shall within six daies of the date hereof be published under the seale of the Collony in Newport by open proclamation to be made there by the Generall Serjant and Read by the Towne Clerke of the said Towne.

Appendix 3

THE RHODE ISLAND TESTIMONY

A Testimony From Us (in Scorn Called Quakers,
But Are) the Children of the Light

24/6M/1675

Christ Jesus the Light of the world, & Prince of peace is come; & hath given an Understanding that is true, & also a being in measure within his Kingdom, which consists of peace, & Joy Everlasting: yea he hath manifested the Root of Bitterness, from whence that plant of Unrighteousness hath Sprung up, which brings forth cursed Fruits, (as Lyeing, Swearing, Envy, Covetousness, Pride, Fightings, Warring with carnall weapons Blood-shed, Killing, Murther, & many more gross Evils in the Kingdoms here below) to the dishonour of God's blessed Name: yea & also he hath called unto the Sons of men to turn from death, & its way, to the Life, the way to God; & this call hath prevailed with a Remnant, though many have rejected it, soe that Judgment hath been set up in the Earth, & the Law of the Spirit of Life, hath taken hold of the bitter Root, & overturned, & is in overturning both Branch & Root: & the Righteousness of the Law fullfilled through Beliefe: & the Kingdom of God & Christ came in men, & his Throne therein Established, & his Sceptor exalted, & swayed over all that thus have passed from death to Life, who have given up their names to Christ the Prince of Peace, under his peaceable Government in a state of Subjection, & Obedience, to abide & dwell in his Kingdom, which consists of Righteousness, Joy, & Peace in the Holy Spirit: We are Witnesses this day, that this work is finished, & in [sic] finishing; & God is tabernacleing in Men, & the Gospel of Peace is preached again; & the voice uttered in the holy City is peace with God, good will towards Men. And therefore this is our Testimony unto all people, that the Gospel of our Lord Jesus Christ is come near in us, & we brought near in Measure to God in it, being reconciled (therein) to God, walking in the

Light with him, in unity where our fellowship one with another is, & the Blood of Jesus Christ Sprinckleth our Conciences dayly, & preserveth us from dead Works, that we serve our God, (even the Liveing God) in newness of Life, & in this his peaceable Kingdom we live, where Strife, Envy, Pride, Covetousness, are not; Fighting, Killing Blood-shed Murther with Carnall Weapons, rendering Evil for Evil, are not; Revenge, Robbing for Concience sake; watching with Guns or Swords to kill the Bodys of Men, though Enemies; Offending, or defending with Carnal weapons of what sort soever to preserve att Liberty Body or Estate are not: for all these things are in the Darkness, Satans Kingdom, which already is past, & Ended; & Humility, Charity, Brotherly Kindness, Peace, & Love are: Faith, Hope, watching for the good of all, & good will towards all, both Friends & Enemies are: Wisdom, & Life Eternall, with the peaceable Fruits of Righteousness, are by all of us possest, who walk in the Light, & are led by Gods Spirit into Obedience to Christ Jesus our Lord & King, in whom wee have believed to the Salvation of our Souls, & by whom we have been Kept & preserved, clean & Liveing to God, in many great Tryalls inwardly & outwardly, & through whose Power we hope to be upheld to the End, Liveing & true Witnesses to the Life of Innocency, to the Gospel, & Kingdom of Peace, & Christ Jesus the Prince of Peace: but against the Murthering hurtful Spirit, Blood-shed, warrs outward, killing men or women; Gods workmanship, Death & him which hath the power thereof the Divel: & in the End, lay down our Heads with God, injoying the fullness of Peace in his blessed Presence, for ever, and evermore.

Our Testimony is, that this Kingdom of Christ, who is our Lord, & Saviour, is not of this world, for if it were, we (his Servants) could (with carnall weapons) fight; but 'tis of another World, where peace and Righteousness dwells for evermore; soo that we (his Servants) cannot (with Swords, Guns, or any carnall Weapons) fight, or make use thereof to hurt or kill our Enemies, or defend our Bodies therewith from our Enemies; but in Obedience to Christ our Master, keep his Command, Love Enemies, bless them that curse you; put thy Sword up into the Sheath; doo good to them that hate you, pray for them that despightfully use you, & persecute you; & wait in the Faith which lays hold on Eternal Life, to outlive Cruelty through suffering; that as we are redeemed out of the Kingdom & Spirit of this World (where the marring of the heavenly Image is, & the killing & destroying of Men & Women his Creatures) & made Partakers of Righteousness & Truth, in the King-dom of God, we follow Christ our Lord, who left us an Example, & drink patiently that Cup; which God (our (Father) giveth us; & though the Hearts of all People are in the Hand of him, in whom we have believed, who is both God & Christ, & that he can change them as pleaseth him, we know, yet we say his will be done; & if he permit the Heathen (which fear not his Name) to come forth against us, & out-wardly spoile us, yet with any carnall Weapons, we may not them resist, nor put Confidence in the Arm of Flesh, but in the Faith, & Patience, of our Gods Hand, in true Love to him, & his Workmanship; & with him in his Kingdom, inwardly Reign, & perfect our Dominion over Destruction & Death, through suffering, & soo be to the Honour of God, his Way, Truth, & Name, thats holy & Perfect for ever; to the encourageing of those, that shall live up (hereafter) to God, in Christ

Jesus, & to the Glory, & Renown, of that prevailing Love & Power of God, which compassed our Spirits, & bore up our minds over the fear of Suffering, or Death, through which obtaining that Crown of Immortall Life.

Lastly Our Testimony is Christ Jesus the Prince of Peace, is in this his Kingdom, that is not of this World, Ruleing over all the Children of Peace, & leads them in & out in the Way of Peace, where they work the Works of God in Peace, & recieve the Rewards of Peace, dwelling with him in his peaceable Kingdom & one with another in Unity & Peace: & that whoever hath known Christ the true Light, & by Faith recieved him the Prince of Peace into their Hearts, & followed him, & dwelt with him in the Light, the way & Covenant of Peace; where Pride, Envy, Fighting, & Warrs, which arise from the Lust, have been subdued, & overcome yet notwithstanding goe out into the dark Spirit of the world again, & lust after the use of Carnall Weapons, in the Kingdom of Contention, & strife (as Guns Swords &c.) to defend their own, or others Bodys, Lives, or Estates, by threatning to Wound; or kill, or by wounding or killing, the Bodyes of their Enemys, or makeing Laws or grant forth Writeings, thereby to Rob, Spoile, or Imprison, any that out of Concience to God-wards, can not make use of Carnall weapons, for their own or others safety, but truely, rely by Faith in God's promise, & pray to God in Faith, for their own, & others preservation, through turning the Hearts of their Enemies from such Wickedness; by his Eternal Power; or Justify, or encourage; by Word or Practice, Killing, Blood-shed, use of carnal Weapons, to preserve Life, by takeing away Life; & Warrs outward either offensive, or defensive, or plead for, or live in, that faith which stands in Carnall Weapons, or the Arm of Flesh, or the unrighteous Liberty, wherein the[y] wound their own Souls, & make sad many Hearts, which God maketh not sad, & pierce in themselves affresh the Righteous Life:

Wee declare all such Works have been, & are against Christ the Truth, his Kingdom of Peace & People; out of the Light, & way of Peace, wrought in darkness, & brought forth in the world, where wickedness abounds, through the Lust of the Flesh, the Lust of the Eye, & the Pride of Life, & with the Light we see them condemnable by the Law of Righteousness, & Judged by Christ our Lord, the Righteous, & Impartiall Judge, & are by us denied. And further we signify to all People, that Christ the Prince of Peace, his Truth, Name, Kingdom & Sanctuary are Clear of all these works, & all other whatsoever, which arise out & from the dark Kingdom of Antichrist; & we (his People) disown such Practices, & Works, & condemn that Spirit, which hath or may lead thereinto: & in the Peaceable Truth we stand, Witnesses for God, his Truth, Name, Kingdom, & Sanctuary; & hope in Innocency, & true Love to be preserved towards all, both Friends & Enemys, & in the holy Righteous ever blessed Life, shine forth more, & more to Gods Eternall Praise, who is over Heaven & Earth, God Blessed for evermore.

From our mens-Meeting att Rhode-Island att Joshua Coggeshalls the Day above dated.

Appendix 4

"THE TASTE OF THE WORLD IN OUR OWN MOUTHS": PROBLEMS OF HISTORICAL INTERPRETATION

W. Alan Cole, Barry Reay, and Christopher Hill, in their studies of English Quakerism, transformed the understanding of the origins of the peace testimony.[1] They concluded that the Quaker peace testimony arose from strategic considerations surrounding the restoration of the monarchy in 1660, and their evidence and arguments have proved so persuasive that their emphases have become a new orthodoxy. But their work and that of those they have influenced, while adding greatly to the knowledge of some aspects of the peace testimony, has somewhat obscured the complexity of Quaker experience and the pertinence of the persistent moral issues. As piety once smoothed the wrinkles from pre-1660 pacifism, so politics has smoothed the other side of that historical divide; where once pacifism was taken for granted "from the beginning," now scholarship is in danger of minimizing peace principles before 1660 and taking them for granted thereafter. In what ways has the new consensus enriched the understanding of Quaker pacifism, and in what respects is it problematical?

The Politics of Peace: A New Consensus

W. Alan Cole's succinct and stunning assertion in 1956 stimulated the new thinking about the peace testimony: "Pacifism was not a characteristic of the early Quakers: it was forced upon them by the hostility of the outside world."[2] In Cole's view, pacifism was a defensive response to persecution, an attempt to diffuse the fears of those powerful enough to punish. Moreover, having seen the failure of a particular army, the army of "God's Commonwealth," Quakers transmuted and generalized this failure of force in experience into a principle that force itself was wrong.[3]

Whether self-conscious or not, then, Cole argued, the development of peace principles was a reactive process. Cole tended to associate pacifism with a realistic awareness of the lack of Quaker power and to confuse pacifism with quietism and retreat. He equated pacifism with the abandonment of active political involvement; quoting Burrough's statement that the Quakers were not "entangled concerning the things of this world," Cole concluded: "Thus the majority of Quakers had now come round to a pacifist position."[4]

Reay's distinguished scholarship, in *The Quakers and the English Revolution,* expanded and refined Cole's groundbreaking political study, persuasively documenting pre-1660 Quaker willingness to be associated with the use of violence. He established the symbiosis between the New Model Army and Quakers—the army as prior profession for many Quakers, as fertile recruiting territory for new adherents, and as protector of Quakers—often a congenial alliance.[5] "Frends is made soe bould that they goe and Reeds [books] . . . in the marketts . . . & some souldiers is made to goe Alonge with them & stand by them," reported Richard Farnworth to Margaret Fell in 1652. Two years later, he described how "the Lord stirred up souldiers to Restraine the Cruelty" when Quaker Thomas Goodaire "had Like to have beene murdered" for disturbing the priest.[6]

By carefully illustrating the reaction to Quakers among the elite and common people alike, Reay laid the foundation for his argument that the collective fears of a fractured society during the frantic political maneuvering of 1659 coalesced into a conviction that Quakers were immediately threatening. Pointing out that the fears were to a degree justified, Reay attributed the Restoration itself more to inchoate fear than love of the monarchy: "fear . . . shaped events."[7] Meanwhile, in 1659, many Quakers energetically enlisted in Rump militias, submitted lists of suitable candidates for office, and otherwise struggled to achieve political ends so long deferred. Interpreted as menace, this activity led to increased suppression and imprisonment.

Charles II returned as monarch in May 1660; the following January, the Fifth Monarchy rising exacerbated anti-Quaker feeling. In response, twelve Quakers issued the Declaration of 1660, designed to defuse the sense of threat they inspired. Reay concurred with Cole's judgment that the leadership's statement was reactive and self-defensive; the peace testimony was codified out of defeat, a tepid triumph of political realism. "The restoration of monarchy in 1660 almost forced pacifism upon the sect, partly through disillusionment, partly because of the simple need to survive; the first declarations of pacifism came with the assault on Quakerism in 1660 and 1661."[8] Moreover, political disappointment in the lack of realization of the Cromwellian promise and the ordeal of persecution were compounded by the death of many Quaker leaders by 1670. Survival demanded organization, which in turn promoted conservatism.[9] For Reay, then, pacifism was reactive to danger, defeat, disappointment; it was essentially conservative.

Christopher Hill has patterned his interpretation of early pacifism on that of Reay and Cole, concentrating on the politics of pacifism.[10] Hill emphasized the heterogeneity of the Quakers before the Declaration of 1660, referring to early Quakers in one study as "pre-pacifist" and describing any Quakers manifesting pacifist tendencies before 1660 on another occasion as "premature pacifists."[11] He has acknowledged, too, that it took time after the "official" declaration in 1660 for pacifism to erase "bellicosity" entirely. His argument rests on a definition of pacifism as a disavowal of war and the military and on pacifism as a collective phenomenon, not on nonviolence as an individual response. Limited in this way, evidence is abundant that many Quakers during the 1650s were indeed not pacifists; they served in the military even after convincement and supported the activities of the army, especially when the army adhered to the righteous values of the Good Old Cause. Hill plausibly postulates that when George Fox explained his refusal of a military commission in 1652 in pacifist terms, it was a retroactive explanation, more compatible with his views at the time he actually prepared his *Journal* many years later. Similarly, he dismissed Fox's 1654 letter to Cromwell denying the use of the carnal sword because Fox had good reasons, other than pacifism, not "to commit himself publicly" either to the army or to Cromwell.[12] Yet Fox in that letter described himself as a "witness against all violence," unwilling to carry a sword against anyone, for an explicit spiritual reason: "my weapons are . . . spirituall & my kingedom is not of this world." This statement, unlike his refusal in the *Journal,* was not a later addition and cannot be as easily dismissed.[13] Hill's restricted definition of pacifism as a phenomenon referring to collective political actions shields him from having to address such individual protestations of nonviolence. After all, even Fox, in addressing Cromwell, was speaking only for himself about his individual intentions.

Like Reay, Hill saw pacifism as arising from profound disillusionment with the Good Old Cause—the oppression and unrighteousness of its leaders, the failure of reform, and the postponement of God's Kingdom—but Hill discerned Quaker disillusionment as far back as the early fifties.[14] He documented many Quaker jeremiads against the betrayal of the Cause during the Commonwealth and Protectorate years, and he described the resurgeance of hope during the turbulent year 1659 and the subsequent, final dashing of Quaker aspirations upon the Restoration. He attributed even instances of "premature pacifism" during the fifties to growing disillusionment, citing, among others, the case of Thomas Lurting, who became a pacifist in 1657. (Lurting, however, was a curious example for one linking politics and pacifism as enthusiastically as Hill, for Lurting's account of his conversion to pacifist ways gives no hint of a political agenda and is almost wholly spiritual.)[15]

The Politics of Peace: Problems of Interpretation

The new orthodoxy, exemplified in *The Quakers and the English Revolution,* has by its very originality and persuasive documentation nevertheless inadvertently contributed to a sometimes uncritical, overstated, and oversimplified understanding of the early peace principles. Reay acknowledged freely that pacifism among individuals had been present before the Restoration and that it "was slower in developing and less universally accepted after 1660 than most historians have assumed."[16] Hill, too, was careful to recognize anomalies, complexities, and speculation. But the central political theme is so assertive that the implications of these acknowledgments are left unexamined; others have been led to a coarsening of the argument. In the course of making more general observations, others, sometimes in an offhand manner, have exaggerated what was only an unfolding trend into fixed doctrine. Thus, T. Canby Jones, noting that by 1659 the Quakers saw there was no hope for the Commonwealth, overstated the issue: "The Friends peace testimony became an anti-government attitude which hardened into monolithic consistency with the Restoration." Characterizing the peace testimony as reactive, "a defense against the suspicions and hostile legislation of the Cavalier Parliament," he observed that henceforth the peace testimony became a "uniform witness supported by all Friends in opposition to the government." After the Declaration of 1660, "no Quaker would knowingly engage in any livelihood or action which involved war or violence."[17] Many have suspended detailed critical consideration of Quaker belief and behavior during much of the succeeding century, assuming that the matter was essentially settled after the early 1660s. The uncritical assessment has appeared in phrases such as "the Quaker peace testimony became indelible only in 1660."[18] Some have acknowledged only political manifestations of the testimony, as expressed by Quaker leaders, ignoring more spiritual experiences of individuals just finding their way. A failure to define terms or a too narrow definition of the peace testimony as a testimony against war alone, ignoring its application in the personal realm, has rendered the peace testimony indistinct. Thus, Richard Vann could write of Quakerism: "None of the 'testimonies' with which it has come to be publicly identified . . . [such as] pacifism itself—were typical concerns of the earliest Friends."[19]

While undeniably true in part, and a crucial antidote to the tendency to analyze religious movements in exclusively religious terms, Reay's thesis—and by extension, Cole's and Hill's—is incomplete. It suffers from a lack of distinction between the individual and the group, private and public; the spiritual and the political, belief and method. It confuses pacifism and quietism and finds invalid causal connections between pacifism, discipline, and organization. It overgeneralizes the English Quaker experience and by default subsumes the colonial experience. Finally, it mischaracterizes aspects of pacifism itself.

The Individual, the Group: Private, Public

By concentrating on the collective expression and slighting the individual expression of pacifism, the political interpretation fails to account for some manifestations and abrogations of peace principles, some central to the testimony and others more peripheral; fails to address some pertinant issues; and leads to inadequate conclusions. Hill, for example, understood pacifism within a context of war and peace, organized violence, and the military—in short, he considered pacifism as a reaction to group behavior, to societal forces. Because he defined pacifism in this truncated way and because there had been no official endorsement of pacifism during the 1650s, he called it a "new principle" when it took a collective form in 1660. Since it had not taken the form of a group phenomenon, it was as if it did not exist. Pacifism was, for him, a political phenomenon, bounded within the social milieu. Thus, he was able to say, "There can, I think, be no doubt that Fox had not committed himself to pacifism before the Restoration."[20] While there appears little doubt that Fox did not commit *others* to pacifism before the Restoration, there is much evidence that he committed *himself* to some pacifist principles. Hill thus by-passed pacifist belief that might be personal, inspired by spiritual revelation, derived from reasoned observation, or emergent from secular moral struggle. He admitted that spirituality may be political but not that politics may also be spiritual.

The argument fails to distinguish between the individual responding to physical abuse and a collection of people plotting to overthrow government—between one person considering her obligations to God's will and a politically sophisticated leadership constructing a national image. By confusing the individual with the collective, the local farmer with the London lobbyist, Reay too cannot evaluate many features of the Quaker witness. It is not credible, for example, that most early Quakers would be calculating how their actions would impact on the Quaker national agenda, to the extent that one existed. They would be concentrating on defusing trouble staring them in the face, not defusing diffuse fears of Quaker subversion. While the Quaker leaders indeed addressed such larger concerns, they cannot explain the motives behind countless small restraints of individual Quakers.[21] The argument ignores, too, the possibility that one individual might come to different conclusions about his religious obligations toward another person in a private capacity and his religious obligations toward others while acting in his capacity as a citizen. When confronted with personal violence, he might react nonviolently; when ordered to serve in the militia, he might comply. Thus, it would have been more accurate to postulate that it was the collective *expression* of a collective position that was a self-defensive maneuver in 1660, not pacifism itself.

We have seen again and again how central is the need for individual commitment to the peace testimony, how it is the individual heart that must be transformed. Not until well into the eighteenth century did Quakers focus more on earthly justice than the "lusts of the heart" removing the cause of war. For the earliest Quakers it was the immediate power of God that was crucial, for he had dominion over that which each person cannot control. George Bishop saw broken links in a great chain: "Here is the ground of all, the spirit that is in man lusteth to envy, boylings are in his heart, revenge is in his breast, he cannot bear an indignity . . . he would have, and he kills to have; he cannot rule his inordinate desires." Without each person seeking the Light within, "bringing into captivity every thought to the obedience of Christ," pacifism is impossible; it was the lack of obedience "which hath been wanting . . . and the want of this hath been the cause why there hath been such Wars." Bishop made it absolutely clear that he was not speaking of people in groups; each person must overcome himself, "which is greater prowess than to overcome strong Cities." For Quakers, the locus of the cause of war and the occasion of fighting and weapons was ultimately within the individual, not in impersonal societal forces. And the power of God was to be found in the one who subdues and destroys the spirit of wickedness, not in he who "fights with mens persons, and kills, and slayes."[22]

The Spiritual, the Political: Belief, Method

The current argument about the origins of the peace testimony does not draw a crucial distinction between belief and method. Granting that the collective expression of the peace principles was a useful strategy in 1660 and that several groups have used nonviolence as a method, divorced from ideology, ever since, it is not true that Quaker pacifism has not also been an intrinsic part of belief itself. Freedom of conscience seemed to be the highest good for early Quakers. For the Quaker leadership in 1660, the peace testimony was also a collective strategy to best *secure* liberty of conscience. But the peace testimony, even before 1660, was, for some, an inherent substantive impulse demanding to be expressed as *part* of conscience. We need only recall such examples as Lurting and Coxere. Neither aspect need be dismissed.

In slighting belief in favor of strategy, historians overlook several other pertinent issues that are components of belief. These issues concern persuading others to pacifism, working out how to act as a pacifist, and pacifism as a process, rhetoric, and providentialism. Because Quaker peace principles were not in essence a political policy subject to being abandoned if unsuccessful but rather were based on obeying God's injunctions about loving one's enemies, the early Quakers made little effort to urge these principles on others. The principles were not to be adopted as a belief system but rather could only proceed from a genuine soul transformation; vigorous persuasion would result in hypocrisy. Had it been otherwise, perhaps those who were developing them within their own lives would have seen a reason to express them earlier. Lurting, as already noted, made a point of his reticence in this matter.

Quakers, then, could be tolerant even of other Quakers serving as soldiers. Reay and Hill relied heavily on Quaker encouragement of military activities in the 1650s to question the consistency of pacifism and even the existence of pacifism. Quoting, for example, Fox's "Let thy soldiers go forth . . . that thou may rock nations as a cradle" and Burrough's "there is some great worke to doe by them, in ye nations, wth their outward sword," Reay and Hill suggest ambivalence, if not outright bellicosity.[23] But it is possible that Fox and Burrough were free to encourage the army as an arm of the magistracy, and/or because they were not in it themselves. Moreover, the Quaker view of magistracy did not change in 1660; they continued to reconcile the measure of violence allotted to magistrates with peace principles under the restored monarchy. When the Declaration of 1660 renounced weapons "for any end, or under any pretence whatsoever," it failed to envision a Quaker magistrate, an oversight that would not go away.

Developing and interpreting the requirements of the peace testimony remained a process, both for the individual Quaker and the movement itself. If consistency is to be the measure of whether or not pacifism exists, there is little difference between Quaker pacifism in the 1650s and at any time thereafter. Because early expressions of pacifism were personal and therefore often appeared inconsistent, as Quakers advocated activities on the part of others they did not feel free to engage in themselves; because then, as thereafter, there was a continuum of responses to pacifism within the Quaker body; and because pacifism was essentially irrational did not mean that it did not exist. Just as belief in millinarianism itself was bifurcated—it encompassed at once a political, collective aspect of a redeemed society and the individualized aspect of the Christ within—so, too, both aspects of pacifism existed from the beginning in the beliefs of individual Quakers and persist as well today. It was not necessarily that they were inconsistent in their pacifism or that pacifism did not exist before 1660 but rather that some newly came to feel that pacifism demanded collective expression, still just applicable within the sect itself. Whether this change was due to strategic considerations, to disappointment, or to a developing sense that peace principles were fundamental to Quakerism undoubtedly varied with the individual.

Some who argue that pacifism during the 1650s was essentially nonexistent rely substantially on a core of evidence derived from providentialist interpretations of immediate past history. Hill, for instance, quoted Fox telling the Protector that had Oliver remained faithful to the Lord's work, "the Hollander had been thy subject and tributary, Germany had given up to have done thy will . . . the King of France should have bowed his neck under thee, the Pope should have withered."[24] God would have rewarded faithfulness, as he had previously in the Civil War battles at Worcester and Dunbar. Fox was not necessarily recommending a crusade; rather, he was describing the logical consequences of obedience to God. Whether Cromwell was to have been a violent agent is left unexamined. Such rhetoric reveals little about pacifism.

Pacifism, Quietism

The political argument also finds inappropriate causal connections between pacifism and other developments within Quakerism. Too often the political argument carelessly associates pacifism with political quietism. "The cause of liberty," Reay wrote, "would not be advanced by militant, political means. Thus we get the first clear declarations of Quaker pacifism."[25] H. Larry Ingle has written that the peace testimony as declared in 1660 embodied a "retreat from politics."[26] "The major rethinking," Hill wrote, "led to the peace principle . . . and to withdrawal from political action."[27] He implied erroneously that Fox after 1661 "came to reject all political action." The overstatement comes from concentrating on Quaker experience in England, and slighting the experience in the colonies, where Fox himself greeted political opportunity with gusto.[28]

Pacifism and political involvement are, of course, not mutually exclusive. Quakers could harmonize some use of violence with their peace principles because of their attitude toward magistracy and because they distinguished between what they did themselves and what others might do. Many activities could be justified as duties of government, including police actions, military activities, and even war itself; again, such justifications were a matter of individual definition. To imply that pacifism necessarily requires opposition to the army, then, is inaccurate. Many early Quakers saw the army as a legitimate instrument to bring in liberty of conscience, for example, or to hasten the arrival of God's Kingdom on earth. Because militias often functioned as civil police, many unequivocally felt justified in being soldiers, or accepting office, because magistracy itself was ordained of God. Fox, for example, when addressing officers and soldiers in 1659, used the explicit biblical vocabulary associated with the magistrate's function:

And you Souldiers . . . for not doing violence to any man, nor accusing any man falsly, *that* differs you from violent doers, and false accusers, whereby your sword is turned against violent doers, and false accusers, and *a terror to the evil doer; and to them that do well, the sword is a praise, and such bear not the sword in vain.*[29]

Obviously, the line between such legitimizations and the familiar and traditional "just war" argument is blurry. Of these same individuals, however, many would not have borne weapons themselves. They were able to envision a righteous agenda for others to carry out, even though, as Quakers, they felt themselves redeemed out of those activities. By so removing themselves, they were, in a measure, pacifists. To insist that in order to be deemed pacifists these early Quakers had to conform to modern ideas of pacifism is to impose an entirely different set of assumptions on the past and to dishonor and misunderstand the foundations of other beliefs.

Pacifism, Organization, Discipline

Those stressing the importance of the 1660 trauma for the introduction of the peace testimony implied too much cause and effect, too, between pacifism and the need for discipline and organization within the movement. "Imposing the peace principle meant organizing, distinguishing, purging," wrote Hill.[30] The evidence does not support his too-close identification of "the Peace Principle and the discipline necessary to enforce it." Organization and discipline had already begun—especially after the Nayler affair when James Nayler, in 1656, succumbed to the temptation of an extravagant bit of street theater and rode into Bristol on the back of a horse, his followers strewing garments in his path and singing hosannah. Organization and discipline were the natural consequences of several factors, the least of which was probably pacifism, which received little disciplinary attention for years, probably because it was so little settled in definition. Rudimentary meeting structure had appeared by 1657; Margaret Fell's Swarthmore Hall had long served as a correspondence clearing house for Quaker ministers, a means of both organization and a certain discipline; and the careful gathering and recording of "sufferings" could not help but define Quaker norms. Christopher Atkinson's 1655 letter to Margaret Fell gives a glimpse of her prior discipline: "Deare sister thy lines I have Received from thy pure love though they sticke in my hart as darts yea ye are sharpe."[31] Thomas Holme took great care to assure Fell in 1656 that he was in "subjection" to Fox and Fell and that he and his wife were keeping asunder.[32] Some leaders were more interested in unity than others. Josiah Coale set people to watch one another in the love of God "and in the Spirit of Love and Meekness exhort and beseech one another."[33] Isaac Penington, in contrast, warned that the spirit of Christ alone must teach, "nothing else exhort, nothing else admonish and reprove, nothing else cut off and cast out."[34] As discipline became more formalized, for the remainder of the century Quakers formulated lists for themselves, reminders of Quaker principles for "walking in the Light."[35] Almost never did these disciplinary lists include reminders about peace principles. Fox set forth a list of "Antient Principles of Truth," a list of thirteen principles. Most were those things Quakers must oppose or resist: the world's fashion, the world's marriages, tithes, priests, repairing of "mass houses," taking oaths, the world's "worships" and religions, defaming others, and "looseness." The rest of the principles were those things Quakers must remember: honesty, to keep to "thou" instead of "you," to make amends to anyone wronged, to make up differences quickly, and to "judge" all bad things immediately so they would not spread. Nowhere on the list was a peace testimony or mention of violence, although some of the principles were obviously directed toward maintaining harmony.[36]

Pacifism, Passivism

Pacifism is all too readily mistaken for passivism. The new consensus, in stressing that pacifism was born in reaction to events, unwittingly reinforces this confusion.

The Colonies

Finally, the colonial experience, as we have seen, does not fit the analysis of the new orthodoxy. The political interpretation, however valid in England, does not explain the behavior and beliefs of Quakers in America. Thus the American experience serves to cast doubt on the validity of the explanation even in England itself. Lest one become overconfident, however, it is well to remember that local records have been barely touched; the study is barely begun; our current understandings are as vulnerable to revision as the old, and new thoughts are eagerly anticipated.

Notes

Introduction

1. William Edmundson, *A Journal of the Life . . . of William Edmundson*, 2d ed. (London, 1715), 87; 93.

2. Arthur J. Worrall, "Toleration Comes to Sandwich," *Seeking the Light: Essays in Quaker History*, ed. J. William Frost and John M. Moore (Wallingford, PA, 1986), 78, n. 6.

3. Fisher, "Abolitionist Biographies," book review, *Journal of African History* 23 (1982): 259.

4. George Fox, Richard Hubberthorne, et al., "Declaration From the Harmless and Innocent People of God," 21/11M/1660, *Journal of George Fox*, ed. John L. Nickalls (Cambridge, England, 1952; reprinted Philadelphia, 1985), 398–404. The Declaration may be found in appendix 1.

5. W. Alan Cole, "The Quakers and the English Revolution," *Past and Present* 10 (November 1956): 42.

6. T. Canby Jones, *George Fox's Attitude toward War* (Richmond, IN, 1984), 8.

7. The following examples typify inappropriate assumptions. Arent Furly was secretary to the commander-in-chief of the English forces in Spain in 1705. Charles R. Simpson wrote, "several of the [military] orders dated in the camp before Bacelona [sic], in 1705, are countersigned by Arent Furly, who, it is clear, must have left the Quakers before he could have accompanied Lord Peterborough." Simpson, "Benjamin Furly, Quaker Merchant, and his Statesmen Friends," *JFHS* 11 (2) (1914): 64. And William L. Saunders acknowledged that there were Quakers who bore arms during Cary's Rebellion, in North Carolina, 1711: "This violation of the principles of their faith was doubtless due to the fact that they were not born Quakers, and were still under the dominion of the natural habit of belligerency." *Colonial Records of North Carolina*, ed. William L. Saunders, vol. 1, *1662–1712* (Raleigh, NC, 1886), xxix.

8. As the sect matured, Quakers formulated short statements of ideal Quaker attitudes and practice called "advices." "Queries" were devised as well to promote both collective and individual consideration of how closely their lives expressed the wisdom contained in the advices. Advices and queries are still regularly introduced in rotation at Quaker meetings.

Rules of Discipline of the Religious Society of Friends, With Advices. . . . 3d ed. (London, 1834), 291. Emphasis added.

9. Samuel Bownas, Journal, 1676–1749, original MSS, vol. 3, Swarthmore College Library, Swarthmore, PA, no p.

10. William C. Braithwaite, *The Beginnings of Quakerism*, 2d ed., rev. Henry J. Cadbury (Cambridge, England, 1955; reprinted York, England, 1981). *The Second Period of Quakerism*, 2d ed., rev. Henry J. Cadbury (Cambridge, England, 1961; reprinted York, England, 1979).

11. Braithwaite, *Second Period*, 608.

12. Braithwaite, *Beginnings*, 440; 183; 358.

13. Braithwaite, *Second Period*, 621.

14. Braithwaite, *Beginnings*, 484.

15. Rufus Jones, *The Quakers in the American Colonies* (London, 1911), 175.

16. Margaret Hirst, *The Quakers in Peace and War: An Account of Their Peace Principles and Practice* (London, 1923).

17. *Ibid.*, 60.

18. Peter Brock, *The Quaker Peace Testimony: 1660–1914* (York, England, 1990), 37. Emphasis added.

19. I examine the work of these historians in detail in appendix 4.

1. "And the Shout of a King Is amongst Us"

1. Douglas Gwyn, *Apocalypse of the Word: The Life and Message of George Fox (1624-1691)* (Richmond, IN, 1986), xxii. Gwyn's exploration of Quaker eschatology is provocative and valuable. This study will use "Truth" to refer to a unified body of absolutes according to the Quaker concept; and "truth" in its usual meaning. Similarly, "Light" will refer to the divine principle Quakers found within.

2. Braithwaite, *Beginnings,* 86. Combined with his *Second Period of Quakerism*, Braithwaite's is the standard history of the early Quakers.

3. Barry Reay has estimated the number of Quakers in England by the early 1660s as thirty-five to forty thousand and perhaps as many as sixty thousand. Between 1660 and 1680, eleven thousand had been imprisoned and 243 had died (presumably as a consequence of punishment); *The Quakers and the English Revolution* (New York, 1985), 27; 106.

4. Isaac Penington, "The Way of Life and Death Made Manifest, and Set Before Men," *The Works of the Long-Mournful and Sorely-Distressed Isaac Penington*, vol. 1, 2d ed. (London, 1761), 50. Penington was the son of the lord mayor of London.

5. George Fox, "[Yoke the Oxen]," 1654, in *"The Power of the Lord is Over All": The Pastoral Letters of George Fox*, ed. T. Canby Jones (Richmond, IN, 1989), 56.

6. Penington, "Way of Life," *Works*, 1:34.

7. Quaker Samuel Fisher recognized too much scriptural inconsistency to be comfortable with scripture as the Word of God. See Christopher Hill, *The World Turned Upside Down* (New York, 1975), chap. 11.

8. Penington, "The Scattered Sheep Sought After," 1659, *Works*, 1:82.

9. See Richard K. Ullmann's discussion of these issues, *Between God and History: The Human Situation Exemplified in Quaker Thought and Practice* (London, 1959), 15–21.

10. Edward Burrough, *The Memorable Works of a Son of Thunder and Consolation* ([London], 1672), 16. In these early days, separation from friends and family was not simply a metaphorical reassignment of one's allegiance. To identify oneself as a Quaker often invited a literal disownment, a possibility for which the convert had to be prepared. However, Phyllis Mack has pointed out that separation was far more characteristic of the male Quaker preacher, undergoing his "solitary quest," than the female, whose conversion was apparently more compatible with her former life. See her "Gender and Spirituality in Early English Quakerism, 1650–1665," in *Witnesses for Change: Quaker Women over Three Centuries*, ed. Elizabeth Potts Brown and Susan Mosher Stuard (New Brunswick, NJ, 1989), 51–2.

11. When Quakers "voluntarily" left their families to serve the Lord, they framed their missions in terms of sacrifice. One cannot help but suspect that it was the spouse left at home, often with children, sometimes for years, who made the greater sacrifice than the one who left fields and responsibilities for a more glorious, if perilous, path. James Nayler, the eloquent Quaker leader, walked abruptly away from wife and three children without bidding them goodbye, when he "was commanded to go into the west," never to return home to live for the remaining eight years of his life. See William G. Bittle, *James Nayler: 1618–1660: The Quaker Indicted by Parliament* (York, England, 1986), 9; 173.

12. See, for example, John 6:32–33: "Moses gave you not that bread from heaven; but my Father giveth you the true bread from heaven. For the bread of God is he which cometh down from heaven, and giveth life unto the world."

13. Fell, "A True Testimony from the People of God . . . of the Doctrines of the Prophets, Christ, and the Apostles," 1660, *A Brief Collection of Remarkable Passages and Occurrences Relating to . . . Margaret Fell . . . Together With Sundry of Her Epistles, Books* (London, 1710), 268–9. To imply that the "Law" of the first covenant was merely legalistic and that spiritual character was not crucial, was, of course, erroneous. It was the purpose of the Law of Holiness in Leviticus, for example, to establish spirituality. The differences, then, derived from means.

14. Isaac Penington, *An Examination of the Grounds or Causes, Which are said to induce the Court of Boston in New-England to make that Order or Law of Banishment upon pain of Death against the Quakers* (London, 1660), 13.

15. Matt. 5:17.

16. Matt. 5:38–39; Matt. 5:43–44; Matt. 5:48. Emphasis added. But see Lev. 19:17: "Thou shalt not hate thy brother in thine heart."

17. "And the shout of a King is amongst us"; "The Epistle," in George Fox, *The Great Mistery of the Great Whore Unfolded: and Antichrists Kingdom Revealed unto Destruction* (London, 1659), no p. See also Num. 23:21; Christopher Holder and John Copeland, quoted in Charles Frederick Holder, *The Holders of Holderness* (n.p., [1902]), 55: "The Lord of Hosts is with us, the shout of a King is amongst us."

18. NEYM Earliest Written Disciplines, MSS, microfilm no. 4, NEYM Collection, RIHS, 14.

19. James Nayler, *A Discovery of the First Wisdom from beneath, and the Second Wisdom from above* (London, 1653), 13–4. See also Eph. 4:13.

20. Matt. 5:48.

21. George Fox in answer to Thomas Moore: "And the work of the Ministry was for the perfecting of the Saints, till they all come unto a perfect man, to the measure of the stature of the fulness of Christ"; *Great Mistery*, 134.

22. Penington, "Scattered Sheep," 1659, *Works*, 1:90.

23. Edward Perry, "Something of the Dealings of the Lord," 1689, *A Memorable Account of the Christian Experiences and Living Testimonies Of that faithful Servant of Christ Edward Perry* ([Philadelphia], 1726), 1; 21.

24. Perry, "Something of the Dealings," 8.

25. Potter, NEYM Disciplines, 14.

26. Geoffrey F. Nuttall has pointed out that without the acknowledgment that they could sin even after conversion, Quakers could easily become subject to "a shallow humanism, in which sin is overlooked, not overcome"; "James Nayler: A Fresh Approach," *JFHS supplement* 26 (1954): 20. But this acknowledgment came about only slowly, when Quakers were faced with the reality of Quaker "backsliding."

27. Penington, "Somewhat Spoken to a Weighty Question, Concerning the Magistrate's Protection of the Innocent," 1661, *Works*, 1:446.

28. 13 June 1660, *Records of the Colony of New Plymouth in New England*, vol. 3, *Court Orders 1651–1661*, ed. Nathaniel B. Shurtleff (Boston, 1855; reprinted New York, 1968), 190. The court somewhat mistrusted the source of this report and did not punish him.

29. William Dewsbury, "A Coppye of the word of the Lord which was Sent unto Oliver Crumwell," Caton Manuscripts, "Quaker Manuscripts Collection from the Library of the Religious Society of Friends (London)," World Microfilms, London, UK, 15 reels, reel 1, 1654–1665, 1.

30. Contrast this view with that of Roger Williams, who saw the magistracy as secular: not of God, but rather "civil" and "humane." People were the origin of laws and government, not God. Williams, quoted in Samuel Brockunier, *The Irrepressible Democrat: Roger Williams* (New York, 1940), 207. "Magistrate" in this study generally refers to government officers of any level, from the most humble to the most powerful, and refers to the inherent power of office in the abstract rather than any particular occupant of the office.

31. Quoted in George Bishop, *A Vindication of the Principles and Practises of the People called Quakers* (n.p., 1665), 5.

32. See 1 Pet. 2:14.

33. Address "To the Protector and his Councell," [1658], from nineteen Quakers, among whom were the controversialist Samuel Fisher, and Edward Byllynge, later leader in West New Jersey. *Extracts from State Papers Relating to Friends, 1654–1672*, ed. Norman Penney (London, 1913), 40.

34. Thomas G. Sanders, *Protestant Concepts of Church and State* (New York, 1964), 156.

35. Matt. 26:52.

36. Sanders, *Protestant Concepts,* 124. For "interim ethic" see Gwyn, *Apocalypse*, xx.

37. George Cartwright, king's commissioner, responding to Roger Williams's complaint that Quakers would not "Act in our government with us," quoted in letter of Richard Scott, in George Fox and John Burnyeat, *A New-England-Fire-Brand Quenched,* The Second Part ([London], 1678), 248.

38. Robert Barclay, *An Apology For the True Christian Divinity, As the same is held for, and preached by the people, Called, in Scorn, Quakers* ([London], 1678), 407.

39. 3/9M/1681, Horsleydown Monthly Meeting (11 b 3)/Southwack MSS, FHL (brackets in original MS), vol. 1, no. 168.

40. General Meeting held in London, 31/3M/1672, *Epistles from the Yearly Meeting of Friends, Held in London, to the Quarterly and Monthly Meetings in Great Britain, Ireland and Elsewhere, from 1681 to 1857,* 2 vols., vol. 1 (London, 1858), xlv.

41. Richard Hubberthorne, *The Good Old Cause Briefly Demonstrated* (London, 1659), 15.

42. Fox and Burnyeat, *A New-England-Fire-Brand Quenched, Being an Answer unto a Slanderous Book, Entituled; George Fox Digged out of his Burrows, &c.,* The First Part ([London], 1679), 225.

43. William Rogers, *The Christian-Quaker, Distinguished from the Apostate & Innovator In Five Parts,* pt. 2, chap. 5 (London, 1680), 30–2.

44. E[dward] B[urrough], *A Declaration Of the Sad and Great Persecution and Martyrdom Of the People of God, called Quakers, in New-England for the Worshipping of God* (London, [1660]), 7–8.

45. James Bowden, *The History of the Society of Friends in America,* vol. 1 (London, 1850), 97.

46. Alice Curwen, *A Relation of the Labour, Travail and Suffering of Alice Curwen* ([London], 1680), 4–5.

47. Quoted in Braithwaite, *Beginnings,* 313.

48. See Craig W. Horle's meticulous study, *The Quakers and the English Legal System: 1660–1688* (Philadelphia, 1988).

49. *Extracts from State Papers,* ed. Penney, 42.

50. Fox, 19/9M/1690, "Epistles Sent, 1683–1702, vol. 1," (transcribed from originals), Friends' House Library, London, 62–3.

51. Fox, Letter to Burlington, 7/6M/1693, "Epistles Sent, 1683–1702, vol. 1," 148.

52. See chapter 5.

53. [Benjamin Newbury of Rhode Island, 1680s?], Newbury-Richardson Commonplace Book, 1687–17–, MS, Newport Historical Society, Newport, RI, n.d., no p.

54. Underhill, *Hell Broke Loose: Or an History of the Quakers Both Old and New*, 2d ed. (London, 1660), 38.

55. John Taylor, *An Account of Some of the Labours, Exercises, Travels and Perils . . . of John Taylor* (London, 1718); reprinted as *Memoir of John Taylor of the City of York* (York, England, 1830), 25.

56. From W. D. [William Dewsbury] to M. F. [Margaret Fell], York, 10/4M/1661, Swarthmore Transcripts, "Letters and Documents of Early Friends," World Microfilms, London, UK, 4 reels, vol. 1, reel 2, 738.

57. William Caton to Margaret Fell, 9/11M/1662, Swarthmore Transcripts, vol. 1, reel 2, 515.

58. Quoted in Henry J. Cadbury, *Friendly Heritage: Letters from the Quaker Past* (Norwalk, CT, 1972), 161–2.

59. William Sewel, *The History of the Rise, Increase, and Progress of the Christian People Called Quakers*, 4th ed., 2 vols., vol. 1 (London, 1799), 578. Francis Bugg, in his anti-Quaker phase, mimicked this Quaker habit and created his own list of misfortunes that had befallen Quakers. John Bolton, for example, was rendered speechless; and "Edward Billing . . . [was] Mad in Bedlam"; Bugg, *The Picture of Quakerism* (London, 1714), 363.

60. Many responses to Quaker behavior were not only completely legal but were also reasonable and responsible from an objective viewpoint. But to Quakers, most opposition appeared to be persecution. It is their interpretation of their treatment that is important, however, not the objective justice of the situation; therefore, I will retain their often unjustified word "persecution."

61. For an exhaustive account of legislation directed against dissenters and the accompanying legal remedies, see Horle.

62. *Praemunire* was a legal device by which the king stripped away and seized one's entire estate. *Minute Book of the Men's Meeting of the Society of Friends in Bristol, 1667–1686*, ed. Russell Mortimer, Bristol Record Society's Publications, vol. 26 ([no p.], 1971), 183, n. 78.

63. Hill, *World,* 348.

64. 1670, Great Book of Sufferings, 44 vols., vol. 1, Friends' House Library, London, 14.

65. Samuel Pepys, *The Diary of Samuel Pepys*, ed. Robert Latham and William Matthews, 10 vols., vol. 5 (Berkeley, CA, 1971), 235.

66. Henry Stubbs, quoted in Hugh Barbour, *The Quakers in Puritan England* (New Haven, 1964), 223.

67. Richard Greaves has made the case for government persecution arising from political concerns rather than theological concerns in *Deliver Us from Evil: The Radical Underground in Britain, 1660–1663* (New York, 1986), 106.

68. "Petition Against Quakers," Great Book of Sufferings, vol. 1, FHL, 499.

69. Wallis, [1672], MS vol. 294/A 43 B (Dix MSS), FHL, no p.

70. Fisher, 18 July 1652, *Depositions from the Castle of York, Relating to Offences Committed in the Northern Counties in the Seventeenth Century*, ed. James Raine, vol. 40, Surtees Society (Durham, England, 1861), 54.

71. 9 September 1652, quoted in *Depositions from the Castle*, 57. It was common to demean opponents by using animal epithets, especially involving the dog. "Men and women that be in the Dogs Nature . . . are biting and devouring them that be in the Power of God," wrote Fox, "And do not you know, that after a Dog hath bitten a Man or a Woman, he is Man-Keen, after he has tasted of his or her Blood?" Fox turned to scripture, to find examples of the dog as persecuting the men of God; of dogs and wolves and swine as despisers of God's power; of Jezebel, she of the dog's nature, whose blood the dogs licked; of Isaiah, calling the false shepherds "greedy dumb Dogs." To call a clergyman "dumb dog," then, not only implied that he was a debased person but also was associated with violence. Fox, 20/11M/1675, *Cain Against Abel, Representing New-England's Church-Hirarchy, In Opposition to Her Christian Protestant Dissenters* ([London?], 1675), 19; 20–1.

72. Wharton, quoted in George Bishop, *New England Judged. The Second Part* (London, 1667), 22.

73. See, for example, Joseph Besse, *A Collection of the Sufferings of the People Called Quakers For the Testimony of a Good Conscience*, 2 vols., vol. 1 (London, 1753), 316; Sewel, *History*, 1:86.

74. [George Fox and John Rous, et al.], *The Secret Workes Of a Cruel People Made Manifest* (London, 1659), 14.

75. William Bayly, "An Answer to a Queerie Published in the Newes Booke Concerning Help Against the Turke," MS, undated, but in answer to item published 12 November 1663, MS vol. 292/45 (Crosse MSS), FHL, 45.

76. James Nayler, "Dying Testimony," in Rufus M. Jones, *Mysticism and Democracy in the English Commonwealth* (Cambridge, MA, 1932), 139–40.

77. 2/2M/1683, Horsleydown Monthly Meeting (11 b 3)/Southwark MSS, vol. 1, no. 192, FHL, no p.

78. "A Brief Relation of the Persecutions," quoted in Braithwaite, *Second Period*, 25.

79. Edmundson, 93.

80. Fox, for example, signed a letter to Oliver Cromwell: "George Fox who is of the world called G. F. who a new name hath wch the world knowes not"; "The Answer of George Fox," Fox to Oliver Cromwell, [1654], MS vol. 321/32–3 (Caton MSS vol. 2), FHL, 32–3.

81. 21/11M/1660. George Fox et al., *A Declaration from the Harmles & Innocent People of God called Quakers. Against all Plotters and Fighters in the World* (London, 1660), 2. See Fox, *Journal*, ed. Nickalls, 398–404; 399. Reminder: this date, January 1660, is according to the Old Style calendar. Others using the New Style refer to this declaration as the Declaration of 1661.

82. Fox, *Journal*, ed. Nickalls, 65; 404. "I lived in the virtue of that life and power that took away the occasion of all wars" was uttered in 1650, when Fox turned down the offer that would have cut short his prison sentence for blasphemy: the offer to be captain of a troop fighting at Worcester. On this occasion, too, he said in words often repeated, "I told them I was come into the covenant of peace which was before wars and strifes were"; 65.

83. The New York Yearly Meeting of the Religious Society of Friends, *Faith and Practice* (New York, 1974), 49; 43.

84. Penington, "Scattered Sheep," 1659, *Works*, 1:91.

85. Those in the Protestant tradition would typically have used the phrase "has come," referring only to the first coming of the historical Jesus portrayed in the scriptures. When Quakers used the phrase "is coming" they did not refer to a singular Second Coming of Christ in the future but to the possibility of an immediate and personal second coming. This sense of "coming" is captured by the Greek *parousia*, meaning "presence," a "being beside." Kenneth S. Wuest, *Studies in the Vocabulary of the Greek New Testament* (Grand Rapids, MI, 1945), 65.

86. Ullmann, *Between God and History*, 30–1.

87. Letter to Skipton General Meeting, quoted in Braithwaite, *Beginnings*, 329.

2. "A Killinge Instrument We May neither Forme, nor Beare"

1. Matt. 5:34; John 18:11.

2. Peter Brock has written a convenient summary of current thinking about the origins of the Quaker peace testimony in *The Quaker Peace Testimony: 1660–1914* (York, England, 1990), chap. 2, 3.

3. 4/3M/1655, quoted in L. V. Hodgkin, *The Shoemaker of Dover: Luke Howard, 1621–1699* (London, 1943), 49. Lilburne declared that he disavowed the sword "not in the least to avoid persecution" or to satisfy "the carnal will of my poor, weak, afflicted wife"; 49.

4. William Smith, *The Banner of Love. Under Which The Royal Army is Preserved, an[d] Safely Conducted. Being a Clear and Perfect Way out of Wars & Contention* (London, 1661), 10.

5. George Fox, "Answer of George Fox," 32–3.

6. [Humphrey Norton], *New-England's Ensigne* (London, 1659), 6.

7. William Dewsbury, "Dear Friends and Gathered of God," undated, with MSS of 1663, MS vol. 292/11 (Crosse MSS), FHL, 11.

8. George Fox, *Journal*, ed. Nickalls, 65.

9. William Ames et al., "To the King, and Counsell," MS vol. 378 (Spence MSS), FHL; now also on microfilm, "Quaker Manuscripts Collection," reel 2 (Spence MSS), vol. 3, 1650–1662, no p. Endorsed "Mf & others to to [sic] the magrastrate 1660."

10. Primarily, historians have had access to the thinking of the leadership, whose writings have been more often preserved. Quakers used the phrase "carnal weapons," meaning earthly weapons, to emphasize the contrast between tainted worldly force and legitimate spiritual force, such as the persuasive power of a righteous life.

11. Anthony Melledge, "A True Relation . . . With the Present Most Unjust Imprisonment of Anthony Mellidge [sic], somtime called a Captain; now in Scorn Caled a Quaker," dated from Dorchester Prison, 25/12M/1656, tract vol. 137/22, FHL, 4. Emphasis added.

12. *The Resurrection of John Lilburne, Now a Prisoner at Dover-Castle, Declared And manifested in these following Lines penned by himself* (London, 1656), 2.

13. Besse, *Collection*, 1:39. By "power to do it," they meant legitimacy rather than force, and they acknowledged that they owed at least passive obedience to government.

14. Fox, *"The Power,"* 6. *Journal,* ed. Nickalls, 127–8. Matt. 5:9; Matt. 5:39.

15. Fox, "Answer of George Fox," 32–3. Much of Fox's exalted vocabulary, here as elsewhere, is taken from scripture. When the letter came to be printed in the *Journal* Nickalls, the editor, enclosed the passage "my kingdom . . ." in quotation marks, as if Fox were quoting the words of Jesus; 198. With Fox's clear vision of himself as being in the Kingdom, to render the rhetoric more orthodox by selectively using quotation marks seems a mere nicety. Six years later, Fox wrote a similar disavowal to the king, in which he said he was "in that [spiritual condition] which was before wars was . . . and my kingdom is not of this world, with carnal weapons I do not fight . . . who am led by the spirit of God, so the son of God, who am not under the law nor its weapons, but am come to the love which fulfills the law"; quoted in Jones, *George Fox's Attitude,* 20. As Jones has noted, this paragraph also has been excised from or modified in the standard versions of Fox's *Journal* because its claims had become an embarassment to later Quakers. In the Nickalls version, 380, much of the paragraph is missing; one phrase has been amended to read, "my kingdom is not of this world, saith Christ." The passage does appear, however, in George Fox, *The Journal of George Fox*, "Cambridge Journal," ed. Norman Penney, 2 vols., vol. 1 (Cambridge, England, 1911), 381. This version of Fox's *Journal* is based largely on the Spence Manuscripts, the autobiographical account that Fox dictated to his stepson-in-law Thomas Lower around 1675. It includes some letters and other material not in the Nickalls revised editions.

16. Christopher Hill portrayed the Bible's cultural permeation of seventeenth-century England in his book *The English Bible and the Seventeenth-Century Revolution* (New York, 1994).

17. See Christopher Hill's discussion of Fisher in *World*, chap. 11. Quaker George Keith, before he returned to the Anglican persuasion, deplored the falling away of biblical knowledge among the next generation of Quakers.

18. [Lilburne], *Resurrection*, 13.

19. *Ibid.,* 10.

20. James 4:1. The other biblical passages are discussed hereafter. [Lilburne], *Resurrection*, 10; 11.

21. M[argaret] F[ell] et al., *A Declaration and an Information From us the People of God called Quakers To the present Governors, the King and Both Houses of Parliament, And all whom it may Concern* (London, 1660), 1; 3–4. The signers were: George Fox, Richard Hubberthorne, Samuel Fisher, Joseph Fuce, Gobert Sikes, Amos Stodert, William Caton, Gerrard Roberts, John Stubbs, Thomas Coveny, Thomas Harte, James Strut [Strutt], Ellis Hookes. *Ibid.,* 8. Margaret Fell was the wife of Judge Thomas Fell, assize judge, of Swarthmoor Hall in Lancashire. She had become convinced at the time of a visit from George Fox. Her home be-

came the clearinghouse of Quaker correspondence and recordkeeping. Judge Fell, while not sharing his wife's convictions, offered protection to the Quaker sect until his death in 1658. Margaret Fell subsequently married George Fox, in 1669.

22. F[ell] et al., *Declaration* , 3–5.

23. F[ell] et al., *Declaration,* 7.

24. George Fox, Richard Hubberthorne, et al., "Declaration From the Harmless and Innocent People of God," 21/11M/1660, Fox, *Journal,* ed. Nickalls, 398–404. The signers were: Fox, Richard Hubberthorne, John Stubbs, Francis Howgill, Gerrard Roberts, John Bolton, Leonard Fell, Samuel Fisher, Henry Fell, John Hinde, John Furley Jr., Thomas Moore. The document is reproduced in appendix 1.

25. The five common signers were George Fox, Richard Hubberthorne, Samuel Fisher, Gerrard Roberts, and John Stubbs.

26. Fox et al., "Declaration," *Journal,* ed. Nickalls, 401–2.

27. Confusion on this point is common in current Quaker historiography and is discussed in appendix 4.

28. J. William Frost, "Religious Liberty in Early Pennsylvania," *PMHB* 105 (4) (October 1981): 441.

29. Jones, *George Fox's Attitude,* 8.

30. Penington, "To Such Who Are Little & Low," MS vol. 292/4 (Crosse MSS), FHL, fol. 4.

31. Fox, *Cain,* 3. This is in reference to Massachusetts Bay Colony hanging four Quakers, 1659–1660. See chapter 4. "Professors" were those ministers and priests who *professed* their interpretive authority on the basis of their training, according to Fox, rather than on experiential knowledge of the truth. See also "Christ . . . never gave order to have men killed *about his truths*" (emphasis added). Penington, "To the Rulers, Teachers, and People of New-England," *Examination,* 8.

32. [George Fox], *To All Kings, Princes, Rulers, Governours, Bishops and Clergy . . . Being a Distinction between the Laws . . . for the Punishment of Evil Doers . . . And the Ordinances . . . concerning Religion and Worship* (London, 1685), 10.

33. Fox, *Caesar's Due Rendred unto Him . . . and God & Christs Due Rendred unto them* ([London], 1679), 21; 22; 27. See Luke 9:51–56 [Jesus]; 1 Chron. 22:7–11 [David]; Acts 20:26 [Paul].

34. Hubberthorne, *Good Old Cause,* 2–3. Emphasis added.

35. *Ibid.,* 7.

36. *Ibid.,* 16; 11.

37. Thomas Taylor, "An Apology from the Harmless against the Unjust. And to the King and his Magistrates against Plotting," 1660, *Truth's Innocency and Simplicity Shining Through* (London, 1697), 115. Cited hereafter as *Works.* Contrast the Fifth Monarchist Christopher Feake, who wrote, "Ploughshares are to be beaten into swords"; quoted in Christopher Hill, *The Experience of Defeat: Milton and Some Contemporaries* (New York, 1984), 57.

38. Ambrose Rigge, epistle, 16/10M/1692, in "A True Relation of Ambrose Rigge, By Way of Journal," *Friends' Library,* 14 vols., vol. 12, ed. William Evans and Thomas Evans (Philadelphia, 1848), 196. "Munition of rocks" is from Isa. 33:16.

39. F[ell], *Declaration* , 7. James 4:1. Penington, *Works,* 1:358.

40. F[ell], *Declaration,* 7. John 18:36. Henry J. Cadbury pointed out that "fight" should more properly be translated "strive"; *Friendly Heritage,* 101.

41. Luke 9:51–56. See also John 12:47, "for I came not to judge the world, but to save the world." F[ell], *Declaration,* 7.

42. Rom. 13:1; 1 Peter 2:13–14.

43. "Answer of George Fox," 33. Historians sometimes have used these admonitions to expose Fox's lack of consistent pacifism without apparently realizing that Fox was directly quoting the instructions John the Baptist delivered to soldiers, Luke 3:14. (See, for example, Hill, *Experience of Defeat,* 157.) Margaret Hirst is an exception: *Quakers in Peace and War,* 58.

John meant that the soldiers should act only within their mandate, just as he instructed tax collectors only to collect that which was properly due. William Dewsbury gave a good example of appropriate military restraint in describing a captain who visited him in prison. The jailor was afraid of the officer and asked him if he was an army commander. The captain replied that it did not matter, for even if he was, "my sword shall not open the Gaol dowers and if thou do not open them I shall not Com in." To Margaret Fell, 15/8M/1655, Swarthmore Transcripts, vol. 1, reel 2, 717. Fox, too, rather than expressing ambivalence, was urging soldiers to act within their proper sphere as extensions of the magistracy. The modern distinction between police functions and military functions was less operable; by approving of soldiers carrying out police functions, Fox was not necessarily being inconsistent with a pacifist position.

44. Matt. 26:51–52.

45. "A Testimony From Us, The People of God, Which The World Call Quakers. To All the Magistrates and Officers of What Sort Soever, From the Highest to the Lowest," MS Port. 24/15, FHL, no d. no p.

46. Matt. 26:53–54. The Book of Mark recounts the cutting off of the ear; here Jesus did not comment (Mark 14:47). The Book of Luke recounts that Jesus' followers asked him "Lord, shall we smite with the sword?" Then one of them cut off the ear, and Jesus said only, "Suffer ye thus far. And he touched his ear, and healed him" (Luke 22:49–51). In the Book of John, the meaning is again made explicit: Jesus' martyrdom was inevitable, because it would fulfill scriptural prophesy; therefore, Peter should not interfere with his arrest. "Then said Jesus unto Peter, Put up thy sword into the sheath: the cup which my Father hath given me, shall I not drink it?" (John 18:10–11) However ambiguous, the texts are evidence that the disciples themselves did not perceive Jesus as a pacifist or they would not have offered violent defense.

47. "Testimony from Us . . . From the Highest to the Lowest," no p.

48. Quakers observed more than once that evil was purposeful: "neither are any able to hurt the hair of your head, except it be permitted by his Power, for your trial." Epistle 6, 1683, in Epistles from the Yearly Meeting (London, 1760), 17.

49. Matt. 10:34; John 2:15.

50. Matt. 5:44.

51. Matt. 5:21–22; 1 John 3:15.

52. "Testimony from Us . . . From the Highest to the Lowest," no p. See Matt. 5:38–39; Luke 6:27–29.

53. "Testimony from Us . . . From the Highest to the Lowest," no p.

54. Matt. 5:43–45.

55. Thomas Maule, Truth Held Forth and Maintained ([New York?], 1695), 137–9; 142.

56. "[Obey Your . . . Commander]", 1654, Fox, "The Power," ed. Jones, 62. Does Fox, by this sectarian reasoning, undercut the universality of the command to "love enemies"?

57. Fox and Burnyeat, New-England-Fire-Brand, The First Part, 228.

58. Micah 4:3; Ambrose Rigge, A Scripture-Catechism for Children, ([London?], 1672), "Early Quaker Writings," reel 4, 32. See also Address from Quakers to Governor Atkins, of Barbadoes, 1677, citing Isaiah, Micah, and the restrictions on David as a man of war. Besse, Collection, 2:312.

59. William Bayly, "A Brief Declaration To All the World . . . concerning Plottings and Fightings with Carnal Weapons Against any People, Men or Nations upon the Earth," A Collection of the Several Wrightings of . . . William Bayly ([London?], 1676), 167(b)–168. This piece is mispaginated throughout.

60. Smith, Banner of Love, 6.

61. Besse, Collection, 2:291–4. These Barbadians were not only living close to the sea but were immigrants, remembering the order on ships, where the captain had unquestioned authority and was perceived as having the destiny of all aboard in his hands; their language and identification with the Israelites reflect their experience.

62. George Bishop, "The Third General Head Concerning Bearing of Arms," *A Looking-Glass for the Times* (London, 1668), 204–5.

63. Perry, "A Testimony Concerning the Lord's Work in my Heart" in *Memorable Account*, 62.

64. Fox to William Fisiold and Laurence Haydock, 7/10M/1675, Lower Virginia Monthly Meeting, Minutes 1673–1756, TMS, Quaker Collection 1116/182, Haverford College Library, Haverford, PA, pt. 2, 99.

65. "'For out of the Heart comes Evil Thoughts, Murders, Adulteries, Fornication, Theft, . . .' (Matt. 15:18–19)." It is "the Uncleanness which proceeds out of the Heart, which defiles the Man"; Fell, "To all the Professors of the World," 1656, *Brief Collection*, 79–80; but "For him that walketh in the Light, as God is in the Light, the Blood of Jesus cleanseth from all Sin"; "A Testimony of the Touch-Stone," 132.

66. Rigge, "True Relation," 196.

67. *Christian Pacifism in History* (Oxford, 1958), 52.

68. Barclay, quoted in *Friends: Some Quaker Peace Documents: 1654–1920* (London, 1939), 26.

69. Thomas Taylor, "A Warning to the Nations," 1667, *Works*, 183.

70. Barclay, 1677, *Friends: Some Quaker Peace Documents*, 25.

71. "Christian and Brotherly Advices," 1693, transcribed by Benjamin Bourne (London, 1756), NEYM Earliest Written Disciplines, MSS, micro. no. 4, NEYM Collection, RIHS, 131. This advice did not pass unnoticed; a critic later commented: "[In] 1693, when we were actually engaged in a war with France, even then did they take care that their people should not be assistant; nay, not so much as to carry guns in their ships"; Francis Bugg, *Quakerism Expos'd to Publick Censure* (London, 1699), 8. And patriotism was not the only issue. Unprotected Quaker ships if captured would make "considerable ships of war"; and "besides they can sail much cheaper than ships of force, which in time will eat all ships of force out of trade if not timely prevented"; 8 November 1672, no. 960, *CSPC, America and West Indies, 1669–1674*, ed. W. Noel Sainsbury, orig. publ. 1889 (reprinted Vaduz, Germany, 1964).

72. "Christian & Brotherly Advices," 132–3.

73. *Rules of Discipline of the Religious Society of Friends, With Advices: Being Extracts from the Minutes and Epistles of Their Yearly Meeting, Held in London, from Its First Institution*, 3d ed. (London, 1834), "Beware," "Behold," 288; "watchful," 293.

74. *Rules of Discipline*, 295. 2 Chron. 32:8.

75. Thomas Taylor, 1672, "A Testimony for Christ Jesus," Broadside, FHL, no p.

3. "Fire at the Mast"

1. See chapter 9. Leverett received Winslow's request at "sixe of the clock this morning," 23 June 1675, John Leverett to Josiah Winslow; 27 June 1675, James Cudworth to Josiah Winslow, Winslow Papers, MSS .L461, Library of the Boston Athenaeum, Boston, no p.

2. A more detailed discussion of this historiography is in appendix 4.

3. In this context, providentialism means a belief in God's *literal* ordination of events, not merely "good fortune" or "luck" in the modern sense. "To crouch to the Spirit of the World": John Burnyeat, Letter to Quakers from Barbados, 30/11M/1670, *The Truth Exalted in the Writings of that Eminent and Faithful Servant of Christ John Burnyeat* (London, 1691), 108.

4. For excellent and copious examples of soldiers and military advocacy of many kinds, see Reay, *Quakers and the English Revolution*; Hirst, *Quakers in Peace and War*; Hill, *Experience of Defeat*, chap. 5. For contemporary views, see *Extracts from State Papers*, ed. Penney.

5. Letter from Lieut.-Col. Nelson to "Dockter Robert Gorge Secretarye," 26 May 1657, quoted in *JFHS* 7 (3): 103–4. Richard Hodden himself bore some responsibility; he "kept a Quaker to preach to his troops"; Reay, *Quakers and the English Revolution*, 50.

6. Parker, 13/11M/1657, Swarthmore Transcripts, vol. 3, reel 3, 39–40; see also Walter Clement letter to Margaret Fell, 1656: "We came to Shrewsbury, where we found some

soudiers . . . newly convinced some of whom are very tender," vol. 1, reel 2, 592. Some soldiers were dismissed for insubordination or for refusing oaths. Thomas G. Sanders has suggested that the expulsion symbolized to Quakers that the army had cut "itself off from the prophetic voice," and Quakers began to question their association with the army on the grounds that it was no longer the agent of God. Sanders, *Protestant Concepts*, 127.

7. This was a common Calvinist explanation for worldly evil. Urian Oakes, minister in Boston and president of Harvard, expressed it clearly in 1677: "[God] is not the *Author*: but He is the *Orderer* of Sin itself"; "Despicable Instruments, sometimes, do great Things in His Hand"; Urian Oakes, *The Soveraign Efficacy of Divine Providence*, Artillery Election Sermon, Cambridge, 10 September 1677 (Boston, 1682), 17; 18.

8. Fisher, quoted in Edward Beckham, Henry Meriton, and Lancaster Topcliffe, *A Brief Discovery of Some of the Blasphemous and Seditious Principles and Practices Of the People, Called Quakers* (London, 1699), 21; 20. Such a view of God's role in war sometimes led to bizarre interpretations of history: Quaker John Archdale, for one, a Carolina governor, endeavored to find higher meanings in the brutal Spanish conquering of the Aztecs. The Aztecs used human sacrifices as part of their religious observances, so while Archdale could not "excuse the Barbarity or Cruelty of the Spaniards towards them," he saw "God's part" in justly giving them "their own Blood to drink, in lieu of what they had . . . shed of their Neighbours." Archdale continued, "And indeed, Providence seemed wholly to design this bloody work for the Spanish nation, and not for the English, who in their natures, are not so cruel as the other; witness the Inquisition, its cruelty being most establish'd in Spain"; John Archdale, *A New Description of that Fertile and Pleasant Province of Carolina* (London, 1707), 2. Reprinted in *Historical Collections of South Carolina*, 2 vols., vol. 2, ed. B. R. Carroll (New York, 1836), 85–120.

9. 3M/1657, Edward Burrough and George Fox, *Good Counsel and Advice* (London, 1659), 3.

10. John Burnyeat, Letter to Quakers from Barbados, 30/11M/1670, *Truth Exalted*, 108.

11. 5M/1659, William Caton, *A Journal of the Life of that Faithful Servant . . . Will. Caton* (London, 1689), 54.

12. 22 October 1656, *Extracts from State Papers*, ed. Penney, 14.

13. [1655?], John Hall to Margaret Fell, Swarthmore Transcripts, vol. 2, reel 2, 283.

14. Cole, "Quakers and the English Revolution," 42.

15. See especially Reay, *Quakers and the English Revolution*; Hill, *Experience of Defeat*; Hill, "Quakers and the English Revolution," *JFHS* 56 (3) (1992): 165–79.

16. According to Henry J. Cadbury, this account, "How the Lord by His Power and Spirit Did Raise Up Friends, etc.," was probably the work of George Fox, the year before he died, in 1691. George Fox, *Narrative Papers of George Fox*, ed. Henry J. Cadbury (Richmond, IN, 1972), 31.

17. Burnyeat, *Truth Exalted*, 108.

18. 12 April 1670, letter to Mr. Jasper Mandit, *Extracts from State Papers*, ed. Penney, 297.

19. Morning Meeting Minutes, 1673–1692, Transcripts, FHL, 6.

20. Braithwaite, *Second Period*, 617.

21. 6M/1692, Kingsbridge MM, *Early Records of Friends in Devonshire*, Friends' House Library Tract 532 (1873), FHL, 52.

22. Fox to Penn, Worcester 10/8M/1674, "Letters to William Penn, from Worcester Prison, 1674," *JFHS* 7 (2) (1910): 73–5. The son led the troop formerly under Lord Fretwell, and was a friend of the duke of Monmouth, King Charles's illegitimate son.

23. See Fox's *A Primer*, cited in Barry Levy, *Quakers and the American Family: British Settlement in the Delaware Valley* (New York, 1988), 77.

24. 30 December 1682, Letter to R. R., in *James Claypoole's Letter Book. London and Philadelphia, 1681–1684*, ed. Marion Balderston, Huntington Library Publications (San Marino, CA, 1967), 174; 170 n.; 13/1M/1682/3, Letter to Benjamin Furly, 197.

25. George Fox "The Younger," *A True Relation of the unlawful and unreasonable Proceedings of the Magistrates of Harwich* (London, 1660), 4–5; *Calendar of State Papers, Domestic Series*,

vol. 11, *1657–1658*, vol. 12, *1658–1659*, ed. Mary Anne Everett Green (reprinted Vaduz, Germany, 1965), 11:240; 478; 414; 12:413.

26. Milton, *Paradise Regained*, 3:401–2, quoted in Steven Marx, "The Prophet Disarmed: Milton and the Quakers," *Studies in English Literature 1500–1900* 32 (1) (winter 1992): 125.

27. *The First Publishers of Truth*, ed. Norman Penney (London, 1907), 89.

28. S. S. [S. Starling?], *An Answer To the Seditious and Scandalous Pamphlet, Entitled, The Tryal of W. Penn and W. Mead* (London, 1671), 15; 20.

29. Edward Coxere, *Adventures by Sea of Edward Coxere*, ed. E. H. W. Meyerstein (New York, 1946), 154.

30. Hookes, quoted in Norman Penney, "Our Recording Clerks. No. 1. Ellis Hookes. c. 1657–1681," *JFHS* 1 (1) (1903–1904): 13.

31. See for example, Fox, *Journal*, ed. Nickalls, 5 [1646]; 64–5 [1651]; 67 [1651]; 459 [1664].

32. George Fox, *To the Councill of Officers of the Armie &c.*, [1659], quoted in Jones, *George Fox's Attitude*, 77.

33. Fox, *Journal*, ed. Nickalls, 64.

34. William Edmundson, "Journal of the Life of William Edmundson," *Friends' Library*, ed. Evans and Evans, 2:110.

35. Rigge, "True Relation," 192.

36. Lurting's account, although written many years later and therefore subject to retrospective coloring, is nevertheless replete with exact details suggesting authentic recollection. He did not write in pious generalities. [Thomas Lurting], *The Fighting Sailor Turn'd Peaceable Christian: Manifested in the Convincement and Conversion of Thomas Lurting*, first published c. 1710 (London, no d.), 13. Lurting did not explain why it was the Quakers that stayed his rod and lash.

37. *Ibid.*, 15.

38. *Ibid.*, 17–8. Providentialism—much of which would be termed "superstition" today— played a prominent role in Quaker accounts. Richard Sellar, a sailor, told of his perilous experience as a pacifist. His account was replete with "magical" happenings, which he interpreted as God's favor, and credited to his own innocence as a martyr. After a brutal beating, for example, he noted that he had no bruises. Sellar was lashed to the capstan; the ropes mysteriously came undone. The mate "thought it was done by an invisible hand." Sellar warned his shipmates of a dangerous sandbank and of an approaching fireship that he had seen in a vision. *An Account of the Sufferings of Richard Sellar, For His Christian Testimony Against War, A Yorkshire Fisherman, Who Was Pressed into the Navy in the Year 1655.*, 1st ed. (London, 1842), 6–7; 15–6.

39. [Lurting], *Fighting Sailor*, 19. The Quaker sailors had been exposed to Quakerism only peripherally: a soldier who had once been to a meeting in Scotland had come on board and conversed with two young sailors, who later became the nucleus of the Quaker six; 13.

40. *Ibid.*, 20–1; 22.

41. Coxere, *Adventures*, 129–30. For date, 176n.

42. "[B]ut left me to the working of the power of the Lord in my own heart"; *ibid.*, 130. The explanation may have been retroactively protective of the two leaders. After all, in May 1659, Fisher and Burrough met with hundreds of soldiers in Dunkirk. Reay, *Quakers and the English Revolution*, 90.

43. "We might fire at the mast," Coxere, *Adventures*, 133–4; 131. Lurting, Coxere, and Knowleman continued to appear in Quaker records in the following years, usually for their "sufferings." See, for example, Besse, *Collection*, 1:297–8; 462; 491–2; *The Second Part of the People's Antient and Just Liberties asserted in the . . . Tryals of . . . Rich. Knowlman* ([London], 1670), 356–7; 359–67; 375. In 1664, Coxere was master of the vessel *Partners*, of which Lurting was mate; Coxere, *Adventures*, 163. Even after church organization took place, resulting in varieties of collective discipline, including censoring and disowning, the principle of individual leading was compelling as against a principle of outward authority. The tension between individual revelation and collective revelation and correction was composed

by the insistence that the individual leading had to be truly "from the Light," which, of course, became a matter of judgement in turn. For a discussion of this problem, see Braithwaite, *Second Period*, chap. 11, especially 305.

44. *A Declaration to the Whole World To try themselves by Gods Witness in them* (London, 1659), 9–11. Strutt signed Fell's *Declaration* of 1660. Strutt's renunciation was temporary and his scruples evolving: in 1672 the clerk of London Yearly Meeting noted with concern that James Strutt's ship as well as those of three other Quakers had been "stopt," presumably because they were sailing without guns. He described the newly issued order that all ships sailing from English ports must have guns, "great gunns if great shipps & small gunns and grenados if small shipps, & must give bond to fight if occasion be." Ellis Hookes to Margaret Fell, 10/10M/1672, Swarthmore Transcripts, vol. 2, reel 2, 444.

45. In addition to its theological basis, the idea of consensus has had practical advantages, for compliance with, and fulfilment of, decisions based on consensus are far more likely than with decisions imposed by a majority, particularly when the issue is difficult, as is pacifism. This may explain, in part, the reason early lists of Quaker disciplines so often were concerned with matters such as speech and dress and why peace principles seldom appeared.

46. "Records of the Yearly Meeting of Aberdeen," 26/2M/1672 and 7/3M/1672, quoted in *JFHS* 8 (1) (1911): 42–3. Those young men who refuse to register with the United States Selective Service at age eighteen or who do so only with the caveat that they are conscientious objectors are engaged with the same principle.

47. Cadbury, *Friendly Heritage*, 27. The map may be found in [Richard Forde], Map of Barbados, Blathwayt Series, no. 32, John Carter Brown Library, Providence, RI.

48. Kenneth L. Carroll, "Quaker Captives in Morocco, 1685–1701," *JFHS* 55 (3, 4) (1985, 1986): 71.

49. [Lurting], *Fighting Sailor*, 17–9.

50. A version of this discussion first appeared in my "Conscience or Compromise: The Meaning of the Peace Testimony in Early New England," *Quaker History* 81 (2) (fall 1992): 73–86; "The Basis of the Early Quaker Peace Testimony," *New Light on George Fox (1624–1691): A Collection of Essays*, ed. Michael Mullett (York, England, 1993), 89–100; and "Henry Pitman," *I Found It At the JCB: Scholars and Sources* (Providence, RI, 1996), 74–5.

51. Henry Pitman, *A Relation of the Great Sufferings and Strange Adventures of Henry Pitman, Chyrurgion to the late Duke of Monmouth* (London, 1689), 4.

52. *Ibid.*, 19.

53. *Ibid.*, 20–1.

54. *Ibid.*, 23.

55. *Ibid.*, 23–4.

56. Howard H. Brinton, *Quaker Journals: Varieties of Religious Experience Among Friends* (Wallingford, PA, 1972), 62. See also [Jonathan Dickinson], *Jonathan Dickinson's Journal or, God's Protecting Providence*, originally published 1699, ed. Charles McLean Andrews and Evangeline Walker Andrews, Yale Historical Publications 19, ed. Leonard Woods Labaree (New Haven, 1945).

57. The Revelation of John. See also Eph. 6: 11–17.

58. Edward Burrough, and fifteen others, *A Declaration From the People Called Quakers, To the Present Distracted Nation of England* (London, 1659), 8–9. One contemporary critic tellingly quoted this passage as an example of Burrough's hypocrisy. It clearly shows ambivalence at least. Bugg, *Picture of Quakerism*, 39.

59. Perhaps they did well to temporize; the next year one Quaker, Thomas Boulton, was "charged with going with some of Lambarts souldiers to take some men after that G. Booths party was routed . . . wther the souldiers did force or Comand them to go I know not"; Alexander Parker to George Fox, 7/6M/1660, Swarthmore Transcripts, vol. 3, reel 3, 57.

60. Fox, "Men in the Fall Are in Wars and Strife," 1656, in *"The Power,"* ed. Jones, 95.

61. Robert Barrow, "Some Account of George Fox's Funeral," letter to John Naughton, Birmingham, England, 20/11M/1691, MS, copy, National Library of Wales, Aberystwyth, Wales, 59–60.

62. Taylor, *Works.*

63. [Katherine Evans and Sarah Chevers], *A Short Relation of some of the Cruel Sufferings . . . In the Inquisition in the Isle of Malta* (London, 1662), 33.

64. George Fox, *Newes out of the North*, 1654, quoted in Jones, *George Fox's Attitude*, 60.

65. George Fox, *For Your Whoredoms*, 1660, quoted in Jones, *George Fox's Attitude*, 61.

66. William Caton, Thomas Salthouse, to Thomas Willon, London, 7/3M/1660, Swarthmore Transcripts, vol. 2, reel 2, 409. They spoke of God punishing the "ould souldiers" for their sins, by subjecting them to contempt and danger under the new monarchy.

67. Fox, *For Your Whoredoms*, 1660, quoted in Jones, *George Fox's Attitude*, 61–2.

68. Many of the early Quaker leaders had served in the Parliamentary forces, such as Nayler, Ames, Dewsbury, Hubberthorne, Bishop, and Edmundson.

69. Howgill, "Letter to G. Fox," 23/1M/[1663 or 1664], *JFHS* 44 (1) (1952): 42–3.

70. Howgill to Fox, 3/7M/1664, "A. R. Barclay MSS," *JFHS* 46 (2) (1954): 78; seventeenth-century meaning of "justice," *OED*, compact ed. 2 vols., vol. 1 (Oxford, 1971), 1524.

71. For accusations that Quakers participated in the Northern Plot, also known as Farnley Wood, see "The Examinations, and Confessions, of the Persons Concerned in the Noted Plot at Farnley Wood," MS, c. 1738, Additional MSS 33,770, British Library, London. For rumors about Quakers, see Greaves, *Deliver Us.* For Monmouth Rebellion, see *Somersetshire Quarterly Meeting of the Society of Friends, 1668–1699*, ed. Stephen C. Morland, Somerset Record Society (Series), vol. 75 ([Yeovil, England], 1978). See also [John Whiting], *Persecution Expos'd, In Some Memoirs Relating to the Sufferings of John Whiting* (London, 1715); and W. McDonald Wigfield, *The Monmouth Rebels 1685*, Somerset Record Society (Series), vol. 79 (Gloucester, England, 1985).

72. Bayly, "A Brief Declaration," 167b.

4. "Bold Boys and Blasphemers"

1. Holder, *The Holders*, 43; 53; 47. Robert Fowler, "A True Relation," quoted in Bowden, *Society of Friends*, 1:63–67. The eleven were Christopher Holder, William Brend, John Copeland, Sarah Gibbons, Mary Weatherhead, Dorothy Waugh (a serving maid), Robert Hodgson, Humphrey Norton, Richard Doudney, William Robinson, and Mary Clark. Of this group, eventually one would be called the Mutilated, four would drown (one of these four shot at sea by a Dutch privateer), one would be branded, and one would be hanged. Charles Holder asserted that Fowler was "innocent" of navigation; Fowler himself said he did not "regard" latitude and longitude." Fox, *Journal*, ed. Penney, 2:336. Holder, *The Holders*, 53; 49.

2. Among them were the first six listed in note 1 preceding. "Missionary" is not a title that early Quakers used; they would have referred to these travelers as "ministers," those who had demonstrated particular "gifts of the spirit." They had no particular "training," nor did they of course accept anything for their services other than hospitality. Quakers in England contributed to the costs of their travel. I will use the term "missionary" here to distinguish those traveling ministers who came from "outside," bringing a novel message to a non-Quaker community, from those spiritual leaders arising within a local Quaker body and largely ministering to them. The distinction between these categories was of course often arbitrary.

3. Date is New Style. Holder, *The Holders*, 22. It is likely that the two women suffered assault when detained, stripped, and searched for witches' marks at Boston: "they were so barbarously misused, that Modesty forbids to mention it"; Joseph Besse, *An Abstract of the Sufferings Of the People call'd Quakers For The Testimony of a Good Conscience* (London, 1733), 1:344–5. Ann Austin reported that she was searched by "a man in womans apparrel"; [Nor-

ton], *New-England's Ensigne*, 7. Mary Fisher is justly celebrated for her extraordinary travels as a missionary, including her effort, after her exile from Boston, to convert the sultan of the Turks. It is less well known that she married a prominent member of the Carolina government, lived in Charleston, and was a leader of the Quakers there. Robert Barrow to his wife, 23/12M/1697, in [Dickinson], *God's Protecting Providence*, ed. Andrews and Andrews, 113.

4. Holder, *The Holders*, 23; 26. Christopher Holder may have been the younger brother of Dr. William Holder, subdeacon of the Chapel Royal and sub-almoner to Charles II who married a sister of Christopher Wren; 14–5; 17. The other Quaker passengers were: Thomas Thurston (age thirty-four), William Brend (forty), John Copeland (twenty-eight), Mary Prince (twenty-one), Sarah Gibbons (twenty-one), Mary Weatherhead (twenty-six), and Dorothy Waugh (twenty); 23.

5. 14 October 1656, *Records of the Governor and Company of the Massachusetts Bay in New England,* ed. Nathaniel B. Shurtleff (reprinted New York, 1968), 3:415–6.

6. Ibid., 3:417–8; Holder, *The Holders*, 39.

7. [William Loddington], *Plantation Work The Work of this Generation* (London, 1682), 12.

8. Fox, *Journal*, ed. Nickalls, 48.

9. Fox, "To Friends in New England and Virginia," 1659, in *"The Power,"* ed. Jones, 144–5.

10. Early Quakers did not relax into the relativist concept of an individualized truth but rather saw the necessity for an individualized search for absolute truth. Today, some people, even Quakers, fail to draw this distinction, misunderstanding a lack of dogma for an easy relativism antithetical to the fundamental Quaker premise.

11. NEYM Earliest Written Disciplines, MSS, microfilm no. 4, NEYM Collection, RIHS, 4.

12. Fox, *Journal*, ed. Nickalls, 624.

13. Fox, "To Friends in the Ministry," 1654, in *"The Power,"* ed. Jones, 55.

14. Quakers would quarrel with this intermingling of the "carnal" and "spiritual."

15. See, for example, the most systematic presentation of this assumption: Frederick B. Tolles, *Quakers and the Atlantic Culture* (New York, 1960). "The ideas of English and American Friends," wrote Tolles, "down at least to the Revolution can be regarded as practically interchangeable"; ix. A fine corroborating study is by Angus J. L. Winchester, "Ministers, Merchants and Migrants: Cumberland Friends and North America in the Eighteenth Century," paper, presented at George Fox Commemorative Conference, Lancaster University, Lancaster, England, March 1991.

16. Thomas Jones, "An Epistle from our Monthly Meeting held at Merion in the Welch Tract in Pennsylvania the 11th of the 3rd month, 1699," MS [copy], Manuscript 6415E, National Library of Wales, Aberystwyth, Wales, 92. Some of the words were sour: Wales Yearly Meeting wrote "we being under a deep sense and consideration of some Friends by their irregular, disorderly and unsavoury proceedings and runnings to Pennsylvania having been cause of great weakening if not total decaying of some meetings." Those who received "such aggravating words" were indignant; 90–2.

17. See Fox's correspondence with Rhode Island Quakers in 1677 in chapter 12.

18. "A Quaker, came naked through the Hall, only very civilly tied about the privities to avoid scandal, and with a chafing-dish of fire and brimstone burning upon his head did pass through the Hall, crying 'Repent! Repent!'" Pepys, *Diary*, 8:360.

19. See, for example, letters in Swarthmore Transcripts, FHL. Available on microfilm, "Letters and Documents of Early Friends," World Microfilms, London, UK, 4 reels.

20. Edward Burrough, *To the Camp of the Lord in England* (London, 1656), 21–2.

21. James Naylor [Nayler], *Love to the Lost: And a Hand Held Forth to the Helpless,* 2nd ed. (London, 1656), 19. Geoffrey F. Nuttall has articulated this reconciliation between harshness and the spirit of love in *Christian Pacifism*, 79.

22. Theodore Eccleston et al., "An Epistle to All Friendly and Impartial Readers," preface to Taylor, *Works*, no p.

23. Eph. 6:11–17. Compare to "It is with the Spiritual Weapons of the Living God, that

you can wrestle with the Principalities and Powers of the Spiritual Wickedness"; Margaret Fell, "An Epistle of M. F. to Friends, 1657," in *Brief Collection*, 193.

24. Francis L. Hawks, *History of North Carolina* (Fayetteville, NC, 1858), 2:222.

25. Edmundson, *Journal*, 58–9.

26. Fox, *Journal*, ed. Nickalls, 642.

27. Fox, *Journal*, ed. Nickalls, 645; 643.

28. Edmundson, *Journal*, 102.

29. As late as 1691, a traveling minister observed that Carolina Quakers were glad to see him, they "not having had any visit by a travelling Friend . . . for several years before"; "A Brief Journal of the Life, Travels, and Labours of Love . . . of . . . Thomas Wilson," *Friends' Library*, 2:325.

30. Again, it is important to stress that in the Quaker view, it was enough to turn their hearers to the Light within, for that Light would eventually give rise to self-evident and inevitable testimonies as an individual's faith matured, independent of any earthly formulation.

31. For example, in 1691, Thomas Wilson "went through woods to Black Creek," no Quaker having been there before; held a meeting; and convinced several, who shortly built a meeting-house and settled a meeting, "which I think is kept there still"; [Wilson], "A Brief Journal," 2:325. The Valiant Sixty was a term used for the early traveling ministers in England.

32. Philip Gura has identified the type as "radical spiritists," those emphasizing the internal spirit of God, experiential modes of religious inquiry, radical transformation of the self, and other characteristic tendencies of those who would become Quakers. *A Glimpse of Sion's Glory: Puritan Radicalism in New England, 1620–1660* (Middletown, CT, 1984).

33. Approximately eighty-seven so-called Public Friends had come to New England to minister by 1700. G. J. Willauer, Jr., "First Publishers of Truth in New England: A Composite List, 1656–1775," *Quaker History* 65 (1) (1976): 35–41.

34. George Wilson, "Written in Virginia in James Citty soe called where I am a prisoner, & was chained to an Indian, wch is in prison for murder; we had our Legs on one boolt made fast to a post with an ox chaine," 20/9M/1661, Wilson Papers, Alderman Library, University of Virginia, Charlottesville, VA, microfilm, no p.

35. *Records . . . New Plymouth*, vol. 3, *Court Orders*, 151. "Freeting," or "fretting," means wasting away by corrosion. *OED*, compact ed., 1:1080.

36. Sewel, *History*, 1:332.

37. The Court of Assistants, characterizing Quakers, 7/7M/1658, quoted in [Norton], *New-England's Ensigne*, 88. Was it cultural habit that made them omit Quaker women from their opprobrium? Most certainly they were aware of the effectiveness and offensiveness of Quaker women.

38. R. A. Lovell, Jr., *Sandwich: A Cape Cod Town* (Sandwich, MA, 1984), 84–5. This work is occasionally unreliable and should be used with caution.

39. October 1657 [?]. Local knowledge of this site is fast disappearing. An unfortunate housing development called Christopher's Hollow, now envelops the glen in the woods. For photograph of the Hollow, see *ibid.*, 88.

40. *Ibid.*, 84.

41. Holder, *The Holders*, 161–2.

42. Davis: *Records . . . New Plymouth*, vol. 3, *Court Orders*, 173; Perry: 173; Dover: *Records . . . Massachusetts*, vol. 4, pt. 2, 69; Whetcombe-Cudworth: *Records . . . New Plymouth*, vol. 3, *Court Orders*, 206; Coggeshall: 204.

43. Cudworth, in [Fox and Rous], *Secret Workes*, 20. Cudworth continued, "as I was no Quaker, so I would be no Persecutor." Restored in 1673, Cudworth led the United Colony forces in King Philip's War. Two of his children were Quakers, Mary and James, Jr.

44. For accounts of New England persecution, see Sewel, *History*; Bowden, *Society of Friends*; Jones, *Quakers in American Colonies*; and especially George Bishop, *New England*

Judged, Not by Man's, but the Spirit of the Lord [The First Part] (London, 1661) and *The Second Part*.

45. [Fox and Rous], *Secret Workes*, 1.

46. See Jonathan M. Chu, *Neighbors, Friends, or Madmen: The Puritan Adjustment to Quakerism in Seventeenth-Century Massachusetts Bay* (Westport, CT, 1985). Chu usefully demonstrates that religious persecution was often a mask for political struggles. Issues of power hid behind the excuse of religious orthodoxy. *Ibid.*, 105–6. Whereas Chu stresses the de jure separation of sedition and heresy in Massachusetts law, Samuel Brockunier, discussing the grounds for Roger Williams's banishment, stresses the de facto identity of political and religious offenses: "heresy and sedition in Massachusetts were inextricably joined"; *Roger Williams*, 71.

47. [Fox and Rous], *Secret Workes*, 3.

48. 9 September 1661, Sewel, *History*, 1:473.

49. Besse, *Abstract*, 1:361.

50. Pembroke Monthly Meeting, Men's Minutes 1741–1801 [*sic*: begins 1676], MSS, microfilm no. 49, NEYM Collection, RIHS, no p. The Pembroke Monthly Meeting incorporated Scituate and Duxbury.

51. Fox was careful to note that about two months after this incident, the Governor died, "distracted, where the vengeance was revealed from heaven upon him for his wickedness." Signed by George Fox, from MS Port. 16/58, FHL, 1674. See also Fox, *Narrative Papers*, 188.

52. Lovell, *Sandwich*, 102.

53. Sewel, *History*, 1:565–6. Gerard Croese wrote that the constables were two brothers named Ruperts, who were in fact the sons of a Quaker. Croese, *The General History of the Quakers: Containing the Lives . . . Of all the most Eminent Quakers*, book 3 (London, 1696), 153.

54. A "Meeting for Sufferings," established in London in 1676, regularized the collection of sufferings, notably preserving the forty-four volumes of the "Great Book of Sufferings," now in Friends House Library, London. The Meeting for Sufferings now acts as the executive body of the Society of Friends in England.

55. John M. Murrin, "The Papers of William Penn," *PMHB* 105 (4) (October 1981): 487. Paul, Silas, and Quakers, for example, all sang in prison. See Acts 16:25.

56. Dennis Holester, Thomas Goulney, and William Rogers, Bristol, England, to Men's Meeting of Friends in Rhode Island, 5/3M/1669, box 39, Newport Historical Society, Newport, RI, fol. 1r.

57. *Ibid.*, fol. 1v.

58. Emphasis added. Elizabeth Hooten, 1665, MS Port. 3, FHL, 1.

59. Rufus Jones, *Quakers in American Colonies*, 201.

60. *Ibid.*, 79.

61. [Fox and Rous], *Secret Workes*, 19.

62. Craig Horle, in *The Quakers and the Legal System*, has corrected the image of the passive Quaker in the face of the justice system in England. He definitively described the Quakers' extensive legal network, which knowledgeably and systematically defended them against the justice system.

63. Emphasis added. Curwen, *Relation*, 50. Her tactic is illustrative of Horle's description of Quakers as strict constructionists. Horle, *Quakers and Legal System*, 171–2. A Massachusetts Assistant was a member of the legislature's upper house.

64. Quoted in *Records . . . New Plymouth*, vol. 3, *Court Orders*, 190.

65. Bishop, *New England Judged*, [The First Part], 84.

66. "So when they had done their bloody Work, they slunck away as a dog when he hath sucked the blood of a Lamb"; Holder, Rous, Copeland, quoted in [Norton], *New-England's Ensigne*, 93–4. Matt. 26:52 quoted 94.

67. Coddington, Letter to "Governor of New England," c. 1674, in Besse, *Collection*, 2:269.

68. Quoted in Bishop, *New England Judged. The Second Part*, 70.

69. *Records . . . Massachusetts*, vol. 4, pt. 1, 390.

70. Coddington, in Besse, *Collection*, 2:207–8.

71. According to Sewel, Adderton (Atherton) said Dyer "hung as a flag." Sewel, *History*, 1:578.

72. Burnyeat, *Truth Exalted*, 55–6.

73. Hooten, quoted in Emily Manners, *Elizabeth Hooten: First Quaker Woman Preacher (1600–1672)* (London, 1914), 45. Note that Hooten places Quakers with Christ in "or [our] Kingdome."

74. Hooten, quoted in *ibid.*, 47.

75. John Callender, *The Early History of Rhode Island. An Historical Discourse, On the Civil and Religious Affairs of the Colony of Rhode-Island* (originally published 1739), 3d ed., ed. Romeo Elton (Boston, 1843), 232–3.

76. *Rhode Island Court Records, Records of the Court of Trials of the Colony of Providence Plantations, 1647-1670*, vol. 1, 1647-1662 (Providence, RI, 1920), 47.

77. A record of sufferings from Maryland circa 1659 provides more evidence that Quakers refused military training in the colonies before the Restoration and the Fifth Monarchist uprising stimulated a formal expression of this belief in England. Richard Keen's refusal to train incited such rage that "the Sheriff drew his Cutlash, and with the point made a thrust at his Breast, and struck him over the shoulders, and said you rogue I could find in my heart to split your brains"; Francis Howgill, "A Declaration of the Sufferings," in *The Deceiver of the Nations Discovered: and his Cruelty Made Manifest* (London, 1660), 20. Another Quaker was under the command of Captain John Odbor, "who declared in the presence of many that they were not fit to be Souldiers that could not swear, be drunk and whore it"; 21.

78. Lovell, *Sandwich*, 91.

79. 21 Oct. 1663, *Records . . . Massachusetts*, vol. 4, pt. 2, 88.

80. 29/7M/1658. [Norton], *New-England's Ensigne*, 99. Samuel Shattuck was an early Quaker convert from Salem, Massachusetts. On 21 July 1657, the missionary Christopher Holder entered the First Church of Salem. While he was speaking, one official tried to force a gag into his mouth. It was Samuel Shattuck who intervened on Holder's behalf. This incident was apparently inscribed upon Shattuck's gravestone, which has since sunk into the ground out of sight. Holder, *The Holders*, 103–4; 108–9.

81. *Court Records, Court of Trials*, vol. 1, 57. There is no independent evidence that the two sons were Quakers; moreover, non-Quakers were certainly capable of failing to train. For the name "Mahorshalelhiashbash," see Isa. 8.

82. [Norton], *New-England's Ensigne*, 45–6. The fines ranged from four shillings to ten shillings except for Jenkins, who was assessed "one pot."

83. 10 March 1675/1676. Maclean W. McLean and Lydia B. (Phinney) Brownson, "Thomas Butler of Sandwich, Mass.," *NEHGR* 127 (1) (1973): 22.

84. Chu, *Neighbors*, 161. April 1674, Old Norfolk County Court Records, MSS, vol. 1, 1648–1678, Peabody Essex Museum, Salem, MA, fol. 121v.

85. 13 June 1660, *Records . . . New Plymouth*, vol. 3, *Court Orders*, 189.

86. 5 June 1658, *Records . . . New Plymouth*, vol. 8, *Miscellaneous Records: 1633–1689*, ed. Nathaniel B. Shurtleff (Boston, 1857; reprinted New York, 1968), 93; 3 December 1658, 95. Lovell, *Sandwich*, 96–7.

87. The record calls Hodgson "Huchin." There is no doubt of his identity. This may have been the occasion when the meeting repaired to Christopher's Hollow. 22 Dec. 1657, *Records . . . New Plymouth*, vol. 3, *Court Orders*, 124–5. One of the two others cited was Joseph Rogers. In 1658, a Joseph Rogers was a member of the Council of War; 153. John Howland, who had come on the Mayflower, was a member of the Plymouth Court when his brother Arthur's case came before it. He absented himself when the case was heard—a legal nicety frequently ignored in legal proceedings of the time. Lovell, *Sandwich*, 84.

88. [Fox and Rous], *Secret Workes*, 5. The Howlands were not comfortable neighbors— Arthur Howland, Jr., "hath disorderly and unrighteously indeavored to obtaine the affec-

tions of Mistris Elizabeth Prence against the mind and will of her parents," *Records . . .
New Plymouth*, vol. 4, *Court Orders 1661–1668*, ed. Nathaniel B. Shurtleff (Boston, 1855;
reprinted New York, 1968), 141. "Mistris Prence" was the daughter of the Plymouth governor who had said, "Quakers were such a people, that deserved to be destroyed." Howland
succeeded in his designs. Lydia S. Hinchman, *Early Settlers of Nantucket*, 2d ed. (Philadelphia,
1901), 78.

89. July 1660, *Sandwich and Bourne Colony and Town Records*, in *Library of Cape Cod History
and Genealogy*, no. 104 (Yarmouthport, MA, 1910), no p.

90. 9 June 1653, *Records . . . New Plymouth*, vol. 3, *Court Orders*, 38; 6 June 1660, 188; 2
March 1657, 130. "Troopers" were provided with "pistals" and "Holstan" but not "soards"
(1667). Many Quakers appeared as town appointees in town records, from William Allen as
a surveyor in 1665, Lodowick Hoxie as a juryman and rater, Henry Dillingham as constable,
William Newland and Edward Perry as financial auditors in 1676, and Stephen Wing as a re-
ceiver of dead blackbirds, when all men and boys were ordered to kill at least twelve of the
pests. *Sandwich and Bourne*, no p.

91. Lovell, *Sandwich*, 85.

92. 2 October 1658, *Records . . . New Plymouth*, vol. 3, *Court Orders*, 153.

93. 5 June 1658, *Records . . . New Plymouth*, vol. 8, *Miscellaneous*, 93. 23/1M/1679, Easton-
Perry marriage, Sandwich MM Birth and Marriage Records, including Marriage Certifi-
cates, 1646–1761, MSS, microfilm no. 44, NEYM Collection, RIHS, 70. Sandwich MM Men's
Minutes, 1672–1818, MSS, microfilm no. 45, NEYM Collection, RIHS, 25.

94. Easton-Perry Marriage, 23/1M/1679; Gifford-Mills Marriage, 16/5M/1683; Sandwich
MM Birth and Marriage Records, including Marriage Certificates, 1646–1761, MSS, microfilm no. 44, NEYM Collection, RIHS, 70; 73.

95. 2 March 1657, *Records . . . New Plymouth*, vol. 3, *Court Orders*, 130; 2 October 1658,
153; 1 May 1660, 185; 6 June 1660, 189.

96. Chu, *Neighbors*, 133; 139. But see also 169.

97. Perry, letter inserted in minutes, after 6/4M/1673 meeting, Sandwich MM Men's Minutes, MSS, microfilm no. 45, NEYM Collection, RIHS, 3. Minutes from 3/8M/1673 refer to a
letter about the peace testimony.

98. George Wilson, 20/1[?]M/1662, to the "heads, mouth, & hand" of Virginia, Wilson
Papers, microfilm, Alderman Library, University of Virginia, Charlottesville, VA, no p.

99. "A Testimony from us (in scorn called Quakers but are) the Children of the Light,"
24/6M/1675, NEYM Earliest Written Disciplines, MSS, microfilm no. 4, NEYM Collection,
RIHS, 47.

100. Sandwich MM Men's Minutes, 1672–1754, MSS, microfilm no. 45, NEYM Collection,
RIHS, 15.

101. "Christian & Brotherly Advices," NEYM Earliest Written Disciplines, MSS, microfilm no. 4, NEYM Collection, RIHS, 131.

5. "The Habitation of the Hunted-Christ"

1. Besse, *Abstract*, 1:382. Humphrey Norton was a man of ardent conviction. In 1656, he
had offered himself up to Cromwell in exchange for the release of Fox from prison. Braithwaite, *Beginnings*, 235–6.

2. [Norton], *New-England's Ensigne*, 14.

3. "Type" is used here in the sense of scriptural typology, where one might stand in for,
or "prefigure" the coming of Christ. See Harry S. Stout, *The New England Soul: Preaching and
Religious Culture in Colonial New England* (New York, 1986), 45. Richard Bailey discussed "celestial inhabitation (the notion that the saints [Quakers] became flesh and bone of Christ)"
in his persuasive and pertinent paper "The Making and Unmaking of a God: New Light on
George Fox and Early Quakerism," presented at the George Fox Commemorative Conference, Lancaster University, Lancaster, England, March 1991. While the Quaker suggestion of

substantive fusion with God was downplayed and eventually undermined by the more conventional rationality of such thinkers as William Penn and Robert Barclay, its effects were formative and lingered to undergird Quaker confidence.

4. Sydney V. James, *Colonial Rhode Island: A History* (New York, 1975), 28.

5. From "aquene" or "aquidne," meaning security, or peace, and "et," meaning place. P. W. Leland, "Algonquin, or Indian Terms, as Applied to Places and Things," *Collections of the Old Colony Historical Society* 1 (3) (1985): 98. It is grimly ironic that the English search for security and peace would all too soon displace Indian security and peace. In this respect Rhode Island was not different from the other New England colonies, in spite of its enlightened religious tolerance.

6. 4 May 1664, General Assembly Minutes, *Records of the Colony of Rhode Island and Providence Plantations, in New England*, 10 vols., ed. John Russell Bartlett, vol. 2, *1664–1677* (Providence, 1857), 57 (hereinafter *Records . . . Rhode Island*). Declaration of Breda, quoted in Horle, *Quakers and Legal System*, 65. Charles II issued the Declaration of Breda on 4 April 1660, just before his restoration. It is interesting to speculate that Christopher Holder may have influenced the issuing of this declaration. Holder traveled in 1660 to England, where he and Samuel Shattuck, Boston Quaker, appealed to the king on behalf of Quakers. Holder, *The Holders*, 163, 164. The Breda and the Rhode Island provisions should be compared with the freedom of conscience Charles II defined in his letter of 28 June 1662 urging Massachusetts to observe liberty of conscience: "We cannot be understood hereby to direct or wish that any indulgence Should be granted to those persons commonly called Quakers, whose principles being inconsistent with any kind of governement[,] wee have . . . [made] a sharpe Law against them." Charles II to Colony of Massachusetts, 28 June 1662, "Trusty and Welbeloved," John Carter Brown Library, fol. 2r. The Second Carolina Charter of 1665 included a provision similar to that of Rhode Island. *Colonial Records of North Carolina*, coll. & ed. William L. Saunders, vol. 1, *1662–1712* (Raleigh, NC, 1886), 114.

7. Hooten, 1665, quoted in Manners, *Elizabeth Hooten*, 44.

8. Hooten, quoted in *ibid.*, 49.

9. Bowden, *Society of Friends*, 96. Holder, *The Holders*, 23.

10. Thomas W. Bicknell, *The History of the State of Rhode Island and Providence Plantations*, vol. 2 (New York, 1920), 536–7. One of their daughters married Christopher Holder, one married Quaker Walter Clarke, later Governor Clarke, and one was the child who was imprisoned at Boston.

11. Croese, *General History*, book 3, 155–6. Dutch Quaker historian William Sewel used the word "knife" rather than "dagger," rendering Hodgson less aggressive. Sewel, *History*, 1:378. Hodgson had traveled aboard the *Woodhouse*.

12. Francis Bugg would delightedly include Thomas Thurston in his anti-Quaker writings as one in his "cage of unclean birds," because Thurston, years later in Maryland, convinced the wife of the absent deputy governor that he "came with a Message from the Lord (as he Horridly pretended)" and got her with child. *Picture of Quakerism*, 198. For long hair, Roger Williams, *The Complete Writings of Roger Williams*, 7 vols., vol. 5, *George Fox Digg'd Out of his Burrowes*, [1676], ed. J. Lewis Diman (New York, 1963), 50.

13. Johan Winsser, "Mary Dyer and the 'Monster' Story," *Quaker History* 79 (1) (1990): 20–34.

14. Maud Lyman Stevens, "The Romance of Newport," *Bulletin of the Newport Historical Society* 24 (January 1918): 12.

15. 1M/1658, quoted in Bowden, *Society of Friends*, 86. This letter bears witness that the missionary effort had taken root because it distinguishes between missionary ("a sort of people") and converts ("divers").

16. The proper name of the colony was "Rhode Island and Providence Plantations." The name "Rhode Island" was ambiguous: sometimes it was shorthand for the colony; as often it was synonymous with Aquidneck Island. I use it here to refer to the colony.

17. Fox wrote that most of those in Narragansett had never before heard Quakers. *Journal*, ed. Nickalls, 623. John Burnyeat and John Stubbs held a Quaker meeting at Richard Smith's house 20/6M/1672, and Fox at Jirah Bull's. It enhanced the power of Quakers in government that they were concentrated near the seat of the colony government at Newport; delegates "from the main" often missed government sessions because of the difficulty of travel, especially during winter and war.

18. Sydney James, "Friends in Colonial Rhode Island Politics," paper presented at George Fox Commemorative Conference, Lancaster University, Lancaster, England, March 1991, 3.

19. Report of Cartwright to Council for Foreign Plantations, 21 June 1671, *CSPC*, *1669–1674*, 232.

20. For constitutional arrangements, see James, *Colonial Rhode Island*, chap. 4.

21. For Carr, see John Osborne Austin, *The Genealogical Dictionary of Rhode Island* (Albany, NY, 1887), 37. Arthur Worrall gives a concise account of the politics behind this upheaval. Arthur J. Worrall, *Quakers in the Colonial Northeast* (Hanover, NH, 1980), 31–4.

22. "Rhode Island General Assembly Proceedings 1646–1715," MSS, vol. 2, Rhode Island Colony Records, 18–9. The original records are at the Rhode Island State Archives, Providence, Rhode Island. Bartlett, the editor of the printed records, left out more and more of the originals with each subsequent volume. The records in his volume 2 are still relatively complete, but from time to time omit names, especially those of deputies.

23. For instructions regarding marriage and marriage certificates, see NEYM Earliest Written Disciplines, MSS, microfilm no. 4, NEYM Collection, RIHS, 11.

24. For "a cage of unclean birds," see Bugg, *Picture of Quakerism*, 198. See also [1655?], John Hall to Margaret Fell, Swarthmore Transcripts, vol. 2, reel 2, 285, where Hall reported he was accused of calling the college at Aberdeen "A Cage of uncleane birds." Babylon was the "cage of every unclean and hateful bird"; Rev. 18:2. Aquidneck in the seventeenth century had two towns: Newport at the southern tip and Portsmouth at the northern tip.

25. [George] Rofe to Richard Hubberthorne, dated Barbados 18/9M/1661, MS vol. 323/62 (A. R. Barclay MSS), FHL, fol. 1r. There had been other meetings in England called general meetings, but they were local in character and met more frequently, corresponding to a "monthly meeting" or a "quarterly meeting." Monthly meetings were meetings for business, sometimes combining several "preparative" meetings from different towns and meeting once a month. Quarterly meetings met four times per year and consisted of people of several area monthly meetings. Yearly (at first called "general") meetings met once per year and encompassed a larger region.

26. Henry J. Cadbury, "The Oldest Yearly Meeting," *Friend* (of London), 24 April 1953, 373–4.

27. Description of William Edmundson: Williams, *George Fox Digg'd*, 57; Fox: 85.

28. Coddington, quoted in Fox and Burnyeat, *New-England-Fire-Brand*, The Second Part, 245.

29. John Stubbs, letter to Margaret Fell, dated Newport, 14/6M/1672, in Fox, *Journal*, ed. Penney, 2:218.

30. Williams, *George Fox Digg'd*, 33. Williams's description of Quaker business dealing is interesting because it is unusual. The common view was that Quaker emphasis on fair dealing, leading to the practice of the fixed price, was so appealing to everyone used to slick dealing in the marketplace that Quaker trade prospered at the expense of the trade of others. Selling liquor to Indians has its modern-day equivalent in the cigarette factories that American companies have scattered in poorer countries, where the factory is sometimes the first—and only—manufacturing establishment in the region. Throckmorton had followed Anne Hutchinson to New Amsterdam, settling near what is now Throg's Neck, named for him, before returning to Rhode Island after an Indian attack in which Hutchinson was killed with all but one of her children.

31. *Ibid.*, 465.

32. Letter of Francis Brinley to Col. Francis Nicholson, dated Newport, 4 November 1709, "Documents Relating to Rhode Island, and Rhode-Islanders: Three Volumes, First Series," Transcripts of MSS in Massachusetts Historical Society, vol. 2, John Carter Brown Library, 59.

33. Nicholson's wife was pregnant, a provocation to some Quakers at Salem, Massachusetts, who advocated celibacy. One of these Quakers, William Brend, deliberately brought his nonpregnant and celibate wife to Rhode Island as a model of purity to counteract Nicholson's bad example. Letter to Margaret Fell, dated Rhode Island, 10/5M/1660, Swarthmore Transcripts, vol. 2, reel 2, 927–30; 929. Norton was intensely mystical, mocking the idea of a historical Christ. Williams, *George Fox Digg'd*, 86.

34. The others were Robert Widders, George Pattison, James Lancaster, and John Cartwright. Fox, *Journal*, ed. Nickalls, 618; 621. George Pattison was a Quaker seacaptain under whom mariner Thomas Lurting served.

35. Letter to Margaret Fell dated RI, 19/4M/1672, in George Fox, Epistles, MSS copies, MS vol. 308, FHL, 252–3.

36. Hooten, MS Port. 3, FHL, fol. 2r. Fox's first recounted "miracle," in which he restored a "roaring" possessed woman, took place in Hooten's house. The aura of the supernatural held a fascination for Quakers, as for others of the seventeenth century. See also *George Fox's "Book of Miracles,"* ed. Henry J. Cadbury (Cambridge, England, 1948). Fox originally set forth on this journey from England with twelve companions, surely a deliberate echo of "The Twelve," the twelve apostles of Jesus.

37. In handwriting of Richard Richardson, 1674 account, MS Port. 16/77, FHL, 180. The quotations are from Fox, *Journal*, ed. Nickalls, 631–2. Jay had been one of the visiting ministers to Rhode Island. He signed a marriage certificate of 22/4M/1672. Rhode Island MM Marriages, MSS, microfilm no. 11, NEYM Collection, RIHS, no p.

38. Rogers, *Christian-Quaker*, pt. 4, 32. Rogers, a Quaker separatist in England, was not present in Rhode Island. It is easy to confuse him with Rhode Islander Roger Williams.

39. Stubbs, to Fell, dated RI, 19/4M/1672, 252–3. The general meeting met in William Coddington's recently built "mansion." Coddington had bought Aquidneck from the Indians in 1637/8 for forty fathoms of white beads. Callender, *Early History*, 214–5.

40. Fox, *Great Mistery.*

41. Fox, "George Fox's American Journey, 1672," MS Port. 9.1, FHL, fol. 3r–3v.

42. A Quaker "minister" was one who had demonstrated special "gifts of the spirit" and who, designated as such by his or her own meeting, was sent forth to travel from meeting to meeting exercising this gift. Although the information about Rhode Island practice comes from antagonist Roger Williams, he would have had nothing to gain by misreporting these practices. Williams, *George Fox Digg'd*, 250; 135.

43. Fox, "American Journey," fol. 3r–3v. George Fox and Margaret Fell established a system of geographically based meetings to introduce some cohesion, discipline, and indeed collective power into the sometimes diffuse, individualized Quaker meetings of the early days and to meet the challenges of persecution.

44. 18/4M/1672, "at Wm Coddingtons," NEYM Earliest Written Disciplines, MSS, microfilm no. 4, NEYM Collection, RIHS, 9; 10n.; 13. Rogers, preface, no p. Quaker schisms were an ongoing problem, far less easily dealt with than individual error. Rogers was a leader of the Wilkinson-Story faction, which formed in reaction to Fox's system of business meetings in the 1660s, strongly objecting to the juxtaposition of collective authority against the authority of individual revelation. Fox had not always been gentle with Rogers: "ratell heades like him self with his healesh paper of lies," Fox to William Penn, 13/11M/1678, *JFHS* 11 (1) (1914): 20. Rogers (and Francis Bugg) figured in an anonymous satirical poem about this schism:

Without spectacles some see your shame
having made yourselves a spectacle, for
Team Rogers, Crisp, Peniman, Bullock and Bug

dark, divel driven, dungy Gods desperately lug
That are ty'd to the taile of their separate schism
Pap-Libertin-Heathen-Juda-Athe-ism[.]

Typescript prepared by Craig Horle (who postulated that the author was Robert Sandi-
lands, writing about 1682); listing of MS vol. 323/1 (A. R. Barclay MSS), FHL, no p.

45. A cautionary note: the phrase "disorderly walking" was often used to conceal the nature of the offense and so protect confidentiality, or deflect outside criticism. Hence some
instances of "disorderly walking" may conceal actual matters relating to violence.

46. Fox, "George Fox's American Journey," fol. 3r. Stubbs to Fell, dated RI, 19/4M/1672,
252–3.

47. Fox, "George Fox's American Journey," fol. 3r. Ann Clayton Easton, the governor's
wife, had been a servant in the household of Margaret Fell, who by 1672 was the wife of
George Fox. As Ann Clayton she was convinced at Swarthmore Hall, the Fell home, in the
early days of Quakerism upon George Fox's first visit; Braithwaite, *Beginnings*, 101.

48. George Fox, "George Fox's Sermon," 25/5M/1672, in J. William Frost, "Quaker versus Baptist: A Religious and Political Squabble in Rhode Island Three Hundred Years Ago,"
Quaker History 63 (1) (spring 1974): 46–7.

49. *Ibid.*, 47. Here Fox has listed the "offices," or functions, of Jesus: Jesus as Priest sancti-
fying the believers, Jesus as Prophet bringing the Word, Jesus as Captain training his soldiers
with the armor of light, the shield of faith, the sword of the spirit, and so on. See Eph.
6:11–17. See also MS of George Fox quoted in *George Fox Speaks for Himself*, ed. Hugh McGregor Ross (York, England, 1991), 69-71.

50. Fox, "Sermon," in Frost, "Quaker versus Baptist," 46–7.

51. T[homas] O[lney] Junior, "Ambition Anatomized," 5/4M/1673, in *ibid.*, 47–52.

52. Olney, in Frost, "Quaker versus Baptist," 52; 48.

53. *Ibid.*, 48.

54. See appendix 4.

55. Olney, in Frost, "Quaker versus Baptist," 48–9. Olney deemed Fox a man "highly
transported with conceit, being blowne up with pride"; 50. If Olney's opinion was more
than jealousy, perhaps Fox had indeed received more adulation than was good for him.
"This is the man who hath benn Adored as a God"; 52.

56. Fox, "George Fox's American Journey," fol. 3r.

57. Williams, *George Fox Digg'd*, 37. Roger Williams, *An Answer to a Letter Sent From Mr.
Coddington of Rode Island, to Governour Leveret of Boston in What Concerns R. W. of Providence*,
originally published 1678, Society of Colonial Wars, RI, pamphlet 38 (Providence, RI, 1946),
4. William Coddington called attention to the fact that Roger Williams's three days of testimony ended with a great eclipse of the sun. Fox and Burnyeat, *New-England-Fire-Brand*, The
Second Part, 246.

58. Williams, *George Fox Digg'd*, 185; 318–9.

59. George Fox, quoting Roger Williams, in Fox and Burnyeat, *New-England-Fire-Brand*,
The Second Part, 34.

60. Others continued to impugn Fox's reputation. One minister, Joshua Hubbard from
Barbados, "published" before the Plymouth General Court that Fox was a "notorious publican or siner, & did exercise severall of his debauched or bestuall practize in Barbadus, with
women ther." Quakers moved quickly to secure affidavits of Fox's good character from Barbados dignitaries. Rhode Island tolerated Hubbard's presence and preaching for an entire
winter. William Coddington reported that some Rhode Islanders evaluated Hubbard as
being a "hoge preist." William Coddington to John Winthrop, Jr., 15/4M/1674, *Massachusetts Historical Society Collections*, 4th series, vol. 7 (Boston, 1865), 293–4.

61. 25 June 1672, Governor and Council Records, 1667–1753, MSS, Rhode Island State
Archives, Providence, RI, 57–8. The Quakers present on this occasion were Nicholas Easton,
his son John Easton, and Joshua Coggeshall; in addition, Benjamin Smith was very likely a

Quaker: his father, Christopher, was termed an ancient Friend of Providence in Quaker records; his nephew "suffered" for not training. Austin, *Genealogical Dictionary*, 376; 379.

62. When Fox suggested a law against fighting and swearing, he was clearly referring to day-to-day disorder among the population, not to organized fighting. Yet the 1673 Exemption was a model of legislation that attempted to meet the needs of all the people, for defense and for freedom of conscience alike, and thus was consonant with the standards Fox had preached about in a more general way. The 1673 Exemption is the subject of chapter 6.

6. "Times of Motion and Danger"

1. Matt. 5:34.
2. *Records . . . Rhode Island*, ed. Bartlett, 2:110–2.
3. 28 September 1667, Joseph Mason to Robert Mason, Lord Proprietor of New Hampshire, *CSPC, America and West Indies, 1661–1668*, ed. W. Noel Sainsbury (London, 1880; reprinted Millwood, NY, 1964), 500.
4. *Records . . . Rhode Island*, ed. Bartlett, 2:114–8.
5. *Ibid.*, 2:118.
6. At this time, the deputy governor, Nicholas Easton, assistants William Reape, John Easton, Benjamin Smith, and deputies Peter Easton, Walter Clark, William Wodell, and possibly John Throckmorton, were Quakers. (Throckmorton was a Quaker at least by 1672.) *Ibid.*, 2:189–90.
7. May 1667, Governor and Council Minutes, *ibid.*, 2:196–7. The council consisted of the governor, deputy governor, and ten assistants.
8. "To the sixth particular the Deputye Governor sayth he cannot consent as to command"; *ibid.*, 2:197. William O. Achtermeier, *Rhode Island Arms Makers and Gunsmiths, 1643–1883* (Providence, RI, 1980), 1; *Records . . . Rhode Island*, ed. Bartlett, 2:196.
9. *Records . . . Rhode Island*, ed. Bartlett, 2:192–3; 194–5; 193–4. "It is also left to the Magistrates of Providence and Warwick to do as they shall think meet, as referring to disarming the Indians among them"; 2:193.
10. *Ibid.*, 2:205; 205–8. Newbury-Richardson Commonplace Book, Newport Historical Society Library, Newport, RI, no p. Although unsigned and undated, it seems likely to date from the 1680s, from the hand of Benjamin Newbury, a Quaker.
11. *Records . . . Rhode Island*, ed. Bartlett, 2:218. The aristocratic aura of the troop of horse may have contributed to the volunteers' enthusiasm. Describing New England troopers generally, William Harris in 1675 wrote, "their Horsemen weare buff-Coats, pistolls, Hangers, & Croslets"; "An Account Taken from Mr. Harris, New England," 29 April 1675, MS, PRO: CO 1/34/170411, fol. 141v [stamped nos].
12. *Records . . . Rhode Island*, ed. Bartlett, 2:199–200.
13. 1666, *ibid.*, 2:158. The activities of the Quaker-dominated Rhode Island governments are detailed in the following chapters.
14. Bruce C. Daniels, *Dissent and Conformity on Narragansett Bay: The Colonial Rhode Island Town* (Middletown, CT, 1983). T. H. Breen has traced this "persistent localism" to the experience that the colonists had carried with them from England. Charles I's excessive attempts to encroach on local affairs, Breen has suggested, had stimulated a defense of local autonomy. This habit of resistance to the centralizing impulse had shaped the New England polity. See his "Persistent Localism: English Social Change and the Shaping of New England Institutions," *WMQ*, 3d series, 32 (1) (January 1975): 3–28.
15. After King Philip's War of 1675–1676, the mainland communities expressed their resentment at their perceived abandonment by the island powers and attributed this indifference to the pacifism of the central Quaker government. Their argument seems based on convenience and scapegoating; the similar neglect by non-Quaker governments, both within and without Rhode Island, belies this complaint.
16. After King Philip's War, Plymouth tried to stimulate the king's guilt for not helping

the colony in its struggles with the Indians in order that the colony might obtain additional territory from the king. On behalf of the Plymouth Court, Nathaniel Morton wrote, "for Wee did always beleive that could your Majestie have known our innocency . . . and our great sufferings, streights and hazards it would have moved your tender heart to have pittyed and your powerfull hands also to have helped us"; New Plymouth, "Letter from New-Plymouth about the Indian Warr," 12 June 1677, MS, PRO: CO 5/904/XC170411, fol. 4r–4v [stamped nos].

17. *Records . . . Rhode Island*, ed. Bartlett, 2:198.

18. *Records . . . New Plymouth*, vol. 4, *Court Orders*, 144; 143–5.

19. Roger Williams supported Philip on this occasion, characterizing the Indian who had reported the rumor as "a very vile fellow." *Records . . . New Plymouth*, vol. 4, *Court Orders*, 165.

20. In 1671 the English Board of Trade estimated that Plymouth had one thousand men able to bear arms, the same estimate as for Rhode Island; 21 June 1671, "An Account about New England from the Board of Trade," MS, Historical Manuscripts from the H. B. M. State Paper Office (Stevens Transcripts), vol. 2, 1666–1682, no. 95, John Carter Brown Library, no p.

21. George M. Bodge, *Soldiers in King Philip's War* (Leominster, MA, 1896), 472–6. The English Board of Trade estimate in 1671 of men able to bear arms in Massachusetts was thirty thousand. "An Account about New England."

22. *Records . . . Massachusetts*, vol. 4, pt. 2, 332–3.

23. "Account Taken from Mr. Harris," fol. 140r–140v.

24. *Records . . . Rhode Island*, ed. Bartlett, 2:490.

25. 31 August 1671, Governor and Council Records, 1667–1753, MSS, Rhode Island Archives, Providence, RI, 53. George Lawton was probably a Quaker by this time.

26. The Council To Captain Greene and Each Town on Rhode Island, Newport, 31 August 1671, "RIHSM.," vol. 1, no. 3, RIHS, fol. 1r.

27. 8 July 1671, *Records . . . New Plymouth*, vol. 5, *Court Orders 1668–1678* (Boston, 1856; reprinted New York, 1968), 70–7.

28. "[T]hen lend a hand": [Newbury?], poem, Newbury-Richardson Commonplace Book, no p.

29. *Records . . . Rhode Island*, ed. Bartlett, 2:489, 492–3; see 2:488–95.

7. "Fighting against the Minde of God"

1. Almost two and a half centuries later, in the early twentieth century, the governments of the United States and of Great Britain were imprisoning men refusing military service on the basis of conscience.

2. Quaker members were: Nicholas Easton, governor; William Coddington, deputy governor; assistants Walter Clarke, Daniel Gould, John Easton, Thomas Harris, Joshua Coggeshall, and Job Almy; deputy and treasurer Peter Easton; deputies Daniel Gould, John Gould, Henry Bull, John Throckmorton, Lawrence Wilkinson, William Wodell, and Robert Dennis. Strong indirect evidence that John Tripp and Walter Todd were Quakers comes through their Quaker wives. Both women appear in Quaker records: Widow Mary Tripp was chastised for nonattendance at meeting and a Margaret Todd, probably Walter's wife, signed several marriage certificates. *Records . . . Rhode Island,* ed. Bartlett, 2:482, 484. Rhode Island MM Marriages, MSS, microfilm no. 11, NEYM Collection, RIHS, no. p.

3. Rhode Island Colony Records 1671–1686, vol. 2, Rhode Island State Archives C#00204, Rhode Island State Archives, Providence, RI, 30. The MSS records will be cited in this chapter as "(MSS)". These records are printed in *Records . . . Rhode Island*, ed. Bartlett, vol. 2. Bartlett makes few errors of significance, with one exception discussed hereafter. The two other committee members were William Harris and Lieutenant William Cadman; 2:488 (MSS, 30).

4. For defense, *Records . . . Rhode Island*, ed. Bartlett, 2:489–91 (MSS, 30–1). For indemnification, 2:492–95 (MSS, 31–2).

5. *Ibid.*, 2:498 (MSS, 33). The exemption provisions are found on 2:495–9 (MSS, 32–4). For clarity the spelling is modernized and the passage abbreviated here. A fuller rendering reads:

> Noe person nor persons (within this Collony), that is or hereafter shall be persuaded in his or their Conscience, or Consciences (and by him or them declared) that he nor they cannot nor ought not to trayne, to learne to fight, nor to war, nor kill any person nor persons . . . shall at any time be Compelled against his or their Judgment and Conscience to trayne, arme or fight, to kill any person . . . nor shall suffer any punnishment.

6. *Ibid.*, 2:495, 498 (MSS, 32, 33).

7. *Ibid.*, 2:499 (MSS, 34). To allow Quakers to watch unarmed was a common solution to the impasse their beliefs often caused. Barbados Quakers, for example, were accorded this accommodation. Quakers of Nevis refused to acquiesce to a similar provision, and Fox rebuked their too-rigorous scruples. Other governments were later to introduce alternative obligations for Quaker service, for example, Antigua in 1705. Peter Brock, *Pioneers of the Peaceable Kingdom* (Princeton, 1968), 54–5; 57–8.

8. Emphasis added. MSS (33–4).

9. The printed version read, "Such said persons who cannot fight . . . it beinge against their conscience[,] to doe and perform civill service to the Collony though not martill service, and can preserve (soo farr as in them lies) lives." *Records . . . Rhode Island*, ed. Bartlett, 2:498. The printed version deleted a crucial qualification and thus has misled historians to believe that while the assembly exempted some from military service, it required civil, alternative service of all. The act in fact excused some from both military and alternative service.

10. Brock, *Pioneers*, 23. The Rhode Island Exemption was not the first provision for objectors, however. Nathaniel Sylvester, a Quaker, bought up the shares in Shelter Island, off Long Island, in 1662. He succeeded in negotiating an agreement by which Shelter Islanders were exempted "forever" from taxes and military duty. Jones, *Quakers in American Colonies*, 226.

11. Worrall, *Quakers*, 37.

12. Jones, *Quakers in American Colonies*, 179.

13. *Records . . . Rhode Island*, ed. Bartlett, 2:496; 495 (MSS, 33; 32).

14. The feverish religious atmosphere of these months, as we have seen, is vividly present in the later written exchanges between Roger Williams and George Fox.

15. *Records . . . Rhode Island*, ed. Bartlett, 2:496 (MSS, 32).

16. *Ibid.*, 2:496 (MSS, 32–3). See also Deut. 28:30, where God retracts these privileges as part of his curse for disobedience: "Thou shalt betroth a wife, and another man shall lie with her: thou shalt build an house, and thou shalt not dwell therein: thou shalt plant a vineyard, and shalt not gather the grapes thereof."

17. Knowledge of this passage, or of the Rhode Island use of it, may have inspired one Nathaniel Byfield, who petitioned the Massachusetts government during King Philip's War to be excused from the press because he was newly married. He argued, "And where as the Law of God is plaine . . . in 24 Dewter: 5: That when a man hath taken a new wife he shall not goe out to warr." 25 April 1676, *Records . . . New Plymouth, Acts of the Commissioners of the United Colonies of New England*, 2 vols., vol. 2, *1653–1679*, ed. David Pulsifer (Boston, 1859; reprinted New York, 1968), 461.

18. Deut. 20:8.

19. *Records . . . Rhode Island*, ed. Bartlett, 2:496–7 (MSS, 33).

20. Arthur Worrall: the Assembly "adopted a biblical justification for pacifism"; *Quakers*, 37.

21. *Records . . . Rhode Island*, ed. Bartlett, 2:497 (MSS, 33):

If persons Excused from war least they be slain and an other dedicate their house they built[,] how much more Excused from learninge war and waringe, least thereby and in their Consciences then beleive they should, if [they] learne war and fight to kill and distroy that house of clay or Tabernacle which God hath built[,] be Excused from war and destroyinge it[,] beinge the Temple of God.

22. *Ibid.*, 2:497 (MSS, 33): "If marryinge of a wife shall Excuse a man from war[,] how much more any such who are perswaded in their Consciences that they are Espoused to Christ, and that if they should learne war or war[,] would occassion a differance and distance between them forever."

23. *Ibid.*, 2:497 (MSS, 33):

Or he that hath planted a vinyard, be Excused from war because he hath not eat of the fruit, how much more rather, a man Excused from war, than whereby he is perswaded if warringe against his Conscience and understanding, he cutts off a branch or limb (which God's Right Hand hath planted), from the vinyard and destroys it.

24. *Ibid.*, 2:496–7 (MSS, 32–3).

25. *Ibid.*, 2:496 (MSS, 33).

26. Brockunier, *Roger Williams*, 225; 227.

27. William Wilkinson, *An Answer to Joseph Jenks's Reply to William Wilkinson's Treatise, Entituled, The Baptism of the Holy Spirit* (London, 1721), iii. The Baptist position fluctuated: around 1680, responding to an accusation that they denied magistracy, Baptists in Boston issued a statement that they were prepared in their persons and estates to do service in defense of their country. Backus, *History,* 338–9.

28. Archdale had been converted by Fox himself, in England. Archdale, *New Description,* preface, no p.

29. *Records . . . Rhode Island,* ed. Bartlett, 2:498 (MSS, 33).

30. *Ibid.*, 2:496 (MSS, 33).

31. *Ibid.*, 2:496. "His Majesty . . . ussith men of other understandings to fight, yet not those . . . who will loose their owne lives rather than distroy other men's lives [who] can noe waies nor by noe meanes be compelled to fight to kill" (MSS, 33).

32. Penington, quoted in John Pennyman, *This is for the People Called Quakers* (London, 1675), 11.

8. "Sin and Flesh"

1. Also written as Zoeth Howland. 31/1M/1676, Rhode Island MM, 1647–1899, Deaths 1647–1875, MSS, microfilm no. 10, NEYM Collection, RIHS, 4. Ann Gidley Lowry, "Quakers and Their Meeting House at Apponegansett," in *Old Dartmouth Historical Sketches*, no. 70 ([New Bedford, MA], 1940), no p. Account taken from *Providence Journal*, October 1, 1933, and found in "Durfee & Stafford Genealogy and Allied Lines from 1600's," assembled in Tiverton, RI, no d., no p. Pocasset, now Tiverton, was on the eastern shore of Narragansett Bay, in Plymouth Colony.

2. The war is named for King Philip, sachem of the Wampanoags. Philip is the English name for Metacom, the son of Massasoit. The traditional assumption has been that Philip was the son of Massasoit. However, the "Council of the Massachusets" called Massasoit Philip's grandfather in 1676. *A Farther Brief and True Narration of the Late Wars Risen in New England, Occasioned by the Quarrelsome Disposition and Perfidious Carriage of the Barbarous and Savage Indian Natives there* (London, 1676), 12. The continuing controversy seems finally to be settled, with Philip as Massasoit's son. Some say the English gave him his English name to honor him; others that the English were mocking him.

3. John Easton, "A Relacion of the Indyan Warre, by Mr. Easton, of Roade Isld., 1675," in *Narratives of the Indian Wars, 1675–1699*, ed. Charles H. Lincoln (New York, 1913), 10–1. The

Wampanoags were located mostly in Plymouth Colony; Philip's home was the Mount Hope peninsula, at the northern end of Narragansett Bay, close to Aquidneck Island.

4. Easton, "A Relacion," in *Narratives*, ed. Lincoln, 13–4.

5. Fox, *Journal*, ed. Penney, 2:250. Under heading "Postscripts of passages to be remembred."

6. Archdale, *New Description*, 2.

7. Easton, "A Relacion," in *Narratives*, ed. Lincoln, 17.

8. Peter Folger, "A Looking-Glass for the Times, or The Former Spirit of New-England Revived in This Generation . . . Relating to the People Called Quakers in New England," 23 April 1676, Sherborn, Nantucket, transcript of book printed in 1763, John Carter Brown Library, no p.

9. [Edward Wharton], *New-England's Present Sufferings Under Their Cruel Neighbouring Indians. Represented In two Letters, lately Written from Boston to London* (London, 1675), 4; [8].

10. [Samuel Groome], *A Glass For the People of New-England, in which They may see themselves and Spirits . . . ever since they usurped Authority to Banish, Hang, Whip and Cut Off Ears* (n.p., 1676), 15.

11. 3 November 1675, *Records . . . Massachusetts*, 5:60.

12. In the provinces of New Hampshire and Maine, a treaty was drawn in spring 1678. Mr. Harris estimated in April 1675, just before the war, that there were seven or eight thousand foot in New England and eight or ten troop of horse, each with sixty to eighty horse. "Account Taken from Mr. Harris," fol. 140r.

13. Russell Bourne, *The Red King's Rebellion: Racial Politics in New England, 1675–1678* (New York, 1990), 36.

14. Michael J. Puglisi, *Puritans Besieged: The Legacies of King Philip's War in the Massachusetts Bay Colony* (Lanham, MD, 1991), 30, n. 31. Puglisi relies on the figures of Sherburne F. Cook; 30, n. 31.

15. *Ibid.*, 59.

16. *So Dreadfull a Judgment: Puritan Responses to King Philip's War, 1676–1677*, ed. Richard Slotkin and James K. Folsom (Middletown, CT, 1978), 3–4.

17. "Genealogy of the Families of Dexters," MS, 17 February 1819, "RIHSM" vol. 7, p. 146, RIHS, fol. 1r.

18. 29 July 1679, Petition of Narragansett Settlers, "Documents Relating to Rhode Island, and Rhode-Islanders: Three Volumes, Second Series," MSS, vol. 6, transcripts of Trumball Papers in Massachusetts Historical Society, in John Carter Brown Library, 152.

19. H. Roger King, *Cape Cod and Plymouth Colony in the Seventeenth Century* (New York, 1994), 240–1.

20. Letter to King Charles II, 4 December 1679, MS, PRO: CO 5/904/XC170411, fol. 7v [stamped nos]. Other estimates implausibly give this figure for Plymouth's costs alone. King estimates the total cost to Plymouth Colony as 11,743 pounds, of which three thousand was the responsibility of the colony government and the remainder that of the towns. King, *Cape Cod*, 240.

21. Renewed agreement found in *Records . . . New Plymouth*, vol. 10, *Acts of the Commissioners*, [vol. 2], 346–51.

22. *Records . . . Rhode Island*, ed. Bartlett, 2:408.

23. *Ibid.*, 2:408–9.

24. *Ibid.*, 2:464.

25. This was at times a matter of Indian perception when English justice superseded Indian practice. See, for example, King Philip's complaint, as reported by John Easton: "[If] 20 of there onest [honest] indians testefied that a Englishmen had dun them rong, it was as nothing, and if but one of ther worst indians testefied against ani indian or ther king when it plesed the English that was sufitiant"; Easton, "A Relacion," in *Narratives*, ed. Lincoln, 11. Rhode Islander William Harris reported in 1676 that the Narragansetts joined in the Indian war partly because the Rhode Island court had refused to condemn for murder an Indian of

Philip's party whom the Narragansetts regarded as culpable, "whereupon the Narragansetts were indignant, and said that before the English came they could do what they list with Philip's party"; William Harris to [Sir Joseph Williamson], 12 August 1676, *CSPC, America and West Indies, 1675–1676,* ed. W. Noel Sainsbury (London, 1893), 442.

26. He himself heard the words of the king's commissioners "Spoken as from King Charles his mouth and hath since Laid it up in his heart That the King did loake upon himselfe & Sucquansh & their Indians as his subjects, together with the English"; 28 July 1669, Governor and Council Records, 1667–1773, MSS, Rhode Island State Archives C#00558, Rhode Island State Archives, Providence, RI, 28.

27. *Records . . . Rhode Island,* ed. Bartlett, 2:487.

28. Thomas Church, *The History of King Philip's War . . . With Some Account of the Divine Providence Towards Col. Benjamin Church,* ed. Samuel G. Drake (Boston, 1825), 18.

29. John Leverett to Josiah Winslow Esq., Boston, 23 June 1675, in Josiah Winslow Papers, MSS .L461, Library of the Boston Athenaeum, Boston, no p.

30. Coddington described his last leave-taking of Winthrop, Sr., who died in 1649, to Winthrop, Jr.: "Wee toucke a very soleme leave one of an other, twice weeping at our parting, which did presage to me that wee should never see one an other in this life"; William Coddington to John Winthrop, Jr., 19 February 1651, *Massachusetts Historical Society Collections,* 281.

31. William Coddington to John Winthrop, Jr., 23/6M/1660, *Massachusetts Historical Society Collections,* 286. His correspondence was not always lugubrious; in 1648, he was writing Winthrop about ten sheep he had sent him: "If yow desire to have more whit sheepe then blacke, then rambe your ewes with whit rambs; if more blacke," and so on; William Coddington to John Winthrop, Jr., 14 October 1648, 280.

32. *Records . . . Rhode Island,* ed. Bartlett, 2:527–8; Rhode Island Colony Records (General Assembly Minutes), MSS, 4–5 May 1675, 2:43. Close associations help to confirm religious affiliation, as do miscellaneous items of information such as marriages, place of burial, phrases in wills. For instance, Thomas Borden's two brothers and his father had been buried in the Friends' burial ground four years earlier. John Tripp, another assistant, also had a Quaker brother. Some may have come to Quakerism later; it is difficult to be exact when one is so dependent on marriage certificates as evidence. For the leaders such as Coddington, the Eastons, Clarke, and others, their identity as Quakers is certain from Quaker minutes.

33. These numbers are of necessity inexact. The Warwick members, for example, were not marked "engaged," the Rhode Island equivalent of having been sworn; they may have been late in arriving or may not have arrived at all. Two of these members would be killed in the war: Toleration Harris and John Wickes. [William Harris], *A Rhode Islander Reports on King Philip's War. The Second William Harris Letter of August, 1676,* trans. and ed. Douglas Edward Leach (Providence, RI, 1963), n. 2, 16–7. Oliver Payson Fuller, *The History of Warwick, Rhode Island, From Its Settlement in 1642 to the Present Time* (Providence, RI, 1875), 24.

34. *Records . . . Rhode Island,* ed. Bartlett, 2:489–92; 531.

35. Douglas Edward Leach, *Flintlock and Tomahawk: New England in King Philip's War* (New York, 1958), 48. Jones, *Quakers in American Colonies,* 175.

36. John Borden was a frequent deputy from Portsmouth. Fuller, in *History of Warwick,* includes an account of this meeting attributed to Borden. Whereas Easton's rendering of the conversation with Philip is unadorned and free from cant, the Borden account, although confirming the basic content of the interchange, is trapped more securely within stereotypical English rhetoric; 72–3.

37. Easton, "A Relacion," in *Narratives,* ed. Lincoln, 9.

38. *Ibid.,* 9–10. Rhode Island had already asked New York to mediate its conflict with its neighbors over land; see New York Council Minutes of 17 Jan. 1675, in *Narratives,* ed. Lincoln, 136–7.

39. Jones, *Quakers in American Colonies,* 182.

40. Brockunier, *Roger Williams*, 116.

41. *Ibid.*, 157.

42. Backus, *History*, 331; 336.

43. To question whether or not Easton's Quakerism provided the impetus for his meeting with King Philip does not lessen the worth of his efforts. His capacity to listen sympathetically to the Indians is reflected in his respectful account of their meeting, where he recorded their grievances without defensive argument. While the meeting apparently had little effect on subsequent events, Easton's description of the encounter provides one of the few glimpses of Indian argument and feelings, unencumbered by overt condescension.

44. Captain James Cudworth to Governor Josiah Winslow, 27 June 1675, Josiah Winslow Papers, MSS .L461, Library of the Boston Athenaeum, Boston, no p.

9. "Midnight Shrieks and Soul-Amazing Moanes"

1. Benjamin Tompson, "New-Englands Crisis," in Peter White, *Benjamin Tompson: Colonial Bard* (University Park, PA, 1980), 97.

2. Warwick Town Records Book A-2 (photostat), Warwick Town Records Collection, Manuscripts Collection, RIHS, 143. Easton, "A Relacion," in *Narratives*, ed. Lincoln, 12. In the seventeenth century, the verb "attend" meant not only to await or watch but also to accompany for hostile purposes, and to render services. In this sense, then, the Rhode Islanders would not merely be passive lookouts for the Plymouth troops but would be rendering more active military service. *OED*, compact ed., 1:137.

3. 23 June 1675, Coddington, quoted in Emily Coddington Williams, *William Coddington of Rhode Island: A Sketch* (Newport, RI, 1941), 72. Dates in this work are unreliable. James Cudworth worried in his letter to Governor Winslow of 27 June 1675 that Coddington's letter to the governor might have never arrived, "because an Indian held up a paper & dared our gard to com over the water from Mr. Sharpes gard to fech a Letter that Came from the governor of Rod Iland." In Josiah Winslow Papers, MSS .L461, Library of the Boston Athenaeum, Boston, no p.

4. James Cudworth to Josiah Winslow, 27 June 1675, in Josiah Winslow Papers, no. p.

5. Leach, *Flintlock*, 40.

6. Roger Williams to Gov. John Winthrop, Jr., 27 June 1675, quoted in Richard Lebaron Bowen, *Early Rehoboth*, 4 vols., vol. 3 (Rehoboth, MA, 1948), 55.

7. Williams to Winthrop, Jr., 27 June 1675, quoted in Bowen, *Early Rehoboth*, 3:55.

8. As reported by Cudworth to Winslow, 27 June 1675, Josiah Winslow Papers, no p.

9. Benjamin Batten, Letter to Sir Thomas Allin, 28 June 1675, 30 June 1675, MS, PRO: CO 1/34/170411, fol. 220v [stamped nos]. James Savage, *A Genealogical Dictionary of the First Settlers of New England*, 4 vols., vol. 1 (Baltimore, 1977), 141. *London Gazette*, 16–19 August 1675, no. 1017, reproduced in Jill Lepore, *The Name of War: King Philip's War and the Origins of American Identity* (New York, 1998), 56. See also Douglas E. Leach, "Benjamin Batten and the *London Gazette*: Report on King Philip's War," *New England Quarterly* 36 (1963): 510–11. Leach did not comment on these modifications.

10. Easton, "A Relacion," in *Narratives*, ed. Lincoln, 12–3. Weetamoo had been married to Philip's brother Alexander, and her sister was Philip's wife.

11. James Cudworth to Josiah Winslow, 27 June 1675, in Josiah Winslow Papers, no p. In the same letter Cudworth relates that a Rhode Island informant named May stimulated Cudworth's suspicions, when he reported that seven of Philip's men, armed, came to Weetamoo's wigwam. When May attempted to enter the wigwam too, in order to have "herd ther discourse," he was prevented from doing so.

12. "Improve" here means "employ to advantage"; hence, it would be of little advantage to employ Rhode Island men to blockade the canoes of the Indians on Mount Hope, if there were so many canoes in Pocasset ready to transport the Indians. Cudworth to Josiah Winslow, 27 June 1675, in Josiah Winslow Papers, no p.

13. Leach, *Flintlock*, 54.

14. *Ibid.*, 54.

15. Easton, "A Relacion," in *Narratives*, ed. Lincoln, 13.

16. Bowen, *Early Rehoboth*, 3:55. See also "hee had sente to Naraganset sachem," James Cudworth to Josiah Winslow, 27 June 1675, Josiah Winslow Papers, no p.

17. Easton, "A Relacion," in *Narratives*, ed. Lincoln, 13.

18. Williams, quoted in Bowen, *Early Rehoboth*, 3:53. A "Foxian" was an adherent of George Fox.

19. Williams to John Winthrop, Jr., 25 June 1675, *The Correspondence of Roger Williams*, ed. Glenn W. LaFantasie, 2 vols., revised from unpublished MS, vol. 2, ed. Bradford F. Swan (Hanover, NH, 1988), 694.

20. It was assumed that the Wampanoags were responsible for these actions. Scot was wounded but later died of his wounds. Williams, quoted in [Harris], *Rhode Islander Reports*, n. 29, 31. For Hubbard, n. 29, 31.

21. W[illiam] Hubbard, *A Narrative of the Troubles with the Indians in New-England, from the first planting thereof in the year 1607. to this present year 1677* (Boston, 1677), 25.

22. Hubbard, *Narrative*, 24.

23. The estimate of "three hundred" was that of Church himself, no doubt enhanced in the retelling. Benjamin Church, *Diary of King Philip's War, 1675–76*, intro. Alan and Mary Simpson, tercentenary ed. (Chester, CT, 1975), 88–9.

24. Brockunier, *Roger Williams*, 275.

25. Leach, *Flintlock*, 61.

26. Brockunier, *Roger Williams*, 265.

27. John Easton wrote that the English army "with out our Consent or informing us came into our coleny" and made an agreement with the Narragansetts. "A Relacion," in *Narratives*, ed. Lincoln, 13.

28. Leach, *Flintlock*, 62; Coddington to Andros, 21 July 1675, in [John Easton], *A Narrative of the Causes which led to Philip's Indian War, of 1675 and 1676, by John Easton, of Rhode Island*, ed. Franklin B. Hough (Albany, NY, 1858), 62–3.

29. [Easton], *Narrative*, ed. Hough, 62.

30. Andros wrote that the government later lent some of this supply to the New England forces when they were fighting in Narragansett country, probably during the Great Swamp Fight. "A Short Accompt of the General Concerns of New Yorke from October 1674 to November 1677," MS, PRO: CO 1/41/116, fol. 1v.

31. 15 December 1675, Coddington to Winslow, quoted in Williams, *William Coddington*, 73–4.

32. *Records . . . Rhode Island*, ed. Bartlett, 2:531–2; 534–7; 537.

33. *Early Records of the Town of Portsmouth*, ed. Clarence S. Brigham and Amos Perry (Providence, RI, 1901), 185; 156; 174.

34. 30 July 1675, Noah Newman to Lieutenant Thomas, quoted in Bowen, *Early Rehoboth*, 3:91.

35. 31 July 1675, Nathaniel Thomas to Capt. Henchman, quoted in *ibid.*, 3:91; 10 August 1675, Nathaniel Thomas to Josiah Winslow, quoted 3:94–5.

36. 10 August 1675, Thomas to Winslow, quoted in *ibid.*, 3:95–6; [Nathaniel Saltonstall] quoted 3:87.

37. [31 July 1675], Daniel Henchman to Governor Leverett, quoted in *ibid.*, 3:89; 10 August 1675, Thomas to Winslow quoted 3:97–8; 7 August 1675, John Pynchon to John Winthrop quoted 3:101; 10 August 1675, Thomas to Winslow quoted 3:99. Henchman returned to Boston, where one hundred men of Roxbury refused to serve under his command; 3:108.

38. Whipple, quoted in *ibid.*, 3:98 n.

39. The phrase is that of Benjamin Tompson, "New-Englands Crisis," in White, *Benjamin Tompson*, 91.

40. None of the Warwick deputies, and only one of the Providence deputies, was marked "engaged," an indication of wartime turmoil. (Taking the engagement, equivalent to an oath, was an indicator of one's presence.) Of the eighteen elected deputies, only eight were present; three of these were Quakers. Since the twelve council members (assistants plus governor and deputy governor) were elected the previous May and took the engagement at that time, there is no way of knowing which were actually present in October; ten of these were Quakers. Assuming all council members were present, thirteen of the twenty assembly members would have been Quakers. Assuming only those council members from Aquidneck were present, six of seven would have been Quakers; a total of nine out of fifteen in attendance at the assembly would have been Quakers. Rhode Island Colony Records MSS, 2:44–5.

41. Leach, *Flintlock*, 120. Massachusetts Council, signed Edward Rawson, Secretary, to [Richard] Smith, 6 November 1675, Film Miscellany 507/68, Manuscripts and Archives Library, Yale University, New Haven, 46 b. Richard Smith, William Coddington, and John Winthrop, Jr., were all good friends. Smith vacillated between Rhode Island and Connecticut in his allegiance.

42. Bowen, *Early Rehoboth*, 3:67 n.

43. *Records . . . New Plymouth*, vol. 10: *Acts of the Commissioners*, vol. 2, *1653–1679*, 357.

44. *Ibid.*, 457–8.

45. Chu, *Neighbors*, 95; 98.

46. Easton, "A Relacion," in *Narratives*, ed. Lincoln, 15. Francis Jennings, in *The Invasion of America: Indians, Colonialism, and the Cant of Conquest* (Williamsburg, VA, 1975), wrote that Rhode Island responded "under menace." He argued that an advance party killing Narragansetts brought reprisals down upon local inhabitants, thereby making Rhode Island dependent on the protection of United Colonies forces; 311. The killing did not take place, however, until December 10, after Rhode Island had committed itself.

47. The assembly was not in session. The governor and council were empowered to meet in the interim; their records do not exist for this period. It is likely that the governor, deputy governor (both from Newport), and whatever assistants were available on Aquidneck took these decisions. Of these seventeen (approx.), ten were Quakers. See order of governor and council, 19 November, cited hereafter.

48. Easton, "A Relacion," in *Narratives*, ed. Lincoln, 15.

49. Walter Clarke, "Loving Friends . . ." 19/9M/1675, "RIHSM," vol. 10, p. 144, Manuscripts Collection, RIHS, fol. 1r.

50. To Captain Arthur Fenner and the Council of War, signed by order of the Governor and Council by John Sanford. "RIHSM," vol. 10, p. 144, Manuscripts Collection, RIHS, fol. 1r. In Walter Clarke's letter of the same date he had written that the council was about to meet.

51. Coddington, quoted in Williams, *William Coddington*, 72–3.

52. Williams, *William Coddington*, 73.

53. Quaker records quoted in Austin, *Genealogical Dictionary*, 100.

54. *Vital Records of Scituate Massachusetts*, vol. 2, *Marriages and Deaths* (Boston, 1909), 11.

55. George Fox to Christopher Holder, 15/4M/1677, in *JFHS* 47 (autumn 1955): 80.

56. His estate of L195/13/00 consisted in part of books, a looking glass, tablecloths and napkins, a silver cup and spoon, five bedsteads, and assorted chairs and tables. "Inventory of the personall or moveable Estate of Robert Hodgson," MS, 16/3M/1696, "RIHSM," vol. 10, RIHS, 89.

57. 2 Mar. 1657, *Records . . . New Plymouth*, vol. 3, *Court Orders*, 130; Lovell, *Sandwich*, 86.

58. In 1810, London Yearly Meeting was to advise that it was inconsistent with the peace testimony "for friends to be in any manner aiding and assisting in the conveyance of soldiers, their baggage, arms, ammunition, or military stores"; *Rules of Discipline*, 293–4.

59. N. S. [Nathaniel Saltonstall], *A Continuation Of the State of New-England; Being a Far-*

ther Account of the Indian Warr . . . 10th of November, 1675 to the 8th of February 1675/6 (London, 1676), 5.

60. Leach, *Flintlock,* 122; 124–5.

61. Bodge, *Soldiers,* 180. It seems likely that the same supply sloops later ferried the wounded from the Great Swamp Fight across the bay to Newport (see hereafter). Bodge's study remains the definitive source for the rosters of Massachusetts soldiers.

62. Fuller, *History,* 74.

63. Benjamin Church, *The History of King Philip's War,* intro. and notes Henry Martyn Dexter (Boston, 1865), 49, n. 121; Samuel Greene Arnold, *History of the State of Rhode Island and Providence Plantations,* 2 vols., vol. 1, *1636–1700* (New York, 1859), 403.

64. Arnold, *History,* 403. The council of war records do not exist, except for those of Warwick, which are unreadable.

65. Thomas Church, *History,* 40.

66. Dated Providence, 18 December 1675, Winthrop Papers, MSS, Massachusetts Historical Society, microfilm, RIHS, Providence, RI, no p. Emphasis added.

67. Bull's house, as the most sizable in the area, often served as a gathering place, as in 1672, when George Fox proselytized there. Jireh Bull, the son of Quaker leader Henry Bull, is always assumed to be a Quaker. See, for example, *A Letter Written by Capt. Wait Winthrop from Mr. Smiths in Narragansett to Governor John Winthrop,* ed. E. A. Burlingame, N. M. Isham, and C. E. Cannon, Society of Colonial Wars in the State of Rhode Island and Providence Plantations Publication no. 12 (Providence, RI, 1919), 31 n. 9. This is by no means certain, however, because he was raised before his father became a Quaker and by a non-Quaker mother and does not appear in Quaker records. He nevertheless had much to do with Quakers, even carrying a message from George Fox to Governor Winthrop of Connecticut. William Coddington to John Winthrop, Jr., 29/4M/1672, in *Massachusetts Historical Society Collections,* 289.

68. Hubbard, *Narrative,* 50.

69. Leach, *Flintlock,* 129.

70. *A Farther Brief and True Narration,* 9.

71. Mather, quoted in *So Dreadfull a Judgment,* ed. Slotkin and Folsom, 381; 10/8M/1675 [October], E. W., *New-England's Present Sufferings Under Their Cruel Neighbouring Indians* (London, 1675), 5. "E. W." may possibly have been Edward Wanton, of Scituate, but was probably Wharton of Salem, who not only had been repeatedly whipped and fined for years but was also banished on the pain of death in 1661 because his hair was too long and he would not remove his hat. Bishop, *New-England Judged. The Second Part,* 20–1.

72. Casualty statistics are extremely precarious for this battle, especially for Indians. Leach declined to choose between widely varied estimates but cited two participants who reported from two to three hundred warriors killed and more than three hundred noncombatant Indians killed. Slotkin and Folsom estimated six hundred Indians killed in all. Leach put English deaths at seventy or eighty; Slotkin and Folsom concurred. Each side had reasons to exaggerate their own and their opponents' losses, accounting for estimates of up to thousands of Indians killed. What is clear, however, is that each side suffered grievously. John Leverett, letter to [Whitehall], 15 June 1676, MS, PRO: CO 1/37/170411, fol. 16r [stamped nos]; Leach, *Flintlock,* 132–3; Slotkin and Folsom, introduction to *So Dreadfull a Judgment,* 32–3; Eric B. Schultz and Michael J. Tougias, *King Philip's War* (Woodstock, VT, 1999), 262–6.

73. Roscoe L. Whitman, *History and Genealogy of the Ancestors and Some Descendants of Stukely Westcott* (no p., 1932), 26. Six of his children, born from 1664 to 1674, are entered in Rhode Island MM, Birth Records, 1638–1812, MSS, microfilm no. 11, NEYM Collection, RIHS, no p. His name usually appears as "Wascoat" in Quaker records. The names of a few other Rhode Island casualties of the Swamp Fight are known: killed were Nicholas Power of Providence (by a member of his own company), Richard Updike of Narragansett; James and Daniel Updike were wounded. Daniel Updike was subsequently captured by Algerine

pirates and ransomed by his uncle Richard Smith, for fifteen hundred gun locks. Austin, *Genealogical Dictionary,* 356; 398.

74. Leach, *Flintlock,* 143.

75. Easton, "A Relacion," in *Narratives,* ed. Lincoln, 15–7.

76. *Ibid.,* 10.

77. *Ibid.,* 17.

78. *Ibid.*

79. [Harris], *A Rhode Islander Reports,* 20.

80. Easton made a tantalizing reference to an exchange between Massachusetts and Rhode Island, date unknown, in which Massachusetts asked for troops, transport, and provisions. Rhode Island refused the request, *giving grounds for refusal.* The refusal letter is lost, the perhaps all-important grounds of refusal lost with it. Subsequently, Rhode Island learned about the 3 November legislation against Quakers. [Easton], *Narrative,* ed. Hough, 132–5.

81. Thomas Budd, *Good Order Established in Pennsilvania and New-Jersey in America* ([Philadelphia], 1685), 34.

82. Leach, *Flintlock,* 131; Leverett to [Whitehall], 15 June 1676, fol. 16r. Perhaps forty men were buried at Smith's in a common grave; a modern stone marks its location.

83. N. S. [Nathaniel Saltonstall], *Continuation,* 7.

84. Bodge, *Soldiers,* 204.

85. For land, 8 March 1675/76, *Early Records . . . Portsmouth,* 185–91. A discussion of Aquidneck as a safe harbor is discussed in more detail in chapter 14.

86. "A Proclamation about the Indyans and Making of Block Houses," 16 September 1675, [Easton], *Narrative,* ed. Hough, 75. Andros offered refuge to mainland Rhode Islanders, as well, sending sloops to Newport in May 1676 and carrying Rhode Islanders to Musceta Cove (Glen Cove). Leach, *Flintlock,* 177.

87. Leach, *Flintlock,* 125.

88. William Coddington to John Winthrop, Jr., 29/4M/1672, *Massachusetts Historical Society Collections,* 289–90.

10. "A Bulit out of Everi Bush"

1. For "abulit out of everi bush," Capt. John Freeman to Gov. Winslow, 3/5M/1675, quoted in Bowen, *Early Rehoboth,* 3:96n. For Warwick, endorsed, "Copie of the towns Letter sent to the governor in the time of warr about releife." Town of Warwick, to Governor of Rhode Island, MS, "RIHSM," vol. 10, RIHS, 152. For Wickes, see Fuller, *History,* 77–8.

2. Bodge, *Soldiers,* 200. The return of the child was part of halfhearted moves toward a temporary truce after the Great Swamp Fight.

3. Those "capacitated" to bear arms were males between the ages of sixteen and sixty. Town of Warwick, 10:152. Barely decipherable in the Warwick town records are the words, "Touching fortifications: First the question was put forth how many houses was fitt to be fortified & . . . was naimed the houses of James Greene John Knowles & Thomas Greenes house to bring into one of the . . . goods . . . the neibors were . . . [sec?]ure with [the women?] and children." Warwick Town Records Book A2 (photostat), 143. I am indebted to Richard D. Stattler, Manuscripts Curator, for help in deciphering this manuscript.

4. The births of his children appear in Quaker records, [ ]/6M/1672, 18/12M/1674, 15/2M/1677; he was a frequent signer of marriage certificates. Rhode Island MM, Births, 1638–1812; Marriages, 1643–1888, MSS, microfilm no. 11, NEYM Collection, RIHS, no p.

5. Walter Clarke to [Arthur] Fenner, Newport, RI, 28/12M/1675, "Letter to Fenner with the Rest Conserned," Providence Town Papers, series 2, vol. 1, p. 107, Manuscripts Collection, RIHS, fol. 1r.

6. Clarke to Fenner, fol. 1r–1v.

7. 13 March 1675/76, Rhode Island Colony Records, MSS, 2:45. *Records . . . Rhode Island,*

ed. Bartlett, 2:533; Bartlett fails to note the special warrant and transcribes "each family . . . wantinge *abiltey* [to have a cow]" as "each family . . . wantinge *a libertye* [to have a cow].") Emphasis added.

8. Assuming that all of the assistants were present as listed, nine or ten of the twelve were Quakers. No deputies from Warwick were listed. Four of the thirteen deputies were Quakers. Rhode Island Colony Records, MSS, 2:45. Beginning with the assembly session of October 1675, the printed records omit the names of deputies. The manuscript records must be consulted for this information.

9. Quoted in Jones, *George Fox's Attitude*, 16. See James 4:1: "From whence come wars and fightings among you? come they not hence, even of your lusts that war in your members?"

10. Quoted in Jones, *George Fox's Attitude*, 16.

11. That some in Providence may have shared Warwick's sense of betrayal as its fellow citizens fled to safety is suggested by the listing in the Providence records of twenty-nine names of "those that went not away." See Bowen, *Early Rehoboth*, 3:18n. Of these, Abraham Mann, wounded in the war, was a Quaker; as was probably Nathaniel Waterman, son of Quaker Richard Waterman. Mann, Lapham–Mann marriage, 6/2M/1673; Rhode Island MM, Births, 1638–1812; Marriages, 1643–1888, MSS, microfilm no. 11, NEYM Collection, RIHS, no p. Richard Waterman, (death) 26/8M/1673; Rhode Island MM, Deaths, 1647–1808, MSS, microfilm no. 10, NEYM Collection, RIHS, 3.

12. Other strategies for saving lives would include negotiation and mediation, fair treatment of others, particularly those in subjection, and removing irritants tending to provoke war, such as poverty, injustice, and oppression. Although Quakers were to become adept at offering all of these strategies, they did not associate social ills with the peace testimony in the early generations.

13. Isaac Penington, "Life and Immortality Brought to Light through the Gospel" [1671], in *Works*, 2:434.

14. For "daingerous hurries," *Records . . . Rhode Island*, ed. Bartlett, 2:531. Benjamin Tompson, *New-Englands Tears for her Present Miseries . . . With an Account of the Battel between the English and Indians upon Seaconk Plain* (London, 1676), 5. Noah Newman of nearby Rehoboth deplored the carelessness of Providence residents, who "exposed a 100 bushells of Corn . . . to the enemys which was all taken away"; Bowen, *Early Rehoboth*, 3:17.

15. *Records . . . Rhode Island*, ed. Bartlett, 2:536. In 1670, the council contracted with five men to supply their boats in the service of the colony, to do such things as transporting officials around the colony on their public duties. These were: Robert Carr, Caleb Carr, Walter Clarke, Jeremiah Browne, and Pardon Tillinghast. Governor and Council Records, 1667-1773, MSS, Rhode Island State Archives C#00558, Rhode Island State Archives, 43.

16. *Records . . . Rhode Island*, ed. Bartlett, 2:537. Roger Williams was not invited to lend his counsel. One of the Quakers was Christopher Holder. The assembly enacted several interesting measures in these two sittings. First, any "man" Indians in the service of any person on Aquidneck were to be counted as if they were "cuntry-men not in warr," for purposes of paying toward the watch; and no Indians in the colony were to be slaves. Second, that "Negro men" were as liable to stand watch as "English men." Rhode Island Colony Records, MSS, 2:46.

17. *Records . . . Rhode Island*, ed. Bartlett, 2:538. The assembly knew it was innovating: it included in the appointment of Major Cranston assurances that when the "extreme troubles" were over, the assembly would see fit to return the selection of military officers to the local militias.

18. Warwick Town Meeting, "Upon Suspition of the Indeans Riseing Against the English," 11 April 1671, MS, "RIHSM" vol. 10, p. 145, Manuscripts Collection, RIHS, fol. 1r.

19. Rhode Island Colony Records, MSS, 2:33–4. As already observed, the published version of these records omitted the phrase "and is not against their Conscience," thus failing to reveal that the 1673 Exemption recognized the inability of some, on the basis of conscience, to perform even civil service connected with war.

20. Records . . . New Plymouth, vol. 5, Court Orders, 202.

21. Records . . . Rhode Island, ed. Bartlett, for kitchen, 2:541; for ammunition, 2:542; for emissaries, 2:543–4. Five of twelve assistants were Quakers; seven or eight of the thirteen deputies probably present. Rhode Island Colony Records, MSS, 2:48.

22. Records . . . Rhode Island, ed. Bartlett, for king's garrison, 2:545; for Fenner, 2:546–8.

23. William Harris to [Sir Joseph Williamson], 12 August 1676, CSPC, America and West Indies, 1675–1676, 442.

24. Records . . . Rhode Island, ed. Bartlett, 2:549. It is obvious why men having to serve in the trained bands resented those who were excused from such service. In 1735, when it was not even wartime, Ezbon Sanford and 111 others persuasively justified such resentment in a petition to the legislature protesting an exemption act: "Some of those persons that have been excused have made it their business to . . . laugh at and jeer those who have been obliged to bear arms, and . . . when the companys have been dismissed, have gone into the taverns with the soldiers to gaming. Now how absurd and unreasonable is it for such persons to be excused . . . for conscience sake, who appear to have no conscience at all"; "Tender Consciences," Newport [Rhode Island] Historical Magazine 5 (1884–1885): 209.

25. Records . . . Rhode Island, ed. Bartlett, 2:498.

26. It had been William Coddington who had insisted that "fines and imprisonments" were "carnal weapons," disavowed by Quakers. Coddington to Governor of Massachusetts, c. 1674, quoted in Besse, Collection, 2:269.

27. See chapter 13.

28. Records . . . Rhode Island, ed. Bartlett, 2:535. For example, Quaker William Wodell bought an Indian captive named Hanah, who had been condemned to perpetual slavery by Plymouth, and secured from her an affidavit indicating her willingness to be his servant, witnessed by Nathanial Thomas of Plymouth; Alderman, the Indian who killed Philip; and a Rhode Islander. While arguably preferable to being sold in the West Indies, it is difficult to judge whether such translations from slavery to servitude were meaningful. Early Records . . . Portsmouth, 433-4. Job Wright, a Quaker of Matinecock Meeting on Long Island, bought an Indian boy as a slave in 1677, probably a captive from the war. John Cox, Jr., Quakerism in the City of New York, 1657–1930 (New York, 1930), 55.

29. 19/7/M/1676, Edmundson to "Friends," NEYM Earliest Written Disciplines, MSS, microfilm no. 4, NEYM Collection, RIHS, 51.

30. B. Church, Diary, intro. Simpsons, 121.

31. Records . . . Rhode Island, ed. Bartlett, vol. 3, 1678–1706 (Providence, RI, 1858), 54. William Clarke was neither a Quaker nor related to the governor.

32. [Richard Hutchinson], The Warr in New-England Visibly Ended (London, 1677), 2. Quartering was the usual punishment for the crime of treason.

33. Charles Fager, Quakers and King Philip's War: 1675–1676 (Falls Church, VA, 1980), 2–3. Stories about Philip's head abound; one of the more curious is that of Patience Faunce, who lived to the age of 105. She told of seeing the head on a pole when she was a girl in Plymouth, and "every spring a wren had nested in it"; William A. Wing, "John Russell," Old Dartmouth Historical Sketches 69 (1935).

34. See, for example, [Harris], A Rhode Islander Reports, 21.

35. "Record of a Court Martial Held at Newport, R. I. in August, 1676, for the Trial of Indians charged with being engaged in Philip's Designs," in [Easton], Narrative, ed. Hough, 173–190.

36. Rhode Island General Court of Trials, Record Book A (transcription), p. 67, August 1676, Indian Court Martial, Judicial Archives, Supreme Court Judicial Records Center, Pawtucket, RI.

37. T. Church, History, 57.

38. The civilian Quakers were: Walter Clarke, John Coggeshall, John Easton, Joshua Coggeshall, Thomas Borden. "Record of a Court Martial," in [Easton], Narrative, ed. Hough, 173–4.

39. *Ibid.*, 187–90.

40. *Ibid.*, 182–9.

41. The case was troubling, necessitating the coroner, Joshua Coggeshall, to dig up the body, whereupon Quaker surgeon Simon Cooper and another reexamined it and reburied it. John Cornell, *Genealogy of the Cornell Family, Being an Account of the Descendants of Thomas Cornell of Portsmouth, R.I.* (New York, 1902), 24. Cornell was convicted on the basis of questionable evidence indeed, including hearsay and a ghostly appearance in a neighbor's dream. In custody, Thomas Cornell was securely fastened to the "greate chaine" until he was "Hanged by the neck untill you are dead dead"; Rhode Island General Court of Trials (transcription), 23–34; 22. Thomas Cornell was a Quaker, although his name does not appear in Quaker records—at least until almost a century had gone by. His mother was a Quaker, his wife was the daughter of a Quaker, his sons were Quakers, and most of the people surrounding him at the time of this incident were Quakers, including those apparently closest to his mother. His mother's death was recorded in Quaker records as "Killed Strangely at Portsmouth." Rhode Island MM, Deaths, 1647–1808, MSS, microfilm no. 10, NEYM Collection, RIHS, 3. For Punnean, see *Records . . . Rhode Island*, ed. Bartlett, 2:485. My paper on this case is in progress.

42. October 1670, *Rhode Island Court Records, Records of the Court of Trials* vol. 2, 1663–1670 (Providence, RI, 1922), 97–8.

43. Rhode Island General Court of Trials (transcription), 68–70.

44. Rhode Island General Court of Trials (transcription), 67.

11. "To Looke to Our Selefs"

1. Easton, "A Relacion," in *Narratives*, ed. Lincoln, 12.

2. 8 May 1680, Peleg Sandford, Answer to Inquiries from Rhode Island, MS, PRO: CO 5/904/XC170411, fol. 35v [stamped nos].

3. Leach, *Flintlock*, 227.

4. Charles T. Burke, *Puritans at Bay: The War against King Philip and the Squaw Sachems* (New York, 1967), 236.

5. Pitman, *A Relation*, 4. Of course, both sides in this conflict were of the same ethnicity.

6. Rhode Island General Court of Trials (transcription), 67.

7. Coddington, as Cudworth reported to Winslow, 27 June 1675, Josiah Winslow Papers, no p. According to Benjamin Batten in his letter to Thomas Allin, Rhode Island had mobilized troops by 30 June 1675. I have found no other contemporary corroborating written evidence of this bit of intelligence. The absence of such corroboration is not altogether surprising, nor does it necessarily negate Batten's assertion. While the Rhode Island Assembly minutes do not record such action, the local councils of war were already empowered to mobilize forces. There are no Rhode Island Council or councils of war records extant.

8. Cotton Mather, *Souldiers Counselled and Comforted. A Discourse Delivered unto some part of the Forces Engaged in the Just War of New-England Against the Northern & Eastern Indians. September 1, 1689* (Boston, 1689), 28.

9. Bowden, *Society of Friends*, 1:306.

10. Edmundson, *Journal*, 82. Coddington and Clarke both signed commissions. Bowden, *Society of Friends*, 1:307–8.

11. Bowden, *Society of Friends*, 1:307–8.

12. *Ibid.*, 1:307.

13. Jones, *Quakers in American Colonies*, 175.

14. Worrall, *Quakers*, chaps. 2, 8.

15. Arthur J. Worrall, "Persecution, Politics, and War: Roger Williams, Quakers, and King Philip's War," *Quaker History* 66 (2) (autumn 1977): 81; 85. Emphasis added.

16. Brock, *Pioneers*, 21–2. For Chu, see for example *Neighbors*: "The peace testimony was not an essential part of Quaker doctrine at this time" and "militia service would seem to

contradict his identification as a Quaker; however, given the fluid nature of Quaker organization and doctrine during this period, militia service would not preclude membership." N. 18, 53; n. 6, 118–9.

17. Nicholas Easton is an exception here, because he could not "consent as to command" the mounting of guns.

18. Virtually every Quaker at this time, commenting on government at any level, used a variant of the "terror . . . praise" phrase to defuse any suggestion that Quakers were anarchists, revolutionaries, or plotters of any kind. See: "For there is no power but of God: the powers that be are ordained of God"; Rom. 13:1. "For rulers are not a terror to good works, but to the evil. . . . Do that which is good, and thou shalt have praise of the same: For he is the minister of God to thee for good. But if thou do that which is evil, be afraid; for he beareth not the sword in vain"; Rom. 13:3–4.

19. And as long as the activities qualified as "terror to evil-doers." A relevant anecdote involves a London Quaker, Humphrey Brewster, who complained to magistrates that soldiers were doing violence toward Quakers during their religious meetings. The magistrates, he argued, were as responsible for the treatment of Quakers as if they acted violently themselves; just as, in the Hebrew scriptures, Ahab was culpable for the blood of Naboth. Although Ahab's wife had issued the death command, Ahab had left his seal carelessly available to her and so he was judged culpable (see 1 Kings 21). Beware of "pulling Innocent blood on your own heads," Brewster warned the London magistrates, "if you shed it or cause it to be shed, it will prove a burthen heavie for you to bear." Because Quakers were innocent rather than evildoers, the magistrates were bearing the sword in vain. Brewster told the officers, too, that if they sent soldiers who shed the blood of Quakers, soldiers and officers both would bear the guilt. Humphrey Brewster, *To the Mayor, Aldermen, Majestrates and Officers of the Military Force in this City of London* ([London, 1662]), 1–2.

20. Backus, *History*, 339.

21. John Austin Stevens, "King Philip's War," in *The First Record Book of the Society of Colonial Wars in the State of Rhode Island and Providence Plantations* (Providence, RI, 1902), 90.

22. Hubbard to Henry Reeve, 1 Nov. 1675, quoted in Austin, *Genealogical Dictionary*, 107. Six Plymouth towns were also unvisited by violence; four of these were geographically isolated, on Cape Cod.

23. *Records . . . Rhode Island*, ed. Bartlett, 2:553–4.

24. *Ibid.*, 2:554.

25. Usually Quakers did not express the desire that all would follow their views on war, except in an abstract sense. This statement, focused on a defined group—their neighbors— is rare for this generation. *Ibid.*, 2:554.

26. *Ibid.*, 2:554–5.

27. *Ibid.*, March 6, 1676/1677, General Court of Trials, 54.

28. *Documents Relating to the Colonial History of the State of New Jersey*, ed. William A. Whitehead, New Jersey Historical Society, vol. 1, 1631–1687 (Newark, NJ, 1880), 400. One George Scot was well aware that Quaker Robert Barclay, governor of the colony (although he never came to America), judged it "unlawful to draw his sword to defend himself against a native, if he were coming to cut his throat." In spite of such "inconveniencies," Scot was confident that Barclay was "more a gentlemen, than ever to be guilty of anything that is base, or unbecoming a gentleman" (such as failing to defend the colony). [George Scot], "The Model of the Government of the Province of East-New-Jersey in America" (Edinburgh, 1685), reprinted in William A. Whitehead, *East Jersey Under The Proprietary Governments*, New Jersey Historical Society *Collections*, vol. 1 ([no p.], 1846), 310–1.

29. *Records . . . Rhode Island*, ed. Bartlett, 2:567–70.

30. *Ibid.*, 2:571. This provision was taken from the traditional "freedom of religion" clause in the charter of 1663.

31. Emphasis added. *Ibid.*, 2:567.

32. 25 August 1686, The Address of the Quakers of Rhode Island and Providence Planta-

tion To His Majesty James the Second, MS, PRO: CO 1/60/170055, fols. 68r–69v [stamped nos]. For governmental changes see J. M. Sosin, *English America and the Revolution of 1688* (Lincoln, Nebraska, 1982), chaps. 2, 3.

33. Governor John Cranston for the General Assembly, Letter to King Charles II, 1 August 1679, MS, PRO: CO 1/43/170819, fol. 183r [stamped nos]. In 1679 Quakers no longer dominated the government, and no Quakers were involved in preparing the report to the king.

34. Cranston, Letter to King Charles II, fol. 183v. The reminder of loyalty was a reference to Rhode Island's posture during the Interregnum, in contrast to the enthusiastic Massachusetts support of fellow Puritan Oliver Cromwell.

35. Randall Howlden and John Greene, "Reply (to the Agents of Boston) and Petition to the Committee of Trade and Plantations," [1679], MS, Historical Manuscripts from H. B. M. State Paper Office (Stevens Transcripts), vol. 2, 1666–1682, no. 149, John Carter Brown Library, no p.

36. Peleg Sanford, Answer to Inquiries, 8 May 1680, PRO: CO 5/904/XC170411, fol. 35v.

37. Richard Smith, "Petition of Richard Smith and others to the King," 3 July 1678, MS, Historical Manuscripts from H. B. M. State Paper Office (Stevens Transcripts), vol. 2, 1666–1682, no. 134, John Carter Brown Library, no p. Richard Smith, the author of the petition, ungratefully neglected to mention that his own wife received shelter on Aquidneck. The troops of the United Colonies greatly reduced Smith's own property when quartered there; when they withdrew, refusing to maintain his garrison, the Indians burned it down the next day ("one of the most delightfull seats in New-England"); [N. S.], *A New and Further Narrative Of the State of New-England, Being A Continued Account of the Bloudy Indian-War, From March till August, 1676* [Boston, July 22, 1676], (London, 1676), 4. Smith was later arrested by Rhode Island, for subversion. In 1684, he was still petitioning the commissioners of the United Colonies to recompense his losses from having billeted the troops. By his account, he had hosted six hundred Massachusetts troops, plus Captain Winthrop's Connecticut troops for eight to ten days, in which time they managed to consume: "26 hed of catell killed and eate by the sowders, with 100 gootes att least, and att least 30 fatt hoggs . . . post and rayle fences being feched and burnt by the sowders"; *Records . . . New Plymouth*, vol. 10: *Acts of the Commissioners* [vol. 2], 1653–1679, 412.

38. Randall Howlden and John Greene, "Answer of the Men of Warwick in Rhode Island to the Petition of R. Smith," 1678, MS, Historical Manuscripts from H. B. M. State Paper Office (Stevens Transcripts), vol. 2, 1666–1682, no. 141, John Carter Brown Library, no p.

39. Easton, quoted in Callender, *Early History*, 134–5 n.

40. *Ibid*. Original italics.

41. Howlden and Greene, "Answer of the Men of Warwick," no p. But petitioning for their own government in 1679, a year later, Narragansett settlers impugned the quality of the sanctuary Rhode Island was so fond of citing. When they retreated to Aquidneck, they claimed, "it cost us one halfe of our Catell to keep the rest . . . so cold was their Charity to their poor distressed neighbours"; 29 July 1679, Documents Relating to Rhode Island, and Rhode-Islanders: Three Volumes, Second Series, MSS, vol. 6, transcripts of Trumball Papers in Massachusetts Historical Society, in John Carter Brown Library, 152.

42. Letter to RI from CT, Hartford, 27 June 1677, *Records . . . Rhode Island*, ed. Bartlett, 2:598.

43. Governor and Council to Secretary of State, 15 July 1680, *The Public Records of the Colony of Connecticut*, 15 vols., vol. 3, 1678–1689, ed. J. Hammond Trumbull (Hartford, CT, 1859), 303.

44. John Allyn to Peleg Sanford, 29 May 1685, MS, photostat from Connecticut Archives, John Allen Papers, Miscellaneous Manuscripts Collection, RIHS, Providence, RI, fol. 1r. In an exasperated postscript, they wrote: "your damage by pilfering &c in your accot how we came to be chargeable wth it is wonderful"; fol. 1r.

45. New Plymouth, "Letter," 12 June 1677, PRO: CO 5/904/XC170411, fol. 5v.

46. *Ibid*. Yet Plymouth effusively praised Captain Roger Goulding of Rhode Island after the war, as "our constant, reall frind in the late warr, and very officious and healpfull as occation hath bine." They granted him land in thanks. *Records . . . New Plymouth*, vol. 5, *Court Orders*, 214.

47. *Records . . . Rhode Island*, ed. Bartlett, 3:23.

48. 30 July 1678, The answer of the Agents of Boston, MS, Historical Manuscripts from the H. B. M. State Paper Office (Stevens Transcripts), vol. 2, 1666–1682, no. 119, John Carter Brown Library, no p.

49. This testimony does not appear in the minute book of the Newport Monthly Meeting, the first entry of which is dated 10M/1676 or in that of the New England Yearly Meeting but was copied into another record book entitled "Ancient Epistles Minutes and Advices," 46–47, now in the NEYM Collection, RIHS, Providence, RI. It is found in NEYM Earliest Written Disciplines, NEYM Collection, RIHS, microfilm no. 4.

12. "Witnesses to the Life of Innocency"

1. The authors called themselves "Witnesses to the Life of Innocency." "A Testimony from us (in scorn called Quakers but are) the Children of the Light," from "our mens-Meeting att Rhode-Island att Joshua Coggeshalls," NEYM Earliest Written Disciplines, MSS, microfilm no. 4, NEYM Collection, RIHS, 46–7. All quotations and references in this chapter refer to this document unless otherwise noted. In order to avoid tedious interruption of the text, page numbers are omitted. As the document is but two pages long, references are easily found; see appendix 3.

2. Lower Virginia Monthly Meeting Minutes, part 1, 1673–1756, TMS, Quaker Collection 1116/182, Haverford College Library, Haverford, PA, 25–9. This copied version is introduced with the date 20/6M/1675, but signed "Given forth at the nationall mens & womans meetings . . . at Dublin the 30 day of the 3rd month 1680."

3. "24th day of 6 month 1675 A Testimony from (us in scorne called Quakers but are) the chidren [sic] of the light," from "our Mans Meeting (on Rhoad Island) att Joshua Coggeshall's," Winthrop Papers [17, fol. 16], Massachusetts Historical Society, (microfilm), RIHS, Providence, RI, no p. The document was published in Massachusetts Historical Society *Proceedings,* vol. 42 (Boston, 1909), 378–81. Even if the testimony did not originate in Rhode Island, it revealed much about the early peace testimony. One may presume that the document was acceptable in its overall content or the meeting would not have incorporated it into its book of disciplines.

4. Linear arrangement imposed, for clarity.

5. Compare Matt. 5:44: "Love your enemies, bless them that curse you, do good to them that hate you, and pray for them which despitefully use you, and persecute you"; John 18:11: "Put up thy sword into the sheath: the cup which my Father hath given me, shall I not drink it?" Matt. 26:52: "Put up again thy sword into his place: for all they that take the sword shall perish with the sword."

6. It is interesting to compare the fussily legalistic diction of this passage with two examples from legislative records: "nor shall suffer any punishment, fine, distraint, pennalty nor imprisonment, who cannot in conscience traine, fight, nor kill any person nor persons"; the 1673 Exemption, *Records . . . Rhode Island*, ed. Bartlett, 2:498. "Use your utmost endeavor to kill, expulse, expell, take and destroy all and every the enemies"; William Coddington, Commission to Major John Cranston, 11 April 1676, 2:538.

7. Easton, "A Relacion," in *Narratives*, ed. Lincoln, 15.

8. The members of the assembly in June, 1676 are listed in Rhode Island Colony Records, MSS, 2:48; although the deputies are omitted from the printed *Records*. Edmundson claimed some responsibility for the stance of Virginia Quakers during Bacon's Rebellion, 1676: "Friends stood neuter, and my being there was not in vain on that account. . . . Friends

were highly commended for keeping clear." Was he revealing that Quakers might have fought if he had not been there? Quoted in *Friends' Library*, ed. Evans and Evans, 2:123. In view of his misperceptions in Rhode Island, however, his judgments must not be viewed as the final authority on the behavior of Virginia Quakers.

9. Rhode Island Colony Records, MSS, 2:51; *Records . . . Rhode Island*, ed. Bartlett, 2:550–1.

10. 12/10M/1676, Rhode Island MM Men's Minutes, 1676–1773, MSS, microfilm no. 12, NEYM Collection, RIHS, no p.

11. 6/12M/1676; 6/1M/1676-7, Rhode Island MM Men's Minutes, 1676–1773, MSS, microfilm no. 12, NEYM Collection, RIHS, no. p.

12. The manner of disciplining wayward Quakers was modeled on the New Testament. Two or three "weighty"—spiritually advanced—Quakers would meet with an offender to explore the substance of his offense and its spiritual consequences and encourage him to acknowledge his fault and to repent. Quaker minutes are extremely discreet about the nature of a person's failings. This discretion resulted from the belief that one might entirely restore oneself by true repentance, in which case a detailed record of the offense would be irrelevant, and from a concern that recording Quaker offenses would offer material for outsiders to condemn the entire body. They were torn between a desire to use such cases as examples to teach and warn their own members and the fear that they would be "teaching" outsiders too.

13. 30/2M/1678, Rhode Island MM Men's Minutes, 1676–1773, MSS, microfilm no. 12, NEYM Collection, RIHS, no p.

14. 29/2M/1679, 27/2M/1680, Rhode Island MM Men's Minutes, 1676–1773, MSS, microfilm no. 12, NEYM Collection, RIHS, no p.

15. 31/11M/1681; meeting at Coggeshall's mentioned 23/3M/1682, Rhode Island MM Men's Minutes, 1676–1773, MSS, microfilm no. 12, NEYM Collection, RIHS, no p. The minutes note that Henry Bull and Joseph Nicholson were reconciled in 1686, Joshua Coggeshall in 1687, about ten years after the disaffections began.

16. Epistle no. 318, received at Newport 20/9M/1675, NEYM Earliest Written Disciplines, MSS, microfilm no. 4, NEYM Collection, RIHS, 32–3. The letter may have been a general epistle, widely distributed. In 1702, the yearly meeting at Rhode Island, as "the daughter" to Quakers in Old England, asked a weighty friend visiting from England for advice about paying taxes for military purposes. Pointing out the "great share" of New Englanders in government, in contrast to the limitations in England, the visitor said, "there is a great disparity between our circumstances and yours here . . . therefore . . . mind your own way in the truth, and look not out"; John Richardson, *An Account of the Life of That Ancient Servant of Jesus Christ, John Richardson*, 4th ed. (London, 1791), 131–2.

17. George Fox to Christopher Holder, London, 15/4M/1677, *JFHS* 47 (2) (autumn 1955): 80.

18. Fox to Holder, 79–81. "And now concerneing Hen: Bull shooting to death soe many horses comeing on his ground *that* he should not have done, but have [im]pounded them, and given them meat to have kept them alive till the owners had released them"; 79. "And I doe hear that An Eason [Ann Easton] soon after that Hen: Bulls wife was deceased that shee should be in Company with H. B. upon which a discourse about Marriage was raised, but I hope better thinges of her and Joshua Coxhall [Coggeshall]"; 80.

19. John Olney would not have been surprised.

20. Edmundson, *Journal*, 82.

21. *Ibid.*, 83.

22. 4/8M/1676, Curwen, *Relation*, 10–1.

23. 19/6M/1679, Rhode Island MM Men's Minutes, 1676–1773, MSS, microfilm no. 12, NEYM Collection, RIHS, no p. (after minutes of 7M/1683). "Disorder" did not mean tumult to Quakers; rather it meant "against the order, or procedures, of Friends."

24. Morning Meeting Minutes 1673-1692, transcripts, FHL, 8.

25. 4/11M/1675, *New-England's Present Sufferings*, 4; 10/8M/1675, 7.

26. *New England's Present Sufferings*, 1–8.

13. "Run the Hazard"

1. "Run the hazard," from Records of the Yearly Meeting of Aberdeen, *JFHS* 8 (1) (1911), 42. *Records . . . Rhode Island*, ed. Bartlett, vol. 1 (Providence, 1856), 154.

2. "The humble petition of Divers of the Church & towne of Sandwich," quoted in Sandwich MM Men's Minutes, 1672–1754, MSS, microfilm no. 45, NEYM Collection, RIHS, 11.

3. 14/3M/167[5 or 6?], Pembroke MM Minutes, 1741–1801 [*sic*], MSS, microfilm no. 49, NEYM Collection, RIHS, no p. The Pembroke Monthly Meeting incorporated Scituate and Duxbury.

4. Curwen, *Relation*, 3–4. Alice and Thomas Curwen mention that Quakers north of Boston, to the "Eastward," had not even met for several months.

5. Ps. 127:1.

6. "Strait is the gate, and narrow is the way, which leadeth unto life, and few there be that find it"; Matt. 7:14.

7. Batten to Thomas Allin, fols. 220r; 221r [stamped nos].

8. The Rhode Island Testimony of 1675, 47.

9. "Account Taken from Mr. Harris," fol. 141v.

10. Exod. 15:3, Nowell, "Abraham in Arms," quoted in *So Dreadfull a Judgment*, ed. Slotkin and Folsom, 274. Nowell was chaplain to the Massachusetts Bay forces at the Great Swamp Fight.

11. Nowell, "Abraham in Arms," 278.

12. 1693. Quoted in "Recent Accessions," *JFHS* 14 (3) (1917): 132.

13. Christine Heyrman has pointed out that the ordinary layperson lagged behind while increased tolerance for Quakers was expressed in law. "Specters of Subversion, Societies of Friends: Dissent and the Devil in Provincial Essex County, Massachusetts," in *Saints and Revolutionaries: Essays on Early American History*, ed. David D. Hall, John M. Murrin, and Thad W. Tate (New York, 1984), 38–74.

14. See, for example, *Records . . . New Plymouth*, vol. 5, *Court Orders*, 198–200.

15. 29 February 1675, *ibid.*, 186–7.

16. 30 December 1675; 29 February 1675, *ibid.*, 185.

17. 7 June 1676, *ibid.*, 198; 200.

18. The fines must be measured against the estimated fines frantically assessed against the Quakers in the perilous years 1658–1660. It has been estimated, for example, that Edward Perry of Sandwich was fined for attending meetings a total of ninety pounds in a thirty-one-month period; William Allen, a total of 126 pounds, William Gifford, a total of seventy-five pounds. Lovell, *Sandwich*, 99. Although many were reduced to penury, these outrageous assessments must have been ultimately futile. On the other hand, when one considers the purchasing power of the pound in 1675, the war-based fines were not negligible. Charles T. Burke, for instance, has estimated that a three-room house with attic cost forty-five pounds; a horse, two pounds; a cow, three pounds. The governor of Plymouth earned fifty pounds per year. Burke, *Puritans at Bay*, 245.

19. 14/3M/167[5 or 6?], Pembroke MM 1741–1801 [sic], MSS, microfilm no. 49, NEYM Collection, RIHS, no p.

20. Any person objecting to fighting who also objected to civil service designed to further the prosecution of war, such as watching unarmed, might be exempted as well.

21. *Records . . . Rhode Island*, ed. Bartlett, 2:531–2. The town records for the period of the war are disappointingly unrevealing or nonexistent. The town records of Newport begin in 1682, for example. The General Assembly confirmed retroactively all acts and orders during the war that town councils, councils of war, or any other officers had enacted,

including verbal orders; 2:550–1. By giving such power to local councils, the central government may have distanced itself from the need to issue difficult orders. The Quakers in the government especially may have appreciated this distance.

22. *Records . . . New Plymouth*, vol. 5, *Court Orders*, 190. The nine were: Daniel Butler, Zachariah Jenkens, Ephraim Allen, William Allen, Zachariah Colman, Joseph Colman, Thomas Colman, John Rance, and John Northy. Three other Quakers neglected to appear in court: Israel Gaunt, Increase Allen, and Obadiah Butler.

23. *Hinckley Papers, Massachusetts Historical Society Collections*, 4th series, vol. 5 (Boston, 1861), 8–9. Here Winslow's choice of words suggested that such men were selfish, but, significantly, he bypassed an opportunity to suggest that they were cowards.

24. 22 February 1675/76, Sandwich Town Meeting Records, 1656–, transcript, Sandwich Historical Society Library, Sandwich, MA, 43. These were likely the Allens, Jenkins, Butlers, and Gaunt in the Plymouth Records as cited in note 22. Sandwich Quakers had a history of refusing military training. Thomas Ewer, Peter Gaunt, Edward Perry, John Jenkins, and Robert Harper were all fined prior to 1659, before the declarations of the peace testimony in England, 1660. [Norton], *New-England's Ensigne*, 45–6.

25. In addition, the petition accused, the minister had tilled only five acres of his designated land when Quakers took it away from him. The petitioners had many grievances: the Quakers were verbally sharp, their "wandering" ones "crept in" among them, their books deceived "the hearts of the simple." Sandwich MM Men's Minutes, 1672–1754, MSS, microfilm no. 45, NEYM Collection, RIHS, 11.

26. "The humble petition," quoted in Sandwich MM Men's Minutes, 1672–1754, MSS, microfilm no. 45, NEYM Collection, RIHS, 11. "Violent in their carriage and voating" did not mean physical violence; it meant provocative, prophetic speech.

27. Sandwich Town Records, 40–1; 55. The number of Quakers is very, but not certainly, reliable. The problem would persist: in 1681, additional names were added to the town list, including Quakers Samuel Swift and John Gifford, who had apparently taken the oath while serving in the military; Sandwich Town Records, 56. This struggle was but a part of ongoing quarrels dating from 1674, in which Sandwich Quakers appealed to the governor for support against the court and to the court for support against their town council and in which, on the local level, those Quakers labeled "none townsmen" exchanged words with the rest of the town at a town meeting. See Sandwich MM Men's Minutes, 1672–1754, MSS, microfilm no. 45, NEYM Collection, RIHS, 5–7.

28. "The humble petition," quoted in Sandwich MM Men's Minutes, 1672–1754, MSS, microfilm no. 45, NEYM Collection, RIHS, 11. Arthur J. Worrall has argued the converse: that the petitioners invoked resentment against Quaker pacifism as a mask for their real grievance—Quaker refusal to pay for the minister. But as I will show hereafter, the Quaker answer to the petition stresses the pacifism issue with obvious energy. Wherever the true focus lay, it is clear that Quaker pacifism was a powerful stimulus of contention. Worrall, "Toleration Comes to Sandwich," in *Seeking the Light: Essays in Quaker History*, ed. J. William Frost and John M. Moore (Wallingford, PA, 1986), 75.

29. Sandwich MM Men's Minutes, 1672–1754, MSS, microfilm no. 45, NEYM Collection, RIHS, 11.

30. The Quakers also responded to other accusations: the matter of the minister's acres had never been definitively decided; only a quarter of those involved in the land seizure had been Quakers, so all Quakers should not have shared blame; they denied that Quakers had ever prevented any vote-taking; nor did Quakers ever "overvote" their neighbors in anything pertaining to the maintenance of their way of worship. Sandwich MM Men's Minutes, 1672–1754, MSS, microfilm no. 45, NEYM Collection, RIHS, 13–4.

31. Sandwich MM Men's Minutes, 1672–1754, MSS, microfilm no. 45, NEYM Collection, RIHS, 14–5. Jer. 17:5.

32. Sandwich MM Men's Minutes, 1672–1754, MSS, microfilm no. 45, NEYM Collection, RIHS, 15.

33. Sandwich MM Men's Minutes, 1672–1754, MSS, microfilm no. 45, NEYM Collection, RIHS, 14–5.

34. *Sandwich and Bourne Records,* 22/12M/1675, no p.

35. 11 April 1676, *Records . . . New Plymouth,* vol. 5, *Court Orders,* 193–4.

36. *Records . . . New Plymouth,* vol. 5, *Court Orders,* 190.

37. N. S. [Nathaniel Saltonstall], "The Present State of New-England with Respect to the Indian War," in *Narratives,* ed. Lincoln, 44.

38. *Records . . . Massachusetts,* 5:72–73; 81; 78–79.

39. N. S. [Nathaniel Saltonstall], "A New and Further Narrative of the State of New-England," in *Narratives,* ed. Lincoln, 86. William Harris told of a woman killed at Providence. [Harris], *Rhode Islander Reports,* 45. This was Quaker Elizabeth Sucklin; see hereafter.

40. Carla Gardina Pestana has stressed the familial and communal ties of the early Quaker sect in Massachusetts. She has attributed the "densely interrelated" character of the groups to the basic radicalism of Quaker belief, inviting consequences from outside for those espousing the belief and making it difficult for any family member to be uninvolved. Carla Gardina Pestana, *Quakers and Baptists in Colonial Massachusetts* (New York, 1991), 68–73.

41. Lydia B. Brownson and Maclean W. McLean, "Lt. John and Elizabeth (Freeman) Ellis of Sandwich, Mass.," *New England Historical and Genealogical Register* 119 (1965): 165.

42. Lovell, *Sandwich,* 102.

43. *Sandwich and Bourne Records.*

44. 5/5M/1672, Sandwich MM Men's Minutes, 1672–1754, MSS, microfilm no. 45, NEYM Collection, RIHS, 1. To "complain" about a member was not unusual; many members fell under complaint at some time.

45. 6/1M/1674, Sandwich MM Men's Minutes, 1672–1754, MSS, microfilm no. 45, NEYM Collection, RIHS, 4; 5/11M/1682, 27–8.

46. Lydia B. Brownson and Maclean W. McLean, "Lt. John and Elizabeth (Freeman) Ellis of Sandwich, Mass," *NEHGR* 119 (July 1965): 167. Sepican is now Rochester. The senior Ellis's age would not necessarily have disqualified him from being a soldier, particularly because he had been an important militia officer. General James Cudworth, for example, was in his seventies; General Winslow was in his fifties. Thomas Savage, Massachusetts commander, was about sixty-seven, Roger Williams seventy-six. However, Ellis's later descendants do not appear to have been Quakers.

47. 2/4M/1676, Sandwich MM Men's Minutes, 1672–1754, MSS, microfilm no. 45, NEYM Collection, RIHS, 8.

48. Under the expedition to Mount Hope is listed "Richard Taylor, Jr."; under the second Narragansett expedition is listed "Richard Taylor." Charles F. Swift, *History of Old Yarmouth,* ed. Charles A. Holbrook, Jr. (Yarmouth Port, MA, 1975), 108–9.

49. Records of Harwich [?], quoted in Conway P. Wing, *A Historical and Genealogical Register of John Wing, of Sandwich, Mass., and His Descendants. 1662–1881* ([Carlisle, PA?], 1881), 53. This source must be used with great caution.

50. Wing, *Register,* 43. In 1676 John Wing was assessed five pounds, sixteen shillings, three pence for the war; 46. Collins-Howland marriage, 20/6M/1675; Eaton-Wing marriage, 12/10M/1684; Jenkins-Allen marriage, 11/10M/1686, Sandwich MM Birth and Marriage Records, including Marriage Certificates, 1646–1761, MSS, microfilm no. 44, NEYM Collection, RIHS, 43; 78; 75.

51. For Ananias Wing: 12/10M/1684, Eaton-Wing marriage, Pembroke MM Births, Deaths, Marriages, MSS, microfilm no. 49, NEYM Collection, RIHS, 78. 11/10M/1686, Jenkins-Allen marriage, Sandwich MM Births, Marriages, MSS, microfilm no. 44, NEYM Collection, RIHS, 75; for Joseph Wing: 3/11M/1710, Wing-Butler marriage, 89; for Taylor: 28/8M/1682, Jenkins-Taylor marriage, 72. Richard Taylor's case illustrates the snares that may attend the search for connections: confusingly, two unrelated Richard Taylors dwelt in the small Yarmouth community, both married to women named Ruth. Since one of them

died in 1674, the soldier of 1675 and the father of the bride in 1682 must have been one and the same. Wing, *Register*, 100–1.

52. Bodge, *Soldiers*, 439. 23/1M/1679, Easton-Perry marriage, Sandwich MM Births, Marriages, MSS, microfilm no. 44, NEYM Collection, RIHS, 70. He is listed as having fought in King Philip's War in Donald G. Trayser, *Barnstable: Three Centuries of a Cape Cod Town* (Hyannis, MA, 1939), 110.

53. 1 June 1675, *Records . . . New Plymouth*, vol. 5, *Court Orders*, 174. Scituate, 25/7M/ 1676, Wanton-Phillips marriage; 4/3M/1683, Howland-Hussey marriage, Pembroke MM Births, Deaths, Marriages, MSS, microfilm no. 49, NEYM Collection, RIHS, no p. Joseph Howland signed many other certificates during these years.

54. Samuel Deane, *History of Scituate, Massachusetts, From Its First Settlement to 1831* (Boston, 1831), 129. *Records . . . New Plymouth*, vol. 5, *Court Orders*, 206. 20/6M/1675, Collins-Howland marriage, Pembroke MM Births, Deaths, Marriages, MSS, microfilm no. 49, NEYM Collection, RIHS , no p.

55. William A. Wing, "Five Johns of Old Dartmouth," *Old Dartmouth Historical Sketches* 25 (1909): 11. Smith's second wife was also a Quaker, daughter of Richard Kirby, one of the original Quakers of Sandwich.

56. *Records . . . New Plymouth*, vol. 5, *Court Orders*, 138. His son Deliverance would suffer imprisonment for refusing to serve in the later Indian wars. Lowry, "Quakers and Their Meeting House,"no p.

57. Joseph Dow, *History of the Town of Hampton, New Hampshire: From its Settlement in 1638, to the Autumn of 1892*, vols. 1, 2 (Salem, MA, 1893), 223–4. See also Bodge, *Soldiers*, 165; 342; 370.

58. Robert Pike, List of Soldiers from Norfolk, MS, 507/68 Massachusetts Archives (microfilm), 185a. Bodge, *Soldiers*, 370. Caleb Perkins was listed as a soldier in King William's War; Dow, *History*, 232. 1674, Old Norfolk County Court Records, vol. 1, 1648–1678, Peabody Essex Museum, Salem, MA, fol. 121v.

59. Pike, List of Soldiers, 185a. 1674, Old Norfolk County Court Records, vol. 1, 1648–1678, fol. 121v. "John Staninge," 10/8M/1682, Salem MM Minutes, 1677–1796, MSS, microfilm no. 83, NEYM Collection, RIHS, 8.

60. Pike, List of Soldiers, 185a. 1674, Old Norfolk County Court Records, vol. 1, 1648–1678, fol. 121v.

61. Bodge, *Soldiers*, 165; Dow, *History*, 224; 228–9; 232. For the nephew Henry Dow, see garrison discussion in chapter 14. English Quaker Thomas Story described his home as "where there was neither gun nor sword . . . but truth [and] faith . . . in a humble and resigned mind." Thomas Story, *A Journal of the Life of Thomas Story* (Newcastle Upon Tyne, 1747), 315.

62. For Ephraim, James, and William as soldiers, Bodge, *Soldiers*, 358; 370; 449. Ephraim was listed for King William's War. Dow, *History*, 232.

63. For William Marston, Sr., Dow, *History*, 56. Dow quotes these words without attribution. The soldiers were probably the grandsons of William Marston, Sr.; 836–8. [Fox and Rous], *Secret Workes*, 7. Marston was fined again for assorted errors in 1658, one of which was possessing John Lilburne's *Resurrection* and William Dewsbury's *Mighty Day of the Lord*. Bishop, *New England Judged*, [The First Part], 70. Sewel, *History*, 1:332. Jonathan Chu pointed out that Marston secured a rebate on his fine by repenting and relinquishing the pamphlets. But Chu implied that Marston continued to be a Quaker in 1669. Chu, *Neighbors*, 59; 138.

64. Bodge, *Soldiers*, 165; 183; 201; 342–7; 370; Dow, *History*, 220–3. For Benjamin Swett, Jr., 4/3M/1683, Howland-Hussey marriage, Pembroke MM Births, Marriages, MSS, microfilm no. 44, NEYM Collection, RIHS, 43. Unfortunately, extant Hampton Quaker records begin only in 1701 (for these families, and for Benjamin and Moses Swett, see Hampton Monthly Meeting Minutes, 1701–1757, MSS, microfilm no. 93, NEYM Collection, RIHS, minutes 1701, 1703; marriage certificate 1705). But some Hampton Quakers appear in earlier quarterly meeting records and on early marriage certificates. For Moses as soldier, Dow, *History*, 232.

65. For Christopher Hussey as Quaker, Chu, *Neighbors,* 111, 161; 1674, Old Norfolk County Court Records, vol. 1, 1648–1678, fol. 121v. As militia officer, Dow, *History,* 223; *CSPC, America and West Indies, 1681–1685,* ed. J. W. Fortescue (London, 1898), 43–4. For John Hussey, 4/3M/1683, 10/8M/1682, Salem MM Minutes, 1677–1796, MSS, microfilm no. 83, NEYM Collection, RIHS, 1, 8.

66. Chu, *Neighbors,* 108; 64. Shapleigh was commissioned major in 1656 and decommissioned in 1663. *Records . . . Massachusetts,* vol. 4, pt. 2, 75–6. The 1659 missionaries were William Robinson and Marmaduke Stevenson, hanged in Boston later that month. *Province and Court Records of Maine,* 6 vols., vol. 2, *York County Court Records,* ed. Charles T. Libbey, Robert Moody, and Neal Allen (Portland, ME, 1931), xxxviii. An earlier writer, James Bowden, thought that missionaries Mary Tomkins and Alice Ambrose of England and Edward Wharton and George Preston of Salem convinced Shapleigh in 1662, when he invited them to his house to dispute with the local minister. Chu's evidence for the earlier conversion makes the more convincing case. Whether Shapleigh's conversion occurred in 1659 or in 1662 is not important, for in either case he continued to serve as major until his commission was annulled in 1663. Bowden, *Society of Friends,* 252; 254.

67. Chu, *Neighbors,* 107.

68. He was "presented" for not commanding his officers to train in 1663—but the same court presented for the same offense three non-Quakers, Ingerson, Hitchcock, and Raynes. *Province . . . Maine,* 2:139–41. For the complexities of Maine politics, see Jonathan M. Chu, *Neighbors.*

69. Bishop, *New England Judged, The Second Part.* Letter from Edward Cranfield to the Committee Touching Waldern, 1 December 1682, *New Hampshire. Provincial and State Papers,* vol. 17, pt. 2, *Miscellaneous Provincial Papers, 1629–1725,* ed. Isaac W. Hammond (Manchester, NH, 1889; reprinted New York, 1973), 572. Title evidence need not always be significant however. Amos Otis wrote that in Barnstable, Plymouth Colony, once someone was an officer, he retained his title thereafter. Amos Otis, *Genealogical Notes of Barnstable Families,* 2 vols., vol. 1, rev. by C. F. Swift (Barnstable, MA, 1888), 377. But many other Quakers who had held military office shed their titles when they became Quakers.

70. Letter to "Worthy Freend," "Passcataway," 20 May 1667, *New Hampshire Provincial . . . Papers,* 513–4. *Province . . . Maine,* 2:177.

71. For wealth, Chu, *Neighbors,* 106. For merchant, *New Hampshire Provincial . . . Papers,* 513–4. For Gorges, Chu, *Neighbors,* 107.

72. Richard Waldron to Captain Frost and Sergeant Neall, *Documents and Records Relating to the Province of New-Hampshire,* vol. 1, ed. Nathaniel Bouton (Concord, NH, 1867), 356. *Records . . . Massachusetts,* 5:72; 88.

73. Edmundson, *Journal,* 78.

74. Ibid., 79–80.

75. Bodge, *Soldiers,* 304. Letter dated Dover, 10 September 1676, *Documents . . . New-Hampshire,* 357–8; Edward Rawson to Major Waldron and Major Pendleton, no d., 365. The terms of the treaty required each settler family to annually give one peck of corn to the Indian "owners" of the land. Jeremy Belknap, *The History of New-Hampshire,* notes by John Farmer, 2 vols., vol. 1 (Dover, NH, 1831), 82–3.

76. N. S., *New and Further,* 5–6.

77. Tompson, "New-Englands Tears For Her Present Miseries," in White, *Benjamin Tompson,* 108.

78. Those killed and wounded in Peirce's Fight were named in Noah Newman's letter to John Cotton, sent the day after the fight. The list may be found in Bowen, *Early Rehoboth,* 3:14–5.

79. I consider the absence of discussion concerning military matters in Quaker records in chapter 14.

80. Sandwich MM Births, Marriages, MSS, microfilm no. 44, NEYM Collection, RIHS, 70. Quaker birth registers are not completely reliable for establishing affiliation at a particu-

lar time, not least because parents often retroactively entered the names of children born before the parents became Quakers.

81. Wing, *Register*, 38.

82. 2 March 1657, *Records . . . New Plymouth*, vol. 3, *Court Orders*, 130. Stephen Wing, Sr., signed a marriage certificate in 1683: 16/5M/1683, Gifford-Mills marriage, Sandwich MM Births, Marriages, MSS, microfilm no. 44, NEYM Collection, RIHS, 73.

83. 27 August 1658, Lovell, *Sandwich*, 85; 90–1.

84. 2 October 1658, *Records . . . New Plymouth*, vol. 3, *Court Orders*, 153.

85. Lovell, *Sandwich*, 104.

86. Elwell Perry, "Quakers in Sandwich," typescript, Sandwich Historical Commission, no d., no p.

87. Sandwich MM Births, Marriages, MSS, microfilm no. 44, NEYM Collection, RIHS, no p. For Samuel, Sandwich MM Men's Minutes, 1672–1754, MSS, microfilm no. 45, NEYM Collection, RIHS, 4. For John and Ebenezer, Collins-Howland marriage, Pembroke MM Marriages, MSS, microfilm no. 49, NEYM Collection, RIHS, no p. For Wing genealogy, Wing, *Register*.

88. 3/4M/1681, Sandwich MM Mens Minutes, 1672–1754, MSS, microfilm no. 45, NEYM Collection, RIHS, 21. After the meeting cited Stephen Wing and Daniel Wing in 1681, they were satisfied with Stephen's answer but not with Daniel's. 1/5M/1681; 21–2. Austin concurs in this identification: "His oldest son, Stephen, Jr., was killed at the memorable fight at Rehoboth." John Osborne Austin, *One Hundred and Sixty Allied Families* (Salem, MA, [1894]), 275.

89. *Vital Records of Rehoboth*, ed. James N. Arnold (Providence, RI, 1897), 919.

90. Otis, *Notes*, 80–1.

91. 7/4M/1678, Sandwich MM Men's Minutes, 1672–1754, MSS, microfilm no. 45, NEYM Collection, RIHS, 10; 2/9M/1688, 44. 23/1M/1679, Easton-Perry marriage, Sandwich MM Births, Marriages, MSS, microfilm no. 44, NEYM Collection, RIHS, 70. Thomas Bourman's own marriage to Mary Harper, 9/6M/1678, took place according to the "good order of Friends," but the General Court seized their certificate, recording that Thomas "Burman" was "marryed in a clandestine way, contrary to the law"; 65. *Records . . . New Plymouth*, vol. 6, *Court Orders*, 6.

92. Bodge, *Soldiers*, 350. 20/6M/1675, Collins-Howland marriage, Pembroke MM Births, Marriages, MSS, microfilm no. 49, NEYM Collection, RIHS, 43.

93. Peirce and his men quartered at Rehoboth the night before their battle. Philip Walker, "Captan Perse & his coragios Company," ed. Diane Bornstein, *Proceedings of the American Antiquarian Society* 83 (1973): 94; 96. Bornstein sometimes refers to the author as "Peter Walker."

14. "The Rectification of the Heart"

1. Jonathan Dymond, *War: An Essay*, with introduction by John Bright, 1829; with introduction by Naomi Churgin Miller (New York, 1973), 44. Dymond's "rectification" referred to bringing one's thoughts to obedience.

2. Roger Williams, letter to John Winthrop, Jr., 27 June 1675, *The Complete Writings of Roger Williams*, vol. 6, *The Letters of Roger Williams, 1632–1682*, ed. John Russell Bartlett (New York, 1963), 371–2. Caleb Carr delivered up to Roger Williams the intelligence that Philip sent the first English heads he cut off to the Narragansetts, "and they gave the bearers a reward"; Harris, *Rhode Islander Reports*, 23; 24 n. 13. Daniel Stanton of Newport was another Quaker who carried news of the war—of the destruction of Dartmouth and the surrender of Indians there—news that Christopher Almy passed along to Captain Daniel Henchman as he ferried him on the way to Nipsachuck, who transmitted it to Governor John Leverett. Henchman to Leverett, 31 July 1675, in Bodge, *Soldiers*, 49.

3. In 1957, for example, Newland protested when Christopher Holder was denied a copy

of the warrant under which he had been detained, an intervention for which Newland was fined ten shillings. Holder, *The Holders*, 77.

4. *Sandwich and Bourne, Records,* June 20, 1676, no p.

5. Bishop, *New England Judged* [The First Part], 37.

6. 23 April 1676, Sherborn, Nantucket, Folger, "Looking-Glass for the Times," no p. Folger was Benjamin Franklin's grandfather.

7. Rom. 12:19.

8. "[Have Salt in Yourselves]," Fox, in *"The Power"*, ed. Jones, 16. Fox did not frame his lines in this manner. I have done so to illuminate his distinctive cadences. (The editor supplied the title.)

9. Norton, to Governor Thomas Prence, Plymouth, 16 June 1658, quoted in Backus, *History,* 256–7.

10. Trask and Smith, 21 December 1660, quoted in Besse, *Collection,* 2:212.

11. Joseph Nicholson, *The Standard Of the Lord lifted up in New-England, In Opposition to the Man of Sin* (London, 1660), 6. See also Mark 9:42: "And whosoever shall offend one of these little ones that believe in me, it is better for him that a millstone were hanged about his neck, and he were cast into the sea."

12. The word "myth" here is not meant to suggest a tale that is untrue but rather a tradition inspired by actual events but transformed in the service of giving voice to a group's sense of itself.

13. Boston, 4/11M/1675, E. W., *New-England's Present Sufferings,* 4.

14. Edmundson, *Journal,* 79; 80. It should be remembered that Edmundson was the one who said in error that Walter Clarke could not issue any commissions because he was a Quaker.

15. 1712, John Farmer, "John Farmer's First American Journey, 1711–1714," ed. Henry J. Cadbury, *Proceedings of the American Antiquarian Society* 53, pt. 1 (1943): 82–3.

16. *Ibid.,* 83.

17. *Ibid.*

18. Story, *Journal,* 315–6.

19. Thomas Chalkley, *A Collection of the Works of that Ancient, Faithful Servant of Jesus Christ, Thomas Chalkley,* 5th ed. (London, 1791), 42–5. The mother who was killed was "the Widow Mussey," "distinguished as a speaker." Dow recounts the story yet again. Another Quaker, and soldier, Thomas Lancaster, was killed on the same occasion. Dow, *History,* 233–4.

20. Brinton, *Sources,* 37.

21. 7 August 1675, *The Pynchon Papers, Letters of John Pynchon, 1654–1700,* 2 vols., vol. 1, ed. Carl Bridenbaugh, Publications of Colonial Society of Massachusetts, vol. 60 (Boston, 1982), 142.

22. Leach, *Flintlock,* 182.

23. Story, [1699], *Journal,* 197.

24. An important exception in Plymouth was the March 1675/76 attack on the Clark garrison, only four miles outside the town of Plymouth, in which ten persons were killed. Bodge, *Soldiers,* 461.

25. Letter of uncertain origin, perhaps written by Roger Williams to his brother Robert, 1 April 1676, *Correspondence of Roger Williams,* 721. Both Elizabeth Sucklin and her husband Thomas were Quakers; 725, n. 4. Elizabeth Sucklin (Sucklyn) signed a letter dated 26/4M/1673 from the "Woemens' Meeting at Rhode Island . . . To our Dear Freinds and Sisters In & about Sandwich"; MS, NEYM Earliest Written Disciplines, microfilm no. 4, NEYM Collection, RIHS, 14. She signed a marriage certificate dated Providence, 6/2M/1673. Rhode Island MM, Births, 1638–1812; Marriages, 1643–1888, MSS, microfilm no. 11, NEYM Collection, RIHS, no p.

26. Lovell, *Sandwich,* 77; map, 46. This Wing house is still standing.

27. Curwen, *Relation,* 5. This might well have been Major Shapleigh's house in Kittery, often used for large gatherings.

28. *Ibid.* In a later war, 1691, Quaker Thomas Wilson told about his experience in a completely matter-of-fact way: "the Indian war being very hot at Hampton . . . it was upon us to go to a garrison, which we did, and had a meeting near it at a Friend's house"; [Wilson], "A Brief Journal," 327.

29. Chu, *Neighbors,* 107. Everett S. Stackpole, *Old Kittery and Her Families* (Lewiston, ME, 1903), 166.

30. Otis and his wife were witnesses, 4/3M/1683, Howland-Hussey marriage, Pembroke MM Births, Marriages, MSS, microfilm no. 44, NEYM Collection, RIHS, 43; Austin, *One Hundred,* 184.

31. In Quaker records his name is given as Zoar. Zoar's son, in turn, became a prominent Quaker minister. Other Quaker settlers were John Smith, Ralph Allen of Sandwich, and Giles Slocum of Portsmouth, whose son married the daughter of Christopher Holder.

32. *A Brief and True Narration of the Late Wars Risen in New-England Occasioned by the Quarrelsom disposition, and Perfidious Carriage of the Barbarous, Savage and Heathenish Natives There,* dated Boston, 7 September 1675 (London, 1675), 5. Later estimates put the number of houses lost at thirty-six. Bourne, *Red King's Rebellion,* 121. A year later, in July 1676, a Dartmouth woman was wounded and captured by the Indians. Since she had once taken care of an Indian child, the Indians dressed her wound and escorted her back, guarding her until she was within the sight of the English. Hubbard, *Narrative,* 133.

33. Bourne, *Red King's Rebellion,* 121. John Russell was probably not a Quaker; he had served as a Plymouth deputy in 1665, for which he would have had to take an oath. But two of his sons married daughters of Quaker Lieutenant John Smith (who would have been tendered the oath in the military; he was perhaps accommodated, or he did not scruple to swear). William A. Wing, "John Russell," *Old Dartmouth Historical Sketches,* no. 69 (1935), no p.

34. Deane, *History of Scituate,* 126. The Ewell house and barn were burned down.

35. John Northy's birth was 6/1M/1674. Pembroke MM Minutes, 13; minutes of 1680 record the "sufferings" of Mrs. Ewell's husband, Henry Ewell, 14/3M/1678.

36. Mary Milles to Thomas and Alice Curwen, Salem, 22/5M/1677, Curwen, *Relation,* 42.

37. Bodge, *Soldiers,* 460–1.

38. Farmer, "First American Journey," ed. Cadbury, 84.

39. New York, 7 March 1675[/1676], Nicolls to Winthrop at Boston, MS, Winthrop Papers, Massachusetts Historical Society, (microfilm), RIHS, no p.

40. Story, [1699], *Journal,* 197.

41. To Henry Reeve, 1 November 1675, Austin, *Genealogical Dictionary,* 107. People from distressed Plymouth towns also moved to Aquidneck. Benjamin Church was ordered to muster troops there, from those who had moved from Swanzey and Dartmouth. *So Dreadfull a Judgment,* ed. Slotkin and Folsom, 421.

42. During the American Revolution, Quakers in Shapaqua Meeting in New York, for example, turned their meeting house into a "hospital" and cared for the wounded from the battle of White Plains, both loyalists and rebels.

43. Winslow, quoted in *A Letter Written by Dr. Simon Cooper of Newport On the Island of Rhode Island to the Governor and Council of the Connecticut Colony,* Society of Colonial Wars in the State of Rhode Island and Providence Plantations publication no. 8 (Providence, RI, 1916), 20.

44. 10 July 1677, *Records . . . New Plymouth,* vol. 5, *Court Orders,* 240. His bill was for eight pounds "or corne equivilent"; 17/3M/1676, *A Letter Written by Dr. Simon Cooper,* 19; 21.

45. June 1682, *Records . . . New Plymouth,* vol. 6, *Court Orders,* 120. See also 27 May 1682, *Hinckley Papers, Massachusetts Historical Society Collections,* 4th ser., 5:67–9.

46. Roger Williams, *An Answer to a Letter Sent from Mr. Coddington of Rode Island* (Providence, RI, 1946), 8.

47. [1679], "Petition from the Inhabitants of the Narragansett Country," in *Records . . . Rhode Island,* ed. Bartlett, 3:59–60.

48. Nabal was a churlish and miserly person who refused food to David (1 Sam. 25.) N. S., *New and Further*, 2.

49. It is a curious sidelight that William Hubbard of Massachusetts, who wrote a contemporary history of the war, did not mention the role Rhode Islanders played in taking care of the wounded after the Great Swamp Fight. His omission may reflect ignorance or instead may represent a parochial unwillingness to acknowledge positive attributes in a despised, if English, people. If his silence was deliberate, and motivated by spleen, it possibly explains why it is so difficult to "see" accurately the Rhode Island role in this war.

50. To "read out of meeting" is the Quaker equivalent to excommunication in other religious groups.

51. Sandwich MM Men's Minutes, 1672–1754, MSS, microfilm no. 45, NEYM Collection, RIHS, 7.

52. "Given forth att a Generall man, & womans meeting att William Coddingtons att Rhode Island the 12th 4th Mo 1676," NEYM Earliest Written Disciplines, MSS, microfilm no. 4, NEYM Collection, RIHS, 35. As noted earlier, the General Meeting was an annual representative meeting of Quakers from all of the New England and Long Island meetings. It carried the most potential authority of any Quaker body in America at that time.

53. The passage was not in list form in the original.

54. Story, *Journal*, 317. He wrote of Thomas Chase, whose house was the meeting place, as "an old . . . dead, dry, and confused preacher . . . and an enemy to the discipline of the church"; 319.

55. Matt. 18:15–17.

56. "Given forth att a Generall man, & womans meeting att William Coddingtons att Rhode Island the 12th 4th Mo 1676." NEYM Earliest Written Disciplines, MS, microfilm no. 4, NEYM Collection, RIHS, 35.

57. Matt. 18:17.

58. NEYM Earliest Written Disciplines, MS, microfilm no. 4, NEYM Collections, RIHS, 36–7.

59. Such variation affects historical generalizations, too. Worrall wrote that King Philip's War was "a war the Plymouth Colony Friends, true to their developing pacifism, refused to fight." Chu, on the other hand, focusing on Salem, Massachusetts and on New Hampshire and Maine communities, observed, "The peace testimony was not an essential part of Quaker doctrine at this time. Quakers . . . served as militia officers." Worrall, "Toleration," 74–5; Chu, *Neighbors*, n. 18, 53.

60. "Questions to a Conscientious Objector and Answers, 1679," ed. Henry J. Cadbury, *Fellowship* 26 (9) (1 May 1960): 29.

61. Salem MM Minutes 1677–1796, MSS, microfilm no. 83, NEYM Collection, RIHS, 17; Story, *Journal*, 266.

62. 12/4M/1702, Minutes, New England Yearly Meeting, 1683–1847, MSS, microfilm no. 1, NEYM Collection, RIHS, 20; 14/4M/1706, 33.

63. Edward Perry, "An Exhortation to Faithfulness," 1688, *A Memorable Account*, 34.

15. "All Things Have Their Beginnings"

1. For a view of later Quaker separateness, see Jon Butler, *Awash in a Sea of Faith: Christianizing the American People* (Cambridge, MA, 1990), 27.

2. Seth B. Hinshaw, *The Carolina Quaker Experience, 1665–1985: An Interpretation* (Greensboro, NC, 1984), 8.

3. *A Discovery of Two unclean Spirits, or two Priests, by their Fruits made manifest to be out of the Way of Truth, and out of the life of Godliness; in the broad way of Destruction, therein working deceitfully the Works of Errour*, cited in Joseph Smith, *A Descriptive Catalogue of Friends' Books*, vol. 1, (London, 1867; reprinted New York, 1970), 963. Trust is a major theme in Sissela Bok, *A Strategy for Peace: Human Values and the Threat of War* (New York, 1989).

4. See, for example, Francis Howgill et al. to Margaret Fell, 17/1M/1655, Swarthmore Transcripts, vol. 2, reel 2, 488.

5. 20/8M/1672, William Coddington, *A Demonstration of True Love Unto You the Rulers of the Colony of the Massachusets* ([n. p.], 1674), 18.

6. Phyllis Mack alerted me to Quaker use of sensual language.

7. James Dickinson, "A Journal of the Life, Travels, and Labours of Love . . . of . . . James Dickinson," *Friends' Library*, 12:384.

8. Burnyeat to Quakers, from Barbadoes, 30/11M/1670, Burnyeat, *Truth Exalted*, 108.

9. Bowen, *Early Rehoboth*, 3:75. *OED*, compact ed., 1:835.

10. [Ann Newbury's hand?] Thomas Richardson's Account Book, 1662–1712, MS, Newport Historical Society Library, Newport, RI, no p. Richardson was a Boston Quaker who moved to Rhode Island in 1712. He married Ann Newbury, also a Quaker, in 1704. The lines appear on the account pages for 1668.

11. I am grateful to Heather Van der Molen for this suggestion. Although not vulnerable to military issues in the same way as men, obviously women were deeply affected by them within their households.

12. Croese, *General History,* book 3, 267–8. Denied envoy status by the queen, Bidley nevertheless made her way to France, delivered her epistle urging the French king to make peace, not war, conversed with the monarch in a public audience, and, according to Croese, returned home "having, with all her endeavours, effected nothing"; 268–9.

13. Different meetings did show distinctly different levels of interest in peace issues, some clearly demanding more scrupulous behavior than others. It is logical that members would influence each other and that some meetings would respond to strong leadership in this area.

14. Reproduced in facsimile with introduction by Francis Fry (London, 1862), quoted in "Recent Accessions," *JFHS* 14 (3) (1917): 132.

15. John Bernstein has discussed the dichotomy in *Pacifism and Rebellion in the Writings of Herman Melville* (The Hague, 1964), 11–2. His examples of the form of pacifism antithetical to rebellion were Ahab and Starbuck in Melville's *Moby-Dick*; his examples of pacifist-revolutionaries were Gandhi and Christ.

16. Woolman, quoted in Edwin H. Cady, *John Woolman*, Great American Thinkers series (New York, 1965), 88.

17. I have profited from many conversations over the years with Carolyn Subin, whose insights on this topic are at once provocative and wise.

18. In his *The Threat and the Glory: Reflections on Science and Scientists*, Peter Medawar compares this "naturalistic" generalization to other dangerous examples: "the doctrines of racial superiority and the metaphysics of blood and soil . . . the belief that warfare between men or classes of men or nations represents a fulfilment of historical laws"; quoted in "Nature as Alibi," *New York Times*, section 7, book review section, 16 September 1990, 43.

19. Sanders, *Protestant Concepts*, 136–7.

20. Hubben, introduction to Cadbury, *Friendly Heritage*, x.

21. Samuel Bownas was explaining the peace testimony to Indians in 1703. The Indians thought it was a good doctrine but commented that few would observe it. Bownas replied, "all Things have their Beginnings, and 'tis now our Duty to embrace this Truth, hoping that others by this Example may do the same"; Bownas, *An Account of the Life, Travels, and Christian Experiences . . . of Samuel Bownas* (London, 1756), 81. "La Lucha Sin Fin," "The Struggle without End," was the name of the farm belonging to Jose Figueres Ferrer, pacifist president of Costa Rica, who dissolved Costa Rica's army in the 1950s. Editorial, *New York Times*, 17 June 1990, section 4, 20.

Appendix 4. "The Taste of the World in Our Own Mouths"

1. Christopher Hill, in *World Turned Upside Down*, generously acknowledged his scholarly debt to Alan Cole's analysis of the early peace testimony. Hill's accounts of the testimony

have remained essentially unchanged since. In his subsequent work, he has continued to attribute his understanding to Cole, as well as to Barry Reay. In the forward to Reay's *Quakers and the English Revolution*, for example, he wrote: "Thanks especially to theses and articles by Alan Cole and Barry Reay, we now know that for the first decade of their existence Quakers . . . were by no means pacifists." In 1992 he introduced an article on the peace testimony with: "Most of what I shall say derives from the work of Barry Reay." Taking his modesty at face value, it is appropriate, then, to credit Cole and Reay with establishing the new direction of scholarship in this area. Hill, *World Turned Upside Down*, 241, n. 49. Reay, *Quakers and English Revolution*, foreword by Christopher Hill, vii. Hill, "Quakers and the English Revolution," *JFHS* 56 (3) (1992): 165.

2. Cole, "Quakers and the English Revolution,"42.

3. Sanders has argued, with Cole, that the peace testimony was an outgrowth of dissatisfaction; *Protestant Concepts*, 128.

4. Cole, "Quakers and the English Revolution," 48.

5. See especially Reay, *Quakers and English Revolution*, 18–9; 49–51.

6. Richard Farnworth to Margaret Fell, Swarthmore Transcripts, vol. 2, reel 2, 18; 55.

7. Reay, *Quakers and English Revolution*, 100.

8. *Ibid.*, 121.

9. *Ibid.*

10. See chap. 5, *Experience of Defeat*, for his full argument. Hill, "Quakers and the English Revolution," 165–79, reproduces a summary lecture based on this chapter.

11. Hill, quoted in Steven Marx, "Prophet Disarmed," 113; *Hill, Experience of Defeat*, 130.

12. Hill, *Experience of Defeat*, 160–1.

13. The original letter still exists. Of course, the fact that Fox explained himself in spiritual terms does not assure that he had no other motives. But such speculations do not advance the argument.

14. Quakers had "long foreseen" defeat. Hill, *Experience of Defeat*, 18–9.

15. Lurting's account, although written many years later and therefore subject to retrospective coloring as well, is nevertheless replete with exact details suggesting authentic recollection. He did not write in pious generalities. See [Lurting], *Fighting Sailor.*

16. Reay, *Quakers and English Revolution*, 108.

17. Jones, *George Fox's Attitude*, 19; 8.

18. Frost, "Religious Liberty," 441.

19. Richard T. Vann, *The Social Development of English Quakerism: 1655–1755* (Cambridge, MA, 1969), 208.

20. Hill, *Experience of Defeat*, 160.

21. Individual Quakers were distinguished far more for principle than pragmatism. Consider the imprisoned Alexander Parker, offered one month's liberty if he engaged to remain peaceful. He undertook the engagement: "my words and actions shall be good and peacable & not by any force of Armes or Carnall weapons of warre to Act any thing prejudiciall to the king." But because he refused to pay prison fees, on principle, he was not released. Parker to Margaret Fell, Swarthmore Transcripts, vol. 3, reel 3, 60.

22. George Bishop, "The Third General Head Concerning Bearing of Arms," *Looking-Glass*, 204–5.

23. Reay, *Quakers and English Revolution*, 42. Hill, "Quakers and the English Revolution," 170.

24. George Fox, in Burrough, *Good Counsel*, 1659, quoted in Hill, *Experience of Defeat*, 157.

25. Reay warned against exaggerating Quaker political passivity, however, pointing especially to colonial experience. Reay, *Quakers and English Revolution*, 107.

26. Ingle, "Richard Hubberthorne and History: The Crisis of 1659," *JFHS* 56 (3) (1992): 197.

27. Hill, *Experience of Defeat*, 130. Cole, however, consistently distinguished clearly between pacifism and quietism.

28. Hill, in comparing one William Sedgewick to Fox, *ibid.*, 115. To illustrate this withdrawal from political action, Hill then quoted Sedgewick's renunciation of war.

29. Emphasis added. George Fox, *To the Councill of Officers of the Armie, and the Heads of the Nation; And for the Inferior Officers and Souldiers to read* ([London?], 1659), 8. See also "governors . . . that are sent by him for the punishment of evildoers, and for the praise of them that do well." 1 Pet. 2:14. "For rulers are not a terror to good works, but to the evil . . . he beareth not the sword in vain." Rom. 13:3–4.

30. Hill, *Experience of Defeat*, 165.

31. Christopher Atkinson to Margaret Fell, 15/1M/1655, Swarthmore Transcripts, vol. 2, reel 2, 582.

32. Thomas Holme to Margaret Fell, 2M/1656, Swarthmore Transcripts, vol. 2, reel 2, 362. Why this had been ordered is not clear. Holme had precipitously married his wife upon his release from prison. "I was emedeatly comanded of thee lord to take hir to wife that day . . . contrary to my will"; Holme to Fell, "abought 1654," 345–6.

33. Coale, "An Epistle to Friends in New-England," London, 21/1M/1665, *Books and Divers Epistles* (no p., 1671), 55.

34. Penington, *Examination*, 1660, 85. One suspects that this predilection is a matter of temperament. See Philip Greven, *The Protestant Temperament* (New York, 1977), for the crucial influence of temperament on belief.

35. In the present day the practice persists, in the form of "advices" and "queries," reminders read and pondered at Quaker business meetings.

36. Fox (no date), recorded in Dartmouth (Plymouth Colony) Monthly Meeting Women's Minutes, 1699–1782, Swarthmore College Library, Swarthmore, PA, microfilm, 8.

Bibliography

Primary Sources: Unpublished

Abraham Redwood Papers. Vol. 1, 1723-1740. MSS. Newport Historical Society, Newport, RI.

"An Account about New England from the Board of Trade." MS. Historical Manuscripts from the H. B. M. State Paper Office (Stevens Transcripts). 5 vols. Vol. 2, 1666–1682, no. 95. John Carter Brown Library, Providence, RI.

"An Account of the Justices Sitting in Quarter Sessions for Rhode Island." 1687. MS. "Rhode Island Historical Society Manuscripts." Vol. 1, p. 5. Rhode Island Historical Society, Providence, RI.

"An Account of the Rebellion of the Duke of Monmouth in a Letter to Dr. James from the Revd Mr. Andrew Poschal." British Library Additional MSS 4162. British Library, London.

"An Account Taken from Mr. Harris, New England." 29 April 1675. MS. PRO: CO 1/34/ 170411, fols. 140–143.

Addington, Isaac. "His Excellency Joseph Dudley . . ." Minutes. 3–7 September 1702. PRO: CO 5/1302/fols. 1–2.

"The Address of the Quakers of Rhode Island and Providence Plantation to His Majesty James the Second." 25 August 1686. MS. PRO: CO 1/60/170055, fols. 68–69.

Address of Rhode Island General Assembly to William and Mary. 25 October 1693. Historical Manuscripts from H.B.M. State Paper Office (Stevens Transcripts). Vol. 4, 1689–1695, no. 301. John Carter Brown Library, Providence, RI.

Allen, John. To Richard Smith. 8 August 1675. MS. Photostat from Connecticut Archives. John Allen Papers. Miscellaneous Manuscripts Collection. Rhode Island Historical Society, Providence, RI.

Allyn, John. To Peleg Sanford. 29 May 1685. MS. Photostat from Connecticut Archives. John Allen Papers. Miscellaneous Manuscripts Collection. Rhode Island Historical Society, Providence, RI.

Ames, William, et al. "To the King and Counsell." MS. Spence Manuscripts. Vol. 3,

1650–1662. Microfilm: "Quaker Manuscripts Collection from the Library of the Religious Society of Friends (London)." World Microfilms, London, UK. 15 reels, reel 2..

Andros, Edmund. "A Short Accompt of the General Concerns of New Yorke from October 1674 to November 1677." MS. PRO: CO 1/41/116, fol. 1.

Answer of the Agents of Boston. 30 July 1678. MS. Historical Manuscripts from H. B. M. State Paper Office (Stevens Transcripts). Vol. 2, 1666–1682, no. 119. John Carter Brown Library, Providence, RI.

Archdale, John. To Friends. 1695. MS [photocopy]. Haverford College Library, Haverford, PA.

———. Papers. 1694–1706. MSS (photocopies, from Library of Congress). North Carolina State Archives, Raleigh, NC.

"At a Meeting of the Commissioners of the United Colonyes." 2 November 1675. Film Miscellany Collection 507 vol. 68. Documents from Massachusetts Archives. Sterling Memorial Library, Yale University, New Haven.

Baily, Richard. To Captain Greene and each town on Rhode Island. Newport, 31 August 1671. MS. "Rhode Island Historical Society Manuscripts." Vol. 1, p. 3. Rhode Island Historical Society, Providence, RI.

A. R. Barclay Manuscript Collection. Manuscript vol. 323. Friends' House Library, London.

Barrow, Robert. "Some Account of George Fox's Funeral." Letter to John Naughton. Birmingham, England, 20/11M/1691. MS [copy]. National Library of Wales, Aberystwyth, Wales.

Batten, Benjamin. To Sir Thomas Allin. 29 June–6 July 1675. MS. PRO: CO 1/34/170411, fols. 220r–222r.

Bayly, William. "An Answer to a Queerie Published in the Newes Booke Concerning Help Against the Turke." MS [undated, but in answer to item published 12 November 1663]. Manuscript vol. 292 (Crosse Manuscripts). Friends' House Library, London.

Biggs, Timothy. "A Narrative of the Transactions Past in the Conty of Albemarle in Carolina . . ." AMS [photocopy]. January 1678. Arents Tobacco Collection. New York Public Library, New York.

"Bond for a Letter of Marque to Captain Isaac Doubt, Mariner; John Brown, Merchant; Peleg Brown, Esq. given by William Greene, Governor of Rhode Island." MS. 15 February 1744. John Carter Brown Library, Providence, RI.

Bownas, Samuel. Journal. 1676–1749. 4 vols. MSS. Friends' Historical Library. Swarthmore College, Swarthmore, PA.

Bradford, William, Captain. To John Cotton at Plimouth. Mount Hope, 21 July 1675. MS. John Carter Brown Library, Providence, RI.

Burrow, Edward [Edward Burrough]. "And Now All Friends and Elect of God . . ." MS. Portfolio 23. Friends' House Library, London.

Burrowe, Edward [Edward Burrough]. "An Information to the . . . Judges and Justices, and to all that handle the Lawe in the Nation of Ireland." 23/8M/1655. Manuscript vol. 321 (Caton Manuscripts vol. 2), 154–7. Friends' House Library, London.

Carr, Robert. "Whereas I am informed . . ." MS. 18 December 1666. Rhode Island Historical Society, Providence, RI.

Cartwright, George. To Colonel Nicoll. 25 January 1664. PRO: CO 1/19/9.

———. To Colonel Nicoll. 3 June 1665. PRO: CO 1/19/72.

Caton Manuscripts. Manuscript vols. 320–1, S. 81. Friends' House Library, London. Microfilm: "Quaker Manuscripts Collection from the Library of the Religious Society of Friends (London)." World Microfilms, London, UK. 15 reels, reel 1.

Caton, William, and Thomas Salthouse. To Thomas Willon. London, 7/3M/1660. Manuscript vol. 356/261 (Swarthmore Manuscripts). Friends' House Library, London.

Charles II, King. To Colony of Massachusetts. 28 June 1662. "Trusty and Welbeloved . . ." Codex England 2. John Carter Brown Library, Providence, RI.

"Christian and Brotherly Advices . . ." 1693. Transcribed by Benjamin Bourne. London,

1756. Men's and Women's Minutes, Epistles. MSS. Microfilm no. 4. New England Yearly Meeting Collection. Rhode Island Historical Society, Providence, RI.

Clarke, Walter. To [Arthur] Fenner. Newport, RI, 28/12M/1675. "Letter to Fenner with the Rest Conserned . . ." MS. Providence Town Papers, series 2, vol. 1, p. 107. Manuscripts Collection. Rhode Island Historical Society, Providence, RI.

———. "Loving friends . . ." 19/9M/1675. "Rhode Island Historical Society Manuscripts." Vol. 10, p. 144. Rhode Island Historical Society, Providence, RI.

Cowell, John. "A Booke wherin are Registered and Recorded The Marriages of Friends, The Births and Deaths of their Children which art not Registered by any Prieste." MS. 1670. Friends' House Library, London. Microfilm.

Cranston, John, Governor. For the General Assembly. Letter to King Charles II. 1 August 1679. MS. PRO: CO 1/43/170819, fols. 183r–184r.

Crosse Manuscripts. Manuscript vol. 292. Friend's House Library, London.

"Cynwyr Ymri, 1682–1747." MSS [copies] of Welsh Meeting Documents. J. R. Hughes Collection, Manuscripts. National Library of Wales, Aberystwyth, Wales.

Dartmouth Monthly Meeting. Men's Minutes. 11M/1698–6M/1770. MSS. Microfilm no. 50. New England Yearly Meeting Collection. Rhode Island Historical Society, Providence, RI.

Dartmouth Monthly Meeting. Women's Meeting Minutes, 1699–1782. MSS. Friends' Historical Library. Swarthmore College, Swarthmore, PA. Microfilm.

"Dear Friends and Brethen." 26/3M/1673. MS. Sundry Ancient Epistles, vol. 47. Friends' House Library, London.

"Depositions Before the Mayor of Dover, 1630–1659." MS. British Library Additional MSS 29624. British Library, London.

"The Despatches of Governor, Sir Jonathon Atkins relating to the Population of the Island of Barbados, A.D. 1679–1680." MS. Barbadoes. Microfilm: Church of Jesus Christ of Latter-Day Saints.

Dewsberry [Dewsbury], Willyam [William]. "Deare Friends and Gathered of God, in His light All Stand Still . . ." [undated, with manuscript from 1663]. Manuscript vol. 292 (Crosse Manuscripts). Friends' House Library, London.

Dewsbury, William. "A Coppye of ye word of ye Lord wch was sent unto Oliver Crumwell . . ." MS. Caton Manuscripts vol. 2. Microfilm: "Quaker Manuscripts Collection from the Library of the Religious Society of Friends (London)." World Microfilms, London, UK. 15 reels, reel 1.

Dix Manuscripts. Manuscript vol. 294. Friends' House Library, London.

Documents Relating to Rhode Island, and Rhode-Islanders: 3 vols., 1st series. Transcripts of MSS in Massachusetts Historical Society. Codex England 122–3. John Carter Brown Library, Providence, RI.

Documents Relating to Rhode Island, and Rhode-Islanders: 3 vols., 2d series. Transcripts of Trumball Papers, in Massachusetts Historical Society. Codex England 124. John Carter Brown Library, Providence, RI.

Dover Monthly Meeting. Births, Deaths, and Marriages, 1678–1862. Friends' Historical Library. Swarthmore College, Swarthmore, PA. Microfilm.

Dublin, John. "Petition to Governor and Magistrates . . . 2 May 1728." MS. Petitions to the Rhode Island General Assembly. Vol. 1, 1725–1729. Rhode Island State Archives, Providence, RI.

Earle, Ralph. "Whereas I, Ralph Earl of Dartmouth . . ." 17 April 1696. MS. Earle Papers. Rhode Island Historical Society, Providence, RI.

Eastern Quarter Perquimans Monthly Meeting [NC]. Vol. 1, 1680-1762. MSS. Quaker Collection. Guilford College Library, Greensboro, NC.

Eastern Quarter Symonds Creek Monthly Meeting [NC]. Records, 1678. MSS. Quaker Collection. Guilford College Library, Greensboro, NC.

Eastern Quarter Symonds Creek Monthly Meeting [NC]. Women's Meeting. Vol. 1, 1715–1768. MSS. Quaker Collection. Guilford College Library, Greensboro, NC.

Easton, John. To Henry Sloughter. 6 May 1691. MS. Gratz Collection. Historical Society of Pennsylvania, Philadelphia, PA.

"Epistles Received, 1683–1706, vol. 1." MSS. Friends' House Library, London.

"Epistles Received, 1705–1738, vol. 2." MSS. Friends' House Library, London.

"Epistles Sent, 1683–1702, vol. 1." MSS [transcribed from originals]. Friends' House Library, London.

"Epistles Sent, 1704–1738, vol. 2." MSS [transcribed from originals]. Friends' House Library, London.

"The Examinations, and Confessions, of the Persons concerned in the Noted Plot at Farnley Wood . . ." MSS. British Library Additional MSS 33770. British Library, London.

"Extract of a Letter from Newport." 7 July 1689. MS. Historical Manuscripts from H.B.M. State Paper Office (Stevens Transcripts). Vol. 4, 1689–1695, no. 259. John Carter Brown Library, Providence, RI.

First-Days Meetings, London, 1682–1683. MSS [copy of original record books]. Manuscript vol. 40. Friends' House Library, London.

Folger, Peter. "A Looking-Glass for the Times, or The Former Spirit of New-England Revived in This Generation . . . Relating to the People Called Quakers in New England." [1676?]. MS [transcript of book printed in 1763]. Codex England 110. John Carter Brown Library, Providence, RI.

[Forde, Richard]. Map of Barbados. Blathwayt Series no. 32. John Carter Brown Library, Providence, RI.

Fox, George. "The Answer of George Fox." To Oliver Cromwell, 1654. Manuscript vol. 321 (Caton Manuscripts vol. 2). Friends' House Library, London.

———. Book of Original Agreements. 1672–1735. MSS. New England Yearly Meeting Collection. Rhode Island Historical Society, Providence, RI.

———. Epistles. Manuscript vol. 308. Friends' House Library, London.

———. "George Fox's American Journey, 1672." MS. Portfolio 9. Friends' House Library, London. [Whether in his handwriting is open to dispute.]

———. "The Word of the Lord to all you Governours, Rulers and Souldiers." 1653. Manuscript vol. 308. Friends' House Library, London.

Freeborn, Susanna, and Esther Palmer. "Journall of Susanna Freeborn and Esther Palmer from Rhoad-Island to and from Pennsylvania." 28/8M/1704. MS. Box X 1/10. Friends' House Library, London.

Friends Records. Births, Deaths. 1638–1812. MSS. Library Special Collections. Newport Historical Society, Newport, RI.

"Friends Visitation Book." MS [photocopy]. 1656–1814. Newport Historical Society, Newport, RI.

"From Our Yearly Meeting Held at Newport . . . 1745 . . . to the Yearly Meeting . . . in London." MS. Portfolio 28. Friends' House Library, London.

"Genealogy of the Families of Dexters." 17 February 1819. MS. "Rhode Island Historical Society Manuscripts." Vol. 7, p. 146. Rhode Island Historical Society, Providence, RI.

Gould, Daniel. To Phineas and Phoebe Pemberton. Newport, 18/8M/1693. MS. Historical Society of Pennsylvania, Philadelphia, PA.

Governor and Council Records [Rhode Island]. 1667–1773. MSS. Rhode Island State Archives C#00558. Rhode Island State Archives, Providence, RI.

Great Book of Sufferings. MSS. 44 vols., vols. 1–7. Friends' House Library, London.

Greene, John. To Thomas Dongan, Governor of New York. Warwick, RI, 8 August 1686. PRO: CO 1/60/24.

———. "To the Freemen of the Towne of Providence . . ." 16 April 1690. MS. "Rhode Island Historical Society Manuscripts." Vol. 5, p. 31. Rhode Island Historical Society, Providence, RI.

Greenwich [Rhode Island] Monthly Meeting. Men's Minutes, 1699—1718. MSS. Microfilm no. 18. New England Yearly Meeting Collection. Rhode Island Historical Society Library, Providence, RI.

Hampton Monthly Meeting. Men's Minutes, 1701—1757. MSS. Microfilm no. 93. New England Yearly Meeting Collection. Rhode Island Historical Society, Providence, RI.

Hinckley, Thomas, Governor of Plimoth. To Henry Sloughter, Governor of New York. 8 July 1691. MS. Simon Gratz Collection. Historical Society of Pennsylvania, Philadelphia, PA.

Historical Manuscripts from H. B. M. State Paper Office (Stevens Transcripts). Vols. 1–5. John Carter Brown Library, Providence, RI.

Holder, Christopher. A Lamentation over New England. A.MS.S. 29 January 1676. Huntington Library, San Marino, CA.

Holester, Dennis, Thomas Goulney, and William Rogers. To Men's Meeting of Friends in Rhode Island. Bristol, England, 5/3M/1669. MS. Box 39. Newport Historical Society, Newport, RI.

Hooten, Elizabeth. Addresses. MS. Portfolio 3, 1653–1671. Friends' House Library, London.

Horsleydown Monthly Meeting (11 b 3)/ Southwark Manuscripts. Vol. 1. Friends' House Library, London.

Howgill, Francis, and Edward Burrough. To Margaret Fell. Caton Manuscripts. 1653–1660. Microfilm: "Quaker Manuscripts Collection from the Library of the Religious Society of Friends (London)." World Microfilms, London, UK. 15 reels, reel 1.

Howlden, Randall, and John Greene. "Answer of the Men of Warwick in Rhode Island to the Petition of R. Smith. . . ." 1678. MS. Historical Manuscripts from H.B.M. State Paper Office (Stevens Transcripts). Vol. 2, 1666–1682, no. 141. John Carter Brown Library, Providence, RI.

———. "Reply (to the Agents of Boston) and Petition to the Committee of Trade and Plantations." [1679] MS. Historical Manuscripts from H. B. M. State Paper Office (Stevens Transcripts). Vol. 2, 1666–1682, no. 149. John Carter Brown Library, Providence, RI.

H[ubberthorne], R[ichard]. To Margaret Fell. London, 26/6M/[1656]. Manuscript vol. S. 81. Friends' House Library, London.

"Humble Adresse, Remonstrance and Petition of the Governor and Company . . . August the 2nd 1692." Ms. Historical Manuscripts from H. B. M. State Paper Office (Stevens Transcripts). Vol. 4, 1689–1695, no. 294. John Carter Brown Library, Providence, RI.

"Indian War Newsletter, 21 December 1675." MS. Codex England 3. John Carter Brown Library, Providence, RI.

"Inventory of the Personall or Moveable Estate of Robert Hodgson." 16/3M/1696. MS. "Rhode Island Historical Society Manuscripts." Vol. 10, p. 89. Rhode Island Historical Society, Providence, RI.

Jamestown, Town of. Proprietor's Records. Vol. 1. 1672–1860. Microfilm: Church of Jesus Christ of Latter-Day Saints.

Jones, Thomas. "An Epistle from our Monthly Meeting held at Merion in the Welch Tract in Pennsylvania the 11th of the 3rd month, 1699." MS. Manuscripts 6415E. National Library of Wales, Aberystwyth, Wales.

Letter to King Charles II. 4 December 1679. MS. PRO: CO 5/904/XC170411, fols. 6v–9r.

Leverett, John. To Josiah Winslow Esq. Boston, 23 June 1675. MS. In Josiah Winslow Papers, .L461. Library of the Boston Athenaeum, Boston.

———. Letter to [Whitehall]. 15 June 1676. MS. PRO: CO 1/37/170411, fols. 16r—17r.

Lower Virginia Monthly Meeting Minutes 1673–1756. Typescript. Quaker Collection 1116/182. Haverford College Library, Haverford, PA.

Marie, R [Queen Mary]. To Colony of Rhode Island. 21 August 1694. Peck Manuscript Collection, 1:14. Rhode Island Historical Society, Providence, RI.

Massachusetts Council, (signed Edward Rawson, Secretary). To [Richard] Smith. 6 November 1675. Film Miscellany 507/68, Documents from Massachusetts Archives. Sterling Memorial Library, Yale University, New Haven, CT.

"Meeting for Sufferings. Account of Sufferings." 1720–1762. MSS. New England Yearly Meeting Archives, Disciplines, box 17. New England Yearly Meeting Collection. Rhode Island Historical Society Library, Providence, RI.

Melledge, Anthony. "A True Relation . . . With the Present Most Unjust Imprisonment of Anthony Mellidge, somtime called a Captain; now in Scorn Caled a Quaker." Dorchester Prison, 25/12M/1656. Tract vol. 137/22. Friends' House Library, London.

Miscellaneous Epistles, 17th and 18th Century. Haverford Quaker Collection. Haverford College Library, Haverford, PA.

Morning Meeting. Minutes 1673–1692. Transcripts. Friends' House Library, London.

Nantucket Monthly Meeting. Men's Minutes. MSS. Microfilm no. 57. New England Yearly Meeting Collection. Rhode Island Historical Society, Providence, RI.

Newbury-Richardson Commonplace Book, 1687–17–. MS. Newport Historical Society, Newport, RI.

New England Yearly Meeting. Earliest Written Disciplines, 1672–1756; Earliest Sufferings, 1720–1762. MSS. Microfilm no. 4. New England Yearly Meeting Collection. Rhode Island Historical Society, Providence, RI.

New England Yearly Meeting. Men's Minutes, 1683–1847. MSS. Microfilm no. 1. New England Yearly Meeting Collection. Rhode Island Historical Society, Providence, RI.

New Plymouth, Colony of. "Letter from New-Plymouth about the Indian Warr." 12 June 1677. MS. PRO: CO 5/904/XC170411, fols. 4–6.

Newport Monthly Meeting of Women Friends. Minutes. MSS. Newport Historical Society, Newport, RI.

Newport Town Meeting Records. Newport Town Council Records. MSS. All extant town records to 1778 at Newport Historical Society, Newport, RI. Microfilm: Church of Jesus Christ of Latter-Day Saints.

New York Yearly Meeting Minutes, 1671–1703. MSS. Friends' Historical Library. Swarthmore College, Swarthmore, PA.

Nicholson, Joseph. To [Oliver Cromwell], undated. Caton Manuscripts. Microfilm: "Quaker Manuscripts Collection from the Library of the Religious Society of Friends (London)." World Microfilms, London, UK. 15 reels, reel 1.

Nicolls, Matthias. To John Winthrop, Jr. 7 March 1675/1676. MS. Winthrop Papers. Massachusetts Historical Society. Microfilm. Rhode Island Historical Society, Providence, RI.

North Carolina Secretary of State Records. Council Minutes, Wills, Inventories, 1677–1706. Vol. 1. North Carolina State Archives, Raleigh, NC.

North Carolina Yearly Meeting. Minutes. Vol. 1, 1704–1793. MSS. Quaker Collection. Guilford College Library, Guilford, NC.

Norton, Humphrey. To John Alden. 16/4M/1658. MS. Peck Manuscript Collection. Rhode Island Historical Society, Providence, RI.

Old Norfolk County Court Records. MSS. Vol. 1, 1648–1678. Peabody Essex Museum, Salem, MA.

Palmer, Esther. "Esther Palmer's Journals." 1704–1705. MS. University of Virginia, Richmond, VA. Microfilm.

Pembroke Monthly Meeting. Men's Minutes 1679–1876 [begins 1676]. Births, Deaths, Marriages 1676–1876. MSS. Microfilm no. 49. New England Yearly Meeting Collection. Rhode Island Historical Society, Providence, RI.

Penington, Isaac. "To Such Who Are Little and Low . . ." [undated, with other documents dated 1663]. Manuscript vol. 292 (Crosse Manuscripts). Friends' House Library, London.

Perrott, John. ["I am not a man of warr."] 1663. Manuscript vol. 292 (Crosse Manuscripts). Friends' House Library, London.

———. To Ed. Crosse, Robt Duncon, and Thom Bayles. Jamaica, 14/4M/1663. ["Deare and Beloved Brethren, I Greet You . . ."] Manuscript vol. 292 (Crosse Manuscripts). Friends' House Library, London.

"Petitions to the Rhode Island General Assembly." Vol. 1, 1725–1729. MSS. Rhode Island State Archives, Providence, RI.

Pike, Robert. List of Soldiers from Norfolk. MS. 507/68 Massachusetts Archives (microfilm). 185a. Rhode Island Historical Society, Providence, RI.

Portsmouth Town Records, 1638-1850. Vol. 1, 1638–1700. Microfilm: Church of Jesus Christ of Latter-Day Saints.

"Quaker Manuscripts Collection from the Library of the Religious Society of Friends (London)." Microfilm: World Microfilms, London, UK. 15 reels. Reel 1: Caton Manuscripts. Reel 2: Spence Manuscripts. Sterling Memorial Library, Yale University, New Haven, CT.

Quary, Robert. To Lord Rochester. New York, 28 June 1709. Codex England 2. John Carter Brown Library, Providence, RI.

Rakestraw, William. "William Rakestraw's Paper." 20/4M/1713. MS. Portfolio 4. Friends' House Library, London.

Randolph, Edward. To Thomas, Earl of Danby. Boston, 17 June 1676. Egerton Manuscripts 3340. British Library, London.

———. "To the Committee for Trade and the Forain Plantations." Boston, "Common Goal," 5 September 1689. MS. Historical Manuscripts from H. B. M. State Paper Office (Stevens Transcripts). Vol. 4, 1689–1695, no. 260. John Carter Brown Library, Providence, RI.

Reading Monthly Meetings (Separatist). Minutes, 1668-1716. Transcribed by Beatrice and Nina Saxon Snell, 1976. Friends' House Library, London.

"The Records of Acts and Orders of the Inhabitants of the Towne of Westerle." 1669–. MS. Clarke Papers 4. Rhode Island Historical Society, Providence, RI.

Records of Marriages. Society of Friends. 1643–1775. MSS. Library Special Collections. Newport Historical Society, Newport, RI.

"Remarkable Occurrences of John Crook." MS [copy]. Manuscript 6415E. National Library of Wales, Aberystwyth, Wales.

"Report from His Majesty's Commissioners for the Affaires of New England in the Year 1665." [14 December] 1665. MS. PRO: CO 1/19/143.

Rhode Island Colony Records. 1646–1669, vol. 1. 1671–1686, vol. 2. 1686–1715, vol. 3. MSS. Rhode Island State Archives, C#00204. Rhode Island State Archives, Providence, RI.

Rhode Island General Court of Trials. Record Book A (transcription). May 1671–September 1704. Judicial Archives, Supreme Court Judicial Records Center, Pawtucket, RI.

[Rhode Island]. Governor and Council Records. 1667–1773. MSS. Rhode Island State Archives C#00558. Rhode Island State Archives, Providence, RI.

"Rhode Island Historical Society Manuscripts." Vol. 10. Rhode Island Historical Society, Providence, RI.

Rhode Island Land Evidences. MSS. Vol. 2 [copies]. Rhode Island Historical Society, Providence, RI.

Rhode Island Monthly Meeting. Births 1638–1812. Marriages 1643–1888. MSS. Microfilm no. 11. New England Yearly Meeting Collection. Rhode Island Historical Society, Providence, RI.

Rhode Island Monthly Meeting. Deaths 1647–1808. MSS. Microfilm no. 10. New England Yearly Meeting Collection. Rhode Island Historical Society, Providence, RI.

Rhode Island Monthly Meeting. Disownments, Testimonies, etc., 1647–1899. MSS. Microfilm no. 10. New England Yearly Meeting Collection. Rhode Island Historical Society, Providence, RI.

Rhode Island Monthly Meeting. Men's Minutes, 1676–1773. MSS. Microfilm no. 12. New England Yearly Meeting Collection. Rhode Island Historical Society, Providence, RI.

Richardson, Thomas. Account Book, 1662–1712. MS. Newport Historical Society, Newport, RI.

———. Letter Book, 1710–1715. MS. Newport Historical Society, Newport, RI.

Richardson, William. To George Fox. West River, MD, 1/5M/1682. MS. Portfolio 4/82. Friends' House Library, London.

Richardson, William and Thomas. Account Book, 1662–1669. MS. Newport Historical Society, Newport, RI.

Rofe, [George]. To Richard Hubberthorne. Barbadoes 18/9M/1661. Manuscript vol. 323:62 (A. R. Barclay Manuscripts). Friends' House Library, London.

Salem Monthly Meeting Men's Minutes 1677–1796. Births and Deaths. Marriage Certificates. MSS. Microfilm no. 83. New England Yearly Meeting Collection. Rhode Island Historical Society, Providence, RI.

Sandford, Peleg, [Governor]. Answer to Inquiries from Rhode Island. To William Blathwaite (Secretary to Committee for Foreign Plantations). Newport, RI, 8 May 1680. MS. PRO: CO 5/904/XC170411, fols. 35–37v.

Sandwich Monthly Meeting. Births and Marriages, 1646-1761. MSS. Microfilm no. 44. New England Yearly Meeting Collection. Rhode Island Historical Society, Providence, RI.

Sandwich Monthly Meeting. Men's Minutes, 1672–1754. MSS. Microfilm no. 45. New England Yearly Meeting Collection. Rhode Island Historical Society, Providence, RI.

Sandwich Monthly Meeting. Women's Minutes, 1677–1709. Typescript. Sandwich Historical Society Library, Sandwich, MA.

Sandwich Town Meeting Records, 1656–. Transcript. Sandwich Historical Society Library, Sandwich, MA.

Scott, John. Deed. 6 February 1666. MS. Potter Papers 1673. Rhode Island Historical Society, Providence, RI.

Secretary of State. Council Minutes; Wills and Inventories, 1677–1701. MSS. North Carolina State Archives, Raleigh, NC.

Shipping Book of Walter Newberry, 1678–1688. MS. Newport Historical Society, Newport, RI.

Smith, Richard. To [?], "Much Hounered Sir . . ." Narragansett, 29 September 1679. PRO: CO 1/43/129.

———. "Petition of Richard Smith and Others to the King." 3 July 1678. MS. Historical Manuscripts from H. B. M. State Paper Office (Stevens Transcripts). Vol. 2, 1666–1682, no. 134. John Carter Brown Library, Providence, RI.

Society of Friends. Book of Discipline. 1719–1777. MSS. [Copies and extracts from Yearly Meeting of Philadelphia and Flushing.] New York Historical Society, New York.

Spence Manuscripts. Friends' House Library, London. Microfilm: "Quaker Manuscripts Collection from the Library of the Religious Society of Friends (London)." World Microfilms, London, UK. 15 reels, reel 2.

Swarthmore Transcripts. (Transcription of Swarthmore Manuscripts, Letters and Documents of Early Friends.) Vols. 1–4. Friends' House Library, London. Microfilm: Swarthmore Transcripts. "Letters and Documents of Early Friends." World Microfilms, London, UK. 4 reels.

Symonds Creek Pascotank Monthly Meeting. Minutes. Vol. 1, 1699–1785. MSS. Quaker Collection. Guilford College Library, Guilford, NC.

"A Testimony from us (in scorn called Quakers but are) the Children of the Light." "From our men's-Meeting att Rhode Island att Joshua Coggeshalls." New England Yearly Meeting, Earliest Written Disciplines. MSS. Microfilm no. 4. New England Yearly Meeting Collection. Rhode Island Historical Society, Providence, RI, 46–7.

"A Testimony from (us in scorne called Quakers but are) the chidren [sic] of the light." From "our Mans Meeting (on Rhoad Island) att Joshua Coggeshall's." Winthrop Papers [17, fol. 16]. Massachusetts Historical Society (microfilm). Rhode Island Historical Society, Providence, RI. Published in "A Testimony," *Massachusetts Historical Society Proceedings*. Boston, 1909. 42: 378–81.

"A Testimony From Us, The People of God, Which The World Call Quakers. To all the Magistrates and Officers of What Sort Soever, From the Highest to the Lowest." N.d. MS. Portfolio 24/15. Friends' House Library, London.

Thatcher, Thomas. "Relation Concerning his Demands of Assistance for Seizing Captain Thomas Payn and Ship." 15 August 1683. MS. PRO: CO 1/55/36/ii.

Thompson, Thomas. "Sufferings of God's People." [1662–1676]. Manuscript vol. 299 (Thomas Thompson Manuscripts.) Friends' House Library, London.

Three Listings of Rhode Island Militia. [17–?] MSS. John Hay Manuscripts. John Hay Library, Brown University, Providence, RI.

To Captain Arthur Fenner and the Council of War. 19 November 1675. "Rhode Island Historical Society Manuscripts." Vol. 10, p. 144. Rhode Island Historical Society, Providence, RI.

"To Friends." Manuscript vol. 47, pp. 1–3. Friends' House Library, London.

Wade, Nathanial. "Account of 1685 on Monmouth's Rebellion." MS. Hart Manuscripts 45. Harleian Manuscripts 6845, 274–82. British Library, London.

Wanton, Edward. "Testimony of Suffering." Scituate, 26/8M/1679. MS. "Rhode Island Historical Society Manuscripts." Vol. 10, p. 84. Rhode Island Historical Society, Providence, RI.

Wanton, Gideon. "To the Sheriff of the County of Newport . . ." 25 June 1745. MS. Box 55. Newport Historical Society, Newport, RI.

Warwick Town Records Book A2 (photostat). Warwick Town Records Collection. Manuscripts Collection. Rhode Island Historical Society, Providence, RI.

Warwick Town Meeting. "Upon Suspition of the Indeans Riseing Against the English." 11 April 1671. MS. "Rhode Island Historical Society Manuscripts." Vol. 10, p. 145. Rhode Island Historical Society, Providence, RI.

Warwick, Town of. To Governor of Rhode Island. N.d. "Rhode Island Historical Society Manuscripts." Vol. 10, p. 152. Rhode Island Historical Society, Providence, RI.

Webb, Elizabeth. Journal of Elizabeth Webb, Called by Her "A Short Account of My Viage Into America with Mary Rogers My Companion." [Voyage 1697–1699]. Edited by Frederick B. Tolles and John Beverley Riggs. Typescript from MS. Haverford Quaker Collection. Haverford College Library, Haverford, PA.

"Westmerland Prisoner Case. For Henry Gouldney . . ." [c. 1694]. MS. Portfolio 36. Friends' House Library, London.

Wilson, George. "The Acceptable Year of the Lord Proclaimed." Originally dated from prison, 20/1M/1662. Transcribed by Warren M. Billings. In "George Wilson: A Quaker in Seventeenth-Century Virginia." Typescript. Temp. Manuscripts 166. Friends' House Library, London.

Wilson Papers. Alderman Library, University of Virginia, Charlottesville, VA. Microfilm.

Winslow, Josiah. Josiah Winslow Papers. MSS. Manuscripts .L461. Library of the Boston Athenaeum, Boston.

Winthrop Papers. Massachusetts Historical Society. Microfilm. RIHS, Providence, RI.

Yearly Meeting Papers [Philadelphia]. 1703–1713. MSS. Haverford Quaker Collection. Haverford College Library, Haverford, PA.

Primary Sources: Published

An Account of Several Passages and Letters Between His Excellency Benjamin Fletcher . . . and the Present Administrators . . . of Connecticut. New York, 1693. Only known copy, John Carter Brown Library, Providence, RI.

An Answer to a Scandalous Paper, Wherein Were Some Queries Given to be Answered. . . . London, 1656.

Archdale, John. A New Description of that Fertile and Pleasant Province of Carolina: With a Brief Account of its Discovery, and Settling, and the Government Thereof to this Time. London, 1707.

A[sh], T[homas]. Carolina; Or a Description of the Present State of that Country. . . . London, 1682. In Historical Collections of South Carolina. Vol. 2. Compiled by B. R. Carroll. New York, 1836.

Backhouse, James. *Memoirs of Francis Howgill, with Extracts From His Writings.* York, England, 1828.

Baker, Daniel. *A Clear Voice of Truth Sounded Forth.* N.p., 1662.

———. "Letter to the Mayor and Recorder of London." Newgate, 17/8M/1659. In *The Prophet Approved, by the Words of His Prophesie Coming to Passe.* London, 1659.

———. *Yet One Warning More, To Thee O England.* London, 1660.

Banks, John. *A Journal of the Life, Labours, Travels, and Sufferings . . . of John Banks.* 2d ed. London, 1798.

Barclay, Robert. *An Apology For the True Christian Divinity, As the same is held forth, and preached by the people, Called, in Scorn, Quakers. . . .* [London], 1678.

Barnwell, John. "Journal of John Barnwell." *Virginia Magazine of History and Biography* 5 (April 1898): 391–402; 6 (July 1898): 42–55.

Baxter, Richard. *The Quakers Catechism, or, the Quakers Questioned. . . .* London, 1655.

Bayly, William. "A Brief Declaration To All the World . . . concerning Plottings and Fightings with Carnal Weapons Against any People, Men or Nations upon the Earth." *A Collection of the Several Wrightings of . . . William Bayly. . . .* [London?], 1676.

Beckham, Edward, Henry Meriton, and Lancaster Topcliffe. *A Brief Discovery of Some of the Blasphemous and Seditious Principles and Practices of the People, Called Quakers. . . .* London, 1699.

Besse, Joseph. *An Abstract of the Sufferings Of the People call'd Quakers For The Testimony of a Good Conscience. . . .* 3 vols. London, 1733–1738.

———. *A Collection of the Sufferings of the People Called Quakers, For the Testimony of a Good Conscience. . . .* 2 vols. London, 1753.

Bishop, George. *A Looking-Glass for the Times.* London, 1668.

———. *New England Judged. The Second Part.* London, 1667.

———. *A Vindication of the Principles and Practises of the People Called Quakers.* N.p., 1665.

Bishope [Bishop], George. *New England Judged, Not by Man's, but the Spirit of the Lord: And the Summe sealed up of New-England's Persecutions.* [The First Part]. London, 1661.

Bond, Sampson. *A Publick Tryal of Quakers in Barmudas, May 1, 1678.* Boston, 1682.

Boston News-Letter. 1704–1711. Sterling Memorial Library, Yale University, New Haven. Microfilm.

Bouton, Nathanial, et al., eds. *Documents and Records Relating to New Hampshire.* Vol. 1. Concord, NH, 1867.

———. *Documents and Records Relating to New Hampshire.* Vol. 40. *New Hampshire Court Records.* Edited by Otis G. Hammond. New Hampshire, 1943.

Bownas, Samuel. *An Account of the Captivity of Elizabeth Hanson. . . .* London, 1787.

———. *An Account of the Life, Travels, and Christian Experiences in the Work of the Ministry of Samuel Bownas.* London, 1756.

———. *The Journals of the Lives and Travels of Samuel Bownas and John Richardson.* [London, 1756]; reprinted Philadelphia, 1759.

[Bowne, John]. *Journal of John Bowne: 1650–1694.* Transcribed and edited by Herbert F. Ricard. New Orleans, 1975.

B[rend], W[illiam]. *A Loving Salutation.* [London?], 1662.

———. *A Short Declaration of the Purpose and Decree of the Everlasting Counsel. . . .* [London?], 1662.

Brewster, Humphrey. *To the Mayor, Aldermen, Majestrates and Officers of the Military Force in this City of London. . . .* [London, 1662].

A Brief and True Narration of the Late Wars Risen in New-England Occasioned by the Quarrelsom disposition, and Perfidious Carriage of the Barbarous, Savage and Heathenish Natives There. Dated Boston, 7 September 1675. London, 1675.

Budd, Thomas. *Good Order Established in Pennsilvania & New-Jersey in America. . . .* [Philadelphia], 1685.

Bugg, Francis. *Battering Rams Against New Rome.* London, 1690–1691.

————. *The Picture of Quakerism*. London, 1714.

————. *The Pilgrim's Progress from Quakerism to Christianity*. . . . London, 1700.

————. *Quakerism Expos'd to Publick Censure*. London, 1699.

Burnyeat, John. *The Truth Exalted in the Writings of that Eminent and Faithful Servant of Christ John Burnyeat*. . . . London, 1691.

B[urrough], E[dward]. *A Declaration Of the Sad and Great Persecution and Martyrdom Of the People of God, Called Quakers, in New-England for the Worshipping of God*. London, [1661].

Burrough, Edward. *The Memorable Works of a Son of Thunder and Consolation*. . . . [London], 1672.

————. *To the Camp of the Lord in England*. London, 1656.

Burrough, Edward, and fifteen others. *A Declaration From the People Called Quakers to the Present Distracted Nation of England*. London, 1659.

Burrough, Edward, and George Fox. *Good Counsel and Advice*. . . . London, 1659.

Burrough, Edward, and Francis Howgill. *Answers to Several Queries Put forth to the despised People called Quakers*. . . . N.p., [1654].

Byllynge, Edward. *A Mite of Affection*. London, 1659.

————. *A Word of Reproof*. London, 1659.

Calendar of State Papers, Colonial Series, America and West Indies, 1661–1668. Edited by W. Noel Sainsbury. London, 1880. Reprinted Millwood, NY, 1964.

Calendar of State Papers, Colonial Series, America and West Indies, 1669–1674. Edited by W. Noel Sainsbury. London, 1889. Reprinted Vaduz, Germany, 1964.

Calendar of State Papers, Colonial Series, America and West Indies, 1675–1676. Edited by W. Noel Sainsbury. London, 1893.

Calendar of State Papers, Colonial Series, America and West Indies, 1681-1685. Edited by J. W. Fortescue. London, 1898.

Calendar of State Papers, Domestic Series. 13 vols. Vol. 11, *1657–1658*. Vol. 12, *1658–1659*. Edited by Mary Anne Everett Green. Reprinted Vaduz, Germany, 1965.

Callender, John. *The Early History of Rhode-Island. An Historical Discourse, On the Civil and Religious Affairs of the Colony of Rhode-Island*. Originally published 1739. 3d ed. Edited by Romeo Elton. Boston, 1843.

Carolina Described More Fully than Heretofore. Dublin, 1684.

Caton, William. *A Journal of the Life of that Faithful Servant . . . Will. Caton*. London, 1689.

Chalkley, Thomas. *A Collection of the Works of that Antient, Faithful Servant of Jesus Christ, Thomas Chalkley*. . . . 5th ed. London, 1791.

Chapin, Howard M., ed. *The Early Records of the Town of Warwick*. Providence, RI, 1926.

The Christian Soldiers Penny Bible, 1693: see "Recent Accessions," *Journal of the Friends' Historical Society* 14 (3) (1917): 132.

Church, Benjamin. *Diary of King Philip's War, 1675–76*. Introduction by Alan and Mary Simpson. Chester, CT, 1975.

————. *The History of King Philip's War*. Introduction and Notes by Henry Martyn Dexter. Boston, 1865.

Church, Thomas. *The History of King Philip's War . . . With Some Account of the Divine Providence Towards Col. Benjamin Church*. . . . Edited with an appendix by Samuel G. Drake. Boston, 1825.

Coale, Josiah. *The Books and Divers Epistles of the Faithful Servant of the Lord Josiah Coale*. . . . N.p., 1671.

Coddington, William. *A Demonstration of True Love Unto You the Rulers of the Colony of Massachusets*. . . . [Originally dated 12/6M/1672 and 20/8M/1672]. N.p., 1674.

————. Letters to John Winthrop, Jr. In *Massachusetts Historical Society Collections*. 4th series. 10 vols. Vol. 7. Boston, 1865, 278–96.

Colonial Records of North Carolina. Collected and edited by William L. Saunders. Vol. 1. *1662–1712*. Vol. 2. *1713–1728*. Raleigh, NC, 1886.

Colonial Records of North Carolina. 2d series. Vols. 2–5. *North Carolina Higher Court Records*. 4

vols. Vol. 1. *1670–1696.* Vol. 2. *1697–1701.* Edited by Mattie Erma Edwards Parker. Raleigh, NC, 1968, 1971. Vol. 3. *1702–1708.* Vol. 4. [called] *Higher Court Minutes. 1709–1723.* Edited by William S. Price, Jr. Raleigh, NC, 1974.

Colonial Records of North Carolina. 2d series. Vol. 7. *Records of the Executive Council, 1664–1734.* Edited by Robert J. Cain. Raleigh, NC, 1984.

Coxere, Edward. *Adventures by Sea of Edward Coxere.* Edited by E. M. W. Meyerstein. New York, 1946.

Croese, Gerard. *The General History of the Quakers: Containing the Lives . . . Of all the most Eminent Quakers. . . .* London, 1696.

Curwen, Alice. *A Relation of the Labour, Travail and Suffering of Alice Curwen.* [London], 1680.

[Davenport, T.]. *A Brief Manifestation of The State and Case of the Quakers presented to all people, but especialy to Merchants, Owners (and Masters) of Ships, and Mariners. . . .* London, 1664.

A Declaration and an Information From us the People of God Called Quakers, 1660: see F[ell], M[argaret], and thirteen others.

A Declaration From the Harmles & Innocent People of God, 1660: see Fox, George, et al.

Denton, Daniel. *A Brief Description of New York, Formerly Called New Netherlands with the Places Thereunto Adjoining.* Originally published London, 1670; new edition with notes by Gabriel Furman, New York, 1845.

Depositions from the Castle of York, Relating to Offences Committed in the Northern Counties in the Seventeenth Century. Edited by James Raine. Vol. 40. Surtees Society. Durham, England, 1861.

Dickinson, James. "A Journal of the Life, Travels and Labours of Love . . . of . . . James Dickinson." In *Friends' Library.* Vol. 12. Edited by William Evans and Thomas Evans. Philadelphia, 1848.

[Dickinson, Jonathan]. *Jonathan Dickinson's Journal; or, God's Protecting Providence.* [Originally published Philadelphia, 1699.] Edited by Charles McLean Andrews and Evangeline Walker Andrews. Yale Historical Publications 19, edited by Leonard Woods Labaree. New Haven, 1945.

Documents and Records Relating to the Province of New-Hampshire. Vol. 1. Edited by Nathaniel Bouton. Concord, NH, 1867.

Documents Illustrative of the History of the Slave Trade to America. Edited by Elizabeth Donnan. 4 vols. Vol. 3. *New England and the Middle Colonies.* Washington, DC, 1930–1935; reprinted New York, 1969.

Documents Relating to the Colonial History of the State of New Jersey. Edited by William A. Whitehead. New Jersey Historical Society. Vol. 1. *1631–1687.* Newark, NJ, 1880.

Dymond, Jonathan. *War: An Essay.* Introduction by John Bright. Originally published 1829; new introduction by Naomi Churgin Miller. New York, 1973.

Early Records of Friends in Devonshire. Friends' House Library Tract 532 (1873). Friends' House Library, London.

Early Records of the Town of Portsmouth. Edited by Clarence S. Brigham and Amos Perry. Providence, RI, 1901.

Early Records of the Town of Providence. Vol. 3. Providence, RI, 1893.

[Easton, John]. *A Narrative of the Causes which led to Philip's Indian War, of 1675 and 1676, by John Easton, of Rhode Island.* Edited by Franklin B. Hough. Albany, NY, 1858.

Edmundson, William. *A Journal of the Life . . . of William Edmundson.* London, 1715.

Ellis, William, and Alice Ellis. *The Life and Correspondence of William and Alice Ellis.* Edited by James Backhouse. Philadelphia, 1850.

Epistles from the Yearly Meeting of Friends, Held in London, to the Quarterly and Monthly Meetings in Great Britain, Ireland and Elsewhere, from 1681 to 1857. . . . 2 vols. Vol. 1. London, 1858.

Epistles from the Yearly Meeting Of the People called Quakers, Held in London, to the Quarterly and Monthly Meetings in Great Britain, Ireland, and Elsewhere; From the Year 1675, to 1759, inclusive. London, 1760.

[Evans, Katherine, and Sarah Chevers]. *A Short Relation of Some of the Cruel Sufferings* . . . *in the Inquisition in the Isle of Malta*. London, 1662.

An Exalted Diotrephes Reprehended, Or the Spirit of Error and Envy in William Rogers against the Truth. London, 1681.

Extracts from State Papers Relating to Friends, 1654–1672. Edited by Norman Penney. Introduction by R. A. Roberts. London, 1913.

F., T. *A Copy of a Letter, Written to the Souldiers that were at Narragansett in the Army. January 1675*. Broadside (facsim.). Boston, 1707. Microfiche: Early American Imprints. First series, no. 39444.

Farmer, John. "John Farmer's First American Journey, 1711–1714." Edited by Henry J. Cadbury. *Proceedings of the American Antiquarian Society* 53, pt. 1 (1943): 79–95.

Farneworth [Farnworth], Richard. *Cesars Penny to be Paid by Cesars Friends*. N.p., [1655].

Farnworth, Richard. *The Scriptures Vindication Against the Scotish Contradictors*. London, 1655.

A Farther Brief and True Narration of the Late Wars Risen in New England, Occasioned by the Quarrelsome Disposition and Perfidious Carriage of the Barbarous and Savage Indian Natives there. London, 1676.

[Fell, John]. [Newsletter, England]. 21 December 1675. John Carter Brown Library, Providence, RI.

Fell, Margaret. *A Brief Collection of Remarkable Passages and Occurrences Relating to* . . . *Margaret Fell* . . . *Together With Sundry of Her Epistles, Books*. . . . London, 1710.

———. *This Was Given to Major Generall Harrison and the Rest*. London, 1660.

[Fell, Margaret]. *To the General Council of Officers*. London, 1659.

F[ell], M[argaret], and thirteen others. *A Declaration and an Information From us the People of God Called Quakers, To the present Governors, the King and Both Houses of Parliament, And all whom it may Concern*. London, 1660.

First Publishers of Truth. Edited by Norman Penney. London, 1907.

Fox, George. *An Answer to Several New Laws and Orders Made by the Rulers of Boston*. [London], 1678.

———. *Caesar's Due Rendred unto Him* . . . *and God & Christs Due Rendred unto them*. . . . London, 1679.

———. *Cain Against Abel, Representing New-England's Church-Hirarchy, In Opposition to Her Christian Protestant Dissenters*. [London?], 1675.

———. *A Collection of Many Select and Christian Epistles, Letters and Testimonies*. . . . London, 1698.

———. *The Great Mistery of the Great Whore Unfolded: and Antichrists Kingdom Revealed unto Destruction*. London, 1659.

———. *The Journal of George Fox*. Edited by John L. Nickalls. Originally published Cambridge, England, 1952; Philadelphia, 1985.

———. *The Journal of George Fox*. "Cambridge Journal." Edited by Norman Penney. Cambridge, England, 1911.

———. *To All Kings, Princes, Rulers, Governours, Bishops and Clergy* . . . *Being a Distinction Between the Laws* . . . *for the Punishments of Evil Doers* . . . *And the Ordinances* . . . *Concerning Religion and Worship*. . . . London, 1685.

———. *To Christopher Holder, 15/4M/1677. Journal of the Friends' Historical Society* 47 (2) (autumn 1955): 79–81.

———. *To the Councill of Officers of the Armie, and the Heads of the Nation; And for the Inferior Officers and Souldiers to read*. [London], 1659.

[Fox, George]. *Narrative Papers of George Fox*. Edited by Henry J. Cadbury. Richmond, IN, 1972.

[———]. *"The Power of the Lord is Over All": The Pastoral Letters of George Fox*. Edited by T. Canby Jones. Richmond, IN, 1989.

[———]. "Some Principles of the Elect People of God, scornfully called, Quakers." In [Isaac

Penington], *Some Principles Of the Elect People of God In Scorn called Quakers*. [London], 1671.

Fox, George, and John Burnyeat. *A New-England-Fire-Brand Quenched, Being an Answer unto a Slanderous Book, Entitled; George Fox Digged out of his Burrows, &c*. [The First Part]. [London], 1678.

———. *A New-England-Fire-Brand Quenched*. The Second Part. [London], 1678.

[Fox, George, John Rous, et al.]. *The Secret Workes Of a Cruel People Made Manifest*. . . . London, 1659.

Fox, George, et al. *A Declaration from the Harmles & Innocent People of God called Quakers. Against all Plotters and Fighters in the World*. London, 1660.

Fox, George, "The Younger." *A True Relation of the Unlawful and Unreasonable Proceedings of the Magistrates of Harwich*. . . . 21/7M/1660. London, 1660.

Friends' Library. Edited by William Evans and Thomas Evans. Vols. 1–14. Philadelphia, 1837–1850.

Friends: Some Quaker Peace Documents: 1654–1920. London, 1939.

A Further Account of New Jersey in an Abstract of Letters Lately Writ from Thence. . . . [London], 1676.

George Fox Speaks for Himself. Edited by Hugh McGregor Ross. York, England, 1991.

George Fox's "Book of Miracles." Edited by Henry J. Cadbury. Cambridge, England, 1948.

Gorton, Samuel. *An Antidote against the Common Plague of the World*. London, 1657.

———. Letters. *Winthrop Papers. Massachusetts Historical Society Collections*. 4th series. Vol. 7. Boston, 1865.

———. *Simplicity's Defence Against Seven-Headed Policy*. [1646]. Notes and appendices by William R. Staples. Providence, RI, 1835.

Gould, Daniel. "True Account of My Travels on Truth's Account in Maryland, Virginia, Written Chiefly for My Own Satisfaction: 27 October 1669–2 October 1693." In Rebecca Gould Mitchell. *The Goulds of Rhode Island*. Providence, RI, 1875.

Great Britain, Public Record Office. *Calendar of State Papers, Colonial Series, 1574–1696*. London, 1860–1908.

Griffith, John. *A Journal of the Life, Travels, and Labours . . . of John Griffith*. London, 1779.

[Groome, Samuel]. *A Glass For the People of New-England, in which They may see themselves and Spirits . . . ever since they usurped Authority to Banish, Hang, Whip and Cut off Ears*. . . . [London], 1676.

Hammett, John. *Vindication and Relation*. Introduction by Jacob Mott, Samuel Bownas, and John Wanton. Newport, RI, 1727.

Harris, William. Letter, in *Collections of the Rhode Island Historical Society* 10: 162–79. Providence, RI, 1902.

———. To [Sir Joseph Williamson]. 12 August 1676. *Calendar of State Papers Colonial. America and West Indies. 1675–1676*. Edited by W. Noel Sainsbury. London, 1893.

[Harris, William]. *A Rhode Islander Reports on King Philip's War: The Second William Harris Letter of August, 1676*. Transcribed and edited by Douglas Edward Leach. Providence, RI, 1963.

[Higgenson, Thomas]. *Glory Sometimes Afar Off, Now stepping in; Or, the great Gospel-Mysterie of the Spirit, or Divine Nature in Saints*. . . . London, [1653].

Hinckley Papers. Massachusetts Historical Society Collections. 4th series. Vol. 5. Boston, 1861.

Historical Collections of South Carolina. 2 vols. Vol. 2. Edited by B. R. Carroll. New York, 1836.

Howgill, Francis. "A. R. Barclay MSS." *Journal of the Friends Historical Society* 46 (2) (1954): 78–9.

———. "A Declaration of the Sufferings of the Inhabitants of the Province of Mariland in Virginia." In *The Deceiver of the Nations Discovered: and his Cruelty Made Manifest*. London, 1660.

———. "Letter to G. Fox." *Journal of the Friends' Historical Society* 44 (1) (1952): 42–3

————. *The Popish Inquisition Newly Erected in New-England.* . . . London, 1659.

Hubbard, W[illiam]. *A Narrative of the Troubles with the Indians in New-England, from the first planting thereof in the year 1607. to this present year, 1677.* Boston, 1677.

Hubberthorne, Richard. *The Good Old Cause Briefly Demonstrated.* London, 1659.

[Hutchinson, Richard]. *The Warr in New-England Visibly Ended.* . . . London, 1677.

James Claypoole's Letter Book. London and Philadelphia, 1681–1684. Edited by Marion Balderston. Huntington Library Publications. San Marino, CA, 1967.

Jennings, Samuel. *The State of the Case . . . betwixt the People called Quakers . . . and George Keith.* . . . London, 1694.

Keith, George. *An Account of the Great Divisions, Amongst the Quakers in Pensilvania . . . The Plea of the Innocent, Against the False Judgement of the Guilty.* London, 1692.

————. *An Account of the Quakers Politicks.* . . . London, 1700.

————. *A Journal of Travels from New-Hampshire to Caratuck.* . . . London, 1706.

[Keith, George]. *A Further Discovery of the Spirit of Falsehood and Persecution in Sam Jennings.* . . . London, 1694.

[Langford, Jonas]. *A Brief Account of the Sufferings of the Servants of the Lord Called Quakers . . . in the Island of Antegoa . . . from the Year 1660, to 1695.* London, 1706.

Lawson, John. *A New Voyage to Carolina.* Edited by Hugh T. Lefler. Originally published 1709; Chapel Hill, NC, 1967.

Leeds Friends' Minute Book, 1692–1712. Edited by Jean Mortimer, and Russell Mortimer. Yorkshire Archeological Society record series, vol. 139. Leeds, England, 1980.

A Letter Written by Capt. Wait Winthrop from Mr. Smiths in Narragansett to Governor John Winthrop. . . . Edited by E. A. Burlingame, N. M. Isham, and C. E. Cannon. Society of Colonial Wars in the State of Rhode Island and Providence Plantations publication no. 12. Providence, RI, 1919.

A Letter Written by Dr. Simon Cooper of Newport On the Island of Rhode Island to the Governor and Council of the Connecticut Colony. Society of Colonial Wars in the State of Rhode Island and Providence Plantations publication no. 8. Providence, RI, 1916.

"Letters to William Penn, from Worcester Prison, 1674." *Journal of the Friends' Historical Society* 7 (2): 73–5.

The Life and Death, Travels and Sufferings of Robert Widders. . . . London, 1688.

[Lilburne, John]. *The Resurrection of John Lilburne, Now a Prisoner at Dover-Castle, Declared And manifested in these following Lines penned by himself.* . . . London, 1656.

[Loddington, William]. *Plantation Work The Work of this Generation.* . . . London, 1682.

Lodowick, Christian. *A Letter from the Most Ingenious Mr. Lodowick to Cotton Mather.* Rhode Island, 1 February 1691. N.p., 1691.

[Lurting, Thomas]. *The Fighting Sailor Turn'd Peaceable Christian Manifested in the Convincement and Conversion of Thomas Lurting.* First published c. 1710; London, no d.

Manuscripts of S. H. LeFleming of Rydal Hall. H. M. C. *Twelfth Report.* Vol. 25, app. pt. 7. London, 1890. (British Library, London.)

[Marvell, Andrew]. *A List of Several Ships Belonging to English Merchants, Taken by French Privateers.* . . . Amsterdam, 1677.

Mather, Cotton. "Decennium Luctuosum: An History of Remarkable Occurrences in the Long War . . . from the year 1688, to the year 1698. . . ." *Narratives of the Indian Wars.* Edited by Charles H. Lincoln. New York, 1913.

————. *Magnalia Christi Americana.* Hartford, CT, 1840.

————. *Souldiers Counselled and Comforted. A Discourse Delivered unto some part of the Forces Engaged in the Just War of New-England Against the Northern & Eastern Indians. September 1, 1689.* Boston, 1689.

Mather, Increase. *Brief History of the War with the Indians in New-England: From June 24. 1675 . . . to August 12. 1676.* . . . London, 1676.

————. *Diary by Increase Mather. March, 1675–December, 1676.* Introduction and notes by Samuel A. Green. Cambridge, [MA], 1900.

————. *A Relation of the Troubles which have hapned in New-England, By reason of the Indians there: From the Year 1614 to the Year 1675*. Boston, 1677.

Maule, Thomas. *New England Persecutors Mauled with Their Own Weapons*. Salem, MA, 1697.

————. *Truth Held Forth and Maintained*. N.p., 1695.

Memoirs of the First Settlement of the Island of Barbadoes, and other the Carribbee Islands. . . . London, 1743.

Middlesex County Records. Vol. 3. *Indictments, Recognizances . . . Certificates of Convictions of Conventiclers*. Edited by John Cordy Jeafferson. London, 1888.

Minute Book of the Men's Meeting of the Society of Friends in Bristol, 1667–1686. Edited by Russell Mortimer. Bristol Record Society publications vol. 26. N.p., 1971.

Minutes of the Provincial Council of Pennsylvania. Pennsylvania Colonial Records. Vol. 1. March 10, 1683–November 27, 1700. Philadelphia, 1852.

Morton, Nathaniel. *New Englands Memoriall*. Edited by Howard J. Hall. [1669]; New York, 1937.

[Mucklow, William]. "From a Little Hidden One of the Flock of Jesus." *A Bemoaning Letter of an Ingenious Quaker, To a Friend of his. Wherein the Government of the Quakers Among Themselves . . . is Brought to Light*. Originally published as *The Spirit of the Hat*, London, 1673; London, 1700.

Narratives of the Indian Wars, 1675–1699. Edited by Charles H. Lincoln. *Original Narratives of Early American History*, J. Franklin Jameson, general editor. New York, 1913.

Narratives of the Insurrections, 1675–1690. Edited by Charles M. Andrews. *Original Narratives of Early American History*, J. Franklin Jameson, general editor. New York, 1915.

Nayler, James. *A Discovery of the First Wisdom from beneath, and the Second Wisdom from above*. London, 1653.

————. *Love to the Lost: And a Hand Held Forth to the Helpless*. . . . 2d ed. London, 1656.

————. *Satans Design Discovered: Who Under a Pretence of Worshipping Christs Person in Heaven, Would Exclude God and Christ, the Spirit and Light, Out of the World: And that He Should No More Dwell in His People as He Hath Done, till Doomsday*. . . . London, 1655.

Nelson, Lieut.-Col., to "Dockter Robert Gorge Secretarye. . . ." 26 May 1657, quoted in *Journal of the Friends' Historical Society* 7 (3): 103–4.

New Hampshire Court Records, 1640–1692. Vol. 40. *State Paper Series*. Edited by Otis G. Hammond. N.p., 1943.

New Hampshire. Provincial and State Papers. Vol. 17, part 2. *Miscellaneous Provincial Papers, 1629–1725*. Edited by Isaac W. Hammond. Manchester, NH, 1889; reprinted New York, 1973.

News from New-England, Being a True and Last Account of the Present Bloody Wars. . . . London, 1676.

New York Yearly Meeting of the Religious Society of Friends. *Faith and Practice*. New York, 1974.

Nicholson, Joseph. *The Standard Of the Lord lifted up in New-England, In Opposition to the Man of Sin*. . . . London, 1660.

North Carolina Under the Lord Proprietors; A Series of Original Documents. . . . London, 1933.

[Norton, Humphrey]. *New-England's Ensigne*. London, 1659.

Nowell, Samuel. "Abraham in Arms." Artillery Election Sermon, 3 June 1678. *So Dreadfull a Judgement: Puritan Responses to King Philip's War, 1667–1677*. Edited by Richard Slotkin and James K. Folsom. Middletown, CT, 1978.

Oakes, Urian. *The Soveraign Efficacy of Divine Providence*. . . . Artillery Election Sermon. Cambridge, 10 September 1677. Boston, 1682.

The Old Indian Chronicle. . . . Introduction and notes by Samuel Gardner Drake. Boston, 1867.

Paskell, Thomas. *An Abstract of a Letter from Thomas Paskell of Pennsilvania To his Friend J. J. of Chippenham*. Last of January 1682/3. London, 1683.

Pastorius, Francis Daniel. "The Matter of Taxes and Contributions briefly examined by

Plain Scripture Testimonies and Sound Reason." Edited by Henry J. Cadbury. *Pennsylvania Magazine of History and Biography* 18 (3) (1934): 255–9.

Penhallow, Samuel. *History of the Wars of New-England, With the Eastern Indians.* Boston, 1726; reprinted, with notes and introduction by Edward Wheelock, Freeport, NY, 1971.

Penington, Isaac. *An Examination of the Grounds or Causes, Which are said to induce the Court of Boston in New-England to make that Order or Law of Banishment upon pain of Death against the Quakers. . . .* London, 1660.

———. Letter dated 26/8M/1670. *Letters of Isaac Penington . . . [and] Letters of Stephen Crisp, William Penn, R. Barclay, William Caton, Josiah Coale, and Others.* London, 1796.

———. *A Voyce out of the Thick Darknesses: Containing in it a Few Words to Christians, About the Late and Present Posture of Spiritual Affairs Among Them.* London, 1650.

———. *The Works of the Long-Mournful and Sorely-Distressed Isaac Penington. . . .* 2d ed. 2 vols. London, 1761.

Penn, William. *A Key, Opening the Way to Every Capacity; How to Distinguish the Religion professed by the People Called Quakers. . . .* London, 1806.

———. *Truth Rescued From Imposture.* [London], 1670.

[Penn, William]. *Correspondence Between William Penn and James Logan, 1700–1750. Publications of the Historical Society of Pennsylvania.* Edited by Edward Armstrong. Philadelphia, 1870.

———. *The Papers of William Penn.* Edited by Richard S. Dunn and Mary Maples Dunn. 4 vols. Vol. 3. *1685–1700.* Edited by Marianne S. Wokeck et al. [Philadelphia], 1986.

Pennyman, John. *The Following is a Copy of a Letter I Sent to George Fox. . . .* 8 August 1671. Broadside. Beinecke Library, Yale University, New Haven.

———. *This is for the People Called Quakers.* London, 1675.

The Peoples Ancient and Just Liberties Asserted, in the Tryal of William Penn, and William Mead. . . . [London], 1670.

Pepys, Samuel. *The Diary of Samuel Pepys.* Edited by Robert Latham and William Matthews. 10 vols. Berkeley, CA, 1970–1983.

Perry, Edward. *A Memorable Account of the Christian Experiences and Living Testimonies Of that faithful Servant of Christ Edward Perry. . . .* [Philadelphia], 1726.

Philalethes. [Thomas Maule?]. *Tribute to CAESAR, How Paid by the Best Christians, And to What Purpose. . . .* N.p., [1715?].

Pitman, Henry. *A Relation of the Great Sufferings and Strange Adventures of Henry Pitman, Chyrurgion to the Late Duke of Monmouth. . . .* London, 1689.

The Present State of New-England, With Respect to the Indian War . . . from the 20th of June, till the 10th of November, 1675. London, 1676.

Pringle, Cyrus. *Record of a Quaker Conscience.* New York, 1918.

The Province and Court Records of Maine. 6 vols. Edited by Charles T. Libbey, Robert Moody, and Neal Allen. Vol. 1. Portland, ME, 1928. Vol. 2. Portland, ME, 1931.

The Public Records of the Colony of Connecticut. 15 vols. Hartford, CT, 1850–1890. Vol. 2, *1665–1678.* Edited by J. Hammond Trumbull. Hartford, CT, 1852. Vol. 3, *1678–1689.* Edited by J. Hammond Trumbull. Hartford, CT, 1859.

Pynchon, John. *The Pynchon Papers: Letters of John Pynchon, 1654–1700.* 2 vols. Vol. 1. Edited by Carl Bridenbaugh. Boston, 1982.

Quarter Sessions Records, 1658–1677. Vol. 6. Edited by J. C. Atkinson. North Riding Record Society. London, 1888.

Quarter Sessions Records for the County of Somerset. Vol. 4. *Charles II, 1666–1677.* Somerset Record Society, vol. 34. London, 1919.

"Questions to a Conscientious Objector and Answers, 1679." Edited by Henry J. Cadbury. *Fellowship* 26 (9) (1 May 1960): 29–31.

Reckitt, William. *Some Account of the Life and Gospel Labours of William Reckitt.* 2d ed. Philadelphia, 1783.

"Record of a Court Martial Held at Newport in August, 1676 for the Trial of Indians

Charged with Being Engaged in Philip's Designs." *Narratives of the Indian Wars. 1675–1699.* Edited by Charles H. Lincoln. New York, 1913.

Records and Files of the Quarterly Courts of Essex County, Massachusetts. Vol. 8. 1680–1683. Salem, MA, 1921.

Records of the Colony of New Plymouth in New England. Vol. 3. *Court Orders 1651–1661.* Vol. 4. *Court Orders 1661–1668.* Vol. 5. *Court Orders 1668–1678.* Edited by Nathaniel B. Shurtleff. Boston, 1855–1856; reprinted New York, 1968.

Records of the Colony of New Plymouth in New England. Vol. 7. *Judicial Acts 1636–1692.* Edited by Nathaniel B. Shurtleff. Boston, 1857; reprinted New York, 1968.

Records of the Colony of New Plymouth in New England. Vol. 8. *Miscellaneous Records: 1633–1689.* Edited by Nathaniel B. Shurtleff. Boston, 1857; reprinted New York, 1968.

Records of the Colony of New Plymouth in New England. Vols. 9–10. *Acts of the Commissioners of the United Colonies of New England.* Edited by David Pulsifer. 2 vols. Vol. 1. *1643–1651.* Vol. 2. *1653–1679.* Boston, 1859; reprinted New York, 1968.

Records of the Colony of New Plymouth in New England. Vol. 11. *Laws 1623–1682.* Edited by David Pulsifer. Boston, 1861; reprinted New York, 1968.

Records of the Colony of Rhode Island and Providence Plantations, in New England. Edited by John Russell Bartlett. Vol. 1. *1636–1663.* Providence, RI, 1856. Vol. 2. *1664–1677.* Providence, RI, 1857. Vol. 3. *1678–1706.* Providence, RI, 1858. Vol. 4. *1707–1740.* Providence, RI, 1859.

Records of the Court of Trials of the Town of Warwick, 1659–1674. Transcribed by Helen Capwell. Providence, RI, 1922.

Records of the Governor and Company of the Massachusetts Bay in New England. 6 vols. in 5. Edited by Nathaniel B. Shurtleff. Boston, 1853–1854; reprinted New York, 1968.

Records of the Proprietors of the Narragansett, otherwise called the Fones Record. Edited by James N. Arnold. Providence, RI, 1894.

Rhode Island Court Records. Records of the Court of Trials of the Colony of Providence Plantations, 1647–1670. 2 vols. Vol. 1, 1647–1662. Providence, RI, 1920. Vol. 2, 1663–1670. Providence, RI, 1922.

"Rhode Island State Papers." *Massachusetts Historical Society Collections.* 2d series. Vol. 7. Boston, 1818.

Richardson, John. *An Account of the Life of That Ancient Servant of Jesus Christ, John Richardson.* 4th ed. London, 1791.

Rigge, Ambrose. "A True Relation of Ambrose Rigge, By Way of Journal." *Friends' Library.* Vol. 12. Edited by William Evans and Thomas Evans. Philadelphia, 1848.

————. *Works.* [London], 1672.

Rogers, William. *The Christian-Quaker, Distinguished from the Apostate & Innovator In Five Parts.* London, 1680.

Rotch, William. *Memorandum Written by William Rotch in the Eightieth Year of His Age.* Boston, 1916.

[Rowlandson, Mary]. *A Narrative of the Captivity, Sufferings and Removes of Mrs. Mary Rowlandson. . . . .* Boston, 1805.

Rules of Discipline of the Religious Society of Friends, With Advices: Being Extracts from the Minutes and Epistles of Their Yearly Meeting, Held in London, from its First Institution. 3d ed. London, 1834.

Salthouse, Thomas. *To all the Christian Congregations. . . .* [dated Cornwall]. N.p., 1662.

S., N. [Nathaniel Saltonstall]. *A Continuation Of the State of New-England; Being a Farther Account of the Indian Warr . . . 10th of November, 1675 to the 8th of February 1675/6.* London, 1676.

[S., N.]. *A New and Further Narrative Of the State of New-England, Being a Continued Account of the Bloudy Indian-War, From March till August, 1676.* [Boston, July 22, 1676]. London, 1676.

[Saltonstall, Nathaniel]. *The Present State of New-England, With Respect to the Indian War . . . from the 20th of June, till the 10th of November, 1675.* London, 1675.

S., S. [S. Starling?] *An Answer To the Seditious and Scandalous Pamphlet, Entitled, The Tryal of W. Penn and W. Mead.* . . . London, 1671.

Sandwich and Bourne Colony and Town Records. In *Library of Cape Cod History and Genealogy,* no. 104. Yarmouthport, MA, 1910.

Sanford, Peleg. *The Letter Book of Peleg Sanford of Newport, Merchant (Later Governor of Rhode Island), 1666–1668.* Providence, RI, 1928.

[Scot, George]. "The Model of the Government of the Province of East-New-Jersey in America." Edinburgh, 1685. Reprinted in William A. Whitehead. *East Jersey under The Proprietary Governments. New Jersey Historical Society Collections.* Vol. 1. [no p.], 1846.

The Second Part of the Peoples Antient and Just Liberties Asserted in the . . . *Tryals of Tho. Rudyard, Francis Moor, Rich. Mew, Rich. Mayfeild, Rich. Knowlman, Gilbert Hutton, Job Boulton, Rich. Thornton, Charles Banister, John Boulton, and William Bayly.* [London], 1670.

Sellar, Richard. *An Account of the Suffering of Richard Sellar, For His Christian Testimony Against War, A Yorkshire Fisherman, Who Was Pressed into the Navy in the Year 1655.* 1st ed. London, 1842.

Sewall, Samuel. *Diary of Samuel Sewall: 1674–1729. Massachusetts Historical Society Collections.* 5th series. Vols. 5–7. Boston, 1878–1882.

Sewel, William. *The History of the Rise, Increase, and Progress of the Christian People Called Quakers.* 2 vols. 4th ed. 1st ed. 1722; London, 1799,1800.

Smith, John. *A Narrative of Some Sufferings for His Christian Peacable Testimony, by John Smith, late of Chester County, Deceased.* Philadelphia, 1800.

Smith, William. *The Banner of Love. Under Which The Royal Army is Preserved, an[d] Safely Conducted. Being a Clear and Perfect Way out of Wars & Contentions.* . . . London, 1661.

So Dreadfull a Judgment: Puritan Responses to King Philip's War, 1676–1677. Edited by Richard Slotkin and James K. Folsom. Middletown, CT, 1978.

Somersetshire Quarterly Meeting of the Society of Friends, 1668–1699. Edited by Stephen C. Morland. Somerset Record Society, vol. 75. [Yeovil, England], 1978.

State Records of North Carolina. Edited by Walter Clark. Vol. 22. *Miscellaneous.* Vol. 23. *Laws 1715–1776.* Vol. 25. Goldsboro, NC, 1904–1907.

Stevenson, Marmaduke. *A Call from Death to Life.* . . . London, 1660.

Story, Thomas. *A Journal of the Life of Thomas Story.* . . . Newcastle Upon Tyne, England, 1747.

Strutt, James. *A Declaration to the Whole World To try themselves by Gods Witness in them.* . . . London, 1659.

Stubbs, John, and William Caton. *A True Declaration of the Bloody Proceedings of the Men in Maidstone in the County of Kent.* . . . London, 1655.

[Taylor, John]. *An Account of Some of the Labours, Exercises, Travels and Perils* . . . *of John Taylor.* . . . London, 1718; reprinted as *Memoir of John Taylor of the City of York,* York, England, 1830.

————. *A Loving and Friendly Invitation to all Sinners to Repent* . . . *With a Brief Account of the Latter Part of the Life of John Perrot.* . . . London, 1683.

Taylor, Thomas. *A Testimony for Christ Jesus.* 1672. Broadside. Friends' House Library, London.

————. *Works.* Originally published as *Truth's Innocency and Simplicity Shining Through.* . . . London, 1697.

A Testimony and Caution to Such as Do Make a Profession of Truth . . . *and More Especially Such Who Profess to be Ministers of the Gospel of Peace, That They Should Not Be Concerned in Worldly Government.* Philadelphia, 1693.

Thomas Shepard's Confessions. Edited by George Selement and Bruce C. Woolley. Colonial Society of Massachusetts *Collections.* Vol. 58. Boston, 1981.

Thurston, Edward, et al. *The Christian Faith of the People of God, Called in Scorn, Quakers in Rhode-Island* . . . *Vindicated.* . . . N.p., n.d.

To the Generals, and Captains, Officers and Souldiers of this Present Army; The Just and Equal Ap-

peal, and the State of the Innocent Cause of Us, Who Have Been Turned Out of Your Army for the Exercise of our Pure Consciences, Who Are Now Persecuted Amongst our Brethren, under the name of Quakers. N.p. [1650s].

Tompson, Benjamin. *New-Englands Tears for her Present Miseries . . . With an Account of the Battel between the English and Indians upon Seaconk Plain. . . .* London, 1676.

A True Account of the Most Considerable Occurrences That Have Hapned in the Warre Between the English and the Indians in New-England, From the Fifth of May, 1676, to the Fourth of August Last. . . . London, 1676.

Trumball Papers. Massachusetts Historical Society Collections. 5th series. Vol. 9.

Underhill, Thomas. *Hell Broke Loose: Or an History of the Quakers Both Old and New.* 2d ed. London, 1660.

Vital Records of Dartmouth Massachusetts. Vol. 1. *Births.* Boston, 1929. Vol. 2. *Marriages.* Boston, 1930. Vol. 3. *Deaths.* Boston, 1930.

Vital Records of Rehoboth. Edited by James N. Arnold. Providence, RI, 1897.

Vital Records of Rhode Island, 1636–1850. Edited by James N. Arnold. First Series. *Births, Marriages and Deaths.* Vol. 7. *Friends and Ministers.* Providence, RI, 1895.

Vital Records of Scituate Massachusetts. Vol. 1. *Births.* Vol. 2. *Marriages and Deaths.* Boston, 1909.

W., E. [Edward Wharton]. *New-England's Present Sufferings Under Their Cruel Neighbouring Indians: Represented in Two Letters, Lately Written from Boston to London.* London, 1675.

Walker, Philip. "Captan Perse and his coragios Company." Edited with introduction by Diane Bornstein. *Proceedings of the American Antiquarian Society* 83 (1973): 67–102.

[Whiting, John]. *Persecution Expos'd, In Some Memoirs Relating to the Sufferings of John Whiting. . . .* London, 1715.

Wilkinson, William. *An Answer to Joseph Jenks's Reply to William Wilkinson's Treatise, Entituled, The Baptism of the Holy Spirit. . . .* London, 1721.

———. *The Baptism of the Holy Spirit.* London, 1718.

Williams, Roger. *An Answer to a Letter Sent from Mr. Coddington of Rode Island, to Governour Leveret of Boston in what concerns R. W. of Providence.* Originally published 1677. Society of Colonial Wars, Rhode Island, publication no. 38. Providence, RI, 1946.

———. *An Answer to a Scandelous Paper Which Came to My Hand from the Massachusetts Clamouring against the Purchase and Slandering the Purchasers of Qunnunnagut Iland, and subscribed by John Easton.* Originally published 1658. Transcribed by Frederick S. Peck. Introduction by Byron Sprague Watson. Providence, RI, 1945.

———. *The Complete Writings of Roger Williams.* Vol. 5. *George Fox Digg'd Out of his Burrowes.* Edited by J. Lewis Diman. New York, 1963.

———. *The Complete Writings of Roger Williams.* Vol. 6. *The Letters of Roger Williams, 1632–1682.* Edited by John Russell Bartlett. New York, 1963.

[———]. *Correspondence of Roger Williams.* Edited by Glenn W. LaFantasie. 2 vols. Revised from manuscript edited by Bradford F. Swan. Vol. 2. Hanover, NH, 1988.

[Wilson, Thomas]. "A Brief Journal of the Life, Travels, and Labours of Love . . . of . . . Thomas Wilson." *Friends Library.* Vol. 2. Edited by William Evans and Thomas Evans. Philadelphia, 1838.

———. *Journals of the Lives, Travels, and Gospel Labours of Thomas Wilson and James Dickinson.* London, 1847.

The Wyllys Papers. Connecticut Historical Society Collections. Vol. 21. Hartford, CT, 1924.

Secondary Sources

Achtermeier, William O. *Rhode Island Arms Makers and Gunsmiths, 1643–1883.* Providence, RI, 1980.

Andrews, Charles M. *The Colonial Period of American History.* 4 vols. New Haven, 1934–1938.

Anscombe, Francis C. *I Have Called You Friends: The Story of Quakerism in North Carolina.* Boston, 1959.

Arnold, Samuel Greene. *History of the State of Rhode Island and Providence Plantations.* 2 vols. Vol. 1. *1636–1700.* New York, 1859.

Austin, John Osborne. *Genealogical Dictionary of Rhode Island.* Albany, NY, 1887.

———. *One Hundred and Sixty Allied Families.* Salem, MA, [1894].

Axtell, James. *After Columbus: Essays in the Ethnohistory of Colonial North America.* New York, 1988.

———. *The Invasion Within: The Contest of Cultures in Colonial North America.* New York, 1985.

Backus, Isaac. *A History of New England. With Particular Reference to the Denomination of Christians Called Baptists.* 2d ed. 2 vols. Vol. 1. Notes by David Weston. Newton, MA, 1871.

Bailey, Richard. "The Making and Unmaking of a God: New Light on George Fox and Early Quakerism." Paper presented at George Fox Commemorative Conference, Lancaster University, Lancaster, England, March 1991.

Bainton, Roland H. *Christian Attitudes toward War and Peace: A Historical Survey and Critical Re-evaluation.* New York, 1960.

Barbour, Hugh. *The Quakers in Puritan England.* New Haven, 1964.

Barbour, Hugh, and Arthur O. Roberts, eds. *Early Quaker Writings, 1650–1700.* Grand Rapids, MI, 1973.

Bartlett, John Russell. *History of the Wanton Family of Newport, Rhode Island. Rhode Island Historical Tracts* no. 3. Providence, RI, 1878.

Bauman, Richard. *For the Reputation of Truth: Politics, Religion and Conflict among the Pennsylvania Quakers 1750-1800.* Baltimore, MD, 1971.

———. *Let Your Words Be Few: Symbolism of Speaking and Silence among Seventeenth-Century Quakers.* Cambridge, England, 1983.

Baylies, Francis. *An Historical Memoir of the Colony of New Plymouth.* Edited by Samuel G. Drake. 2 vols. Boston, 1866.

Belknap, Jeremy. *The History of New-Hampshire.* Notes by John Farmer. 2 vols. vol. 1. Dover, NH, 1831.

Bernstein, John. *Pacifism and Rebellion in the Writings of Herman Melville.* The Hague, 1964.

Bicknell, Thomas W. *The History of the State of Rhode Island and Providence Plantations.* 3 vols. New York, 1920.

———. *Sowams.* New Haven, CT, 1908.

Bigelow, Bruce. "The Walter Newbury Shipping Book." In *Rhode Island Historical Society Collections* 24 (2) (1931): 79–81.

Billings, Warren M. "A Quaker in Seventeenth-Century Virginia: Four Remonstrances by George Wilson." *William and Mary Quarterly,* 3d series, 33 (1) (1976): 127–40.

Bittle, William G. *James Nayler: 1618–1660: The Quaker Indicted by Parliament.* York, England, 1986.

Bjorkman, Gwen. *Quaker Marriage Certificates.* Bowie, MD, 1988.

Black, Jeannette. *The Blathwayt Atlas.* Vol. 2. *Commentary.* Providence, RI, 1975.

Boddie, John Bennett. *Seventeenth Century Isle of Wight County, Virginia.* Chicago, 1938.

Bodge, George M. *Soldiers in King Philip's War.* Leominster, MA, 1896.

Bok, Sissela. *A Strategy for Peace: Human Values and the Threat of War.* New York, 1989.

Bonomi, Patricia U. *Under the Cope of Heaven: Religion, Society, and Politics in Colonial America.* New York, 1986.

Bourne, Russell. *The Red King's Rebellion: Racial Politics in New England, 1675–1678.* New York, 1990.

Bowden, James. *The History of the Society of Friends in America.* 2 vols. London, 1850, 1854.

Bowen, Richard Lebaron. *Early Rehoboth.* 4 vols. Vol. 2. Rehoboth, MA, 1946. Vol. 3. Rehoboth, MA, 1948.

Braithwaite, Alfred W. "Early Friends' Testimony against Carnal Weapons." *Journal of the Friends' Historical Society* 52 (2) (1969): 101–5.

Braithwaite, Constance. "Legal Problems of Conscientious Objection to Various Compulsions Under British Law." *Journal of the Friends' Historical Society* 52 (1) (1968): 3–18.

Braithwaite, William C. *The Beginnings of Quakerism*. 2d ed. Revised by Henry J. Cadbury. Cambridge, England, 1955; reprinted York, England, 1981.

———. *The Second Period of Quakerism*. 2d ed. Prepared by Henry J. Cadbury. Cambridge, England, 1961; reprinted York, England, 1979.

Breen, T. H. "Persistent Localism: English Social Change and the Shaping of New England Institutions." *William and Mary Quarterly*, 3rd series, 32 (1) (January 1975): 3–28.

Bridenbaugh, Carl. *Fat Mutton and Liberty of Conscience: Society in Rhode Island, 1636–1690*. Providence, RI, 1974.

Brinton, Howard H. *Quaker Journals: Varieties of Religious Experience among Friends*. Wallingford, PA, 1972.

———. *Sources of the Quaker Peace Testimony*. Pendle Hill Historical Studies no. 2. Wallingford, PA, [1941].

Brock, Peter. "Colonel Washington and the Quaker Conscientious Objectors." *Quaker History* 53 (1964): 12–26.

———. *Pacifism in Europe to 1914*. Princeton, NJ, 1972.

———. *Pacifism in the United States: From the Colonial Era to the First World War*. Princeton, NJ, 1968.

———. "The Peace Testimony in 'A Garden Enclosed.'" *Quaker History* 54 (2) (1965): 67–80.

———. *Pioneers of the Peaceable Kingdom*. Princeton, 1968.

———. *The Quaker Peace Testimony: 1660–1914*. York, England, 1990.

———. *The Roots of War Resistance: Pacifism from the Early Church to Tolstoy*. Nyack, NY, 1981.

Brockbank, Elizabeth. *Richard Hubberthorne of Yealand*. London, 1929.

Brockunier, Samuel. *The Irrepressible Democrat: Roger Williams*. New York, 1940.

Bronner, Edwin B. "Intercolonial Relations among Quakers Before 1750." *Quaker History* 56 (1) (1967): 3–17.

Brown, Elizabeth Potts, and Susan Mosher Stuard. *Witnesses for Change: Quaker Women over Three Centuries*. New Brunswick, NJ, 1989.

Brown, Marley Roberts, III. "'Among Weighty Friends': The Archaeology and Social History of the Jacob Mott Family, Portsmouth, Rhode Island, 1640–1800." Ph.D. diss. Brown University, 1987.

Brownson, Lydia B., and Maclean W. McLean. "Lt. John and Elizabeth (Freeman) Ellis of Sandwich, Mass." *New England Historical and Genealogical Register* 119 (July 1965): 161–73.

———. "Thomas Butler of Sandwich, Mass." *New England Historical and Genealogical Register* 127 (1) (January 1973): 18–26; 127 (2) (April 1973): 108–13.

Burke, Charles T. *Puritans at Bay: The War against King Philip and the Squaw Sachems*. New York, 1967.

Burlingame, Edwin Ailsworth, Norman Morrison Isham, and Charles Edward Cannon. *A Preliminary Report on the Excavations at the House of Jireh Bull on Tower Hill in Rhode Island*. Society of Colonial Wars, Rhode Island, publication no. 10. Providence, RI, 1917.

Butler, Jon. *Awash in a Sea of Faith: Christianizing the American People*. Cambridge, MA, 1990.

———. "The Future of American Religious History: Prospectus, Agenda, Transatlantic Problématic." *William and Mary Quarterly*, 3d series, 42 (2) (April 1985): 167–83.

Butler, Lindley S., and Alan D. Watson. *The North Carolina Experience: An Interpretive and Documentary History*. Chapel Hill, NC, 1984.

Cadbury, Henry J. "The Captain of Shelter Island." *Friend* (London) 3 (20 March 1953): 257–8.

———. *Friendly Heritage: Letters from the Quaker Past*. Introduction by William Hubben. Norwalk, CT, 1972.

———. "The Oldest Yearly Meeting." *Friend* (London) 3 (24 April 1953): 373–4.

Cady, Duane L. *From Warism to Pacifism : A Moral Continuum*. Philadelphia, 1989.

Cady, Edwin H. *John Woolman*. Great American Thinkers Series. New York, 1965.

Capp, Bernard. *Cromwell's Navy: The Fleet and the English Revolution 1648-1660*. Oxford, 1989.

Carpenter, Daniel H. "Rhode Island Families Who Went to Long Island, 1676, during King Philip's War." *Rhode Island Historical Magazine* 6 (1885–1886): 213–6.

Carroll, Kenneth L. "Quaker Captives in Morocco, 1685–1701." *Journal of the Friends' Historical Society* 55 (3, 4) (1985–1986): 67–79.

Cartland, Fernando G. *Southern Heroes; or Friends in War Time*. Cambridge, MA, 1895.

Catalogue of the Thomason Tracts: 1640-1661. Vol. 1. Preface by G. K. Fortescue. London, 1908.

Chalmers, George. *Introduction to the History of the Revolt of the American Colonies*. Boston, 1845.

———. *Political Annals of the Present United Colonies, From their Settlement to the Peace of 1763*. Book 2. In *Collections of the New-York Historical Society for the Year 1868*. New York, 1868.

———. "Political Annals of the Province of Carolina." In *Historical Collections of South Carolina*. Vol. 2. Compiled by B. R. Carroll. New York, 1836.

Chapin, Howard M. *Privateer Ships and Sailors: The First Century of American Colonial Privateering 1625–1725*. Toulon, France, 1926.

———. *Rhode Island Privateers in King George's War, 1739–1748*. Providence, RI, 1926.

Chu, Jonathan M. *Neighbors, Friends, or Madmen: The Puritan Adjustment to Quakerism in Seventeenth-Century Massachusetts Bay*. Westport, CT, 1985.

Clifton, Robert. *The Last Popular Rebellion: The Western Rising of 1685*. New York, 1984.

Cole, W. Alan. "The Quakers and the English Revolution." *Past and Present* 10 (November 1956): 39–54.

Cornell, John. *Genealogy of the Cornell Family, Being an Account of the Descendants of Thomas Cornell of Portsmouth, R.I.* New York, 1902.

Cox, John, Jr. *Quakerism in the City of New York, 1657–1930*. New York, 1930.

Daniels, Bruce C. *Dissent and Conformity on Narragansett Bay: The Colonial Rhode Island Town*. Middletown, CT, 1983.

Davidson, Robert L. *War Comes to Quaker Pennsylvania, 1682–1756*. New York, 1957.

Deane, Samuel. *History of Scituate, Massachusetts, From Its First Settlement to 1831*. Boston, 1831.

Ditsky, John. "Hard Hearts and Gentle People: A Quaker Reply to Persecution." *Canadian Review of American Studies* 5 (1974): 47–51.

Douglass, James W. *The Non-Violent Cross: A Theology of Revolution and Peace*. New York, 1966.

Dow, Joseph. *History of the Town of Hampton, New Hampshire: From its Settlement in 1638 to the Autumn of 1892*. 2 vols. Salem, MA, 1893.

Drake, Thomas. "Patterns of Influence in Anglo-American Quakerism." *Friends' Historical Society Journal Supplement* 28 (1958).

Duganne, Augustine Joseph Hickey. *The Fighting Quakers, A True Story of the War for our Union*. New York, 1866.

Dunn, Mary Maples. *William Penn: Politics and Conscience*. Princeton, NJ, 1967.

Dunn, Richard S., and Mary Maples Dunn, eds. *The World of William Penn*. Philadelphia, 1986.

Durfee, Thomas. *Gleanings from the Judicial History of Rhode Island*. Rhode Island Historical Tracts, no. 18. Providence, RI, 1883.

Duvall, Ralph G. *The History of Shelter Island, 1652–1932*. New York, 1932.

Ekrich, Roger. *"Poor Carolina": Politics and Society in Colonial North Carolina, 1729–1776*. Chapel Hill, NC, 1981.

Ellis, George W., and John E. Morris. *King Philip's War*. New York, 1906.

Endy, Melvin. *William Penn and Early Quakerism*. Princeton, 1973.

Erikson, Eric H. *Gandhi's Truth: On the Origins of Militant Nonviolence*. New York, 1969.

Fager, Charles. *Quakers and King Philip's War, 1675–1676*. Falls Church, VA, 1980.

Felt, Joseph B. *The Ecclesiastical History of New England*. Vol. 2. Boston, 1862.

Feola, Maryann S. *George Bishop: Seventeenth-Century Soldier Turned Quaker*. York, England, 1996.

Ferling, John E. *The Wilderness of Miseries: War and Warriors in Early America*. Westport, CT, 1980.

Firth, C. H. *Cromwell's Army*. London, 1962.

Fisher, Humphrey J. "Abolitionist Biographies." *Journal of African History* 23 (1982).

Fiske, John. *The Dutch and Quaker Colonies in America*. Vol. 2. Boston, 1899.

Flanders, Louis W. "The Garrisons of Ancient Dover, NH." *Old-Time New England* 17 (2) (October 1926): 51–62.

Ford, J. Massyngberde. *My Enemy is My Guest: Jesus and Violence in Luke*. Maryknoll, NY, 1984.

Foster, William E. *Stephen Hopkins. Rhode Island Historical Tracts*, no. 10. Providence, RI, 1874.

Freeman, Frederick. *The History of Cape Cod: Annals of the Thirteen Towns of Barnstable County*. Vol. 1. Boston, 1869. Vol. 2. Boston, 1862.

"Friends and the Press-Gang." *Journal of the Friends' Historical Society* 24 (1932): 61.

Frost, J. William. "Quaker versus Baptist: A Religious and Political Squabble in Rhode Island Three Hundred Years Ago." *Quaker History* 63 (1) (spring 1974): 39–52.

———. "Religious Liberty in Early Pennsylvania." *Pennsylvania Magazine of History and Biography* 105 (4) (October 1981): 419–51.

Fuller, Oliver Payson. *The History of Warwick, Rhode Island, From Its Settlement in 1642 to the Present Time. . . .* Providence, 1875.

Fussell, Paul. *Wartime: Understanding and Behavior in the Second World War*. New York, 1989.

Gardiner, Samuel Rawson. *History of the Commonwealth and Protectorate, 1649–1656*. Vol. 4. *1655–1656*. Originally published London, 1903; reprinted New York, 1965.

Genealogies of Rhode Island Families, from the New England Historical and Genealogical Register. Vol. 1. Selected by Gary Boyd Roberts. Baltimore, 1989.

George Fox's "Book of Miracles." Edited by Henry J. Cadbury. Cambridge, England, 1948.

Gilpin, Thomas. *Exiles in Virginia*. Philadelphia, 1848.

Gove, William Henry. *The Gove Book, History and Genealogy*. Salem, MA, 1922.

Greaves, Richard L. *Deliver Us from Evil: The Radical Underground in Britain, 1660–1663*. New York, 1986.

Greene, Jack P. *The Quest for Power: The Lower Houses of Assembly in the Southern Royal Colonies, 1689–1776*. Chapel Hill, NC, 1963.

Greven, Philip. *The Protestant Temperament*. New York, 1977.

Grimes, J. Bryan. *North Carolina Wills and Inventories*. Raleigh, NC, 1912.

Gummere, Amelia Mott. *The Quaker in the Forum*. Philadelphia, 1910.

Gura, Philip F. *A Glimpse of Sion's Glory: Puritan Radicalism in New England, 1620–1660*. Middletown, CT, 1984.

Gwyn, Douglas. *Apocalypse of the Word: The Life and Message of George Fox (1624–1691)*. Richmond, IN, 1986.

Hall, David D. *Worlds of Wonder, Days of Judgement: Popular Religious Belief in Early New England*. New York, 1989.

Hallie, Philip. *Lest Innocent Blood Be Shed*. New York, 1979.

Hallowell, Richard P. *The Pioneer Quakers*. Boston, 1887.

———. *The Quaker Invasion of Massachusetts*. Boston, 1883.

Hambrick-Stowe, Charles E. *The Practice of Piety: Puritan Devotional Disciplines in Seventeenth-Century New England*. Chapel Hill, NC, 1982.

Hathaway, J. R. B., ed. *North Carolina Historical and Genealogical Register*, Vols. 1, 3. Edenton, NC, 1900.

Hawks, Francis L. *History of North Carolina*. Vol. 2. Fayetteville, NC, 1858.

Hazard, Caroline. *The Narragansett Friends' Meeting*. Boston, 1899.

———. *Thomas Hazard, Son of Rob't, Call'd College Tom*. Boston, 1893.

Heiss, Willard C. *Quaker Genealogies*. Boston, 1985.

Hershberger, Guy. "The Pennsylvania Quaker Experiment in Politics, 1682–1756." *Mennonite Quarterly Review* 10 (1936).

Heyrman, Christine. *Commerce and Culture: The Maritime Communities of Colonial Massachusetts; 1690–1750.* New York, 1984.

———. "Specters of Subversion, Societies of Friends: Dissent and the Devil in Provincial Essex County, Massachusetts." In *Saints and Revolutionaries,* edited by David D. Hall, John M. Murrin, and Thad W. Tate. New York, 1984.

Higginbotham, Don. "The Early American Way of War: Reconnaissance and Appraisal." *William and Mary Quarterly,* 3d series, 44 (2) (April 1987): 230–73.

Hill, Christopher. *The English Bible and the Seventeenth-Century Revolution.* London, 1993.

———. *The Experience of Defeat: Milton and Some Contemporaries.* New York, 1984.

———. *Milton and the English Revolution.* New York, 1978.

———. "Quakers and the English Revolution." *Journal of the Friends' Historical Society* 56 (3) (1992): 165–79.

———. *The World Turned Upside Down.* New York, 1975.

Hinchman, Lydia S. *Early Settlers of Nantucket.* 2d ed. Philadelphia, 1901.

Hinshaw, Seth B. *The Carolina Quaker Experience, 1665–1985: An Interpretation.* Greensboro, NC, 1984.

Hinshaw, William Wade. *Encyclopedia of American Quaker Genealogy.* Vol. 1. Ann Arbor, MI, 1936.

Hirst, Margaret E. *The Quakers in Peace and War: An Account of Their Peace Principles and Practice.* London, 1923.

Historical Data Relating to Counties, Cities and Towns in Massachusetts. Boston, 1975.

Hodgkin, L. V. *The Shoemaker of Dover: Luke Howard. 1621–1699.* London, 1943.

Holder, Charles Frederick. *The Holders of Holderness.* N.p., [1902].

Holifield, E. Brooks. *Era of Persuasion: American Thought and Culture, 1521–1680.* Boston, 1989.

Horle, Craig W. *The Quakers and the English Legal System: 1660–1688.* Philadelphia, 1988.

Horowitz, David. *The First Frontier: The Indian Wars and America's Origins 1607–1776.* New York, 1978.

Hutchinson, J. R. *The Press-Gang, Afloat and Ashore.* London, 1913.

"The Indians of Southern Virginia, 1650–1711." *Virginia Magazine of History and Biography* 7 (April 1900): 337–52; 8 (July 1900): 1–11.

Ingle, H. Larry. *First among Friends: George Fox and the Creation of Quakerism.* New York, 1994.

———. "George Fox as Enthusiast: An Unpublished Epistle." *Journal of the Friends' Historical Society* 55 (8) (1989): 265–70.

———. "Richard Hubberthorne and History: The Crisis of 1659." *Journal of the Friends' Historical Society* 56 (3) (1992): 197.

Interpreter's One-Volume Commentary on the Bible. Edited by Charles M. Laymon. Nashville, TN, 1971.

James, Sydney V. *Colonial Rhode Island: A History.* New York, 1975.

———. "Friends in Colonial Rhode Island Politics." Paper presented at George Fox Commemorative Conference, Lancaster University, Lancaster, England, March 1991.

———. *A People among Peoples: Quaker Benevolence in Eighteenth Century America.* Cambridge, MA, 1963.

Jeffrey, William, Jr. "Early New England Court Records—A Bibliography of Published Materials." *American Journal of Legal History* 1 (1957): 119–46.

Jenkins, Charles F. *Tortola: A Quaker Experiment of Long Ago in the Tropics.* London, 1923.

Jennings, Francis. *The Invasion of America: Indians, Colonialism, and the Cant of Conquest.* Chapel Hill, NC, 1976.

Jones, Matt Bushnell. "Thomas Maule, the Salem Quaker, and Free Speech in Massachusetts Bay, with Bibliographical Notes." *Essex Institute Historical Collections* 72 (1) (January 1936): 1–43.

Jones, Rufus M. *Mysticism and Democracy in the English Commonwealth.* Cambridge, MA, 1932.

————. *The Quakers in the American Colonies*. London, 1911.

Jones, T. Canby. *George Fox's Attitude toward War*. Richmond, IN, 1984.

Jordan, David W. "'Gods Candle' within Government: Quakers and Politics in Early Maryland." *William and Mary Quarterly*, 3rd series, 39 (4) (October 1982): 628–54.

Journal of the Friends' Historical Society. London, 1903–present.

Juricek, John T. "Indian Policy in Proprietary South Carolina, 1670–1693." M.A. thesis, University of Chicago, 1962.

Keegan, John. *A History of Warfare*. New York, 1993.

Kelsey, Rayner W. *Friends and the Indians, 1655–1917*. Philadelphia, 1917.

Kern, John. "The Politics of Violence: Colonial American Rebellions, Protests, and Riots, 1676–1747." Ph.D. diss. University of Wisconsin, 1976.

Ketcham, Ralph L. "Conscience, War, and Politics." *William and Mary Quarterly*, 3rd series, 20 (1963): 416–39.

King, H. Roger. *Cape Cod and Plymouth Colony in the Seventeenth Century*. New York, 1994.

Klein, Randolph Shipley. *Portrait of an Early American Family: The Shippens of Pennsylvania Across Five Generations*. N.p., 1975.

Leach, Douglas E. "Benjamin Batten and the *London Gazette*: Report on King Philip's War." *New England Quarterly* 36 (1963): 502–17.

————. *Flintlock and Tomahawk: New England in King Philip's War*. New York, 1958.

————. "The Military System of Plymouth Colony." *New England Quarterly* 24 (3) (September 1951): 342–64.

————. *The Northern Colonial Frontier, 1607–1763*. New York, 1966.

Lee, Lawrence E. *Indian Wars in North Carolina, 1663–1763*. Raleigh, NC, 1963.

Lefler, Hugh Talmadge. *North Carolina History, Told by Contemporaries*. Chapel Hill, NC, 1965.

Lefler, Hugh T., and William S. Powell. *Colonial North Carolina*. New York, 1973.

Leland, P. W. "Algonquin, or Indian Terms, as Applied to Places and Things." *Collections of the Old Colony Historical Society* 1 (3) (1985): 83–103.

Lepore, Jill. *The Name of War: King Philip's War and the Origins of American Identity*. New York, 1998.

Levy, Barry. *Quakers and the American Family: British Settlement in the Delaware Valley*. New York, 1988.

Lloyd, Arnold. *Quaker Social History, 1669–1738*. London, 1950.

Lonn, Ella. *The Colonial Agents of the Southern Colonies*. Chapel Hill, NC, 1945.

Lovejoy, David S. *Religious Enthusiasm in the New World: Heresy to Revolution*. Cambridge, MA, 1985.

Lovell, R. A., Jr. *Sandwich: A Cape Cod Town*. Sandwich, MA, 1984.

Lowry, Ann Gidley. "Quakers and Their Meeting House at Apponegansett." *Old Dartmouth Historical Sketches*, no. 70. [New Bedford, MA], 1940.

Mack, Phyllis. "Gender and Spirituality in Early English Quakerism, 1650–1665." In *Witnesses for Change: Quaker Women over Three Centuries*, edited by Elizabeth Potts Brown and Susan Mosher Stuard. New Brunswick, NJ, 1989.

————. *Visionary Women: Ecstatic Prophecy in Seventeenth-Century England*. Berkeley, CA, 1992.

Maclear, James F. "Quakerism and the End of the Interregnum: A Chapter in the Domestication of Radical Puritanism." *Church History* 19 (4) (December 1950): 240–71.

MacMaster, Richard Kerwin. *Conscience in Crisis: Mennonites and other Peace Churches, 1739–1789: Interpretation and Documents*. Scottdale, PA, 1979.

Main, Jackson Turner. "The Distribution of Property in Colonial Connecticut." In *The Human Dimensions of Nation Making*, edited by James Kirby Martin. Madison, WI, 1976.

Malone, Patrick M. *The Skulking Way of War: Technology and Tactics among the New England Indians*. Baltimore, 1991.

Manners, Emily. *Elizabeth Hooten: First Quaker Woman Preacher (1600–1672)*. Notes by Norman Penney. London, 1914.

Marietta, Jack D. "Conscience, the Quaker Community, and the French and Indian War." *Pennsylvania Magazine of History and Biography* 95 (1) (January 1971): 3–27.

———. *The Reformation of American Quakerism.* Philadelphia, 1984.

———. "William Rakestraw: Pacifist Pamphleteer and Party Servant." *Pennsylvania Magazine of History and Biography* 98 (1) (January 1974).

Marley, Branson. "Minutes of the General Court of Albemarle, 1684." *North Carolina Historical Review* 19 (1) (January 1942): 48–58.

Martin, David A. *Pacifism: An Historical and Sociological Study.* London, 1965.

Marx, Steven. "The Prophet Disarmed: Milton and the Quakers." *Studies in English Literature 1500–1900* 32 (1) (winter 1992).

The Mayflower Descendant. [Journal]. Boston, 1913.

McCormick, Jo Anne. "The Quakers of South Carolina, 1670-1807." Ph.D. diss. University of South Carolina, 1984.

McLean, Maclean W., and Lydia (Phinney) Brownson. "Lt. John Ellis of Sandwich, Mass." *New England Historical and Genealogical Register* 119 (1965): 161–73.

———. "Thomas Butler of Sandwich, Mass." *New England Historical and Genealogical Register* 127 (1973): 18–26.

McLoughlin, William G. "The Dartmouth Quakers' Struggle for Religious Liberty, 1692–1734." *Quaker History* 78 (1) (spring 1989): 1–23.

McPartland, Martha R. *The History of East Greenwich, Rhode Island, 1677–1960.* East Greenwich, RI, 1960.

McPherson, Elizabeth Gregory, ed. "Nathanial Batts, Landholder on Pasquotank River, 1660." *North Carolina Historical Review* 43 (winter 1966): 66–81.

Mekeel, Arthur J. "New York Quakers in the American Revolution." *Bulletin of Friends Historical Association* 29 (1940): 47–55.

———. *The Relation of the Quakers to the American Revolution.* Washington, DC, 1979.

Miller, Perry. *The New England Mind: The Seventeenth Century.* Cambridge, MA, 1954.

Mitchell, Rebecca Gould. *The Goulds of Rhode Island.* Providence, RI, 1875.

Morgan, Edmund S. *Roger Williams: The Church and the State.* New York, 1967.

Murrin, John M. "The Papers of William Penn." *Pennsylvania Magazine of History and Biography* 105 (4) (October 1981): 483–87.

Nash, Gary B. *Quakers and Politics: Pennsylvania, 1681–1726.* Princeton, NJ, 1968.

Nelson, Jacquelyn S. "The Military Response of the Society of Friends in Indiana to the Civil War." *Indiana Magazine of History* 81 (June 1985): 101–30.

New England Diaries: 1602–1800. A Descriptive Catalogue of Diaries, Orderly Books and Sea Journals. Compiled by Harriette Merrifield Forbes. N.p., 1923.

New Light on George Fox, 1624–1691. Edited by Michael Mullett. York, England, 1993.

Norton, Mary Beth. "The Evolution of White Women's Experience in Early America." *American Historical Review* 89 (1984): 593–619.

"Notes and Queries." *Journal of the Friends' Historical Society* 3 (1) (1906): 2–6.

Nuttall, Geoffrey F. *Christian Pacifism in History.* Oxford, 1958.

———. "James Nayler: A Fresh Approach." *Friends' Historical Society Journal Supplement* 26 (1954).

———. *Studies in Christian Enthusiasm.* Pamphlet. Wallingford, PA, 1948.

Oldmixon, John. *History of the British Empire in America.* London, 1741.

Onderdonk, Henry, Jr. *The Annals of Hempstead; 1643 to 1832; Also, The Rise and Growth of the Society of Friends on Long Island and in New York 1657 to 1826.* Hempstead, NY, 1878.

Otis, Amos. *Genealogical Notes of Barnstable Families.* Barnstable, MA, 1888.

Parker, Mattie Erma E. "Legal Aspects of 'Culpepper's Rebellion.'" *North Carolina Historical Review* 45 (2) (April 1968): 111–27.

Parramore, Thomas C. "The Tuscarora Ascendancy." *North Carolina Historical Review* 59 (4) (October 1982): 307–26.

Penhallow, Samuel. *The History of the Wars of New-England.* Cincinnati, 1859.

Penney, Norman. "Our Recording Clerks, No. 1, Ellis Hookes, c. 1657–1681." *Journal of the Friends' Historical Society* 1 (1) (1903–1904): 12–22.

———. ed. *First Publishers of Truth.* London, 1907.

Penrose, E. Josephine. "Edmund Peckover, Ex-Soldier of the Commonwealth, and Quaker." *Journal of the Friends' Historical Society* 2 (3) (1904): 88–90.

Perry, Elwell. "Quakers in Sandwich." Typescript, Sandwich Historical Commission, Sandwich, MA. N.p., n.d.

Pestana, Carla Gardina. "Neighbors, Friends, or Madmen: The Puritan Adjustment to Quakerism in Seventeenth-Century Massachusetts Bay." *Essex Institute Historical Collections* 122 (July 1986): 259–62.

———. *Quakers and Baptists in Colonial Massachusetts.* New York, 1991.

Powell, William Stevens. "Colonial North Carolina, 1585–1764." In *Writing North Carolina History,* edited by Jeffrey J. Crow and Larry E. Tise. Chapel Hill, NC, 1979.

———. *North Carolina: A Bicentennial History.* New York, 1977.

Pratt, Harvey H. *The Early Planters of Scituate.* Scituate, MA, 1929.

"Present State of the Nonconformists." [Stowe Manuscripts, vol. 186, 1672]. *Journal of the Friends' Historical Society* 4 (3), (1907): 122–4.

Preston, Howard Willis. *Rhode Island and the Sea.* State Bureau of Information historical publication no. 4. Providence, RI, 1932.

Price, Jacob M. *Overseas Trade and Traders.* Aldershot, England, 1996.

Puglisi, Michael J. *Puritans Besieged: The Legacies of King Philip's War in the Massachusetts Bay Colony.* Lanham, MD, 1991.

Quaker Crosscurrents: Three Hundred Years of Friends in the New York Yearly Meetings. Edited by Hugh Barbour et al. Syracuse, NY, 1995.

Quaker History. Haverford, PA, 1906–present.

Raimo, John W. *Biographical Directory of American Colonial and Revolutionary Governors, 1607–1789.* Westport, CT, 1980.

Rankin, Hugh F. *Upheaval in Albemarle: The Story of Culpeper's Rebellion, 1675–1689.* Raleigh, NC, 1962.

Reay, Barry. *The Quakers and the English Revolution.* New York, 1985.

"Recent Accessions." *Journal of the Friends' Historical Society* 14 (3) (1917): 132.

"Records of the Yearly Meeting of Aberdeen." *Journal of the Friends' Historical Society* 8 (1) (1911): 40–46.

Rediker, Marcus. *Between the Devil and the Deep Blue Sea: Merchant Seamen, Pirates, and the Anglo-American Maritime World, 1700–1750.* New York, 1987.

Richman, Irving Berdine. *Rhode Island: Its Making and Its Meaning.* Vol. 2. New York, 1902.

Rider, Sidney S. *The Lands of Rhode Island as They Were Known to Caunounicus and Miantunnomu When Roger Williams Came in 1636.* Providence, RI, 1904.

Robinson, W. Stitt. *The Southern Colonial Frontier, 1607–1763.* Albuquerque, NM, 1979.

Rowntree, John Wilhelm. *Essays and Addresses.* Edited by Joshua Rowntree. London, 1905.

Russell, Chester. *Was Jesus a Pacifist?* Nashville, TN, 1871.

Sanders, Thomas G. *Protestant Concepts of Church and State.* New York, 1964.

Savage, James. *A Genealogical Dictionary of the First Settlers of New England.* Vol. 2. Baltimore, MD, 1977.

Scales, John. *Colonial Era History of Dover, New Hampshire.* [Manchester, NH], 1923.

Schlissel, Lillian D., ed. *Conscience in America: A Documentary History of Conscientious Objection in America, 1757–1967.* New York, 1968.

Schultz, Eric B., and Michael J. Tougias. *King Philip's War: The History and Legacy of America's Forgotten Conflict.* Woodstock, VT, 1999.

Selleck, George A. *Quakers in Boston: 1656–1964: Three Centuries of Friends in Boston and Cambridge.* Cambridge, MA, 1976.

Schroeder, Betty Groff. "The True Lineage of King Philip (Sachem Metacom)." *New England Historical and Genealogical Register* 144 (July 1990): 211–4.

Sharp, Morrison. "Leadership and Democracy in the Early New England System of Defense." *American Historical Review* 50 (2) (January 1945): 244–60.

Sharpless, Isaac, and A. Gummere. *A History of Quaker Government in Pennsylvania*. Vol. 1. *A Quaker Experiment in Government*. Philadelphia, 1902.

Sheeran, Michael J. *Beyond Majority Rule: Voteless Decisions in the Religious Society of Friends*. Philadelphia, 1983.

Sheffield, William P. *An Address Delivered by William P. Sheffield, Before the Rhode Island Historical Society*. Newport, RI, 1883.

Simmons, William S. *Spirit of the New England Tribes: Indian History and Folklore, 1620–1984*. Hanover, NH, 1986.

Simpson, Charles R. "Benjamin Furly, Quaker Merchant, and His Statesmen Friends." *Journal of the Friends' Historical Society* 11 (2) (1914): 62–70.

Sloan, David. "'A Time of Sifting and Winnowing': The Paxton Riots and Quaker Non-Violence in Pennsylvania." *Quaker History* 66 (1) (1977): 3–22.

Slotkin, Richard. *Regeneration Through Violence: The Mythology of the American Frontier, 1600–1860*. Middletown, CT, 1973.

Smith, Joseph. *Bibliotheca Anti-Quakeriana*. Originally published 1873; reprinted New York, 1968.

———. *A Descriptive Catalogue of Friends' Books*. 2 vols. Originally published London, 1867; reprinted New York, 1970. *Supplement*. Originally published London, 1893; reprinted New York, 1970.

Smith, Joseph Jencks, comp. *Civil and Military List of Rhode Island, 1647–1800*. Providence, RI, 1900.

Smith, Samuel. *The Colonial History of New Jersey*. Trenton, NJ, 1890.

Soderlund, Jean R. *Quakers and Slavery: A Divided Spirit*. Princeton, NJ, 1985.

Sosin, J. M. *English America and the Revolution of 1688*. Lincoln, NE, 1982.

Spindel, Donna. *Crime and Society in North Carolina, 1663–1776*. Baton Rouge, LA, 1989.

Stackpole, Everett S. *Old Kittery and Her Families*. Lewiston, ME, 1903.

———. *Swett Genealogy*. Lewiston, ME, [no date].

Stannard, William G. "The Indians of Southern Virginia, 1650–1711: Depositions in the Virginia and North Carolina Boundary Case." *Virginia Magazine of History and Biography* 7 (April 1900): 345-8.

Staples, William R. *Annals of the Town of Providence*. Providence, RI, 1843.

Stevens, John Austin. "King Philip's War." *The First Record Book of the Society of Colonial Wars in the State of Rhode Island and Providence Plantations*. Providence, RI, 1902: 81–90.

Stevens, Maud Lyman. "The Romance of Newport." *Bulletin of the Newport Historical Society* 24 (January 1918): 1–30.

Stout, Harry S. *The New England Soul: Preaching and Religious Culture in Colonial New England*. New York, 1986.

Surtees, Robert. *The History and Antiquities of the County Palatine of Durham*. Vol. 2. London, 1820.

Swift, Charles F. *History of Old Yarmouth*. Edited by Charles A. Holbrook, Jr. Yarmouth Port, MA, 1975.

"Tender Consciences." *Rhode Island Historical Magazine* 5 (1884–1885): 205–10.

Terrell, Thomas E. Jr. "Some Holsom Exhortation! Henry White's Seventeenth Century Southern Religious Narrative in Verse." *Early American Literature* 18 (1983): 31–44.

"A Testimony." 24/6M/1675. *Massachusetts Historical Society Proceedings*. Boston, MA, 1909. 42: 378–81.

Thistlethwaite, W. P. *Yorkshire Quarterly Meeting (of the Society of Friends) 1665–1966*. Harrogate, England, 1979.

Thornton, John Wingate. *Mementos of the Swett Family*. Roxbury, [MA], 1851.

Tolles, Frederick B. *Quakers and the Atlantic Culture*. New York, 1960.

Trayser, Donald G. *Barnstable: Three Centuries of a Cape Cod Town*. Hyannis, MA, 1939.

Trevett, Christine. *Women and Quakerism in the Seventeenth Century.* Sessions Book Trust. York, England, 1991.

Trueblood, E. Elton. *Studies in Quaker Pacifism.* Philadelphia, 1934.

Turner, H. E. "Jeremy Clarke's Family: An Address before the Rhode Island Historical Society, March 1879." Reprinted from *Newport Historical Magazine,* 1881. Newport Historical Society, Newport, RI.

Turner, Henry E. *Settlers of Aquidneck, and Liberty of Conscience.* Newport, RI, 1880.

———. *William Coddington in Rhode Island Colonial Affairs.* Rhode Island Historical Tracts, no. 4. Providence, RI, 1878.

Ullmann, Richard K. *Between God and History: The Human Situation Exemplified in Quaker Thought and Practice.* London, 1959.

Ulrich, Laurel Thatcher. *Good Wives: Image and Reality in the Lives of Women in Northern New England, 1650–1750.* New York, 1982.

Underdown, David. *Revel, Riot, and Rebellion: Popular Politics and Culture in England: 1603–1660.* Oxford, 1985.

———. *A Freeborn People: Politics and the Nation in Seventeenth-Century England.* Oxford, 1996.

Updike, Daniel B. *Richard Smith.* Boston, 1937.

Vann, Richard T. *The Social Development of English Quakerism: 1655–1755.* Cambridge, MA, 1969.

Washburn, Wilcomb E. "Seventeenth-Century Indian Wars." In *Handbook of North American Indians,* vol. 15, *Northeast,* edited by Bruce G. Trigger. Washington, DC, 1978.

Webb, Stephen Saunders. *1676: The End of American Independence.* Cambridge, MA, 1985.

Weddle, Meredith Baldwin. "The Basis of the Early Quaker Peace Testimony and its Implications for Behaviour." In *New Light on George Fox (1624–1691): A Collection of Essays,* edited by Michael Mullett, 89–100. York, England, 1993.

———. "Conscience or Compromise: The Meaning of the Peace Testimony in Early New England." *Quaker History* 81 (2) (Fall 1992): 73–86.

———. "Henry Pitman." In *I Found It At the JCB: Scholars and Sources,* 74–5. Providence, RI, 1996.

Weeks, Stephen B. *Southern Quakerism and Slavery: A Study in Institutional History.* Baltimore, 1896.

Wellenreuther, Hermann. "The Political Dilemma of the Quakers in Pennsylvania, 1681–1748." *Pennsylvania Magazine of History and Biography* 94 (1970): 135–72.

Wetherill, Charles. *History of the Religious Society of Friends Called by Some the Free Quakers in the City of Philadelphia.* N.p., 1894.

Wheeler, E. Milton. "Development and Organization of the North Carolina Militia." *North Carolina Historical Review* 41 (July 1964): 307–23.

Wheeler, John Hill. *Historical Sketches of North Carolina, from 1584 to 1851.* Philadelphia, 1851.

White, Peter. *Benjamin Tompson: Colonial Bard.* University Park, PA, 1980.

White, Stephen Jay. "From the Vestry Act to Cary's Rebellion: North Carolina Quakers and Colonial Politics." *Southern Friend: Journal of the North Carolina Friends Historical Society* 8 (2) (1986): 3–26.

———. "North Carolina Quakers in the Era of the American Revolution." M.A. thesis, University of Tennessee, Knoxville, TN, 1981.

Whitman, Roscoe L. *History and Genealogy of the Ancestors and Some Descendants of Stukely Westcott.* N. p., 1932.

Wigfield, W. McDonald. *The Monmouth Rebels 1685.* Somerset Record Society, vol. 79. Gloucester, England, 1985.

Willauer, G. J., Jr. "First Publishers of Truth in New England: A Composite List, 1636–1775." *Quaker History* 65 (1) (1976): 35–44.

Williams, Emily Coddington. *William Coddington of Rhode Island: A Sketch.* Newport, RI, 1941.

Winchester, Angus J. L. "Ministers, Merchants and Migrants: Cumberland Friends and

North America in the Eighteenth Century." Paper presented at George Fox Commemorative Conference, Lancaster University, Lancaster, England, March 1991.

Wing, Conway P. *A Historical and Genealogical Register of John Wing, of Sandwich, Mass., and his Descendants, 1632–1888*. Carlisle, PA, 1881.

Wing, William A. "Five Johns of Old Dartmouth." *Old Dartmouth Historical Sketches* 25 (1909).

———. "John Russell." *Old Dartmouth Historical Sketches* 69 (1935).

———. *Some Wings of Old Dartmouth and Their Homes*. N.p., [1905].

Winship, Michael P. *Seers of God: Puritan Providentialism in the Restoration and Early Enlightment*. Baltimore, MD, 1996.

Winslow, Ellen Goode. *History of Perquimans County*. Raleigh, NC, 1931.

Winsser, Johan. "Mary Dyer and the 'Monster' Story." *Quaker History* 79 (1) (1990): 20–34.

Worrall, Arthur J. "Persecution, Politics, and War: Roger Williams, Quakers, and King Philip's War." *Quaker History* 66 (2) (autumn 1977): 73–86.

———. *Quakers in the Colonial Northeast*. Hanover, NH, 1980.

———. "Toleration Comes to Sandwich." In *Seeking the Light: Essays in Quaker History,* edited by J. William Frost and John M. Moore. Wallingford, PA, 1986.

Wright, Edward N. *Conscientious Objectors in the Civil War*. Philadelphia, 1931.

Wuest, Kenneth S. *Studies in the Vocabulary of the Greek New Testament*. Grand Rapids, MI, 1945.

Yarnall, Charles. "John Bowne of Flushing, 1627–1695." *Bulletin of Friends' Historical Society* 2 (2) (1908): 44–67.

Index

Bourman [Bowerman], Thomas, 210, 301n.91

Bowden, James, 172–3

Bownas, Samuel, 8, 305n.21

Bowne, John, 103, 106 fig. 5.2

Bradford, [William], Major, 166

Bradstreet, Simon, 89

Braithwaite, William C., 9

Brayton, Francis, 117

Brend, William, 86, 88, 106, 276n.33
    missionary, 29, 100, 268n.1

Briar, Joseph, 102 fig. 5.1

Brinton, Howard, 70, 216

Brock, Peter, 9–10, 173

Budlong, Francis, 159

Buffum, [Joshua], 89

Bull, Henry, 101, 111, 136, 138, 192,
    279n.2

Bull, Jireh, 101, 144, 154, 155 fig. 9.2, 167,
    275n.17, 287n.67

Burnyeat, John, 59, 91, 104, 110, 227,
    275n.17

Burrough, Edward, 17, 29, 41, 57, 63

Butler, Daniel, 93–4, 297n.22

Butler, Obadiah, 297n.22

Callender, John, 180

Camm, John, 17

Canonchet, 137, 146

Canonicus, 137

capital punishment, 84, 86, 88–91, 167

carnal weapons, 59, 145, 177, 186–7, 200
    defined broadly, 70–1, 90–1, 214
    on ships, 53–4, 59–61, 163, 264n.71
    vs. spiritual weapons, 70–1, 96

Carolina, 82–3, 255n.7

Carr, Caleb, 101, 145, 163, 212

Cary's Rebellion, 255n.7

Caton, William, 31, 57, 261n.21

centralization, of military measures, 163

Chalkley, Thomas, 216

Charles II (king of England), 18, 43, 86, 95

Charter of 1663, Rhode Island, 99, 101, 114,
    148

Chase, Abraham, 206

Christopherson, Wenlock, 94

Chu, Jonathan, 173

Church, Benjamin, 137, 147, 154, 166–7

Clarke, Latham, 167

Clarke, Walter, 101, 102 fig. 5.1, 117, 138,
    279n.2

as governor, 167, 172, 193, 290n.38
    wartime activities of, 152, 161–5

Clarke, Weston, 101, 138, 159–60, 167, 204

Clarke, William, 166

Claypoole, James, 59–60

clergy, 20, 133–4, 156

Clifton, Thomas, 102 fig. 5.1, 138

Coale, Josiah, 100

Coddington, Ann, 91, 102 fig. 5.1

Coddington, William, 101, 104, 120, 226,
    279n.2
    as governor, wartime Rhode Island, 138,
    220
    and military activities, 55, 144–8, 153, 163,
    180, 193
    as Quaker, 90, 102 fig. 5.1, 115, 158, 192,
    218–9

Coggeshall, John, 116–7, 138, 163, 290n.38

Coggeshall, Joshua
    as magistrate, 101, 138, 167, 277–8n.61,
    279n.2, 290n.38
    as Quaker, 86, 102 fig. 5.1, 182–3, 189 fig.
    12.1, 192

Cole, W. Alan, 7–8, 58, 245–6

Colman, [Ann], 207

Colman, Joseph, 199–200, 297n.22

Colman, Thomas, 199–200, 297n.22

Colman, Zachariah, 199–200, 297n.22

commentary from England, 184, 192

commissioners, king's, 91–2, 113–5, 148

Conventicle Acts (1664, 1670), 18, 33, 44

conversion, 21–2, 82, 232, 257n.26

convincement, 21–2, 62–3, 82

Cooper, Simon, 102 fig. 5.1, 219, 291n.41

Copeland, John, 29, 90, 210

Cornell, Thomas, 167, 291n.41

Corporation Act (1661), 33

courage, 52, 60, 63, 228

covenant, first, 22, 49, 129, 257n.13

covenant, new, 22, 48–9, 197. *See also*
    scriptures, New Testament

cowardice, 227

Coxere, Edward, 63–5

Cram, Thomas, 206

Cranston, John, 150, 163, 165, 171

Cromwell, Oliver, 18, 25, 42, 57, 59, 162

Cromwell, Richard, 18, 42

Cudworth, James, 86, 144, 146, 153, 227

Cudworth, Mary, 86

Curwen, Alice, 29, 89

Curwen, Thomas, 29

universalism, 17, 20, 78
Upshall, Nicholas, 77–8

violence, 227
    causes of, 52–3, 162
    consequences of, 52–4, 96, 188
    forms of, 4, 40, 90
    Quakers and, 40, 54, 59, 61, 72, 85 fig. 4.1
    victims of, 96–7, 128, 187–8, 229, 231

Waldron, Richard, 87 fig. 4.2, 207–8
Walker, Philip, 210
Waller, William, 61
Wallis, John, 33–4
Wampanoags, 55, 137, 145–6, 166, 281–2n.3
Wanton, Edward, 88–9
Ward, William, 61
Warde, Cornet, 58
Wardel, Eliakim, 90
Warwick, 159–63
    military affairs of, 123, 154
Waterman, Nathaniel, 289n.11
Waterman, Richard, 289n.11
weapons. *See* carnal weapons
Wecopeak, 167
Weetamoo, 136–7, 145–7, 284n.10
Wenanaquabin, 167
Westcott, Robert, 155, 204
Wharton, Edward, 34, 155, 194–5
Whetcombe, Robert, 86
Whipple, Eleazer, 150
Wickes, John, 159, 283n.33
Wickford, 101, 119, 147

Wilkinson, Lawrence, 279n.2
Wilkinson-Story controversy, 107
Willett, Hezekiah, 218
Willett, Thomas, 218
Williams, John, Jr., 95
Williams, Robert, 129
Williams, Roger, 99–100, 119, 140, 147, 258n.30
    and Quakers, 27, 104–5, 110–1, 220
    and view of Quaker pacifism, 85 fig. 4.1, 110–1, 154
Wilson, George, 84, 96–7
Wing, Ananias, 205–6
Wing, Daniel, 205, 210, 213
Wing, Ebenezer, 210
Wing, John, Jr., 210
Wing, John, Sr., 205, 210
Wing, Joseph, 205
Wing, Samuel, 210
Wing, Stephen, Jr., 209–10
Wing, Stephen, Sr., 94–5, 205, 210, 217
Winslow, Josiah, 55, 138, 144, 153, 174, 219
Winthrop, John, Jr., 111, 138, 154, 184, 191, 217–9
Winthrop, John, Sr., 138, 140
Winthrop, Samuel, 138
Wodell, William, 101, 138, 176, 278n.6, 279n.2
Woodworth, Benjamin, 206
Woodworth, John, 206
Wooley, Emanuel, 116
Worrall, Arthur J., 173, 304n.59
Wright, H., 203–4